Mastering Windows™ Programming with Borland® C++ 4

Tom Swan

PUBLISHING

A Division of Prentice Hall Computer Publishing
201 West 103rd Street, Indianapolis, Indiana 46290

To Anne.

Publisher
Richard K. Swadley

Associate Publisher
Jordan Gold

Acquisitions Manager
Stacy Hiquet

Acquisitions Editor
Gregory Croy

Development Editor
Dean Miller

Editors
Fran Hatton
Mitzi Foster Gianakos

Editorial Coordinator
Bill Whitmer

Editorial Assistants
Carol Ackerman
Sharon Cox
Lynette Quinn

Technical Editor
Gary Walker

Cover Designer
Kathy Hanley

Production Director
Jeff Valler

Imprint Manager
Juli Cook

Book Designer
Michele Laseau

Production Analysts
Dennis Clay Hager
Mary Beth Wakefield

Proofreading Coordinator
Joelynn Gifford

Indexing Coordinator
Johnna VanHoose

Graphics Image Specialists
Tim Montgomery
Dennis Sheehan
Sue VandeWalle

Production
Lisa Daugherty
Angela P. Judy
Greg Kemp
Jenny Kucera
Stephanie J. McComb
Jamie Milazzo
Shelly Palma
Ryan Rader
Amy Schatz
Susan Shepherd
Tonya R. Simpson
Becky Tapley
Suzanne Tully
Alyssa Yesh

Indexers
Rebecca Mayfield
C. Small

Overview

Contents

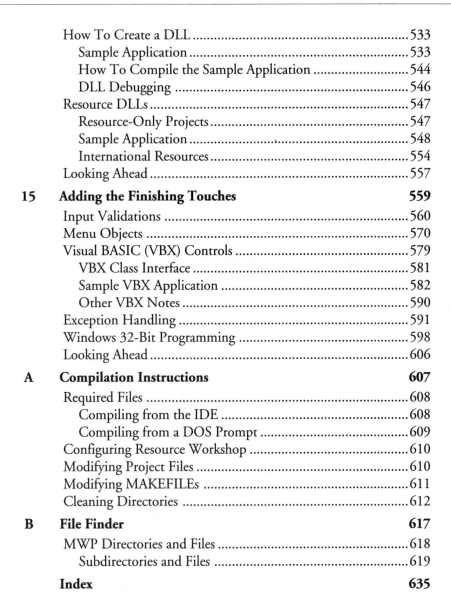

Acknowledgments

Many friends and associates helped make this book possible. I owe special thanks to the editors, proofreaders, and other hard workers at Sams, especially Greg Croy, Jordan Gold, Fran Hatton, Dean Miller, Richard Swadley, Keith Davenport, and Mitzi Foster Gianakos. Gary Walker reviewed the manuscript, weeded out numerous mistakes, and made many helpful suggestions. My agent, Bill Gladstone, and his capable staff at Waterside Productions, kept the business side of this project intact, so I could concentrate on writing. I owe special thanks also to my friends at A & B Marina in Key West, Florida, for patiently enduring a flurry of packages and phone calls while this book was edited. Thank you all!

Introducing Windows Programming

Whether you're a seasoned veteran or just getting started in Windows programming, it's tough to master the techniques behind features that users take for granted. To be competitive, modern Windows software must take every possible advantage of multitasking, 32-bit code generation, graphics, custom and VBX controls, toolbars, status lines, and a host of other exotic components.

This book can help. Borland C++ 4 (BC4) and the ObjectWindows class library 2.0 (OWL) are designed to help you create reliable 16- and 32-bit Windows applications without wasting months of your time just getting up to speed. In the coming chapters, you learn how to use BC4, and you focus on ObjectWindows techniques for performing tasks that, at the moment, might seem impossibly complex—like how to create a toolbar of icons, how to customize dialogs and controls, how to program a popup menu, how to print text and graphics, how to validate control data, and dozens of other topics.

This is a how-to book with a one-track purpose: to help you save time writing applications with features that Windows users demand. To help you get started, this chapter provides an overview of the ObjectWindows library. The next chapter covers the BC4 integrated development environment (IDE), preparing you for in-depth looks at Windows programming throughout the rest of the book.

In this chapter, you learn:

- Different approaches to solving the complexity problem in Windows development.
- Why a class library can simplify writing Windows software.
- How to write a simple Windows program.
- How to construct an application object.
- Types of classes for Windows programming.
- How to use BC4's header files.
- The benefits of encapsulation and inheritance to Windows programming.

> **NOTE**
>
> Please feel free to use the sample listings in this book in any way you wish. *You do not need special permission to incorporate my sample programs into your own compiled code.*

The Complexity Problem

Writing Windows software in straight C or assembly language is possible, of course, but at what cost? Applications such as Microsoft Excel have consumed an estimated *five hundred* combined programmer years in development—an investment that lone developers and small software shops cannot afford.

The solution for most Windows developers is to save time by using third-party libraries and development systems to build applications. The real question then becomes: Which of the many available software tools should you use? A few possible solutions follow.

The Straight C Approach

According to the popular press, C and Windows fit hand in glove. The truth, however, is that *straight C* was never designed to handle the event-driven, highly complex, world of Windows programming. For most developers, it's too time-consuming to write and debug reliable code written in C. As soon as you finish and test your application, some other programmer with more efficient tools might come along and scarf up your customers. How long can you wait to bring your code to market?

The Application Generator Approach

To save time, some developers turn to an *application generator*. Typically, these products create program source code files from selected menu commands, dialogs, controls, and other options. When the source file shell is finished, the developer fills in the blanks with the application's code.

An application generator is a good way to create prototypes, database entry screens, and similar applications in a hurry. All generators, however, have two main failings. First, you still have to write the heart of your program. No application generator can do that for you. Second, when the time comes to upgrade your code, the generator may be unable to help. Experience teaches that automatically generated applications are usually rewritten from scratch at upgrade time. Can you afford to rewrite your program for every new release?

> **NOTE**
>
> BC4 includes the AppExpert application generator, which suffers from the same disadvantages discussed here. AppExpert might be useful in some cases, but I suggest you learn how to program Windows applications from scratch before using AppExpert. That way, you'll have a better appreciation for the generated code, and you stand a better chance of being able to reuse that programming for your program's upgrades. See Chapter 2, "Introducing Borland C++ 4," for more information about AppExpert.

The Visual Plug-and-Play Approach

The *visual programming* approach is highly appealing for some types of applications. Products such as Visual Basic and ToolBook offer plug-and-play objects that interpret instructions when selected, or are linked in some way to other objects and preprogrammed operations.

Visual Basic is suitable for database entry screens, calendars, and similar small-scale utilities. For general-purpose application development, however, the plug-and-play approach doesn't cut the mustard. When performance matters (when doesn't it?), and when you cannot afford to be restricted by the limited range of capabilities offered in a visual programming system, you need powerful tools and a general-purpose development language such as C or C++.

> **NOTE**
>
> BC4 includes classes for interfacing with Visual Basic controls, also called *VBX controls*. With these classes, you can incorporate plug-and-play modules into Windows programs yet still use C++ as your development language. For more information on VBX controls, see Chapter 15, "Putting On the Finishing Touches."

The Class Library Approach

That brings us to what is probably the best approach for Windows programming—using C++ and a class library such as ObjectWindows. This solution offers programmers two key advantages over the preceding methods.

One, C++ classes model the Windows architecture far better than straight C. A window class, for example, *encapsulates* data and functions. *The class automatically takes care of internal requirements that you have to provide explicitly in C.* In addition to encapsulation, by using *response tables,* class member functions can respond directly to Windows messages, simplifying the difficult task of writing code for an event-driven operating system.

Two, a class library such as OWL provides an *application framework* on which you build programs. Through *inheritance,* you derive new classes based on those that BC4 provides to which you add the capabilities you need. With C++, you *reuse existing code,* which saves development time, minimizes debugging, and improves your application's reliability.

OWL isn't the only Windows class library on the market. Some products such as the Microsoft Foundation Class Library provide *wrapper classes* that serve as stand-ins for Windows functions. Wrapper-class libraries make it possible to use C++ rather than straight C for Windows programming, but they offer little or no savings in development and debugging time. OWL has wrapper classes, and it also provides a framework that helps direct, mold, and shape application design.

Other products offer single-source compilation for different operating systems. You can purchase a library, for example, with identical classes that target the Macintosh and Windows operating systems. Unfortunately, you pay a high price in lost performance for this level of compatibility. Functions in multiplatform libraries must be translated into low-level subroutine calls for Macintosh and Windows, which wastes time. OWL makes *direct* calls to the Windows API (application programming interface). Many such calls are compiled as inline statements—not, in other words, as nested subroutines. Because of BC4's extensive use of inline code, using the library adds practically no appreciable runtime overhead to the final application. Many expert programmers claim that because a class library helps organize programs more efficiently, the final program usually performs better than straight code written from scratch. That's a difficult claim to prove, but those who are familiar with OWL generally confirm that using a class library does not necessarily degrade runtime performance, which you can expect with interpreted languages such as Visual Basic.

> **NOTE**
>
> OWL 2.0 is written to conform to the latest ANSI C++ standard, raising the possibility that future editions of OWL will be available for other operating systems. So far, OWL is available only for Windows, but it stands to reason that Borland didn't insist on OWL's ANSI C++ compatibility for no reason at all.

Say Hello to ObjectWindows 2.0

That's enough background for now. A sample program demonstrates some of the advantages of using a class library to program Windows applications. Listing 1.1, HOWL.CPP (*Hello OWL*), is the ObjectWindows equivalent of the "hello world" example traditionally used to introduce C programming. Compile and run the listing to say "Hello to OWL programming." Figure 1.1 shows HOWL's display.

FIGURE 1.1.
HOWL's display.

> **NOTE**
>
> There are two ways to compile and run HOWL.CPP. Using the BC4 integrated environment, switch to the HOWL directory, open the HOWL.IDE project, and

press Ctrl+F9. Or, from a DOS prompt, change to the HOWL directory and type **make**, then use the File Manager to select HOWL.EXE. Compile and run all of this book's sample programs in the same way. *Remember, to compile programs in the IDE, you must open their .IDE project files.* If you have trouble compiling programs, see Appendix A, "Compilation Instructions," for help.

Listing 1.1. HOWL.CPP.

```
#include <owl\applicat.h>

int
OwlMain(int argc, char* argv[]) {
  TApplication app("Hello World from OWL 2.0!");
  return app.Run();
}
```

Though simple-minded, HOWL.CPP demonstrates four key elements found in every Windows program:

- An #include directive refers to a header file such as APPLICAT.H. There are many such headers located in the OWL subdirectory in the compiler's default include-file path (usually C:\BC4\INCLUDE). To use OWL classes, simply include the headers that declare them.

- The OwlMain function receives the same two arguments that a standard C program's main function receives. Also like main, OwlMain returns an int value (written above the function name in the style that many C++ programmers prefer). Parameter argc of type int indicates the number of command line arguments passed to the program. Parameter argv, a character-pointer array, addresses those arguments as null-terminated strings. The expression argv[0] addresses the program's name, argv[1] addresses the first string argument, argv[2] addresses the second, and so on.

- OwlMain defines an *application object* of the TApplication class. The application object encapsulates the entire application—there is only one TApplication object in a program. You can initialize the object with a string for the program's main window title, but as you will learn, there are other, and probably better, ways to construct application objects. The method shown here, however, is handy for quick demos and tests.

● OwlMain calls the application's Run member function to activate the program's message loop. At this point, the program leaves its startup phase and enters normal operation. Chapter 3, "Starting Up and Shutting Down," discusses operations you can perform during an application's early moments, and also explains what happens when the program ends. The Run function returns an integer status value that OwlMain returns.

Unused Arguments

When you compile HOWL.CPP, you may notice two warning messages that tell you argc and argv are not used in OwlMain. Normally, the compiler tells you when a function defines but does not use an argument or variable. Not using a defined variable wastes memory, but not using a variable that has to be declared anyway because of OWL's design is a minor problem that you can safely ignore.

For your own functions, when you receive an unused argument warning, you probably should delete the unused parameter or other variable. When using supplied functions such as OwlMain, though, the arguments are passed to the functions whether the code uses the parameters or not. In that case, you have two options: ignore the warning or disable it by inserting this line above OwlMain:

```
#pragma argsused
```

The #pragma argsused directive disables the compiler's warning about *unused arguments*, but only for the next function. You can also disable the warning by surrounding selected function parameters with comment brackets:

```
int
OwlMain(int /*argc*/, char* /*argv*/[])
```

That's usually better because it makes you account for the use of each parameter. The #pragma option affects *all* unused parameters and variables in the function. Sample programs in this book use both techniques.

A Shorter *OwlMain*

It's possible to shorten OwlMain in HOWL.CPP to one statement, a technique you may see in other published OWL programs (most notably, for example, BC4's example OWL applications). OwlMain can create and execute a TApplication object, and call its Run member function, with this lone statement:

```
return TApplication("Hello World from OWL 2.0!").Run();
```

To try the alternate code, replace OwlMain's two statements with that one. It constructs a temporary TApplication object on the stack, calls its Run member function, and returns that function's result. The object is automatically destroyed when OwlMain ends.

There's no advantage of the single-line method over that shown in Listing 1.1—I prefer the longer method of constructing objects and then using them. The single-line method is tricky, and it provides no practical benefits. Sample programs in this book use the longer, and more readable, technique shown in HOWL.CPP.

Module-Definition Files

Windows programs are rarely composed of a single file such as HOWL.CPP. Even this simple example, for instance, uses a *module-definition file*, which specifies linker options that affect the type of module created, and that configure some module settings. Listing 1.2, HOWL.DEF, lists the sample program's module-definition file.

Listing 1.2. HOWL.DEF.

```
EXETYPE WINDOWS
CODE PRELOAD MOVEABLE DISCARDABLE
DATA PRELOAD MOVEABLE MULTIPLE
HEAPSIZE 4096
STACKSIZE 8192
```

BC4 does not require a module-definition file to create Windows applications and libraries. If you don't specify a .DEF file, the linker uses a default file, a fact the linker also warns you about. You also can select linker settings by using IDE commands.

> **NOTE**
>
> BC4's default module-definition file, DEFAULT.DEF, is located in the C:\BC4\LIB directory.

Even so, module-definition files have many possible settings—too many to explain fully in this introduction. Some options differ depending on whether you are creating a 16- or a 32-bit program, and many options won't make any sense until you learn about the associated programming, so I'll skip a complete overview here. For more information about module-definition files, look them up in the BC4 User's Guide. Following, however, are some notes about options you may want to use now.

The first line of a module-definition file for 16-bit applications (32-bit programs don't need this) is always:

```
EXETYPE WINDOWS
```

There is only one type of executable code file for 16-bit Windows, so there aren't any other options in the EXETYPE statement. The next line in the file is usually a CODE statement, which has the following syntax:

```
CODE
  [FIXED¦MOVEABLE]
  [DISCARDABLE¦NONDISCARDABLE]
  [PRELOAD¦LOADONCALL]
```

The brackets indicate items that are optional. (All the ones shown here are optional, but of course, if you didn't include any settings, there'd be no reason to have a CODE statement.) The vertical bar means "or." So, you can specify a CODE segment to be either FIXED or MOVEABLE, but not both. The CODE statements options are:

- FIXED—Segment remains at a fixed address.*
- MOVEABLE—Segment can be moved to make room in memory.*
- DISCARDABLE—Segment can be swapped out of memory to make room.
- NONDISCARDABLE—Segment cannot be swapped.
- PRELOAD—Segment is loaded into memory when application is executed.
- LOADONCALL—Segment is loaded into memory only when an item in the segment is referenced.

> **NOTE**
>
> The FIXED and MOVEABLE settings have little meaning in the world of 386-enhanced, protected-mode execution, in which segments can be moved but still *appear* to be fixed for the purposes of calling functions, referring to variables, and so on. There's practically no reason to use the FIXED setting. You might as well make code segments MOVEABLE—they are anyway.

The 32-bit linker, TLINK32, recognizes only the PRELOAD and LOADONCALL code segment settings. It also recognizes two others:

- EXECUTEONLY—Segment can be executed.
- EXECUTEREAD—Segment can be executed and read (by another process, for example).

A DATA statement in a module-definition file specifies attributes for a program or library's data segments. The DATA statement has the following syntax:

```
DATA
   [NONE|SINGLE|MULTIPLE]
   [READONLY|READWRITE]
   [PRELOAD|LOADONCALL]
   [SHARED|NONSHARED]
```

- NONE—No data segment (used only by DLLs).
- SINGLE—Single data segment shared by all processes (the default for DLLs).
- MULTIPLE—Multiple data segments (the default for executable code files).
- READONLY—Data in segment can be read only, not changed.
- READWRITE—Data in segment can be read and changed.
- PRELOAD—Segment is preloaded automatically into memory.*
- LOADONCALL—Segment is loaded into memory when referenced.*
- SHARED—One copy of data segment is shared by all processes (the default for 16-bit DLLs).
- NONSHARED—A copy of the data segment is loaded for each process (the default for applications and for 32-bit DLLs).

> **NOTE**
>
> 32-bit applications linked by TLINK32 ignore the PRELOAD and LOADONCALL options.

A description statement inserts text into a code file, usually to embed a copyright notice. You may insert a DESCRIPTION statement such as the following in a module-definition file.

```
DESCRIPTION 'Copyright (c) 1994 by Your Name'
```

HEAPSIZE and STACKSIZE statements set the size of the local heap and the program's stack. Only an executable code file has a stack—a DLL shares the host application's stack.

A STUB statement inserts a DOS program into the Windows .EXE code file. It is never used for a library. If you don't specify a STUB program, BC4 automatically inserts WINSTUB.EXE into the finished .EXE file. The default file is located in C:\BC4\BIN. From a DOS prompt, switch to that directory, and type WINSTUB to execute the program. On screen, you see the familiar message:

```
This program must be run under Microsoft Windows.
```

Actually, in this case, that's a lie because you just executed WINSTUB from DOS! Seriously, however, the stub is there just to do something if a user attempts to run a Windows program from DOS, which, of course, is a no-no. If you don't like the default message, write your own DOS .EXE file, and specify it in the module-definition file's STUB statement:

```
STUB mystub.exe
```

The stub is supposed to display a message and quit, but some programmers use this trick to create .EXE code files that can run the same program under DOS and Windows. Each part of the dual-purpose code file is still a separate program with its own copies of any library functions and so on.

Other module-definition options include a NAME statement for 32-bit applications, plus EXPORTS and IMPORTS statements for dynamic link libraries, and SEGMENTS for defining multiple segment options. With BC4, and especially when using the integrated development environment, there are easier methods to create 32-bit programs and libraries, so you may never need these settings.

The ObjectWindows Class Library

By the time you reach the end of this book, you will have met most of OWL's many classes, which encompass the following main areas:

- *Windows:* The TWindow class provides a base-class interface to window elements such as dialog boxes, controls, child windows, and others.

- *Frame windows:* The TFrameWindow class, derived from TWindow, is typically used to construct a program's main window object. A TFrameWindow can own a client window that performs the window's visual antics. (Programs that use a dialog as their main window benefit greatly from this arrangement.)

- *MDI windows:* Three classes fully support the multiple document interface (MDI): TMDIFrame, TMDIClient, and TMDIChild. MDI child windows are instances of the TMDIChild class.

- *Graphics classes:* The entire Windows graphics device interface (GDI) is encapsulated in a set of device-context classes such as TClientDC, TPrintDC, TPaintDC, and others. To draw in a window, or to print text and graphics, you simply construct a device-context object and call a member function in reference to that object.

- *GDI object classes:* All objects such as pens, brushes, color palettes, fonts, icons, cursors, bitmaps, and others have associated GDI classes. A Windows pen is an object of the TPen class; a brush is a TBrush instance, and so on. To use these items, you first select them into a device context object. Next, you call class member functions that output graphics using the selected tools. Because the device context *knows* about the graphics objects it owns, the context automatically deletes objects when you are done using them, a feature that helps reduce memory leaks caused by failing to delete pens and brushes—common problems in conventional Windows programs.

- *Decorated windows:* These classes simplify programming toolbars, status lines, and other *window decorations.* Define a window's layout with `TLayoutWindow` and `TLayoutMetrics`. Insert self-adjusting client windows with `TDecoratedFrame` and `TDecoratedMDIFrame`. Add *tiled gadgets* with `TGadgetWindow` and `TGadget`. All of these classes dress up windows with features especially appreciated by power users.

- *Dialog boxes:* The `TDialog` class interfaces with Windows dialogs designed as resources with *Resource Workshop* or in *resource script files.* `TDialog`'s *data transfer mechanism* makes it easy to copy information to and from dialog controls.

- *Common dialogs:* These classes provide class interfaces for all common Windows dialogs. These classes include file choosers (`TOpenSaveDialog`, `TFileOpenDialog`, and `TFileSaveDialog`), a font selector (`TChooseFontDialog`), a color picker (`TChooseColorDialog`), a printing options interface (`TPrintDialog`), and three search-and-replace prompters (`TFindReplaceDialog`, `TFindDialog`, and `TReplaceDialog`).

- *Control classes:* The `TControl` class constructs control objects that simplify communicating with control elements in windows. OWL 2.0 offers three types of controls: standard Windows controls, Widgets (custom sliders, for example, written entirely in C++), and decoration controls (toolbars and status lines). OWL 2.0 also supports 16- and 32-bit versions of Borland Windows Custom Controls (BWCC) as well as Microsoft 3-D controls.

- *Printing classes:* `TPrinter` and `TPrintout` perform single and multipage printing. You never have to use archaic (and cranky) Windows "escapes" for printing text and graphics.

- *Module and application classes:* `TModule` forms the basis for the `TApplication` class, which encapsulates the application's global functions such as startup tasks, message loops, and error handling. The `TDll` class provides a similar base for developing dynamic link libraries (DLL).

- *Document and view classes:* Classes `TDocManager`, `TDocument`, and `TView` provide a document-view model that molds data for input and output purposes. In simple terms, these classes make it possible to design I/O services that function independently of the accessed information. You can associate any number of views with a specific document—representing graphics visually, for example, or as a list of coordinate values that can be edited as text.

● *Other classes:* OWL is peppered with miscellaneous classes. TRect and TPoint simplify display-coordinate handling. Menu classes help you create dynamic and popup menus. The TClipboard class simplifies passing information to and from the Windows clipboard. Validation classes facilitate prompting for and verifying formatted data.

● *VBX classes:* Use these classes to access Visual Basic controls, fast becoming the standard in plug-and-play object programming. VBX classes let you take advantage of "smart" controls, but still use C++ to develop your application.

● *Class library:* Borland's container class library has also been completely revised, and is now entirely template based. (For an introduction to C++ templates, see my forthcoming book, *Mastering Borland C++ 4.*) OWL 1.0 used a similar, but less versatile, object-class library. OWL 2.0 uses only the newer template container and string classes. I discuss these classes as needed by this book's sample programs.

Header Files

Like all programming libraries in C and C++, OWL's declarations are stored in *header files* such as APPLICAT.H and WINDOW.H. Most headers names resemble their declared classes. The TGadget class, for example, is declared in the header file GADGET.H. (The T in the class name stands for *Type.*)

OWL header files are stored in the OWL subdirectory, located in the default INCLUDE path where standard headers such as STDIO.H and STDLIB.H are found, usually C:\BC4\INCLUDE. Specify this directory with a command-line -I option, or by using BC4's *Options\Project...* command and selecting *Directories* from the *Topics* list. Installing BC4 automatically sets the default directories for the integrated development environment and command line tools. Unless you rename your BC4 directory (never a wise move), you should be able to compile all of this book's sample programs without having to change default directory settings.

To reduce the number of individual paths the compiler searches, rather than add OWL's directory to the list of default paths, specify the OWL path name in the #include directive:

```
#include <owl\gadget.h>
```

Most OWL source files have numerous such directives for each class (or class category) the program uses. It's also possible to include all OWL classes with a single directive:

```
#include <owl\owlall.h>
```

The OWLALL.H file is the Superman of OWL headers. It makes every class available, but it also takes a long time to compile. Including OWLALL.H might save compilation time for large applications that use *precompiled headers* (binary representations of header files stored in .CSM *compiled symbol* files). Small applications and demonstrations, however, such as those in this book, should include individual headers as needed. You might also include a subset of commonly OWL used classes with the following directive, which also works well with precompiled headers:

```
#include <owl\owlcore.h>
```

To include a standard header, because those files are stored in the default path, just specify the header name prefaced with no path:

```
#include <stdlib.h>
```

To use a container class, include a header from the CLASSLIB subdirectory. This, for example, makes array containers available to the program:

```
#include <classlib\arrays.h>
```

The ANSI C++ `string` class, fully supported by BC4 and OWL, is part of the standard C++ library. To use this class, include its header, CSTRING.H, from the default include path:

```
#include <cstring.h>
```

The standard C null-terminated string library, containing functions such as `strlen` and `strcpy`, is still available. The `string` class is compatible with these time tested subroutines, and you may use the class and standard string functions in the same program. Include the standard string functions with the directive

```
#include <string.h>
```

Don't confuse CSTRING.H and STRING.H. The former (CSTRING.H) declares the ANSI C++ `string` class. The latter (STRING.H) declares null-terminated (also called C-style) string functions that address character data with `char*` pointers. You may use either or both of these headers and string types.

Encapsulation and Inheritance

For writing object-oriented Windows programs, your primary programming tools are *encapsulation* and *inheritance*. Almost every operation you program in a Windows application will make use of these C++ object-oriented programming techniques.

This isn't the time or place for a course in C++. Understanding encapsulation and inheritance, however, is critical to your success with OWL. The next two sections go over some key points as a refresher course. (C++ experts should at least skim this material.)

Encapsulation

A class encapsulates data members and member functions. They are called *members* to distinguish them from data and functions outside of a class.

The `TApplication` class is a good example of encapsulation. Create an instance of the class, also called a *class object*, like this:

```
TApplication app("Window Title");
```

The app object encapsulates data and functions for a Windows application. To obtain a data member from the object, you normally call a member function that returns the value you want. For example, if you need the application's instance handle (an integer assigned by Windows that identifies the running application), call the `GetInstance` member function:

```
HINSTANCE hInstance = app.GetInstance();
```

The app object doesn't contain the `GetInstance` function—a common misconception. Rather, the function is defined for all objects of the class. One way to make the concept clearer is to think of GetInstance as a command or a message that is *applied* to the object. You are in effect saying to the app object, "do your GetInstance thing, whatever that may be." You might similarly command another object of the same class.

You can also construct a dynamic instance of a class with the C++ new operator:

```
TApplication* papp = new TApplication("Window Title");
```

If that fails, the statement *throws an exception* that is *caught* by an *exception handler*. In the recent past, all such statements would be followed with a test of papp's value. If papp is null, there wasn't enough memory available for new to construct the requested object, and the program would call an Error function. Because of ANSI C++ exceptions, however, it is pointless to test whether papp is null. With exceptions, the statement either succeeds or an error handler takes over. The next statement can therefore safely assume that the preceding memory allocation was successful.

Programming with exceptions takes care, and if you are new to the subject, you'll find it difficult at first. Chapter 3 explains more about exception handling in C++. For now, just be aware that critical errors are handled by this new technique.

Call class member functions for a dynamic object by using a pointer dereference operator (->):

```
papp->SetName("New Application Name");
```

By the way, for 16-bit programming, you might need to preface literal strings with LPSTR, casting the string's address to a far pointer:

```
papp->SetName((LPSTR)"New Application Name");
```

In 32-bit applications, such casts are not needed because all pointers are far by definition. There are no near (segment and offset) pointers in a 32-bit program.

Encapsulation's main benefit is the elimination of logical errors caused by passing the wrong data to a function. A typical example is a misused window handle. In conventional Windows programs, you obtain a window handle and pass it to an API function. If hWindow represents the window's handle, you might use programming such as:

```
RECT r;
GetClientRect(hWindow, &r);
```

Calling the Windows function GetClientRect fills a RECT structure r with the client area's dimensions—the space inside the window's menu, title bar, and borders. Even simple function calls like that, however, can cause a world of trouble if the program passes the wrong or an *uninitialized* handle argument. OWL virtually eliminates such errors because the window object encapsulates the handle. The preceding code is better written as:

```
TRect r;
winObject.GetClientRect(&r);
```

Rather than RECT, the sample uses the TRect class. Instead of calling the API GetClientRect function, the statement calls the member function of that name for winObject. There is no need to pass the window handle to the function because the handle is encapsulated inside that object.

Many functions such as GetClientRect that accept address-arguments such as &r (the address of r) are overloaded to return a value or reference of that type. The preceding sample code is even safer when written like this:

```
TRect r;
r = winObject.GetClientRect();
```

Or, inside another TFrameWindow (or derived class) function, you can simply call member functions directly:

```
TRect r = GetClientRect();
```

You may still call API functions directly, but to prevent name conflicts, you might have to preface statements with a scope resolution operator:

```
RECT r;
::GetClientRect(hWindow, &r);
```

The :: operator tells the compiler to look in the global scope for GetClientRect. (All API functions are in the global scope.) Whenever possible, this book's sample programs call encapsulated member functions. All direct calls to API functions are prefaced with a scope resolution operator even when unnecessary so you can tell what kind of function is being used in each case.

Inheritance

The second key C++ technique you will use frequently is *inheritance*. To add new operations and data, you derive new classes from supplied classes and insert the data and functions you need. You also override existing member functions, either to replace them completely, or to enhance what they do.

For example, you can create a derived window class like this:

```
class TDerived: public TFrameWindow {
public:
```

```
    TMyClass(TWindow* parent, const char* title);
    // ...
};
```

The new class, TDerived, inherits the data and functions from TFrameWindow, known as the *base class,* or sometimes, the *ancestor class.* TDerived must define a constructor to initialize objects of the class. The constructor is typically implemented something like this:

```
TDerived::TDerived(TWindow* parent, const char* title)
  : TFrameWindow(parent, title),
    TWindow(parent, title)
{
  // ...
}
```

The first line declares the constructor's implementation. The second and third lines call the base class constructors. TFrameWindow is virtually derived from TWindow so that, in cases where a derived class might inherit TWindow from many different paths, only one TWindow object exists in the derived result. This fact means you must call TDerived's immediate base class constructor (TFrameWindow) and also the virtual base class (TWindow).

> **NOTE**
>
> Some classes are abstract; that is, they declare pure virtual member functions that end with = 0. You cannot create objects of an abstract class, which serves as a kind of schematic for designing other classes. You must instead derive a new class using the abstract class as a base and provide finished versions of all pure virtual member functions. The TSlider class, for example, is an abstract class. To use it, you must derive a new class from TSlider and provide implementations for each pure virtual member function.

A derived class usually overrides inherited virtual member functions. For example, all classes derived from TWindow or TFrameWindow inherit a member function declared as

```
virtual BOOL CanClose();
```

The program calls CanClose to determine whether it is safe to close a window. Normally, CanClose returns true. To replace the existing function with a new model that returns false—if a file is still open, for instance—derive a class from TFrameWindow and override the virtual function (shown in bold here):

```
2class TDerived: public TFrameWindow {
  BOOL fileIsOpen;  // True if file is open
```

```
public:
  TMyClass(TWindow* parent, const char* title);
  virtual BOOL CanClose();
  // ...
};
```

Implement the replacement CanClose function to return false if the fileIsOpen flag indicates a file is open, in which case the window must not be permitted to close (assume this flag is set by other member functions in the class):

```
BOOL
TDerived::CanClose()
{
  if fileIsOpen {
    // display error message
    return FALSE;
  } else
    return TRUE;
}
```

Users are now forced to save their work before they can close the window. Best of all, you programmed that feature without having to consider the many possible ways in which a window might be closed. You can be confident that the class *always* calls CanClose to determine if it is safe to close the window, so there's no need to track down all events that might cause that to happen. You simply override functions and trust classes to perform as expected.

Looking Ahead

In the next chapter, you tour BC4's integrated development environment—a necessary first step before digging more deeply into Windows programming. If you pick up new software commands easily, you can probably skim Chapter 2 and then turn to Chapter 3.

Introducing
Borland C++ 4

Before digging deeper into Windows programming with Borland C++, you need to take a side trip into BC4's many commands and features. This chapter gives tips and suggestions for using the integrated development environment (IDE), text editor, built-in and external debuggers, project manager, and the AppExpert automatic application generator. This chapter also introduces command-line compilers, linkers, and other tools.

In this chapter, you learn:

- IDE commands and tools.
- How to create and use projects.
- Configuration options.
- 16- and 32-bit code generation.
- How to create resources using Resource Workshop.
- How to create resources using resource script files.
- Automatic application generation with AppExpert and ClassExpert.

- Command-line compilation techniques.
- How to build Windows applications with the Make utility.
- Debugging and browsing techniques using the IDE and command-line Turbo Debuggers.

HINT

BC4 comes with extensive online help. Select any item and press F1, or use the commands in the *Help* menu and follow instructions on screen. You may also want to install the Acrobat Reader, from Adobe Systems Incorporated, which is supplied on CD-ROM with the BC4 development system. You can then browse, search, and view most of the printed BC4 reference manuals on your computer.

Integrated Development Environment

If you have used Borland's IDEs before, you'll be *almost* right at home in the BC4 environment. There are many similarities to past versions, but there are also dozens of new features to master. The most important difference is that BC4's IDE requires Microsoft Windows—this is the first Borland compiler that does not come with a DOS-based editor. You must have Windows to run BC4's IDE. Continue reading this section for configuration tips and some options you might want to select.

Parts and Pieces

Figure 2.1 shows the BC4 integrated display. You can probably figure out most commands on your own—you don't need me to tell you what *File|Open...* does. Rather than go through each command in reference style, then, I'll discuss only the IDE features that may have less than obvious purposes.

If you want to follow along, you must have installed Borland's example listings. If you have not installed them, do that now. Then, start BC4 and select the *Project|Open project...* command. Change to this directory (be sure to select the OWLAPPS—not the OWLAPI—subdirectory):

```
C:\BC4\EXAMPLES\OWL\OWLAPPS\MDIFILE
```

You should see the file MDIFILE.IDE in the window pane at left. (MDI stands for *multiple document interface.*) Select MDIFILE.IDE. (Highlight the name and press Enter, click OK, or double-click the name.) Opening an IDE project file creates a *Project* window, illustrated at the bottom of Figure 2.1. Inside the project window are all the files associated with the application. To open one of the files, select it in one of these ways:

- Cursor to the file and press Enter.

- Point to the filename and double-click the left mouse button.

- Point to the filename and click the right mouse button to open a popup window. Select the *View* command to open a subwindow, then select a method for viewing the file's information.

FIGURE 2.1.

The Borland C++ 4.0 IDE.

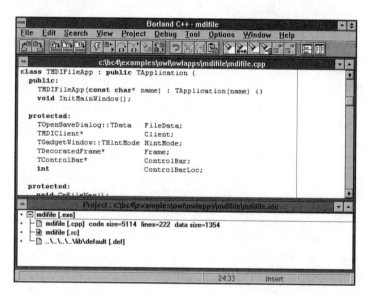

Try the first or second method to open MDIFILE.CPP. These are the easiest ways to open text files in a project. Use *Window\Tile horizontal* to position the windows as shown in Figure 2.1. After opening the file, you can switch to its window and edit the text. I won't go into the IDE's text editing commands here. You can easily pick them up by trial and error and by browsing BC4's documentation. The commands for inserting, cutting, pasting, and performing other jobs are standard Windows issue.

HINT

If you prefer a different key arrangement, select the *Options*/*Environment...* command, set *Topics* to *Editor,* and select one of the *Editor SpeedSettings* at mid-screen. Or, highlight *Editor* and click the plus sign (or press the spacebar) to see more options for this category. Select one of the listed options and choose the individual features you want. For example, I select 2-space indents and no embedded tabs. Under *Editor|Display*, I select *BRIEF Cursor Shapes*, which gives me an underbar cursor. Feel free to experiment with other options. You might want to spend a moment customizing *Syntax Highlighting*, one of the IDE's most attractive features. Click or press the spacebar on that topic's plus sign, then select *Customize*. You can select and color individual syntax elements as you like. Watch out, though. It's easy to waste hours getting the display "just right!" For the time being, you might want to select one of the factory-supplied options in the *Syntax Highlighting* dialog. My favorite is *Classic*, but at night, I sometimes switch to *Twilight* to reduce my screen's brightness.

Views

Switch back to the *Project* window (just click anywhere inside the window, or press Ctrl+F6 to view successive windows until the window you want becomes active.) Use the cursor keys to highlight the MDIFILE.RC resource script file, but don't open that file yet. (If you do that accidentally, Resource Workshop runs. Wait a moment, then quit RW to continue.) Click the right mouse button or press Alt+F10 to open a popup menu of local commands that you can apply to this selected entry.

There are several possible choices. You can add new project *nodes,* build selected nodes (rather than build the entire project), compile resource files, and select a host of project manager options, some of which I cover later in this chapter. The popup menu's commands change for different types of files. Try it, for example, on the .EXE and .CPP project window entries.

You may want to view specific kinds of files in different ways. For example, to edit the MDIFILE.RC script file as ASCII text, highlight the filename in the project manager window, click the right mouse button (or press Alt+F10), select the *View* command from the local popup menu, and choose *Text Edit*. That opens MDIFILE.RC in an IDE text editor window.

At other times, you might want to open MDIFILE.RC as a resource file, using Resource Workshop (RW) to edit bitmaps, construct menus interactively, and perform other resource magic. To open MDIFILE.RC in RW, select the filename in the project window as before, then use the *View|Edit Resource* command, or highlight the file and press Enter. In a moment, you should see the compiled resources in RW. When you are done fooling around, exit RW, which returns you to the IDE.

Compiling Projects

To compile and run a project, open its .IDE file and press Ctrl+F9. Or, you can compile using one of the following alternate methods, then run the program using the File Manager, or drag its .EXE code file to a Program Manager window and select the icon.

> **WARNING**
>
> Never use the *File/Open...* command to open a project's .IDE file. Doing that and then saving the file as text permanently damages the project file. Always use the *Project/Open project...* command to open .IDE files.

Try these methods. First, open the *Project* menu, then:

- choose *Compile* (or press Alt+F9) to compile the project, but not run the resulting .EXE file,

- or, choose *Project\Make all* (or press F9) to compile out of date files only, saving time by recompiling only the files you modified,

- or, choose *Project\Build all* (no equivalent key) to recompile every file, whether necessary or not. You might use this command to rebuild an application just before release.

> **HINT**
>
> You can also use the IDE's speedbar buttons to compile, make, and build applications (see Figure 2.1). The three buttons under the *Edit* and *Search* menus correspond to the preceding three *Project* commands. Select the lightning symbol to "Make and run" the current project.

Configurations

In addition to selecting editor features, you can also choose from an overwhelming list of compiler and linker options. Your BC4 reference manuals and online help files list every option with (mostly) clear descriptions. Some options you may want to select for the sample programs in this book include the following:

- Select *Options\Project...* and choose one of several *Topics* to configure. (Hint: If you have trouble compiling programs, make sure the Include and Library directories are set correctly. All supplied projects assume you installed the compiler in C:\BC4.)

- Note the descriptions of each outer-level topic that appear in the large window pane. Scan each of these for an overview of the project options you can select.

- Topics preceded by plus signs have sublevels that you can open by clicking the plus symbol or by highlighting the topic and pressing the spacebar. After you open a topic, its plus sign changes to minus. Click the minus sign or press the spacebar to collapse a topic's sublevels.

- I prefer to use the large memory model for my programs, though other choices might be okay for most programs in this book. To select a memory model, open the *16-bit Compiler* topic, choose *Memory Model,* and select one of the radio buttons labeled *Tiny, Small, Medium, Compact, Large,* or *Huge.* OWL programs may use only *Small, Medium,* or *Large* memory models. There are no memory models selections for 32-bit applications, which are capable of using all available memory.

- You might also want to choose *80386* or *i486* for the *16-bit Compiler* topic's *Processor* options. It may also be a good idea to select *Word* data alignment to place byte-size data at even addresses. This can help improve runtime speeds of some types of programs.

- Under *Optimizations,* you'll see the button *Disable all optimizations.* Make sure this button is selected—it simplifies debugging, and it enables the compiler to run as fast as possible. For your own programs, you may want to begin debugging optimized code when the program nears completion. In a project's early stages, however, and for the sample programs in this book, it's best not to use any optimizations.

- For most projects, you should enable *precompiled headers* to save compilation time. Select *Options\Project...,* open the *Compiler* topic, and highlight *Precompiled headers.* Toggle on the *Generate and use* option for the programs in this book. Toggle *Use but do not generate* if you have a precompiled header file (perhaps generated by compiling a program that includes OWLALL.H) that you want the compiler to use, but not recreate. Toggle the third option, *Do not generate or use,* to disable precompiled headers. When enabled, precompiled headers store header file declarations in binary .CSM (compiled symbol) files for fast loading. These files take lots of disk space—several megabytes per project is typical—but greatly speed compilation. You can also specify a filename in which to store precompiled headers, but it's usually just as well to let the IDE name the file for you.

Insert the command `#pragma hdrstop` after the last header `#include` directive you want to add to the precompiled header file. For example, you might use these directives in a source code file:

```
#include <owl\applicat.h>
#pragma hdrstop
#include "filename.h"
```

That places APPLICAT.H into the precompiled .CSM header file, but not the program's FILENAME.H header. Any changes to FILENAME.H do not cause the compiler to regenerate the precompiled header file, saving time, especially in programs that use many headers. Without the `#pragma` directive, a change to FILENAME.H will cause the compiler to recreate the precompiled header file even though APPLICAT.H hasn't changed. Using `#pragma hdrstop` can also help trim .CSM precompiled header files to more reasonable sizes.

It is difficult—if not impossible—to recommend a set of IDE options that will suit all readers. Plan to set aside some time to experiment with the effects of various options on this book's sample programs. You can use the *Options* menu to set default options for all projects. Or, open any .IDE file, select the .EXE (or other) node in the project window, and use the local popup menu's *Edit local options...* to select options for an individual project entry.

When BC4 is not running, you can double-click any .IDE file in the File Manager to start BC4 and open a project. Or, you also can drag .IDE files to a Program Manager window, and then select them. Unfortunately, BC4 isn't smart enough to close an existing project when it receives a command to open another. If BC4 is already running, you must use the *Project* menu to open .IDE projects.

16- and 32-Bit Code Generation

To generate 32-bit applications, highlight the project's .EXE file (MDIFILE.EXE if you are following along). Open the local menu (click the right mouse button or press Alt+F10), and choose *TargetExpert*. A *target* represents the type of application you want to create. For a 32-bit code file, change *Platform* in the *TargetExpert* dialog to *Win32*. Close the dialog, and rebuild. What could be easier?

A Win32 project creates an .EXE code file that can run natively under Windows NT and also as a 32-bit application under Windows 3.1 with the help of the Win32s NT subset, provided with BC4 along with a sample 32-bit application, FreeCell, a solitaire card game. (This book would have been published earlier if I hadn't wasted so many hours playing that game!) The Win32s files and demonstration program are the same as those packed with Microsoft's 32-bit Windows software development kit (SDK). Win32s *extends* Windows 3.1, adding the ability to run NT Win32 applications. With BC4, you have all you need to create 32-bit applications—you do not need the SDK.

If you are confused by all this business of 16- and 32-bit Windows, Windows NT, and Win32s development, take some comfort in the fact that you are in good company. Actually, though, the choices are simpler than you might think. There are only two kinds of Windows applications: 16-bit code files that run natively under Windows 3.1 (and as tasks in Windows NT), or 32-bit code files that run natively under Windows NT (or in Windows 3.1 using Win32s extensions). There is no such thing as a Win32s application.

Before compiling 32-bit code, however, be sure you need to do that. Don't make the common mistake of assuming that 32-bit programs automatically run faster than their 16-bit counterparts. Good reasons to generate 32-bit applications include the following:

- Your program already relies heavily on 32-bit integer values (long variables, for example) that would benefit from being stored in 32-bit registers. Storing 16-bit integer values in 32-bit registers is wasteful and produces no increase in performance.

- Your program makes relatively few API function calls—that is, most of your program's critical code is internal to your application. Win32s add an additional "thunking" layer to function calls, translating many API calls to their 16-bit equivalents, wasting time that you can otherwise save by calling those same functions directly.

- Your program uses large data structures that would benefit from a flat memory model. All addresses and pointers in 32-bit programs are *far*. There are no *near* pointers in 32-bit code. There is no need to select an appropriate memory model, as there is in a 16-bit application.

- Your program does not use a lot of floating point math, and it does not depend on a math coprocessor. Math coprocessor instructions are the same for 16- and 32-bit programs. Programs that spend most of their time executing math coprocessor instructions gain little when compiled for 32-bit operation.

- Your program will be executed only under Windows NT. 32-bit code runs more efficiently than 16-bit code under NT.

- You want to take advantage of new API functions available only to Windows NT programs.

The most important rule is: *Don't create 32-bit applications just because they are the latest rage.* The results may not be as good as you expect. Here are some poor reasons to generate 32-bit applications:

- You have heard that 32-bit code automatically runs twice as fast as 16-bit code. This is not true. Programs that use 16-bit values gain nothing by storing those values in 32-bit registers.

- You have heard that Windows NT will replace Windows 3.1. This is unlikely. Windows NT is expected to capture only 10 to 20 percent of the total Windows market. A future version of Windows, code-named *Chicago,* is expected to replace DOS 6 and Windows 3.x sometime in 1995.

- You have heard that preemptive multitasking in Windows NT eliminates bugs in Windows 3.1. This is wishful thinking. All software has bugs, including Windows NT. Programs can and do run correctly in a nonpreemptive operating system such as Windows 3.1. BC4 is a good example.

Project Manager

As you have seen, a project lists the various components of a Windows application. Project files, ending in .IDE, also store options for the project and for its individual nodes. Some projects might have only a few files; others can have dozens of component nodes. You add, edit, and subtract nodes, and specify their attributes, using the IDE's project manager.

The next few paragraphs describe the steps for creating a new project from scratch—a good way to learn how to use the IDE project manager, which differs greatly from Borland and Turbo C++ project managers in past compiler versions. (Project files originally began as plain text files that listed a project's filenames, and until BC4's release, .PRJ was the default filename extension.) To try some project features, start BC4, then follow these steps (some selections affect other choices, so do these in order until you know your way around):

- Create a temporary, empty directory to hold the project files. I'll use C:\PROJECT, but any other name will do just fine. Create the directory using the File Manager, or type an MD command from a DOS prompt.

- In the BC4 IDE, use the *Project|Close project* command to close the current project. Also use the *Window* menu to close any windows that may be open.

● Select *Project\New project...*, which brings up an extensive *New Project* dialog box listing various options. Select the *Browse* button, and change to C:\PROJECT (or another directory). Click inside the *File Name* input box, and enter **myproj** (or whatever you want to call your program). Usually, the project's target name should be the name of your application—the same as the filename of its main module. The IDE automatically adds .IDE to the project filename. Close the *Browse* dialog by clicking the OK button. This returns you to the *New Project* window.

● Choose one of six target types for your application. Table 2.1 lists the types of projects you may create.

Table 2.1. Project target types.

Target type	Extension	Description
Application	.EXE	Builds a Windows application. Most of the programs in this book use this setting.
Dynamic Library	.DLL	Builds a dynamic link library (DLL) containing functions, data, and resources that multiple applications can share.
EasyWin	.EXE	Builds an EasyWin application that runs in a text-only window. Use this target to run sample programs from C or C++ tutorials, and for short tests that do not need to be fully equipped Windows applications. Only standard input and output functions may be used. Special text mode commands (such as declared in CONIO.H) and graphics (such as in GRAPHICS.H) are not allowed in EasyWin programs.
Static Library	.LIB	Builds a static library of .OBJ files. This can help speed compilation of large programs by opening a single file rather than dozens of separate .OBJ files. You don't need this option for the programs in this book.
Import Library	.LIB	Builds an import library used by a dynamic link library.
Windows Help	.HLP	Builds an online Windows help file.

- Under *Standard Libraries,* choose OWL for all ObjectWindows programs. Because OWL programs use the Borland container class and standard runtime libraries, these two items are selected automatically for OWL applications. Select *BWCC* only if your program uses Borland Custom Controls. (You can add BWCC controls later, so leave the option unchecked if you are unsure.)

> **TIP**
>
> Select standard libraries from top to bottom. For example, deselect *OWL* to enable the *Class library* setting. Deselect *that* setting to enable the *Runtime* option.

- Just below *Standard Libraries,* choose **Dynamic** to use the dynamic link library forms of OWL, the container class library, and the standard runtime library. Choose **Static** to insert the compiled library code directly into your program's .EXE code files. For this book's programs, select *Dynamic* to save disk space. Select *Static* for production code unless you are prepared to distribute and properly install the library .DLL files in your customers' WINDOWS\SYSTEM directory.

- With **Dynamic** libraries selected, you may use only the Large memory model for 16-bit applications. With *Static* selected, you may select among small, medium, compact, and large models, unless you are writing OWL programs, which cannot use the compact model. Try various settings to see the models available for different targets and libraries. Non-OWL *Win32* applications may choose between *GUI* (graphical user interface) and *Console* (text mode) target models. OWL *Win32* applications must run in *GUI* mode. Unless you are creating Windows NT applications, however, you should select *GUI* for all *Win32* applications. The Windows 3.x Win32s subset cannot run console-mode 32-bit applications.

> **TIP**
>
> Statically linked OWL code files are much larger than those that use dynamic libraries, but they load faster because it takes time to read and initialize DLLs. To have the best of both worlds, run a small application such as HOWL.EXE from Chapter 1, shrink it to an icon, and leave it on the Windows desktop while you compile and run other sample programs from this book. This trick keeps OWL, container, and runtime DLLs in memory, greatly improving startup times of applications that use these libraries, while conserving disk space.

Finally, after selecting your project's features, you may now select the *New Project* dialog's OK button to create the new project. A project window opens, showing the nodes illustrated in Figure 2.2.

FIGURE 2.2.

A newly created project.

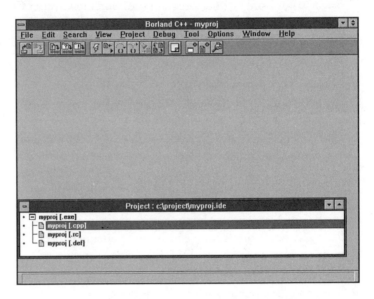

Starting a new project does not create any files in the current directory. It is still your job to create .CPP, .RC, .DEF, and other files for your program's source code, resources, and other components. (The AppExpert application generator extends the project manager, and in addition, creates source code and other files for new projects—but more on that later.)

After creating a new project, you can select the .CPP and other files to begin typing your program's commands. Or, you can do what most Windows programmers do—copy common parts and pieces from another application and use the *Search* menu's commands to replace identifiers with your application's name. You can do this before or after creating the new project.

To add a new module to a project, activate the Project window, and click the right mouse button to open the local popup menu, or press Alt+F10. Select *Add node* and choose a file to add, or *Delete node* to remove a project entry. (A dialog box requests confirmation before deleting a node.)

TIP

The Project menu lacks a *Save* command, a strange omission that many developers find disconcerting (me too). The *only* way to save a project is to close it. I suggest you do that immediately after creating or editing a project!

Resources

Resources are binary data elements stored inside a program's .EXE file. Menu commands, for example, are constructed as resources that the program loads at runtime. Resources save time by reducing the amount of setup work a program has to perform, and they also conserve memory because the binary resources remain on disk until needed.

Using a resource editor such as *Resource Workshop* (RW), supplied with BC4, you design your program's resources as you would paint a picture, edit a word processor document, or draw an architectural diagram. RW is an *interactive* resource editor—what you see on screen is what your final resources will look like in the finished application. Figure 2.3 shows RW editing an icon resource.

FIGURE 2.3.

Resource Workshop icon editor.

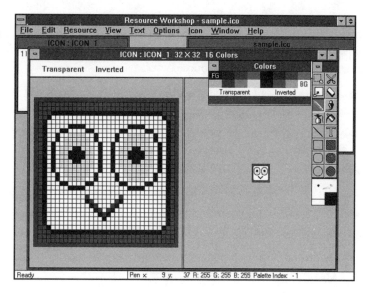

33

You can also use the BC4 text editor (or RW) to create *resource script files,* ending in .RC. A resource script file contains ASCII text commands that describe resource elements—much in the same way that C++ source code statements describe a program's actions and data. Resource script files provide the source code for binary resources. To use a resource script file, you compile it to a binary file ending in .RES, which is then linked into the application's .EXE code file. The resources are then loaded into memory from the .EXE code file when the program needs them.

> **TIP**
>
> Resource Workshop and BC4 can compile .RC resource scripts directly to binary form and combine the resulting resources into an application's .EXE code file. Just add the .RC filename to the project window, and BC4 will issue the necessary commands. The entire process is more complicated to describe than it is to use!

The next sections give hints for using Resource Workshop and for working with resource script files. You'll meet these subjects again throughout this book as you learn how to use different types of Windows resources.

Resource Workshop

Borland's Resource Workshop can create and edit all types of Windows resources. RW knows about the following resource types:

- *Accelerators*—Identify accelerator keys, also called *hot keys,* which are typically associated with menu commands.
- *Bitmap*—General purpose bitmaps, either stored directly in resource files, or copied from .BMP bitmap files.
- *Cursor*—Bitmaps used for cursor shapes.
- *Dialog*—Modal and modeless dialog boxes boxes and their controls.
- *Dlginit*—Initialization data for custom dialog box controls.
- *Font*—Raster font patterns.
- *Icon*—Bitmaps used for icon symbols.
- *Menu*—Menus and commands.
- *RCData*—User-defined resource data.
- *StringTable*—Error messages, online hints, and other strings.
- *VersionInfo*—Version and copyright information, typically used by an automatic installation utility and displayed in an about-box dialog.

In addition to those types, you also can create new resource types of your own designs. A *user defined resource* may contain string and integer data in any format. It is the program's responsibility to load a user-defined resource and interpret the data appropriately.

RW uses the term *resource project* to describe all of an application's resources. Simple resource projects might be stored in a single .RC file, but more involved application resources might be stored in several different files. A resource project might include resource script files, bitmap files, icon files, text data files, header files, and other resource data. To distinguish between an application's IDE project and a resource project, I use the term *resource project* or just *resources* for RW's project files.

> **TIP**
>
> You can store a resource project directly in binary form, using RW to create and edit .RES files, but it is usually best to have RW create .RC script files for your resource projects. For minor editing—fixing a misspelling in a string or a button label, for example—it's often easier to edit a resource script file using the BC4 text editor than it is to restart RW just to make small adjustments.

To configure RW, start the program and select its *File\Preferences...* command *before* opening or creating a resource project. A few settings are disabled when a project is open, and you must remember to choose them beforehand. A few other settings, though, are enabled only when a project is open. You can, for example, choose whether to save a project in .RES binary form or to edit resources directly in an executable .EXE code file. You can run RW from the Program or File Managers, or you can select *Resource Workshop* from the IDE's *Tool* menu.

> **WARNING**
>
> For application development, always store and edit resource projects in .RC script files or in .RES binary files (or both). You may use RW to view and edit resources stored in .EXE code files, but any changes you make will be discarded the next time you compile that application.

Be sure RW's *Include path* (using the *File\Preferences...* command) is set to the default BC4 include path as also specified in the IDE. (The IDE and RW path names are distinct—you must set both of them individually.) You may use a *relative pathname* such as ..\..\..\..*include;* so you can move your projects easily to other drives and base directories. Or, you can use a *fixed pathname* such as *C:\BC4\INCLUDE;* (recommended) if you don't expect to move your project's files. Notice that the pathname ends with a semicolon.

RW can generate resource identifiers automatically, though most developers probably won't use this feature. If you want to create your own identifiers such as a menu command name, `CM_VIEWBITMAP`, turn off this check box in the *Preferences* dialog.

You may also select a *Target Windows version*. Binary resources are version dependent, so if you are using RW to edit resources in .RES binary or .EXE code files, you must select *Windows 3.0, Windows 3.1,* or *Win32* as appropriate for your application. Choosing *Win32* also lets you select target languages for creating *multiple language resources.* You can, for example, create English, Spanish, German, Swedish, French, and Japanese (among other) versions of your resources for a truly international Windows application. For 16-bit applications, you need to create separate resources for each language version of your code.

After selecting RW's preferences, you can create a new resource project. In general, I begin my resource projects by following these steps:

1. Select *File\New project...* and pick *.RC* from the *Project file type* list. Use the other types to create or edit individual resource components—an icon stored in a file ending in .ICO, for example. New resource projects should always be type *.RC.*

2. Use the *File\Add to project...* command to attach a header file to the project for storing resource identifiers using `#define` directives. The resulting *Add file to project* dialog box appears automatically for a new project if RW's preferences specify *Generate identifiers automatically;* otherwise, you must use the *File* menu command to open the dialog. Select the file type *RH, H c Header* and enter a file name. A resource header file typically ends in .RH, and it may be included in source code and in resource script files. Always perform this step before creating any resources. If you forget, your identifiers will be stored in the .RC file, making it difficult for the program to include them for referring to resources in statements. *All resource identifiers should be stored in a .RH header file.*

3. Use the *Resource\New...* command to select a resource to add to the project. Use this command for each new resource you want to create. Select *MENU,* for example, to create a menu resource.

4. Selecting a new resource type runs the RW editor for that type. All RW editors are tailor made for each resource kind. Some commands are common to all

editors; others are unique. A good way to learn RW's many commands is to open sample resource scripts provided with BC4 and with this book's sample programs.

> **HINT**
>
> If know your way around Windows, you can learn most RW commands on your own. To save time, try each of the editors and look up unfamiliar commands in BC4's User's Guide.

5. After creating a new resource, I always use the **Resource\Rename** command to change the name assigned automatically by RW. For instance, RW assigns the string *MENU_1* to the program's first menu resource. I prefer to rename the resource using an integer identifier ID_MENU, assigned the value 100 (or a similar small value). That identifier is stored in the .RH header file attached to the resource project. The program's source files can include that header and use the constant identifiers to refer to individual resources. In large programs, this method results in faster resource loading because it takes longer for Windows to search for resources named using strings.

> **TIP**
>
> Whenever you create a new identifier, RW asks permission to do that, then prompts for a value. Type in the value you want, and be sure the *File* entry in the *New identifier* dialog refers to the resource project's .RH file, *not* to the .RC script. If you accidentally store a resource identifier in the script, close the resource project and use BC4 to transfer the #define directive from the .RC script to the .RH header.

Resource Script Files

A resource script file is just a text file containing source code statements for an application's resources. Resource script commands are fully documented in BC4's online help—browse this information, or search for specific resource type names for more information. Listing 2.1 shows a sample resource script for a simple menu. (I extracted this file from one of the sample programs on disk. Don't bother typing this—it's listed here just to illustrate a resource script's format.)

Listing 2.1. Typical resource script.

```
#include <owl\window.rh>
#include "filename.rh"
ID_MENU MENU
BEGIN
  POPUP "&Demo"
  BEGIN
    MENUITEM "&Erase", CM_ERASE
    MENUITEM "E&xit", CM_EXIT
  END
END
```

Note that the resource script includes a resource header file, WINDOW.RH, from the OWL subdirectory in the default include path (usually C:\BC4\INCLUDE). Many OWL classes have associated resources that you can use by including the appropriate resource header. The sample script also includes the program's own resource header, FILENAME.RH, containing #define directives for resource identifiers. Source code files also should include FILENAME.RH. The OWL resource header, WINDOW.RH, is automatically included along with OWL class headers such as WINDOW.H.

The resource command begins with a resource identifier such as ID_MENU followed by a resource type, MENU in this example. Resource script statements are surrounded by BEGIN and END key words, making a resource script file resemble a Pascal program. (A version of RW changed to braces in favor of these keywords, but the more traditional BEGIN and END are still recognized.) Various statements in the resource create a popup menu and two commands, *Erase* and *Exit,* identified by constants CM_ERASE and CM_EXIT. (In the next chapter, you learn how to write programs that respond to menu commands using their identifiers.)

Other resource script commands can become highly complex, containing positioning and size information, window attributes, control elements, and a host of other details. As I mentioned, it's usually best to have RW store a resource project in a resource script file, ending in .RC. The script may contain all of a program's resources, and it also can refer to bitmap, icon, cursor, and other binary files—similar to the way a C++ program can be composed of modules.

AppExpert

Application generators are better thought of as application *shell* generators. An application generator creates source code for common program features such as menus, multiple document interface (MDI) windows, about-box dialogs, tool bars, and so on. It doesn't write the full application—that's still your job. (Someday, some bright programmer is going to write the ultimate application generator and put us all out of work!)

BC4 has a sophisticated application generator, AppExpert, built into the IDE. The generator is capable of creating numerous types of OWL source code shells for a variety of common application features. You might consider using AppExpert to:

- Build prototype applications in a hurry. With AppExpert, you can have a sample program up and running in an hour or so, complete with toolbars, windows, text editing, file handling, and other features.

- Learn more about OWL programming techniques. AppExpert generates object-oriented, OWL code. To study an OWL method, you can create a sample AppExpert applications and read the source code to discover how the application generator implements a particular feature.

- Start new applications in a hurry. AppExpert can construct all the necessary files, resources, bitmaps, and other elements needed by many applications. Rather than invent these features from scratch, you can use AppExpert to build program shells to which you add your own code.

Don't be lulled into thinking that AppExpert will write your applications for you (though you undoubtedly will see such demonstrations at computer shows). Building new AppExpert applications is simple, as I show in a second. Before creating applications, however, you need to be aware of some major deficiencies that plague all application generators:

- After creating the application shell, it is your responsibility to add your program's code. AppExpert cannot write your program's statements for you. Comments are embedded in generated files, suggesting where you can insert statements of different kinds.

- If you fail to select a feature using AppExpert from the start, you cannot go back and add that operation later. AppExpert can create only fresh application shells. It does not keep track of changes you make to those shells, and it cannot modify the files it creates. Starting over too many times can cost you more time than writing the application from scratch in the first place.

- You may not agree with the selection of identifiers and source file styles generated by AppExpert. It may take many long sessions to update the generated code to suit your preferred programming style.

The best way to get the most out of AppExpert is to postpone using the generator until you gain more experience programming with OWL. The better you understand OWL's classes, the better you'll be able to modify AppExpert-generated source files. You also stand a better chance of making good selections before generation—remember, after generating and modifying an application, you cannot use AppExpert to add new features. It is your responsibility to insert all new operations to generated applications.

Despite its deficiencies, AppExpert can be extremely useful for getting prototypes and demos up and running in hurry. Follow these numbered steps for a demonstration of how to use AppExpert for building a sample application:

1. Create a new directory named C:\SAMPLE to hold generated files. (You may use a different name and drive if you want.) Make sure you have *at least* five megabytes of available disk space. A typical AppExpert application consists of several dozen files, and can consume gobs of disk space. *Never construct new applications in a root directory or inside an existing subdirectory. Always create a new, empty directory to hold a generated application.*

2. Start BC4 and close any open projects and windows. Always start fresh when generating a new AppExpert application.

3. Select *Project\AppExpert...* to bring up the *New Project* dialog, the same one you use to create application projects. (An AppExpert application is an extended project that includes source code generation. AppExpert runs the BC4 IDE much as you do when creating your own projects, but of course, at a much faster speed.) Change to the C:\SAMPLE directory you created in step one and enter `sample` into the *File Name* input line. Close the *New Project* dialog by selecting the *OK* button (or just press Enter after typing `sample`).

4. You now see the *AppExpert Application Generation Options* dialog in Figure 2.4. Use this dialog's commands to select the features you want to include in your application.

5. The plus signs in the *Topics* window pane indicate that these items have one or more sublevels. To open a sublevel, single-click the plus sign, or highlight the topic and press the spacebar. Take a moment to open and highlight each sublevel for each of the three topics—*Application, Main Window,* and *MDI Child/View*—and to read the resulting options in the main window pane at right.

6. There are many possible kinds of AppExpert applications—it is impossible to recommend a set of options that will suit every need. You might want to set aside an afternoon to try different setups, and if you have enough disk space, to save raw generated applications for future reference. For demonstration

purposes, highlight the *Advanced Options* sublevel (the second choice in the *Application* topic), and select *BWCC* in the *Control style* window pane. Also highlight the *Admin Options* sublevel and enter your name and other copyright information for the program's about-box dialog.

FIGURE 2.4.

The AppExpert
Application
Generation Options
dialog.

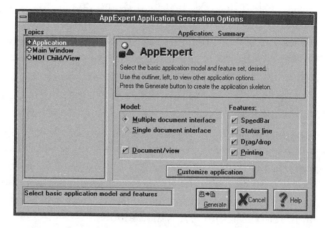

> **WARNING**
>
> Do not type quotes marks around strings in the *Admin Options* section. Use *My Program* rather than *"My Program"* or RW will not be able to read the resulting resource script.

7. To modify the program's main window title, select the *Main Window* topic and enter the name you want under *Window title* in the main window pane at right. You can select a background color for the window and you can customize its style attributes. For the demonstration, use the default settings.

8. AppExpert is especially useful for generating *Document-View* applications. Select the *MDI Child/View* topic's *Basic Options* sublevel to see the kinds of document-view options you can select. For this demonstration, use the default settings of TEditView and TFileDocument.

9. When you are done choosing AppExpert features, select the *Generate* button to create the application. Answer Yes to the resulting dialog, cover your ears, don your protective goggles, and stand back while AppExpert creates your application's source code, resource script, and .IDE project files. This takes a while.

41

10. After a few moments, and a lot of disk activity, BC4 displays the generated application's Project window. Select the plus sign next to SAMPLE.EXE to see a list of files that AppExpert created. (If you instead see a minus sign, the file list is already shown under SAMPLE.EXE.)

11. Select the first file, SMPLAPP.CPP, and press Enter to open and view some of the application's source code. AppExpert inserts #include directives, declares classes, implements member functions, and writes comments that you can browse to learn more about the generated code. AppExpert even adds your name and copyright notice to every source file.

12. Change back to the *Project* window and select file SAMPLAPP.RC to open the program's resources in Resource Workshop. (It takes a little while for RW to compile the script. Future uses of RW for this project will go faster after this initial compilation.) After RW finishes loading the project's resources, select a resource identifier (the sample menu is a good one) to view it in a RW editor. Exit RW to return to the IDE. (If you previously switched to another program, however, it may appear instead of the IDE. Just switch to BC4 as you normally do to select other programs in Windows.)

> **NOTE**
>
> RW has an age-old bug in it that prevents its name from appearing in the Windows task list when the menu editor's sample menu view is active. If RW seems to disappear when you press Alt+Tab to change to another program, press Ctrl+Esc instead to bring up the Windows *Task List* dialog, then select Resource Workshop from there. You can also minimize all open windows and find RW's icon on the desktop.

13. When you are finished viewing the files that AppExpert created, select BC4's *Project\Make all* command (or just press F9) to compile and link the application. This will take several minutes, even on a fast 80486 system.

14. After compilation, use the Windows File Manager to run the SAMPLE.EXE code file. Figure 2.5 shows the generated application's display.

The finished application comes complete with a text editor (I opened two of the program's source files), a toolbar of icons, full printing capabilities, and a status bar at bottom. Point the mouse cursor at the toolbar icons and read their descriptions in the status bar. The figure also shows the application's about-box dialog, which needs some adjustments. The Copyright notice, for example, should be displayed on a single line, and the program's icon should be displayed in place of the default symbol. The generated application is unfinished, and much work remains to turn it into *your* program. But AppExpert certainly gives you an impressive flying start toward that ultimate goal.

FIGURE 2.5.

Sample AppExpert-generated application.

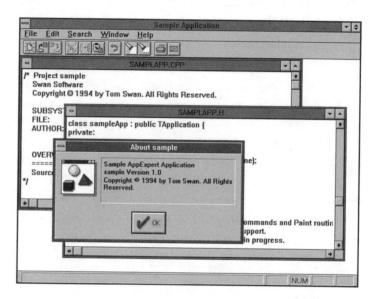

ClassExpert

In conjunction with the AppExpert application generator, you can also use ClassExpert to design classes more or less automatically. You may do this at any time after generating an AppExpert application.

Start by opening an AppExpert project, such as the one you generated in the preceding section. Select the .EXE file target filename in the project window, and either double click or use the local *View* command. This opens the project's ClassExpert dialog, from which you may select events and member functions to add to various classes. Of course, you can do the same simply by typing the function declarations in .CPP and .H text files—ClassExpert simply inserts the declarations for you.

Until you become intimately familiar with OWL, you will have little use for ClassExpert. Knowing which member functions to add to classes is the key to using OWL effectively. After you finish this book and examine its sample listings, you might want to try ClassExpert along with AppExpert to generate OWL source files. Until you can write your own OWL application, ClassExpert will be more confusing than helpful.

Debugging and Browsing

Debugging is one of those chores that every programmer loves to hate. Unfortunately, unless you are a better programmer than the rest of us (including me), you'll spend a great deal of time chasing down bugs and fixing errors.

To make debugging relatively painless (if not enjoyable), BC4 comes with four types of debuggers and one symbol browser. These are:

- A built-in debugger is incorporated in the IDE's graphical user interface. Use this debugger by selecting menu commands, just as you use other IDE features. You may debug 16- and 32-bit Windows programs and also DOS programs with the IDE debugger.
- A 16-bit Windows debugger, *Turbo Debugger for Windows (TDW)*, operates in stand-alone mode to debug compiled Windows programs.
- A 32-bit Windows debugger, *Turbo Debugger for Win32 (TD32)*, also operates in stand-alone mode to debug compiled 32-bit Windows programs.
- A DOS debugger, *Turbo Debugger (TD)*, works like the original TD supplied with Borland languages for several years. Use this debugger to analyze DOS-only programs.
- A built-in symbolic browser, which you can use to view class declarations, step through class hierarchies, view source files, and more.

In addition, you can also run the stand-alone debuggers in remote mode, attaching two computer serial ports with an RS-232 cable. The code runs on one computer, while the debugger's output appears on the other. To use this feature, assuming you have the appropriate hardware, run the *Remote Debugging* and *Remote Setup* programs.

All of BC4's debuggers recognize similar commands—learn one, and you get the others for free. Because this book teaches Windows programming techniques, however, the following notes concentrate on the IDE and Windows debuggers. See my book, *Mastering Borland C++ 4*, for more information on DOS programming and debugging.

You will probably use the IDE debugger for most debugging chores. It's convenient and always ready to single step code, examine variables, and set breakpoints. For complex programs and difficult bugs, you can switch to one of the more capable stand-alone debuggers, either the 16- or 32-bit version, depending on your application's target operating system. Of course, if you don't use the IDE to develop your programs, you'll probably use a stand-alone debugger exclusively.

Setting Up BC4's Debuggers

There are two steps for configuring BC4's debuggers, which you should do before using the programs. First, you need to select a video output mode for displaying the debugger's output. Because the debugger takes control of Windows and a target program, it has special video switching needs that require special handling. Second, you need to run a debugger configuration program to select among its operational defaults.

Run *TD Video Configuration* from the Windows Program Manager. The program, TDWINI.EXE, known internally as the "TD Weenie Program" (just kidding), searches for a single copy of file TDW.INI, which should be stored in the WINDOWS directory. TDW.INI is a text file that lists various configuration options for Windows Turbo Debuggers. If more than one copy of this file exists, the results could cause display problems. Delete all existing copies of TDW.INI before selecting a video configuration.

You should see a list of *Available Video DLLs*. Select a driver that takes best advantage of your computer's display card or built-in capabilities. There are currently four drivers. (Check with Borland for the availability of others.) The four stock drivers are:

- DUAL8514.DLL—Select this driver if your system has an 8514 video display card, and you are using two monitors. The debugger's output appears on one monitor while you view your program on the other.

- STB.DLL—Select this driver if your system has an STB MTP-2 or MVP-4 video card, with two or more Tseng Laboratory ET-4000 VGA ports. The driver displays the debugger's output on one screen while you view your program on the other.

- SVGA.DLL—Select this driver for most coprocessor enhanced VGA cards, often known as *Super VGA*. This driver displays the debugger's screen in text mode (the same text mode used by plain DOS), while the Windows display and the target program hide in the background. You must switch back and forth from the debugger screen to Windows to see both displays. Some video cards, especially Tseng and ATI non-coprocessor cards, do not support the subroutines required by this driver.

● TDWGUI.DLL—Select this driver to display the debugger's output in any Windows-compatible display. If none of the other drivers works, use this one. (I use this driver, for example, on my laptop, which has a standard-issue 640-by-480 VGA color display.) With this driver, the debugger's display appears in a graphical window while your program runs as it normally does in Windows. Be sure to select a font (see text after following note) that is appropriate for your display's resolution. By the way, it's no easy trick to write a GUI debugger—Borland programmers worked for *two years* in developing a GUI debugger that would work properly with all Windows compatible displays.

NOTE

For more information and help in selecting an appropriate debugger video driver, select the Help button in the *TD Video Configuration (TDWINI.EXE)* program.

After selecting a video driver, click the *Settings...* button to see more options. You can read the online help for most of these—they select window border width and display position (for technical reasons, it's a fixed window that doesn't move like a regular Windows window). If you are using the GUI display driver, click the *Position...* button and drag the debugger display where you want it. Press Esc to cancel; Enter to save the debugger's position. Click the *Font...* button and select a font size. (I use choice #3, 6-by-8, with a 9-point font, which looks especially good when configuring the debugger's output for 43/50 lines as I explain later.) All GUI debugger screens use fixed fonts, which cannot be scaled to arbitrary sizes. You cannot specify a TrueType font for a debugger screen—the listed choices are the only ones available.

HINT

After selecting a font, use the *Position...* button to see a sample of the debugger's display. This is easier than using the *Test* button in the main TDWINI.EXE window.

After configuring the debugger's video output, you need to configure each of the stand-alone debuggers you plan to use. (The IDE debugger requires no additional configuration.) From the Program Manager, run one or more of these programs to finish configuring BC4's debuggers:

- *TDW Configuration*—Run this program to configure the 16-bit Windows debugger.
- *TD32 Configuration*—Run this program to configure the 32-bit Windows debugger.
- *TD Configuration*—Run this program to configure the DOS-only debugger.

Each debugger configuration utility runs in a text screen (they are all DOS programs), and each offers similar choices. You can customize display colors, select various display options, select default directories, configure a video mode (which may be preempted by using a GUI display driver), and so on. Many of these options have obvious purposes, and all are documented in Borland's references (online and on paper). The only change that I make to the default settings is to select 43/50 screen lines with the *Display...* menu command.

Select the *Save* command to save your settings. You may save them to a configuration file or you may choose to change the default settings in the debugger's code file. The only reason to save to a configuration file is if you plan to keep more than one configuration on disk, perhaps using different setups for different applications in development. Store the debugger's .CFG file in the application's directory. If you plan to use the same configuration for all debugging sessions, you can save your options to the debugger's .EXE code file.

Finally, try all three stand-alone debuggers, and make sure you can see their displays. If you are running a debugger in a text-screen on a single computer, press Alt+F5 to switch between the debugger and normal views. Exit each debugger before running another. To make the debuggers more accessible, hold down the Ctrl button while you click and drag their icons into another Program Manager window. You can then do as I do: re-name the icons TDW, TD32, and TD, which are easier to locate in a busy display.

NOTE

The DOS debugger, TD, always runs in text mode. It does not use a Windows display driver as do the Windows debuggers. To have TD's display appear in a Windows graphical window, run the Program Manager's PIF Editor, and open the TD.PIF file in C:\BC4\BIN. Select the *Windowed* radio button under *Display Usage:* When you next run TD, its output appears in a graphical window. The program is still running in DOS mode—just as a DOS prompt window does. To further configure the display, run TD, and maximize its window. Next, select the window system button (at upper-left) and use the *Fonts...* dialog to pick an appropriate font and screen resolution for the display.

This option is not available, however, with all Windows video drivers. If your window's system menu (the one *Restore*, *Move*, and other window commands) doesn't have a *Fonts...* command, you cannot select a different font. You may, however, still run TD in a graphical window.

Code Preparations

The first step in using any of BC4's debuggers is to add debugging information to the compiled code. Do this in the IDE by selecting *Options\Project...*, open the *Compiler* topic, and highlight the *Debugging* sublevel. Make sure **Debug information in OBJs** is checked, which copies debugging information to compiled object-code files. Also open the *Linker* topic, highlight *General,* and make sure *Include debug information* is checked, which copies debugging information from object-code files to the final .EXE code file. You must select *both* options (one for the compiler and one for the linker) to debug compiled programs.

NOTE

Turn off debugging information and recompile your application before shipping it to customers. Debugging information takes space, and turning it off can shrink .EXE code file sizes significantly. Rather than recompile an application, you may also run it through the DOS utility TDSTRIP.EXE (for 16-bit programs) or TDSTRP32.EXE (for 32-bit programs), provided with BC4. The programs remove all traces of debugging information from compiled .EXE code files.

When using command-line tools or the Make utility, specify option -v for the compiler and linker to add debugging information to object- and executable-code files. The same option is recognized by the 16- and 32-bit compilers (BCC and BCC32) and linkers (TLINK and TLINK32).

Adding debugging information provides the debuggers with facts about the compiled program—such as its symbols, code-segment structure, entry points, and so on. If you debug a program and, instead of a source-level display that shows your program's statements, you see a CPU screen that displays processor registers and assembly language, you probably did not select the correct options during compilation. You can debug programs in CPU mode, which you may want to do on occasion to investigate how the raw, compiled assembly language operates. But for most debugging sessions, you want to see your program's *statements,* not the compiler's output. For that, you must add debugging information to the compiled code.

BC4's debuggers have numerous commands, which are documented in Borland's references. The following hands-on demonstrations help you get started using the IDE and stand-alone debuggers.

> **NOTE**
>
> This book's sample .IDE project files automatically add debugging information to all compiled programs. Take a moment to learn how to run programs in the debugger—it's a marvelous way to investigate how programs operate inside.

IDE Debugging

The IDE debugger is fully integrated into BC4's editor. You can single-step program statements, set breakpoints at strategic locations, inspect variables, and so on, all by typing a few function keys or selecting commands from menus. For a quick tour of the IDE debugger, start BC4 now and close any open projects and windows, then follow these step-by-step instructions:

> **NOTE**
>
> If the key strokes in this section don't match those in your IDE, you may be using a different key binding. Open the menu commands to learn the assigned keys. Use *Options/Environment...* to select **IDE** *classic* key bindings if you are familiar with previous IDE versions. Keys listed here are for the default BC4 bindings.

- Use the *Project\Open project...* command to open the SKETCH.IDE project in the SKETCH directory, created by installing this book's disk. Even though you haven't learned about the commands and features in this program (I cover the program in a later chapter), it serves as a useful demonstration of the built-in debugger's commands.

- Compile and run the program by pressing Ctrl+F9, or by clicking the *Make and run* toolbar button (the sixth button with a Thunder Bolt icon). This step isn't strictly necessary—if you attempt to debug a program that isn't compiled, the IDE compiles the program before starting the debugger. The sample program lets you sketch with a mouse inside the window. Click and drag the mouse pointer, double click to erase your drawing (or use the sample's *Erase* command), then exit the program, returning to the IDE.

● Next, you will run the same program one step at a time using the debugger's *single-step* command. Press F8. In a few seconds, you see the program's source code open in a window, with the following line highlighted:

```
OwlMain(int argc, char* argv[])
```

At this point, the debugger has executed the program's startup code, and is paused before executing `OwlMain`. Use this opportunity to inspect the function's two arguments. Cursor to `argc` and press Alt+F10 to open the window's local menu, then press I to inspect this argument's value. (It should equal 1.) Close the window (pressing Esc is easiest). You can also click the right mouse button on `argc` and select *Inspect object* from the popup menu to inspect variables.

● Use one of the preceding techniques to inspect also the second argument, `argv`, passed to `OwlMain`. This argument is an array of string pointers, displayed in a two-pane inspector window. Expand the window so you can see the string in the rightmost pane—it should equal the program's path and fiiename, always passed in `argv[0]`. Close this inspector window before continuing.

● Press F8 one time to step to `OwlMain`'s first statement, which constructs an object app of the class `TSketchApp`. Cursor up a few lines to the statement that constructs the program's main window object:

```
MainWindow = new TSketchWin(0, "Click and Drag the Mouse");
```

To pause the program *before* that statement executes, set a breakpoint on the statement by pressing F5, or by using the *Debug\Toggle breakpoint* command. (Press Ctrl+F8 if you are using classic IDE key mappings. Press F2 in the stand-alone debuggers.) The line turns bright red (on color monitors only, of course), indicating that a breakpoint is set here.

● To run the program up to the next breakpoint, press Ctrl+F9. In a brief moment, the breakpoint statement is highlighted normally, indicating that it is the next one to execute. When the debugger pauses at a statement such as this one that calls a function or constructs an object with a constructor, you have two options: you can *step over* the statement, or you can *step into* the function. Press F7 now to *step into* the constructor that creates the `TSketchWin` object.

> **NOTE**
>
> If you make a mistake following the instructions here, use *Debug/Terminate program* to halt a program at any stage in its execution. Cursor to any statement, set a breakpoint there, and press Ctrl+F9 to run the program up to that spot.

- You should now see the program source code paused at the entrance to the main window class's constructor. Press F8 a few times to step over (that is, to execute but not step into functions) until the assignment to `dragging` is highlighted. Cursor to any character in `dragging`, and press Alt+F10 or click the right mouse button to open a local menu of commands. Select *Set **watch*** to add `dragging` to a *Watch* window that can show the values of one or more variables while the code runs.

- Move the *Watch* window aside so you can see the source code, then cursor down in the program until you reach the assignment to `dragging` inside function `EvLButtonDown`, in the `TSketchWin` class (line 70). Set a breakpoint (press F5 or Ctrl+F8) on this assignment statement inside the `if` statement:

  `dragging = TRUE;`

- Press Ctrl+F9 to run the program up to that assignment. The program is now running full force. Click the right mouse button inside the sample window as you did to begin drawing when you ran the program without the help of the debugger. This time, the IDE reappears, and the assignment to `dragging` is highlighted. You have halted the program inside the function that responds to a message generated by clicking the mouse.

- Make sure you can see the *Watch* window, then press F8 to execute the assignment. The value of `dragging` changes from 0 to 1 in *Watch,* reflecting the assignment to that variable. You have just completed the most common techniques for tracking down bugs: setting a breakpoint, pressing Ctrl+F9 to run the program to that point, adding variables to a *Watch* window, then pressing F8 or F7 to execute statements one at a time while you view their effects on those variables.

- To switch to the program's output window, press Alt+Tab, or use whatever means you normally use to switch to other windows. For programs paused inside the debugger, moving the mouse pointer to the program's window changes the cursor to a *stop sign.* Try not to leave programs paused this way. When you are finished debugging, terminate the program or run it to completion.

● To run SKETCH to completion, first clear all breakpoints by selecting the *View\Breakpoint* command, then selecting the resulting window's *Delete all* local command. (Remember, press Alt+F10 or click the right mouse button to open a local command menu.) You might also want to try the other commands at the bottom of the *View* menu. You can view the *Watch* window, breakpoints, call stack, processor registers, and an event log showing a program's execution history—all powerful weapons in the battle against bugs.

● After clearing all breakpoints, press Ctrl+F9 to continue running SKETCH. You might discover at this point that the mouse button seems *stuck* in the down position—a normal, and unavoidable, conflict caused by the use of the mouse in the IDE and in the program under investigation. Click the left mouse button to get back in sync, then exit the sample program. (Don't worry about such conflicts—they are usually harmless. If, however, mouse conflicts interfere with your ability to debug your code, you can resolve the problem by debugging with two computers via an RS-232 serial cable.)

> **NOTE**
>
> Don't wait for me to suggest using the built-in debugger to investigate how this book's sample programs operate. Go through the preceding instructions to become familiar with the debugger's commands, then use them to inspect variables, set breakpoints, and single-step statements for any of this book's sample programs.

Stand-Alone Debugging

You don't need to use BC4's stand-alone 16- and 32-bit debuggers with the programs in this book. For learning how to program Windows with BC4, the built-in IDE debugger is sufficiently powerful. You might, however, want to use a stand-alone debugger to analyze your own projects, and you can do the same if you want with the programs in this book. The commands in the stand-alone debuggers are much the same as those built into the IDE, but the external debuggers also have features that take advantage of the processor's hardware debugging registers. The debuggers also can communicate over a serial line for remote debugging.

I won't go into those features here—they are too far afield of this book's mandate to teach Windows programming techniques. Still, the stand-alone debuggers are extremely valuable tools, and you should know how to operate them. Follow these steps for a quick look at debugging using the stand-alone Turbo Debugger for Windows (TDW).

- If the SKETCH.IDE project is not open from the preceding section, open it now. If the program is paused in mid execution, use the *Debug\Terminate program* command to reset. Close other applications to make as much memory available as possible and to guard against losing unsaved files.

- Select the IDE's *Tool\Turbo Debugger* command to transfer to Turbo Debugger for Windows (TDW). (The IDE *Tool* menu automatically selects the correct debugger for 16- or 32-bit applications.) Normally, you should have a project loaded before selecting this command. If necessary, the IDE compiles the program, and in a moment, switches to TDW's text-only display. If you selected a GUI video driver, you see the debugger's screen on top of other windows. If you selected a text display, you see only the debugger.

- Don't be fooled by TDW's text-only display—the program is a Windows application, but it takes over total control of your system. Windows and the application are still running over in the graphics screen; you are seeing a special text display available only through TDW. This means you cannot use the usual ways to switch to other windows, as you can with the built-in IDE debugger. Also, the mouse cursor is changed to a block, not an arrow, even in GUI display mode, and the cursor cannot be moved beyond the debugging window's borders.

- You can now follow the steps in the preceding sample, beginning with the commands that inspect argc and argv. All TDW commands work the same as the built-in debugger's, but the key assignments follow the classic IDE settings, not the default IDE keys as listed in this chapter. Press F8 and F7 to single-step statements. Press F2 to toggle breakpoints. Press F9 rather than Ctrl+F9 to run the program. Some menus and windows are arranged differently, but for the most part, once you know how to use the IDE debugger, you should be able to run the stand-alone versions.

When you complete SKETCH, the debugger shows you the value returned from OwlMain. (Windows doesn't use this value, but you can view it as an indication of the program's success.) Close the final window and exit the debugger to return to the IDE and normal Windows operation.

NOTE

Always run programs to completion when executing them under control of a stand-alone debugger. Because the debugger takes total control over the system, exiting the debugger before an application finishes is potentially dangerous, and might leave DOS or Windows in an unstable state. If you must exit early, or if a bug causes serious trouble, close all files, exit Windows, reboot, and restart before using any other commands. If you must do that frequently, try using the IDE debugger which permits you to terminate a program before it ends, or consider purchasing a separate debugging system, the only reliable way to protect your development computer from harm caused by application bugs.

IDE Browsing

Though it's not technically a debugger, the IDE *Browser* is often useful for investigating a program's bugs and inner workings. Like BC4's debuggers, the browser requires special information to be inserted into compiled code. You must insert that information, and you must compile a program successfully, before you can browse its symbols.

To add the necessary browsing information (automatically inserted by this book's sample projects), select *Options\Project...*, open the *Compiler* topic, and highlight the *Debugging* sublevel. Make sure *Browser reference information in OBJs* is checked. Compiling with this option adds the information needed to browse the program's symbols.

As with BC4's debuggers, the IDE browser has many commands and features that are best learned by using them. The following suggestions demonstrate some of the ways to browse symbols in the sample programs in this book. (Don't wait for me to suggest using the browser—use it frequently as you learn new OWL techniques in the coming chapters!)

- Start BC4, and close any open projects and windows.
- Use the *Project\Open project...* command to open the SKETCH.IDE project in the SKETCH directory. Press F9 or use the *Project\Make all* command to compile and link the program. (If you see "Success," it is already compiled.)
- Open the program's SKETCH.CPP file (it may already be open), and cursor down to the word TSketchWin (at line 25). The browser is a *context-sensitive* tool—it reads the symbol under the cursor. Place the cursor at any character in TSketchWin, then select *Search\Browse symbol...* Press Enter to select the name shown in the resulting input window. Or, for faster browsing, press Alt+F10 or click the right mouse button on TSketchWin, and choose the *Browse symbol* local command to display the *Browse* window, illustrated in Figure 2.6.

FIGURE 2.6.

The IDE's Browse window.

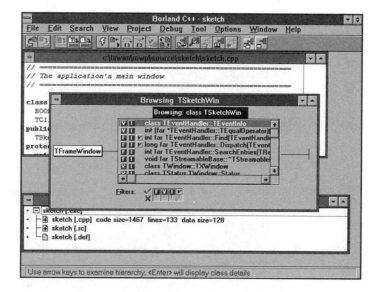

NOTE

This is a good time to remind you that menu hot-key settings depend on the selected key mapping in the IDE. If the keys mentioned in this chapter are different from the ones listed in menus, select *Options/Environment...*, highlight the *Editor* topic, and select the *Default keymapping* button.

- Select one or more *Filters* to view **F**unctions, **V**ariables, **I**nherited data and functions, and **V**irtual functions. (Hint: the first **V** filter selects variables; the second **V** filter (shown in slanted italic style) selects virtual functions only if **F** is also toggled on.) All filters are on by default.

- Select any symbol in the Browse window's main section and click the right mouse button, or press Alt+F10, for a local popup menu of additional commands. To switch to a symbol's source code, select the *Edit source* command. To see a class's position in its hierarchy, select the *Browse class hierarchy* command. Try some of the other options in this menu, and make a mental note of their mnemonic control keys. After you are done fooling around, get back to the Browse window (you may have to repeat the preceding instructions), highlight the TSketchWin class, and press Ctrl+C to display a graph of the program's classes, showing where TSketchWin fits into its family tree (see Figure 2.7).

FIGURE 2.7.

A class hierarchy displayed by the IDE Browser.

Borland C++ - sketch - [Browsing Objects]

File   Edit   Search   View   Project   Debug   Tool   Options   Window   Help

opstream — ofpstream

pstream — ipstream — ifpstream

fpbase

TFrameWindow — TSketchWin

TEventHandler — TWindow

TModule — TApplication — TSketchApp

TStreamableBase

tagPOINT — TPoint

ios — ostream
      — istream

streambuf — filebuf

Use arrow keys to examine hierarchy, <Enter> will display class details

- To browse a class's declarations, highlight the class name in the hierarchy graph, and press Enter. Toggle off the **I**nherited filter to see only new and replaced declarations in a derived class. With that filter on, the Browse window shows *all* declarations, including those inherited from ancestor classes.

- From the Browse window (press enter on a symbol in the hierarchy, or repeat these instructions to get back to the Browse window), you can select the local command *Edit source* (or press Ctrl+E) to bring up an item's source declaration in an editor window. This is a very handy method for locating a function in a large source file. Just browse to that function's name—perhaps starting with the use of that function somewhere in the program—and then select *Edit source* to go straight to the function's implementation. Try this on several different kinds of symbols—it's one of the most useful browsing capabilities, but it takes a few minutes to get the hang of the commands.

- Be careful when editing source with the browser. *The Browser sometimes opens OWL's source code files and headers.* Editing an OWL class in a supplied header file may permanently damage that file, causing you to lose the ability to compile programs. If you accidentally make changes to OWL's header files, you may have to reinstall BC4 to recover. After using the browser's *Edit source* command, it's a good idea to check the window title before editing class declarations. If the window refers to an OWL header or to an OWL source code file in a C:\BC4 directory, you may view the file, but you should close it as soon as possible to prevent accidents.

> **TIP**
>
> Using Browse commands to view and edit source also closes the Browse window. To make the window stay open, select *Options/Environment...,* highlight the *Browser* topic, and select *Multiple windows* under *Browser window behavior.* Using browser commands will now open new windows rather than replacing the existing window, but you will have more windows to close when you are done browsing. Try both settings to see which you prefer.

Command-Line Tools

Many professional developers prefer to use command-line tools to build applications. BC4 comes with command-line compilers, linkers, and other programs that you can use to construct Windows applications without using the IDE. In fact, if you always use command-line tools, you can delete BC4.EXE and related files from C:\BC4\BIN. Don't do that, however, unless you are absolutely sure you will never use the IDE. (I've never been a big fan of IDEs, and I've used the Brief text editor and command-line tools for most of my programming. BC4's IDE is worlds better than in past compilers, however, and I used it to write all of this book's programs.)

This section explains some of the options and features you can use with BC4's command-line development tools. To run these programs, open a DOS prompt window. Or, enter the suggested commands from DOS. You don't even have to run Windows to compile applications, a fact that may appeal to programmers who are not Windows users.

> **NOTE**
>
> Some programmers keep a DOS-only development system for programming and a separate computer, running Windows, for testing and debugging. This setup protects the development system and the program's source files, but obviously, a two-computer development system isn't practical for everyone.

The Command-Line Compilers

There are two command-line compilers supplied with BC4 4.0: BCC.EXE for 16-bit code-file generation and BCC32.EXE for 32-bit code. In general terms, a command-line compiler reads .CPP source files and translates statements in those files into *object code,* stored in .OBJ files. Those files must be linked to produce the final executable .EXE code file.

You will soon discover, however, that using the command-line compiler is complicated by hundreds of possible options, some of which are required for Windows and OWL applications. A few options are available *only* with command-line compilation—the compiler can generate assembly language statements rather than object code, for example (use option -S). You can't do that with the IDE's built-in compiler.

To demonstrate how to use BC4's command-line compilers, in the next sections, you rebuild the HOWL.CPP program from Chapter 1 using only command-line tools to create 16- and 32-bit application code files.

NOTE

Follow these suggestions if you receive out of memory errors when using BC4's command-line tools. If you are using a Windows DOS prompt, close it (type **exit** at the prompt) and run the PIF Editor utility (its icon is in a Program Manager window). Open the DOSPRMPT.PIF file located in C:\WINDOWS. Under *EMS Memory,* set *KB Limit* to at least 1024. Under *XMS Memory,* set *KB Limit* to at least 4096 (four megabytes). Set *KB Required* for both EMS and XMS memory to 0. Save the DOSPRMPT.PIF file. You should now have enough memory to run command line tools from a Windows DOS prompt.

If you are *not* running Windows, follow these steps instead. *Do not issue these commands in a Windows DOS prompt! Use the following suggestions only if you are not running Windows.* Create a swap file with BC4's MAKESWAP utility. Specify the number of kilobytes to set aside for swapping. For example, to create a 12 megabyte swap file, enter this command at a DOS prompt:

```
makeswap 12000
```

The resulting file, EDPMI.SWP, is created in the current directory. To use that file, add the following command to AUTOEXEC.BAT (change the drive and path as needed to refer to the location of EDPMI.SWP):

```
set DPMI32=SWAPFILE C:\EDPMI.SWP
```

To disable the swap file, which you might have to do before running other DPMI-aware programs such as Paradox, issue the command:

```
set DPMI32=
```

> You may issue either command as many times as needed to enable and disable swapping. Again, do not take these steps if you compile from a Windows DOS prompt. Create a swap file *only* if you are not running Windows.

16-Bit Compilation

From a DOS prompt, change to the HOWL directory. Make sure C:\BC4\BIN is in your system PATH (type **path** to check). To compile and link HOWL.CPP to a 16-bit .EXE code file, enter this command:

```
bcc -W -ml howl.cpp bidsl.lib owlwl.lib
```

> **NOTE**
>
> When you compile HOWL.CPP using the suggested commands in this section, you receive two warnings about `argv` and `argc` not being used. As explained in Chapter 1, you may ignore these warnings, or to fix them, comment out the parameters or insert a `#pragma argsused` directive above `OwlMain`. (I purposely left the warnings in so you would see them.)

The -W option specifies a Windows code file; -ml selects the large memory model (the default model is small). The source filename, HOWL.CPP, can be shortened to HOWL—the compiler automatically appends the .CPP extension. Because this is an OWL application, you also have to specify two library files: BIDSL.LIB (part of Borland's container class library) for miscellaneous ancestor classes used by some OWL classes, and OWLWL.LIB containing OWL's complied code. The "L" before the period in those two library filenames stands for the large memory model, the one specified by the -ml option. If you compiled the program using a different model (-ms for small, for instance), you would have to specify the appropriate libraries (BIDSS.LIB and OWLWS.LIB in that case). In general, library files are named XXXS.LIB for the small model, XXXM.LIB for medium, XXXL.LIB for large, and so on.

32-Bit Compilation

To compile and link HOWL as a 32-bit application for Win32 is even easier. Run the BCC32.EXE compiler by typing this DOS command:

```
bcc32 -W howl.cpp bidsf.lib owlwf.lib
```

If nothing seems to happen for a while, be patient—it takes longer to compile 32-bit code than it does to compile 16-bit programs. The command runs BC4's 32-bit compiler, BCC32, specifying the -W option to create a Windows target code file. Here again, HOWL.CPP could be shorted to HOWL—the compiler looks for source files ending with .CPP by default. At a minimum, all 32-bit OWL applications use the same two library files: BIDSF.LIB for the container class library, and OWLWF.LIB for OWL's 32-bit compiled code. The "F" in these filenames stands for *flat memory model*, the only model available to 32-bit applications. Because there is only one memory model, you don't have to use the -m option as you do when compiling 16-bit code.

Compiling with Batch Files

Typing manual compilation commands as you have done for the preceding two examples is not too inconvenient for building small tests and demonstrations from the command line. The commands to create most Windows applications, however, are too unwieldy to be typed manually. Instead, you can build a batch file with the necessary commands, and then run that file to compile your programs. (Experienced programmers realize that there are other ways to build applications—I'll get to the Make utility, for example, a bit later. But don't discount batch files for simple projects. They are quick and easy to use, especially for tests and demos for which you don't want to create a Make file.)

To demonstrate how to use batch files to compile 16- and 32-bit Windows programs, change to the HOWL directory on this book's disk. There you find two files: Listing 2.2, CHOWL16.BAT and Listing 2.3 CHOWL32.BAT. Run either of the batch files to compile and link the application, using some new options. (Hint: copy either file to C.BAT, then just type C to compile.) The files also demonstrate how to run the compiler and linker separately—before, you used BCC and BCC32 to compile and link the program. Performing those two steps separately is sometimes advantageous. You might, for example, compile only one of several modules, then reissue the link command to link all .OBJ files into the final .EXE code file. That way, you save time by not recompiling modules that haven't changed.

> **NOTE**
>
> Enter the last three lines of CHOWL16.BAT on one line. Enter the last two lines of CHOWL32.BAT on one line. Those lines are separated here to fit on the page. The disk files, of course, are correctly formatted.

Listing 2.2. CHOWL16.BAT.

```
bcc -IC:\BC4\INCLUDE -c -WS -w -xd -ml howl.cpp
tlink -LC:\BC4\LIB -Twe -x -c -C -E c0wl.obj howl.obj,
  howl.exe,,bidsl.lib owlwl.lib cwl.lib import.lib
  mathwl.lib,howl.def
```

Listing 2.3. CHOWL32.BAT (for HOWL).

```
bcc32 -IC:\BC4\INCLUDE -c -w -xd howl.cpp
tlink32 -LC:\BC4\LIB -Tpe -x -c c0w32.obj howl.obj,howl.exe,,
  bidsf.lib owlwf.lib import32.lib cw32.lib,howl.def
```

For demonstration purposes, I added some additional command-line options and libraries to the two batch files beyond what is absolutely necessary. In CHOWL16.BAT, -Ixxxx specifies the default path (*xxxx*) for header files—overriding any path specified in TURBOC.CFG. The -c option tells the compiler to *compile only*—that is, to produce an object-code .OBJ file, but not create a finished .EXE code file. Use this option to compile multiple modules that you can then link into the final code. The -w option turns on all warning messages (usually a good idea). The -xd option selects automatic destructor calls for class objects left on the stack due to an exception error. The -ml option specifies the large memory model. HOWL.CPP is, of course, the name of the file to compile. The BCC command in CHOWL16.BAT compiles that file, and stores the resulting object code in HOWL.OBJ.

After compiling, HOWL.OBJ file must be linked to various other components to create the final .EXE code file. To perform this step, a lengthy TLINK command first specifies –Lxxxx as the default path (*xxxx*) for library files, overriding any path listed in a TLINK.CFG configuration file. Option –Twe creates a Windows .EXE file (use –Twd for a DLL). The -x option switches off map-file generation. (A map file shows the locations of code segments, public symbols, and other details of the code's structure, which are sometimes useful for debugging.) The -c and -C options specify case-sensitivity options, needed by most programs. The -E option enables extended dictionaries in library files for faster object-code loading.

After these options are several .OBJ and .LIB files, and also the output file's name, HOWL.EXE, and a module-definition file, HOWL.DEF. As you can see, compiling and linking a windows application—even one as simple as HOWL—is no easy matter.

CHOWL32.BAT (Listing 2.3) shows the equivalent commands for compiling HOWL as a 32-bit application. The 32-bit compiler understands similar options, but as I've said, memory models (to name one example) are not required, so there's no -ml option. The -Lxxxx option specifies the path (*xxxx*) to BC4's library files, overriding any similar setting in a TLINK32.CFG configuration file. The TLINK32 command links the object code to various 32-bit libraries, creating the finished HOWL.EXE code file. To run it, you must have installed Win32s. (Or, you can run the code file under Windows NT.)

The foregoing options and libraries are by no means sacred. Every program has its requirements, and it's impossible to give one example that covers all the bases. Consider all of the sample compilation and linking commands in this chapter as starting places. You probably will need to specify other options and files to compile and link your applications.

Use CHOWL16.bat and CHOWL32.BAT to create general-purpose batch files capable of compiling tests and demonstrations. Just replace "howl" in each listing with the batch-file substitution command %1. Listings 2.4, C16.BAT, and 2.5, C32.BAT, show the final results. Type the final three lines of C16.BAT on one line. Type the final two lines of C32.BAT on one line. The disk files are correctly formatted. Both files are stored in the MISC directory on this book's disk.

Listing 2.4. C16.BAT (general).

```
bcc -IC:\BC4\INCLUDE -c -WS -w -xd -ml %1.cpp
tlink -LC:\BC4\LIB -Twe -x -c -C -E c0wl.obj %1.obj,
  %1.exe,,bidsl.lib owlwl.lib cwl.lib import.lib
  mathwl.lib,%1.def
```

Listing 2.5. C32.BAT (general).

```
bcc32 -IC:\BC4\INCLUDE -c -w -xd %1.cpp
tlink32 -LC:\BC4\LIB -Tpe -x -c c0w32.obj %1.obj,%1.exe,,
  bidsf.lib owlwf.lib import32.lib cw32.lib,%1.def
```

To use the C16.BAT and C32.BAT files, copy them to a directory on your system path. I keep a directory, C:\BATCH, in which I store various batch files. I insert C:\BATCH in a PATH statement in AUTOEXEC.BAT so I can run my batch files from any other directory. If you don't want to create a separate directory, you can copy C16.BAT and C32.BAT into C:\BC4\BIN. If you reinstall the compiler, however, those files will be deleted. Keep backup copies elsewhere.

You can now compile simple examples such as HOWL.CPP with the two batch files. For example, from a DOS prompt, change to the HOWL directory. To compile the program as a 16-bit application, enter the command:

```
c16 howl
To compile HOWL as a 32-bit application, enter:
c32 howl
```

Automatic Compilation with Make

Supplied with BC4, *Make* is a command-line tool that runs *other* command-line tools, compilers, linkers, and so on. Many professional developers—especially those who use programmer's editors such as *Brief* or *Codewrite for Windows*—use Make to compile programs. Make compares the dates and times of source text files to the dates and times of compiled object- and executable-code files (if they exist), and then issues the minimum number of commands required to compile and link an application's .EXE code file. In short, if your program is divided into four modules A, B, C, and D, and if you change only modules A and B, Make compiles those two modules, then links the object code files (C.OBJ and D.OBJ didn't change, and therefore, don't require recompilation), creating the finished .EXE code file.

This isn't the proper time nor place to go into Make's many intricate features, some of which you may never need. Rather than provide a complete Make tutorial (which you receive with BC4's documentation), this section explains how to create Make files using the IDE, and how to compile programs using the Make files supplied with this book's disk and with BC4's example programs. I also list Make file shells you can adapt to your own 16- and 32-bit Windows programs.

Using Make Files

You can store Make files under filenames ending in .MAK, or you can name them MAKEFILE with no extension. You need to use .MAK files only if you keep several projects in the same directory. If you follow the "one-directory, one-application" rule (usually a wise plan), you can name all of your Make files MAKEFILE. All Make files supplied with this book's disk are named MAKEFILE.

A Make file is a plain text file that you can edit using any text editor or the BC4 IDE. The IDE can create Make files automatically, or you can type them from scratch (a job made easier by using one of the Make file shells listed later in this chapter). Using the IDE is the simplest method. Follow these steps to create a Make file for the HOWL.CPP program from Chapter 1:

1. Start BC4 and close any open projects and windows.
2. Open the HOWL.IDE project using the *Project|Open project...* command.
3. Be sure you can compile the project. Press F9 to check. If successful, continue with step 4; otherwise, you must fix the problem (most likely an error in configuration or the system PATH) before you can create the Make file.
4. Select the *Project|Generate makefile* command.

That's all you need to do to create a Make file for any project. The file is opened in a window, and is named the same as the project or main program file plus the extension .MAK. In this example, the resulting window is named HOWL.MAK. You may examine or edit this file. To use it, you must save the file to disk. Until you do that, the generated Make file is stored only in memory—if you decide not to keep the generated file, close the window and answer No when asked whether to save your changes. If you are following along, save the HOWL.MAK file now. Listing 2.6, HOWL.MAK, shows the resulting file. (The file is not included on the book's disk—you need to create the file using the IDE.) If you've never seen a Make file before, the listing probably looks like mush. Don't worry about that—I explain some of its parts and pieces later in the chapter.

Listing 2.6. HOWL.MAK.

```
#
# Borland C++ IDE generated makefile
#
.AUTODEPEND


#
# Borland C++ tools
#
IMPLIB  = Implib
BCC     = Bcc +BccW16.cfg
TLINK   = TLink
TLIB    = TLib
BRC     = Brc
TASM    = Tasm
#
# IDE macros
#


#
# Options
#
IDE_LFLAGS =  -LC:\BC4\LIB
IDE_RFLAGS =  -IC:\BC4\INCLUDE
LLATW16_howldexe =  -Twe -C -c
RLATW16_howldexe =  -31
BLATW16_howldexe =
LEAT_howldexe = $(LLATW16_howldexe)
REAT_howldexe = $(RLATW16_howldexe)
BEAT_howldexe = $(BLATW16_howldexe)

#
# Dependency List
#
Dep_howl = \
   howl.exe

howl : BccW16.cfg $(Dep_howl)
  echo MakeNode howl
```

continues

Listing 2.6. continued

```
Dep_howldexe = \
   howl.obj

howl.exe : $(Dep_howldexe)
  $(TLINK)   @&&|
 /v $(IDE_LFLAGS) $(LEAT_howldexe) +
C:\BC4\LIB\c0wl.obj+
howl.obj
$<,$*
C:\BC4\LIB\bidsi.lib+
C:\BC4\LIB\owlwi.lib+
C:\BC4\LIB\import.lib+
C:\BC4\LIB\crtldll.lib
howl.def
|

howl.obj :  howl.cpp
  $(BCC)    -c $(CEAT_howldexe) -o$@ howl.cpp

# Compiler configuration file
BccW16.cfg :
   Copy &&|
-R
-v
-vi
-X-
-H
-IC:\BC4\INCLUDE
-H=howl.csm
-ml
-WS
-H"owl\owlpch.h"
-D_RTLDLL;_BIDSDLL;_OWLDLL;_OWLPCH;
| $@
```

After saving HOWL.MAK, exit BC4. You don't need the IDE any longer—all necessary command-line commands and options are now stored in the Make file. Follow these
steps to compile the HOWL project using HOWL.MAK:

1. Open a DOS prompt window from the Program Manager. Or, you may quit
   Windows and compile from a plain DOS environment. *See the note earlier in
   this chapter about configuring memory using the Windows PIF Editor or the DOS-
   only MAKESWAP utility.*

2. Change to the HOWL directory by typing a command such as

```
cd c:\mwp\howl
```

3. Enter the following Make command to process the generated Make file (do *not* type a space between -f and the HOWL.MAK filename):

```
make -fhowl.mak
```

That tells Make to read HOWL.MAK and execute the file's commands. Because you already compiled the HOWL program, the command doesn't do much. Make is smart— it issues only the minimum number of commands necessary to compile a program's modules. To rebuild HOWL from scratch using Make, first delete the program's .OBJ and .EXE code files:

```
del howl.obj
del howl.exe
```

For simplicity, you can also rename HOWL.MAK to MAKEFILE, which the Make utility automatically recognizes. Type this command (but first delete any exiting MAKEFILE in the current directory):

```
rename howl.mak makefile
```

You can now run Make to build the program. First, however, you might want to study the commands that Make will issue, but not actually give those commands. To do that, use the Make utility's -n option like this:

```
make -n
```

You don't need to specify a filename because Make automatically looks for a file named MAKEFILE in the current directory. In this case, however, because you specified the -n option, Make simply displays the commands it would have issued. On screen, you see these lines:

```
Copy MAKE0001.@@@ bccw16.cfg
Bcc +BccW16.cfg  -c  -ohowl.obj howl.cpp
TLink @MAKE0000.@@@
echo MakeNode howl
```

The first line copies a temporary file, MAKE0001.@@@, which is created by Make, to a configuration file BCCW16.CFG. That file contains various compiler and linker options specified in the Make file. The second line calls the command-line compiler, BCC, passes it the configuration filename, and compiles HOWL.CPP to create HOWL.OBJ. The third line links object-code modules, listed in another temporary file, MAKE0000.@@@, to create the finished .EXE code file. The final line displays a confirming message.

Table 2.2 lists some other Make file options that I find useful. You can list all options by typing **make -?**. Option letters are case-sensitive (you must type then in upper- or lowercase as shown). For example, rather than delete .EXE and .OBJ code files in the directory, you can rebuild an application by entering the command:

```
make -B
```

Table 2.2. Some Make file options.

Option	Effect
-? or -h	Lists all Make options with brief descriptions.
-B	Builds the application (compiles all modules, even those that are apparently up to date). Use this option to prepare shipping versions of applications.
-K	Keeps temporary files created by Make. Use this option to save files such as MAKE0001.@@@. After Make finishes, you can examine the temporary files using a text editor. They may help you fix MAKEFILE bugs.
-S	Swaps Make in and out of memory to make more room for command-line tools. Use this command only as a last resort if you run out of memory—it addes extra time to compilation and linking.
-m	Displays the date and time of each file.
-n	Displays, but does not execute, commands. Use this option to preview what Make will do when you run the program without the -n option.
-q	Causes Make to return 0 if the target is completely up to date (in which case Make issues no commands, but may still display some messages), or to return a nonzero value if one or more commands are needed to bring the target project up to date. Use this command when running Make from a batch file so you can display a message about the state of a project.
-s	Silences most (not all) of Make's on-screen messages. Also known as the *shut up* option.

You may combine multiple Make options. For example, to view all commands required to build a project from scratch, but not actually issue those commands, type:

```
make -B -n
```

You can also direct Make's output to a temporary file, which you may print or view using a text editor:

```
make -B -n>build.txt
```

The resulting BUILD.TXT file shows all the commands needed to build the program. By the way, redirecting Make's output this way is the only way you can silence the program's on-screen messages completely.

NOTE

Most of the programs supplied on this book's disk have Make files that you can use to compile the programs from a DOS prompt. All such files are named MAKEFILE, and were created using the IDE's *Project/Generate makefile...* command. To use the supplied Make files, go to a DOS prompt, change to one of the book-disk's directories, and type **make**. If you receive errors, you may have to reconfigure the .IDE project directories, set aside more XMS memory, create a swap file, modify your PATH statement, or edit the paths in the default .CFG configuration files stored in C:\BC4\BIN. Reread this and the preceding chapter for details. You can then regenerate the Make files using the Project menu's command. Remember that this command creates a file ending in .MAK. Rename that file to MAKEFILE after deleting the old file of that name.

Make File Components

Many readers probably already know how to create and use Make files, but I receive many requests for this information, so the following reviews some of the basics. If you are familiar with Make-file components, skip ahead to *Writing Your Own Make Files*. A Make file consists of several elements (see the sample HOWL.MAK listing). Common elements include the following:

- *Comments* preceded with #.
- *Macros,* giving names to directory paths, or selecting options such as adding debugging information to compiled code.
- *Explicit rules,* listing a target file (such as MYPROG.OBJ), the files on which it depends (MYPROG.CPP and MYPROG.H, for example), and the compiler or linker commands required to create the target.

- *Implicit rules,* for compiling or linking files ending in a certain extension.
- *Directives,* selecting Make options and choosing selected Make file statements based on the values, presence, or absence of certain macros.

Comments

A Make file *comment* is any text beginning with a pound sign, #, and it extends to the end of that line. For example, HOWL.MAK begins with the comment:

```
#
# Borland C++ IDE generated makefile
#
```

Macros

A Make file *macro* is a named string that you may use throughout a Make file's other lines. Several macros appear in the *Options* section of HOWL.MAK. For example, the following creates a macro named IDE_RFLAGS:

```
IDE_RFLAGS =  -IC:\BC4\INCLUDE
```

To use the macro, type a dollar sign and insert the macro name in parentheses. Make replaces the construction with the macro's contents. For instance, Make processes this command:

```
BCC $(IDE_RFLAGS) howl
```

as though you wrote:

```
BCC -IC:\BC4\INCLUDE howl
```

Explicit Rules

An *explicit rule* tells Make that a certain target file depends on the status of another file, usually one that contains declarations or statements. For example, an explicit rule might state that HOWL.OBJ depends on HOWL.CPP. In other words, if the date and time of HOWL.CPP is *later* than HOWL.OBJ (or if the object code file doesn't exist), the source code file must be recompiled to update the object code. If HOWL.OBJ's date and time is the same or *later* than HOWL.CPP, however, then Make assumes no changes were made to the source file, and it skips the commands needed to recompile the object code. This process saves time, especially for programs composed of many modules, only some of which require recompiling at any one time. Here's a sample explicit rule from HOWL.MAK:

```
howl.obj : howl.cpp
  $(BCC)   -c $(CEAT_howldexe) -o$@ howl.cpp
```

The rule is on the first line. It states that HOWL.OBJ depends on HOWL.CPP. If the source code file's date and time is *later* than the object code file, or if HOWL.OBJ does not exist, Make issues the command given on the next one or more lines, each of which must begin with at least one blank character. In the command (the second line in the preceding example), the macros $(BCC) and $(CEAT_howldexe) are replaced with their associated text. The -c option means "compile only, don't link" and the -o option names the resulting object-code file HOWL.OBJ, using the shorthand $@, which Make translates to HOWL. (That option is superfluous in this example, but the IDE adds it anyway.)

Implicit Rules

Implicit rules work something like DOS wild cards—they issue generic commands for all files ending with a particular extension. For example, a single implicit rule can compile all .CPP files in the current directory, creating .OBJ code files for each out of date module. HOWL.MAK contains no implicit rules. Here's a sample of one from a listing to be explained later in this chapter:

```
.cpp.obj:
  $(CC) -c {$< }
```

The command tells the compiler that all files ending in .OBJ depend on files of the same name ending in .CPP. The second line gives a compile only (-c) command, using the compiler named by macro CC, and specifying the filename with the shorthand expression {$< }. The result is a command that compiles all .CPP modules in the current directory.

Directives

Make-file *directives* work like conditional directives in C and C++. They process or skip sections of a Make file depending on whether a symbol is defined (that is, a symbol that Make knows to exist). HOWL.MAK has no directives. Here's a sample directive from a listing to be presented later in the chapter:

```
!if $d(DEBUG)
!undef DEBUG
DEBUG=-v
!endif
```

Directives begin with an exclamation point. The first line in the sample causes Make to process subsequent lines, up to the end mark !endif, if a symbol DEBUG is defined. If that symbol is defined, the next line undefines it, and the third line assigns the option -v to DEBUG. Such symbols are macros, thus if DEBUG exists, it is translated to the associated text, -v. If it doesn't exist, it translates to thin air. The command:

```
BCC $(DEBUG) filename.cpp
```

is therefore translated to one of the following:

```
BCC filename.cpp
BCC -v filename.cpp
```

To define a symbol, give it a value:

```
DEBUG=1
```

Or, you can define a symbol when running Make by using the -D option (don't type a space after D):

```
make -DDEBUG
```

Writing Your Own Make Files

Automatically generated Make files are like automatically generated applications—they may or may not include all the options, or be written in the style, that you need. For simple programs, automatically generated Make files are certainly convenient. In fact, some programmers like to build prototypes of their applications using the IDE, then after receiving a green light to begin serious development, they generate a Make file and start using command-line tools and editors, perhaps on a DOS-only development system.

That approach is fine, but if you are going to use command-line tools, you may as well create your own Make files. This is not easy task, so I've included three sample files that you can use as guides. Listing 2.7, MAKEFILE (in the MAKEDEMO directory) shows a working example of a Make file that I wrote from scratch, using one of two Make-file templates listed later in this section.

> **NOTE**
>
> MAKEFILE is stored in directory MAKEDEMO along with a sample multifile application named DEMO, not listed here. Unlike other programs in this book, DEMO does not have an .IDE project file. To compile the program, open a DOS window if you are running Windows, then change to the MAKEDEMO directory, and type **make**. A copy of this same file is stored in MAKE16.MAK, also in the MAKEDEMO directory.

Listing 2.7. MAKEFILE (in MAKEDEMO directory).

```
#*  ================================================================ *#
#*   makefile -- Multi-file Make file shell                          *#
#*  ================================================================ *#
#*                                                                    *#
#*   To add an object-code file to project:                          *#
#*     1. Add .OBJ filename to LDEPENDS macro                        *#
#*     2. Add same .OBJ filename to object-code file list            *#
#*     3. Optionally add explicit dependency for file                *#
#*                                                                    *#
#*   To add a library file to project:                               *#
#*     1. Add .LIB filename to library file list                     *#
#*                                                                    *#
#*   To use:                                                          *#
#*     make                        normal make                       *#
#*     make -DDEBUG                 add debugging info                *#
#*     make -DMEM=x                 memory model x = s, m, or l       *#
#*     make turboc.cfg              make TURBOC.CFG file only         *#
#*     make tlink.cfg               make TLINK.CFG file only          *#
#*     make clean                   erase miscellaneous files        *#
#*                                                                    *#
#*  ================================================================ *#
#*      Copyright (c) 1994 by Tom Swan. All rights reserved.         *#
#*  ================================================================ *#


# ================================================================
#  Various macros
# ================================================================
# BC4ROOT      Borland C++ for Windows installation directory
# CC           Compiler filename (bcc or bcc32)
# LINK         Linker filename (tlink or tlink32)
# RC           Resource compiler (brcc)
# RLINK        Resource linker (rlink)
# CFG          Compiler configuration file (turboc.cfg)
# LCFG         Linker configuration file (tlink.cfg)
# LISTOBJ      File containing object-code filenames
# LISTLIB      File containing library filenames
# LIBPATH      Path(s) to library (.lib) files
# INCPATH      Path(s) to include (.h) files
# MEM          Memory model (s,m,c, or l) OPTIONAL
# DEBUG        Include debugging/browsing information OPTIONAL
# COPTS        Compiler options
# LOPTS        Linker options
# RCOPTS       Resource compiler options
# RLOPTS       Resource linker options

BC4ROOT=C:\bc4
CC=bcc
LINK=tlink
RC=brcc
```

continues

Listing 2.7. continued

```
RLINK=rlink
CFG=turboc.cfg
LCFG=tlink.cfg
LISTOBJ=obj.lst
LISTLIB=lib.lst
LIBPATH=$(BC4ROOT)\lib
INCPATH=$(BC4ROOT)\include

!if !$d(MEM)
MEM=l
!endif

!if $d(DEBUG)
!undef DEBUG
DEBUG=-v
!endif

COPTS=-WS -w -xd -m$(MEM) $(DEBUG)
LOPTS=-Twe -x -c -C -E $(DEBUG)
RCOPTS=-31
RLOPTS=-31

# ===============================================================
#  Linker dependencies (i.e. files that DEMO.EXE depends on)
# ===============================================================

LDEPENDS=$(LISTOBJ) $(LISTLIB) $(LCFG)\
 demo.res\
 demo.obj\
 demowin.obj\
 demo.def

# ===============================================================
#  Implicit dependency rules
# ===============================================================

.c.obj:
  $(CC) -c {$< }

.cpp.obj:
  $(CC) -c {$< }

# ===============================================================
#  Explicit dependencies and rules
# ===============================================================

demo.exe: $(LDEPENDS)
  $(LINK) @$(LISTOBJ),demo.exe,demo.map,@$(LISTLIB),demo.def
  $(RLINK) $(RLOPTS) demo.res demo.exe
```

```
demo.obj: $(CFG) demo.cpp demo.h

demowin.obj: $(CFG) demowin.cpp demowin.h

demo.res: $(CFG) demo.rc demo.rh
  $(RC) -i$(INCPATH) -fodemo.res $(RCOPTS) demo.rc


# =================================================================
#  Create object-code file list for linker
#  Insert .OBJ filenames between "¦" delimiters
# =================================================================

$(LISTOBJ): makefile
  copy &&¦
c0w$(MEM).obj+
demo.obj+
demowin.obj+
¦ $(LISTOBJ)


# =================================================================
#  Create library file list for linker
#  Insert .LIB filenames between "¦" delimiters
# =================================================================

$(LISTLIB): makefile
  copy &&¦
bids$(MEM).lib+
owlw$(MEM).lib+
cw$(MEM).lib+
import.lib+
mathw$(MEM).lib
¦ $(LISTLIB)


# =================================================================
#  Create linker configuration file
#  Insert linker options between "¦" delimiters
# =================================================================

$(LCFG): makefile
  copy &&¦
-L$(LIBPATH)
$(LOPTS)
¦ $(LCFG)


# =================================================================
#  Create compiler configuration file
#  Insert compiler options between "¦" delimiters
# =================================================================

$(CFG): makefile
  copy &&¦
```

continues

75

Listing 2.7. continued

```
-I$(INCPATH)
-L$(LIBPATH)
-H=header.csm
$(COPTS)
| $(CFG)

# =================================================================
#  Delete backups, obj, exe, and miscellaneous files
#  Enter MAKE CLEAN to use
# =================================================================

clean:
  @if exist *.bak del *.bak
  @if exist *.obj del *.obj
  @if exist *.exe del *.exe
  @if exist *.map del *.map
  @if exist *.res del *.res
  @if exist *.rws del *.rws
  @if exist *.dll del *.dll
  @if exist *.csm del *.csm
  @if exist *.dsk del *.dsk
  @if exist *.tdr del *.tdr
  @if exist *.tdw del *.tdw
  @if exist *.scr del *.scr
  @if exist *.err del *.err
  @if exist lib.lst del lib.lst
  @if exist obj.lst del obj.lst
```

My custom MAKEFILE begins with a large comment that explains how to insert new code-file modules, libraries, and options. Just under this comment are several macros, in all capital letters. Edit these macros as needed for your system. Be sure to set the path in BC4ROOT correctly.

The CC and LINK macros specify the names of the compiler and linker—BCC and TLINK for Borland C++ for Windows. RC and RLINK select Borland's resource compiler (BRCC) and resource linker (RLINK). CFG and LCFG are assigned the names of two configuration files, TURBOC.CFG and TLINK.CFG. You don't have to create these files—MAKEFILE does that automatically. LISTOBJ and LISTLIB specify two other files, OBJ.LST and LIB.LST, also created by MAKEFILE. Two other macros list compiler and linker pathnames. Modify the directory names as needed in LIBPATH and INCPATH.

Two !if directives set macro MEM to the letter l (for *large*) if MEM is not defined. To use a different memory model, assign a different letter to MEM in a -D directive at a DOS prompt or in a batch file command:

```
make -DMEM=s
```

Use that command to compile DEMO for the small memory model. Or you can modify MEM's setting in MAKEFILE. Set MEM to m for the medium model. (Remember, however, that OWL programs can use only small, medium, or large models.) To add debugging and browsing information to the compiled code, define the DEBUG macro with the command:

```
make -DDEBUG
```

Or, enter this macro definition command near the beginning of MAKEFILE:

```
DEBUG=1
```

The next four macros—COPTS, LOPTS, RCOPTS, and RLOPTS—define options for the compiler, linker, resource compiler, and resource linker. You may add or subtract any options you like in these sections. The default options create an nonoptimized, statically linked, 16-bit Windows .EXE code file for Windows 3.1.

The next section defines a macro LDEPENDS that lists all files on which the program's .EXE code file depends. In other words, if any one of these files is out of date relative to the program's .EXE file, Make relinks the program to update the code. The notation $() means "replace the symbol in parentheses with the macro's value." Thus Make replaces $(LCFG) with TLINK.CFG, the value assigned to the LCFG macro.

The LDEPENDS macro should list every .OBJ, .RES, .DEF, and .LIB file used by the program (but not system .LIB files). The program's definition file, DEMO.DEF, must be last. Separate multiple entries with a single space, or place them on separate lines ending with a backslash as shown here. The backslash must be the last character on the line.

The next section defines two implicit dependency rules—shorthand commands that apply to all files ending with certain extensions. For example, the .c.obj rule translates .C files to compiled .OBJ code files. The .cpp.obj rule does the same for .CPP files. The command in each case is:

```
$(CC) -c {$< }
```

which isn't so odd when you pick it apart. Make replaces $(CC) with the compiler name (BCC in this case), -c means compile don't link, and {$< } expands to one or more filenames—the ones that need compiling.

> **NOTE**
>
> No other options are required in MAKEFILE's implicit dependency rules because *all* compiler and linker options are stored in the configuration files, TURBOC.CFG and TLINK.CFG, created by MAKEFILE *before* the implicit rules' commands are issued.

You can remove the braces from {$< } to issue individual compilation commands. With the braces, Make *batches* multiple files together, giving commands such as the following (don't type this, however; it's just for show):

```
bcc -c file1.cpp file2.cpp file3.cpp
```

This trick saves time by not reloading the compiler into memory for each file, but it may not work for projects with too many files to specify on one line.

Explicit dependency rules come next in MAKEFILE, listing files that depend on more than one other file. For example, the command that begins with *demo.exe* lists the files needed to link the final .EXE code file. Because of MAKEFILE's design, this same dependency rule should work with most programs. Simply replace all instances of *demo* with your program's name. You do not have to specify other object-code filenames or options here.

The next two rules (beginning with .OBJ filenames) list the names of each program module that depends on more than one other file. For example, DEMO.OBJ depends on $(CFG) (expanded to TURBOC.CFG), DEMO.CPP, and DEMO.H. Modifying any of those files causes Make to recompile DEMO.CPP, in this case using the implicit .cpp.obj rule, to recreate DEMO.OBJ.

The final dependency rule (the two lines beginning with *demo.res*) calls Borland's resource compiler, BRCC.EXE, to compile the program's resources. The second rule under *demo.exe* calls Borland's resource linker, RLINK.EXE, to bind the resulting DEMO.RES binary resource file into the finished DEMO.EXE code file.

> **NOTE**
>
> Because of MAKEFILE's design, you can edit a program's resources and bind them into the finished code file using a minimum of commands. Try this: first type **make** to be sure the program is up to date. Then, enter **touch demo.rc** to update that file's directory entry to the current date and time, simulating a change to a resource script command. (You could also load DEMO.RC into a text editor, make an arbitrary change, and save the file

to change its date and time.) Next, type **make**, and watch the commands issued to rebuild the program's resources and bind them into the program. Notice that Make does not recompile the program, which hasn't changed since the last compilation.

Four key sections in the sample MAKEFILE come next. To adapt MAKEFILE for your own projects, you may have to edit a few lines in these parts. Each section uses a technique that creates a temporary text file, then copies that file to another named file. This line, for example:

```
$(LISTOBJ): makefile
```

states that the file identified by LISTOBJ depends on MAKEFILE. If MAKEFILE is updated (to add a new compiler option, for example), Make issues the commands that follow, beginning with:

```
copy &&¦
```

On processing that line, Make issues a DOS COPY command, replacing && with a unique temporary filename that Make invents. The vertical bar can be any unused character (an exclamation point also works). Everything between this character and the next occurrence of that *same* character is stored in the file. The final line:

```
¦ $(LISTOBJ)
```

ends the parade, copying the preceding lines to the file identified by the LISTOBJ macro—OBJ.LST in this example. The result is a *response file* containing the program's object-code filenames that MAKEFILE passes to the linker.

In the next section, MAKEFILE creates a similar file named LIB.LST, containing library filenames. This response file is also passed to the linker. There's no defined limit to the number of object-code and library files you can link using these response-file techniques.

Next in MAKEFILE are two sections that create two more files, TLINK.CFG and TURBOC.CFG. Don't edit these files directly; instead, let MAKEFILE create them from the options macros LOPTS and COPTS. You may also insert explicit compiler and linker options in MAKEFILE between the vertical bars in the sections beginning with $(LCFG) and $(CFG).

Finally in MAKEFILE is a small section that begins with *clean:*. This undocumented trick causes MAKEFILE to issue optional commands, in this case, to delete all files ending in the extensions shown, and also the individual files LIB.LST and OBJ.LST. To purge the directory of these files (perhaps as a prelude to rebuilding the entire program from scratch), type *make clean* on the DOS command line. Then type **make** to rebuild.

One neat trick I use frequently is to display a report of the commands that Make will issue. Try this. Delete all .OBJ files in the MAKEDEMO directory, then type `make -n` on the command line. On screen, you see all the commands that typing x alone will give.

16-Bit Make File Template

A copy of MAKEFILE in Listing 2.7 is stored in MAKE16.MAK, also in the MAKEDEMO directory. Use MAKE16.MAK to create your own Make files for 16-bit, Windows programs. Follow these steps to edit MAKE16.MAK (which you can rename MAKEFILE) for a new project:

1. Edit the pathnames and other macros as needed. Most should require no changes.
2. Delete DEMOWIN.OBJ from the LDEPENDS macro. Rename all instances of DEMO in this section to your program's main filename.
3. In the "Explicit dependencies" section, delete the line beginning with DEMOWIN.OBJ. Rename every instance of DEMO in this section to your program's main filename.
4. In the object-code file list, delete DEMOWIN.OBJ, then rename DEMO.OBJ to your program's object-code main filename. All filenames except the last should end with a plus sign.
5. Modify linker (LOPTS) and compiler (COPTS) options to suit your requirements.

To add a new module to your modified MAKEFILE, follow these three steps:

1. Add the module's .OBJ filename to the LDEPENDS macro.
2. Add that same .OBJ filename to the object-code file list.
3. Insert a dependency for any module that depends on multiple files. Use the line that begins with DEMOWIN.OBJ as a guide.

That's all you need to do to add a new module to a project. Steps 1 and 2 are required. Step 3 is needed only if the module depends on more than one other file. For example, if X.OBJ depends on X.CPP and X.H—in other words, if you enter changes in either of those two files, and you want Make to recreate X.OBJ—add this line to the "Explicit dependencies" section:

```
x.obj: $(CFG) x.cpp x.h
```

The $(CFG) macro expression is optional, but causes Make to recompile the module if you change an option in MAKEFILE that creates a new TURBOC.CFG configuration file.

My MAKEFILE creates configuration files that make it easy to compile programs directly from another editor for different platforms. For example, before editing programs, I enter this DOS command:

```
make turboc.cfg
```

This creates the TURBOC.CFG configuration file containing all MAKEFILE options and paths. I can then load a source file into Brief and use that program's compilation command (Alt+F10) to compile .CPP files with the command bcc -c filename.cpp. That *same* command works with DOS files and with earlier compiler releases such as Borland C++ 3.1. By storing specific options in TURBOC.CFG (such as the options required to create Windows object-code), I can use the same editor command for DOS and Windows development.

32-Bit Make File Template

Listing 2.8, MAKE32.MAK, is similar to MAKE16.MAK (see listing 2.7), but compiles the MAKEDEMO application for 32-bit Windows NT or Win32s. This also demonstrates that, by using OWL, you can write 16- and 32-bit versions of Windows programs without requiring any changes to your source code. (You must use only 16-bit Windows functions, however. If you use 32-bit specific features, or if you write code that assumes integers are 32-bits long, for example, then your code will compile only as a 32-bit application.) After the listing, I explain how to use MAKE32.MAK to compile MAKEDEMO as a 32-bit application.

81

Listing 2.8. MAKE32.MAK.

```
#* ============================================================ *#
#*   makefile -- Multi-file Make file shell 32-bit OWL programs *#
#* ============================================================ *#
#*                                                              *#
#*   To add an object-code file to project:                     *#
#*      1. Add .OBJ filename to LDEPENDS macro                  *#
#*      2. Add same .OBJ filename to object-code file list      *#
#*      3. Optionally add explicit dependency for file          *#
#*                                                              *#
#*   To add a library file to project:                         *#
#*      1. Add .LIB filename to library file list              *#
#*                                                              *#
#*   To use:                                                    *#
#*      make                      normal make                  *#
#*      make -DDEBUG              add debugging info            *#
#*      make bcc32.cfg            make BCC32.CFG file only      *#
#*      make tlink32.cfg          make TLINK32.CFG file only    *#
#*      make clean                erase miscellaneous files    *#
#*                                                              *#
#* ============================================================ *#
#*      Copyright (c) 1994 by Tom Swan. All rights reserved.   *#
#* ============================================================ *#


# ==================================================================
#   Various macros
# ==================================================================
# BC4ROOT       Borland C++ for Windows installation directory
# CC            Compiler filename (bcc32)
# LINK          Linker filename (tlink32)
# RC            Resource compiler (brcc32)
# CFG           Compiler configuration file (bcc32.cfg)
# LCFG          Linker configuration file (tlink32.cfg)
# LISTOBJ       File containing object-code filenames
# LISTLIB       File containing library filenames
# LIBPATH       Path(s) to library (.lib) files
# INCPATH       Path(s) to include (.h) files
# DEBUG         Include debugging/browsing information OPTIONAL
# COPTS         Compiler options
# LOPTS         Linker options
# RCOPTS        Resource compiler options

BC4ROOT=C:\bc4
CC=bcc32
LINK=tlink32
RC=brcc32
CFG=bcc32.cfg
LCFG=tlink32.cfg
LISTOBJ=obj32.lst
```

```
LISTLIB=lib32.lst
LIBPATH=$(BC4ROOT)\lib
INCPATH=$(BC4ROOT)\include

!if $d(DEBUG)
!undef DEBUG
DEBUG=-v
!endif

COPTS=-w -xd $(DEBUG)
LOPTS=-Tpe -x -c $(DEBUG)
RCOPTS=-W32

# =================================================================
#  Linker dependencies (i.e. files that DEMO.EXE depends on)
# =================================================================

LDEPENDS=$(LISTOBJ) $(LISTLIB) $(LCFG)\
 demo.res\
 demo.obj\
 demowin.obj\
 demo.def

# =================================================================
#  Implicit dependency rules
# =================================================================

.c.obj:
  $(CC) -c {$< }

.cpp.obj:
  $(CC) -c {$< }

# =================================================================
#  Explicit dependencies and rules
# =================================================================

demo.exe: $(LDEPENDS)
  $(LINK) @$(LISTOBJ),demo.exe,demo.map,@$(LISTLIB),demo.def,demo.res

demo.obj: $(CFG) demo.cpp demo.h

demowin.obj: $(CFG) demowin.cpp demowin.h

demo.res: $(CFG) demo.rc demo.rh
  $(RC) -i$(INCPATH) -fodemo.res $(RCOPTS) demo.rc

# =================================================================
#  Create object-code file list for linker
#  Insert .OBJ filenames between "¦" delimiters
# =================================================================
```

continues

Listing 2.8. continued

```
$(LISTOBJ): makefile
  copy &&¦
c0w32.obj+
demo.obj+
demowin.obj
¦ $(LISTOBJ)


# =================================================================
#  Create library file list for linker
#  Insert .LIB filenames between "¦" delimiters
# =================================================================

$(LISTLIB): makefile
  copy &&¦
bidsf.lib+
owlwf.lib+
cw32.lib+
import32.lib
¦ $(LISTLIB)


# =================================================================
#  Create linker configuration file
#  Insert linker options between "¦" delimiters
# =================================================================

$(LCFG): makefile
  copy &&¦
-L$(LIBPATH)
$(LOPTS)
¦ $(LCFG)


# =================================================================
#  Create compiler configuration file
#  Insert compiler options between "¦" delimiters
# =================================================================

$(CFG): makefile
  copy &&¦
-I$(INCPATH)
-L$(LIBPATH)
-H=header.csm
$(COPTS)
¦ $(CFG)


# =================================================================
#  Delete backups, obj, exe, and miscellaneous files
#  Enter MAKE CLEAN to use
# =================================================================
```

```
clean:
  @if exist *.bak del *.bak
  @if exist *.obj del *.obj
  @if exist *.exe del *.exe
  @if exist *.map del *.map
  @if exist *.res del *.res
  @if exist *.rws del *.rws
  @if exist *.dll del *.dll
  @if exist *.csm del *.csm
  @if exist *.dsk del *.dsk
  @if exist *.tdr del *.tdr
  @if exist *.tdw del *.tdw
  @if exist *.scr del *.scr
  @if exist *.err del *.err
  @if exist lib.lst del lib.lst
  @if exist obj.lst del obj.lst
  @if exist lib32.lst del lib32.lst
  @if exist obj32.lst del obj32.lst
```

Before using MAKE32.MAK, first erase any compiled object-code and executable files from the MAKEDEMO directory. Change to that directory and enter the command:

```
make clean
```

That deletes any 16-bit files from preceding compilations (you cannot mix 16- and 32-bit object code files). Next, enter the following command to compile the demonstration as a 32-bit application:

```
make -fmake32.mak
```

The same Make utility can create 16- and 32-bit code. You can also rename MAKE32.MAK as MAKEFILE (but first delete the existing MAKEFILE). You can then simply type **make** to compile.

To use MAKE32.MAK for your own projects, follow the suggestions given earlier for 16-bit code. The only significant differences are the library filenames (OWLWF.LIB, for example, and CW32.LIB), and the absence of a MEM macro, which isn't needed by flat-memory model 32-bit applications. Other features in the 32-bit Make file work the same as they do in the 16-bit version.

Other Tools

BC4 comes with several other tools and utilities, which deserve at least a mention here. Some tools are DOS-only programs, many of which have been supplied with Borland development systems for many years. The GREP.COM program, for example, searches text files for string patterns; TOUCH.COM updates file dates and times, and so on.

This book is about Windows programming, so I'll mention only Windows tools here. BC4's miscellaneous utilities, all of which you find in a Program Manager window, are:

- WinSpector
- WinSight
- FConvert
- Hot-Spot Editor

WinSpector

Run this program to install a background process that traps *Unexpected Application Errors,* also known as the dreaded UAEs. Such errors might be caused by programs referring to code or data outside of their allotted memory bounds, and are usually indications of serious trouble. UAEs may also be caused, unfortunately, by poorly written or incompatible device drivers, and by conflicts between the hardware and Windows. If you receive a UAE, it may indicate an error in your code, but it might also indicate a problem in your development system. Figure 2.8 shows WinSpector's display.

FIGURE 2.8.
WinSpector's display.

You can install WinSpector permanently by dragging its icon (click and drag while holding down Ctrl to drag a *copy* of the icon) to the *Startup* Program Manager window. When you next run Windows, WinSpector is automatically installed in the background. Run the program a second time after installation to view its window and to select various options.

WinSight

The WinSight utility is a kind of runtime Windows debugger that you can use to trace message activity, and to view various aspects of a program's runtime operations. WinSight is an investigative tool of a class usually called *spy programs.* Use WinSight to spy on a program's runtime actions, to view the messages received by windows, to inspect their handles and other settings, and so on.

Figure 2.9 shows a sample of WinSight's display. The top pane lists active processes and window handles. The bottom pane, opened by using a *Messages* menu command, lists message activity for a selected window, in this case, the Sketch program on this book's disk. Being able to trace messages sent to and from a window is highly valuable, and you should spend some time getting to know this important program.

FIGURE 2.9.
WinSight's display.

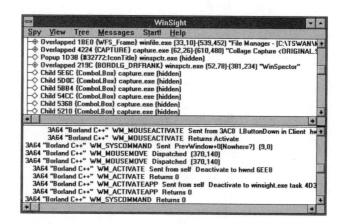

FConvert

This small program converts text files from OEM to ANSI character sets. If you have text files with extended ASCII text, you might be able to convert them for use in Windows using this tool. Or, you can convert ANSI text files to OEM versions. Be sure to save backup copies of all files before conversion, which is irreversible.

Hot-Spot Editor

Use this editor to create context-sensitive bitmaps for online help files. You can assign strings to locations in bitmaps, and select options for jumping to help topics when users click in bitmaps. Read the editor's online help for an overview of this tool. Writing help files is a topic that could fill a book (and has), so I'll skip full coverage of the Hot-Spot Editor.

Looking Ahead

That's enough background on using BC4. Now that you are comfortable with the IDE, and have configured BC4's debuggers, you're ready to dig into this book's main topic. Turn the page to begin learning how to use the ObjectWindows library to write Windows software.

Starting Up and Shutting Down

Every computer program goes through three main stages. There's a beginning, an end, and then there's everything else that goes on in between. The rest of this book deals with stage three. This chapter, however, covers the actions that a program takes when starting up and shutting down—two key aspects of Windows programming that are too often neglected in the rush to get to meatier subjects. Don't skip this important area of Windows development! Getting an application up and running correctly, and shutting it down properly, helps build a solid foundation on which your program's other code may depend.

In this chapter, you learn:

- Application startup and shutdown techniques.
- Windows startup and shutdown techniques.
- How to pass command-line arguments to Windows programs.
- How to detect first and subsequent program instances.
- How to load an accelerator table resource.

- How to display a window normally, as an icon, or full-screen.
- How to enable Borland Custom Controls and Microsoft 3-D controls.
- Application and window constructors and destructors.
- How to construct an ANSI C++ string object.
- How to use the CanClose function for safe window closing.
- How to display prompts and messages with the MessageBox function.
- Error handling techniques using ANSI C++ exceptions.

Application Startups

Every ObjectWindows Library (OWL) program begins with the first statement inside OwlMain, introduced in Chapter 1. OwlMain receives two arguments—argc and argv, the same two arguments passed to a common C program's main function. A typical OwlMain function looks like this:

```
int
OwlMain(int argc, char* argv[])
{
  TApplication app("AppName");
  return app.Run();
}
```

OwlMain has two primary duties: it must construct an *application object* of the TApplication class (or a class derived from TApplication), and it must call that object's Run member function. OwlMain may optionally return the status value returned by Run, or OwlMain can simply return zero (meaning no errors):

```
int
OwlMain(int argc, char* argv[])
{
  TApplication app("AppName");
  app.Run();
  return 0;
}
```

Resist the urge to add too many other statements and function calls to OwlMain. Because OWL programs are object-oriented, they should be initialized using class constructors and other techniques covered in this chapter and those that follow. Most programs, no matter how complex, have minimal OwlMain functions similar to those shown here.

Command-Line Arguments

Windows programs are often passed command-line arguments, similar to what happens when you execute a DOS program by typing

```
myprog filename.txt
```

That passes *filename.txt* to myprog. In Windows, a similar effect occurs in one of two ways: when you specify a *Command Line* option with the Program Manager's *File\Properties...* command, or when you associate an application and filename extension in the File Manager and you open a file of that type. Either way, OwlMain receives one or more arguments in its argv character-pointer array. Parameter argc indicates the number of arguments received—always at least one, since argv[0] addresses the program's pathname string.

In Borland C++, any function can access a program's command-line arguments by using the global variables, _argc and _argv. Each variable name is preceded by an underscore—the mark generally used for *system* variables. Only OwlMain, however, receives argc and argv parameters. Because the global _argc and _argv variables are available to all parts of a program, there is never any good reason to pass OwlMain's parameters as arguments to other functions or to class constructors.

Listing 3.1 demonstrates how to use command-line options. The demonstration's OwlMain function sets the program's main window title to *[untitled]* if no arguments are passed, or to the first argument if one is specified. You might use the program as a shell for a simple file processor (the demonstration doesn't actually open any files).

> **NOTE**
>
> Use the BC4 IDE *Project/Open project...* command to open ARGS.IDE in the ARGS directory on this book's disk. Press F9 to compile the program. Or, from a DOS prompt, change to the ARGS directory and type **make**. Then, follow instructions after the listing to run the program.

Listing 3.1. ARGS.CPP.

```
/* ============================================================ *\
** args.cpp -- Demonstrate command-line arguments             **
** ============================================================ **
**                                                             **
** ============================================================ **
```

continues

Listing 3.1. continued

```
#include <owl\applicat.h>
#include <owl\framewin.h>


// ============================================================
// The application class
// ============================================================

class TArgsApp: public TApplication {
public:
  TArgsApp(const char far* title)
    : TApplication(title) {};
  void InitMainWindow();
};

// Initialize the program's main window
void
TArgsApp::InitMainWindow()
{
  char far* title = "[untitled]";
  if (_argc > 1)
    title = _argv[1];
  MainWindow = new TFrameWindow(0, title);
}

#pragma argsused

// Main program
int
OwlMain(int argc, char* argv[])
{
  TArgsApp app(argv[0]);
  return app.Run();
}
```

To pass arguments to ARGS.EXE, you must run the program using the Windows File or Program Manager *File\Run...* commands. Select one of those commands, and enter **args** to run the program and display the main window title *[untitled]*. Or, enter **args filename.txt** to run the program and change the main window title to *filename.txt* (it doesn't have to refer to a real file).

Just to be different, I passed the program's path name to the TArgsApp constructor. Usually, you should pass a literal application title such as "ArgsApp" or another string when constructing the application object. TArgsApp is derived from TApplication, providing the means to tap into the application's startup sequence. In this case, the derived class provides two elements: a constructor and a replacement function for `InitMainWindow`, which constructs the application's main window object.

The `TArgsApp` constructor doesn't have much to do. It merely passes the `title` string argument to its ancestor `TApplication` constructor. `InitMainWindow` constructs an object of the `TFrameWindow` class, typically used for a program's main window. To obtain the string passed to the application object in `OwlMain`, `InitMainWindow` uses the global `_argc` and `_argv` variables to assign either *[untitled]* or a command-line argument string to the window's title.

Right away, you can see there's a lot more going on than meets the eye—even with this relatively simple application. The `TApplication` class is derived from `TModule`, and therefore, `TArgsApp` inherits all member functions and data from both of its ancestors. You can obtain the application's name by calling the inherited `GetName` function, which returns the string passed to the `TApplication` constructor in `OwlMain`:

```
char far* s = GetName();
```

> **TIP**
>
> To understand how to use a new class, you often need to examine the declarations in more than one class. Use the IDE browser to inspect a class's inheritance for a complete list of all inherited functions and data members. Chapter 2 explains how to use the browser.

By the way, ARGS.CPP includes the APPLICAT.H header, which declares the `TApplication` class. Because `TApplication` is derived from `TModule`, including APPLICAT.H automatically includes MODULE.H. You don't have to include both headers explicitly. OWL's headers are designed to include ancestor class declarations as needed by derived classes.

Application and Instance Initializations

Like lighting a fuse, constructing an application object in `OwlMain` ignites a string of actions that initializes the program and ends with a bang—the appearance of the program's main window. A `TApplication` object embodies the application's functions and data that would be defined globally in a typical non-OWL program.

TApplication is derived from TModule, which is sometimes used in the creation of dynamic link libraries (DLLs). TModule defines the fundamental properties of *modules*—applications and libraries that contain executable code. TApplication adds additional items needed only by Windows applications. The TApplication class declares two constructors, the simplest of which is:

```
TApplication(const char far* name = 0,
  TModule*& gModule = ::Module);
```

Normally, you should pass the application's name to the constructor's first parameter (as the preceding OwlMain examples show). The second parameter refers to the application's module (providing a context for other code to find the application), and rarely needs to be altered. Because both TApplication constructor parameters have default values, you can also create an unnamed application object like this:

```
TApplication app;
```

If you've done any Windows programming before, you may realize that WinMain is the function where a non-OWL program begins. Actually, OWL programs also have a WinMain function, but it's hidden and normally not referenced directly. Instead, OWL programs use OwlMain to initialize applications. If for some reason you need to use WinMain, you must initialize the program's TApplication object using the class's alternate constructor:

```
TApplication(const char far* name,
            HINSTANCE        hInstance,
            HINSTANCE        hPrevInstance,
            const char far* cmdLine,
            int              cmdShow,
            TModule*&        gModule = ::Module);
```

The first parameter represents the application's name. The next two are *instance handles*—hInstance represents the current program instance and hPrevInstance equals a previous instance if, for example, you restart the same program without closing all other invocations. The cmdLine parameter addresses the unparsed command-line string passed to the program, and cmdShow indicates whether to display the application's window normally, as an icon, or zoomed to full screen. The final parameter refers to the application module, and is rarely altered.

Use TApplication's alternate constructor to begin an OWL program in a WinMain function rather than OwlMain:

```
int
PASCAL WinMain(HINSTANCE, hInstance, HINSTANCE hPrevInstance,
  LPSTR lpszCmdLine, int nCmdShow)
{
```

```
TApplication app("name", hInstance, hPrevInstance,
  lpszCmdLine, nCmdShow);
return app.Run();
}
```

You normally shouldn't initialize applications like that, but the technique might be useful for converting straight C programs to OWL. All straight C Windows programs have a WinMain function. To convert them, rewrite WinMain as shown here. Programs written like that do not require an OwlMain function. Your application's class, derived from TApplication, must include a constructor with the parameters listed here, and it must call the alternate TApplication constructor. If your derived class is named TAnyApp, you might declare it as follows (along with other declarations of course):

```
class TAnyApp: public TApplication {
public:
  TAnyApp(const char far* name,
          HINSTANCE        hInstance,
          HINSTANCE        hPrevInstance,
          const char far*  cmdLine,
          int              cmdShow)
    : TApplication(name, hInstance, hPrevInstance, cmdLine,
      cmdShow) {};
...
};
```

You can then construct an instance of TAnyApp in WinMain as demonstrated for TApplication in the preceding example.

Whatever method you use to construct an application object (obviously, using OwlMain is simpler), calling a TApplication constructor activates three virtual member functions that you can override to tap into the program's startup phase. The functions are called automatically—you don't call them in statements; you simply replace them in your application's derived class. The three startup functions are:

```
virtual void InitApplication();
virtual void InitInstance();
virtual void InitMainWindow();
```

OWL calls InitApplication for the first program instance only. InitApplication is *not* called if the same program is run again without first closing the initial instance. That makes InitApplication the perfect place to perform global initializations and other tasks needed once and only once no matter how many copies of a program are run.

OWL calls InitInstance for *every* program instance. Use this function to perform local initializations and other tasks required every time the program runs. OWL calls InitApplication before calling InitInstance.

OWL calls InitMainWindow to construct the program's main window object. See "Main Window Startups" later in this chapter for more information on this subject. OWL calls InitMainWindow only after successfully calling InitApplication (for the first program instance only) and InitInstance.

To detect whether an application is a first or subsequent instance, you can inspect the application's hPrevInstance handle of type HINSTANCE declared in the TApplication class. All classes derived from TApplication inherit this handle, so any TApplication or derived-class function may refer to hPrevInstance. A good place to do that is in the InitInstance function because that function is called for every program instance:

```
if (hPrevInstance == 0)
  // code for first instance;
else
  // code for subsequent instance(s)
```

Outside of a TApplication derived class, hPrevInstance is not directly available. You can find this instance handle, however, using another technique that's only slightly more complicated. First call the global GetApplicationObject function (not a member of a class, but defined in MODULE.H) to obtain a pointer to the application object constructed in OwlMain. For example, any function may execute the following code:

```
TApplication* ap = GetApplicationObject();
if (ap->hPrevInstance == 0)
  MessageBox(ap->GetName(), "First Instance");
else
  MessageBox(ap->GetName(), "Subsequent Instance");
```

The first line defines a pointer, ap, to a TApplication object. The pointer is initialized to the result of GetApplicationObject, after which it addresses the object constructed in OwlMain. Using the pointer, you can inspect hPrevInstance as shown in the if statement. If the instance handle is zero, this is the first instance; otherwise, the program was restarted. You can use this technique inside window objects, for example, to take different actions for first and subsequent instances of a program.

InitInstance is the correct place to load an accelerator table resource, designating the program's function keys. Always do this in InitInstance because each program instance needs its own copy of the table. First, derive a new class from TApplication:

```
class TYourApp: public TApplication {
public:
  TYourApp(const char far* name)
    : TApplication(name) {};
  void InitInstance();
};
```

The derived class, TYourApp, inherits all members of TApplication and its ancestor TModule. The new class provides a constructor, which simply passes the name argument to initialize the base class portion of the object. The new class also *overrides* the virtual InitInstance member function. You may precede void with the virtual keyword, but you don't have to. TYourApp is the end of the line. In this example, no additional classes are derived from the class, so the overridden virtual member functions do not need to be redeclared virtual.

The reason for overriding InitInstance is to add additional capabilities to the inherited function. For example, to load an accelerator resource, implement InitInstance like this:

```
void
TYourApp::InitInstance()
{
  TApplication::InitInstance();  // Call ancestor function
  HAccTable = LoadAccelerators(ID_ACCEL);  // Load table
}
```

First, InitInstance calls its base-class ancestor function because you don't want to replace the function completely; you merely want to enhance what the function does. In this example, the enhancement is a statement that loads the accelerator table resource, bound into the program's .EXE code file. HAccTable is a data member of type HACCEL (handle to accelerator table resource) declared in TApplication. LoadAccelerators is a member function inherited from TModule. The function is passed the resource identifier (string or integer) assigned when the table was created—by Resource Workshop, for example, or in the program's resource script.

It's important to understand that LoadAccelerators is an *encapsulated application function*. Windows has a similar *global API* function of the same name. To call the global function, you could rewrite the preceding code as:

```
HAccTable = ::LoadAccelerators(GetInstance(),
  MAKEINTRESOURCE(ID_ACCEL));
```

Because LoadAccelerators is a member function, to call the global API function of that same name, you must precede the function identifier with a scope resolution operator, telling the compiler to look for LoadAccelerators in the global scope.

Perhaps you've seen similar statements in straight C applications. In OWL, the application's instance handle is encapsulated in the application object, so there's no need to pass it to LoadAccelerators. Also, the member function can handle integer and string resource identifiers, so there's also no need to call MAKEINTRESOURCE to fool the function into accepting an integer resource identifier in the offset portion of a far char pointer—

an unfortunate trick required by all Windows resource loading functions. OWL uses C++ classes, function overloading, and default parameter values to eliminate the need to play those kinds of tricks.

Listings 3.2 (APPSTART.RH), 3.3 (APPSTART.RC), and 3.4 (APPSTART.CPP) create an application that demonstrates the sequence that all OWL applications follow when they begin. Use the IDE to open APPSTART.IDE in the APPSTART directory, and press F9 to compile. Run the program from the File Manager, then start a second instance while the first is still running. The first instance's window title, *First Instance*, changes to *Other Instance* for subsequent instances, demonstrating how a program can detect if it is the first or another instance.

You can run only a single instance of a program from the IDE. To run more than one, you must start the program using the File or Program Manager. To run a second instance of a program from the IDE, start the first one using the File or Program Manager. Switch back to the IDE, and press Ctrl+F9 to start the second instance. You might use this technique to debug a second program instance using the built-in IDE debugger.

> **NOTE**
>
> 32-bit applications always run as distinct tasks, and therefore, they appear as "first" instances no matter how many times you restart them. Multiple 16-bit application instances share the same code, but they have distinct data segments. The inability of 32-bit applications to share executable code files is one negative aspect of Windows NT and Win32s that must be considered if your application needs to be started more than once. In such cases, a 16-bit version of your program might use memory more efficiently.

Listing 3.2. APPSTART.RH.

```
// appstart.rh -- Resource header file

#define ID_ACCEL 100
```

Listing 3.3. APPSTART.RC.

```
#include <owl\window.rh>
#include "appstart.rh"
```

```
ID_ACCEL ACCELERATORS
{
 "x", CM_EXIT, ASCII, ALT
 "X", CM_EXIT, ASCII, ALT
}
```

Listing 3.4. APPSTART.CPP.

```
/* ============================================================ *\
** appstart.cpp -- Demonstrate OWL application startups        **
** ============================================================ **
**                                                             **
** ============================================================ **
**      Copyright (c) 1994 by Tom Swan. All rights reserved.   **
\* ============================================================ */

#include <owl\applicat.h>
#include <owl\framewin.h>
#pragma hdrstop
#include <cstring.h>
#include "appstart.rh"

// ============================================================
// The application class
// ============================================================

class TStartApp: public TApplication {
public:
  TStartApp(const char far* name);
  ~TStartApp();
  void InitApplication();
  void InitInstance();
  void InitMainWindow();
private:
  string* title;  // Pointer to string object
};

// Constructor
TStartApp::TStartApp(const char far* name)
  : TApplication(name)
{
  title = new string("Other Instance");
}
```

continues

Listing 3.4. continued

```
// Destructor
TStartApp::~TStartApp()
{
  delete title;
}

// Initialize the application (first instance)
void
TStartApp::InitApplication()
{
  TApplication::InitApplication();
  *title = "First Instance";
  EnableBWCC();
  EnableCtl3d();
}

// Initialize this instance (and all instances)
void
TStartApp::InitInstance()
{
  TApplication::InitInstance();
  HAccTable = LoadAccelerators(ID_ACCEL);
}

// Initialize the program's main window
void
TStartApp::InitMainWindow()
{
  MainWindow = new TFrameWindow(0, title->c_str());
}

#pragma argsused

// Main program
int
OwlMain(int argc, char* argv[])
{
  TStartApp app("AppStart");
  return app.Run();
}
```

APPSTART's resource script in Listing 3.3 defines an accelerator table with two hot keys, Alt+x and Alt+X, both of which issue the command indentifier CM_EXIT, a symbol defined in the resource header file WINDOW.RH. (Upper and lowercase keys X and x are specified, so they work even if the CapsLock key is on. If you don't care about that, you may define only the lowercase key.)

Loading the accelerator table into the application's `InitInstance` function enables users to press Alt+X to exit the program—an expected Windows standard. `InitInstance` is the correct startup function to use in this case because accelerator tables must be loaded for each program instance.

To identify which instance is running, the `TStartApp` class uses a pointer to a C++ object of the `string` class declared in CSTRING.H. The class constructor initializes the `title` pointer with the statement:

```
title = new string("Other Instance");
```

There are other ways to construct `string` objects, but using the `new` operator is the most common. The class destructor deletes the object with:

```
delete title;
```

It may seem backwards for the constructor to initialize the object to the string *Other Instance,* but examine the `InitApplication` function. Remember, this function is called only for the *first* program instance. After calling the ancestor `InitApplication`, the derived class function reassigns the string object addressed by `title`:

```
*title = "First Instance";
```

In that way, only the first instance has that title; all others remain set to *Other Instance.* By the way, being able to assign strings using the = operator—a privilege formerly granted only to Pascal and BASIC programmers, but not to C developers—is just one of many advantages gained by using the ANSI C++ `string` class. You'll see other uses of the `string` class throughout this book.

To assign the window's title using the `string` object addressed by `title`, the `TStartApp` class overrides another function, `InitMainWindow`. OWL calls that function to construct the program's main window object, usually of `TFrameWindow` or a derived class. In APPSTART, `InitMainWindow` executes the single statement:

```
MainWindow = new TFrameWindow(0, title->c_str());
```

That constructs an object of the `TFrameWindow` class, and assigns the object's address to `MainWindow`, a `TFrameWindow*` pointer declared in `TApplication`. The 0 argument indicates that this window has no parent. (That's always true for main windows, but not child windows, as you learn in future chapters.) Because the `TFrameWindow` constructor expects a window title of type `const char far*`, it isn't possible to pass the `string` object addressed by `title`. Instead, the program calls the `c_str` function in the `string` class to obtain a C-style `char*` pointer to the string data in the object. Though inconvenient, converting `string` class objects to C-style strings is outweighed by the advantages of using the `string` class to store character data.

101

HINT

Now that you are familiar with APPSTART's listing, run the program under the control of the IDE's debugger (or the external Turbo Debugger for Windows). Set breakpoints in the TStartApp constructor and destructor, and in each of the functions InitApplication, InitInstance, and InitMainWindow, then run the program by pressing Ctrl+F9 (or F9 in TDW). (If you receive an error that debug information isn't available, choose **Build all** in the **Project** menu.) Running the demonstration in the debugger shows you the order in which the startup application functions are called before the program's main window appears. You might also want to inspect the string object addressed by title to see its contents. To learn more about the string class, use the IDE browser to examine its members.

Other Startup Tasks

There are a couple of other miscellaneous tasks you might want to perform in a TApplication derived class. For example, changing the value of a TApplication int data member, nCmdShow, determines whether the program's main window starts as an icon, normally, or zooms to full screen on its own.

Load the APPSTART.IDE project from the preceding section into BC4, then add this statement to InitInstance *before* the call to the ancestor's InitInstance function:

```
nCmdShow = SW_SHOWMAXIMIZED;
```

To display the window as an icon, assign SW_SHOWMINIMIZED to nCmdShow. InitInstance calls InitMainWindow to construct the program's main window object, so that statement must come before calling the ancestor function. Alternatively, you can add that statement to InitMainWindow *after* the assignment to MainWindow.

HINT

For a better understanding of main window initialization, examine the source code for TApplication::InitInstance in file APPLICAT.CPP, located in C:\BC4\SOURCE\OWL. As you can see, InitInstance calls InitMainWindow, after which if MainWindow is not null, the object is flagged as the program's main window, the Create function is called to create the Windows element associated with the window object, and the Show function displays the window, using the value of nCmdShow. At any time before these events take place, you may change nCmdShow to affect the main window's initial appearance. Get used to reading OWL's source code to answer questions you have about how a function works, and in what order various tasks occur. If you did not install BC4's source code files, you might want to do that now. OWL's source files may not be as thrilling as a Tom Clancy novel, but they are invaluable reading material for learning how to use OWL in Windows programming.

If you want to use Borland Window Custom Controls (BWCC) or Microsoft's 3-D control library—both of which give a chiseled-steel appearance to dialog boxes and buttons—initialize these libraries in your application class's InitApplication function:

```
void
TYourApp::InitApplication()
{
  TApplication::InitApplication();
  EnableBWCC();
  EnableCtl3d();
}
```

You may initialize either or both libraries. Use EnableBWCC if your dialog resources specify BWCC controls and dialog styles. Use EnableCtrl3d to give other dialogs such as standard message boxes a chiseled-steel look. (I explain more about BWCC and Ctrl3d control libraries later in this book along with other dialog and control programming techniques. See especially Chapters 10 and 11.)

Main Window Startups

To your program's users, there may seem to be little difference between the "application" and its window. For Windows software users, an application and the program's window are one and the same. For a programmer, however, understanding the relationship between the application and its main window object is vital for getting started on the right foot with OWL programming.

Window Elements

As you have seen, the application class, typically derived from TApplication, can override the member function InitMainWindow to tap into the process that constructs the application's main window object. The term *window object* refers to an object of the TWindow class (or of a derived class such as TFrameWindow). The term *window element* refers to the Windows structure associated with that object. In OWL programs, a window object serves as an *interface* to the internal Windows element.

You might think of window objects as C++ *views* of window elements. Any Windows programming language refers to window elements, as these are created and maintained by the operating system. Only C++ OWL programs, however, have window objects.

Rather than call functions and refer directly to window elements (as you would do in a straight C program), in OWL, you call member functions declared by the window object's class. In other words, you access a window element through its higher level window-object view. This technique takes advantage of C++ programming features (especially encapsulation and inheritance), and provides a cleaner way to implement and use windows. Using window objects also helps eliminate errors caused by passing incorrect or uninitialized *window handles* to API functions. In OWL, window objects *encapsulate* their handles, which are automatically used at the appropriate times. You have to try very hard to pass the wrong window handle to a function in an OWL program!

Window Object Construction

Several key events occur when you construct a main window object in the application object's `InitMainWindow` function. First, derive a new class from `TFrameWindow`, which merely creates a blank window that is barely useable. (In practice, you never construct `TFrameWindow` objects. You always derive a class from `TFrameWindow` and construct the object of your own class.) At the minimum, the derived class must declare a constructor. Here's a sample:

```
class TYourWin: public TFrameWindow {
public:
  TYourWin(TWindow* parent, const char* title);
};
```

Insert initialization statements in the constructor's implementation. Study the following sample implementation closely—you will use similar programming throughout your own code:

```
TYourWin::TYourWin(TWindow* parent, const char* title)
  : TFrameWindow(parent, title),
    TWindow(parent, title)
{
  // ... Initialize window object here
}
```

`TFrameWindow` is *virtually derived* from `TWindow`, and for that reason, the derived class constructor must call both its immediate ancestor's constructor (`TFrameWindow`) and the constructor for the virtual base class (`TWindow`). That's because OWL uses *multiple inheritance*, a C++ technique that derives some classes from multiple base classes. Due to this design, it is conceivable that a derived class could inherit multiple copies of TWindow data members—but that's not allowed because there can be only one associated window element for a window object. To prevent the possibility of a conflict, OWL declares TWindow as a virtual base class of TFrameWindow, ensuring that derived-class objects receive only one copy of TWindow's data members. That eliminates the potential conflict introduced by multiple inheritance, but now also requires all derived classes to *explicitly* initialize TWindow by calling its constructor as shown here.

If you don't follow why that's necessary, think of the situation this way. Because of multiple inheritance, there might be several different paths *back* to TWindow, thus there are several potential ways to initialize the TWindow portion of a derived class object. But only one TWindow object is allowed—so, it makes no sense to permit that object to be initialized multiple times. The final derived class must therefore call TWindow's constructor, ensuring that this *and only this* call initializes the TWindow portion of the object. All of this means that a class derived from TYourWin (which is derived from TWindow) still must call the TWindow constructor even though the TYourWin base class appears to do that. For example, a class derived from TYourWin must call the TWindow constructor, and despite appearances to the contrary, that is the *only* place where the TWindow portion of the object is initialized (see the line in bold):

```
class TMoreDerivedWin: public TYourWin {
public:
  TMoreDerivedWin(TWindow* parent, const char* title)
    : TYourWin(parent, title),
      TWindow(parent, title) {}
};
```

SetupWindow Function

A TWindow or TFrameWindow constructor performs only half of the steps required to initialize a window object. Somewhere along the way, the class has to tell Windows to create a window element to be associated with the window object under construction. That action happens in a virtual member function, SetupWindow—the source of much confusion among OWL programmers.

Simply stated, the constructor builds the base object; SetupWindow completes the object's construction for any tasks requiring access to the object's associated window element. It's useful to think of SetupWindow as an *extension* to the class constructor, though technically, it is not a constructor. In most cases, you will use both the constructor and SetupWindow to completely initialize window objects, performing some tasks in the constructor and others in the function.

Listing 3.5 demonstrates the important differences between a window constructor and SetupWindow. As a side benefit, the program also shows how to display an application's main window centered onscreen, regardless of display resolution. (Windows seems to bring up new windows in the strangest sizes and locations, and I prefer to wrest control over the process. I assume there's an algorithm somewhere deep inside Windows that determines where the next window goes, but rather than figure it out, I just put my windows where I want them.)

Listing 3.5. WINSIZE.CPP.

```
/* ============================================================ *\
** winsize.cpp -- Predetermine window size and location    **
** ============================================================ **
**                                                          **
** ============================================================ **
**    Copyright (c) 1994 by Tom Swan. All rights reserved.  **
\* ============================================================ */

#include <owl\applicat.h>
#include <owl\framewin.h>


// ============================================================
// The application's main window
// ============================================================

class TWinSizeWin: public TFrameWindow {
public:
  TWinSizeWin(TWindow* parent, const char far* title);
  BOOL FileClosed();
protected:
  void SetupWindow();
  BOOL CanClose();
};

// Constructor
TWinSizeWin::TWinSizeWin(TWindow* parent, const char far* title)
  : TFrameWindow(parent, title),
    TWindow(parent, title)
{
  Attr.X = GetSystemMetrics(SM_CXSCREEN) / 8;
  Attr.Y = GetSystemMetrics(SM_CYSCREEN) / 8;
  Attr.H = Attr.Y * 6;
  Attr.W = Attr.X * 6;
}

// Finish window initialization
void
```

```
TWinSizeWin::SetupWindow()
{
  TFrameWindow::SetupWindow();
  MessageBox(
    "Inside SetupWindow",
    GetApplicationObject()->GetName());
}

// Pseudo file-close function for demonstration
BOOL
TWinSizeWin::FileClosed()
{
  return TRUE;  // return FALSE to simulate file error
}

// Return TRUE if okay to close window
BOOL
TWinSizeWin::CanClose()
{
  BOOL result = TFrameWindow::CanClose();
  int userResponse =
    MessageBox(
      "Save Changes? (demo only--any answer is okay)",
      GetApplicationObject()->GetName(),
      MB_YESNOCANCEL | MB_ICONQUESTION
    );
  if (userResponse == IDCANCEL)
    return FALSE;  // Window close cancelled
  else if (userResponse == IDYES) {
    if (!FileClosed()) {
      MessageBox(
        "Error closing file! (demo only)",
        GetApplicationObject()->GetName(),
        MB_OK | MB_ICONSTOP);
      return FALSE;  // Window close cancelled
    }
  }
  return result;
}

// ============================================================
// The application class
// ============================================================

class TWinSizeApp: public TApplication {
public:
  TWinSizeApp(const char far* name)
    : TApplication(name) {};
  void InitApplication();
```

continues

Listing 3.5. continued

```
  void InitMainWindow();
};

// Initialize first instance
void
TWinSizeApp::InitApplication()
{
  TApplication::InitApplication();
  EnableCtl3d();  // Enable Microsoft 3-D control library
}

// Initialize the program's main window
void
TWinSizeApp::InitMainWindow()
{
  MainWindow = new TWinSizeWin(0, "Front and Center");
}

#pragma argsused

// Main program
int
OwlMain(int argc, char* argv[])
{
  TWinSizeApp app("WinSize");
  return app.Run();
}
```

Load the WINSIZE.IDE project from the WINSIZE directory and press Ctrl+F9 to compile and run the program. Rather than a main window, you see the message dialog in Figure 3.1, displayed by the derived TWinSizeWin class's SetupWindow function, proving that this function is called *before* the main window becomes visible.

FIGURE 3.1.

SetupWindow displays this dialog in WINSIZE.

In the application's InitMainWindow function, as in most OWL programs, the following statement constructs the main window object:

```
MainWindow = new TWinSizeWin(0, "Front and Center");
```

As a result, the `TWinSizeWin` constructor builds an object of type `TWinSizeWin`, derived from OWL's `TFrameWindow`. Take a look at the class constructor's implementation in WINSIZE.CPP. Four statements assign values to fields `X`, `Y`, `H`, and `W`, setting the window's position and size. The calls to `GetSystemMetrics` return the X and Y screen sizes, used to center the window in any resolution.

Following the window object's construction, OWL calls `SetupWindow` to finish the job of initializing the object. In `TWinSizeWin`, `SetupWindow` first calls the ancestor class's `SetupWindow`, which creates the window element associated with this window object. After `SetupWindow` calls its ancestor function, you may call any API function that requires a window handle. Before that time, the window element has not been created, and you can call only API functions that do not require a window handle. In this case, the overridden function in `TWinSizeWin` then calls the `MessageBox` function to display the note shown in the figure.

`MessageBox` is an *API wrapper function*—a function in OWL that is encapsulated in a class. There's also a global `MessageBox` function in the Windows API. To call the global function requires passing the window element's handle, and for that reason, the wrapper is easier to use. To call the global function, you can replace the `MessageBox` statement in `SetupWindow` with:

```
::MessageBox(HWindow,
  "Inside SetupWindow",
  GetApplicationObject()->GetName(),
  MB_OK);
```

You'll rarely need a window element handle in OWL programs, but if you do, it is available as shown here in the `HWindow` member of any `TWindow` class function. You also need to supply `MB_OK` (or another combination of `MB_` constants) to display an OK button in the dialog. That argument isn't needed by the wrapper function, which assigns a default parameter value to this argument if unsupplied. Many other wrapper functions use default arguments that simplify their use.

HINT

Examine OWL's header files to find default argument values for API wrapper functions. For example, open WINDOW.H in the OWL subdirectory of C:\BC4\INCLUDE using BC4 or a text-file viewer, and search for the `MessageBox` function. You may have to view more than one file to find the function you want. In this case, `TFrameWindow` inherits `MessageBox` from `TWindow`, therefore WINDOW.H, not FRAMEWIN.H, is the right header to view.

Main Window Shutdowns

What goes up, must come down. Likewise, what *starts* up must *shut* down, and in addition to considering what happens when windows are constructed, you also need to pay attention to the steps that OWL takes when windows close. In most cases, however, a program's shutdown duties are easier to program than startup chores.

In OWL, a single member function plays a key role in a window's demise. All TWindow-derived classes inherit a virtual function, CanClose that indicates whether it is safe for a window object to close. To use CanClose, override it in any class derived from TWindow (or a descendant such as TFrameWindow):

```
class TAnyWin: public TFrameWindow {
public:
  TAnyWin(TWindow* parent, const char far* title);
protected:
  BOOL CanClose();  // This overrides the inherited function
};
```

CanClose is a virtual function, and its replacement may be prefaced with the keyword virtual if other classes will be derived from that one. If you derive no other classes from TAnyWin, CanClose does not have to be declared virtual. Normally, CanClose returns true, indicating that the window may close. CanClose may return false to prevent closing the window. Implement the function something like this:

```
BOOL
TAnyWin::CanClose()
{
  if (condition)
    return FALSE;  // Window may not close
  else
    return TRUE;   // Window may close
}
```

The first rule in using CanClose is to be certain to return true for at least *one* possible condition. If, for example, a file is open and not saved, the window can return false from CanClose until the user saves the file or decides to discard changes.

A better way to use CanClose, however, is to return false only to *cancel* a window close command. WINSIZE (see Listing 3.5) demonstrates how CanClose can prompt users to save changes to a file. First, the function calls its ancestor CanClose, saving the result of any close operations performed on this window's children (if any). Next, a MessageBox statement prompts the user to save changes. (You might do that if a flag is set to true; the demonstration always displays the prompt.) Note the MB_ constants used to display *Yes, No,* and *Cancel* buttons in the message dialog, along with a question mark icon (see Figure 3.2).

FIGURE 3.2.
In WINSIZE,
CanClose *prompts*
whether to save a file.

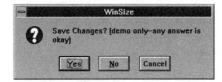

MessageBox returns a value indicating which button was selected. If that value equals IDCANCEL, CanClose returns false to cancel the window close operation. If the *Yes* button is selected, the program calls FileClosed, a pseudo file-closing function that I programmed to return true. Change that function's return value to see what happens if the file can't be saved. In that case, the only way to end the program is to discard the modified file. (Of course, this is only a simulation—there's no data to lose.)

You might think of CanClose as the mirror image of SetupWindow, which as you recall, initializes a window object (and creates the associated window element) after the class constructor builds the object. The window's constructor also has a destructor, which destroys the window object after it's no longer needed. In general, a destructor is responsible for deleting pointers, closing files, and performing other cleanup chores required at the end of an object's useful existence.

The most common use for a destructor is to delete memory allocated by the class's constructor or another member function. Consider this example of TAnyClass, derived from TFrameWindow:

```
#include <cstring.h>
class TAnyClass: public TFrameWindow {
  string* anyString;  // Pointer to string object
public:
  TAnyClass(TWindow* parent, const char far* title);
  ~TAnyClass();
};
```

The class constructor allocates memory for a string object addressed by the anyString member pointer:

```
// Constructor
TAnyClass::TAnyClass(TWindow* parent, const char far* title)
  : TFrameWindow(parent, title),
    TWindow(parent, title)
{
  anyString = new string(title);  // Allocate string object
}
```

You might use that code to store in a C++ string object a copy of the title string passed to the constructor. When a TAnyClass object is destroyed or goes out of scope, the class destructor deletes the allocated memory:

```
// Destructor
TAnyClass::~TAnyClass()
{
  delete anyString;
}
```

Because allocated memory is global, if the destructor did not delete anyString, the memory addressed by that pointer would remain in RAM, and there would be no way to find its location.

> **NOTE**
>
> The C++ delete operator ignores null pointers, so there's no need to test whether anyString is null. Also, in ANSI C++, a destructor is called only if the constructor runs successfully to completion, thus it is always safe to delete anyString as shown here. In cases where a member function allocates memory to a pointer, however, the constructor for that class must set the pointer to null so the delete statement doesn't accidentally dispose of an uninitialized pointer. You can't go wrong if you remember always to allocate memory (or assign null) to all pointers in the class constructor, and to delete those pointers in the destructor.

Application Shutdowns

An OWL application's shutdown isn't nearly as complex as its startup. Because most items in an OWL program are class objects, destructors carry out all necessary chores of deleting pointers, disposing of child windows, and doing what's necessary to clean up before the program ends. You need to worry only about the objects your own code creates. OWL pretty much takes care of itself.

For each class you derive from an OWL class, think carefully about the jobs needed to destroy an instance of the class, and insert the necessary code in the class destructor. If you do that correctly in every case, an application's shutdown will be automatic.

As you have seen, the final task in an OwlMain function returns an integer value, indicating the success or failure of the program. Usually, it's best to return the value passed back by the Run function in TApplication:

```
int
OwlMain(int argc, char* argv[])
{
  TApplication app("AppName");
  return app.Run();
}
```

Unfortunately, Windows ignores OwlMain's return value. Turbo Debugger, however, displays the return value when a program ends, which might be useful for indicating error conditions (0 means no error).

Despite the Run function's apparent simplicity, it is responsible not only for running the program, but also for ensuring a proper appication shutdown. Most shutdown activities occur *before* OwlMain returns. One way to learn more about application shutdown sequences is to examine Run's source code in file APPLICAT.CPP (provided with BC4 in directory C:\BC4\SOURCE\OWL). Search for TApplication::Run. As you can see from Run's TRY and CATCH statements, the function uses C++ *exceptions*—a recent addition to ANSI C++ that OWL employs for error handling. (The next section introduces exceptions for readers who are unfamiliar with the technique.)

> ### NOTE
>
> OWL defines uppercase macros TRY, CATCH, and THROW that correspond to the lowercase C++ keywords try, catch, and throw. To disable exception handling in OWL, define the macro NO_CPP_EXCEPTIONS and rebuild OWL following directions at the beginning of file MAKEFILE, located in C:\BC4\SOURCE\OWL. With the macro defined, the TRY, CATCH, and THROW macros are nulled, removing their effects and associated statements from OWL. Error handling reverts to normal C and C++ methods—new returns null if out of memory, for example, and it is your responsibility to examine function return values. (You must rebuild OWL from the DOS command line. You can't build it using the IDE.)

Run executes OWL applications by executing this short piece of code:

```
int status;
TRY {
  if (!hPrevInstance)
    InitApplication();
  InitInstance();
  status = MessageLoop();
}
```

Remember, TRY is equivalent to the try C++ keyword. If TRY is not defined, the block is compiled as three common statements with no exception handling. The TRY block attempts to call InitApplication unless the hPrevInstance handle indicates that this is not the first instance of the program. The block also attempts to call InitInstance, initializing *every* program instance. (InitInstance calls MainWindow to create the program's main window object. InitInstance also calls SetupWindow to initialize that object and create its associated window element.) Finally, the try block assigns to status the result returned by MessageLoop, the function responsible for obtaining and dispatching messages intended for this application. You might think of MessageLoop as the *heartbeat* of an OWL program.

If any of the preceding operations fail, and if exceptions are enabled, the TRY block exits, and one of several subsequent CATCH statements handle the condition that caused a problem—in other words, the *exception*. Those statements can *rethrow* the exeception to retry the same operations, or they can simply display an error message and allow the program to end—OWL's default method for dealing with errors. Examine Run's source code for examples of CATCH statements.

Exceptions

Because OWL uses exceptions to handle error conditions, it's important that you understand the basics of this relatively new ANSI C++ feature. Because they are so new, exceptions are not covered in most C++ tutorials. In fact, Borland C++ 4.0 is one of the first compilers to implement exceptions, and OWL is probably the first (and possibly the only) major class library to use exceptions extensively for error handling.

Exceptions come with their own terminology and concepts. Following are some overviews that will help you to read and understand this section:

- An exception is just that—an *exceptional condition* that requires special handling. Exceptions are best used for a program's error handling, but they are not limited to that use.

- To create an exception, a statement *throws* an object that describes the nature of the exception. The object can be a literal value, a string, an object of a class, or any other object. (An *exception object* is not necessarily a *class* object.)

- To handle an exception, a statement *catches* a condition thrown by some other process. Statements that catch exceptions are called *exception handlers*.

- Programs prepare to catch exceptions by *trying* one or more processes that might throw exceptions. In general, to use execptions, you *try* one or more statements and *catch* any exceptions that those statements *throw*.

Now, let's see what exceptions actually look like in C++. Upon detecting an error condition, a function can *throw an exception,* which has two effects:

- It announces that an error has occurred.
- It requests that an exception handler deal with the problem.

You throw an exception using a `throw` statement:

```
throw 1;
```

Usually, however, you shouldn't throw literal integers around—they don't mean much out of context. A better object to throw is a string:

```
throw "overflow";
```

That's more meaningful. Elsewhere in the program, a handler could catch and display this error message:

```
catch (char* message) {
  cout << "Error! -- " << message << endl;
}
```

What happens at this point is up to you (or to the library module that catches the exception). The program could continue, it could end, it could restart the condition that caused the problem, and so on. An exception is a mechanism for reporting and dealing with an exceptional condition. Exceptions don't dictate a course of action when errors occur. That's still your job.

NOTE

Exceptions are not limited to a program's error handling. For instance, an empty list object could report its bare cupboards as an exceptional condition. Whether that condition is an "error," though, is open to interpretation, and depends on your definition of what errors are. You would probably agree that not being able to open a file is an error. But is the absence of a specific string inside that file an error, or is that merely one of many possible, and *unexceptional,* results of a search process? Depending on your answer, exceptions may or may not be appropriate for dealing with failed searches or empty lists.

Because of their potential for ambiguous application, exceptions are probably best used for dealing with actual errors—those that force the program to cancel a process, or those conditions that if ignored, would cause the program to fail or to produce faulty output. Limiting exceptions to these truly exceptional conditions helps separate a program's normal statements from those that perform critical error handling—one of the most difficult goals to acheive in any but the smallest of programs. This division of labor adds clarity to the source code, and can also help prevent bugs caused by a hodgepodge of other error methods such as special function return values and global error flags—common techniques that are employed, but often ignored or misused.

Newcomers to exceptions might question what exactly an exception is. The answer is simple: Exceptions are *objects* that closely resemble function arguments. Exceptions can be objects of any type, but they are most conveniently represented as instances of a class. For example, you might declare an Overflow class—it doesn't need any substance, just a name:

```
class Overflow { };
```

You can then throw an instance of this class as an exception:

```
throw Overflow();
```

That constructs an object of the Overflow class, and it throws that object back to whatever process called the one that detected a problem. Elsewhere, the program can catch the exception in a catch statement:

```
catch (Overflow) {
  cout << "Overflow detected!" << endl;
}
```

Be sure to understand that the throw statement throws an *object of the Overflow class,* which is caught by the catch statement at another place in the program (never mind exactly where for the moment). It isn't just the class name that's thrown around—that would be impossible because, like structs, class names exist only in source code, not in the compiled program. The concept might be easier to fathom by giving the caught object a name, using the same syntax employed in function parameter lists:

```
catch (Overflow overObject) {
  // ...
}
```

That statement catches an exception object of type Overflow, and it gives that object the name, overObject. Other statements inside the catch statement may use overObject in exactly the same way as a function parameter.

Typically, an exception object provides member functions for various purposes. For example, class Overflow could declare a member function Report:

```
class Overflow {
  void Report()
    { cout << "Error: overflow" << endl; }
};
```

The catch statement can call Report for the thrown exception object to display an error message:

```
catch (Overflow overObject) {
  overObject.Report();
}
```

Now it's time to toss in another wrinkle—*try blocks,* which seem to confuse everybody the first time they use them. First, however, we need a function that throws a couple of exceptions. Here's a hypothetical example:

```
int AnyFunction()
{
  if (conditionA) throw "Big trouble!";
  if (conditionB) throw Overflow();
  return 123;  // normal return
}
```

If conditionA is true (whatever that is), the function throws a string exception, reporting *Big trouble!* If conditionB is true, the function throws an object of the Overflow class, constructed by calling that object's default class constructor. If the function detects no error conditions, it returns normally, passing a return value 123 to its caller. The three most important lessons to learn from the example are:

- Functions can throw one or more exceptions of various types representing different exceptional conditions.

- Throwing an exception immediately terminates the function.

- *An exception provides functions with an alternate return mechanism.*

The last point is key. The preceding sample function normally returns an int value, but if an exception occurs, it returns either a string or an object of the Overflow class. These special return values can *only* be used in catch statements. If no exceptions are thrown, the function returns normally, optionally passing a value of the function's declared type.

> **NOTE**
>
> Exceptions eliminate the need to reserve special error return values. For example, a function that returns int might specify that a return value of -1 indicates an error; otherwise, the return value is legitimate. Sometimes, this technique works, but reserving a special value isn't always possible. Consider a function that sums a list of integers. In that case, all return values must be legitimate, and it is impossible to reserve any single value as a special case. Most programmers solve that kind of impasse by defining a global error flag or variable, which the program must check to detect errors after function calls. Exceptions do away with that sort of messy error handling by returning objects that represent exceptional conditions without conflicting with a function's normal return values.

Getting back to the preceding example, a program can call `AnyFunction` in the usual way:

```
int x = AnyFunction();
```

In this case, the program ignores any exceptions thrown by `AnyFunction`—usually, not a wise decision. In small programs or tests, however, you might call `AnyFunction` that way. Unhandled exceptions normally cause the program to end—similar to the way a divide-by-zero error or a stack overflow aborts a program. If the program continues after the call to `AnyFunction`, you can be sure that x holds a valid return value. You do *not* need to test x for validity.

Production-quality code must do better. To trap errors, insert the call to `AnyFunction` inside a try block:

```
try {
   int x = AnyFunction();
}
```

A try block contains one or more statements for which you want to catch exceptions. The most important rule to remember about try blocks is that `catch` statements *must* follow them immediately. You cannot have a try block in one place and your `catch` statements in another. That would be like having a ball game's pitcher in one stadium and the catcher in another. In all cases, you must follow a try block with one or more `catch` statements that catch any exceptions thrown by the tried statements. Both kinds of statements must play in the same ballpark. Outside of the try block you can write other statements as you normally do. Multiple try blocks and their associated `catch` statements also can be nested.

Some addtional examples help clarify what try blocks are and how to use them. A try block may have multiple statements (and it usually does):

```
try {
  cout << "Here we go! << endl;
  int x = AnyFunction();
  cout << "x == " << x << endl;
}
```

Translating that to English, the try block first displays a message. Next, it calls `AnyFunction`, assigning the function's result to an int variable, x. If `AnyFunction` throws an exception, *the try block immediately ends.* Any exceptional conditions, in other words, skip the assignment to x and the final output statement.

A try block must be followed by one or more `catch` statements (otherwise, there's no reason to use try). Here's a more complete example:

```
try {
  cout << "Here we go! << endl;
  int x = AnyFunction();
  cout << "x == " << x << endl;
}
catch (char* message) {
  cout << "Error! -- " << message << endl;
}
catch (Overflow) {
  cout << "Overflow!" << endl;
}
```

The expanded code first *tries* to call AnyFunction. If the function returns normally, its result is assigned to x, which a subsequent statement writes to the standard output. If no exceptions are thrown, the catch statements are skipped because there are no errors to catch. If AnyFunction throws an exception, however, *the try block is immediately terminated,* and the object thrown is caught by an appropriate catch statement.

You may insert one, two, three, or more catch statements after a try block to catch exceptions of different types. In this example, two catch statements handle string and Overflow exceptions. Any other types of exceptions not handled are *passed upward in the call chain.* Suppose, for instance, that AnyFunction also throws an exception of type NewException. If a function g() had called the preceding code, that exception is passed upwards to g() since only char* and Overflow exceptions are handled here.

Exceptions in Practice

A sample program demonstrates how to write and use C++ exceptions. To avoid conflicts with OWL's exception handlers, and to keep the demonstration as simple as possible, I wrote it as an *EasyWin application.* An EasyWin program is a Windows application like any other, but it lacks a menu and other features found in full-featured applications. EasyWin programs consist of a simple text-only output window that resembles the capabilities of a DOS text display. Actually, output is even more limited than in DOS because EasyWin doesn't support colors, direct video, or graphics. Even so, EasyWin programs are useful for short tests and demonstrations.

Listing 3.6, EXCEPT.CPP, demonstrates exceptions and EasyWin applications. The program is located in the EXCEPT directory on this book's disk. To compile and run with BC4's IDE, load the program's .IDE project file and press Ctrl+F9. To compile with the command-line compiler, use the -W switch (the W must be uppercase) in a command such as **bcc -W except**. To compile as a DOS program, enter **bcc except**. (The sample program has no MAKEFILE. Non-Windows programs are automatically compiled on the command-line as EasyWin applications when you specify the -W option.)

> **NOTE**
>
> For demonstration purposes, EXCEPT.CPP has a statement that never executes, causing the compiler to warn you that line 88 contains *Unreachable code.* Ignore this expected warning.

Listing 3.6. EXCEPT.CPP.

```
/* =========================================================== *\
**   except.cpp -- Demonstrate ANSI C++ exceptions             **
** =========================================================== **
**                                                             **
**   To compile as an EasyWin Windows application:             **
**     bcc -W except                                           **
**   To compile as a DOS application:                          **
**     bcc except                                              **
**                                                             **
** =========================================================== **
**     Copyright (c) 1994 by Tom Swan. All rights reserved.    **
\* =========================================================== */

#include <iostream.h>
#include <math.h>

class Error;

double Pow(double b, double e);

// Alternate prototype form:
// double Power(double b, double e);

// Better prototype form specifies exception type:
double Power(double b, double e) throw(Error);

class Error {
  double b;     // Base
  double e;     // Exponent
public:
  Error()
    { cout << "Error in source code!" << endl; }
  Error(double bb, double ee)
    : b(bb), e(ee) { }
  void Report();
};

int main()
{
```

```
  cout << "Power Demonstration\n\n";
  cout << "This program displays the result of raising\n";
  cout << "a value (base) to a power (exponent). To\n";
  cout << "force an exception, enter a negative base\n";
  cout << "and a fractional exponent (e.g. -4 and 1.5)\n";
  cout << "Or, enter a zero base and an exponent less than\n";
  cout << "zero.\n\n";
  try {
    double base, exponent, result;
    cout << "base? ";
    cin >> base;
    cout << "exponent? ";
    cin >> exponent;
    result = Power(base, exponent);
    cout << "result == " << result << endl;
  }
  catch (Error& e) {
    e.Report();
    return -1;
  }
  return 0;
}

// Subfunction to Power
double Pow(double b, double e)
{
  return exp(e * log(b));
}

// Final b raised to the e power
double Power(double b, double e) throw(Error)
{
  if (b > 0.0) return Pow(b, e);
  if (b < 0.0) {
    double ipart;
    double fpart = modf(e, &ipart);
    if (fpart == 0) {
      if (fmod(ipart, 2) != 0)  // i.e. ipart is odd
        return -Pow(-b, e);
      else
        return Pow(-b, e);
    } else
      throw Error(b, e);
  } else {
    if (e == 0.0) return 1.0;
    if (e < 1.0) throw Error(b, e);
    return 0.0;
  }
```

continues

121

Listing 3.6. continued

```
  throw Error();   // Unreachable code warning expected
}

// Display values that caused an exception
void
Error::Report()
{
  cout << "Domain error:"
    << " base:" << b
    << " exponent:" << e
    << endl
    << "Press Enter to continue...";
  char c;
  char buffer[80];
  if (cin.peek() == '\n') cin.get(c);
  cin.getline(buffer, sizeof(buffer) - 1);
}
```

EXCEPT includes a `Power()` function that can raise any real number to any real-number power. Two exceptional conditions, however, cause the function to throw an exception:

● Raising a negative base to a fractional exponent.

● Raising zero to an exponent less than zero.

Those conditions are exactly the kind of problems that exceptions are best at handling. The alternatives are: halt the program (not pretty), return a special value (not practical), or set a global error flag (not good programming).

Instead of those relatively poor error-handling solutions, `Power` throws an exception as an object of an `Error` class. For example, on attempting to raise a negative base to a fractional exponent, `Power` executes the statement

```
throw Error(b, e);
```

That constructs an object of the `Error` class, initialized with the values of b and e. The `Error` object is caught in the main program, which tries to call `Power` in a `try` block, repeated in part here:

```
try {
  double base, exponent, result
  // ... prompt for base and exponent
  result = Power(base, exponent);
  cout << "result == " << result << endl;
};
```

If Power throws an exception, the final output statement is skipped and the try block immediately ends. The error condition is caught by a catch statement immediately following the try block:

```
catch (Error& e) {
  e.Report();
  return -1;
}
return 0;
```

If Power throws an exception, Error object e is caught by reference. Although you can throw and catch objects by value, using a reference is usually best when class objects are involved because it saves stack space. The catch statement calls Error's Report member function for the exception e, displaying the values that caused Power to fail.

At this point, the program has complete control over how to handle the exception. The example returns -1 for errors, or 0 if no exceptions occurred. This is standard practice, even though DOS and Windows ignore program return values.

The important observation is that returning -1 for an exceptional condition *is your choice.* You might instead repeat the process that led to the problem, or you could display a Window message dialog. Exceptions give you total control over the program's error handling, far superior to the methods used by standard library functions such as pow. If you have used pow, you probably know how difficult it can be to deal with "DOMAIN" errors that halt your code with no advance warning. Exceptions give *you* control over OWL's error handling.

Declared Exceptions

Using an alternate function declaration format, you can declare exactly the types of exceptions that a function is permitted to throw. This format can be valuable in libraries such as OWL where you need to know what kinds of exceptions you can catch. A function AnyFunction, for example, can state its exception types:

```
void AnyFunction() throw(Error);
```

AnyFunction might throw an Error object, but more importantly, the declaration states that AnyFunction *is not permitted to throw exceptions of any other kind.* A function can also state that it throws exceptions of multiple types:

```
void AnyFunction() throw(Error, char*, OtherType);
```

Use this alternate (and highly recommended) design in function prototypes. For instance, in EXCEPT.CPP, the Power function is prototyped like this:

```
class Error;
double Power(double b, double e) throw(Error);
```

Predeclare Error as an incomplete class so its name can be used in Power's function prototype. (Or, you could declare the entire class before the function prototype.) Given these declarations, which might appear in a header file, you can write try blocks and catch statements to deal with all possible exceptions generated by Power. You don't need to look at Power's source code to find out what the function does in case of trouble. You *do* need the source code, or good documentation, to find the kinds of errors thrown by functions that do not specify their exceptional conditions in prototypes.

Unhandled Exceptions

You might wonder: What happens to exceptions that are thrown but not caught? The answer is simple and logical. Unhandled exceptions are passed upwards in the call chain until they are handled by a catch statement, or until there are no more exception handlers left. In that case, one of three global functions are called to deal with the exception: abort, terminate, or unexpected:

- Exceptions that are not handled by a catch statement call the unexpected function. By default, unexpected calls terminate, explained next.

- Exceptions that detect a corrupted stack or that result from a destructor throwing an exception (a dangerous practice to be reserved only for the most critical of problems) call the terminate() function. By default, terminate calls abort, explained next.

- The abort function is lowest on the totem pole. As you might expect, abort ends the program immediately. It is never called directly.

Obviously, unexpected, terminate, and abort are intimately related, and in fact, all three have the identical effect of terminating the program for unhandled exceptions. You can, however, replace the first two of these functions with your own versions to deal with unhandled exceptions in whatever way you wish. In some programs, for example, it might make sense to replace unexpected with a default error handler. In others, you might want to replace terminate to sweep the floors and dust the rugs (and close open files) in case a program ends prematurely. You cannot replace abort. It always ends the program with no ifs, ands, buts, or tomorrows.

An unexpected function may throw an exception, in which case the search for an exception handler (that is, a catch statement) begins at the location that originally caused unexpected to be called. A terminate function may *not* throw an exception. Neither unexpected nor terminate may return normally to their callers. A call to terminate is truly the beginning of the end.

Call set_terminate and set_unexpected to replace the terminate and unexpected functions with your own versions. For example, given this function

```
void MyUnexpected()
{
  // ...
}
```

you can direct unhandled exceptions to MyUnexpected by adding this statement to the program:

```
set_unexpected(MyUnexpected);
```

You can similarly replace terminate with your own version:

```
void MyTerminate() { }
set_terminate(MyTerminate);
```

Exceptions and Local Objects

Using a special compiler option, local objects left on the stack following an exception are automatically destroyed—that is, their destructors are called. To enable autodestruction, specify -xd for the command-line compiler. Or, in the IDE, select *Options\Project...*, open the *C++ Options* topic, and select the topic-sublevel *Exception handling/RTTI.* (RTTI stands for *Runtime Type Information.*) Make sure *Enable exceptions* and *Enable destructor cleanup* are selected. You *must* enable automatic destructor cleanups for OWL programs.

In general, autodestruction is required for functions that:

● Construct a local object

● Throw an exception after constructing the object

A simple example illustrates why you should be concerned about those two issues. The following function might leave an object of the AnyClass class floating on the stack:

```
int AnyFunction()
{
  AnyClass object(123);
  // ...
  if (condition) throw Error();
  return object.Value();
}
```

The AnyClass object is constructed on the stack by the function. In the normal course of events, when the function ends, object's destructor is called to perform any needed cleanup chores. If, however, an exeption ends the function, object's destructor is *not* called, which in some cases might cause serious problems—if dynamic variables owned by object are not deleted, for instance.

Using the -xd switch or equivalent IDE setting certifies that in cases such as this, object's destructor is called if the function ends via an exception. Normally, this effect is desirable, but the switch adds a certain amount of overhead that you can eliminate if you don't have any local objects in functions that throw exceptions. (Remember, however, you must use autodestruction in OWL programs.)

Notice that pointers to objects *are not automatically deleted*. If you construct a dynamic object, before throwing an exception, it's your responsibility to delete the object:

```
int AnyFunction()
{
  AnyClass *p = new AnyClass(123);
  // ...
  if (condition) {
    delete p;          // You MUST delete p here!
    throw Error();
  }
  delete p;
  return 123;
};
```

The only way to prevent duplicating the use of delete is to postpone checking for errors until after all dynamic objects are disposed:

```
int AnyFunction()
{
  AnyClass *p = new AnyClass(123);
  // ...
  delete p;
  if (condition) throw Error();
  return 123;
}
```

Use a flag such as condition to indicate any errors, delete all dynamically allocated objects, then throw the exception.

Exceptions and Constructors

Class constructors may throw exceptions to indicate that they cannot successfully construct an object. Up until now, C++ had no capability of indicating a faulty object construction other than by calling a member function that returns true or false based on whether the object was properly constructed.

To throw an exception inside a constructor, use the `throw` keyword as shown in other examples:

```
class AnyClass {
public:
  AnyClass()
    { if (condition) throw Error(); }
  ~AnyClass() { }
};
```

The key concept here is that if a constructor throws an exception—meaning that the constructor ends abnormally—*that object's destructor is not called.* Only fully constructed objects are destroyed by destructors, a fact that has especially important consequences in classes that own objects of *other* classes. Consider this case:

```
class AnyClass {
  OtherClass x;
public:
  AnyClass(): x(123)
    { if (condition) throw Error(); }
  ~AnyClass() { }
};
```

Object x of type `OtherClass` is constructed by `AnyClass`'s constructor *before* the constructor's statements are executed. If the `OtherClass` constructor throws an exception, then `AnyClass`'s constructor statements *are not executed.* Because that code never runs, the `AnyClass` object is not constructed, and therefore, the `AnyClass` destructor is also not called. The same mechanism applies in classes that own multiple objects:

```
class AnyClass {
  OtherClass a, b, c;
public:
  AnyClass: a(), b(), c() { }
  ~AnyClass() { }
};
```

If object b's constructor throws an exception, object c *is not constructed,* and neither is the `AnyClass` object. Object a's destructor is called normally (because a was fully constructed before b threw an exception), but the destructors, if any, in b, c, and `AnyClass` are not called.

Looking Ahead

In future chapters, you learn how OWL uses exceptions for error handling. You can also use the preceding techniques in your own code independently of OWL's exception handling. For the moment, however, it's best to put exceptions on the back burner while you become more familiar with OWL's classes and techniques, especially resources and message-response tables, introduced next.

4

Programming with Resources and Response Tables

Programming for Windows requires many related skills. You have to know how to create and use *resources,* and you must write code that responds to *event-driven* processes identified by *messages.* Mastering these skills throws many programmers for a loop—and I'm not talking about a *while* loop.

Because resources are central in Windows programming, they make a useful platform for introducing a few more key OWL features such as *response tables,* which programs can use to respond to event-generated messages. This chapter introduces resources and response tables. You learn:

- How to use Resource Workshop to create resource files.
- How to access resources from inside an OWL program.
- How to create and use message response tables.
- How to respond to commands in a menu resource.

- How to add accelerator *hot keys* to a menu.
- How to attach a system icon to an OWL application.

Programming with Resources

Most programmers create resources using a resource editor such as Resource Workshop (RW), which is included with BC4, but you also can type resource script commands into a text file with the extension .RC. You can then compile the script with Borland's resource compiler BRCC.EXE (or BRCC32.EXE for 32-bit programs). Or, just add the script's filename to an IDE project. Figure 4.1 shows RW's menu editor in action.

FIGURE 4.1.

Resource Workshop's menu editor.

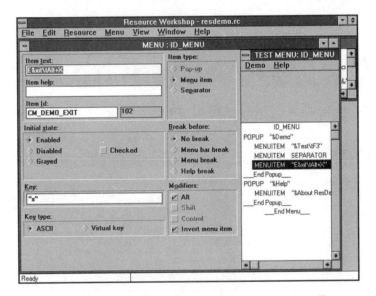

Whatever method you use to create resources, the end result is the same—a resource script file ending in .RC that you compile to create another file, ending in .RES, containing the program's resources in binary form. During—or just after—linking an application, the binary resources are bound into the finished .EXE code file, from which those resources are loaded at runtime. A menu command, for example, is stored in a resource and loaded when the program constructs its main window object. A dialog box is stored and displayed, usually in response to a menu command. An accelerator table is attached to the application to generate messages when designated keys are pressed.

NOTE

This book's disk includes .RC files for all sample programs that use resources (most do). Load these files into Resource Workshop (RW), and examine the individual resources to inspect their formats. This is the best way to learn your way around RW's commands.

OWL makes handling resources easy, and in future chapters I'll explain more about creating and using them. If this is your first introduction to using resources, however, they may seem a bit mysterious. To demonstrate some of the principles involved, and to show how to use resources with OWL, the next three listings construct an application that uses four types of resources:

- Menu commands
- An icon
- Keyboard accelerators (also called *hot keys*)
- A dialog box

Creating Resources

The first step is to create the resources—in fact, that's usually a good way to begin *all* Windows programs. I usually start new programs by constructing a menu. I might also add an About-box dialog describing the program, its version number, and so on. Listing 4.1 shows a sample resource script, created by Resource Workshop, with the elements similar to those that I typically use when starting a new program. (I modified the listing so the lines would fit on this page, and I deleted a large comment at the file's beginning, but RW created the text.) Load this file into RW to view the resources as they appear in the final program.

Listing 4.1. RESDEMO.RC.

```
#include "resdemo.rh"

ID_MENU MENU
BEGIN
  POPUP "&Demo"
  BEGIN
    MENUITEM "&Test\tF3", CM_DEMO_TEST
    MENUITEM SEPARATOR
    MENUITEM "E&xit\tAlt+X", CM_DEMO_EXIT
  END
```

continues

Listing 4.1. continued

```
  POPUP "&Help"
  BEGIN
    MENUITEM "&About ResDemo...\tF1", CM_HELP_ABOUT
  END
END

ID_ICON ICON "resdemo.ico"

ID_ACCELERATORS ACCELERATORS
BEGIN
  VK_F3, CM_DEMO_TEST, VIRTKEY
  "x", CM_DEMO_EXIT, ASCII, ALT
  VK_F1, CM_HELP_ABOUT, VIRTKEY
END

ID_ABOUT DIALOG 18, 18, 159, 95
STYLE DS_MODALFRAME ¦ WS_POPUP ¦ WS_CAPTION ¦ WS_SYSMENU
CAPTION "About ResDemo"
{
 CTEXT "A Resource Demonstration", -1, 10, 38, 138, 8
 CTEXT "Written for Borland C++ 4.0 and OWL 2.0", -1, 10, 49, 138, 8
 CTEXT "Copyright \xA9 1994 by Tom Swan", -1, 10, 60, 138, 8
 ICON ID_ICON, -1, 14, 13, 16, 16
 CTEXT "ResDemo v1.00", -1, 46, 18, 69, 8
 PUSHBUTTON "Ok", IDOK, 119, 76, 24, 14
}
```

As you can see from RESDEMO.RC, a resource script uses a unique language that seems to resemble a mixture of C and Pascal with some BASIC thrown in for good measure. Actually, however, resource script commands lack control statements and other features such as mathematical expressions that general-purpose languages require. Unlike statements in C++, resource script commands don't perform actions; they describe the formats of binary data elements, created by a resource compiler such as RW or BRCC. The exact nature of each binary resource format isn't important—you never have to deal with resources in their binary forms (unless, that is, you are writing a resource compiler). Furthermore, if you use Resource Workshop to create resources, you don't need to bother learning resource-script commands at all. Just use RW's editors to create all of your program's resources.

> **TIP**
>
> On the other hand, sometimes it is just as well to edit a resource script than it is to load the file into RW just to make simple changes such as altering a string, correcting a misspelled control label, or changing the name of an icon file. For this reason, it's best to save RW's output to an .RC script file rather than saving resources in .RES binary form (which RW can do perfectly well). By saving resources in .RC files, you can edit the scripts using the IDE or another text editor, but you also can use RW to make more difficult changes—adding a new dialog box, for example, which is far easier to do with RW's dialog editor than by typing the equivalent script commands.

To better understand how to create resources, you might want to re-create RESDEMO.RC in Listing 4.1 using Resource Workshop. Follow these steps (or, if you know how to use RW, skip to the next section, *Identifying Resources)*:

1. Start RW either from the Program or File Managers, or after closing any open project and other windows, by using BC4's *Tool\Resource Workshop* command. From RW's menu, select *File\New project...* and choose .RC as the project file type.

2. Before creating any resources, I like to save the project in order to give it a name. Select *File\Save project*, change to your program's directory (or to a temporary one) and enter a filename such as **test**. RW automatically appends the .RC filename extension. In RW's terms, the named resource is called a *resource project*.

3. Add a *resource header file* to the project for saving resource identifiers. The resource script and program source files can include the header file and use its defined symbols to access each resource. To create the file, select *File\Add to project...*, select a *File type* of *RH, H c Header,* type the *File name* TEST.RH (you must supply the extension), press Enter, and answer Yes to the prompt that requests permission to create TEST.RH. (In programs with only one header file, you can store identifiers along with other symbolic constants in FILENAME.H, but it's usually best to store resource identifiers separately in FILENAME.RH as most programs in this book do.)

4. You can now add new resources to the project. For example, select *Resource\New...* and choose *MENU* from the offered list of resource types. These notes explain how to create only menu resources, but the steps for other resources are the same. Specific commands differ, of course, for menu, icon, accelerator, and other resource editors, but these are mostly intuitive.

5. RW initially names resources using strings such as MENU_1 and ICON_9. I prefer to give my resources integer "names." When using a lot of resources, string names take more time for Windows to locate, slowing resource loading. Integer resource identifiers load faster and take less space. To rename a resource, select *Resource\Rename...*, and enter a symbolic name such as ID_MENU (my preferred name for a menu identifier). Press Enter to continue.

6. At this point, RW asks permission to create a new identifier. Answer Yes (or just press Enter). Then, type a value into the resulting dialog box. You can use any small integer values to identify resources—I usually use 100 for no particular reason. All resources of the same type must have unique identifying values. (Multiple icons might be numbered 100, 101, 102, and so on.) Other resources of different types can reuse the same numbers. Only resources of the *same type* must be uniquely identified. Notice that the *New identifier* dialog lists the project's TEST.RH or other header file. When you give the resource identifier a value, RW inserts a #define statement into that header. The program's source files and the resource script include this file so they can refer to resources by identifiers such as ID_MENU.

7. If you are following along, you are looking at RW's menu editor. (If you don't see the editor, enter 100 as the resource name value, and select the *OK* button in the *New identifier* dialog.) Use the menu editor to enter menu commands. Give each one a symbolic *Item id*. I use names such as CM_DEMO_TEST and CM_DEMO_EXIT, where the CM means command, the next word is the menu name, and the final word is the command (or an abbreviation). In time, you'll see how this naming convention simplifies writing functions to respond to menu commands—but more on that later. As when identifying the menu resource, you must give each command a unique value (100, 101, 102, and so on). For each CM symbol and value, RW inserts a #define statement into the project's header (TEST.RH if you are following along).

8. Save the project. (You can leave the menu editor open, or you can close it.) Always remember to save the resource project, or any changes you make won't be included in the compiled program. To prevent troubles, I try to save my resource projects before switching away from RW to another program—that way I never forget to save them. (At least, I *usually* never forget.)

9. Exit RW when you are done entering resources. If you started from the IDE, you are transferred back to there.

There's plenty more to the process of creating resources, but in most cases, RW's commands are intuitive, and you shouldn't have any trouble figuring out how to use them on your own.

TIP

RW creates a file ending in .RWS for each resource project. This file contains various settings along with an internally formatted binary representation of all resource images. RW can load .RWS files much more quickly than it can translate the equivalent .RC files. Both files, however, contain the same resource information, and you may delete .RWS files without harm. To conserve disk space, only .RC files are included on this book's disk. To create faster-loading .RWS files, load each .RC file into RW and select *File:Save project...* .

Identifying Resources

You must identify each resource with a unique string or integer value. As I mentioned, I prefer to use integers associated with symbolic constants such as ID_MENU and ID_ICON. Some resources have subcomponents that are similarly identified, but only with integers, not strings. A menu resource, for example, has one or more commands, each identified by a unique name and number such as CM_DEMO_EXIT.

That and other symbols are best stored in a resource header file for including into programs and resource script files. Listing 4.2 shows the RESDEMO.RH header file created by Resource Workshop for the RESDEMO program. When writing resource script files using a text editor, you may want to create a similar file manually. Usually, however, it's easier to let RW create the file for you.

Listing 4.2. RESDEMO.RH.

```
// resdemo.rh -- Resource header file

#define ID_ABOUT 100
#define ID_ACCELERATORS 100
#define ID_MENU 100
#define ID_ICON 100
#define CM_DEMO_TEST 101
#define CM_DEMO_EXIT 102
#define CM_HELP_ABOUT 201
```

RW inserts a statement to include RESDEMO.RH into RESDEMO.RC (see the first line of RESDEMO.RC in Listing 4.1). Including the RESDEMO.RH header file makes defined symbolic constants available to the resource compiler and to RW.

Program source modules can also include the header file for loading and communicating with resources by their symbolic names. For example, the program's source file listed in the next section includes RESDEMO.RH with the statement:

```
#include "resdemo.rh"
```

Using Resources

After creating the program's resources (you can always add more resources later, and you can always edit existing ones), and after identifying resources symbolically in a header file, you are ready to begin writing the program. Listing 4.3, RESDEMO.CPP, uses the resource and header files in the preceding two listings to display and respond to simple menu commands. One of those commands displays an About-box dialog, shown in Figure 4.2.

FIGURE 4.2.

RESDEMO's window and About-box dialog.

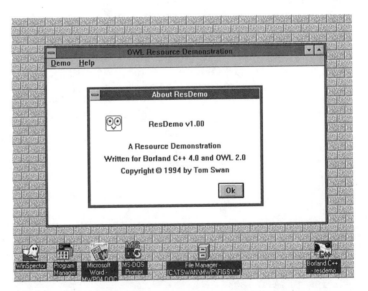

TIP

Using the IDE, first open RESDEMO.IDE using the *Project*/*Open project...* command, then open the RESDEMO.CPP file by selecting its name from the project window (or make the RESDEMO.CPP window active if it's already open). Next, cursor to any character in the quoted RESDEMO.RH filename in the fourth #include directive. Press Alt+F10 or click the right mouse button and select *Open source* to open RESDEMO.RH in an editor window. This is a great way to browse header files that are included into a source file listing.

Listing 4.3. RESDEMO.CPP.

```cpp
/* ============================================================= *\
**   resdemo.cpp -- Resource demonstration                      **
** ============================================================= **
**                                                              **
** ============================================================= **
**      Copyright (c) 1994 by Tom Swan. All rights reserved.    **
\* ============================================================= */

#include <owl\applicat.h>
#include <owl\framewin.h>
#include <owl\dialog.h>
#pragma hdrstop
#include "resdemo.rh"


// ============================================================
// The application's main window
// ============================================================

class TResDemoWin: public TFrameWindow {
public:
  TResDemoWin(TWindow* parent, const char far* title);
protected:
  void CmDemoTest();
  void CmDemoExit();
  void CmHelpAbout();
DECLARE_RESPONSE_TABLE(TResDemoWin);
};

DEFINE_RESPONSE_TABLE1(TResDemoWin, TFrameWindow)
  EV_COMMAND(CM_DEMO_TEST, CmDemoTest),
  EV_COMMAND(CM_DEMO_EXIT, CmDemoExit),
  EV_COMMAND(CM_HELP_ABOUT, CmHelpAbout),
END_RESPONSE_TABLE;

// Constructor
TResDemoWin::TResDemoWin(TWindow* parent, const char far* title)
  : TFrameWindow(parent, title),
    TWindow(parent, title)
{
  AssignMenu(ID_MENU);
}

// Respond to Demo¦Test menu command
void
TResDemoWin::CmDemoTest()
{
  MessageBox(
    "Demo¦Test command selected!",
```

continues

137

Listing 4.3. continued

```
    "Message Box Dialog",
    MB_ICONINFORMATION | MB_OK);
}

// Respond to Demo|Exit menu command
void
TResDemoWin::CmDemoExit()
{
  CmExit();
}

// Respond to Help|About menu command
// Display About-box dialog
void
TResDemoWin::CmHelpAbout()
{
  (new TDialog(this, ID_ABOUT))->Execute();
}

// ===========================================================
// The application class
// ===========================================================

class TResDemoApp: public TApplication {
public:
  TResDemoApp(const char far* name)
    : TApplication(name) {};
  void InitMainWindow();
};

// Initialize the program's main window
void
TResDemoApp::InitMainWindow()
{
  MainWindow = new TResDemoWin(0, "OWL Resource Demonstration");
  MainWindow->Attr.AccelTable = ID_ACCELERATORS;
  MainWindow->SetIcon(this, ID_ICON);
}

#pragma argsused

// Main program
int
OwlMain(int argc, char* argv[])
{
  TResDemoApp app("ResDemo");
  return app.Run();
}
```

Picking apart RESDEMO.CPP one piece at a time demonstrates several key techniques for using resources and for responding to messages. As in the other sample OWL programs you have examined, RESDEMO begins with some #include and #pragma directives:

```
#include <owl\applicat.h>
#include <owl\framewin.h>
#include <owl\dialog.h>
#pragma hdrstop
#include "resdemo.rh"
```

You saw the first two headers before: APPLICAT.H declares the TApplication class; FRAMEWIN.H declares TFrameWindow. The third header, DIALOG.H, is new. To display a dialog box, the program creates an object of the TDialog class, declared in DIALOG.H. The fourth header file, RESDEMO.RH, makes resource identifiers available to statements.

> **NOTE**
>
> The directive #pragma hdrstop tells the compiler to stop collecting precompiled header file information into RESDEMO.CSM (compiled *symbol* file). The directive also tells the compiler that changes to headers following the directive (RESDEMO.RH, for example) do not require reprocessing of preceding header files. Precompiled header files speed compilation by storing precompiled information that is loaded into memory during compilation. You may safely delete RESDEMO.CSM at any time to save disk space. If the file is missing, the compiler automatically re-creates it.

After its #include directives, RESDEMO derives a class, TResDemoWin, from TFrameWindow, for the program's main window. The class declares several of its own items. First is a required constructor:

```
TResDemoWin(TWindow *parent, const char far* title);
```

That declaration is similar to the derived class constructors you examined in other sample listings. In addition to a constructor, TResDemoWin also declares three new protected member functions:

```
void CmDemoTest();
void CmDemoExit();
void CmHelpAbout();
```

Each function returns void (that is, nothing), and declares no parameters. Because the class declares the functions in a protected section, only members of TResDemoWin or of a derived class may call them. If a bug develops in one of the functions, it's relatively easy to trace all calls to the routine because those calls *must* have come from other class members. (Easier debugging and improved reliability through isolation of functions in classes are two primary benefits of using protected members.)

> **NOTE**
>
> The class constructor is usually best declared in a public section so that objects of the class may be created by statements outside of the class. It is possible, but rarely useful, to declare constructors as protected or private members.

From their names, you can probably figure out what the three protected member functions do. Each corresponds to one of the program's three menu commands. Pay close attention to the naming convention. Function CmDemoTest is associated with the menu command identified by the symbolic constant CM_DEMO_TEST defined in RESDEMO.RH. The other two functions are similarly associated with other CM constants.

> **TIP**
>
> Another good reason to adopt a consistent naming convention is that some OWL classes define ready-made functions for responding to common menu commands (such as *Exit*) and to other Windows messages.

Programming with Response Tables

The final declaration in the derived TResDemoWin class (see file RESDEMO.CPP) is a macro, which may seem a bit odd at a first meeting. Here it is again for reference:

```
DECLARE_RESPONSE_TABLE(TResDemoWin);
```

The DECLARE_RESPONSE_TABLE macro requires the name of a class that declares one or more *message-response* member functions. The macro must be placed inside the class declaration to which it refers. Usually, the class declaration is written in a header file, but it may be written directly in a source file as in this demonstration. By convention, the macro is normally the last item in the class, and it may be inserted after a public, protected, or private access specifier. (The macro determines its own access status.) The macro inserts a few private and public members into the class that enable a *response table* to call class member functions in response to Windows messages.

When the program receives a certain message from Windows, the response table indicates which member function should be called to perform an action. Essentially, a response table is simply a table of Windows messages and class member function addresses. When the program receives a message (generated, for example, by selecting a menu command or by clicking a mouse button), the program automatically calls the associated member function.

In addition to telling the compiler that the class needs a response table, you also have to specify which member functions to associate with specific message values. To implement a response table, follow the class declaration with another macro, named DEFINE_RESPONSE_TABLEx, where x is a magic number I'll explain in a moment. The response table's implementation must appear in a source code file, never in a header, and it may not appear inside a function, a class, or any other declaration. For reference, here's a sample response-table macro from RESDEMO minus the macro's contents:

```
DEFINE_RESPONSE_TABLE1(TResDemoWin, TFrameWindow)
...
END_RESPONSE_TABLE;
```

Replace the x in DEFINE_RESPONSE_TABLEx with the number of base classes in the derived class's inheritance list that also have response tables. (A base class has a response table if the class's declaration uses the DECLARE_RESPONSE_TABLE macro.) In this case, TResDemoWin inherits one base class, TFrameWindow, which declares its own response table, so x is set to 1. Never mind the fact that TFrameWindow is derived from another base class, TWindow, which is derived from two other classes, TEventHandler and TStreamableBase. The total number of base classes doesn't matter. To calculate the correct value for x, *count only the number of immediate base classes that have response tables (or are derived from classes that have response tables) and that are actually listed in the derived class's inheritance list.* The same rule also applies to virtual base classes. In the macro, specify the derived and base class names separated by commas. End the response table macro with the symbol END_RESPONSE_TABLE.

A few examples help clear up any questions you may have about how to declare and define response tables. (They are a bit strange on a first meeting, so don't worry if you don't understand them fully at this stage.) In the following code snippets, assume that class Derived inherits from three base classes: Base1, Base2, and Base3. All classes except Base2 have response tables of their own. Here's the Derived class declaration:

```
class Derived: public Base1, public Base2, public Base3 {
public:
  // ... public class members
protected:
  // ... protected class members
private:
  // ... private class members
DECLARE_RESPONSE_TABLE(Derived);
};
```

Members of class Derived respond to one or more Windows messages, so the class declares a response table using the DECLARE_RESPONSE_TABLE macro, listing the class name in parentheses. In this example, I inserted the macro into a private section, but I could have inserted it after a public or protected specifier. You may place the Derived class declaration in a program .CPP module or in a header file.

Somewhere after the class declaration (or, in a separate .CPP file if the class is declared in a header file), define the response table using the DEFINE_RESPONSE_TABLEx macro. In this example, only two classes, Base1 and Base3, have response tables. Base2 has none, and therefore, the magic number x is set to 2:

```
DEFINE_RESPONSE_TABLE2(Derived, Base1, Base3)
...
END_RESPONSE_TABLE;
```

The table's definition doesn't list the Base2 class because it doesn't have a response table of its own. Only the classes with response tables are listed so that the compiler can generate the proper code and internal pointers that enable locating all response tables for related class objects at runtime. This means that OWL handles specific messages by the correct member functions in the proper classes without *you* having to write a single scrap of code. (Of course, you have to construct the response tables, but that's usually easier than using lengthy switch statements and other code to respond to Windows messages as plain C programs commonly do.)

> In simple examples such as those in this chapter, it's difficult to demonstrate the benefits of response tables. In fact, it might seem easier just to use a `switch` or an `if` statement to respond to Windows messages. Have faith. In larger programs with many related classes and member functions responding to scads of Windows messages, response tables simplify the program's organization and add clarity to the source code.

Inside the response table, other macros tell the compiler to relate specific message values and member functions. In this case, the program needs to associate menu commands with `TResDemoWin` member functions, and for that, OWL provides another macro `EV_COMMAND` (EV for "Event"). Use this macro to relate a menu-resource command identifier with a function name. Here's the finished table again for reference:

```
DEFINE_RESPONSE_TABLE1(TResDemoWin, TFrameWindow)
  EV_COMMAND(CM_DEMO_TEST, CmDemoTest),
  EV_COMMAND(CM_DEMO_EXIT, CmDemoExit),
  EV_COMMAND(CM_HELP_ABOUT, CmHelpAbout),
END_RESPONSE_TABLE;
```

That's a complete response table—one of many similar tables you will see throughout this book. Each of the `CM` menu-resource command identifiers defined in RESDEMO.RH is associated with the appropriate member function in `TResDemoWin`. From this association, the program automatically calls the proper functions in response to menu commands. An OWL program is object oriented, but it also is an *event-table-driven application.*

Be sure that you understand the basic steps for declaring and defining response tables. In general, to create a response table for any class, follow these three simple steps:

1. Use the `DECLARE_RESPONSE_TABLE` macro in the class declaration, which may appear in a source (.CPP) or header (.H) file.

2. Use the `DEFINE_RESPONSE_TABLEx` macro in a source file to define the declared table. Replace x with the number of base classes that also have response tables.

3. Insert event and other macros such as `EV_COMMAND` in the defined table to associate class member functions with Windows messages. When the program receives a designated message, OWL calls the associated function automatically.

Attaching a Menu Resource

In designing a window class, I usually implement its constructor before writing any other code. In this example, the constructor has only one job to perform: attaching a menu resource to the window. As usual, the TResDemoWin constructor calls the virtual base class constructors for classes TFrameWindow and TWindow. In addition, the constructor calls AssignMenu to attach the menu resource:

```
AssignMenu(ID_MENU);
```

The AssignMenu function is a member of TFrameWindow. To attach a menu to an object of that class, simply call AssignMenu and pass it a menu resource identifier. The identifier can be a string or, as it is here, an integer defined by a symbolic constant such as ID_MENU.

Responding to Menu Commands

Of course, you also need to provide programming to respond to selected menu commands. The response table prepares your program to call the proper functions in response to menu-command messages. It's still your job to write those functions to perform your program's actions.

The first message-response function, CmDemoTest, displays a message dialog, verifying the command was selected.

```
void
TResDemoWin::CmDemoTest()
{
  MessageBox(
    "Demo¦Test command selected!",
    "Message Box Dialog",
    MB_ICONINFORMATION ¦ MB_OK);
}
```

When you run RESDEMO and select the *Demo|Test* command, Windows issues a WM_COMMAND message that identifies the selected command as CM_DEMO_TEST. That message causes the program to call the function associated with the command in a response table, in this case, CmDemoTest.

NOTE

Actually, CM_DEMO_TEST isn't a Windows message. It's a *component* of the WM_COMMAND message that Windows issues for every menu command selection. CM_DEMO_TEST identifies which command was chosen—the value is just an integer passed along with the WM_COMMAND message. OWL understands these facts, and it's therefore easier to think of CM_DEMO_TEST as a message. As a result of OWL's understanding, you do not need to decode or respond to WM_COMMAND messages directly, though you may do so if necessary. You can instead associate CM_DEMO_TEST with a class member function in which you insert statements to perform menu command operations.

The CmDemoTest function calls MessageBox to display the window shown in Figure 4.3. To MessageBox, the program passes two strings—one for the window title and the other for the message inside. The program also passes the logical OR combination of the two Windows constants MB_ICONINFORMATION and MB_OK, specifying an icon and an *OK* button.

FIGURE 4.3.

RESDEMO's message box.

TIP

Look up other MB constants and the MessageBox function in BC4's online help. Use RESDEMO's CmDemoTest function to experiment with other message box styles by altering the constants used in the third MessageBox argument.

MessageBox is an example of an *encapsulated API function*. In this case, MessageBox is inherited from the TWindow class, from which TFrameWindow is partially derived. Any member function of the derived class can call MessageBox.

As you may know, the Windows API also has a MessageBox function, but in most cases, OWL programs should call encapsulated functions like MessageBox to help prevent common errors such as passing the wrong or an uninitialized window handle. TFrameWindow objects encapsulate a window handle named HWindow as a data member, which the MessageBox member function passes to the API function of the same name. By using the encapsulated function rather than the Windows API function, it is virtually impossible to pass a faulty window handle argument, a common error that can lead to hard-to-find bugs.

Don't think, however, that encapsulated functions prohibit you from calling Windows API subroutines. You can always do so! Although it's usually best to use OWL's encapsulated member functions, for demonstration, here's how to modify RESDEMO to call the API MessageBox function. Replace CmDemoTest with this modified version:

```
// This calls the Windows API MessageBox function
void
TResDemoWin::CmDemoTest()
{
  ::MessageBox(HWindow,
    "Demo¦Test command selected!",
    "Message Box Dialog",
    MB_ICONINFORMATION ¦ MB_OK);
}
```

There are only two differences in the function's MessageBox statement. First, a scope resolution operator (::) precedes the function name. Second, the statement passes the window handle HWindow as the first argument, telling the function to which window it should attach itself. When you compile and run the modified program, you won't see any change in results. Internally, however, the function now calls the Windows API MessageBox function directly rather than the TWindow member.

> **TIP**
>
> When you need a window handle for any object of the TWindow class (or of a derived class such as TFrameWindow or one of your own derivations), always use the HWindow data member declared by the TWindow class.

Because the two MessageBox functions are named the same, you must preface the API function with a scope resolution operator (::). The operator tells the C++ compiler to look for the function's name in the global scope, where all API function names are situated. The notation also reminds you that a statement calls a native function rather than a class member, a fact that can be useful during debugging. For that reason, even when an API function has no encapsulated member in an OWL class, it's a good idea to preface its name with a scope resolution operator, which costs nothing in runtime performance.

Ending an OWL Application

Getting back to RESDEMO.CPP, another response function, CmDemoExit, ends the demonstration program. Here it is for reference:

```
void
TResDemoWin::CmDemoExit()
{
  CmExit();
}
```

Calling the CmExit member function for an object of the TWindow class used as the program's main window is one good way to end a program. Another is to call TWindow's CloseWindow member function. (Windows programs end when their main windows are closed.) To do that, replace the CmExit statement with this:

```
CloseWindow();
```

Or, there's an even simpler method for ending OWL programs. Use the predefined CM_EXIT symbol from WINDOW.RH to identify the program's *Exit* command in a *File* or other menu resource. (Many of the programs in this book have a *Demo* menu with an *Exit* command created this way.) When you select the command, OWL automatically calls CmExit in the TWindow class. That way, you don't need to write a response function such as CmDemoExit. The necessary code is already inside OWL. To save space, from now on, most sample programs in this book use the predefined CM_EXIT symbol, along with other predefined command constants.

> **NOTE**
>
> Some programmers prefer to create a response function for *every* menu command rather than use a mix of predefined functions such as CmExit along with their own functions. If you want to define a response function as I did in RESDEMO to exit programs, that's fine. If not, just use the CM_EXIT symbol to identify your program's *Exit* command in the menu resource and leave the rest to OWL. It's entirely your choice. Also note the style used in the function's name—the Cm preface in CmExit indicates that this function responds to a menu-resource command identified as CM_EXIT. The function name infers the symbolic constant. If you know one, you can figure out the other—a subtle but valuable convention that helps sort out numerous identifiers in big programs.

Bringing Up a Dialog Box

The third and final response function in RESDEMO shows how to bring up a dialog box—in this case, an "About-box" dialog that identifies the program. All Windows programs should have an About-box dialog—a familiar element in most graphical user interfaces, and a good place to toot your horn and to list programmers on your team (or just your own name if you happen to be your "team's" only member).

For reference, here's the CmHelpAbout function extracted from RESDEMO.CPP:

```
void
TResDemoWin::CmHelpAbout()
{
  (new TDialog(this, ID_ABOUT))->Execute();
}
```

OWL calls the CmHelpAbout message-response function when you select the *Help\About ResDemo...* command or when you press the accelerator key F1. That automatic response is possible because the response table for the TResDemoWin class associates the CM_HELP_ABOUT menu-resource command identifier with the CMHelpAbout function.

> **TIP**
>
> If you are still a little fuzzy on how response tables work, examine the response table definition in the sample listing. Don't be concerned at this stage with *how* messages are processed. Just be sure to understand that, simply by relating a message and member function in a response table, the function is automatically called to perform an action in response to receiving that message.

The CmHelpAbout function executes a single statement that demonstrates how to create and activate a simple dialog box. The statement has three important effects:

- It creates a dynamic object of the TDialog class.
- It tests whether that object is constructed successfully.
- It calls the TDialog object's Execute function.

Operator new constructs a dynamic instance of the TDialog class—the proper way to construct most objects, especially large ones with many data members. Every dialog box should be similarly encapsulated in a TDialog object. To enhance a dialog's capabilities, you can derive a new class from TDialog. You can then construct an object of your own class using the same method demonstrated in CmHelpAbout. You'll see many examples of this technique throughout this book.

Purists in the crowd may howl about three apparent errors in CmHelpAbout's lone statement:

- The fact that new's result is not saved in a pointer.
- The lack of a corresponding delete statement to reclaim the memory allocated for the TDialog object.
- The lack of any error checking on new's result.

Let's take each of these important concerns one at a time. There's nothing wrong with the way the statement as written, but its unusual style may seem odd at first.

First, new's result is not saved because, in creating the TDialog object, the statement passes this to the dialog's constructor. The this pointer addresses the TResDemoWin object that declares the CmHelpAbout function. In other words, TResDemoWin represents the dialog's *parent window*. When the dialog window closes, its parent automatically detaches and deletes the TDialog object.

That also explains the second concern about a lack of a delete statement. In general, whenever you pass a this pointer to a constructor that creates an object of the TWindow class (from which TDialog and many other classes are derived), that object is deleted automatically when the window is closed.

The third concern requires additional explaining. It is not necessary to test whether new returns a valid pointer because OWL uses *exception handling* to deal with errors. As I mentioned in Chapter 3, This new feature of ANSI C++ programming goes a long way to simplifying code by eliminating the need to insert explicit error checks after every use of new and other functions.

All of this discussion about CmHelpAbout ignores the real effect of the function's lone statement—displaying a dialog box window. That action requires a separate step, making it possible to construct a dialog object at one place in a program and then use that object later. Usually, however, the steps are combined in a single statement as they are in CmHelpAbout:

```
(new TDialog(this, ID_ABOUT))->Execute();
```

You can also break the steps apart and write them individually as shown here:

```
TDialog *p;
p = new TDialog(this, ID_ABOUT);
// ... Perform other actions
if (p) p->Execute();
```

## FOUR

Variable p is defined as a pointer to a TDialog object, which is created by new. The address of the object is saved in p for later. After other unspecified actions, the TDialog Execute function displays and activates the dialog. As before, the object is automatically deleted when its window is closed—an explicit delete statement is not needed.

The sample statements illustrate how to create a *modal dialog*—one that must be closed before any other program operation can be used. (When a modal dialog is active, you can switch to *another* application, but you must close the dialog before continuing to use the application's other commands.) Modeless dialogs look like modal ones, but do not preempt other program activities. (I return to modal and modeless dialogs in Chapter 10.)

Attaching Application Resources

As in all OWL applications, RESDEMO also declares an application class, TResDemoApp, derived from TApplication. The derived class is nearly the same as others you have seen, but its InitMainWindow member function has a couple of new statements that attach application-wide resources to the program. In this case, the program uses two such resources:

- An accelerator table.
- A system icon.

The accelerator table programs "hot keys" that, when pressed, send command messages to the current window. The program handles the messages exactly as it does menu-resource commands. The program also displays the system icon when you minimize the main window on the Windows desktop.

To try out these resources, run RESDEMO and minimize its window. Redisplay the window normally, then press F1 to bring up the About-box dialog, or press F3 to display a sample message box. You can also press Alt-X to end the program. The program handles these actions simply by creating appropriate accelerator keys that issue the same CM_ constant values associated with menu commands. Accelerator keys can also operate independently of menus, but they usually correspond to menu commands to provide hot keys that users can press to select familiar operations quickly.

As you may recall, InitMainWindow's job is to construct an application's main window object (of a TFrameWindow class), and assign the address of that object to MainWindow. This time, however, the function also performs two other common chores. First, it loads the keyboard accelerator table, using the statement:

```
MainWindow->Attr.AccelTable = ID_ACCELERATORS;
```

Actually, the program loads the table later. Simply assigning the resource identifier, ID_ACCELERATORS, to the AccelTable data member in the Attr structure of the window object attaches the table to the window. AccelTable is an object of the TResId class, which can be initialized with string or integer resource names.

> **TIP**
>
> A TResId object is a good place to store a resource identifier, especially to accommodate both string and integer IDs (as a shared library of classes might need to do).

Programmers who aren't familiar with OWL 2.0 might be tempted to write resource statements something like this:

```
MainWindow->Attr.AccelTable = MAKEINTRESOURCE(ID_ACCELERATORS);
```

TResID makes such code completely unnecessary. If you have programmed Windows using C, you probably know that MAKEINTRESOURCE is a "fooler" macro that permits integer resource names like ID_ACCELERATORS to be passed to char pointer function parameters— one of many quirks that have given Windows programming a bad name. The macro inserts a 16-bit integer value into one half of a 32-bit char pointer and sets the other half to zero.

Forget about such error-prone "magic tricks." Instead, initialize TResId objects with integer or string resource names. The class properly uses the correct resource identifier form, eliminating the need for MAKEINTRESOURCE.

> **TIP**
>
> With TResId, it should be possible to change a resource identifer from an integer to a string, or vice versa, and simply recompile. No other changes are needed. The resulting benefits are tremendously useful when preparing class libraries that use shared resources, which are probably best identified with strings because they are less likely to conflict with other resource identifiers used in the program. Still, programmers who use the library may want to change the string identifiers to integers, which load faster. If you use TResId consistently, such a change is relatively easy to make.

RESDEMO's InitMainWindow function also demonstrates how to attach a system icon to an application. Do that with the statement:

```
MainWindow->SetIcon(this, ID_ICON);
```

151

Pass a `TModule*` pointer to `SetIcon`'s first parameter, identifying the module in which the icon resource is stored. Usually, you should perform that task in the application class's `InitMainWindow` function; that way, `this` refers to the object of the application class derived from `TApplication`. At runtime, the icon is loaded from the program's .EXE code file. If you store an icon in another module (a DLL, for instance), and if you can obtain its `TModule` pointer, you can pass that pointer to `SetIcon` to load an icon from there.

You should now have a clearer picture about how to write Windows applications. There's a lot more to come, but you have examined most of the basics. Nearly all other aspects of Windows programming involve preparing resources, deriving classes, replacing selected member functions, and constructing message-response tables. That's another benefit of using a class library such as OWL—you program widely differing tasks using similar techniques.

Looking Ahead

Next up are graphical methods—among the most important of Windows programming techniques. Whether you write business (that is, *serious)* software or games, you will use many graphics statements in your code. Graphics programming also makes an ideal training ground for learning more about how Windows works. The next chapter explains how to use OWL along with the *Windows graphics device interface.*

5

Introducing the GDI

Great-looking graphics are as hard to find as a good restaurant. Some programs have mouth-watering displays; others look like fried mush and beans. Fortunately, the Windows graphics device interface (GDI) can produce spectacular visual effects even for programmer's like me who, in real life, can't remember which end of a brush to hold.

Regardless of your artistic skills, graphics are a good place to begin learning how to write Windows software. Graphics give instant visual feedback of a program's events. Besides, in Windows, *all* visual elements, even text, are drawn graphically. Whether you write computer games or serious business applications, learning GDI techniques is a key step in mastering the art of Windows programming.

In this chapter, you learn:

- How to respond to WM_PAINT messages.
- How to use the TWindow class's Paint function to draw shapes in a window.
- How device context objects work.
- How to use location and size classes TRect, TPoint, and TSize.

- How to select colors using the TColor class.
- How to use graphics objects such as TPen and TBrush.
- How to display graphics that automatically adjust themselves when a window's size changes.
- More about message-response member functions.

Drop-of-a-Hat Graphics

In Windows programming, graphics throw an additional monkey wrench into the works. (Or, maybe it's a monkey *brush*.) You must design your program's windows to maintain the illusion of a three-dimensional desktop. It's not enough simply to design and draw a program's graphics. You must fashion code that can draw *and redraw* graphical output at the drop of a hat.

In this case, the drop of a hat is the receipt of a WM_PAINT message, an event that requires a window to paint all or a portion of its contents. For example, Windows issues a WM_PAINT message when you move one window aside and uncover another window below (see Figure 5.1). The WM_PAINT message tells the window to repair its newly uncovered space, an area known as the *invalid region*. Windows also issues WM_PAINT messages at other times—when a program creates and displays a new window, for instance, or when a minimized window is restored to normal size.

FIGURE 5.1.

When one window uncovers another, the uncovered window is required to redraw its exposed region.

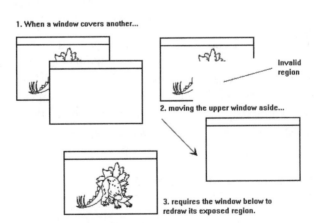

1. When a window covers another...

Invalid region

2. moving the upper window aside...

3. requires the window below to redraw its exposed region.

Beginners to Windows programming often mistakenly assume that Windows saves a bitmap of the pixels that are visually "behind" other windows on screen. At times, it's true that Windows does exactly that. For example, Windows saves relatively small bitmaps when you open a pull-down menu, covering a portion of the display. When you close the menu, Windows quickly restores the uncovered area by repainting the saved pixels, an operation that happens so rapidly you barely see it.

At most times, however, that obvious method for managing overlapping windows is impractical because saving every obscured portion of the display for every window in every application would take an enormous amount of memory. Instead, Windows requires programs to be able to recreate their displays on demand, a technique that conserves memory but requires careful programming.

Store Now, Paint Later

Rather than draw graphics and forget about them, Windows programs typically save graphics *parameters* such as line-end coordinates, color values, circle diameters, bitmap patterns, and so on. When a window receives a WM_PAINT message, the program draws images using the stored parameter values. You might call this principle *store now, draw later*. It's one of the key techniques in event-driven, graphical user interface programming.

Here are some other related definitions and concepts you need to know:

- A window's *client area* is where a program's output normally appears. Borders, the title bar, the menu, scrollers, and so on are outside of a window's client area. Windows automatically clips output by not drawing any objects outside of a window's client area. You never have to worry about accidentally drawing on top of a menu bar or a scroller.

- A window's *update region* is the portion of the window's client area that requires drawing or redrawing. When you move a window and uncover another window below, Windows adds the exposed area to the uncovered window's update region. Windows automatically redraws the window's borders and other attachments such as scrollers and buttons as needed. You never have to do that.

- A window's update region is said to be *invalid,* or in need of redrawing. *Invalidating* a window—or a portion of a window—tells Windows that some or all of the window's contents must be redrawn.

- For displaying new graphical output, a program has two options. It can draw graphics directly in the window and save the new drawing's parameters, or it can save graphics parameters and force an *update event* by invalidating the window (or the portion containing the new graphics). Sample listings in this chapter demonstrate both techniques.

- When no other messages are pending for the window, if that window has any invalid regions, Windows issues a WM_PAINT message, telling the window to redraw itself. The generation of the message is also called an *update event.* Along with WM_PAINT, Windows passes the coordinates of the window's update region.

- Programs do not have to limit drawing to the update region's coordinates. In response to a WM_PAINT message, a program can simply draw its entire display. Windows automatically *clips* graphical output to the update region, so only the necessary portions of a drawing are actually redrawn.

- Rather than rely on Windows' clipping services, however, programs can optionally limit drawing to the update region. This method, which you might call *self clipping,* is a key technique in maintaining high display speeds, especially for windows that use horizontal and vertical scrollers.

- Windows GDI functions operate independently of any specific output device—the main characteristic of *device-independent graphics.* Programs use the same functions to display graphics in windows as they do to print on paper or to draw on a plotter. In Windows, you should never directly access output devices. Instead, you should call GDI functions that produce similar results on *any* compatible device. Alas, all devices are not equal. A plotter, for example, might not be able to print bitmap images or use TrueType fonts.

The *Paint* Member Function

The TWindow class declares a member function named Paint that programs can use to update window contents. Simply stated, Paint's job is to respond to a WM_PAINT message, and in doing so, to keep a window's visual content up-to-date. Paint is a central element in the visual appearance of all types of windows. Classes derived from TWindow, for example, compose main windows, child windows, toolbars, status bars, dialog controls, and so on. Every one of those objects' classes inherits a Paint function from TWindow. To update the windows' contents, you simply replace the inherited Paint and insert the drawing statements you need.

A simple example demonstrates how to use Paint to display graphics in a window. The program also introduces the related concept of a *device context,* a term that is the source of much confusion in Windows programming. Listings 5.1 (PDEMO.RH), 5.2 (PDEMO.RC), and 5.3 (PDEMO.CPP) show the program's main files. Figure 5.2 shows PDEMO's window.

NOTE

Another file in the PDEMO directory, PDEMO.DEF, is identical to DEFAULT.DEF located in C:\BC4\LIB, and is not listed here. From now on, I list .DEF files only if they differ from the default settings. As with other sample programs in this book, use the IDE's *Project* menu to open PDEMO.IDE, then press Ctrl+F9 to compile and run. Or, from a DOS prompt, type **make** to compile with command-line tools using the supplied MAKEFILE. By now, you should be comfortable loading projects and compiling programs, so I won't repeat these instructions again.

FIGURE 5.2.

PDEMO's window.

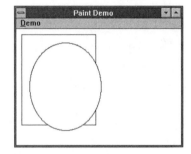

Listing 5.1. PDEMO.RH.

```
// pdemo.rh -- Resource header file

#define ID_MENU 100
```

Listing 5.2. PDEMO.RC.

```
#include <owl\window.rh>
#include "pdemo.rh"

ID_MENU MENU
BEGIN
  POPUP "&Demo"
  BEGIN
    MENUITEM "E&xit", CM_EXIT
  END
END
```

157

Listing 5.3. PDEMO.CPP.

```cpp
/* ============================================================ *\
**   pdemo.cpp -- Demonstrate Paint() function                **
** ============================================================ **
**                                                             **
** ============================================================ **
**      Copyright  1994 by Tom Swan. All rights reserved.      **
\* ============================================================ */

#include <owl\applicat.h>
#include <owl\framewin.h>
#include <owl\dc.h>
#pragma hdrstop
#include "pdemo.rh"

// ============================================================
// The application's main window
// ============================================================

class TPDemoWin: public TFrameWindow {
public:
  TPDemoWin(TWindow* parent, const char far* title);
  virtual void Paint(TDC& dc, BOOL erase, TRect& rect);
};

// Constructor
TPDemoWin::TPDemoWin(TWindow* parent, const char far* title)
  : TFrameWindow(parent, title),
    TWindow(parent, title)
{
  AssignMenu(ID_MENU);
}

// Paint or repaint shapes in the window
void
TPDemoWin::Paint(TDC& dc, BOOL /*erase*/, TRect& /*rect*/)
{
  dc.Rectangle(10, 10, 150, 175);
  dc.Ellipse(25, 25, 160, 185);
}

// ============================================================
// The application class
// ============================================================

class TPDemoApp: public TApplication {
public:
  TPDemoApp(const char far* name)
```

```
         : TApplication(name) {};
    void InitMainWindow();
};

// Initialize the program's main window
void
TPDemoApp::InitMainWindow()
{
    MainWindow = new TPDemoWin(0, "Paint Demo");
}

#pragma argsused

// Main program
int
OwlMain(int argc, char* argv[])
{
    TPDemoApp app("Sketch");
    return app.Run();
}
```

In addition to the usual APPLICAT.H and FRAMEWIN.H header files, PDEMO also includes DC.H, which declares *device context* classes that encapsulate GDI functions and data. Before you can generate graphics output, you must obtain or create a device context object, usually referred to simply as a *DC*. Think of a DC as a *device interface* through which Windows directs graphical output to its final destination—a window, for example, or a printer or plotter.

In traditional Windows programming, you obtain a *handle* to a DC, an object of type HDC. Actually, a device-context handle is just an integer that programs can use to refer to the actual DC structure stored internally by Windows. You may use DC handles, as well as handles to other items, but it's usually more convenient and much safer to use class objects for device contexts rather than integer handles.

A good example of how to use device context objects appears in PDEMO's Paint function, declared in the PDemoWin class as

```
virtual void Paint(TDC& dc, BOOL erase, TRect& rect);
```

PDemoWin inherits Paint from TFrameWindow (which inherits the function from its TWindow ancestor class). To override the inherited function—and therefore to receive all WM_PAINT messages sent to the window—PDemoWin redeclares Paint as shown here.

NOTE

I'm not telling the entire truth of Paint's relationship to WM_PAINT. Below decks, a response table that belongs to TWindow calls *another* function that calls Paint. That other function responds to WM_PAINT messages, but you can ignore this detail for now and think of Paint as the message-response function for redrawing window contents. Later in this chapter, I explain exactly how window objects call Paint for update events.

Paint receives three parameters: a reference dc to an object of type TDC, a BOOL true or false value erase, and TRect reference rect. The dc reference represents the device context—in other words, the destination for graphical output. The erase value is true if the WM_PAINT message requests the function to clear old graphics from the update region. The rectangle defines the region that could use some paint. (More on the TRect class in a bit.) In this example, Paint uses only the first parameter, dc, so I turned the other two into C-style comments, shown in bold here:

```
void
TPDemoWin::Paint(TDC& dc, BOOL /*erase*/, TRect& /*rect*/)
```

TIP

"Comment-out" unneeded function parameters to eliminate warnings from the compiler that parameters such as erase and rect are unused. You still must specify the parameter types (Bool and TRect& in the example) because Paint is already defined to receive argument values of those types, but you need to give names to only the parameters the function uses.

Paint's function body executes these two statements:

```
dc.Rectangle(10, 10, 150, 175);
dc.Ellipse(25, 25, 160, 185);
```

Running PDEMO shows the results of calling the Rectangle and Ellipse functions encapsulated in the device context object referenced by dc. Of course, it doesn't take a genius to figure out that Rectangle draws a rectangle and Ellipse draws an ellipse. The Rectangle's arguments are coordinate values relative to the window's client area. The Ellipse function uses similar coordinates to define a rectangle in which the ellipse is drawn to fit. Try different values to see how they change the program's output. Also try covering and uncovering the demo window—every time the window requires repainting, Windows issues a WM_PAINT message, causing Paint to update the display.

The important observation to make from examining PDEMO's Paint function is that GDI functions such as Rectangle and Ellipse *are called in reference to a device context object.* In conventional Windows programming, Paint's statements might look like this:

```
Rectangle(hDC, 10, 10, 150, 175);
Ellipse(hDC, 25, 25, 160, 185);
```

The hDC argument represents a handle to the device context to which you want to send graphical output. You almost never need to write statements like those because most GDI functions are encapsulated in device context classes. Instead of passing device context handles to GDI functions, you simply call encapsulated functions for a device context object such as dc:

```
dc.Rectangle(10, 10, 150, 175);
dc.Ellipse(25, 25, 160, 185);
```

The end results are the same, but the class object method helps eliminate common errors caused by using the wrong or uninitialized device context handles. The handles are already in the DC objects, making it almost impossible to use the wrong handles.

The encapsulation of GDI functions in the TDC class provides another advantage over standard Windows programming techniques. By using the C++ property of *function overloading,* TDC provides several different forms of Rectangle that take arguments of other types, not only the four integer coordinate values shown here.

The standard Windows Rectangle function requires four integer arguments, but the encapsulated function makes it possible to draw rectangles in a variety of ways. Simply select the kinds of arguments that are most convenient for your program. For example, you can define a TRect object and use it to draw a rectangle. To do that, replace the first statement in PDEMO's Paint function with:

```
TRect myRect(10, 10, 150, 175);
dc.Rectangle(myRect);
```

The first statement defines an object, myRect, that specifies the integer coordinate values of an imaginary rectangle's top-left and bottom-right corners. That object is passed by reference to the overloaded Rectangle member function for the dc device-context object. To perform a similar job in standard Windows is more difficult. For example, you might define a RECT structure, fill it with values, and then call Rectangle:

```
RECT myRect;
HDC hDC;   // Initialized somewhere else
...
myRect.left = 10;
myRect.top = 10;
myRect.right = 150;
myRect.bottom = 175;
Rectangle(hDC, myRect.left, myRect.top, myRect.right, myRect.bottom);
```

The overloaded Rectangle function, though it might not operate any faster or more efficiently than the standard approach, helps simplify graphics programming by using class functions and objects. Many other GDI functions are similarly encapsulated and overloaded in device context classes. The next section introduces OWL's graphics classes and shows some of the functions you can use to draw output in windows.

> **NOTE**
>
> OWL defines many encapsulated GDI functions *inline*, which compile directly to equivalent Windows API statements. You pay nothing in lost performance by calling inline encapsulated GDI functions.

Graphics Classes

Before digging into OWL's graphics classes, be sure to understand these concepts introduced in the preceding sections:

- Windows creates the illusion of a desktop primarily by issuing WM_PAINT messages to windows that require updating. There really is no such thing as an "overlapping window." It's your job as a programmer to provide the smoke and mirrors that make windows *appear* to sit on top of one another.

- An object of a class derived from TWindow can respond to WM_PAINT messages by providing a replacement Paint function. Insert statements in Paint to draw (and redraw) the window's contents.

- A device context class encapsulates GDI functions such as `Rectangle` and `Ellipse`. A `Paint` function calls encapsulated functions for the device-context object passed by reference in parameter `TDC& dc`. Whenever possible, you should call encapsulated GDI functions for a device-context object rather than call standard Windows graphics functions.

Keep those fundamental concepts in mind as you explore OWL's graphics classes. There are four main categories:

- Location and size classes
- Color classes
- Graphics-object classes
- Device-context classes

The first two categories provide support classes with broad applications in Windows programming. You will use location, size, and color classes in graphics, but you can also use them in a variety of other programs. The last two categories form the core of OWL's support for the Windows GDI. In general terms, graphics-object classes provide pens, brushes, and other tools for drawing in windows. Device-context classes provide interfaces between programs and output devices such as displays, printers, and plotters. The following sections describe the classes in each of these four categories.

Location and Size Classes

Location and size classes produce no visible effects; they merely define parameters used by other graphical operations. An object of the `TRect` class, for example, stores coordinate values that define a rectangular area in a window. `TRect` objects do not *display* rectangles. To draw a rectangle in a window, you can define a `TRect` object and then pass it to the `Rectangle` function, which draws the shape. You might also pass `TRect` to other functions (`Ellipse`, for instance) that require rectangular location and size arguments.

`TRect` is one of three location and size classes declared in the header file POINT.H. Table 5.1 lists and briefly describes these three classes.

Table 5.1. Location and size classes.

Class name	Base class	Alias	Used for
TPoint	tagPOINT	POINT	Single coordinates
TRect	tagRECT	RECT	Rectangular areas
TSize	tagSIZE	SIZE	Offsets and relative directions

Each class in Table 5.1 is derived from a Windows struct. The tagPOINT structure, for example, is the base class for the TPoint class. For simplicity, Windows defines aliases such as POINT for struct tagPOINT. If you are familiar with Windows programming in plain C, you probably use the aliases in the table rather than real structure names—a fact that's of little consequence except in understanding the associated class declarations. POINT and struct tagPOINT are one and the same.

> **NOTE**
>
> In C++, classes are merely specialized extensions of C structs; therefore, classes may be derived using structs as base classes.

Because the TPoint, TRect, and TSize classes are derived from structures, objects of those types are compatible with their ancestor Window structs. You can use a TPoint class object, for example, where a POINT structure might be called for in standard Windows programming. A TPoint object *is* a POINT structure, extended for object-oriented programming by the TPoint class.

Why, you might wonder, should you use classes if they are so closely related to Windows structures? Why not use the structures instead? The answer requires belief in the advantages of object-oriented programming, but the classes are far more capable than their standard structural counterparts. There are, for instance, many different ways to define and initialize TPoint objects. Here's one way:

```
TPoint p1(10, 20);
```

That statement initializes object p1 with the coordinate values 10 and 20. Suppose, however, that you want to copy a TPoint object. In that case, you can use the one object to define the other:

```
TPoint p2(p1);
```

That effectively clones p1 to a new object p2. Now, both p1 and p2 refer to the same coordinate. You can also define a TPoint object, and then initialize it by assignment:

```
TPoint p3;
//...
p3 = p2;
```

You can also compare TPoint objects as in the following if statement, which calls a fictitious function DoSomething if p1 and p3 represent the same location:

```
if (p1 == p3)
  DoSomething();
```

Replace == with != to call DoSomething if the two points are not equal.

To obtain the values of a TPoint object, you may refer directly to the base struct x and y integer members:

```
int x2 = p1.x + 5;
int location = p2.y * 100;
```

Object-oriented purists might expect TPoint to provide member functions to access x and y, but in this case, direct access is permitted so that TPoint remains compatible with its ancestor POINT structure, defined as:

```
typedef struct tagPOINT {
  int x;
  int y;
} POINT;
```

It's important to realize that TPoint inherits its x and y data members from POINT. TRect and TSize similarly inherit their data members (look up RECT and SIZE in a Windows reference or in BC4's online help files). A TPoint object is not merely a look-alike POINT structure. A TPoint class object *is* a Windows POINT structure in object-oriented form.

There are several other operations you can perform on TPoint objects. For example, the following statement offsets the location represented by a point p1 by 10 coordinate values horizontally and 20 vertically:

```
p1.OffsetBy(10, 20);
```

The OffsetBy member function in the TPoint class encapsulates an operation commonly performed on POINT structures, in this case adding values to the object's x and y members. A program loop could perform a similar operation for a series of coordinates, beginning from a fixed location:

```
TPoint p(STARTX, STARTY);
for (int i = 0; i < 10; ++i) {
  p.OffsetBy(i, 0);
  DoSomething(p);
}
```

Or, you can instead use the similar Offset function to create a *new* point object that refers to a location at a relative distance:

```
TPoint pStart(10, 20);
// ...
TPoint pEnd = pStart.Offset(10, 20);
```

Use negative values to offset points in the reverse direction. The following statements, for instance, initialize a point to the coordinate (10, 20), then move it to (8, 16):

```
TPoint p1(10, 20);
p1.OffsetBy(-2, -4);
```

I've hardly scratched the surface in the versatile TPoint class! You can subtract one point object from another, moving the result a relative distance that depends on the subtracted value:

```
TPoint presult = p1 - p3;
```

I could go on, but let's stop. My "point" here isn't to list all you can do with TPoint objects, but to hammer home a vital concept: *Most class objects are data types—use them as you do other types such as int and float.* Assign point objects, compare them, add, and subtract them just as you do simple unstructured integers and floating point values.

TIP

Before rushing to consult reference manuals about what you can do with a TPoint object, try the operation in your program. For example, if you have a TSize object s1 and you want to add it to a TPoint object p1, try the expression p1 = p1 + s1 (or, even better, p1 += s1). Remember, C++ classes are data types. Chances are, your intuitions about how to use class objects in expressions will be correct, and you can move on to other programming tasks without wasting time looking up declarations and browsing through source code files.

In addition to TPoint, OWL also provides TRect, a derived class from the Windows tagRECT structure (used in programs as the alias RECT). A TRect object stores two coordinate pairs, representing the top-left and bottom-right corners of an imaginary rectangle. As with TPoint, you can use TRect in a variety of ways. You can define TRect objects like these:

```
TRect r1(10, 20, 100, 200);
TRect r2(r1);
TRect r3(p1, p2);
TRect r4(p1, s1);
```

The first line assigns literal values to r1's left, top, right, and bottom data members inherited from RECT. The second line clones a TRect object r2 using r1. Line three defines r3 using two TPoint objects, p1 and p2. The last line defines r4 with its upper-left corner at point p1 and its lower-right corner at a location offset from p1 by the relative values in a TSize object s1.

> **TIP**
>
> Functions that use `TRect` or `RECT` members typically list them in `left`, `top`, `right`, and `bottom` order. After mixing up these values countless times, I finally memorized the sequence with a simple association that takes some explaining. In my neck of the woods there's a popular beer, Rolling Rock, brewed in Latrobe, PA. One day, on quenching my thirst after a long programming session, I realized that `left`, `top`, `right`, and `bottom` form the acronym LTRB, which forever after I remembered as *Latrobe*. If that doesn't work for you, try *Late Trains Run Backward*. Well, anyway, try *something* to keep `left`, `top`, `right`, and `bottom` in the right order.

Like `TPoint` objects, `TRect` rectangles provide a number of operations that come in handy for defining screen areas. To change a `TRect` object's values, you can use the `Set` function:

```
r.Set(100, 200, 300, 400);
```

A "full" rectangle defines a region that encloses at least one display unit (a pixel for instance); an "empty" rectangle's left and right sides, or its top and bottom sides, or both, refer to the *same* location, and therefore, it defines no space. Empty rectangles have many practical uses—you can, for example, draw a sequence of shapes in a shrinking rectangle, ending the loop when the rectangle snuffs itself out. Initialize an empty rectangle like this:

```
r.SetEmpty();
```

To test whether a rectangle is empty, use the `IsEmpty()` member function, which returns true if the rectangle does not enclose at least one display unit:

```
if (r.IsEmpty()) return;
```

You can also compare two rectangles for equality (`DoSomething` represents any operation):

```
if (r1 == r2 && r2 == r3)
  DoSomething();
```

Or, use the `Contains` and `Touches` functions to determine whether one rectangle is inside another, whether they overlap, and so on:

```
if (r1.Contains(r2))
  DoSomething();
if (r1.Touches(r2))
  DoSomething();
```

Need I explain what those obvious statements do? You can also test whether a rectangle contains a specific coordinate represented by a TPoint object (the Contains function, in other words, is overloaded to accept TRect or TPoint arguments):

```
if (r1.Contains(p1))
  DoSomething();
```

Blow up a rectangle like a balloon by inflating it:

```
r1.Inflate(10, 10);
```

Or, create a TSize object and use it like a pump to expand the object by a specified size:

```
TSize s1(10, 10);
r1.Inflate(s1);
```

To shrink a rectangle, let out some of its air by passing negative values to the Inflate function:

```
r1.Inflate(-10, -20);
```

Those are just a very few of many things you can do with TPoint, TRect, and TSize objects. These are three versatile classes of immeasurable value. For more samples, hunt through this book's listings and also those provided with BC4.

TIP

Here are a couple more hints for getting the most from TPoint, TRect, and TSize classes. Rather than define coordinate variables such as HisX and HerY, use a TPoint object. Rather then use the ubiquitous x1, y1, x2, y2 integer values for rectangular areas, use a TRect object. Rather than keep delta values such as dx and dy, use TSize. Get in the habit of using location and size classes—your programs will be easier to understand, and you'll be able to take advantage of encapsulation and inheritance as you write and revise your code. Also, many member functions in other classes accept TPoint, TRect, and TSize arguments. Using the classes will make other class operations more accessible and easier to learn.

Color Classes

Windows has come to represent *the wonderful world of color* in PC computing. Color is a natural element of the visible world, and it's only natural for color to be an important ingredient in well written software. Where color dresses up text-only DOS displays, it becomes an essential element in graphical user interfaces.

Windows programs typically express colors in one of two ways: as unsigned 32-bit integer values such as 0x0448844L (quick, what color is that?), or as red, green, and blue byte values in the range of 0 to 255. Windows provides several data types that make working with colors of both varieties easier and more descriptive than using hexadecimal values. OWL also provides classes for working with colors in an object-oriented way. Table 5.2 lists color classes declared in header file COLOR.H.

Table 5.2. Color classes.

Class name	Base class	Use
TColor	none	General-purpose color values; use in place of COLORREF values.
TPaletteEntry	tagPALETTEENTRY	Entries in TPalette class objects; equivalent to struct PALETTEENTRY.
TRgbQuad	tagRGBQUAD	32-bit red-green-blue structures; equivalent to struct RGBQUAD.
TRgbTriple	tagRGBTRIPLE	24-bit red-green-blue structures; equivalent to struct RGBTRIPLE.

Class TColor is the rough equivalent of a COLORREF value in conventional Windows programming. Because COLORREF is simply a 32-bit unsigned integer, not a struct, the TColor class is not derived from COLORREF. Instead, TColor contains a private COLORREF value.

> **TIP**
>
> TColor defines a COLORREF operator, so you can use TColor objects wherever a COLORREF value is expected.

Like most OWL classes, TColor has numerous capabilities. You can create a TColor object by specifying literal red, green, and blue byte values:

```
TColor redColor(255, 0, 0);
```

Because redColor's red component equals the highest value, and its green and blue values are zero, redColor represents the reddest possible red. As you can probably figure out, the following statements define green and blue color objects:

```
TColor greenColor(0, 255, 0);
TColor blueColor(0, 0, 255);
```

You can use any values you like in defining color objects. Because, however, typical

Windows displays support only 16 or 256 colors at a time, some combinations of values are likely to give the same visible hues:

```
TColor c1(255, 124, 62);
TColor c2(255, 124, 64);
```

Because color objects c1 and c2 differ only slightly in their blue components, they may or may not produce the same visible color, depending on the type of display hardware. If Windows is unable to provide an exact color for a set of RGB values, it uses the color that matches as closely as possible. Keep that fact in mind when comparing two TColor objects:

```
if (c1 == c2)
  DoSomething();
```

In that statement, function DoSomething() is called only if c1 and c2 specify the exact same color *values,* but not necessarily the same visible hue, which depends on the hardware.

To obtain a TColor object's individual RGB values, call the Red, Green, and Blue member functions:

```
BYTE redComponent = c.Red();
BYTE blueComponent = c.Blue();
BYTE greenComponent = c.Green();
```

A mix of all colors produces white; the absence of color is black. Using TColor, you can define whiteColor and blackColor objects using these statements:

```
TColor whiteColor(255, 255, 255);
TColor blackColor(0, 0, 0);
```

So you don't have to define standard colors in every application, TColor provides a set of static objects ready to go:

```
static const TColor Black;
static const TColor LtGray;
static const TColor Gray;
static const TColor LtRed;
static const TColor LtGreen;
static const TColor LtYellow;
static const TColor LtBlue;
static const TColor LtMagenta;
static const TColor LtCyan;
static const TColor White;
```

These color objects are `static` class members (you can't reference them directly by name as you can `TColor` variables) and they also are `const` (you can't change their values). To use the objects, preface their names with `TColor::`

```
ChangeColor(TColor::LtCyan);
```

If you forget to preface `LtCyan` with `TColor::`, the program will not compile.

NOTE

C++ permits programs to use static class members in reference to objects of the same class, but this questionable technique can lead to confusing code. For example, given a `TColor` object `myColor`, this statement is technically correct:

```
ChangeColor(myColor.LtCyan);
```

In effect, that passes `LtCyan` to the function, effectively bypassing `myColor`'s color. Don't use this questionable method to access static `TColor` objects. Always use the more sensible expressions `TColor::LtCyan`, `TColor::Black`, and so on.

The three other color classes (refer back to Table 5.2) are relatively simple in design. `TPaletteEntry` is used in conjunction with color palettes (see "Graphics Object Classes" in this chapter).

The `TRgbQuad` class stores four `BYTE` values representing red, green, and blue color components plus a reserved byte that fills the structure to 32 bits. `TRgbTriple` is almost the same as `TRgbQuad`, but lacks a fourth filler byte. Use `TRgbQuad` in place of the conventional Windows `RGBQUAD` structure; use `TRgbTriple` in place of `RGBTRIPLE`. In most cases, however, you can represent colors as `TColor` objects. Use `TRgbQuad` and `TRgbTriple` only when called for (for passing arguments to functions, for instance).

Graphics Object Classes

In conventional Windows programming, graphics objects are a hodgepodge of internal structures, inconsistently referenced by handles or pointers. In OWL, there are two kinds of graphics objects: those that store graphical information (a bitmap, for instance) and those that define graphical properties (the color of a logical pen, for example, used to draw a shape's outline).

All of OWL's graphics objects are instances of classes derived from `TGdiObject`, declared in the header file GDIOBJEC.H. Because all graphics objects are derived from the same base class, you use them all in similar ways. Learn how to use one class, and you master the others at no extra charge. Table 5.3 lists OWL's graphics object classes declared in GDIOBJEC.H.

Table 5.3. Graphics object classes.

Class name	Base class	Use
TBitmap	TGdiObject	Device-dependent, in-memory bitmaps
TBrush	TGdiObject	Background and fill colors, and patterns
TCursor	TGdiObject	Small bitmaps used as mouse cursors
TDib	TGdiObject	Device-independent, file-based bitmaps
TFont	TGdiObject	Text styles and sizes
TGdiObject	TGdiBase	Abstract base class
TIcon	TGdiObject	Small bitmaps used as icons
TPalette	TGdiObject	Indexed color tables
TPen	TGdiObject	Foreground colors and line styles
TRegion	TGdiObject	Shape outlines and areas

TGdiObject is one of the few abstract classes in OWL. TGdiObject inherits miscellaneous capabilities such as a GDI graphics object handle and exception handling member functions from TGdiBase.

Before you investigate TGdiObject, you must understand the nature and purpose of an abstract class. Because the subject may be unfamiliar to many readers, following is a quick review. (C++ wizards can skim the next few paragraphs.)

An abstract class is any class (or any derived class) that defines one or more unfinished member functions of the form:

```
virtual void f() = 0;
```

A member function that ends with = 0 is called a *pure virtual function*. It is an unfinished function—one with only a declaration, but no implementation. Statements may call pure virtual functions (permitting code to be written in advance of the class's use), but you may not construct objects of an abstract class. An abstract class is an *incomplete* class. It cannot be instantiated (that is, used to define objects).

Think of an abstract class as a kind of paint-by-numbers picture, a mere sketch that you are expected to fill in. To use an abstract class, follow these two steps:

1. Derive a new class that specifies the abstract class as a base.
2. In the derived class, provide finished function declarations and implementations for all pure virtual member functions.

Precompiled code inside of OWL calls the abstract class's pure virtual member functions. You provide the statements that carry out what those calls are supposed to do. In many cases, you may also write statements that call the completed functions, but you won't always do so. *The purpose of completing pure virtual functions is to provide actual programming for reserved capabilities of a class.*

The other classes in Table 5.3 do exactly that, inheriting common functions and data members from TGdiObject and completing that class's pure virtual member functions. Also, as a consequence of their common heritage, all classes in Table 5.3 may be addressed by TGdiObject pointers. (That's another C++ rule: base class pointers may address objects of the base class or of any class derived from the base.)

Except for their common base, however, the classes in the table have distinct uses. TPen objects, for example, define foreground colors used to draw shape outlines (among other tasks). Usually, you define a TPen object using an object of the TColor class:

```
TColor redColor(255, 0, 0);
TPen pen(redColor);
```

The two statements define a TPen object named pen initialized to the color specified by object redColor. For simplicity, you might want to combine the two steps into one statement:

```
TPen pen(TColor(255, 0, 0));
```

That way, you don't need to define a named TColor object. The object constructed by the expression TColor(255, 0, 0) is a *temporary object*, and is automatically destroyed after use. Alternatively, you can specify a pen's color by using one of TColor's static color objects:

```
TPen pen(TColor::Red);
```

It's also possible to construct a pen object from a pen handle of type HPEN obtained from a Windows function:

```
HPEN hp = SomeFunctionThatReturnsHPEN();
TPen pen(hp);
```

Of course, there's no function in Windows named SomeFunctionThatReturnsHPEN. I mean only to show how you can combine conventional Windows techniques (such as obtaining a handle to a pen) with OWL's classes. In this case, the handle hp initializes a TPen object—a good example also of class-constructor overloading, which provides many ways to construct an object of the TPen class.

Remember, however, that for every TPen class object, there's an internal windows element for which the object serves as an interface. (I've mentioned this principle before— every TWindow object, for example, has a corresponding window element that Windows constructs and maintains.) This raises an important question. Should objects be responsible for destroying their associated Windows element, or should you do that? In other words, when the TPen class object pen goes out of scope or is otherwise destroyed, should the object automatically destroy the Windows pen associated internally with the HPEN handle?

There's no single correct answer. In some cases, you may want the object to destroy the associated Windows element; in other cases you don't. In the following example, for instance, if you obtained the pen handle from a function that destroys the associated Windows pen element, the object must not perform that same delete operation. (Deleting the same Windows pen element twice would likely cause hard-to-find bugs.) In such cases, you should define the object like this:

```
TPen pen(hp, NoAutoDelete);
```

That's the default action for TPen objects constructed from HPEN handles, so you don't have to specify NoAutoDelete unless you want to for clarity. If you *do* want the pen object's destructor to destroy the Windows pen element, use this alternative statement to define the object:

```
TPen pen(hp, AutoDelete);
```

A third way to construct a pen object is to define a LOGPEN (logical pen) structure, or to call a function that returns a pointer to a LOGPEN structure, and pass the pointer to TPen's constructor:

```
LOGPEN* lpenPtr = FunctionThatReturnsLOGPEN();
TPen pen(lpenPtr);
```

You can also perform the reverse operation, dumping a TPen object's contents into a LOGPEN structure:

```
LOGPEN logpen;
TPen pen(TColor::LtCyan);
pen.GetObject(&logpen);
```

After that, you can examine the pen object's style, width, and color values taken from logpen.

Other TGdiObject classes are used in similar ways. For example, you can create a TBrush object, typically used to paint window backgrounds and to fill shapes with colors or patterns:

```
TBrush brush(TColor::White);
```

That creates a brush object of type TBrush initialized to the static White color defined by the TColor class. You might use brush to fill an area in a window with white—but more on such operations in a bit. You can also construct brushes with colors and patterns:

```
TBrush brush(TColor::Red, HS_CROSS);
```

You can use other HS_ (hatch style) constants such as HS_BDIAGONAL, HS_DIAGCROSS, and HS_VERTICAL to create different brush shapes. (Search for other hatch style constants in a Windows API reference.)

Other graphics object classes—TFont, TPalette, TBitmap, TIcon, TCursor, TDib, and TRegion—all have their own idiosyncrasies that are best explained in the context of examples. The foregoing merely introduces graphics-object techniques and shows some possible uses. (I tried to pick examples that also would help you to discover more capabilities on your own by reading the class references.) In this and in future chapters, you'll meet many more examples of graphics-object classes that will explain them further.

Device Context Classes

The final category of GDI classes are those derived from TDC. These are known as *device context classes*. Technically speaking, they determine the contexts in which graphics are formed, but it's often easier just to think of them as destinations to which graphics are sent. By selecting an appropriate device context, you can direct graphical output to a window, to an offscreen bitmap, to the printer, to a plotter, or to another device.

Device context classes encapsulate GDI functions. To draw a rectangle, for example, you first construct or obtain a device context and then call the Rectangle member function for that object. In OWL programs, you don't pass device context handles to GDI functions, as you do in conventional C programming. Instead, you call GDI functions that are members of the context—a cleaner and more object-oriented way to keep graphics looking good and, more important, to direct graphical output to the right windows or other destinations.

TDC is the fundamental class on which all device context classes are based. Table 5.4 lists and briefly describes device context classes declared in header file DC.H.

Table 5.4. Device context classes.

Class name	Base class	Use
TDC	none	Base class for other device context classes; encapsulates GDI functions as class members.
TIC	TDC	Information-only device context; not for use in producing graphical output. For more about this class's capabilities, look up CreateIC in a Windows API reference.
TWindowDC	TDC	Provides access to an entire window.
TScreenDC	TDC	Provides access to the entire display.
TDesktopDC	TDC	Drawing in the desktop's client area.
TClientDC	TDC	Drawing in a window's client area.
TPaintDC	TDC	Drawing in a Paint function or in response to a WM_PAINT message.
TMemoryDC	TDC	Drawing to an offscreen bitmap.
TDibDC	TDC	Provides access to device-independent bitmaps; requires the Borland DIB.DRV driver.
TMetaFileDC	TDC	Provides access to a device context associated with a metafile.
TPrintDC	TDC	Provides access to a printer; to print, a program draws into a TPrintDC object.

TIP

The TDC class provides an HDC operator that permits objects of type TDC (or of a derived class) to be passed to any function requiring a conventional Windows HDC device context handle. To extract the device context handle from a device context object (tdc), simply assign the object to an HDC variable:

HDC hdc = tdc;

Calling encapsulated GDI member functions correctly takes practice—as a programming technique, the method may seem awkward at first, especially to programmers accustomed to writing non-object-oriented code. In general terms, the process of using one of OWL's device context classes to produce graphical output involves four steps:

1. Obtain or construct a device context object using one of the classes from Table 5.4.

2. Construct a graphics object (refer back to Table 5.3)—a TPen or TBrush object, for example. Select the object *into* the device context by calling the SelectObject member function. You can select only one object of a type at a time into a device context. The same context, for example, cannot own two pens.

3. Call one or more member functions for the device context object. The functions use any graphics objects such as pens and brushes selected into the device context in step 2.

4. Restore the original pens, brushes, and other graphics objects selected into the device context. In conventional C programming, this step is vital; in OWL, objects are restored automatically in many cases, though you still need to be careful not to leave pens and brushes lying around inside devices.

> **NOTE**
>
> In Windows jargon, you *select* a pen *into* a device context. I would rather say *insert* than *select*, but fighting the accepted jargon is worse than fighting city hall. So, with apologies to my English teacher, *select into* is the phrase I'll use to describe the process of inserting graphics objects into device contexts.

If those four steps seem unnecessarily complex, keep in mind that one of the GDI's primary goals is to provide *device-independent graphics*. The operations of displaying and printing graphics use the identical GDI functions in different contexts. To display graphics in a window, you call GDI functions in reference to a TClientDC or to another window-access context; to print, you call *the same functions* in reference to a TPrintDC context. Achieving device independence might seem burdensome, but in the long run, the results are simpler to manage than if you had to call a different set of functions for displaying and printing the same shapes. Furthermore, new devices such as high resolution video displays can easily be supported by existing software through the installation of an appropriate output device driver.

The basic steps for using device contexts might be clearer from a few examples. Imagine that you are writing a member function in a class derived from TFrameWindow. You want to display a red box with the coordinates (45, 65) and (250, 200), perhaps to outline a key section of the program's main window. Here's how you might construct the function (to keep the steps clear, I made no attempt to shorten or optimize the statements):

```
void TMyWindow::DrawRedBox()
{
  TClientDC dc(HWindow);
  TRect rect(45, 65, 250, 200);
  TColor color(255, 0, 0);
  TPen pen(color);
  dc.SelectObject(pen);
  dc.Rectangle(rect);
  dc.RestorePen();
}
```

The function begins by constructing a device context object of type TClientDC, initialized with the window handle HWindow inherited by class TMyWindow from TFrameWindow. This is the most general way to use a device context class. To draw inside a window, simply construct a TClientDC using the window's handle. In a more complete example, you would also save the graphics parameters so a Paint function can repaint the same shape in case the window is covered or another event causes Windows to send a WM_PAINT message to the window.

The sample function also constructs three other objects of classes TRect, TColor, and TPen. Object rect defines the location and size of the rectangle. Object color defines the color red. Object pen uses color to create a red pen. This statement selects the pen into the device context:

```
dc.SelectObject(pen);
```

Selecting a pen into a device context is how you specify a foreground drawing color in Windows. Next, call a GDI function such as Rectangle to draw a shape using the selected pen color:

```
dc.Rectangle(rect);
dc.RestorePen();
```

Calling RestorePen removes the most recent pen object selected into the device context. This step is important because Windows device contexts are shared resources, and therefore, programs must create and dispose of them repeatedly. A device context can only be deleted, however, if it has no selected objects, thus you should always call RestorePen to remove any selected pen before the device context is deleted. (Object dc is local to a function in this example, and it is automatically deleted when the function ends.)

> **NOTE**
>
> Actually, calling `RestorePen` is unnecessary in this example because the `dc` object is local to a function. When the function ends, the object's destructor automatically removes any selected objects. Similarly, other functions such as `RestoreBrush`, `RestorePalette`, and `RestoreFont` remove any selected `TBrush`, `TPalette`, or `TFont` objects respectively from a device context.

In the next section, you explore various techniques for using device context objects along with other graphics classes.

Graphics Objects

A few sample listings demonstrate some of the techniques for using OWL's graphics classes. The samples also show a few tips and tricks that you might want to use in your own code.

Pens, Brushes, and Colors

It's hard to imagine a Windows program that doesn't use pens, brushes, and colors. These common objects have practical uses in all sorts of Windows software from games to serious business applications.

Listings 5.4 (BAR.RH), 5.5 (BAR.H), 5.6 (BAR.RC), and 5.7 (BAR.CPP) demonstrate how to use pens, brushes, and colors to draw the bar chart shown in Figure 5.3. The program also demonstrates how to create *relative* graphics that automatically adjust for changes in window size. To see how this works, expand and shrink BAR's window. As you can see, no matter how large or small, the bar chart automatically adjusts itself to fit inside the window's borders. (When the window is very small, however, the chart's labels may be difficult to read.)

Listing 5.4. BAR.RH.

```
// bar.rh -- Resource header file

#define ID_MENU 100              // Menu resource identifier
```

FIGURE 5.3.
Bar chart drawn by the BAR.CPP program.

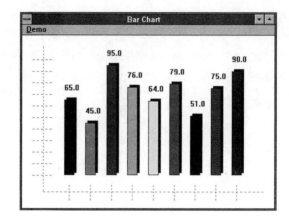

Listing 5.5. BAR.H.

```
// bar.h -- Header file for bar.cpp

// Symbolic constants
#define NUMCLRS 16              // Number of colors in colorArray
#define NUMDATAPOINTS 9         // Number of points in data array
#define SPACEATBOTTOM  60       // Reserved pixels below chart
#define SPACEATLEFT  80         // Reserved pixels to left of chart
#define SPACEATTOP 40           // Reserved pixels at top of chart
#define SPACEATRIGHT 40         // Reserved pixels at right of chart
#define YSCALEMAX 100.0         // Maximum Y scale value
#define YSCALEINCREMENT 10.0    // Increment for Y scale markers

// Constant expressions
#define SPACEVERTICAL (SPACEATTOP + SPACEATBOTTOM)
#define SPACEHORIZONTAL (SPACEATLEFT + SPACEATRIGHT)
#define HALFSPACEATBOTTOM (SPACEATBOTTOM / 2)
#define HALFSPACEATRIGHT (SPACEATRIGHT / 2)
#define YSCALEMARKERS (YSCALEMAX / YSCALEINCREMENT)
#define YAXISX (SPACEATLEFT / 2)
#define YAXISY (SPACEATTOP / 2)
#define YMARKERX1 (SPACEATLEFT / 4)
#define YMARKERX2 (YMARKERX1 + (SPACEATLEFT / 2))
```

Listing 5.6. BAR.RC.

```
#include <owl\window.rh>
#include "bar.rh"

ID_MENU MENU
```

```
BEGIN
  POPUP "&Demo"
  BEGIN
    MENUITEM "E&xit", CM_EXIT
  END
END
```

Listing 5.7. BAR.CPP.

```
/* ============================================================ *\
** bar.cpp -- Display bar chart and demonstrate Paint()       **
** ============================================================ **
**                                                            **
** ============================================================ **
**      Copyright  1994 by Tom Swan. All rights reserved.     **
\* ============================================================ */

#include <owl\applicat.h>
#include <owl\framewin.h>
#include <owl\dc.h>
#include <owl\gdiobjec.h>
#include <stdio.h>
#include <string.h>
#include "bar.h"
#include "bar.rh"

// ============================================================
// Global definitions
// ============================================================

// Color values (assumes NUMCLRS == 16)
static TColor colorArray[NUMCLRS] = {
  0x0000000L, 0x0FFFFFFL, 0x0FF0000L, 0x000FF00L,
  0x00000FFL, 0x0FFFF00L, 0x000FFFFL, 0x0FF00FFL,
  0x0880000L, 0x0008800L, 0x0000088L, 0x0888800L,
  0x0008888L, 0x0880088L, 0x0448844L, 0x0884488L
};

// Sample data array
static double data[NUMDATAPOINTS] =
  {65.0, 45.0, 95.0, 76.0, 64.0, 79.0, 51.0, 75.0, 90.0};

// ============================================================
// The application's main window
// ============================================================
```

continues

181

Listing 5.7. continued

```cpp
class TChartWin: public TFrameWindow {
  int xMax, yMax;      // Maximum client area coordinates
  int xBase, yBase;  // X and Y coordinate base for chart
  int xIncrement, yIncrement, width, widthD2;  // Miscellaneous
public:
  TChartWin(TWindow* parent, const char far* title);

// Inherited functions
  virtual void SetupWindow();
  virtual void Paint(TDC& dc, BOOL erase, TRect& rect);

// New functions
  void SetMaxCoordinates();
  int YData(int n);
  void DrawGrid(TDC& dc);
protected:

// Inherited response function
  void EvSize(UINT sizeType, TSize& size);

DECLARE_RESPONSE_TABLE(TChartWin);
};

DEFINE_RESPONSE_TABLE1(TChartWin, TFrameWindow)
  EV_WM_SIZE,
END_RESPONSE_TABLE;

// Constructor
TChartWin::TChartWin(TWindow* parent, const char far* title)
  : TFrameWindow(parent, title),
    TWindow(parent, title)
{
  AssignMenu(ID_MENU);
  Attr.X = GetSystemMetrics(SM_CXSCREEN) / 8;
  Attr.Y = GetSystemMetrics(SM_CYSCREEN) / 8;
  Attr.H = Attr.Y * 6;
  Attr.W = Attr.X * 6;
}

// Initialize window coordinates (requires window handle)
void
TChartWin::SetupWindow()
{
  TWindow::SetupWindow();
  SetMaxCoordinates();
}

// Paint or repaint bar chart in current window size
void TChartWin::Paint(TDC& dc, BOOL /*erase*/, TRect& /*rect*/)
{
```

```
    TBrush* brush;
    int i, x1, y1, x2, y2;
    char szBuf[10];

    DrawGrid(dc);
    for (i = 0; i < NUMDATAPOINTS; i++) {
      x1 = SPACEATLEFT + (xIncrement * i);
      y1 = YData(i);
      x2 = x1 + width;
      y2 = yBase;
      sprintf(szBuf, "%0.1f", data[i]);  // Create label
      dc.TextOut(x1, y1 - 30, szBuf, strlen(szBuf));
      brush = new TBrush(colorArray[0]);  // Black
      dc.SelectObject(*brush);
      dc.Rectangle(x1 + 4, y1 - 4, x2 + 4, y2 - 4);
      dc.RestoreBrush();
      delete brush;
      brush = new TBrush(colorArray[(i + 2) % NUMCLRS]);
      dc.SelectObject(*brush);
      dc.Rectangle(x1, y1, x2, y2);
      dc.RestoreBrush();
      delete brush;
    }
}

// Set up maximum coordinate values
void
TChartWin::SetMaxCoordinates()
{
  TRect rect;

  GetClientRect(rect);
  xMax = rect.right;
  yMax = rect.bottom;
  yBase = yMax - SPACEATBOTTOM;
}

// Return Y coordinate for data point n
int
TChartWin::YData(int n)
{
  return (yBase - (data[n] / YSCALEINCREMENT) * yIncrement);
}

// Draw grid and initialize bar chart variables
void
TChartWin::DrawGrid(TDC& dc)
{
  int i, k, y1, y2;
  TPen pen(TColor::Gray, 1, PS_DOT);
```

continues

Listing 5.7. continued

```cpp
  dc.SelectObject(pen);
  xIncrement = (xMax - SPACEHORIZONTAL) / NUMDATAPOINTS;
  yIncrement = (yMax - SPACEVERTICAL) / YSCALEMARKERS;
  width = xIncrement / 2;
  widthD2 = width / 2;
  xBase = SPACEATLEFT + widthD2;
  y2 = yBase + HALFSPACEATBOTTOM;          // Draw axes
  dc.MoveTo(YAXISX, YAXISY);
  dc.LineTo(YAXISX, y2);
  dc.LineTo(xMax - HALFSPACEATRIGHT, y2);
  for (i = 0; i <= YSCALEMARKERS; i++) { // Draw Y-axis markers
    k = yBase - (i * yIncrement);
    dc.MoveTo(YMARKERX1, k);
    dc.LineTo(YMARKERX2, k);
  }
  y1 = yMax - (SPACEATBOTTOM / 4);        // Draw X-axis markers
  y2 = y1 - HALFSPACEATBOTTOM;
  for (i = 0; i < NUMDATAPOINTS; i++) {
    k = xBase + (i * xIncrement);
    dc.MoveTo(k, y1);
    dc.LineTo(k, y2);
  }
  dc.RestorePen();
}

void
TChartWin::EvSize(UINT sizeType, TSize& size)
{
  TFrameWindow::EvSize(sizeType, size);
  SetMaxCoordinates();
  Invalidate();
  UpdateWindow();   // Optional
}

// ============================================================
// The application class
// ============================================================

class TChartApp: public TApplication {
public:
  TChartApp(const char far* name)
    : TApplication(name) {};
  void InitMainWindow();
};

// Initialize the program's main window
void
TChartApp::InitMainWindow()
{
```

```
  MainWindow = new TChartWin(0, "Bar Chart");
}

#pragma argsused

// Main program
int
OwlMain(int argc, char* argv[])
{
  TChartApp app("Bar");
  return app.Run();
}
```

BAR.CPP includes four OWL headers: APPLICAT.H, FRAMEWIN.H, DC.H, and GDIOBJEC.H. In addition, STDIO.H makes the standard function sprintf available for preparing labels. The STRING.H header makes standard string functions such as strlen available. Notice that these two headers do not begin with the path name owl\ because, as standards, they are located in the default C:\BC4\INCLUDE directory.

> **TIP**
>
> Windows programs may call functions in the standard C library by including the appropriate headers such as STRING.H, MATH.H, and STDLIB.H. Before calling a standard function, however, check in your BC4 reference whether the function is supported under Windows. If not, Windows may have a similar API function that you can use.

BAR.CPP also includes the BAR.H header file, using double quotes to indicate that this file is located in the current directory (that is, the same one that also holds BAR.CPP). The header file defines several constants and macro expressions used in calculating bar positions and sizes.

Two static global arrays hold color objects and sample bar-chart data. (A more sophisticated program might read data from a file—I used a static array just for simplicity.) The colorArray holds a set of TColor objects, initialized with 32-bit values that are equivalent to COLORREF values typically used in conventional C programs:

```
static TColor colorArray[NUMCLRS] = {
  0x0000000L, 0x0FFFFFFL, 0x0FF0000L, 0x000FF00L,
  // ...
};
```

This isn't the only way to construct an array of TColor objects. You could also declare colorArray as a class member:

```
TColor colorArray[NUMCLRS];
```

and then, perhaps in the class constructor, fill the array with TColor objects:

```
colorArray[0] = TColor(0, 0, 0);
colorArray[1] = TColor(255, 0, 0);
// ...
colorArray[15] = TColor(128, 64, 128);
```

There are many ways to use TColor objects. How you define and store them is up to you. When defining large color arrays, however, you might want to allocate dynamic memory using programming such as this:

```
TColor* bigArray;
bigArray = new[] TColor[512];
for (int i = 0; i < 512; ++i)
  InitializeColor(bigArray[i]);
// ...
delete[] bigArray;
```

When constructing arrays of TColor objects (or of other classes), use the ANSI C++ new[] and delete[] operators as shown to ensure that the arrayed constructors and destructors are properly called. (The new[] operator is *brand* new, and replaces new without brackets for the purpose of defining dynamic memory for arrays. The delete[] operator has been in C++ longer—always use delete[] to dispose of memory allocated with new[].)

> **NOTE**
>
> TChartWin's eight int members are private by default. Some C++ programmers prefer to define private data members at the bottom of a class below a private: access specifier. The end result is the same—use whichever style you prefer.

TChartWin's member functions demonstrate several techniques that you'll want to use in your own Windows programs. The following sections describe each function. (The functions are declared in a different order than discussed here. Though function declaration order is usually not important in C++ classes, I like to separate inherited and new functions. This makes perfectly clear which functions are inherited from base classes and which are declared fresh in the derived class.)

TChartWin Constructor

TWindow constructors typically perform three kinds of jobs: initializing class data members, calling OWL functions to perform tasks like attaching a menu resource, and calling Windows API functions (or their encapsulated equivalents inherited from TWindow).

In this case, TWindow's constructor calls AssignMenu to attach the menu resource to the program's main window. The constructor also assigns size and location values to fields in the Attr structure. Calling GetSystemMetrics as shown is a handy way to ensure that the program's window begins dead center, with the same amount of relative space on all sides.

When deciding what tasks to insert in a TWindow constructor, keep in mind that at this point, the associated *Windows* window element has not yet been created. Only the object is being constructed, so you must limit the constructor's tasks to those that directly affect your class data members. A TWindow constructor must never call any function that requires a window handle—the HWindow handle inherited from TWindow is not yet initialized.

SetupWindow

You might ask: What if you have to call an initializing function that requires a window handle? If that statement can't go in a TWindow constructor, where *should* it go? The answer is: insert the task into a replacement SetupWindow function, inherited from TWindow. SetupWindow creates the window object's associated window element. You may therefore insert into SetupWindow statements that require a window handle.

As its first step, SetupWindow should always call its ancestor function as shown in BAR. In the sample listing, SetupWindow also calls the next function to initialize some data members that require a window handle.

SetMaxCoordinates

This function initializes the xMax, yMax, and yBase data members of the TChartWin class. The function also resets these values when the window size changes so the chart remains centered inside the window's borders. SetMaxCoordinates is a new function; it's not inherited from a base class.

To determine the window's size, the function calls GetClientRect, passing a TRect object, rect, by reference as an argument. GetClientRect fills rect with the coordinates of the window's client area. Because GetClientRect requires a window handle, this function cannot be called from a TWindow constructor. It may be called from SetupWindow (as it is here), or at any time after the window becomes visible.

> **NOTE**
>
> The Windows API function, GetClientRect, requires an initial HWND argument, making it obvious that this function requires a window handle. The encapsulated GetClientRect declared in TWindow automatically passes the object's HWindow handle, and therefore it is no longer obvious from the source code that this function needs the handle! Before calling Windows functions from constructors and in SetupWindow (or from another function called by a constructor or SetupWindow), it's a good idea to look up the API function to determine whether the function requires a window handle.

Paint

Paint responds to a WM_PAINT message sent to the program's main window. To draw inside the window, the function uses the device context dc, passed by reference to Paint. This device context is supplied ready to use. You can select graphics objects such as pens and brushes into dc, call GDI member functions, and so on. The other two arguments, erase and rect, aren't needed here, so I turned them into comments.

TChartWin's Paint defines a pointer to a TBrush object. It's up to you whether to define pointers to graphics objects, or just define the objects directly. I used a pointer here merely to demonstrate the technique, not because a pointer is required.

Paint begins by calling another function, DrawGrid, which plunks down the bar chart's vertical and horizontal axes. Notice how Paint passes dc to DrawGrid, which can then call GDI functions in reference to that object. Another function might pass a *different* device context object (perhaps of type TPrint) and, in that way, direct the function's output to another device or window.

To draw the bar chart, Paint uses a for loop. First, several local variables are initialized to position each bar. The standard sprintf prepares text labels in a local char array, szBuf. (The "sz" is an abbreviation for "zero-terminated string," also known as a null-terminated string.) Paint displays each label with the statement:

```
tdc.TextOut(x1, y1 - 30, szBuf, strlen(szBuf));
```

The first two arguments specify the starting position for the string's first character, the next argument is a pointer to a char array (or it can be a literal string), and the final argument specifies the string's length by calling the standard strlen function.

When you run BAR, you see that each bar in the chart is displayed on top of a black "shadow" that gives a pseudo three-dimensional look to the graphics. To draw the shadows, Paint executes the following statements:

```
brush = new TBrush(colorArray[0]);  // Black
dc.SelectObject(*brush);
dc.Rectangle(x1 + 4, y1 - 4, x2 + 4, y2 - 4);
dc.RestoreBrush();
delete brush;
```

First, the program creates a dynamic TBrush object, colored black. The first statement also assigns the object's address to the brush pointer. SelectObject selects the brush into the device context, dc, passed by reference to Paint. Notice the asterisk prefacing *brush. You must pass the *object* to SelectObject, not the pointer, and therefore, you must dereference the pointer when calling SelectObject. It is also your responsibility to delete the brush object as this sample does in its last statement. Before then, calling Rectangle for the device context object dc paints a black-filled bar—the shadow that appears behind the colored bars in the chart. RestoreBrush deselects the brush object from the device context so the brush can be deleted. Never delete objects selected into a device context. Always deselect them first.

> **TIP**
>
> When a device context object is deleted, or when it goes out of scope, its destructor automatically restores all selected graphics objects. You do not have to call RestoreBrush, for example, if you are sure the device context will be deleted. It doesn't hurt to call RestoreBrush needlessly, however, so it's better to err on the side of safety.

A similar sequence of statements draws each colored bar:

```
brush = new TBrush(colorArray[(i + 2) % NUMCLRS]);
dc.SelectObject(*brush);
dc.Rectangle(x1, y1, x2, y2);
dc.RestoreBrush();
delete brush;
```

Those statements are almost the same as the ones that draw the bar shadows. In this case, however, the program selects a color from colorArray, using a formula that assigns each bar a different color. The program selects the brush object into the device context, draws the rectangle filled with the selected brush color, calls RestoreBrush, and deletes the brush.

YData

This simple function, which is new, not inherited, returns the vertical coordinate for a data point passed as an argument. BAR uses the function in calculating axis markers, and also for drawing the chart's bars. The YData function is important to this application's design because the function returns a coordinate that is sized relative to the window. You might want to consider writing similar functions in other programs that need to display automatically-sized graphics.

> **NOTE**
>
> The Windows Paintbrush application is another good example of a program that resizes its graphics to fit. Run that program and expand its window. Notice how the toolbars at left and at bottom resize automatically to fit. Notice also that if you make Paintbrush's window very small, the resized toolbars are difficult to use—a relatively minor problem with this technique.

DrawGrid

This function, which is new, not inherited, draws the axis markers to the left and bottom of the bar chart. Paint calls DrawGrid, passing a reference to a device context, ready to be used for drawing inside the window. Passing device context objects by reference is a good way to divide a graphics program's duties among two or more functions. You don't have to insert every output statement into Paint. You can delegate some responsibilities to other functions and call them from Paint.

To draw the axis markers using a different color from the default (usually black), DrawGrid constructs a dotted, gray, TPen object:

```
TPen pen(TColor::Gray, 1, PS_DOT);
```

Past examples constructed pen objects with only a TColor argument. The second argument specifies a line width of 1. The third argument specifies a pen style, in this case dotted. Look up other PS_ pen styles in a Windows API reference. PS_DASH, for instance, draws a dashed line. Unfortunately, the line width must be 1 to use these alternate pen styles. Wider lines are always solid.

DrawGrid calls two GDI functions you haven't seen before. These two statements, for example, draw a line:

```
dc.MoveTo(YAXISX, YAXISY);
dc.LineTo(YAXISX, y2);
```

MoveTo positions an internal GDI location pointer to the given coordinate. LineTo draws a line, using the selected pen, for the device context object dc. The internal location is set to the end of the line, so you can follow this statement with another call to LineTo to continue drawing.

In conventional C programs, you must pass two integer values to MoveTo and LineTo. In OWL, you may instead pass a TPoint object. These statements give the same results as the preceding two:

```
TPoint pt1(YAXISX, YAXISY);
TPoint pt2(YAXISX, y2);
dc.MoveTo(pt1);
dc.LineTo(pt2);
```

In this case, that's more work, but in another, using TPoint objects instead of X and Y coordinate values might be more convenient.

> **TIP**
>
> Most functions in device context classes that accept two integer coordinate values will also accept a TPoint object. Most functions that accept four coordinate values (Rectangle, for instance), will accept two TPoint arguments or a single TRect object.

EvSize

Though it may seem insignificant, the EvSize function plays a major role in the BAR program's window handling. Examine the function's declaration in the TChartWin class:

```
void EvSize(UINT sizeType, TSize& size);
```

EvSize is an example of an inherited response function, one of several provided by the TWindow class. (Hint: To find similar functions, search for EvSize in file WINDOW.H in directory C:\BC4\INCLUDE\OWL.) The BAR program replaces EvSize to detect when the main window size changes. This permits the program to adjust the variables that control the bar chart's position and size.

EvSize is called in response to the window receiving a WM_SIZE message from Windows. To ensure that EvSize is called at the correct time, TChartWin declares that it requires a response table:

```
DECLARE_RESPONSE_TABLE(TChartWin);
```

Following the TChartWin declaration, the program defines a response table for the class:

```
DEFINE_RESPONSE_TABLE1(TChartWin, TFrameWindow)
  EV_WM_SIZE,
END_RESPONSE_TABLE;
```

TChartWin has only one immediate base class, TFrameWindow, which also uses a response table, so the DEFINE_RESPONSE_TABLE1 macro is the correct one to use. The table has only one entry, another macro named EV_WM_SIZE. OWL defines this macro to associate the Windows message WM_SIZE with the TWindow function EvSize. (Note the naming convention used by the macro and function—other response functions and macros are named similarly.)

With these preparations out of the way, the replacement EvSize function in TChartWin will be called every time the window receives a WM_SIZE message. At that time, the replacement function executes these statements:

```
TFrameWindow::EvSize(sizeType, size);
SetMaxCoordinates();
Invalidate();
UpdateWindow();  // Optional
```

First, the replacement calls its inherited function to perform default actions required by the window. `SetMaxCoordinates` then adjusts `TChartWin`'s data members according to the new window's size. In this program, any change to the window means redrawing the entire window because the graphics must be refitted to the window's new borders. To update the window, the program calls `Invalidate`, which invalidates the entire client area. This condition instructs Windows to issue a `WM_PAINT` message, causing the window's `Paint` function to be called. Windows issues `WM_PAINT` only when the window has no other pending messages. To force Windows to issue the message immediately, follow `Invalidate` with `UpdateWindow` as shown here. This step is optional, but can sometimes improve display speed (at the possible expense of delaying other events).

> **TIP**
>
> Some response functions such as `EvSize` require you to call their ancestors; others do not. To tell the difference, look up the function in file WINDOW.H. If the function has an `inline` definition that calls `DefaultProcessing`, it does *not* require a replacement function to call its inherited base-class version. If, however, the function has a body in file window.cpp, then it does require a replacement to call its base-class version. Even in that case, though, you may choose to replace the function completely and not call the base-class version if you don't want the replacement function to perform its default actions.

Message Crackers

In addition to a variety of default response functions like `EvSize`, OWL also provides ready-made response-table macros such as `EV_WM_SIZE`. The macro name indicates that it relates a function with a message, in this case `WM_SIZE`. The `EV` preface stands for "event." The macros and others like it are known as *message crackers* because they *crack open* the parameters passed with the message. In conventional Windows programming, you will find numerous instances of function parameters named `wParam` (word parameter) and `lParam` (long parameter). OWL cracks these parameter values into their components, which in the old days of Windows programming, you would have to do manually. Take another look, for example, at `EvSize`'s declaration:

```
void EvSize(UINT sizeType, TSize& size);
```

The function receives two cracked parameters: an unsigned integer named `sizeType`, and a reference to a `TSize` object, `size`:

- sizeType is set to one of several SIZE_ constants such as SIZE_MAXIMIZED or SIZE_MINIMIZED, which indicate whether the window is displayed full screen or is shown as an icon. A program might inspect sizeType to avoid wasting time preparing variables that won't be used anyway when users reduce the window to a desktop icon.

- size provides the width and height of the window in a TSize object, the object-oriented equivalent to the Windows SIZE structure. Use the object's cx and cy data members to determine the windows width and height respectively.

TIP

A good way to learn the purposes of cracked message parameters is to read the documentation on a Windows message. For example, look up WM_SIZE in BC4's online help. As you can see, the message's wParam and lParam values contain uncracked values that indicate the size information provided in more convenient form by EvSize. Similar message crackers in OWL help prevent bugs that are typically caused by improperly decoding raw data values passed along with Windows messages.

Window Classes

Normally, the device context object passed to a Paint function is primed with the system's foreground and background colors. Unless you select pens and brushes of different colors in the device context, graphics automatically use the system's default colors.

Those colors, however, might not suit every application. In a simulation of a night sky, for example, using a default background color of light pink probably won't win you any awards. To force the background to jet black, you could paint the client area with a black brush in a Paint function, but there's a better way: change the *window class* to use a black brush for the window's background.

The window class is not a C++ class. It's the internal structure that Windows uses to store a window's characteristics. Multiple window elements can be created from the same window class, which must be identified by a unique name. A TWindow OWL class *registers* a window class with Windows, so that, when you construct an object of that class, it is associated with the proper window element.

Changing a fundamental window characteristic, then, requires making a change to one of the parameters in the window class. In any OWL class derived from TWindow, do this by replacing function GetWindowClass, declared as:

```
virtual void GetWindowClass(WNDCLASS& wndClass);
```

Always call the inherited GetWindowClass to initialize the wndClass parameter, passed by reference to the function. You can then modify one or more fields in wndClass to change the window class characteristics. (You may completely initialize wndClass's fields if you prefer, in which case, you do not have to call the inherited function.) For example, to change the default window background to black, implement GetWindowClass like this:

```
void
TAnyWin::GetWindowClass(WNDCLASS& wndClass)
{
  TFrameWindow::GetWindowClass(wndClass);
  wndClass.hbrBackground =
    (HBRUSH)GetStockObject(BLACK_BRUSH);
}
```

WNDCLASS is a Windows structure, not a class object. Assigning a new background color to the hbrBackground field therefore requires calling the Windows API GetStockObject function to obtain a brush handle, and using the type cast expression (HBRUSH) in the assignment.

When redefining GetWindowClass, you can also give the *Windows* window-class a new name, which must be unique among all the windows your program registers. TWindow automatically creates a window class name equal to the module name plus the word "Window." The BAR program's main window, for example, is registered under the name "BARWindow." To assign a different name to a window class, override TWindow's GetClassName function, declared as:

```
virtual char far *GetClassName();
```

> **NOTE**
>
> The Windows window-class name is a string that is stored internally by Windows for identifying the internal window element structure that defines a window's properties. The C++ window-class name is the name you give to a class in your program's text. The two names are not related.

It's usually easiest to reprogram an inline version of GetClassName in a class derived from TWindow (or a derivative such as TFrameWindow). I usually do this just below a declaration for GetWindowClass. That way, I never forget to assign a new class name to my window classes. It's probably okay to use TWindow's default window class names, but modules that declare multiple classes derived from TWindow, should always define a new GetClassName function in any instance where GetWindowClass modifies a window class field. OWL uses class names to determine whether to register a window class with Windows. If you don't give your modified window classes unique names, they won't be registered, and your modified parameters won't be used.

Listings 5.8 (WBACK.RH), 5.9 (WBACK.RC), and 5.10 (WBACK.CPP) demonstrate how to use GetWindowClass and GetClassName to create a window with a black background. The program displays a small sample window in "reversed video," a term that in computing's past used to mean black graphics on white backgrounds, but in Windows usually means the opposite.

Listing 5.8. WBACK.RH.

```
// wback.rh -- Resource header file

#define ID_MENU 100      // Menu resource identifier
```

Listing 5.9. WBACK.RC.

```
#include <owl\window.rh>
#include "wback.rh"

ID_MENU MENU
BEGIN
  POPUP "&Demo"
  BEGIN
    MENUITEM "E&xit", CM_EXIT
  END
END
```

Listing 5.10. WBACK.CPP.

```
/* ============================================================ *\
**   wback.cpp -- Modify window background color               **
** ============================================================ **
```

```
**                                                            **
** ========================================================== **
**      Copyright   1994 by Tom Swan. All rights reserved.    **
\* ========================================================== */

#include <owl\applicat.h>
#include <owl\framewin.h>
#include <owl\dc.h>
#include <owl\gdiobjec.h>
#include "wback.rh"

// ==========================================================
// The application's main window
// ==========================================================

class TBackWin: public TFrameWindow {
public:
  TBackWin(TWindow* parent, const char far* title);
protected:
  virtual void GetWindowClass(WNDCLASS& wndClass);
  virtual char far* GetClassName() { return "TBackWin"; }
  virtual void Paint(TDC& dc, BOOL erase, TRect& rect);
};

// Constructor
TBackWin::TBackWin(TWindow* parent, const char far* title)
  : TFrameWindow(parent, title),
    TWindow(parent, title)
{
  AssignMenu(ID_MENU);
}

// Modify background color in window class
void
TBackWin::GetWindowClass(WNDCLASS& wndClass)
{
  TFrameWindow::GetWindowClass(wndClass);
  wndClass.hbrBackground = (HBRUSH)GetStockObject(BLACK_BRUSH);
}

// Paint or repaint the window's client area
void
TBackWin::Paint(TDC& dc, BOOL /*erase*/, TRect& /*rect*/)
{
  TPen whitePen(TColor(255, 255, 255));
  TBrush blackBrush(TColor(0, 0, 0));
  char s[] = "Reversed video display";

  dc.SelectObject(whitePen);              // White outline
  dc.SelectObject(blackBrush);            // Black fill
```

continues

Listing 5.10. continued

```
  dc.Rectangle(10, 10, 100, 100);         // Draw rectangle
  dc.SetBkColor(TColor(0, 0, 0));         // Black txt background
  dc.SetTextColor(TColor(255, 255, 0));   // Yellow txt foreground
  dc.TextOut(10, 120, s, sizeof(s) - 1);  // Draw text
  dc.RestorePen();                        // Restore default pen
  dc.RestoreBrush();                      // Restore default brush
}

// ==============================================================
// The application class
// ==============================================================

class TBackApp: public TApplication {
public:
  TBackApp(const char far* name)
    : TApplication(name) {};
  void InitMainWindow();
};

// Initialize the program's main window
void
TBackApp::InitMainWindow()
{
  MainWindow =
    new TBackWin(0, "Window Background Demonstration");
}

#pragma argsused

// Main program
int
OwlMain(int argc, char* argv[])
{
  TBackApp app("Back");
  return app.Run();
}
```

WBACK's TBackWin class, derived from TFrameWindow, declares a constructor and three replacement functions: GetWindowClass, GetClassName, and Paint. Notice how the inline GetClassName returns the address of a literal string equal to the class name. Any string will do, but the class name is unique (otherwise the module wouldn't compile), so it's usually convenient to use the same name for the C++ and the *Windows* window-class.

You can also implement `GetClassName` as a non-inline function:

```
char far* GetClassName()
{
  return "TBackWin";
}
```

Or, you can define a `char` array, assign it a string, and return the array's address. Keep in mind, however, that a pointer to the string returned by `GetClassName` is saved in the window class `lpszClassName` field in the `WNDCLASS` structure, which is given to Windows to register the window's class information prior to creating window elements. For that reason, be sure to define the string array `static` so it isn't deleted when the function ends. This works:

```
#include <string.h>
#define HISNAME "Bill"
#define HERNAME "Hillary"
char far* GetClassName()
{
  static char className[33];
  strcpy(className, HISNAME);
  strcat(className, HERNAME);
  return className;
}
```

Looking Ahead

I could go on and on about Windows graphics—and, in fact, I do go on some more in Chapter 7, "Painting with Graphics Objects," and in Chapter 8, "Managing Icons, Cursors, and Bitmaps." All of those graphics items can take up a lot of display real estate, so before getting back to graphics, in the next chapter you investigate how to use scrollers to increase a window's apparent client area and, in doing so, effectively expand the window's display space without forcing users to purchase larger CRTs.

6

Scrolling
Window Views

Few documents fit entirely onscreen. Even if computers had wall-size monitors, you'd still have to provide scrollers or use other methods to present information too large to show all at once.

In Windows, *scrollers* are your primary tools for viewing large amounts of data in relatively small spaces. Scrollers give users the means to browse through lengthy documents, whether they contain text, graphics, or both.

In this chapter, you learn:

- How to use the TScroller class to add scrollers to a window.
- How to set a scroller's units, page, and other internal values.
- How to take advantage of TScroller's capability to work in conjunction with TWindow's Paint function, providing automatic scrolling with very little programming required.
- How to adjust scrollers (and why you must do that) when the window size changes and at other times.
- How to optimize scrolling to maintain high scrolling speeds.

Fundamentals of Scrolling

Don't confuse *scrollers* with general purpose *scrollbars,* which can appear anywhere inside a window or dialog. Scrollers are specialized window extensions that, when enabled, are always attached to a window's right and bottom borders. Scrollers and scrollbars look the same, but have different programming requirements (see Figure 6.1). This chapter investigates scrollers. Chapter 11 covers scrollbar controls.

FIGURE 6.1.
Scrollers and scrollbars.

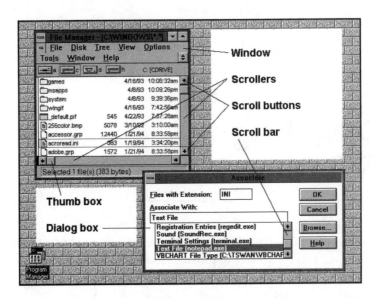

A scroller's main purpose is to expand a window's apparent client area. Using scrollers, a window becomes a kind of viewer or magnifying glass that can "move" over a document's larger surface. Of course, the window doesn't actually move, but when you click a scroller's buttons or drag its thumb box, the effect is the same as if the window moved to a new position on top of a document below. By "document," I mean any information that can be shown in a window. Scrollers work the same for text and graphics.

Scroller Classes

The TScroller class, defined in SCROLLER.H, declares fundamental scroller functions and data. For example, TScroller's ScrollTo function adjusts the scroller thumb boxes to place a specified coordinate at upper left. Use TScroller to attach horizontal, vertical, or both kinds of scrollers to a window. First include the SCROLLER.H header file:

```
#include <owl\scroller.h>
```

Next, in a `TWindow` or `TFrameWindow` class constructor, modify the window's style to include scrollers:

```
Attr.Style |= WS_VSCROLL | WS_HSCROLL;
```

If you don't need both kinds of scrollers, you can specify vertical (`WS_VSCROLL`) or horizontal (`WS_HSCROLL`) constants alone. The constants tell Windows to draw scrollers on the window, and to adjust the window's client area to exclude the scroller images.

Next, to provide an interface object for communicating with scrollers, construct an object of the `TScroller` class. Do that in the window class constructor:

```
Scroller = new TScroller(this, 1, 1, 200, 300);
```

`Scroller` is a pointer of type `TScroller*` in the `TWindow` class, and every class derived from `TWindow` inherits a `Scroller` pointer. Normally, the pointer is set to null. To enable scrollers, construct a `TScroller` object as shown here and assign its address to `Scroller`.

TScroller Parameters

The `TScroller` constructor requires five parameters. The `this` pointer passes the address of the window object to the `TScroller` object. As a result, the window *owns* the scrollers, so you do not have to delete `Scroller` as you do most other objects created by `new`.

> **TIP**
>
> I mentioned this before, but it deserves a reminder. When you pass `this` to a class constructor, it indicates that the object addressed by `this` owns the new object being constructed and will delete that object automatically.

The other four integer parameters passed to `TScroller`'s constructor initialize the scroller's *units* and *ranges*. A unit is the smallest increment by which a scroller's thumb can move. A range is the maximum distance that the scroller's thumb can travel from one end of the scroller to the other. In the preceding example, horizontal and vertical units are set to 1—the smallest possible increment. The horizontal range is set to 200 and the vertical range to 300.

Use the `TScroller` function `SetRange` to change a scroller's range of travel—usually necessary when loading a new document or to respond to a change in the window's size. Use `SetUnits` to adjust the scroller's minimum increments.

Scrollers also have other values that affect their use. A scroller's *position* represents the relative location of its thumb box within its defined range. Its *lines* represent the number of units to move the scroller for each line of movement; its *pages* represent the number of units to move for each page. The meanings of the terms *lines* and *pages* depend on the type of information shown in a window, and are expressed in the scroller's units. For most purposes, you can set the scroller's unit and range values and let the class figure out the others. Use SetPageSize to adjust a scroller's page value. Strangely, there is no function to set a scroller's line increment—to change those quantities, you have to assign values directly to TScroller's XLine and YLine data members.

TScroller Data Members

TScroller implements automatic scrolling. To use this feature, position the mouse pointer inside a window, click and hold the mouse button, then drag the pointer outside of the window's borders. The farther away you drag the mouse, the faster the contents scroll. You must have a mouse to use automatic scrolling.

If you don't want automatic scrolling, at any time after constructing the window's TScroller object, set data member AutoMode to false:

```
Scroller->AutoMode = FALSE;
```

To reenable automatic scrolling, change AutoMode back to its default value, TRUE.

Tracking is another automatic scrolling operation that you might want to disable. Normally, when you drag a scroller's thumb box, it automatically scrolls the window's contents as you move the mouse pointer. When displaying complex data, automatic tracking can cause an effect that you might call "scroller stutter." As you drag the thumb box, activity pauses and then the window seems to jump to a new page of information. The lag between jumps is caused by the amount of time it takes for the program to respond to the WM_PAINT messages issued during automatic tracking. When the amount of time lag becomes excessive, it's time to optimize scrolling (as I explain later), or you can turn off automatic tracking by setting TrackMode false:

```
Scroller->TrackMode = FALSE;
```

Change TrackMode back to true to reenable automatic tracking. Another data member you can change is AutoOrg. Use the following statement to disable TScroller's automatic window-origin adjustments during an update event (that is, the generation of a WM_PAINT message):

```
Scroller->AutoOrg = FALSE;
```

TScroller normally shifts the window's origin so that you can display text and graphics at document coordinates, but have the correct data appear in the window relative to the scrollers' current positions. Set AutoOrg false when you *don't* want TScroller to adjust the window's origin this way. In most programs, you can leave AutoOrg set to true.

You can inspect other data members such as XPos and YPos, but you should not change their values, which represent relative thumb box positions. For example, to set a long value Y to the horizontal scroller thumb box position, use the statement

```
Y = Scroller->YPos;  // Get vertical thumb position
```

You can similarly examine other data members such as XLine, YLine, XPage, YPage, XRange, and YRange. They are adjusted automatically as needed. Never change these values directly, or you might give your scrollers serious psychological problems.

TScroller Member Functions

The TScroller class has several member functions, but most programs use only a few main ones. Call the functions described here to make scroller adjustments at any time after constructing a window's TScroller object.

To change the number of units, call SetUnits. For example, to set scroller resolutions to 16 horizontal and 8 vertical display units, use the statement

```
Scroller->SetUnits(16, 8);  // Change XUnit and YUnit
```

To change one scroller but not the other, use this statement:

```
Scroller->SetUnits(Scroller->XUnit, 8);  // Change YUnit only
```

Changing a scroller's units increases scroll speed, but also increases scrolling *granularity.* In other words, if you set the vertical scroller to eight units, then it will not be possible for users to scroll data in smaller increments. The display is limited to scrolling in the scrollers' unit values. A large granularity might not be acceptable in graphics programs in which fine control over document positioning is often desirable.

Calling SetUnits automatically adjusts the scroller XPage and YPage settings—the amounts by which data scrolls when you click the mouse pointer inside the scrollbar to either side of a thumb box. For finer control over these values (but always *after* calling SetUnits), you can assign values directly to XPage and YPage:

```
Scroller->XPage = 8;
Scroller->YPage = 16;
```

In most cases, however, you should not set these values manually. Changing scroller units by calling SetUnits automatically adjusts page sizes via SetPageSize. (There's probably no need to call SetPageSize in applications.)

Another member function that you may need is SetRange. Use it to update scrollers whenever a document's size changes. Suppose, for example, that the program has already constructed the window's TScroller object. Later, another function loads a different document. To adjust the scrollers, call SetRange like this:

```
Scroller->SetRange(documentWidth, documentHeight);
```

When loading a new document, you might also want to reposition the window to its topmost position. To do that, call ScrollTo with two 0 arguments:

```
Scroller->ScrollTo(0, 0);
```

You can pass other values to ScrollTo, which forces a document to scroll to a specific location. To scroll to a document's end, use the statement

```
Scroller->ScrollTo(0, Scroller->YRange);
```

To scroll from the current position to a new position a relative distance away, call ScrollBy. Here's how, for instance, you might simulate a scroll up operation:

```
Scroller->ScrollBy(0, -1);
```

ScrollBy calls ScrollTo to reposition the document inside the window, in this case by one display unit up from the current position. ScrollBy is typically used to implement keyboard support for scrolling, as I'll explain a bit later in this chapter.

> **NOTE**
>
> In discussing scrollers, up, down, left, and right are ambiguous terms. To lessen confusion, it helps to refer to the directions that scroller *thumb boxes* travel, rather than the direction the data appears to move. "Scroll up," for example, means that the vertical scroller's thumb moves upward. (The document appears to move down.) "Scroll right" means that a horizontal scroller's thumb moves to the right. (The document moves left.) The window's contents move in the *opposite* direction of the scroller's thumbs.

Window Views

Before using TScroller, it helps to understand a few more concepts, starting with a window's *view*. Think of a view as a logical rectangle through which a portion of a document is visible inside the window's client area. If a document were a large chart spread on a table, a window view works as though you cut a rectangle in a piece of cardboard and positioned it over the page. Sliding the cardboard over the chart brings different information into view.

When you scroll a window, it appears as though the document moves, but the movement is an illusion. Actually, the document remains in place; only the window's *origin* changes. The window's origin—the document coordinate at the window's upper-left corner—determines what portion of the data shines through the window's client area. Scrolling the window shifts the origin and thus makes new data come into view.

There are some other low-level details about scrolling that you can safely ignore at this stage. In conventional C programming, for instance, a chief concern is how to determine where to display data relative to a window's origin. The TScroller class eliminates the need to calculate origin offsets by automatically adjusting the window's origin relative to the scrollbar thumb positions. This means that, with TScroller, you can always draw text and graphics at their *document* coordinates and be assured that data will appear correctly in the window. Windows and TScroller take care of the low-level details that scroll the window's contents up, down, left, or right.

Simple Scroller Example

Adding and using scrollers in OWL windows is not difficult, and for small windows, TScroller's default settings and operations are probably adequate. Listings 6.1 (SCROLL.RH), 6.2 (SCROLL.H), 6.3 (SCROLL.RC), and 6.4 (SCROLL.CPP) demonstrate scrollers for a fictitious 48-line document created "on the fly" just for show. Run the program and use the scrollers to scroll the sample text up, down, left, and right.

> **TIP**
>
> I listed the program's resource script file, SCROLL.RC, to demonstrate a method for using resource header files such as WINDOW.RH. Some classes (TWindow in this case) have associated resource identifiers such as CM_EXIT declared in a file ending with .RH. You may use Resource Workshop (RW) to attach the headers to a resource project. Select *File*/*Add to project...* and choose a resource header file from C:\BC4\INCLUDE\OWL. That command inserts a *relative pathname* into the resource script, something like this:
>
> ```
> #include "..\..\..\..\bc4\include\owl\window.rh"
> ```

Relative pathnames are not always desirable because they assume the resource script
file will never move to a directory at a different level. I prefer to add the necessary
#include directive manually to my resource script text files, changing RW's relative
directive to this:

```
#include <owl\window.rh>
```

That makes RW look for WINDOW.RH in the OWL subdirectory of the default include
path. All resource scripts in this book use this method so that you can install the book's
listings in any drive or directory. Be sure, however, that RW's *Include path* is set to
C:\BC4\INCLUDE (run RW and select *File*|*Preferences...* to check).

Listing 6.1. SCROLL.RH.

```
// scroll.rh -- Resource header file

#define ID_MENU 100            // Menu resource identifier
```

Listing 6.2. SCROLL.H.

```
// scroll.h -- Header file for scroll.cpp

#define MAX_LINES 48           // Number of text lines in window
```

Listing 6.3. SCROLL.RC.

```
#include <owl\window.rh>
#include "scroll.rh"

ID_MENU MENU
BEGIN
  POPUP "&Demo"
  BEGIN
    MENUITEM "E&xit", CM_EXIT
  END
END
```

Listing 6.4. SCROLL.CPP.

```
/* ========================================================== *\
**   scroll.cpp -- Demonstrate window scrollers               **
** ========================================================== **
**                                                            **
** ========================================================== **
**     Copyright (c) 1994 by Tom Swan. All rights reserved.   **
\* ========================================================== */

#include <owl\applicat.h>
#include <owl\framewin.h>
#include <owl\scroller.h>
#include <owl\point.h>
#include <owl\dc.h>
#include <string.h>
#pragma hdrstop
#include "scroll.h"
#include "scroll.rh"


// ==========================================================
// The application's main window
// ==========================================================

class TScrollWin: public TFrameWindow {
  int textHeight;    // Height of text lines including spacing
  TSize increment;   // Amount to shift each line down and right
public:
  TScrollWin(TWindow* parent, const char far* title);
protected:
  void SetupWindow();
  void EvSize(UINT sizeType, TSize& size);
  void Paint(TDC& dc, BOOL erase, TRect& rect);
DECLARE_RESPONSE_TABLE(TScrollWin);
};

DEFINE_RESPONSE_TABLE1(TScrollWin, TFrameWindow)
  EV_WM_SIZE,
END_RESPONSE_TABLE;

// Constructor
TScrollWin::TScrollWin(TWindow* parent, const char far* title)
  : TFrameWindow(parent, title),
    TWindow(parent, title)
{
  AssignMenu(ID_MENU);
  Attr.Style |= WS_VSCROLL | WS_HSCROLL;
  Scroller = new TScroller(this, 0, 0, 0, 0);
}
```

continues

209

Listing 6.4. continued

```
// Perform initializations that require a window handle
void
TScrollWin::SetupWindow()
{
  TFrameWindow::SetupWindow();
  TClientDC dc(*this);
  increment = dc.GetTextExtent((LPSTR)"M", 1);
  increment.cy *= 2;   // Double-spaced lines
  Scroller->SetUnits(increment.cx, increment.cy);
}

// Respond to WM_SIZE messages
void
TScrollWin::EvSize(UINT sizeType, TSize& size)
{
  TFrameWindow::EvSize(sizeType, size);
  Scroller->SetRange(MAX_LINES, MAX_LINES);
  Scroller->ScrollTo(0, 0);
  Invalidate(FALSE);
}

// Paint or repaint bar chart in current window size
void TScrollWin::Paint(TDC& dc, BOOL /*erase*/, TRect& /*rect*/)
{
  char buffer[80];         // Holds output strings
  TPoint location(0, 0);   // Text location relative to window
  int ln;                  // Line number

  for (ln = 1; ln <= MAX_LINES; ++ln) {
    location += increment;
    wsprintf(buffer, "This is line #%d", ln);
    dc.TextOut(location, buffer, strlen(buffer));
  }
}

// ===============================================================
// The application class
// ===============================================================

class TScrollApp: public TApplication {
public:
  TScrollApp(const char far* name)
    : TApplication(name) {};
  void InitMainWindow();
};
```

```
// Initialize the program's main window
void
TScrollApp::InitMainWindow()
{
  MainWindow = new TScrollWin(0, "Simple Scrollers");
}

#pragma argsused

// Main program
int
OwlMain(int argc, char* argv[])
{
  TScrollApp app("Scroll");
  return app.Run();
}
```

The sample program's TScrollWin class, derived from TFrameWindow, adds the WS_VSCROLL and WS_HSCROLL flags to the windows style. (See the class constructor.) After doing that, the constructor constructs an object of the TScroller class and assigns the object's address to the Scroller pointer inherited from TFrameWindow. This statement is a little different from the earlier example:

```
Scroller = new TScroller(this, 0, 0, 0, 0);
```

I set the scroller units and ranges to zero because I plan to adjust those values later on. If you know the scroller unit and range values in advance, you can supply them when you construct the TScroller object. In this case, I initialize the scroller's units in a SetupWindow replacement function, which is called before the window becomes visible, and therefore before the scrollers come into view. To determine the unit values, SetupWindow creates a TClientDC device context object, then calls the encapsulated GDI function GetTextExtent for the single character string *M*. Assigning that function's result to a TPoint object, increment, provides the width and height of text in the current font (automatically selected into a device context object by default). To provide space between lines, SetupWindow doubles the text height (increment.cy). The SetUnits function then sets the scroller units to the values in increment.

> **NOTE**
>
> Setting a scroller's units to a value greater than 1 greatly improves the scroller's speed by moving the window relative to its data at a greater rate. In this case, I set the vertical scroller's units to a value twice the height of the character M. Consequently, clicking the vertical scroller buttons scrolls text two lines at a time (one text line and one blank space).

Scrollers and Window Size

Most windows should adjust their scrollers when the window size changes. Expanding a window to full screen, for example, changes the amount of information displayed in the window, and therefore requires adjustments to thumb positions and other values.

In SCROLL.CPP, EvSize responds to WM_SIZE messages, issued when the window's size changes. At that time, the program calls two TScroller functions: SetRange (not strictly required in this case because the document's size doesn't change along with the window), and ScrollTo. Calling ScrollTo with arguments 0, 0 repositions the document to its extreme upper-left corner, thus ensuring that the scroller thumb boxes are positioned correctly.

> **TIP**
>
> The scroller thumb boxes must be resynchronized when the window size changes so that the thumbs always show the relative position of the information currently in view. Calling ScrollTo(0, 0) to accomplish that goal is "cheating," a quick and dirty solution that works, but makes the window difficult to use. Later in this chapter, I show a better way to reposition scroller thumb boxes when the window receives a WM_SIZE message.

As usual, the SCROLL program's Paint function updates the window display in response to a WM_PAINT message. In this case, Paint calls the GDI TextOut function to display sample lines of text (48 of them unless you change MAX_LINES). The for loop simulates the display of a document's lines, perhaps stored in an array.

> **TIP**
>
> The techniques of scrolling apply equally well to graphical shapes and text. For example, try inserting a few rectangles or other objects into SCROLL's Paint function. You don't have to perform any special magic to make scrollers work with graphics and text. To display a scrollable rectangle, for example, add this statement to the Paint function in SCROLL.CPP:
>
> ```
> dc.Rectangle(10, 10, 100, 250);
> ```

Most important in the SCROLL program is the fact that Paint displays the *entire* document, regardless of the position of the scroller thumbs. That's possible because EvPaint (the TWindow response function that calls Paint) automatically takes scroller positions into account. To implement scrolling, you simply draw text or graphics anywhere on your window's *logical surface.* You don't have to shift information or call any functions to cause the document to appear to move. Because of the way `TWindow` and `TScroller` work together, the window always shows only the portion of that document relative to the positions of any scrollers, and as a result, the motion of scrolling (an illusion, of course) is automatic. As I mentioned, Windows clips any output outside of the window's client area—you don't have to "paint inside the lines."

This method of implementing scrolling works pretty well for small documents with uncomplicated display requirements. Larger documents with busy displays and many shapes require a different strategy for fast scrolling—an important goal, especially in graphical user interfaces, which are slower by nature than text-only consoles. Almost nothing is more aggravating than trying to use a text editor or graphics program that scrolls in ponderous, wave-like motions for each click of a mouse button.

Fortunately, with careful programming, it's possible to maintain good scrolling speed even in programs with complex displays. The next section demonstrates one approach for optimizing scrollers in a text-file lister that exhibits lightning-fast scrolling regardless of document size.

Optimized Scrolling

Slow scrolling is mostly caused by displaying too much information during an update event. Because Windows clips drawing to a window's update region, a `Paint` function can simply draw every shape or line of text and let Windows clip the output to show only what's necessary to update the window. Also, as explained in the preceding section, `TWindow` and `TScroller` cooperate to show the correct portion of a document relative to the scroller thumb boxes.

Drawing a large document's every shape or line of text, however, wastes time, resulting in slow window updates, and consequently, relatively slow scrolling. By carefully constructing `Paint` to limit output to the bare minimum, the function runs faster, improving scroll speed.

Listings 6.5 (WLIST.RH), 6.6 (WLIST.H), 6.7 (WLIST.RC), and 6.8 (WLIST.CPP) demonstrate how to optimize scrolling for large text documents. (The same methods work for graphics.) The program also introduces several new Windows programming techniques explained after the listing. Run WLIST and use the *File|Open* command to view any text document. Or, pass a filename to the program with the File Manager's *File|Run...* command—enter `wlist wlist.cpp`, for example, to view the program's source file. Try the scrollers. Click and drag the scroller thumbs to scroll. To use autoscrolling, click and drag the mouse in the document while you drag the pointer away from the window. (Try dragging in a circle *around* the window.) As you can see, no matter how large the document, scrolling speed remains fast—a direct result of the optimization techniques used in the window's Paint function.

Listing 6.5. WLIST.RH.

```
// wlist.rh -- Resource header file

#define ID_MENU 100         // Menu resource identifier
#define CM_FILE_OPEN 101    // Menu command identifier
```

Listing 6.6. WLIST.H.

```
// wlist.h -- Header file for wlist.cpp

#define SARRAY_HIGH 249     // Initial high sArray index
#define SARRAY_LOW  0       // Initial low sArray index
#define SARRAY_DELTA 125    // sArray expansion amount
```

Listing 6.7. WLIST.RC.

```
#include <owl\window.rh>
#include "wlist.rh"

ID_MENU MENU
BEGIN
  POPUP "&File"
  BEGIN
    MENUITEM "&Open...", CM_FILE_OPEN
    MENUITEM "E&xit", CM_EXIT
  END
END
```

Listing 6.8. WLIST.CPP.

```cpp
/* =============================================================== *\
**   wlist.cpp -- list text files                                 **
** =============================================================== **
**                                                                **
** =============================================================== **
**      Copyright (c) 1994 by Tom Swan. All rights reserved.      **
\* =============================================================== */

#include <owl\applicat.h>
#include <owl\framewin.h>
#include <owl\color.h>
#include <owl\dc.h>
#include <owl\gdiobjec.h>
#include <owl\scroller.h>
#include <owl\opensave.h>
#include <classlib\arrays.h>
#include <classlib\stdtempl.h>
#include <stdio.h>
#include <cstring.h>
#include <string.h>
#include <mem.h>
#pragma hdrstop
#include "wlist.h"
#include "wlist.rh"


// =============================================================
// The application's main window
// =============================================================

class TListWin: public TFrameWindow {
public:
  TListWin(TWindow* parent, const char far* title,
    BOOL autoOpen);
  ~TListWin();
protected:
  void SetupWindow();
  void AdjustSettings();
  void AdjustScrollers();
  BOOL ReadFile();
  void EvSize(UINT sizeType, TSize& size);
  void EvKeyDown(UINT key, UINT repeatCount, UINT flags);
  void OpenNamedFile();
  void CmFileOpen();
  void Paint(TDC& dc, BOOL erase, TRect& rect);
private:
  TIArrayAsVector<string> sArray;  // Array of string objects
  TColor fontColor;        // Window text color
  int fontPointSize;       // Window text size
```

continues

Listing 6.8. continued

```cpp
  long width, height;        // Size of window in display units
  int numRows, numCols;      // Number of text file rows and columns
  int rowSep, colSep;        // Units separation between characters
  int glyphW, glyphH;        // Character glyph width and height
  TFont* font;               // Pointer to font object
  string* filename;          // Pointer to filename string object
  TOpenSaveDialog::TData filenameData; // Common file dialog data
DECLARE_RESPONSE_TABLE(TListWin);
};

DEFINE_RESPONSE_TABLE1(TListWin, TFrameWindow)
  EV_WM_SIZE,
  EV_WM_KEYDOWN,
  EV_COMMAND(CM_FILE_OPEN, CmFileOpen),
END_RESPONSE_TABLE;

// Constructor
TListWin::TListWin(TWindow* parent, const char far* title,
  BOOL autoOpen)
  : TFrameWindow(parent, title),
    TWindow(parent, title),
    sArray(SARRAY_HIGH, SARRAY_LOW, SARRAY_DELTA),
    filenameData(OFN_FILEMUSTEXIST|OFN_PATHMUSTEXIST,
      "All files (*.*)|*.*|Text files (*.txt)|*.txt|",
      0, "", "*")
{
  AssignMenu(ID_MENU);
  Attr.Style |= WS_VSCROLL | WS_HSCROLL;
  Scroller = new TScroller(this, 0, 0, 0, 0);
  fontColor = ::GetSysColor(COLOR_WINDOWTEXT);
  fontPointSize = 10;
  width = height = 0;
  numRows = numCols = 0;
  rowSep = colSep = 0;
  glyphH = glyphW = 0;
  font = 0;
  if (!autoOpen)
    filename = new string;
  else {
    filename = new string(title);
    if (!ReadFile())
      numRows = 0;
  }
}

// Destructor
TListWin::~TListWin()
{
  delete font;
  delete filename;
}
```

```
// Perform window initializations that require a window handle
void
TListWin::SetupWindow()
{
  TFrameWindow::SetupWindow();
  int yUnits = (new TClientDC(*this))->GetDeviceCaps(LOGPIXELSY);
  font = new TFont(
    "Courier New",           // facename
    -::MulDiv(fontPointSize, yUnits, 72),  // height
    0, 0, 0,                 // width, escapement, orientation
    FW_NORMAL,               // weight
    FIXED_PITCH,             // pitchAndFamily
    FALSE, FALSE, FALSE,     // italic, underline, strikeout
    ANSI_CHARSET,            // charSet
    OUT_TT_PRECIS,           // outputPrecision
    CLIP_DEFAULT_PRECIS,     // clipPrecision
    PROOF_QUALITY            // quality
  );
  AdjustSettings();
}

// Adjust document and font settings, and call AdjustScrollers
void
TListWin::AdjustSettings()
{
  if (!font) return;   // No font; no settings!
  TEXTMETRIC tm;       // Text (font) information
  TClientDC* dc;       // Needed for gathering text info
//
// Get facts using a device context
  dc = new TClientDC(*this);
  dc->SelectObject(*font);
  dc->GetTextMetrics(tm);
  colSep = dc->GetTextCharacterExtra();
  delete dc;  // Done with context, so delete it ASAP
//
// Get other facts and call AdjustScrollers
  glyphW = tm.tmMaxCharWidth;
  glyphH = tm.tmHeight;
  rowSep = tm.tmExternalLeading;
  width = colSep + ((numCols + 1) * (glyphW + colSep));
  height = rowSep + ((numRows + 1) * (glyphH + rowSep));
  AdjustScrollers();
}

// Adjust scroll bars to match document and font settings
void
```

continues

217

Listing 6.8. continued

```
TListWin::AdjustScrollers()
{
  TRect r;      // Rectangle for client area dimensions
  long h, w;    // Document size minus window in display units

  if (numRows == 0) return;  // No document; no scrollers!
  Scroller->SetUnits(glyphW + colSep, glyphH + rowSep);
  GetClientRect(r);                      // Get client area dimensions
  w = width - (r.right - r.left);    // Width LESS client width
  h = height - (r.bottom - r.top);   // Height LESS client width
  w /= Scroller->XUnit;              // Scroller horizontal range
  h /= Scroller->YUnit;              // Scroller vertical range
  Scroller->SetRange(w, h);         // Set scroller ranges
//
// Synchronize horizontal and vertical thumbs
  SetScrollPos(SB_HORZ, (int)Scroller->XPos, TRUE);
  SetScrollPos(SB_VERT, (int)Scroller->YPos, TRUE);
}

// Read file (filename) into string array (sArray)
BOOL
TListWin::ReadFile()
{
  FILE *fp;
  char buffer[256];
  int len;

  fp = fopen(filename->c_str(), "r");
  if (!fp) return FALSE;
  sArray.Flush();
  numRows = numCols = 0;
  while (fgets(buffer, 256, fp)) {
    len = strlen(buffer);
    if (len > 0 && buffer[len - 1] == 0x0A)
      buffer[--len] = 0;
    if (len > numCols)
      numCols = len;
    sArray.Add(new string(buffer));
    numRows++;
  }
  fclose(fp);
  return TRUE;
}

// Respond to WM_SIZE messages
void
TListWin::EvSize(UINT sizeType, TSize& size)
{
  TFrameWindow::EvSize(sizeType, size);
```

```
  if (!IsIconic()) {
    AdjustSettings();
    Invalidate(FALSE);
  }
}

// Respond to WM_KEYDOWN messages
void
TListWin::EvKeyDown(
  UINT key, UINT /*repeatCount*/, UINT /*flags*/)
{
  int xLine = Scroller->XLine;
  int yLine = Scroller->YLine;
  int yPage = Scroller->YPage;
  switch (key) {
    case VK_UP:
      Scroller->ScrollBy(0, -yLine);
      break;
    case VK_DOWN:
      Scroller->ScrollBy(0,  yLine);
      break;
    case VK_LEFT:
      Scroller->ScrollBy(-xLine, 0);
      break;
    case VK_RIGHT:
      Scroller->ScrollBy( xLine, 0);
      break;
    case VK_PRIOR:
      Scroller->ScrollBy(0, -yPage);
      break;
    case VK_NEXT:
      Scroller->ScrollBy(0,  yPage);
      break;
    case VK_HOME:
      Scroller->ScrollTo(0, 0);
      break;
    case VK_END:
      Scroller->ScrollTo(0, numRows);
      break;
    default: DefaultProcessing();
  }
}

// Open file named by data member filename
void
TListWin::OpenNamedFile()
{
  const char* sp =
    filename->c_str();  // Get C-style string pointer
  if (ReadFile()) {
```

continues

219

Listing 6.8. continued

```
      SetWindowText(sp);        // Change window title
      AdjustSettings();         // Adjust variables and scrollers
      Invalidate(TRUE);         // Redisplay everything
      Scroller->ScrollTo(0, 0); // Show new file from the top
  } else {
    MessageBox(sp, "Error opening file",
      MB_ICONSTOP ¦¦ MB_OK);
    numRows = 0;  // Safety measure--"no file loaded"
  }
}

// Respond to CM_FILE_OPEN menu-command messages
void
TListWin::CmFileOpen()
{
  if ((new TFileOpenDialog(this,
    filenameData))->Execute() == IDOK) {
    if (filenameData.Error == 0) { // no error and not cancelled
      delete filename;
      filename = new string(filenameData.FileName);
      OpenNamedFile();
    }
  }
}

// Display text in window
// Optimize scrolling by limiting output to bare minimum
void TListWin::Paint(TDC& dc, BOOL /*erase*/, TRect& /*rect*/)
{
  TRect r;  // Dimensions of clipping region
  int startRow, endRow, row, x, y;
  const char* cp;

  if (numRows == 0) return;  // Exit if nothing to display
  dc.SetTextColor(fontColor);
  dc.SetBkColor(::GetSysColor(COLOR_WINDOW));
  dc.SelectObject(*font);
  dc.GetClipBox(r);
  startRow = max(0, r.top / Scroller->YUnit - 1);
  endRow = min(numRows, r.bottom / Scroller->YUnit + 1);
  for (row = startRow; row < endRow; ++row) {
    x = colSep;
    y = rowSep + Scroller->YUnit * row;
    cp = sArray[row]->c_str();
    dc.TextOut(x, y, cp, strlen(cp));
  }
  dc.RestoreFont();
}
```

```
// ===============================================================
// The application class
// ===============================================================

class TListApp: public TApplication {
public:
  TListApp(const char far* name)
    : TApplication(name) {};
  void InitMainWindow();
};

// Initialize the program's main window
// Use a command-line argument as a filename if present
void
TListApp::InitMainWindow()
{
  const char far* title;   // Initial window title string
  BOOL autoOpen;           // True if cmdLine is a filename

  if (_argc <= 1) {
    title = "[untitled]";
    autoOpen = FALSE;
  } else {
    title = _argv[1];
    autoOpen = TRUE;
  }
  MainWindow = new TListWin(0, title, autoOpen);
}

#pragma argsused

// Main program
int
OwlMain(int argc, char* argv[])
{
  TListApp app("WList");
  return app.Run();
}
```

WLIST's main window class, TListWin, derived as usual from TFrameWindow, adds a third parameter to its constructor, BOOL autoOpen. To see how this parameter is used, skip to the end of the listing at function InitMainWindow. The function uses the global _argc and _argv variables to detect whether WLIST was passed a command-line argument. If so, autoOpen is set true, telling the window to open a file by that name. (If the file doesn't exist, the program opens a bare window.)

221

Command-line arguments are valuable in applications associated with specific document types. For example, you can use the File Manager's *File\Associate...* command to associate .TXT files with WLIST.EXE. Selecting any .TXT file from then on automatically runs WLIST with a command-line argument equal to the file's path name. As I mentioned, you can also use the File Manager's *File:Run...* command to run WLIST. Enter a command such as **wlist myfile.txt** to list the named file.

Containers

Skip to TListWin's constructor. After calling the required TFrameWindow and TWindow base class constructors, TListWin initializes two data members: a container sArray and a common-dialog object filenameData. The sArray container is declared as a private class member:

```
TIArrayAsVector<string> sArray;
```

To use the TIArrayAsVector and other array-like container-class templates, include the ARRAYS.H header file from the CLASSLIB subdirectory:

```
#include <classlib\arrays.h>
```

The TIArrayAsVector template is used to construct an actual class capable of storing data of a specified type. Initialize the array with three values: a maximum number of objects, a minimum index value, and a delta value that specifies by how many objects a full array should grow to hold more data (container arrays can expand dynamically). Don't specify a delta value if you want a fixed array. For example, you can construct and initialize sArray to store up to 25 ANSI C++ string objects:

```
TIArrayAsVector<string> sArray(25, 0, 10);
```

Use sArray as you do other arrays in C. Or, you can call the container's member functions. For example, do the following to add string object to the array:

```
string* sp = new string("Any text");
sArray.Add(sp);
delete sp;
```

Or, you can combine the two steps into one:

```
sArray.Add(new string("Any text"));
```

The same technique is often useful for transferring a char buffer to a string object in the array:

```
char buffer[80] = "Any text";
sArray.Add(new string(buffer));
```

You may also use indexing operations with sArray. This copies the fourth string object from the array to a new string object cleverly named newString:

```
string newString = *sArray[3];
```

Because I specified an *indirect* (TI) container class, string *pointers* are stored in sArray, so it's necessary to dereference those pointers to extract objects stored in the array.

Nested Class Declarations

Examine also the declaration of filenameData in the TListWin class. The declaration is a good example of how to define objects of a nested class declaration:

```
TOpenSaveDialog::TData filenameData;
```

That declares filenameData as an object of type TData, a nested class declared inside TOpenSaveDialog. Dialogs are discussed in a future chapter, so I'll explain them only briefly here. The TOpenSaveDialog class, declared in OPENSAVE.H, provides an object-oriented interface to a *common dialog,* one of several such dialogs provided by Windows in the COMMDLG.DLL dynamic link library. (If you have trouble running WLIST, make sure you have that DLL file in your C:\WINDOWS\SYSTEM directory.)

The TData class nested in TOpenSaveDialog provides several members for selecting options in a file-open dialog. To initialize the members, construct the TData object as demonstrated in the TListWin constructor:

```
filenameData(OFN_FILEMUSTEXIST¦OFN_PATHMUSTEXIST,
  "All files (*.*)¦*.*¦Text files (*.txt)¦*.txt¦",
  0, "", "*")
```

Look up the individual members in your OWL reference for the meaning of each field, and try making changes to selected arguments. The second line provides two entries for the dialog's *List Files of Type:* list box (see Figure 6.2). The vertical bar characters are separators for this string's individual parts, and are replaced with nulls by the TData class, forming a set of individual strings.

After constructing the filenameData object, the TWlistWin constructor passes a menu resource identifier to AssignMenu, adds the scroller flag values to Attr.Style, and constructs a TScroller object. I specified 0 for the scroller's unit and range values because the program adjusts those values when opening a document, so their initial settings are unimportant.

The constructor assigns the system's window text color setting to an object, fontColor, of type TColor. Use the technique to display text in the color selected by the Control Panel's Color applet:

```
fontColor = ::GetSysColor(COLOR_WINDOWTEXT);
```

GetSysColor is not encapsulated, so this statement must call the global API function directly. (In general, only API functions that require window or other element handles are encapsulated in classes.) Look up other COLOR_ constants that you can pass to the function for obtaining other element colors. The constant COLOR_CAPTIONTEXT, for example, represents the system's color for title bars, size buttons, and scroller arrows.

FIGURE 6.2.

The WLIST program's file-open dialog.

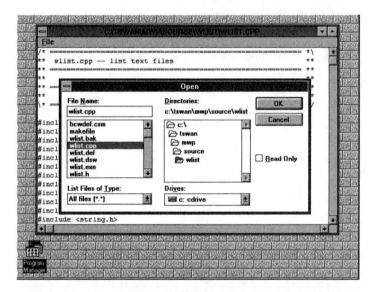

TIP

If you base all your program's display elements on system COLOR_ settings, users will be able to use the Control Panel to select colors for your application. You might, for instance, state that objects of a certain type are colored the same as button text (COLOR_BTNTEXT). This technique avoids having to provide a custom color-selection editor for adjusting application color settings.

TListWin's constructor initializes other data members to zero. It then assigns the window title passed to the constructor to filename, an object of the ANSI C++ string class. This statement creates an empty string:

```
filename = new string;
```

This statement constructs a `string` object using the null-terminated string addressed by `title`:

```
filename = new string(title);
```

The main advantage in using `string` objects rather than `char` pointers is the encapsulation of string functions in the class. For example, in C you might obtain a null-terminated string's length with a statement like this:

```
int len = strlen(title);
```

Using the ANSI C++ `string` class, you can instead write:

```
int len = filename.Length();
```

There are many other encapsulated functions in `string` that I won't go into here. Using `string` takes practice, but the class can prevent many common errors associated with the standard library's string functions. You may, however, use `string` objects and standard null-terminated string library functions. To obtain a standard `char*` pointer for a `string` object, call the `c_str` function like this:

```
const char* sp = filename.c_str();
```

You can then pass `sp` to a standard function, as demonstrated in WLIST.CPP. There is one complication, however, that may cause you some trouble. The `char` pointer returned by the `string` class's `c_str` member function is `const` to prevent you from changing the internal characters stored in the `string` object. To make such a change, you must instead use a `string` member function. Consider the pointer returned by `c_str` to be *read-only*.

WLIST also demonstrates how to use a font for displaying text in a window. Function `SetupWindow` in the `TWListWin` class initializes a font pointer, of type `TFont*`, with the statement:

```
font = new TFont(
  "Courier New",           // facename
  -::MulDiv(fontPointSize, yUnits, 72),   // height
  0, 0, 0,                 // width, escapement, orientation
  FW_NORMAL,               // weight
  FIXED_PITCH,             // pitchAndFamily
  FALSE, FALSE, FALSE,     // italic, underline, strikeout
  ANSI_CHARSET,            // charSet
  OUT_TT_PRECIS,           // outputPrecision
  CLIP_DEFAULT_PRECIS,     // clipPrecision
  PROOF_QUALITY            // quality
);
```

`TFont`'s constructor is a busy affair, requiring a variety of values and constants that initialize a font. The comments explain each item. First comes the face name. I specified a

TrueType font *Courier New,* but you can use any other monospace font for WLIST. (If you don't use TrueType fonts, change the face name to *Courier.*)

The second parameter specifies the font's size in typesetting points. A positive value represents the font's *cell* height; a negative value specifies the *character* height, equal to the cell height minus any internal leading. ("Leading," pronounced *led-ing,* refers to extra space added to a character. Programs such as WLIST that perform their own line and character spacing express text size as negative point sizes, avoiding spacing conflicts with a font's internal leading.)

To determine the font size, SetupWindow calls the global MulDiv Windows function. This function multiplies its first two arguments and divides the result by the third, and is frequently used to select a font's height to produce similar-looking text regardless of display resolution. The 72 in the equation refers to one typesetter point, approximately 1/72 inch. The yUnits value equals the number of display units in one logical inch (not necessarily the same as a real-size inch), obtained by calling GetDeviceCaps:

```
int yUnits =
  (new TClientDC(*this))->GetDeviceCaps(LOGPIXELSY);
```

Take a moment to pick this statement apart—it shows how to find out all sorts of interesting information about the computer's capabilities (abbreviated "Caps" in GetDeviceCaps). The statement uses the new operator to construct a TClientDC device context object, passing *this as an argument—equivalent in this case to the window object's HWindow handle. The statement calls GetDeviceCaps, passing LOGPIXELSY as an argument. (Look up the function in a Windows API reference for other constants you can use to obtain different information.)

The single statement in SetupWindow actually performs five individual operations, which are easier to see when written separately:

```
TClientDC* tcdc;
tcdc = new TClientDC(*this);
int yUnits = tcdc->GetDeviceCaps(LOGPIXELSY);
delete tcdc;
```

Wrapping those individual statements into one is convenient when you need to call only one function for a device context, and avoids having to define and delete a pointer variable. The single-statement version automatically deletes the TClientDC when that object goes out of scope after the statement finishes, but it is admittedly harder to read and understand.

That completes WLIST's initializations. Now, let's take a look at how the program optimizes its scrollers. Locate the Paint function's implementation in the TListWin class.

The function begins by checking if there is any information to display. If not, and numRows is zero, Paint has nothing to do; otherwise, Paint sets the foreground and background text colors with the statements:

```
tdc.SetTextColor(fontColor);
tdc.SetBkColor(::GetSysColor(COLOR_WINDOW));
```

I used two different techniques just to show different ways to select text colors. You can store a color in a TColor object such as fontColor, or you can just call GetSysColor for a system color as shown here.

The next job is to select the TFont object into the device context. Paint does this with the statement:

```
tdc.SelectObject(*font);
```

Dereferencing the font pointer passes the TFont *object,* not its address, to SelectObject. After that step, Paint reveals the key secret behind optimized scrolling:

```
tdc.GetClipBox(r);
startRow = max(0, r.top / Scroller->YUnit - 1);
endRow = min(numRows, r.bottom / Scroller->YUnit + 1);
```

GetClipBox fills a TRect object (r here) with the dimensions of the window's clipping region. Limiting Paint's output to this location usually reduces the amount of work that Paint has to perform, and as a result, scrolling is faster than if Paint relies upon Windows to clip output to this same area. In this example, Paint uses the clipping rectangle to compute two values, startRow and endRow, representing the first and last lines of text that must be displayed to update the window. Lines (or other graphics) outside of the clipping rectangle are not disturbed; therefore, these do not require redrawing.

> **NOTE**
>
> I made no attempt to optimize horizontal scrolling in this version of Paint. When you run WLIST, you may notice that scrolling left and right is noticeably slower than scrolling up and down. This might be caused by a variety of reasons—the row-order arrangement of bytes in your system's video refresh buffer, for example. In general, however, optimizing horizontal scrolling requires computing the left and right character positions of lines inside the clipping rectangle. This takes extra work, and is usually not necessary for most text documents, since their lines probably fit within the window width anyway.

With all its preliminary work out of the way, Paint uses a simple for loop to display the lines of text that require repainting. Two variables, x and y, represent line spacing in pixels. A char* pointer cp is assigned the address of the string in the sArray container, using the c_str function to extract the string object's C-style string information. Finally, TextOut displays the text.

Using a character pointer such as cp isn't strictly necessary, but I wanted to show the technique because it's commonly required when using the string class. Alternatively, you could replace the last two statements in Paint's for loop with:

```
tdc.TextOut(x, y, sArray[row]->c_str(), sArray[row]->length());
```

If (like me) you don't trust compilers to optimize the two redundant indexing expressions, you can instead define a string* pointer:

```
string* sp = sArray[row];
tdc.TextOut(x, y, sp->c_str(), sp->length());
```

Scroller Adjustments

It's always important to consider the effects of changes in window size or document dimensions on scrollers. Loading a new document into WLIST requires adjustments to the window's scrollers, especially their ranges.

I designed two functions for those situations. AdjustSettings initializes class data members for a new document. AdjustScrollers performs whatever actions are necessary to keep the window's scrollers in sync with the current document and window sizes. You could use one function to do these jobs, but dividing the responsibilities between two functions helps make their purposes clear.

In WLIST, AdjustSettings calls GetTextMetrics to obtain information about the program's font. Some of the facts in the resulting TEXTMETRIC structure help calculate the font's *glyph* width and height. (A glyph is the visible portion of a font character.) AdjustSettings also calculates the document width and height, and then calls AdjustScrollers to resync the scrollers and thumb boxes according to the new settings.

AdjustScrollers returns with no action if there is no document to display (numRows == 0). In that case, the window has no scrollers, so there's nothing to adjust. If there is a document, the function calls SetUnits to change the scroller units to the size of the font's characters plus some column and row separation. In this case, the program uses a fixed font, but you would perform this operation if it were possible to select different fonts for the window. (I cover this elsewhere in this book.)

AdjustScrollers also calls SetRange to adjust the distance that the scroller thumb boxes can travel. Too many programmers get this step wrong, a fact that's obvious by scrolling windows as far down as possible. If the last line of text disappears, leaving a blank window, the scroller ranges were not set correctly. As shown in WLIST's AdjustScrollers function, you must take the current window size into account when setting the range.

Another less than obvious requirement is to resynch the scroller thumb boxes every time you adjust the scroller's unit or range values. This is especially critical when resizing a window, which potentially causes a different amount of information to be shown in the window. Because the thumb boxes represent a document's relative position, they must be reset if the document's viewable information changes.

The easiest way to satisfy that requirement is to call the encapsulated SetScrollPos function inherited from TWindow. Pass SB_HORZ or SB_VERT to select horizontal or vertical scrollers, the new thumb position in units within the scroller range value, and TRUE if you want the scroller to be repainted (usually you do).

> **TIP**
>
> SetScrollPos requires a window handle, and is therefore encapsulated in the TWindow class. It is not a member of TScroller, though it probably could have been.

By the way, properly keeping track of a document's size and adjusting scrollers as demonstrated here automatically enables another feature required by well written Windows software. When a window is large enough to show all of a document vertically, horizontally, or both, the corresponding scroller should be removed. This important visual feedback tells users that they are looking at their entire document. The *presence* of scrollers, in other words, should indicate that there is more information to view.

Fortunately, you don't have to perform any special incantations to cause scrollers to disappear at the correct times. Just adjust the scroller units and ranges as shown in AdjustScrollers, and if the range includes the entire document, TScroller automatically removes any unnecessary scrollers from the window.

Keyboard Scrolling Keys

One major deficiency in the TScroller class is the lack of keyboard support. Keyboard scrolling is easy to add, but you must do so for every program that uses scrollers. Most do, so its hard to understand why this capability wasn't included in TScroller or provided as an option.

The first step in keyboard scrolling is to direct WM_KEYDOWN messages to the window. To interrupt the event, which indicates a key press, declare an *event-handler* function, EvKeyDown, in your class (see TListWin in WLIST.CPP):

```
void EvKeyDown(UINT key, UINT repeatCount, UINT flags);
```

Also add the EV_WM_KEYDOWN macro to the class's response table. Like other response-table macros you have seen, this one "cracks" a Windows message (WM_KEYDOWN) and calls the preceding function, which you must declare exactly as shown.

> **NOTE**
>
> Message response-table macros are defined in the WINDOWEV.H header file, located in the OWL subdirectory of C:\BC4\INCLUDE. You don't have to include this header in your programs. It's automatically included by other library headers. Examine the file for the names of other macros you can use to respond to various Windows messages. For the formats of *event-handler* functions associated with specific Windows messages, search for the strings *EV_WM_xxx* and *EV_xxx macros* in the IDE's online help.

Function EvKeyDown receives three arguments. The unsigned integer key represents the pressed keys *virtual key code*. If key equals VK_UP, for instance, the user pressed the up arrow key. (Search BC4's online help for "Virtual Key Codes" for a complete list of other key values.)

The second argument passed to EvKeyDown indicates how many times a key was pressed or held down and repeated. You can ignore the value for the purpose of scrolling—it might be useful, however, in editors that implement repeated key input.

The third and final EvKeyDown parameter is another unsigned integer, flags. For more information on these values, which are used with special mode keys like CapsLock and to determine key states, see your Windows online or printed reference for message WM_KEYDOWN. (WLIST ignores the parameter.)

To finish the job, implement EvKeyDown as shown in the listing. The sample function here is probably the bare minimum design. You are free to add other virtual key values, to perform special actions when the Ctrl key is held down, and so on. To simplify the code, I extract three key values from the scrollers:

```
int xLine = Scroller->XLine;
int yLine = Scroller->YLine;
int yPage = Scroller->YPage;
```

The XLine and YLine data members addressed by Scroller represent the amount of information to scroll the window a line at a time. As mentioned, I prefer not to use these values, but instead, to set the scroller units to the size of a line's height in display units (pixels in this case). Here, XLine and YLine equal 1. Scrolling one line therefore scrolls the window by one unit value. You could do the reverse—setting units to 1 and using XLine and YLine to represent the number of units for each line-oriented operation. The choice is yours.

I also save the YPage value for the PgUp and PgDn keys. If you implement paging left and right (perhaps with Ctrl+Left and Crtl+Right keys), you would also need the XPage scroller value.

Armed with these values, a switch statement calls the scroller ScrollBy function to reposition the document depending on which key is pressed. Pressing the down arrow key, for instance, sets key to VK_DOWN, calling ScrollBy with arguments 0 and yLine, thus scrolling the document down by that amount.

Reading a File

WLIST also demonstrates how a Windows program can open and read a file using standard DOS techniques (see function ReadFile). Each line is read into a char buffer, and the Windows end of line value if present (0x0A) is deleted. (The character shows up as an empty box under most fonts.) The buffer is then inserted as a string object into the array sArray. ReadFile also keeps track of the number of columns and rows used by the document—critical values in calculating scroller ranges.

Two other related functions display the program's file-open dialog and call ReadFile. Function CmFileOpen is called when you select the *File* menu's *Open* command. (Examine the response table entry that makes this happen.) CmFileOpen calls the TFileOpenDialog's Execute function, passing as an argument the current window pointer and the filenameData object initialized in the TListWin constructor. If Execute returns IDOK, it's safe to assume that the user selected or entered a valid filename. To open and read the file, CmFileOpen assigns the file's name to the filename string object, and calls another function, OpenNamedFile.

TIP

Use a separate function rather than opening files in CmFileOpen message-response method. That way, other operations can open files without displaying the file-open dialog—a drag-and-drop function, for example.

OpenNamedFile calls ReadFile to read a text file's lines into memory. If that's successful, the function changes the window's title by calling SetWindowText. AdjustSettings is then called to update the program's variables, and to adjust the scrollers. Calling Invalidate causes Windows to issue a WM_PAINT message at the next opportunity when the window has no other messages to process. Finally, ScrollTo positions the new document to its beginning.

Looking Ahead

In the next chapter, you return to exploring GDI graphics, and you learn more programming techniques such as rubberbanding, fonts, and timers—important tools for all kinds of Windows software.

7

Painting with Graphics Objects

With the basic GDI and scrolling skills introduced in the preceding two chapters, you are ready to branch out into more interesting graphics subjects that demonstrate more about Windows programming. Painting with GDI graphics involves a lot more than simply drawing a few shapes in a Paint function. You also need to learn how to write code that interacts graphically with a variety of Windows events.

In this chapter, you learn:

- How to respond directly to WM_PAINT messages without using a Paint function.
- How to program clicking-and-dragging operations for a mouse input device—a task known as *capturing the mouse.*
- How to implement *rubberbanding,* a key technique for selecting items on screen with a captured mouse.
- How to respond to system messages that affect an application's graphics and colors.

- How to implement advanced graphics techniques for using color palettes, special drawing modes, and fonts.
- How to use timers to create animated graphics that run in the background, a technique that can also be used to create other nongraphical background processes.

WM_PAINT Maneuvers

Sophisticated Windows programs might need to respond directly to WM_PAINT messages rather than using a Paint function. The default function in TWindow performs a number of essential operations, so you shouldn't take this step without good reason—to eliminate one function call, for example, in an application that absolutely must do everything possible to improve display speed. Learning the method is useful also to gain a better understanding of how Paint works—knowledge that will improve your understanding of Windows message handling.

The following two sections take a close look at the insides of Paint, and then explain how to write your own functions to respond directly to WM_PAINT messages.

Inside the *Paint* Function

Up to now, I've told you that Paint responds to WM_PAINT messages. That's only half of the story, however, because Paint is not an event-handler function. Actually, Paint is called by *another* function, EvPaint, which is the real event-handler for WM_PAINT. The function's Ev preface is the key to understanding this important difference—all functions prefaced with Ev, by design, respond to Windows *events*.

You might wonder why TWindow has two functions to respond to a single message. The answer goes to the heart of object-oriented programming. The TWindow class declares EvPaint as:

```
void EvPaint();
```

Function EvPaint expects no arguments and it returns no value. The TWindow class also tells the compiler that it uses a response table:

```
DECLARE_RESPONSE_TABLE(TWindow);
```

The TWindow module defines the class's response table, a portion of which is reproduced here:

```
DEFINE_RESPONSE_TABLE(TWindow)
  EV_WM_CREATE,
```

```
EV_WM_SIZE,
EV_WM_PAINT,
// ...
END_RESPONSE_TABLE;
```

> **NOTE**
>
> File WINDOW.CPP located in C:\BC4\SOURCE\OWL contains the full definition for TWindow's response table. You don't need to study it, but you might want to scan the text while you read this section.

The response table includes several *message-cracker* macros such as EV_WM_CREATE and EV_WM_SIZE, which have corresponding response functions EvCreate and EvSize. Pay special attention to the naming convention. Without looking in a reference, you can easily determine that the macro EV_WM_PAINT associates the Windows message WM_PAINT with the message-response function EvPaint. That function is called, then, when a TWindow based window receives a WM_PAINT message.

You might want to examine EvPaint's source code in file WINDOW.CPP, located in C:\BC4\SOURCE\OWL. The function calls DefaultProcessing for non-OWL window objects constructed from an existing window handle, perhaps returned from a DLL. (Most TWindow objects are not of this variety.) The function calls some Scroller functions to keep any scrollers attached to the window in shape during WM_PAINT events. EvPaint also constructs a TPaint device context object named dc:

```
TPaintDC dc(*this);
```

The argument *this is a reference to the TWindow object for which EvPaint was called—the window, in other words, that needs painting. Several important actions now take place that might not be evident from reading the function's source code:

- The TWindow class defines an operator function named HWND. Because of that function, the argument *this passed to the TPaintDC constructor, which requires an argument of type HWND, is translated to the window object's handle. (Operator functions have been rightly criticized for their tendancy to encourage obscure code, and this is a prime example. It's hardly obvious that *this would satisfy a function's HWND parameter.)

- The TPaintDC constructor calls the global Windows API function BeginPaint—a requirement for all functions that respond to WM_PAINT messages.

- EvPaint calls the *virtual* Paint function, passing the constructed TPaintDC device context object as an argument. This is the dc object that you receive in your own Paint functions.

235

- When Paint returns, EvPaint ends (it first tells any scrollers, however, that the update event is over). The device context object goes out of scope, causing TPaintDC's destructor to be called.

- TPaintDC's destructor calls the global Windows API function EndPaint— required by any task that calls BeginPaint in response to WM_PAINT.

Don't be concerned about every nuance of the preceding descriptions. Just be aware of these key facts:

- EvPaint calls the virtual Paint function. The easiest way to respond to WM_PAINT messages, then, is to replace Paint in a derived class.

- EvPaint constructs a device context object of the TPaintDC class. That object is passed by reference to Paint's dc parameter.

- The TPaintDC object automatically satisfies the Windows rule that BeginPaint and EndPaint must be called in response to WM_PAINT.

Those facts give you the necessary information to write functions that respond directly to WM_PAINT, as explained next.

Outside the *Paint* Function

Follow these guidelines to direct WM_PAINT messages to your own derived class's EvPaint message-response function:

- Declare a replacement EvPaint function in the class.
- Define a response table using the EV_WM_PAINT macro.
- Construct an object of the TPaintDC class.

Just declaring a replacement EvPaint function isn't enough because the function is not virtual, and therefore, it won't be called in response to WM_PAINT messages unless you also associate the function and message in a response table. You must also construct an object of the TPaintDC class. You can use that object to select pens, to call encapsulated GDI functions, and to perform other graphical tasks.

Listings 7.1 (PAINTER.RH), 7.2 (PAINTER.RC), and 7.3 (PAINTER.CPP) demonstrate how to write a function that responds directly to WM_PAINT messages. The program also introduces several GDI techniques explained after the listing.

Listing 7.1. PAINTER.RH.

```
// painter.rh -- Resource header file

#define ID_MENU     100
```

Listing 7.2. PAINTER.RC.

```
#include <owl\window.rh>
#include "painter.rh"

ID_MENU MENU
BEGIN
  POPUP "&Demo"
  BEGIN
    MENUITEM "E&xit", CM_EXIT
  END
END
```

Listing 7.3. PAINTER.CPP.

```
/* ============================================================ *\
**  painter.cpp -- Respond directly to WM_PAINT messages       **
** ============================================================ **
**  Most TWindow-derived classes should respond to WM_PAINT    **
**  by using a Paint function. Use the method demonstrated in  **
**  this program only if you are sure it is necessary to       **
**  respond directly to WM_PAINT messages.                     **
** ============================================================ **
**      Copyright (c) 1994 by Tom Swan. All rights reserved.   **
\* ============================================================ */

#include <owl\applicat.h>
#include <owl\framewin.h>
```

continues

Listing 7.3. continued

```
#include <owl\dc.h>
#include <owl\gdiobjec.h>
#include <owl\point.h>
#include <owl\color.h>
#pragma hdrstop
#include "painter.rh"


// ================================================================
// The application's main window
// ================================================================

class TPaintWin: public TFrameWindow {
  TPen blackPen, redPen, greenPen, bluePen;
  TBrush blueGreenBrush;
public:
  TPaintWin(TWindow* parent, const char far* title);
  void DrawEllipse(TDC& dc, TRect& cr);
protected:
  void EvPaint();
  void EvSize(UINT sizeType, TSize &size);
DECLARE_RESPONSE_TABLE(TPaintWin);
};

DEFINE_RESPONSE_TABLE1(TPaintWin, TFrameWindow)
  EV_WM_PAINT,
  EV_WM_SIZE,
END_RESPONSE_TABLE;

// Constructor
// Note how private member class objects are constructed
TPaintWin::TPaintWin(TWindow* parent, const char far* title)
  : TFrameWindow(parent, title),
    TWindow(parent, title),
    blackPen(TColor::Black),        // Construct private
    redPen(TColor::LtRed),          //   member-object
    greenPen(TColor::LtGreen),      //   pens and brush.
    bluePen(TColor::LtBlue),
    blueGreenBrush(TColor::LtCyan)
{
  AssignMenu(ID_MENU);
}

// Draw a filled, outlined, colored ellipse
// Demonstrates that other functions can draw shapes
// dc == reference to a TDC device-context object
// cr == reference to client window dimensions class object
void
TPaintWin::DrawEllipse(TDC& dc, TRect& cr)
```

```
{
  TColor foreground(255, 0, 128);
  TColor background(0, 128, 255);
  TPen pen(foreground);
  TBrush brush(background);
  dc.SelectObject(pen);
  dc.SelectObject(brush);
  TPoint origin((cr.right / 4) * 3, cr.bottom / 4);
  TSize size(cr.right / 5, cr.bottom / 5);
  TRect dimensions(origin, size);
  dc.Ellipse(dimensions);
  dc.RestorePen();
  dc.RestoreBrush();
}

// Respond to WM_PAINT messages
void
TPaintWin::EvPaint()
{
// Construct a device context object
  TPaintDC dc(*this);

// Get client area dimensions
  TRect cr;                         // Define rectangle
  GetClientRect(cr);                // Set cr to client area

// Erase window background
  TBrush whiteBrush(TColor::White);  // Create white brush
  dc.FillRect(cr, whiteBrush);       // Paint window white

// Shrink a copy of rectangle cr 10 pixels on all sides
  TRect outline(cr);                // Construct copy of cr
  outline.Inflate(-10, -10);        // Shrink copy

// Draw a red rectangle using dimensions in TRect outline
  dc.SelectObject(redPen);          // Use red pen in dc
  dc.Rectangle(outline);            // Draw the rectangle

// Draw a black rectangle the "hard way"
  dc.SelectObject(blackPen);        // Use black pen in dc
  dc.Rectangle(25, 25, 150, 175);   // Draw the rectangle

// Draw a green rectangle using TPoint arguments
  TPoint p1(20, 20);                // Construct a couple of
  TPoint p2(60, 80);                //  TPoint objects.
  dc.SelectObject(greenPen);        // Use green pen in dc
  dc.Rectangle(p1, p2);             // Draw the rectangle

// Draw a filled rectangle using TPoint and TSize arguments
  TPoint p3(30, 90);                // Construct TPoint object
```

continues

239

Listing 7.3. continued

```
  TSize s(48, 32);                   // Construct TSize object
  dc.SelectObject(bluePen);          // Use blue pen in dc
  dc.SelectObject(blueGreenBrush);   // Use blue-green brush
  dc.Rectangle(p3, s);               // Draw the rectangle

// Draw colored lines
  for (int i = 0; i < 3; ++i) {
    // Construct line start and stop points
    TPoint startLine(cr.right / 2 + i * 8, cr.bottom / 2);
    TPoint stopLine(startLine.x, cr.bottom - 20);
    if (i == 0)
      dc.SelectObject(redPen);       // Use red pen in dc
    else if (i == 1)
      dc.SelectObject(greenPen);     // Use green pen in dc
    else
      dc.SelectObject(bluePen);      // Use blue pen in dc
    dc.MoveTo(startLine);            // Move to start of line
    dc.LineTo(stopLine);             // Draw to end of line
  }

// Restore original pen and brush in the device context
  dc.RestorePen();
  dc.RestoreBrush();

// Call a program function to draw an ellipse
// It's okay to pass the TPaintDC object, dc, to
// the function's TDC& paramter because TPaintDC is
// derived from TDC.
  DrawEllipse(dc, cr);
}

// Respond to WM_SIZE message
// Forces window to be redrawn completely if its size changes
void
TPaintWin::EvSize(UINT sizeType, TSize &size)
{
  TFrameWindow::EvSize(sizeType, size);  // Default actions
  Invalidate();   // Force update of window's client area
}

// ==============================================================
// The application class
// ==============================================================

class TPaintApp: public TApplication {
public:
  TPaintApp(const char far* name)
    : TApplication(name) {};
```

```
  void InitMainWindow();
};

// Initialize the program's main window
void
TPaintApp::InitMainWindow()
{
  MainWindow = new TPaintWin(0, "Paint Demonstration");
}

#pragma argsused

// Main program
int
OwlMain(int argc, char* argv[])
{
  TPaintApp app("Painter");
  return app.Run();
}
```

The program's main window class, TPaintWin, derived from TFrameWindow, declares EvPaint and EvSize response functions. The formats of these and other response functions are predefined by TWindow, and as I mentioned, are associated with message-cracker macros, in this case EV_WM_PAINT and EV_WM_SIZE. You must use the predefined function forms for EvPaint and EvSize as shown in TPaintWin's class because the corresponding macros are designed for functions only in those forms.

In addition to declaring EvPaint and EvSize, the program defines a response table, using the macros for the functions:

```
DEFINE_RESPONSE_TABLE1(TPaintWin, TFrameWindow)
  EV_WM_PAINT,
  EV_WM_SIZE,
END_RESPONSE_TABLE;
```

The TPaintWin class also declares several private pens and one brush. For better speed when painting in windows, it's often a good idea to define graphics objects ahead of time rather than in a Paint or EvPaint function.

TPaintWin's constructor demonstrates the correct way to initialize private class objects that are data members in a class. (The constructor is located immediately after the class's response table.) In addition to calling the base-class TFrameWindow and TWindow constructors, the TPen and TBrush objects are constructed by calling these class constructors in a similar way.

241

Next in the listing is a subfunction, DrawEllipse, that demonstrates an important aspect of using device context objects. The function requires a reference to a TDC object and also a TRect parameter that indicates the size and location of the ellipse. The TDC parameter enables the program to pass other kinds of device context objects to DrawEllipse, and in that way, to direct the function's output to other destinations. For example, you could pass a TPrintDC or a TDesktopDC object to DrawEllipse's TDC parameter because these classes are all derived from TDC.

EvPaint shows how to respond directly to WM_PAINT messages. A critical step is to define a TPaintDC object as the function's first statement:

```
TPaintDC dc(*this);
```

The TPaintDC class takes care of Windows' requirement that programs call the API function BeginPaint before drawing in a window in response to WM_PAINT. When the dc object is destroyed—which happens automatically when EvPaint ends—the TPaintDC destructor calls EndPaint, also required by Windows.

EvPaint shows one way to erase a window to a predetermined color, which you might need to do when responding to WM_PAINT messages. The following statements fill a TRect object with the client area's dimensions, create a pen and brush, and then call FillRect to paint the window's insides white. In this case, the whiteBrush is not selected into the device context because FillRect uses a TBrush argument:

```
TRect cr;
GetClientRect(cr);
TBrush whiteBrush(TColor::White);
dc.FillRect(cr, whiteBrush);
```

WM_PAINT and *Paint* Parameters

The WM_PAINT message has no parameter values, and therefore, EvPaint also needs no parameters. As you have seen in other sample listings, however, (such as BAR.CPP), a Paint function has three parameters. Where do Paint's parameters come from and how do you use them? To answer those questions, let's take a final close-up look at Paint and its parameters:

```
virtual void Paint(TDC& dc, BOOL erase, TRect& rect);
```

When a TWindow object receives a WM_PAINT message, it calls the EvPaint function. That function constructs a TPaintDC device context and passes that object by reference to Paint's dc parameter. To draw in the window, you then call encapsulated GDI functions in reference to dc.

The other two parameters, erase and rect, are created when EvPaint constructs the device context. The parameters are actually copies of two PAINTSTRUCT fields, fErase and rcPaint, that Windows fills in when the TPaintDC constructor calls BeginPaint—required by any task that responds to WM_PAINT. If erase is true, Paint is expected to fill in the window's background using the coordinate values in rect, which specifies the upper-left and lower-right corners of the rectangle that requires painting.

If you assign a brush to be used for the window background, erase will always be false, and you can ignore it because BeginPaint has already taken care of painting the background. You may always ignore rect, but for speed, you might want to limit output to coordinates within the update rectangle.

> **TIP**
>
> In a Paint function, the expression dc.Ps refers to the original PAINTSTRUCT structure filled in by BeginPaint. In the rare event that you need the Windows HDC (handle to device context) created by BeginPaint, it is available as dc.Ps.hdc where dc is a TPaintDC object or reference.

Advanced Graphics Techniques

Many volumes have been published on advanced graphics techniques, and my aim here is not to cover every possible angle, but to introduce a few select topics that will help you discover on your own more of what OWL can do in the graphics art department.

I begin with color palettes, one of the subjects that seems to confuse many programmers. After that, I describe how to relate mouse activity with graphics, using a simple but effective method called *capturing the mouse*. Using that method, I also explain *rubberbanding*, a way to select multiple objects in windows using the mouse. Finally, just for fun, I end the chapter with a graphics animation that runs in the background. The example isn't entirely frivolous—you can use similar methods to run other background tasks in "serious" software.

Color Palettes

Of all the subjects in Windows graphics, color palettes are among the most confusing. The first rule to remember is that palettes are hardware-device resources. Some output devices support color palettes; other's don't. The purpose of Windows palettes is to provide programs with device-independent techniques for using a *logical palette* regardless of whether a *physical palette* is available on a given output device.

Palettes are typically used on output devices that can support many different colors, but not all at the same time. A high-quality display, for example, might be able to show 250,000 colors, but only 256 of those colors at once. On the hardware level, a color palette stores the 256 colors currently in use. On the software level, as Figure 7.1 illustrates, programs specify colors, not as red-green-blue quantities, but as indexes into a 256-element array. A fictitious function, `SetColor`, shows how a program might specify the color green as an index value 2.

FIGURE 7.1.

A hardware color palette stores color values.

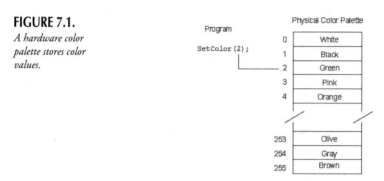

Figure 7.1 illustrates only half the palette story. Suppose window A's program uses the index value 4 to specify orange. Then, suppose window B's program *changes* that color to purple. Suddenly, the programmer may become red-faced when all of window A's oranges turn into grapes.

To help eliminate such conflicts, Windows *maps* logical and physical palette entries. In the program, a logical palette specifies the colors that the program intends to use. Windows maps those colors to entries in the physical palette. Another program can use its own logical palette, which Windows again maps to entries in the physical table. Some of the mapped colors might be the same; others might be unique. The mapping of logical palettes permits two or more programs to *share* the same physical palette in most cases without conflict.

Figure 7.2 shows conceptually how Windows maps logical and physical palette entries. Program A selects the color orange by using an index value 2 into A's logical three-color palette. Windows maps that color to the fifth physical palette entry (index 4), also orange, a perfect match. Program B uses a second three-color logical palette. Because the physical palette lacks a red entry, Windows maps the logical palette's red color to the nearest match, in this case, the fourth physical entry, pink (index 3). If the palette had any unused positions, Windows would attempt to add red to the physical palette so an exact match could be made. When all physical palette entries are filled, Windows makes the closest match that it can between a logical and a physical color.

FIGURE 7.2.

Windows maps logical and physical palette color entries.

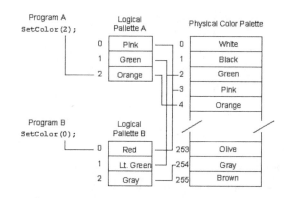

Windows reserves 20 palette colors for a default palette used for mapping its own colors. That way, windows and menus are unaffected by the use of a color palette in applications.

To use color palettes, first construct an array of class TPaletteEntry objects. The objects have red, green, and blue components, plus a fourth value that selects options for each color's use. (For more information, see the Windows PALETTEENTRY structure, from which TPaletteEntry is derived.) First include the COLOR.H header, which declares TPaletteEntry:

```
#include <owl\color.h>
```

Also create a constant for the number of colors you want to define:

```
#define NUMCOLORS 32
```

Then, declare the array as a TPaletteEntry pointer, perhaps in a TWindow-derived class:

```
TPaletteEntry* palentries;
```

Somewhere in the program (in a class constructor, for instance), allocate memory for the number of colors the program needs and assign the memory's address to the TPaletteEntry pointer:

```
palentries = (TPaletteEntry*)
  new char[sizeof(TPaletteEntry) * numColors];
```

Initialize the palette entries using whatever method suits your needs. To choose colors at random, for example, you could use a for loop:

```
for (int i = 0; i < numColors; ++i) {
  palentries[i].peRed = random(256);
  palentries[i].peGreen = random(256);
  palentries[i].peBlue = random(256);
  palentries[i].peFlags = PC_RESERVED;
}
```

The PC_RESERVED flag tells Windows that this color is subject to frequent change. PC_NOCOLLAPSE tells Windows to insert the color into an unused physical palette entry. PC_EXPLICIT indicates that the low-order word of the color is actually a hardware palette index. Don't use PC_EXPLICIT unless you must have direct access to a hardware palette (in a specialized drawing program, for instance, designed for a specific display device).

To create the logical color palette from the array of TPaletteEntry values, declare a second pointer of type TPalette*:

```
TPalette* palette;
```

Use the new operator to allocate the logical palette of type TPalette with the array of TPaletteEntry color values and flags:

```
palette = new TPalette(palentries, numColors);
```

Your program now has a logical color palette that it can use to select color values—in a Paint function, for instance, or in any other function that generates graphical output. As with all graphical objects, to use the color palette, you must select it into a device context. For example, a Paint function might begin with the statements:

```
dc.SelectObject(*palette);
dc.RealizePalette();
```

The first line selects the logical color palette addressed by the palette pointer into the TPaintDC object referenced by dc. The second statement tells Windows to *realize* the palette—or, in plain English, to map the logical palette entries to colors in the physical palette. The program can now select a color by specifying an index value for the logical palette rather than red-green-blue color components. For example, these statements fill a rectangle with the logical color value 3:

```
TColor color(3);
TRect rect(10, 10, 150, 250);
dc.FillRect(rect, color);
```

That maps color value 3 to the fourth logical palette entry, which is in turn mapped to an entry in the physical palette. If luck and the force are with you, the actual color you see on screen will be the one you expected, but at least, the final color should be *something* like the one you want.

Capturing the Mouse

When you click the mouse, or when you click and drag it, Windows issues a variety of mouse messages to the current window. By responding to those messages and displaying appropriate graphics, a program provides a level of interaction that isn't possible on text-only displays. For example, Windows users quickly learn the technique of *rubberbanding* for selecting items in windows by clicking and dragging the mouse, drawing a stretchy rectangle over the items they want. The method requires careful programming, but the illusion is well worth the effort.

The key element in the technique is known as *capturing the mouse,* a method that temporarily provides a window with total control over all mouse events. While captured, the mouse cannot be used to select other windows or pull down menu commands. During that time, drawing lines or rectangles at the mouse pointer's position makes it seem as though you really can use the mouse to pick up items, drag them around, and so on.

Fortunately, the programming requires no mouse traps or cheese—only a couple of message response functions. Listings 7.4 (SKETCH.RH), 7.5 (SKETCH.RC), and 7.6 (SKETCH.CPP) show the basic steps in capturing the mouse. Run the program, then click and drag the mouse pointer inside the window to sketch lines. Double-click the left mouse button to erase your drawings and start over.

> **NOTE**
>
> SKETCH breaks the cardinal rule that Windows programs should store graphical information for redrawing images at the drop of a hat. Because of this problem, covering SKETCH's window with another erases any sketches below. To fix this bug, you need to learn techniques introduced in the next chapter, so for now, consider the problem to be a "feature." (You've heard that excuse before, right?)

Listing 7.4. SKETCH.RH.

```
// sketch.rh -- Resource header file

#define ID_MENU  100
#define CM_ERASE 101
```

Listing 7.5. SKETCH.RC.

```
#include <owl\window.rh>
#include "sketch.rh"

ID_MENU MENU
BEGIN
  POPUP "&Demo"
  BEGIN
    MENUITEM "&Erase", CM_ERASE
    MENUITEM "E&xit", CM_EXIT
  END
END
```

Listing 7.6. SKETCH.CPP.

```
/* =============================================================== *\
**   sketch.cpp -- Mouse clicking and moving demonstration         **
** =============================================================== **
**   Click and drag the mouse inside the sample window to draw     **
**   a sketch. Double-click the left button to erase. This         **
**   program requires a mouse.                                     **
** =============================================================== **
**      Copyright (c) 1994 by Tom Swan. All rights reserved.       **
\* =============================================================== */

#include <owl\applicat.h>
#include <owl\framewin.h>
#include <owl\dc.h>
#pragma hdrstop
#include "sketch.rh"

// =============================================================
// The application's main window
// =============================================================

class TSketchWin: public TFrameWindow {
  BOOL dragging;    // True if clicking and dragging the mouse
```

```
    TClientDC* cdc;    // Pointer to client-window device context
  public:
    TSketchWin(TWindow* parent, const char far* title);
  protected:
    void CmErase();
    void EvLButtonDown(UINT modKeys, TPoint& point);
    void EvMouseMove(UINT modKeys, TPoint& point);
    void EvLButtonUp(UINT modKeys, TPoint& point);
    void EvLButtonDblClk(UINT modKeys, TPoint& point);
  DECLARE_RESPONSE_TABLE(TSketchWin);
  };

  DEFINE_RESPONSE_TABLE1(TSketchWin, TFrameWindow)
    EV_COMMAND(CM_ERASE, CmErase),
    EV_WM_LBUTTONDOWN,
    EV_WM_MOUSEMOVE,
    EV_WM_LBUTTONUP,
    EV_WM_LBUTTONDBLCLK,
  END_RESPONSE_TABLE;

  // Constructor
  TSketchWin::TSketchWin(TWindow* parent, const char far* title)
    : TFrameWindow(parent, title),
      TWindow(parent, title)
  {
    AssignMenu(ID_MENU);
    dragging = FALSE;
  }

  // Erase drawing in window
  void
  TSketchWin::CmErase()
  {
    Invalidate();    // "Window needs updating"
    UpdateWindow();  // "Do it now!" (optional but faster)
  }

  // Note: The commented /*modKeys*/ parameters in the next three
  // functions eliminate warnings from the compiler that these
  // items are not used.

  // Respond to mouse-click WM_LBUTTONDOWN message
  // Begin mouse click-and-drag operation
  void
  TSketchWin::EvLButtonDown(UINT /*modKeys*/, TPoint& point)
  {
    if (!dragging) {
      dragging = TRUE;
      SetCapture();
      cdc = new TClientDC(HWindow);
```

continues

249

Listing 7.6. continued

```cpp
    cdc->MoveTo(point);
  }
}

// Respond to mouse-move WM_MOUSEMOVE message
// Leave trail behind mouse as user drags it
void
TSketchWin::EvMouseMove(UINT /*modKeys*/, TPoint& point)
{
  if (dragging)
    cdc->LineTo(point);
}

// Respond to mouse-release WM_LBUTTONUP message
// End click-and-drag operation
void
TSketchWin::EvLButtonUp(UINT /*modKeys*/, TPoint& /*point*/)
{
  if (dragging) {
    ReleaseCapture();
    delete cdc;
    dragging = FALSE;
  }
}

// Respond to mouse double-click WM_LBUTTONDBLCLK message
// Erase any drawing in window
void
TSketchWin::EvLButtonDblClk(UINT /*modKeys*/, TPoint& /*point*/)
{
  CmErase();
}

// ============================================================
// The application class
// ============================================================

class TSketchApp: public TApplication {
public:
  TSketchApp(const char far* name)
    : TApplication(name) {};
  void InitMainWindow();
};

// Initialize the program's main window
void
TSketchApp::InitMainWindow()
```

```
{
  MainWindow = new TSketchWin(0, "Click and Drag the Mouse");
}

#pragma argsused

// Main program
int
OwlMain(int argc, char* argv[])
{
  TSketchApp app("Sketch");
  return app.Run();
}
```

Three message-response functions are the essential ingredients for all click-and-drag operations. These functions are EvLButtonDown, EvMouseMove, and EvLButtonUp. The TWindow class provides these functions along with their message-cracker macros EV_WM_LBUTTONDOWN, EV_WM_MOUSEMOVE, and EV_WM_LBUTTONUP. The corresponding Windows messages are, as usual, the same as the macro names minus the EV_ prefixes.

To respond to left mouse-button clicks, declare function EvLButtonDown and add the associated macro to the window's response table. Do the same for the other two functions and macros as shown in SKETCH's TSketchWin class. You also need a flag, dragging, to indicate the current mouse state. If the flag is true, the user has clicked and is dragging the mouse; otherwise, the program ignores mouse movements.

SKETCH's implementation of EvLButtonDown shows the first step in capturing the mouse. If the dragging flag is false, set the flag true and call the encapsulated SetCapture member function. After this step, all mouse messages are sent to the window, and it is not possible for users to switch to other windows. SKETCH also prepares a TClientDC device-context object, cdc, for drawing in the window, and calls MoveTo to position the internal graphics location to the mouse position, passed to EvLButtonDown in the point parameter.

> **TIP**
>
> The program can't use TPaintDC here because the function does not respond to a WM_PAINT message. Instead, TClientDC provides a device context object for drawing inside the window.

When you move the mouse, Windows issues a WM_MOUSEMOVE message to the window. SKETCH responds to these messages in function EvMouseMove, which first checks whether the `dragging` flag is true. If so, function `LineTo` draws a line from the last known position to the current one passed to the function in `point`.

Finally, when you release the left mouse button, Windows issues a third message, `WM_LBUTTONUP`. SKETCH responds to this message in function `EvLButtonUp`, which again checks `dragging` to determine if a click-and-drag operation is in progress. If so, `ReleaseCapture` counteracts the preceding call to `SetCapture`, releasing the poor mouse to scurry off on its business (and letting you again select other windows and menus). At this time, the click-and-drag operation is over, and `EvLButtonUp` deletes the device context `cdc` and sets the `dragging` flag to `FALSE`.

Rubberbanding

Using the basic methods outlined in the preceding section, you can add *rubberband selection* to a window. Rather than sketch lines during click-and-drag operations, the program erases and displays a rectangle, making it appear to stretch and shrink as though it were made of rubber.

The sample listings in this section also demonstrate a good way to build and refine general-purpose tools using C++ classes. One of the most difficult aspects of object-oriented programming is choosing which operations to insert into specific classes. For example, I could have written a single program to demonstrate rubberbanding—as many Windows tutorials do. Instead, I divided the job into three distinct operations:

- Clicking and dragging
- Rubberbanding
- Object selection

The first two of these operations are *generalizations* of the methods used in SKETCH to sketch inside a window. Always be ready to pounce on similar cases where you can generalize a concept from a specific action. Here, clicking, dragging, and rubberbanding, are generalizations of the methods used to draw lines in the earlier sketch program. As such, those generalizations make excellent C++ classes that you can refine to provide specific tools—one that, in this example, you can use to select objects in a window by dragging a rubberband outline with the mouse. The same classes could also be used in other ways—to divide a window, select text, zoom a portion of a bitmap, and so on.

Listing 7.7, DRAG.H, declares a class, `TDragWin`, derived from `TFrameWin`, that generalizes the concepts of clicking and dragging the mouse.

252

Listing 7.7. DRAG.H.

```
// drag.h -- Header file for drag.cpp

#ifndef __DRAG_H
#define __DRAG_H   // Prevent multiple includes

#ifndef __OWL_FRAMEWIN_H
  #include <owl\framewin.h>
#endif

#ifndef __OWL_DC_H
  #include <owl\dc.h>
#endif

// Abstract click-and-drag class
class TDragWin: public TFrameWindow {

public:
  TDragWin(TWindow* parent, const char far* title);
  ~TDragWin();

protected:
// Pure virtual functions (derived class must provide)
  virtual void BeginDragging(
    TDC& dc, UINT modKeys, TPoint& mousePt) = 0;
  virtual void DragMouse(
    TDC& dc, UINT modKeys, TPoint& mousePt) = 0;
  virtual void EndDragging(
    TDC& dc, UINT modKeys, TPoint& mousePt) = 0;

// Inherited response functions
  void EvLButtonDown(UINT modKeys, TPoint& pt);
  void EvMouseMove(UINT modKeys, TPoint& pt);
  void EvLButtonUp(UINT modKeys, TPoint& pt);

private:
  BOOL dragging;     // True when clicking and dragging
  TClientDC* cdc;    // Passed to pure virtual functions
```

continues

253

Listing 7.7. continued

```
DECLARE_RESPONSE_TABLE(TDragWin);

};

#endif  // __DRAG_H
```

The DRAG.H header file begins by defining the symbol _ _DRAG_H, unless it is already defined, in which case the file's declarations are skipped. This device prevents accidentally including the same header (thus wasting time) in programs with many modules that share the same classes.

A related technique saves time when including OWL and other header files such as FRAMEWIN.H and DC.H, which declare items used by TDragWin. The conditional statement:

```
#ifndef __OWL_FRAMEWIN_H
  #include <owl\framewin.h>
#endif
```

includes FRAMEWIN.H only if that header was not included by another file during compilation of a multiple-file program. You don't have to use this method. You could delete the #ifndef and #endif directives because, like DRAG.H, FRAMEWIN.H begins by checking whether symbol _ _OWL_FRAMEWIN_H is defined. Performing the test in *every* file as demonstrated here, however, saves the compiler the trouble of opening the same headers over and over just to determine that they were already included. In small examples, the benefits of these gyrations are nil, but in large programs with many files, you can save a lot of compilation time by opening only the header files that have not already been included.

Next in DRAG.H, the TDragWin class declares a constructor and destructor in its public section. The class also declares three *pure virtual functions* in a protected section. A derived class must supply bodies for these functions. TDragWin is an unfinished class—it provides a skeleton for building other classes, but it cannot be used directly to define objects.

The class also replaces three inherited message-response functions, the same ones you saw in SKETCH. These functions call the pure virtual functions, and in that way, provide derived classes with *hooks* into the process of clicking and dragging. To implement clicking and dragging, the derived class simply provides bodies for the three pure-virtual functions—the underlying class, TDragWin, takes care of the messy details of capturing the mouse, responding to Windows messages, and so on.

In addition to its member functions, TDragWin also declares two data members. BOOL dragging is true during click-and-drag operations; TClientDC pointer cdc addresses a device context object for use at that time.

The purpose of each member function will be clearer after you examine the class's implementation in Listing 7.8, DRAG.CPP.

Listing 7.8. DRAG.CPP.

```
/* ============================================================ *\
** drag.cpp -- Implement TDragWin class                        **
** ============================================================ **
**                                                             **
** ============================================================ **
**      Copyright (c) 1994 by Tom Swan. All rights reserved.   **
\* ============================================================ */

#include "drag.h"

// ============================================================
// TDragWin
// ============================================================

// Message-response table
DEFINE_RESPONSE_TABLE1(TDragWin, TFrameWindow)
  EV_WM_LBUTTONDOWN,
  EV_WM_MOUSEMOVE,
  EV_WM_LBUTTONUP,
END_RESPONSE_TABLE;

// Constructor
TDragWin::TDragWin(TWindow* parent, const char far* title)
  : TFrameWindow(parent, title),
    TWindow(parent, title)
{
  dragging = FALSE;
  cdc = 0;
}

// Destructor
TDragWin::~TDragWin()
{
  if (dragging) delete cdc;
}

// Respond to WM_LBUTTONDOWN
void
```

continues

Listing 7.8. continued

```
TDragWin::EvLButtonDown(UINT modKeys, TPoint& pt)
{
  if (!dragging) {
    cdc = new TClientDC(*this);
    SetCapture();
    dragging = TRUE;
    BeginDragging(*cdc, modKeys, pt);
  }
}

// Respond to WM_MOUSEMOVE
void
TDragWin::EvMouseMove(UINT modKeys, TPoint& pt)
{
  if (dragging)
    DragMouse(*cdc, modKeys, pt);
}

// Respond to WM_LBUTTONUP
void
TDragWin::EvLButtonUp(UINT modKeys, TPoint& pt)
{
  if (dragging) {
    EndDragging(*cdc, modKeys, pt);
    ReleaseCapture();
    delete cdc;
    cdc = 0;  // So cdc isn't deleted again in destructor
    dragging = FALSE;
  }
}
```

File DRAG.CPP implements the TDragWin class declared in header file DRAG.H. Because files with dozens of classes are difficult to maintain and debug, it's often best to declare each class in a separate header file and define its member functions in a separate module. Later in this chapter, you'll see how to combine DRAG with other modules to create a finished program.

Notice that, when separating class declarations and definitions into separate files, any response table must be defined in the .CPP module, never in the header. In this case, the response table lists the three message-cracking macros for the mouse button and movement messages you saw in SKETCH.

The implemented constructor calls the base class TFrameWindow and TWindow constructors, then sets dragging to FALSE. The constructor also sets pointer cdc to null (using a literal 0, not the NULL macro, as recommended for ANSI C++). This pointer won't be used until later, but it is still important to initialize the pointer because, if an object of type TDragWin were destroyed before that pointer is ever used, deleting the pointer would most likely corrupt the heap and cause serious bugs. In this example, TDragWin's destructor prevents that undesirable possibility by deleting cdc only if dragging is true (indicating that cdc addresses a valid device context object). Still, it doesn't hurt to play safe. If you always initialize all variables, your code will never catch a bug caused by using an uninitialized object.

The implementations for the class's three response functions follow the destructor. Compare these functions with those in SKETCH.CPP—they are similar, but more general versions of the same programming. Here, a TClientDC device context is created for use during click-and-drag operations. Also, each response function calls one of the pure virtual functions declared in the class. EvLButtonDown calls BeginDragging; EvMouseMove calls DragMouse; and EvLButtonUp calls EndDragging. These actions create the hooks I mentioned before. A derived class's replacements for the three pure virtual functions are called by TDrawWin's response functions.

The next two listings demonstrate how to create a derived class to hook into those operations. Listing 7.9, RUBBER.H, declares class TRubberWin, derived from TDragWin. The base class provides the most general level of the task—clicking and dragging. The derived class, TRubberWin, inherits from and refines its base class to implement rubberbanding, a more specific example of the generalized technique.

Listing 7.9. RUBBER.H.

```
// rubber.h -- Header file for rubber.cpp

#ifndef _ _RUBBER_H
#define _ _RUBBER_H  // Prevent multiple includes

#ifndef _ _DRAG_H
  #include "drag.h"
#endif

#ifndef _ _OWL_POINT_H
  #include <owl\point.h>
#endif

#ifndef _ _OWL_DC_H
  #include <owl\dc.h>
#endif

#ifndef _ _OWL_GDIOBJEC_H
  #include <owl\gdiobjec.h>
#endif
```

continues

Listing 7.9. continued

```
class TRubberWin: public TDragWin {
public:
  TRubberWin(TWindow* parent, const char far* title);
  virtual void OutlineSelect(TRect outline, UINT modKeys);
protected:
  void RubberBand(TDC& dc)
    { dc.Rectangle(startPt, endPt); }
  virtual void BeginDragging(
    TDC& dc, UINT modKeys, TPoint& mousePt);
  virtual void DragMouse(
    TDC& dc, UINT modKeys, TPoint& mousePt);
  virtual void EndDragging(
    TDC& dc, UINT modKeys, TPoint& mousePt);
private:
  int oldMode;
  TPoint startPt, endPt;
  TPen dragPen;
};

#endif // __RUBBER_H
```

As in DRAG.H, the RUBBER.H header file defines a symbol, _ _RUBBER_H, that pre-vents the file's declarations from being included more than once. The header also in-cludes DRAG.H, POINT.H, DC.H, and GDIOBJEC.H, in each case testing whether those files are already included. (I'll stop using this technique in most future listings for clarity and to save space in the book, but as I mentioned, it's a great way to save time when compiling large programs that include many of the same headers in various modules.)

TRubberWin declares two public functions, a constructor and a virtual function, OutlineSelect. A small number of public functions is usually a good sign that a derived class is doing a good job of refining more general, inherited operations. In this case, OutlineSelect is passed a rectangle giving the final location and dimensions of a rubberband outline. The function is also passed a value that indicates if any keys are held down when the mouse button is released—but more on that later. Important here is the idea that, simply by basing another class on TRubberWin and providing a replace-ment for the OutlineSelect function, you can add rubberbanding to any window.

TRubberWin's four protected member functions implement the class's duties. The inline RubberBand draws a rectangle. The other three functions implement the pure virtual functions inherited from TDragWin. Remember, these functions are called in response to mouse-click and -move messages received by the base class. The derived TRubberWin class does not recognize any new Windows messages, so it doesn't need a response table of its own. All message handling is performed in the base class.

TRubberWin also declares several private data members. Integer oldMode is used to reset the device context's drawing mode, which is changed during rubberbanding to use *exclusive OR drawing,* a technique that permits erasing images (in this case, a rectangle) without disturbing other images. Two TPoint objects, startPt and endPt, record the locations of the rubberband's upper-left and lower-right coordinates. A TPen object, dragPen, defines the color and style of the rubberband rectangle.

Listing 7.10, RUBBER.CPP, implements the TRubberWin class. As you read through the listing, keep in mind that rubberbanding is just one of many possible refinements of clicking and dragging—the general operations inherited from the TDragWin base class. In another program, you might derive a different class from TDragWin and refine those operations to perform a different job.

Listing 7.10. RUBBER.CPP.

```
/* ============================================================ *\
** rubber.cpp -- Implement TRubberWin class **
** ============================================================ **
** **
** ============================================================ **
** Copyright (c) 1994 by Tom Swan. All rights reserved. **
\* ============================================================ */

#include "drag.h"
#include "rubber.h"

// ============================================================
// TRubberWin
// ============================================================

// Constructor
TRubberWin::TRubberWin(TWindow* parent, const char far* title)
  : TDragWin(parent, title),
    TWindow(parent, title),
    dragPen(TColor::Black, 1, PS_DOT)
{
}

// Placeholder function called by EndDragging()
void
TRubberWin::OutlineSelect(TRect /*outline*/, UINT /*modKeys*/)
{
}
```

continues

259

Listing 7.10. continued

```
// Begin to select area with rubberband
void
TRubberWin::BeginDragging(TDC& dc,
  UINT /*modKeys*/, TPoint& mousePt)
{
  startPt = mousePt;
  endPt = mousePt;
  oldMode = dc.SetROP2(R2_NOTXORPEN);
  dc.SelectObject(dragPen);
//  RubberBand(dc);
}

// Continue selecting area
void
TRubberWin::DragMouse(TDC& dc,
  UINT /*modKeys*/, TPoint& mousePt)
{
  RubberBand(dc);  // Erase existing outline
  endPt = mousePt;
  RubberBand(dc);   // Draw new outline
}

// End selecting area
void
TRubberWin::EndDragging(TDC& dc,
  UINT modKeys, TPoint& /*mousePt*/)
{
  if (startPt != endPt)   // If outline is NOT empty,
    RubberBand(dc);       // erase the outline
  dc.SetROP2(oldMode);
  dc.RestorePen();
  TRect outline(startPt, endPt);
  outline.Normalize();
  OutlineSelect(outline, modKeys);
}
```

TRubberWin's constructor calls its base class constructors, and also constructs the dragPen object. You can use a different color and style if you want, but a black dotted line is traditional. Notice that the constructor calls its immediate base class constructor, TDragWin, but also calls the virtual base class TWindow. All virtually inherited base classes such as TWindow must be called explicitly by all derived classes. In a class derived from TRubberWin, for example, the constructor must call the TRubberWin *and* the TWindow constructors.

Placeholder function OutlineSelect exists only to provide a shell that other functions can call. I could have designed OutlineSelect as a pure virtual function, as I did the three functions in TDragWin. That would make TRubberWin an abstract class, requiring derived classes to implement OutlineSelect. Perhaps that would be a good idea, since after all, there's no reason to use TRubberWin unless you plan to implement rubberbanding. I wanted to show, however, that classes can use pure virtual and placeholder functions similarly to provide hooks for attaching new processes in derived classes.

> **TIP**
>
> It's often unclear which is better: a pure virtual function or a placeholder do-nothing function such as OutlineSelect. As a rule of thumb, if there is any chance that a class will be used to construct an object, use a placeholder; otherwise use a pure virtual function.

The file ends with implementations of the three pure virtual functions inherited from TDragWin. BeginDragging starts the show, saving the mouse location passed in mousePt in the two TPoint objects, startPt and endPt. In other words, at the beginning of a rubberband operation the selection outline is empty. The function also calls the encapsulated SetROP2 GDI function for device context dc, passed to BeginDragging. ("ROP" is short for "raster operation.") Option R2_NOTXORPEN selects negative, exclusive OR, drawing. With this mode, redrawing an object erases it, restoring any background image below. BeginDragging ends by selecting dragPen into the device context, preparing it to begin drawing rubberbands.

The drawing begins in the next function, DragMouse, called by the base class's EvMouseMove response function during clicking and dragging. DragMouse is not called at other times, so there's no need to use a flag to differentiate between clicking and dragging and other mouse movements, as there was in the SKETCH program. DragMouse simply calls the inline RubberBand function to erase any existing outline and then, after saving the new mouse pointer location in endPt, calls RubberBand again to draw a new outline. By erasing and redrawing the rectangle, these three functions animate the rubberband, making it appear to stretch as you move the mouse.

The final function, EndDragging, is called when you release the mouse button. If the outline is not empty, RubberBand is called to erase the final rubberband image. (The Rectangle function never draws empty rectangles—those that don't define a space of at least one display unit.) EndDragging restores the device context's saved drawing mode, and also restores the original pen. It's always wise to restore drawing modes and graphics objects such as pens and brushes when you are done using a device context. Even though device context objects can clean up after themselves (unlike standard Windows device contexts), restoring selected modes and objects helps prevent conflicts with other functions that might use the same device contexts.

The final three statements in EndDragging create a TRect object, outline, from the saved startPt and endPt objects that were used to draw the rubberband outline. The outline object is then *normalized* by calling the TRect member function, Normalize. This swaps the rectangle's coordinates so that outline.left is less than outline.right, and that outline.top is less than outline.bottom. If the rectangle were not normalized, its coordinates might be reversed, or it might even be upside down if the mouse had been drug upward instead of down in the usual way. You don't have to normalize TRect objects, but they tend to be easier to use.

Finally, EndDragging calls the virtual placeholder function, OutlineSelect, passing the final rubberband coordinates in outline along with modKeys, which indicates whether any keys were held down during the click-and-drag operation. Deriving a class from TRubberWin and replacing OutlineSelect is all that's needed to provide a rubberband selection tool in a window. Listings 7.11 (TESTRUB.RH), 7.12 (TESTRUB.H), 7.13 (TESTRUB.RC), and 7.14 (TESTRUB.CPP) show how.

Listing 7.11. TESTRUB.RH.

```
// testrub.rh -- Resource header file

#define ID_MENU 100     // Menu resource identifier
```

Listing 7.12. TESTRUB.H.

```
// testrub.h -- Header file for testrub.cpp

#define NUM_SHAPES 4     // Number of objects in window
```

Listing 7.13. TESTRUB.RC.

```
#include <owl\window.rh>
#include "testrub.h"

ID_MENU MENU
BEGIN
  POPUP "&Demo"
  BEGIN
```

```
      MENUITEM "E&xit", CM_EXIT
  END
END
```

Listing 7.14. TESTRUB.CPP.

```
/* ============================================================ *\
** testrub.cpp -- Demonstrate rubberbanding                   **
** ============================================================ **
**                                                            **
** ============================================================ **
**      Copyright (c) 1994 by Tom Swan. All rights reserved.  **
\* ============================================================ */

#include <owl\applicat.h>
#include <owl\framewin.h>
#include <owl\dc.h>
#include <owl\gdiobjec.h>
#include <owl\color.h>
#pragma hdrstop
#include "drag.h"
#include "rubber.h"
#include "testrub.h"
#include "testrub.rh"


// ============================================================
// TShape
// ============================================================

class TShape: public TRect {
public:
  TShape(): TRect(), selected(FALSE) { }
  TShape(int L, int T, int R, int B)
    : TRect(L, T, R, B), selected(FALSE) { }
  BOOL Selected() { return selected; }
  void Select(BOOL tf) { selected = tf; }
  void Draw(TDC &dc);
private:
  BOOL selected;  // True if shape is selected
};

// Draw shape in window. Fill with light cyan if
// shape is selected; else fill it with white.
void
TShape::Draw(TDC &dc)
{
  TBrush *brush;
```

continues

263

Listing 7.14. continued

```
  if (Selected())
    brush = new TBrush(TColor::LtCyan);
  else
    brush = new TBrush(TColor::White);
  dc.SelectObject(*brush);
  dc.Ellipse(*this);
  dc.RestoreBrush();
  delete brush;
}

// ============================================================
// The application's main window
// ============================================================

class TMainWin: public TRubberWin {
public:
  TMainWin(TWindow* parent, const char far* title);
  virtual void OutlineSelect(TRect outline, UINT modKeys);
  virtual void Paint(TDC& dc, BOOL erase, TRect& rect);
private:
  TShape shapes[NUM_SHAPES];   // Array of shapes
};

// Constructor
TMainWin::TMainWin(TWindow* parent, const char far* title)
  : TRubberWin(parent, title),
    TWindow(parent, title)
{
  AssignMenu(ID_MENU);
  TShape r(50, 100, 100, 150);
  TSize s(100, 0);
  for (int i = 0; i < NUM_SHAPES; ++i) {
    shapes[i] = r;
    r += s;
  }
}

// Select items within outline's dimensions
void
TMainWin::OutlineSelect(TRect outline, UINT /*modKeys*/)
{
  BOOL sflag;   // Selection flag--true if outline contains object

  for (int i = 0; i < NUM_SHAPES; ++i) {
    if (outline.IsEmpty())
      sflag = FALSE;
    else
      sflag = outline.Contains(shapes[i]);
```

```
    shapes[i].Select(sflag);
  }
  Invalidate(FALSE);  // Show new selections
  UpdateWindow();
}

// Paint shapes in the window
void
TMainWin::Paint(TDC& dc, BOOL /*erase*/, TRect& /*rect*/)
{
  for (int i = 0; i < NUM_SHAPES; ++i)
    shapes[i].Draw(dc);
}

// ============================================================
// The application class
// ============================================================

class TRubberApp: public TApplication {
public:
  TRubberApp(const char far* name)
    : TApplication(name) {};
  void InitMainWindow();
};

// Initialize the program's main window
void
TRubberApp::InitMainWindow()
{
  MainWindow = new TMainWin(0, "Drag mouse to select items");
}

#pragma argsused

// Main program
int
OwlMain(int argc, char* argv[])
{
  TRubberApp app("TestRub");
  return app.Run();
}
```

The final test program includes various headers along with DRAG.H, RUBBER.H, TESTRUB.H. File TESTRUB.RH defines a resource identifier for the program's menu. Compile the program by opening the TESTRUB.IDE project file, or run MAKE as explained in Chapters 1 and 2. Run TESTRUB.EXE, then click and drag the mouse to select one or more of the four circles as shown in Figure 7.3. You must completely enclose each circle with the rubberband outline to select it. To deselect objects, click the left mouse button, or select other objects (or, you can select empty space in the window).

FIGURE 7.3.

Click and drag the mouse to select the TESTRUB program's sample graphic objects.

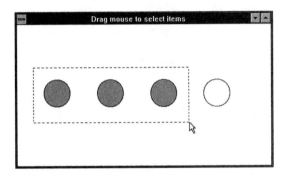

Though simple, the TESTRUB program demonstrates one of the basic operations used in object-drawing programs, and others such as databases and forms designers. In TEST, the four circles are instances of class TShape, derived from TRect. TShape has only one non-inline function, Draw. As you might expect, this function draws the shape, in this case, a simple circle. The other functions construct TShape objects and set or return the value of private member selected, which indicates whether a shape is selected.

The Draw function selects a brush color in the device context object, dc. If the object is selected, the program uses a light cyan brush; otherwise, it uses white. GDI function Ellipse draws the shape.

> **NOTE**
>
> Don't let the *this argument passed to Ellipse throw you. TShape is derived from TRect, or to say that another way, *a TShape object is also a TRect object*. The encapsulated GDI function Ellipse can accept a TRect argument for drawing a circle or ellipse within that rectangle's imaginary outline. So, because a TShape object is also a TRect object, you can pass either type of object to Ellipse.

The rest of the sample TESTRUB program should be familiar. The program's main window class, however, is derived from TRubberWin rather than the usual TFrameWin. The TRubberWin constructor calls its base class constructors (including, as always, the virtual base class TWindow constructor), assigns the menu resource identified by ID_MENU, and creates a few shapes, storing coordinate values in the shapes array. This isn't necessarily the best way to create and store graphical shapes—a more sophisticated drawing program could use a container class. (An example container appears later in this chapter.)

> **TIP**
>
> Study how TMainWin's constructor uses TShape and TSize classes. The expression r += s in the for loop adjusts the coordinates in a TShape object (remember, TShape is derived from TRect) by the amounts specified in TSize. Adding TSize objects to TRect objects is a good way to move a rectangle to another relative location. Many similar calculations involving TRect, TPoint, and TSize objects are possible.

Skip down to the TMainWin class's Paint function—it simply calls the Draw function for each TShape object stored in the shapes array. A simple Paint function is usually desirable. Rather than draw shapes directly in Paint, as I did in earlier listings, here *the objects literally draw themselves.* Remember also, if a shape is selected, it is drawn in light cyan; otherwise it is filled with white. Paint doesn't *decide* which way to draw the objects. The objects do that on their own, a good example of how object-oriented programming simplifies the code. TMainWin's simple Paint function can draw a thousand shapes as easily as four.

Now, skip back to function OutlineSelect, where the test program's most interesting code resides. This function is called as a result of the TDragWin and TRubberWin implementations of clicking and dragging, and also rubberbanding. When you release the mouse button, OutlineSelect receives a rectangle, outline, indicating the rubberband's final location and size. It's a simple matter to use this outline to discover whether it surrounds any shapes on display in the window. If the outline is empty, TRect's IsEmpty returns true, and nothing is selected. If the outline is not empty, then function Contains determines whether a shape is inside the outline, setting the shape's selected flag true or false accordingly.

These actions change the conditions of the program's shapes, necessitating an update event. OutlineSelect therefore ends by invalidating the window, passing FALSE as an argument so the window is not first erased. (The shapes don't move, so erasing the window isn't necessary.) This action causes Windows to issue a WM_PAINT message, in turn causing Paint to redraw the sample shapes, and also changing their colors to show which are selected. Notice that there is no code to "turn off" deselected objects. The same selection programming selects and deselects objects.

> **TIP**
>
> In general, to test whether one rectangle is inside another, use programming such as:
>
> TRect a, b;
> //...
> if (a.Contains(b)) { }
>
> The expression a.Contains(b) works like it sounds. It's true only if rectangle a completely surrounds rectangle b. You can also pass TPoint objects to Contains to determine whether a single coordinate is inside a rectangle. Another related function, Touches, returns true if any part of one rectangle touches another. These functions have obvious value in games, where objects "hit" others, requiring a reaction of some kind. They also have value in serious applications, however, as demonstrated by the rubberband program.

Background Animations

Finally in this chapter, is an animation that is admittedly frivolous, but introduces the important technique of running background tasks. The method uses a timer to call a function periodically, a simple technique that works in all versions of Windows. Though used here to animate a window's graphics, you can use similar programming for other jobs—printing in the background, for example, sorting a big file, or performing a lengthy search of a database. Listings 7.15 (POLYFLOW.RH), 7.16 (POLYFLOW.H), 7.17 (POLYFLOW.RC), and 7.18 (POLYFLOW.CPP) display the window illustrated in Figure 7.4. (Black-and-white doesn't do justice to the program's colorful display.) Compile and run POLYFLOW (load its IDE project file), then partially cover its window with another. As you can see, the animation continues to run in the background while you perform other tasks. (As a test, I ran POLYFLOW in the background all day while I wrote portions of this chapter.) You can also start multiple instances of the program.

Listing 7.15. POLYFLOW.RH.

```
// polyflow.rh -- Resource header file

#define ID_MENU    100      // Menu resource identifier
```

FIGURE 7.4.

Sample output from
POLYFLOW.

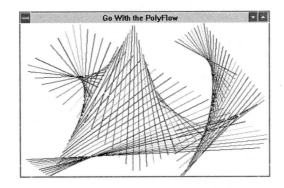

Listing 7.16. POLYFLOW.H.

```
// polyflow.h -- Header file for polyflow.cpp

#define TIMER_ID 1        // Any integer will do
#define TIMER_RATE 10     // Frequency in milliseconds (approx)
#define NUM_SHAPES 100    // Number of shapes
```

Listing 7.17. POLYFLOW.RC.

```
#include <owl\window.rh>
#include "polyflow.rh"

ID_MENU MENU
BEGIN
  POPUP "&Demo"
  BEGIN
    MENUITEM "E&xit", CM_EXIT
  END
END
```

Listing 7.18. POLYFLOW.CPP.

```
/* ============================================================ *\
** polyflow.cpp -- Timer-controlled graphics demonstration   **
** ============================================================ **
**                                                            **
** ============================================================ **
```

continues

Listing 7.18. continued

```
**      Copyright (c) 1994 by Tom Swan. All rights reserved.      **
\* ============================================================ */

#include <owl\applicat.h>
#include <owl\framewin.h>
#include <owl\dc.h>
#include <owl\gdiobjec.h>
#include <owl\color.h>
#include <classlib\arrays.h>
#include <stdlib.h>
#pragma hdrstop
#include "polyflow.h"
#include "polyflow.rh"

// Returns -1 if n is negative, else +1
inline int sign(int n)
{
  return (n < 0) ? -1 : 1;
}

// ============================================================
// TShape base class
// ============================================================

class TShape {
public:
  TShape();
  void SetParameters(TDC& dc, TRect& rect);
  void Draw(TDC& dc);
  int operator ==(const TShape& shape) const;
protected:
  void NewColor(TDC& dc);
  void NewCoord(int &c, int &delta, int max);
  void DrawShape(TDC& dc);
  BOOL IsValid() { return p1.x != -1; }  // True if shape valid
private:
  TColor color;            // Shape pen color
  TPoint p1, p2;           // Shape coordinates
  TSize delta1, delta2;    // Changes in p1, p2 respectively
};

// Constructor
TShape::TShape()
  : p1(-1, 0),             // Initialize p1 ("shape is not valid")
    p2( 0, 0),             // Initialize p2
    delta1(4, 10),         // Arbitrary values--change if you want
    delta2(3,  9)          // Arbitrary values--change if you want
{
}
```

```
// Modify shape coordinates and color
void
TShape::SetParameters(TDC& dc, TRect& rect)
{
  NewCoord(p1.x, delta1.cx, rect.right);
  NewCoord(p1.y, delta1.cy, rect.bottom);
  NewCoord(p2.x, delta2.cx, rect.right);
  NewCoord(p2.y, delta2.cy, rect.bottom);
  NewColor(dc);
}

// Nonvirtual function draws any shape
void TShape::Draw(TDC& dc)
{
  TPen pen(color);                        // Construct pen
  dc.SelectObject(pen);                   // Select pen into dc
  int iOldROP = dc.SetROP2(R2_XORPEN);    // Set drawing mode
  if (IsValid())                          // If shape is valid,
    DrawShape(dc);                        //   draw it.
  dc.RestorePen();                        // Restore dc's pen
  dc.SetROP2(iOldROP);                    // Restore drawing mode
}

// Implement == operator required by TIArrayAsVector container
// Notice that parameter shape is const (it can't be changed)
// and that the function is const (it doesn't change the
// object for which it is called).
int
TShape::operator ==(const TShape& shape) const
{
  return (this == &shape);
}

// Select a shape color not equal to the background
void
TShape::NewColor(TDC& dc)
{
  do {
    color = dc.GetNearestColor(
      TColor(random(256), random(256), random(256)));
  } while (color == dc.GetBkColor());
}

// Select shape coordinates
void
TShape::NewCoord(int &c, int &delta, int max)
{
  int t = c + delta;
  if ((t < 0) || (t > max))
```

continues

271

Listing 7.18. continued

```
    delta = sign(-delta) * (3 + random(12));
  else
    c = t;
}

// Draw the shape (line, rectangle, or whatever you want)
void
TShape::DrawShape(TDC& dc)
{
  dc.MoveTo(p1);
  dc.LineTo(p2);
}


// ============================================================
// The application's main window
// ============================================================

class TFlowWin: public TFrameWindow {
  TIArrayAsVector<TShape> shapes;  // Array of TShape pointers
  int index;        // shapes array index
  BOOL erasing;     // True if erasing old shapes
public:
  TFlowWin(TWindow* parent, const char far* title);
  ~TFlowWin();
  virtual void SetupWindow();
  virtual void Paint(TDC& dc, BOOL erase, TRect& rect);
protected:
  void GetWindowClass(WNDCLASS &wndClass);
  void EvSize(UINT sizeType, TSize& size);
  void EvTimer(UINT timerId);
DECLARE_RESPONSE_TABLE(TFlowWin);
};

DEFINE_RESPONSE_TABLE1(TFlowWin, TFrameWindow)
  EV_WM_SIZE,
  EV_WM_TIMER,
END_RESPONSE_TABLE;

// Constructor
TFlowWin::TFlowWin(TWindow* parent, const char far* title)
  : TFrameWindow(parent, title),
    TWindow(parent, title),
    shapes(NUM_SHAPES)
{
  AssignMenu(ID_MENU);
  for (int i = 0; i < NUM_SHAPES; ++i)
    shapes[i] = 0;
}
```

```
// Destructor
// Halts timer if set
TFlowWin::~TFlowWin()
{
  KillTimer(TIMER_ID);   // Stop sending WM_TIMER messages
}

// Initialize timer to send WM_TIMER messages to window
void
TFlowWin::SetupWindow()
{
  TFrameWindow::SetupWindow();
  SetTimer(TIMER_ID, TIMER_RATE);
}

// Force window to use a black background
void
TFlowWin::GetWindowClass(WNDCLASS& wndClass)
{
  TFrameWindow::GetWindowClass(wndClass);
  wndClass.hbrBackground = (HBRUSH)::GetStockObject(BLACK_BRUSH);
}

// Respond to changes in the window's size
void
TFlowWin::EvSize(UINT sizeType, TSize& size)
{
  TFrameWindow::EvSize(sizeType, size); // Default actions
  shapes.Flush();                       // Destroy old shape objects
  index = 0;                            // Initialize array index
  erasing = FALSE;                      // Not erasing old shapes yet
  for (int i = 0; i < NUM_SHAPES; ++i)  // Construct TShape objects,
    shapes[i] = new TShape();           //   and insert into array
  Invalidate();                         // Generate WM_PAINT message
  UpdateWindow();                       // Update window NOW!
}

// Animate graphics in response to a timer event
void
TFlowWin::EvTimer(UINT /*timerId*/)
{
  TRect cr;               // Client area dimensions
  TClientDC cdc(*this);   // Client area device context

  if (IsIconic()) return; // Exit if window is iconic
  GetClientRect(cr);        // Get client area dimensions
  for (int i = 0; i < 10; i++) {  // Loop ten times for extra speed
    int oldIndex = index++;       // Save current index for erasing
    if (index >= NUM_SHAPES) {    // If index is past end of array,
```

continues

273

Listing 7.18. continued

```
        index = 0;                      //  reset index to beginning, and
        erasing = TRUE;                 //  start erasing old shapes
    }
    if (erasing)                        // If erasing old shapes,
      shapes[index]->Draw(cdc);         //  then erase it.
    *shapes[index] = *shapes[oldIndex];       // Copy current shape
    shapes[index]->SetParameters(cdc, cr);    // Animate new shape
    shapes[index]->Draw(cdc);                 // Draw new shape
  }
}

// Repaint window contents as needed
void
TFlowWin::Paint(TDC& dc, BOOL /*erase*/, TRect& /*rect*/)
{
  for (int i = 0; i < NUM_SHAPES; i++)
    shapes[i]->Draw(dc);
}


// ================================================================
// The application class
// ================================================================

class TFlowApp: public TApplication {
public:
  TFlowApp(const char far* name)
    : TApplication(name) {};
  void InitMainWindow();
};

// Initialize the program's main window
void
TFlowApp::InitMainWindow()
{
  MainWindow = new TFlowWin(0, "Go With the Polyflow");
}

#pragma argsused

// Main program
int
OwlMain(int argc, char* argv[])
{
  TFlowApp app("PolyFlow");
  return app.Run();
}
```

Most of POLYFLOW's statements should be familiar—you've seen many of the techniques in one form or another in other listings. I'll describe only new items here. Comments in the listing help explain the other parts not discussed here.

POLYFLOW uses a TShape class to store the coordinates and color of each line drawn in the window. To draw other shapes, modify the class's DrawShape function. For example, to use rectangles for the animation, change DrawShape's two statements to:

```
dc.Rectangle(p1, p2);
```

The two TPoint objects, p1 and p2, keep track of each shape's starting and ending coordinates. Many shapes—rectangles, ellipses, circles, and even triangles—can be defined by only two TPoint values (or a single value of type TRect).

The program's main window class, TFlowWin, stores pointers to TShape objects in an array, using the TIArrayAsVector template from Borland's container class library. The array, named shapes, is declared as

```
TIArrayAsVector<TShape> shapes;
```

That may seem to be an odd construction if this is your first introduction to templates. (My forthcoming book, *Mastering Borland C++ 4* introduces C++ templates.) The TIArrayAsVector class can store pointers to objects of any class type. Here, the expression <TShape>, creates a real class from the template that can store pointers to TShape objects. Templates are like schematics that the compiler uses to create a real class. That class's name, in this example, is TIArrayAsVector<TShape>.

TIArrayAsVector and other class library templates require that objects can be compared in expressions. For this reason, you must define an operator== function in your class, or the program will not compile. TShape satisfies this rule by declaring:

```
int operator ==(const TShape& shape) const;
```

The overloaded operator function is implemented as

```
int
TShape::operator ==(const TShape& shape) const
{
  return (this == &shape);
}
```

The simplest way to implement this function in another class is to replace each instance of TShape with the class name. As written here, the function assumes that two objects are equivalent if they have the same address. Two distinct objects are considered to be different even if they have identical values. If that doesn't make sense in your application, you'll have to write an `operator==` function that returns true for whatever condition means "these two objects are the same."

The `shapes` array is initialized in the class constructor's declaration (above the opening function brace) using the statement:

```
shapes(NUM_SHAPES)
```

Because the container is *indirect* (a fact indicated by the "I" in `TIArrayAsVector`), it stores *pointers* to objects, not the objects themselves. Constructing the container as shown here creates an empty vessel of pointers. It is still necessary to create the objects and store their addresses in the array. POLYFLOW does that in a `EvSize` response function, causing a new animation to begin when the window size changes (and when it is created for the first time). This deletes any objects in the container:

```
shapes.Flush();
```

This constructs new `TShape` objects and stores their addresses in the `shapes` array:

```
shapes[i] = new TShape();
```

`Paint` uses similar programming to draw each shape stored in the container:

```
for (int i = 0; i < NUM_SHAPES; i++)
  shapes[i]->Draw(dc);
```

POLYFLOW's animation is controlled by a Windows timer, initialized in function `SetupWindow` in the `TFlowWin` class. Setting a timer requires using a window handle, so `SetupWindow` is the right location for the job. Never set a timer for a `TWindow` object in a constructor, in which `HWindow` is not yet initialized. In this case, `SetupWindow` creates a timer with the statement:

```
SetTimer(TIMER_ID, TIMER_RATE);
```

The ID value is just for convenience so the program can refer to this same timer later on. In POLYFLOW, `TIMER_ID` equals 1, but it could be another integer. `TIMER_RATE` is in milliseconds, equal to 10 in this program, or about 0.01 second. The maximum rate is 65,535 milliseconds—about one minute plus change.

After the program calls `SetTimer`, Windows begins issuing `WM_TIMER` messages at the specified frequency. POLYFLOW intercepts these messages with a response function, `EvTimer`, in the `TFlowWin` class. The class also inserts the message-cracking macro `EV_WM_TIMER` in a response table. To stop the timer, the `TFlowWin` destructor calls `KillTimer`, passing `TIMER_ID` as an argument. You can set and kill timers at other places in a class, except as I mentioned, in a `TWindow` or derived class constructor.

Function `EvTimer` is called when the window receives a `WM_TIMER` message. Because this happens even when another application's window is active, POLYFLOW continues to run in the background no matter what else is going on. Some critical operations, however, such as disk accesses and window dragging temporarily stop background processing implemented using timers.

`EvTimer` calls the `TWindow` function, `IsIconic`, which returns true if the window is minimized as an icon on the desktop. It's possible to draw into iconic windows, though most applications don't need to do that. If you want to draw inside an icon, obtain its client area dimensions with the statement:

```
Parent->GetClientRect(tr);
```

The programming in `EvTimer` is straightforward. To keep the animation running reasonably fast, but not interfere too much with other background and foreground processes, a `for` loop displays 10 shapes for each timer event.

> **TIP**
>
> Keep this trick in mind for other background processing tasks—it's usually faster to execute 10 statements every second (giving the program a kind of super burst at regular intervals) than it is to create a timer that goes off every tenth of a second.

Looking Ahead

As I mentioned several times, writing graphics programs is a great way to learn Windows programming techniques. Even if you plan to write business software, you'll find many uses for graphics objects such as icons, cursors, and bitmaps, introduced in the next chapter.

8

CHAPTER

Managing Icons, Cursors, and Bitmaps

Icons, cursors, and bitmaps play well known roles in Windows software. Icons identify programs and files. Cursors show the mouse location. Bitmaps serve many needs, from providing window backgrounds to painting custom button faces. No matter what kind of programs you write, you'll find numerous uses for one or more of these graphical objects.

In this chapter, you learn:

- How to use the TIcon class.
- How to use the TCursor class.
- How to assign a cursor to a window.
- How to use the TBitmap class.
- How to create, use, and display bitmap resources and .BMP files.
- How to write a Paint-style program that draws into an offscreen bitmap.

Icons

It takes skillful imagination to design good-looking icons in a space no bigger than a postage stamp. Fortunately, though, you don't have to be Picasso to add good-looking icons to your programs. Thousands of icon images are available for purchase or in public-domain libraries posted on bulletin boards and networks. It's easy to incorporate icons of many kinds into your programs, whether you draw them yourself or extract them from an icon library.

System Icons

Every Windows program should have a unique system icon, displayed when you minimize the program's window on the desktop. Start by creating an icon with Resource Workshop (RW). You can draw a new icon or open an icon file ending in .ICO. You can also open .EXE or .DLL files with RW and extract any icons stored as resources in those files.

Name your icon resource (I use an integer symbol such as ID_ICON) and save the image to disk. You can save icons directly in resource script files ending in .RC, but I prefer to store icons separately. I then insert a command in the resource script to load the icon as a resource:

```
ID_ICON ICON "myicon.ico"
```

Resource Workshop enters a similar command into the resource script if, while editing a program's resource project, you create and save an icon to a .ICO file. To identify the icon as the program's system icon, insert the following statement into the application class's InitMainWindow function after constructing the main window object:

```
MainWindow->SetIcon(this, ID_ICON);
```

The this argument refers to the TApplication object for the module in which the icon resource is stored (that is, the program's .EXE code file). SetIcon is inherited from TFrameWindow.

TIP

To tell whether a window is minimized, you can call the TWindow BOOL function IsIconic. If the function returns true, the window is currently displayed as the icon selected by SetIcon.

TIcon Class

Except for system icons, which are managed more or less automatically, it's best to represent general-purpose icons as objects of the TIcon class. The class provides a consistent interface for icon images that you can initialize in a variety of ways—from a .ICO file, for example, as a resource, or as a collection of bits constructed by a program operation. Derived from TGdiBase, the TIcon class is declared in GDIOBJEC.H. (TGdiObject is derived from TGdiBase, which provides fundamental functions and data for all GDI objects.) Any program that uses TIcon must include this header file:

```
#include <owl\gdiobjec.h>
```

Create a TIcon object in one of several ways. The most common method is to load an icon image from a file, usually ending in .ICO, but you can use the same method with .EXE and .DLL files that contain icon resources. To load an icon image from a file, create a TIcon object this way:

```
TIcon icon(GetApplicationObject()->GetInstance(),
  "MYICON.ICO", 0);
```

The first argument specifies the application's instance handle, needed by Windows to associate icons with the modules that create them. The second argument is the file that contains one or more icon images—it can be a code file (.EXE), a dynamic link library (.DLL), or an icon file (.ICO). The third argument specifies the icon's index for files that store multiple icons. An index value of 0 refers to the first icon in a file; 1 refers to the second icon; 2 to the third, and so on.

Constructing a TIcon object from a file calls the Windows 3.1 ExtractIcon function. It's probably best to construct TIcon objects rather than call this function directly, but you can use it as follows to determine how many icons are in a file:

```
int nIcons = (int)::ExtractIcon(
  GetApplicationObject()->GetInstance(), (LPSTR)"MYICON.ICO", -1);
```

An index value of -1 causes the function to return the number of icons in the specified file, but doesn't load those icons into memory. You can't use this same technique with the TIcon class—you must call the global API function directly as shown. Because the function returns an icon handle of type HICON, its result must be cast to int.

memory model. If you dislike having to cast literal strings as much as I do, compile your programs with the large model so that all pointers are far by default. If you do that, you can delete the (LPSTR) cast.

You can also construct a TIcon object from an icon resource, named either with a string or an integer. You can specify resource names directly:

```
HINSTANCE hInstance = GetApplicationObject()->GetInstance();
TIcon icon1(hInstance, "ICONNAME");
TIcon icon2(hInstance, ICON_ID);
```

Or, you can construct resource identifier objects, and pass them to the TIcon constructor:

```
TResID iconID("ICONNAME");
TIcon icon3(hInstance, iconID);
```

If you already have an icon handle of type HICON, construct a TIcon object like this:

```
TIcon icon(iconHandle);
```

It is your responsibility to delete the Windows icon element associated with the TIcon object, usually by calling DeleteObject. If you want the TIcon class to delete the icon element automatically, construct the object like this:

```
TIcon icon(iconHandle, TDC::AutoDelete);
```

You must include the DC.H header file to use the TAutoDelete enumerated constant AutoDelete declared in the TDC class.

You can also construct TIcon objects from other TIcon objects:

```
TIcon iconDup(hInstance, icon);
```

And, finally, you can construct a TIcon object "the hard way," by specifying its size and bitmap components:

```
TSize size;  // Size of icon image
int planes;  // Number of bitmap color planes
int bitsPixel;  // Number of bits per pixel
const void far * andBits;  // Pointer to AND mask
const void far * xorBits;  // Pointer to XOR mask
// ... initialize preceding variables, then ...
TIcon icon(hInstance,
  size, planes, bitsPixel, andBits, xorBits);
```

It's up to you to specify each component correctly. Windows uses the AND mask (addressed by andBits) to "punch a hole" in the display, leaving a blank space into which the icon's foreground image (the XOR mask addressed by xorBits) is dropped. The two-step display process makes the icon appear to float on top of the background.

The TIcon class contains no callable member functions. It defines an operator of type HICON, however, making it possible to pass TIcon objects to any function that requires an icon handle argument. Use the operator to extract an icon handle from any TIcon object:

```
TIcon icon(hInstance, "MYICONS.ICO", 4);
HICON iconHandle = (HICON)icon;  // Get icon handle from object
```

Related Icon Functions

To draw an icon, call TDC's DrawIcon functions. There are two overloaded varieties:

```
BOOL DrawIcon(int x, int y, const TIcon& icon);
BOOL DrawIcon(const TPoint& point, const TIcon& icon);
```

Use the first DrawIcon to paint an icon image at a specified coordinate. Use the second with coordinate values stored in a TPoint object. For example, a Paint function might call DrawIcon like this:

```
dc.DrawIcon(10, 50, icon);
```

Or, you can define a TPoint object and pass it to DrawIcon:

```
TPoint location(10, 50);
dc.DrawIcon(location, icon);
```

You aren't limited to drawing icons in a Paint function. Use a TWindowDC device-context object to draw icons anywhere in a window, not only inside its client area. In any function of a class derived from TWindow, use statements such as:

```
TWindowDC dc(*this);
dc.DrawIcon(0, 100, icon);
```

Use device-context objects of types TClientDC, TWindowDC, TDesktopDC, and so on to draw icons at various locations.

Cursors

Cursors differ from icons in two ways: they always use monochrome bitmaps, and they define a *hot spot* for identifying one pixel inside a cursor as the location of the mouse. (The tip of an arrow pointer, for example, is its hot spot.)

Window Cursors

Like icons, cursors may be stored in separate files, usually ending in .CUR, and are most easily created using Resource Workshop. Because cursors are always monochrome images, their bitmaps don't take up much room, and you can also store them directly in .RC resource script files.

Cursors are commonly associated with a program's windows. When the mouse pointer moves over the window's client area, the cursor changes shape, indicating that a specific operation is available, perhaps by clicking the mouse button. (Using the popular lingo, you might say the cursor *morphs*.) Moving the mouse pointer over a menu item or a scroller changes the cursor back to the familiar arrow, suggesting that clicking the mouse button performs a system task. Well-designed cursors that automatically morph into different shapes can provide valuable feedback that, in the hands of expert users, can help make programs easier to use. But don't overdo the feature. Too many different cursors might be more confusing than helpful.

To assign a cursor to a window, call the window object's SetCursor function, inherited from TWindow. For example, add this statement to your application class's InitMainWindow function:

```
MainWindow->SetCursor(this, ID_CURSOR);
```

As usual, you can specify an integer resource identifier (ID_CURSOR), or you can name your resource using a string:

```
MainWindow->SetCursor(this, "CursorName");
```

You can also call SetCursor in a SetupWindow function, or at any time after constructing the window object. When the mouse pointer moves over the window's client area, the cursor shape automatically changes. This same technique works for *all* kinds of windows—including buttons, child windows, and main windows.

TIP

Internally, the SetCursor function uses an interesting technique to determine whether a coordinate (a cursor's hot spot, for example) is inside a window's client area. You might use the same method to detect any object's presence in a window. Given a TPoint object p that specifies the target coordinate, the following if statement calls a function doSomething() (or it could perform another action) if that point is inside the window's client area:

```
if (GetClientRect().Contains(p))
  doSomething();
```

TCursor Class

Except for self-adjusting window cursors, for more general purpose uses, it's best to represent cursors as objects of the TCursor class, derived from TGdiObject. TCursor objects are constructed using statements similar to those explained for the TIcon class. To construct a TCursor object from a resource, use the statement:

```
TCursor cursor(hInstance, ID_CURSOR);
```

You can also construct a cursor from another TCursor object:

```
TCursor dup(hInstance, cursor);
```

Or, you can use a Windows cursor handle of type HCURSOR (perhaps returned by another function) to construct a TCursor object:

```
TCursor cursor(cursorHandle);
```

Add a second argument if you want the object to delete the cursor element stored by Windows when the cursor object is deleted or goes out of scope:

```
TCursor cursor(cursorHandle, TDC::AutoDelete);
```

As with the TIcon class, you can also construct cursor objects the hard way, specifying their individual components. The process is nearly the same as it is for TIcon, but uses an additional TPoint argument to designate the cursor's hot spot, relative to the image's upper-left corner. Also, because cursors are always monochrome bitmaps, the constructor doesn't require color plane and bits-per-pixel values:

```
TSize size;  // Size of cursor image
TPoint hotSpot;  // Relative hotspot coordinate
const void far * andBits;  // Pointer to AND mask
const void far * xorBits;  // Pointer to XOR mask
// ... initialize preceding variables, then ...
TCursor cursor(hInstance,
  hotSpot, size, , andBits, xorBits);
```

Bitmaps

Bitmaps are general-purpose images that can range from simple monochrome pictures to multicolor works of art. Bitmaps come in an overwhelming variety of internal formats, sizes, and color values. But just figuring out how to load a bitmap file into memory has tried the patience of countless Windows programmers.

Lucky for us, with the TBitmap and TDib classes, using bitmaps has never been easier. All of the complexity of recognizing bitmap formats is encapsulated in classes—all you have to do is learn a few tricks for creating and using bitmap objects. The objects all work the same regardless of the bitmap's internal format.

285

This section introduces bitmap classes, and explains the difference between *device-dependent* and *device-independent* bitmaps. I also show how to load and display bitmap files and resources. Finally, I explain the useful, but not well documented, technique of drawing into an offscreen bitmap.

Device-Independent and -Dependent Bitmaps

A *device-independent bitmap* (DIB) is exactly what its name implies. It's an image that is stored in a device-independent manner. Any Windows display device that supports bitmaps can display DIBs. The final outcome might look best on the same devices that were used to create the original image, but when an icon is stored in DIB form, its image may be sent to any compatible device.

A *device-dependent bitmap* (DDB) is also exactly what it seems—an image that can be used *only* by a specific device. Obviously, storing a bitmap in DDB form limits the image's use to a specific hardware, and therefore, DDBs are not recommended for keeping bitmaps on disk.

Which bitmap format is the right one to use? For most uses, bitmap files are best stored in DIB (device-independent) form. To use a bitmap, a program can read the DIB image from disk and convert it to a DDB (device-dependent) image in memory. That image is then ready for use. It's okay to store device-dependent bitmaps in memory because the system's display isn't likely to change while the program is running. On disk, however, bitmaps are best stored in DIB form so they can be shown on different displays and used with other output devices that support bitmaps.

> ### TIP
>
> The internal formats of device-dependent bitmaps (DDBs) depend on the current output device, and for that reason, DDBs typically display faster than their DIB equivalents. For the best output speed, it's usually best to convert DDBs into DDBs for temporary in-memory storage.

TDib and *TBitmap* Classes

Use the TDib class for device-independent bitmaps (DIBs), as stored, for example, in disk files ending in .BMP. Use the TBitmap class for in-memory device-dependent bitmaps (DDBs). The TDib class is also useful for bitmaps created with Resource Workshop and stored as resources in the module's code file.

TDib is derived from TGdiBase, while TBitmap is derived from TGdiObject. Because of this relationship—that is, because the two classes have the same ultimate parent in TGdiBase—they are called *siblings*. TDib and TBitmap are not otherwise related. (If TDib were derived from TGdiObject, then TDib and TBitmap would be true siblings. Borland probably could have organized the classes this way, but for unexplained reasons, didn't.)

Most of the time, you'll take a two-step approach to loading and using a bitmap image. First, construct a TDib object from a device-independent bitmap. You might, for example, load a .BMP file from disk:

```
TDib dib("MYBITS.BMP");
```

Object dib now refers to the DIB image loaded in memory. Because the object's bitmap image is in device-independent form, it can't be used directly with an output device. To make that possible, convert the dib object to device-dependent form, using the TBitmap class:

```
TBitmap bitmap(dib);
```

You can now display, shrink, stretch, and perform other operations on the bitmap object. These steps are all you need to load and use any .BMP file.

> **NOTE**
>
> The TDib class also recognizes old-style *PM bitmaps,* also called *core bitmaps,* from OS/2. (PM stands for *Presentation Manager,* OS/2's graphical user interface.) Windows programs should use the superior DIB format supported by the TDib class. To convert a PM bitmap to a DIB image, load it into the Paintbrush utility and save the image to a .BMP file.

There are several other ways to create TDib and TBitmap objects. You can construct a TDib object from a resource:

```
HINSTANCE hInstance = GetApplicationObject()->GetInstance();
TDib dib(hInstance, ICON_ID);
```

As usual, you can specify an integer resource identifier such as ICON_ID (my preferred method), or you can use a string to name your resources. You can also create a TDib object from a TBitmap. If bitmap is a TBitmap object, this initializes a TDib object dib with the device-dependent image:

```
TDib dib(bitmap);
```

To attach a different color palette to the bitmap, add a TPalette argument to the preceding statement:

```
LOGPALETTE* lpal;
// ... initialize lpal, then...
TPalette myPalette(lpal);
TDib dib(bitmap, myPalette);
```

Or, you can construct a TDib object from another object of the same type:

```
TDib clone(dib);
```

To create a fresh TDib, specify its width, height, number of colors, and optional mode:

```
TDib dib(width, height, ncolors, mode);
```

The first three arguments are type int; the last is a WORD. If you don't specify a mode, it defaults to DIB_RGB_COLORS, a Windows constant that indicates the bitmap color table contains literal RGB (red, green, blue) color values of type COLORREF. Set mode to DIB_PAL_COLORS to indicate that the bitmap's color table contains 16-bit index values into a device-context's realized color palette.

If you happen to have a global handle of type HGLOBAL to a DIB, you can construct a TDib object with the statement:

```
TDib dib(hglobal);
```

As with many other classes, when constructing objects from existing elements that were created by other processes, it is your responsibility (or that of the other process) to delete the element. If you want the TDib class to delete the associated element when the object is deleted or goes out of scope, add a second argument:

```
TDib dib(hglobal, TDC::AutoDelete);
```

You can also construct a TDib object from data stored in the clipboard. Given a TClipboard object named clipboard, you can extract a bitmap with:

```
TDib dib(clipboard);
```

TDib Member Functions

There are a number of TDib member functions you can use to access and change information in a device-independent bitmap. Call the Width and Height functions to determine a DIB's size. If more convenient, call Size to obtain a TSize object with that same information. You can assign the returned object to a TSize variable such as size in the following example:

```
int width = dib.Width();    // Obtain width
int height = dib.Height();  // and height,
TSize size = dib.Size();    // or get a TSize object
```

Call NumColors for a long integer value that indicates how many colors the bitmap uses. Call NumScans for an int value equal to the number of scan lines—that is, pixel rows.

These and other functions are mostly intuitive. TDib also has several functions for working with a bitmap's color table. GetColor returns a color table entry that you can use to initialize a TColor object:

```
TColor color = dib.GetColor(5);
```

SetColor inserts a new color into the bitmap's color table. In the following, I specify a static TColor value, LtCyan, indexed with 6:

```
dib.SetColor(6, TColor::LtCyan);
```

To find a specific color's index in a bitmap, call FindColor like this:

```
int colorIndex = dib.FindColor(TColor::LtBlue);
if (colorIndex == -1) ColorNotFound();
```

FindColor returns -1 if it can't find the specified color (static LtBlue in the sample) in the bitmap's color table.

TBitmap Member Functions

Like TDib, the TBitmap class sports several member functions that you can use to access and change device-dependent bitmaps. Start by constructing a TBitmap object, perhaps after loading a TDib device-independent bitmap from disk:

```
TDib* dib = new TDib("MONALISA.BMP");
TBitmap bitmap(dib);
delete dib;
```

The sample code first loads a bitmap file such as MONALISA.BMP (or any other .BMP file) into a dynamically allocated TDib object addressed by a pointer, dib. That object is then used to create a device-dependent bitmap object, named bitmap, of type TBitmap. After that step, the original device-independent image addressed by dib is no longer needed, so I delete dib. The image is available in bitmap. You could, however, keep both the independent and dependent images if necessary.

Whatever method you use to construct a TBitmap object, you can call its Width and Height functions for the bitmap's dimensions:

```
int width = bitmap.Width();
int height = bitmap.Height();
```

The Width and Height functions in TBitmap have the same names as the similar functions in the TDib class, but are otherwise unrelated. (Remember: TBitmap and TDib are siblings—one is not a derivative of the other.) You can use Width and Height to display bitmaps and to adjust scrollers that display large bitmaps. (Sample programs that show these techniques come later in the chapter.) You can also fill a TSize object with a bitmap's dimensions:

```
TSize size;
bitmap.GetBitmapDimension(size);
```

Unfortunately, TBitmap doesn't have a Size function as found in TDib. (In a perfect world, TBitmap and TDib member functions would be more compatible.) To determine the number of color planes and bits per pixel used by a TBitmap object, call these functions:

```
BYTE numPlanes = bitmap.Planes();
BYTE bitsPerPixel = bitmap.BitsPixel();
```

For a copy of a bitmap's bits, call GetBitmapBits, which returns a DWORD value that represents the number of bytes in the bitmap. If this value equals the number of bytes requested, the function was successful; otherwise, something went wrong with the operation:

```
DWORD size;
void far* bp;
// ... initialize size and bp, then ...
if (bitmap.GetBitmapBits(size, bp) != size)
  Error();
```

You can also copy bits to a bitmap, but remember, because a TBitmap object is in device-dependent form, assuming anything at all about the information in the object is dangerous. You might use the preceding code, however, to make a temporary copy of a bitmap, then use the following statements to restore the image:

```
// ... modify bits addressed by bp, then ...
if (bitmap.SetBitmapBits(size, bp) != size)
  Error();
```

> **NOTE**
>
> GetBitmapBits and SetBitmapBits in the TBitmap class call the global API functions of the same names. Refer to a Windows API reference for more information about these functions.

TDib and *TBitmap* Brushes

In an earlier chapter, you learned how to construct a TBrush object for painting graphics shapes. You can also construct a brush from a TDib or TBitmap object. For example, this fragment constructs two TBrush objects named brush1 and brush2, initialized from a bitmap stored in a disk file:

```
TDib dib("MYDIB.BMP");
TBitmap bitmap(dib);
TBrush brush1(dib);      // Construct brush from bitmap
TBrush brush2(bitmap);   // Same as above
```

You can then select brush1 or brush2 into a device context and draw a filled object using that brush as a background pattern.

TDib Color Palettes

Device-independent bitmaps have color tables that specify either RGB color values, or indexes into a realized color table. To extract a bitmap's color table, simply construct a TPalette object using a TDib object:

```
TDib dib("PICTURE.BMP");
TPalette dibColors(dib);
```

Those two statements load a device-independent bitmap file, PICTURE.BMP, and then use that information to construct a dib object. The second line extracts the bitmap's color-table into a TPalette object, dibColors. If you make any changes to the palette, you can construct a new bitmap object using the updated colors:

```
TDib newDib(dib, dibColors);
```

TDib File Handling

With the TDib class, bitmap file handling is almost too easy to believe. As you have seen, simply constructing a TDib object with a filename loads any .BMP file into memory. Because bitmap files can be large, it's often best to allocate memory dynamically to a TDib object. TDib objects should probably not be created as automatic function variables or passed by value to function parameters. You might create global TDib objects, but if you do, you risk using a significant amount of the program's data space.

Avoid those problems by allocating memory for TDib objects using the new operator. The following, for example, loads a file named PICTURE.BMP into a TDib object addressed by a pointer, pdib:

```
TDib* pdib;  // Define pointer to a TDib object
pdib = new TDib("PICTURE.BMP");  // Construct object
```

You probably know this, but if the filename has any path information, be sure to double up on the directory separators (otherwise known as backslashes):

```
pdib = new TDib("C:\\MYDIR\\YOURDIR\\PICTURE.BMP");
```

> **NOTE**
>
> If I had a nickel for every time I forgot that a backslash is C's escape character for embedded control codes (such as "\n" for a newline and "\t" for a tab), turning strings like "c:\temp\name.bmp" into gibberish, I could have retired long before writing this book and you might not be reading these words. You might also try using forward slashes as in "c:/temp/name.bmp" though this trick might not work with other compilers and it might cause problems with third-party library functions that parse file pathnames.

You can also write any TDib object to disk, creating a new .BMP file or overwriting an existing one. (To preserve existing files, check whether the file exists *before* executing the following.) To write the TDib object addressed by pdib, use a statement such as:

```
if (!pdib->WriteFile("NEWFILE.BMP"))
  Error();
```

The TDib member function, WriteFile, returns a BOOL value that indicates whether it was successful. The Error() function represents any action you might take for an unsuccessful write.

In between the time you read a .BMP file into a TDib object and write that object to disk, you probably want to perform various operations on the bitmap image. OWL makes such operations no more difficult than drawing in a window. First, include the DC.H header file:

```
#include <owl\dc.h>
```

Then, using your TDib object, construct an object of type TDibDC:

```
TDibDC dibdc(*pdib);
```

This creates dibdc, a device context for a TDib, device-independent bitmap. This special device context (there's no equivalent in standard Windows programming) uses a device driver supplied with BC4, DIB.DRV, located in C:\BC4\BIN.

The great advantage of the TDibDC device-context class is that it lets you use all GDI drawing functions to manipulate device-independent bitmaps. For example, to draw a rectangle in a TDib object, you can write:

```
dibdc.Rectangle(10, 20, 100, 150);
```

Typically, you would do that while mimicking the same action for a `TPaintDC` object (in a `Paint` function, for example), or for a `TClientDC` object outside of `Paint`:

```
TClientDC clientdc(*this);
dibdc.Rectangle(10, 20, 100, 150);
clientdc.Rectangle(10, 20, 100, 150);
```

Drawing the image twice—once for each device context—saves in the device-independed bitmap a mirror image of the onscreen drawing. You can also save the object to disk, preserving the onscreen image, which can be reloaded at any time by constructing a new `TDib` object (perhaps as part of a program's undo capabilities):

```
dib->WriteFile("SAVE.BMP");
delete dib;
// ... time passes, then ...
dib = new TDib("SAVE.BMP");
```

The convenience of being able to call GDI functions to draw in device-independent bitmaps can't be overstated. In fact, with the `TDib` class's file-handling capabilities and the DIB.DRV driver, you have the raw materials for a Paint-type drawing program. Combined with a few more techniques for displaying bitmaps and working with offscreen images—subjects described next—you can manipulate bitmap images in any way you can imagine.

Bitmap Listings

This chapter ends with three sample programs that show the `TIcon`, `TCursor`, `TDib`, and `TBitmap` classes (and relatives) in action. The programs are:

- RESBIT: Demonstrates icon, cursor, and bitmap resources.
- SHOWBIT: Displays any bitmap file and shows how to use scrollers in bitmap windows.
- DRAWBIT: Shows how to draw into an offscreen bitmap, a technique used by Paint-style graphics programs.

To run the sample programs, switch to their directories (named the same as the programs), and open their .IDE project files with the *Project|Open project...* menu command. Press Ctrl+F9 to compile and run.

RESBIT (Bitmap Resources)

Listing 8.1, RESBIT.RH, defines resource identifiers for RESBIT's resource script, Listing 8.2, RESBIT.RC. The program's source file (listed later) also includes RESBIT.RH. The script file in Listing 8.2 demonstrates how to directly and indirectly specify icon, cursor, and bitmap resources.

Listing 8.1. RESBIT.RH.

```
// resbit.rh -- Resource header file

#define ID_MENU 100        // Menu resource identifier
#define ID_ICON 100        // Icon resource identifier
#define ID_BITMAP 100      // Bitmap resource identifier
#define ID_CURSOR 100      // Cursor resource identifier
```

Listing 8.2. RESBIT.RC.

```
#include <owl\window.rh>
#include "resbit.rh"

ID_MENU MENU
BEGIN
  POPUP "&Demo"
  BEGIN
    MENUITEM "E&xit", CM_EXIT
  END
END

ID_ICON ICON "resbit.ico"

ID_BITMAP BITMAP
BEGIN
  '42 4D 76 08 00 00 00 00 00 00 76 00 00 00 28 00'
  '00 00 40 00 00 00 40 00 00 00 01 00 04 00 00 00'
  '00 00 00 08 00 00 00 00 00 00 00 00 00 00 00 00'
  '00 00 10 00 00 00 00 00 00 00 00 00 80 00 00 80'
  '00 00 00 80 80 00 80 00 00 00 80 00 80 00 80 80'
  '00 00 80 80 80 00 C0 C0 C0 00 00 00 FF 00 00 FF'
  '00 00 00 FF FF 00 FF 00 00 00 FF 00 FF 00 FF FF'
  '00 00 FF FF FF 00 FF FF FF FF FF FF FF FF FF FF'
  'FF FF FF FF FF FF FF FF FF FF FF FF FF FF FF FF'
  'FF FF FF FF FF FF FF FF FF FF FF FF FF FF FF FF'
  'FF FF FF FF FF FF FF FF FF FF FF FF FF FF FF FF'
  'FF FF FF FF FF FF FF FF FF FF FF FF FF FF FF FF'
  'FF FF FF FF FF FF FF FF FF FF FF FF FF FF FF FF'
  'FF FF FF FF FF FF FF FF FF FF FF FF FF FF FF FF'
```

```
'FF FF FF FF FF FF FF FF FF FF FF FF FF FF FF FF'
'FF FF FF FF FF FF FF FF FF FF FF FF FF FF FF FF'
'FF FF FF FF FF FF FF FF FF FF FF FF FF FF FF FF'
'FF FF FF FF FF FF FF FF FF FF FF FF FF FF FF FF'
'FF FF FF FF FF FF FF FF FF FF FF FF FF FF FF FF'
'FF FF FF FF FF FF FF FF FF FF FF FF FF FF FF FF'
'FF FF FF FF FF 7F FF FF FF FF FF FF FF FF FF FF'
'FF FF FF FF FF FF FF FF FF FF FF FF FF FF FF FF'
'FF FF FF FF FF 77 FF FF FF FF FF FF FF FF FF FF'
'FF FF FF FF FF FF FF FF FF FF FF FF FF FF FF FF'
'FF FF FF FF F7 77 FF FF FF FF FF FF FF FF FF FF'
'FF FF FF FF FF FF FF FF FF FF FF FF FF FF FF FF'
'FF FF FF FF F7 77 FF FF FF FF FF FF FF FF FF FF'
'FF FF FF FF FF FF FF FF FF FF FF FF FF FF FF FF'
'FF FF FF FF F7 77 7F FF FF FF FF FF FF FF FF FF'
'FF FF FF FF FF FF FF FF FF FF FF FF FF FF FF FF'
'FF FF FF FF 7F 7F 7F FF FF FF FF FF FF FF FF FF'
'FF FF FF FF FF FF FF FF FF FF FF FF FF FF FF FF'
'FF FF FF FF 7F 7F 77 FF FF FF FF FF FF FF FF FF'
'FF FF FF FF FF FF FF FF FF FF FF FF FF FF FF FF'
'FF FF FF FF 7F 7F 77 FF FF FF FF FF FF FF FF FF'
'FF FF FF FF FF FF FF FF FF FF FF FF FF FF FF FF'
'FF FF FF FF 7F 7F 7F 7F FF FF FF FF FF FF FF FF'
'FF FF FF FF FF FF FF FF FF FF FF FF FF FF FF FF'
'FF FF FF F7 FF 7F F7 F7 FF FF FF FF FF FF FF FF'
'FF FF FF FF FF FF FF FF FF FF FF FF FF FF FF FF'
'FF FF FF F7 FF 7F F7 F7 FF FF FF FF FF FF FF FF'
'FF FF FF FF FF FF FF FF FF FF FF FF FF FF FF FF'
'FF FF FF F7 FF 7F F7 FF 7F FF FF FF FF FF FF FF'
'FF FF FF FF FF FF FF FF FF FF FF FF FF FF FF FF'
'FF FF FF 7F FF 7F F7 FF F7 FF FF FF FF FF FF FF'
'FF FF FF FF FF FF FF FF FF FF FF FF FF FF FF FF'
'FF FF FF 7F FF 7F F7 FF F7 FF FF FF FF FF FF FF'
'FF FF FF FF FF FF FF FF FF FF FF FF FF FF FF FF'
'FF FF FF 7F FF 7F FF 7F FF 7F FF FF FF FF FF FF'
'FF FF FF FF FF FF FF FF FF FF FF FF FF FF FF FF'
'FF FF F7 FF FF 7F FF 7F FF F7 FF FF FF FF FF FF'
'FF FF FF FF FF FF FF FF FF FF FF FF FF FF FF FF'
'FF FF F7 FF FF 7F FF 7F FF F7 FF FF FF FF FF FF'
'FF FF FF FF FF FF FF FF FF FF FF FF FF FF FF FF'
'FF FF F7 FF FF 7F FF 7F FF FF 7F FF FF FF FF FF'
'FF FF FF FF FF FF FF FF FF FF FF FF FF FF FF FF'
'FF FF F7 FF FF 7F FF 7F FF FF F7 FF FF FF FF FF'
'FF FF FF FF FF FF FF FF FF FF FF FF FF FF FF FF'
'FF FF 7F FF FF 7F FF F7 FF FF F7 FF FF FF FF FF'
'FF FF FF FF FF FF FF FF FF FF FF FF FF FF FF FF'
'FF FF 7A AA AA AA FF F7 FF 88 88 78 FF FF FF FF'
'FF FF FF FF FF FF FF FF FF FF FF FF FF FF FF FF'
'FF FA AA AA AA AA AA F7 88 88 88 88 88 FF FF FF'
'FF FF FF FF FF FF FF FF FF FF FF FF FF FF FF FF'
```

continues

295

Listing 8.2. continued

```
'FF AA AA AA AA AA AA 88 88 88 88 88 88 88 FF FF'
'FF FF FF FF FF FF FF FF FF FF FF FF FF FF FF FF'
'FA AA AA AA AA AA A8 88 88 88 88 88 88 88 8F FF'
'FF FF FF FF FF FF FF FF FF FF FF FF FF FF FF FF'
'AA AA AA AA AA AA A8 88 88 88 88 88 88 88 8F FF'
'FF FF FF FF FF FF FF FF FF FF FF FF FF FF FF FF'
'AA AA AA AA AA AA 88 88 88 88 88 88 88 88 88 FF'
'FF FF FF FF FF FF FF FF FF FF FF FF FF FF FF FA'
'AA AA AA AA AA AA 88 88 88 88 88 88 88 88 88 FF'
'FF FF FF FF FF FF FF FF FF FF FF FF FF FF FF FA'
'AA AA AA AA AA A8 88 88 88 88 88 88 88 88 88 8F'
'FF FF FF FF FF FF FF FF FF FF FF FF FF FF FF FA'
'AA AA AA AA AA A8 88 88 88 88 88 88 88 88 88 8F'
'FF FF FF FF FF FF FF FF FF FF FF FF FF FF FF FA'
'AA AA AA AA AA A8 88 88 88 88 88 88 88 88 88 8F'
'FF FF FF FF FF FF FF FF FF FF FF FF FF FF FF FA'
'AA AA AA AA AA A8 88 88 88 88 88 88 88 88 88 8F'
'FF FF FF FF FF FF FF FF FF FF FF FF FF FF FF 44'
'AA AA AA AA AA A8 88 88 88 88 88 88 88 88 88 8F'
'FF FF FF FF FF FF FF FF FF FF FF FF FF FF 44 44'
'AA AA AA AA AA AA 88 88 88 88 88 88 88 88 88 FF'
'FF FF FF FF FF FF FF FF FF FF FF FF FF F4 44 44'
'4A AA AA AA AA AA 88 88 88 88 88 88 88 88 88 FF'
'FF FF FF FF FF FF FF FF FF FF FF FF FF 44 44 44'
'44 AA AA AA AA AA A8 88 88 88 88 88 88 88 8F FF'
'FF FF FF FF FF FF FF FF FF FF FF FF F4 44 44 44'
'44 4A AA AA AA AA A8 88 88 88 88 88 88 88 86 6F'
'FF FF FF FF FF FF FF FF FF FF FF FF F4 44 44 44'
'44 44 4A AA AA AA EE 88 88 88 88 88 88 88 66 66'
'FF FF FF FF FF FF FF FF FF FF FF FF 44 44 44 44'
'44 44 44 EE EE EE EE EE 88 88 88 88 88 66 66 66'
'FF FF FF FF FF FF FF FF FF FF FF FF 44 44 44 44'
'44 44 44 4E EE EE EE E6 66 88 88 88 66 66 66 66'
'6F FF FF FF FF FF FF FF FF FF FF FF 44 44 44 44'
'44 44 44 4E EE EE EE E6 66 66 66 66 66 66 66 66'
'6F FF FF FF FF FF FF FF FF FF FF FF 44 44 44 44'
'44 44 44 44 EE EE EE 66 66 66 66 66 66 66 66 66'
'66 FF FF FF FF FF FF FF FF FF FF FF 44 44 44 44'
'44 44 44 44 EE EE EE 66 66 66 66 66 66 66 66 66'
'66 FF FF FF FF FF FF FF FF FF FF FF 44 44 44 44'
'44 44 44 44 4E EE EE 66 66 66 66 66 66 66 66 66'
'66 FF FF FF FF FF FF FF FF FF FF FF F4 44 44 44'
'44 44 44 44 44 FE EE 66 66 66 66 66 66 66 66 66'
'66 FF FF FF FF FF FF FF FF FF FF FF F4 44 44 44'
'44 44 44 44 44 FF FE 66 66 66 66 66 66 66 66 66'
'66 FF FF FF FF FF FF FF FF FF FF FF FF 44 44 44'
'44 44 44 44 4F FF FF 66 66 66 66 66 66 66 66 66'
'66 FF FF FF FF FF FF FF FF FF FF FF FF F4 44 44'
'44 44 44 44 FF FF FF F6 66 66 66 66 66 66 66 66'
```

```
'6F FF FF FF FF FF FF FF FF FF FF FF FF FF 44 44'
'44 44 44 4F FF FF FF F6 66 66 66 66 66 66 66 66'
'6F FF FF FF FF FF FF FF FF FF FF FF FF FF FF 44'
'44 44 4F FF FF FF FF FF 66 66 66 66 66 66 66 66'
'FF FF FF FF FF FF FF FF FF FF FF FF FF FF FF FF'
'FF FF FF FF FF FF FF FF 66 66 66 66 66 66 66 66'
'FF FF FF FF FF FF FF FF FF FF FF FF FF FF FF FF'
'FF FF FF FF FF FF FF FF F6 66 66 66 66 66 66 6F'
'FF FF FF FF FF FF FF FF FF FF FF FF FF FF FF FF'
'FF FF FF FF FF FF FF FF FF F6 66 66 66 66 6F FF'
'FF FF FF FF FF FF FF FF FF FF FF FF FF FF FF FF'
'FF FF FF FF FF FF FF FF FF FF F6 66 66 6F FF FF'
'FF FF FF FF FF FF FF FF FF FF FF FF FF FF FF FF'
'FF FF FF FF FF FF FF FF FF FF FF FF FF FF FF FF'
'FF FF FF FF FF FF FF FF FF FF FF FF FF FF FF FF'
'FF FF FF FF FF FF FF FF FF FF FF FF FF FF FF FF'
'FF FF FF FF FF FF FF FF FF FF FF FF FF FF FF FF'
'FF FF FF FF FF FF FF FF FF FF FF FF FF FF FF FF'
'FF FF FF FF FF FF FF FF FF FF FF FF FF FF FF FF'
'FF FF FF FF FF FF FF FF FF FF FF FF FF FF FF FF'
'FF FF FF FF FF FF FF FF FF FF FF FF FF FF FF FF'
'FF FF FF FF FF FF'
END

ID_CURSOR CURSOR
BEGIN
'00 00 02 00 01 00 20 20 02 00 10 00 0F 00 30 01'
'00 00 16 00 00 00 28 00 00 00 20 00 00 00 40 00'
'00 00 01 00 01 00 00 00 00 00 00 02 00 00 00 00'
'00 00 00 00 00 00 00 00 00 00 00 00 00 00 00 00'
'00 00 FF FF FF 00 00 00 00 00 00 00 00 00 00 00'
'00 00 00 00 00 00 00 00 00 00 00 00 00 00 00 00'
'00 00 00 00 00 00 00 00 00 00 00 00 00 00 00 00'
'00 00 00 00 00 00 00 00 00 00 00 00 00 00 00 00'
'00 00 00 00 00 00 00 00 00 00 00 00 00 00 00 00'
'00 00 00 00 00 00 00 00 00 00 00 00 00 00 00 00'
'00 00 00 00 00 00 00 00 00 00 00 00 00 00 00 00'
'00 00 00 00 00 00 00 00 00 00 00 00 00 00 00 00'
'00 00 00 00 00 00 FF F0 0F FF FF 8F 71 FF FE 7F'
'7E 7F FD FF 7F BF FB FF 7F DF F7 FF 7F EF EF FF'
'7F F7 DF FF 7F FB DF FF 7F FB BF FF 7F FD BF FF'
'7F FD BF FF 7F FD 7F FF 7F FE 7F FF 7F FE 7F FF'
'7F FE 7F FF 7F FE 00 00 00 00 7F FF 7F FE 7F FF'
'7F FE 7F FF 7F FE BF FF 7F FD BF FF 7F FD BF FF'
'7F FD DF FF 7F FB DF FF 7F FB EF FF 7F F7 F7 FF'
'7F EF FB FF 7F DF FD FF 7F BF FE 7F 7E 7F FF 8F'
'71 FF FF F0 0F FF'
END
```

RESBIT.RC defines three kinds of bitmap resources. The first is an icon, identified by the constant ID_ICON, defined in the resource header file, RESBIT.RH:

```
ID_ICON ICON "resbit.ico"
```

Compiling the resource script creates an icon resource from the icon bitmap image stored in file RESBIT.ICO. Following that statement is another way to create a device-independent bitmap as an array of hexadecimal byte values, identified by ID_BITMAP. The hexadecimal data includes header information, a color table, and the bit patterns that make up the image. Obviously, creating a bitmap byte-by-byte is a taxing business, but don't get the idea that I slaved day and night to bring you this listing. I actually drew the image using Resource Workshop, which created the hexadecimal script statements.

I created the cursor resource the same way. Cursors are similar to icons in format but are always stored as monochrome bitmaps.

> **NOTE**
>
> My book, *Windows File Facts,* Sams 1993, describes the file formats of icon, cursor, and bitmap files and resources.

Listing 8.3, RESBIT.H, declares symbolic constants used by the RESBIT program. The program's source code in Listing 8.4, RESBIT.CPP, demonstrates how to use icon, cursor, and bitmap resources. Figure 8.1 shows the program's display.

FIGURE 8.1.

RESBIT's window, showing icon, cursor (the circle with a cross inside), and bitmap resources.

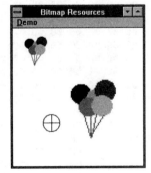

Listing 8.3. RESBIT.H.

```
// resbit.h -- Header file for resbit.cpp

#define BITMAP_W 64        // Our bitmap resource width
#define BITMAP_H 64        // and height
```

Listing 8.4. RESBIT.CPP.

```cpp
/* ============================================================ *\
** resbit.cpp -- Resource bitmaps, icons, and cursors          **
** ============================================================ **
**                                                             **
** ============================================================ **
**     Copyright  1994 by Tom Swan. All rights reserved.       **
\* ============================================================ */

#include <owl\applicat.h>
#include <owl\framewin.h>
#include <owl\dc.h>
#include <owl\gdiobjec.h>
#pragma hdrstop
#include "resbit.h"
#include "resbit.rh"


// ============================================================
// The application's main window
// ============================================================

class TResBitWin: public TFrameWindow {
public:
  TResBitWin(TWindow* parent, const char far* title);
  ~TResBitWin();
protected:
  void Paint(TDC& dc, BOOL erase, TRect& rect);
private:
  TBitmap* bitmap;    // Pointer to bitmap object
};

// Constructor
TResBitWin::TResBitWin(TWindow* parent, const char far* title)
  : TFrameWindow(parent, title),
    TWindow(parent, title)
{
  AssignMenu(ID_MENU);
  bitmap = new TBitmap(
    GetApplicationObject()->GetInstance(),  // Instance handle
    ID_BITMAP);  // Load resource bitmap
}

// Destructor
TResBitWin::~TResBitWin()
{
  delete bitmap;
}
```

continues

299

Listing 8.4. continued

```cpp
// Paint or repaint bar chart in current window size
void TResBitWin::Paint(TDC& dc, BOOL /*erase*/, TRect& /*rect*/)
{
  TMemoryDC memdc(dc);
  memdc.SelectObject(*bitmap);

  dc.BitBlt(
    10, 10,                  // Destination X,Y coordinate
    BITMAP_W, BITMAP_H,      // Bitmap width and height
    memdc,                   // Source device context
    0, 0,                    // Source X,Y coordinate
    SRCCOPY);                // Raster display operation

  dc.StretchBlt(
    BITMAP_W + 20,           // Destination X coordinate
    BITMAP_H + 20,           // Destination Y coordinate
    BITMAP_W * 2,            // Destination width (stretched)
    BITMAP_H * 2,            // Destination height (stretched)
    memdc,                   // Source device context
    0, 0,                    // Source X,Y coordinate
    BITMAP_W, BITMAP_H,      // Source width and height (normal)
    SRCCOPY);                // Raster display operation

  memdc.RestoreBitmap();     // Not strictly necessary
}

// ============================================================
// The application class
// ============================================================

class TResBitApp: public TApplication {
public:
  TResBitApp(const char far* name)
    : TApplication(name) {};
  void InitMainWindow();
};

// Initialize the program's main window
void
TResBitApp::InitMainWindow()
{
  MainWindow = new TResBitWin(0, "Bitmap Resources");
  MainWindow->SetIcon(this, ID_ICON);
  MainWindow->SetCursor(this, ID_CURSOR);
}

#pragma argsused
```

```
// Main program
int
OwlMain(int argc, char* argv[])
{
  TResBitApp app("ResBit");
  return app.Run();
}
```

For referring to its bitmap resource, RESBIT's main window class, TResBitWin, declares a private TBitmap pointer:

```
TBitmap* bitmap;
```

That's usually the best way to maintain bitmap information in a class object. In this case, TResBitWin's constructor creates the TBitmap object by specifying its resource identifier:

```
bitmap = new TBitmap(
  GetApplicationObject()->GetInstance(),
  ID_BITMAP);
```

Don't forget the all important step of deleting the TBitmap object when you are done using it. TResBitWin's destructor deletes the memory addressed by bitmap:

```
delete bitmap;
```

The window's Paint function demonstrates two common ways to display a bitmap resource. (The same methods work with bitmaps loaded from DIB files and converted to DDB TBitmap objects.) Paint begins with two key statements that construct and initialize a *memory device context:*

```
TMemoryDC memdc(dc);
memdc.SelectObject(*bitmap);
```

You never display bitmaps directly. Instead, you select a bitmap object into a memory device context (or another kind of context), then transfer the object from that context to another by calling one of two Windows functions: BitBlt or StretchBlt. (Contrary to popular opinion, *Blt* does not mean "bacon, lettuce, and tomato." It's an abbreviation for "block transfer." A *bit blit* function such as BitBlt and StretchBlt performs a bit-block-transfer of a bitmap's bits from one context to another.)

If the destination context is attached to a window, the result of calling BitBlt or StretchBlt is a visual representation of the bitmap. If the destination is a memory device context, the result is a *copy* of the bitmap in the destination. Get used to thinking in terms of transferring information from one context to another rather than "showing" or "displaying" bitmaps, and these steps will make more sense.

301

Paint displays the sample balloon bitmap in two ways. Function BitBlt shows the image in normal size. Function StretchBlt shows the image twice as large by specifying double width and height arguments. If the destination width and height are smaller than the original, the image is shrunk to that size. If the destination height and width are the same as the original, StretchBlt works the same as BitBlt.

> **TIP**
>
> StretchBlt takes a lot more time than BitBlt, so it's usually best to use BitBlt for better output speed. For more information about these two functions, look them up in a Windows API reference or in BC4's online help. The API functions work the same as their encapsulated counterparts in TDC device-context classes.

The last statement in Paint isn't strictly necessary, but after selecting a bitmap object into a device context, it's "good form" to deselect that object by calling RestoreBitmap:

```
memdc.RestoreBitmap();
```

In this case, the memdc object goes out of scope when Paint ends, and at that time, the TMemoryDC class automatically restores and deletes any bitmaps or other selected graphical objects such as pens and brushes. If memdc had been supplied by another function, however, it might be necessary to include programming to call RestoreBitmap as shown here. Don't leave bitmaps or other objects inside device contexts unless you have a good reason for doing so.

RESBIT also shows how to load icon and cursor resources provided by a resource script file, RESBIT.RC. To give the program a system icon, the application class's InitMainWindow function calls SetIcon after constructing the program's window and assigning its address to MainWindow:

```
MainWindow->SetIcon(this, ID_ICON);
```

The this argument refers to the module in which the icon is stored—in this case, in the program's .EXE code file. The ID_ICON argument specifies the icon's resource identifier. Minimize RESBIT on the Windows desktop to see the system icon.

InitMainWindow also calls SetCursor to load the program's cursor resource:

```
MainWindow->SetCursor(this, ID_CURSOR);
```

Move the mouse pointer over the main window's client area to see the cursor loaded by this statement. Moving the mouse beyond the client area causes the cursor to change back to its default arrow. These actions are automatic and require no additional programming.

SHOWBIT (Display Bitmap File)

Displaying a bitmap file is simple, but the steps might seem confusing until you've tried them a few times. In general, you need to perform these actions:

1. Load a device-independent bitmap file into a TDib object.
2. Construct a device-dependent bitmap TBitmap object using the TDib object from step 1.
3. Add a Paint function to the window class.
4. In Paint, construct a memory device context of type TMemoryDC.
5. Select the TBitmap object into the memory device context.
6. Call BitBlt or StretchBlt to transfer the bitmap from the memory device context to the TPaintDC context passed to Paint.
7. Optionally call RestoreBitmap for the memory device context, removing the selected bitmap.

Listings 8.5 (SHOWBIT.RH), 8.6 (SHOWBIT.H), 8.7 (SHOWBIT.RC), and 8.8 (SHOWBIT.CPP) demonstrate those seven basic steps. The program displays a bitmap file named PICTURE.BMP located in the DATA subdirectory created by installing this book's disk. To display a different bitmap, change the filename in SHOWBIT.H. The program also shows how to add scrollers to a window that displays a bitmap image.

> **TIP**
>
> SHOWBIT's scrollers demonstrate the TScroller's automatic scrolling features. Click and drag a thumb box to adjust the bitmap's position as you move the mouse. Or, click and drag the mouse pointer from inside to outside of the window. The farther away you move the mouse pointer, the faster the image scrolls in that direction. These features come at no extra charge—just use the TScroller class as shown in the SHOWBIT.CPP listing.

Listing 8.5. SHOWBIT.RH.

```
// showbit.rh -- Resource header file

#define ID_MENU 100
```

Listing 8.6. SHOWBIT.H.

```
// showbit.h -- Header file for showbit.cpp

#define FILENAME "..\\data\\picture.bmp"
```

Listing 8.7. SHOWBIT.RC.

```
#include <owl\window.rh>
#include "showbit.rh"

ID_MENU MENU
BEGIN
  POPUP "&Demo"
  BEGIN
    MENUITEM "E&xit", CM_EXIT
  END
END
```

Listing 8.8. SHOWBIT.CPP.

```
/* ============================================================ *\
**   showbit.cpp -- Display a device-independent bitmap (DIB)   **
** ============================================================ **
**   Also demonstrates how to use scrollers in a bitmap window  **
** ============================================================ **
**      Copyright  1994 by Tom Swan. All rights reserved.       **
\* ============================================================ */

#include <owl\applicat.h>
#include <owl\framewin.h>
#include <owl\dc.h>
#include <owl\gdiobjec.h>
#include <owl\scroller.h>
#pragma hdrstop
#include "showbit.h"
#include "showbit.rh"
```

```
// ===========================================================
// The application's main window
// ===========================================================

class TShowBitWin: public TFrameWindow {
public:
  TShowBitWin(TWindow* parent, const char far* title);
  ~TShowBitWin();
  void AdjustScrollers();
  virtual void Paint(TDC& dc, BOOL erase, TRect& rect);
protected:
  void EvSize(UINT sizeType, TSize& size);
private:
  TBitmap* bitmap;
DECLARE_RESPONSE_TABLE(TShowBitWin);
};

DEFINE_RESPONSE_TABLE1(TShowBitWin, TFrameWindow)
  EV_WM_SIZE,
END_RESPONSE_TABLE;

// Constructor
TShowBitWin::TShowBitWin(TWindow* parent, const char far* title)
  : TFrameWindow(parent, title),
    TWindow(parent, title)
{
  AssignMenu(ID_MENU);
  Attr.Style |= WS_VSCROLL | WS_HSCROLL;
  TDib* pdib = new TDib(FILENAME);  // Load DIB file
  bitmap = new TBitmap(*pdib);      // Convert DIB to DDB bitmap
  delete pdib;                      // Done with DIB, so delete it
  Scroller = new TScroller(this,
    1, 1, bitmap->Width(), bitmap->Height());
}

// Destructor
TShowBitWin::~TShowBitWin()
{
  delete bitmap;
}

// Paint or repaint window contents
// Scrolling is automatic
void
TShowBitWin::Paint(TDC& dc, BOOL /*erase*/, TRect& /*rect*/)
{
  TMemoryDC memdc(dc);
  memdc.SelectObject(*bitmap);
  dc.BitBlt(0, 0,
    bitmap->Width(), bitmap->Height(), memdc, 0, 0, SRCCOPY);
}
```

continues

Listing 8.8. continued

```cpp
// Respond to WM_SIZE message
// Limit scroller ranges to window and bitmap sizes
void
TShowBitWin::EvSize(UINT sizeType, TSize& size)
{
  TFrameWindow::EvSize(sizeType, size);
  AdjustScrollers();
}

// Adjust horizontal and vertical scroller ranges
void
TShowBitWin::AdjustScrollers()
{
  TRect tr;    // Rectangle for client area dimensions
  long H, W;   // Document size minus window in display units

  GetClientRect(tr);
  W = bitmap->Width() - (tr.right - tr.left);
  H = bitmap->Height() - (tr.bottom - tr.top);
  Scroller->SetRange(W / Scroller->XUnit, H / Scroller->YUnit);
  SetScrollPos(SB_HORZ, (int)Scroller->XPos, TRUE);
  SetScrollPos(SB_VERT, (int)Scroller->YPos, TRUE);
}

// ============================================================
// The application class
// ============================================================

class TShowBitApp: public TApplication {
public:
  TShowBitApp(const char far* name)
    : TApplication(name) {};
  void InitMainWindow();
};

// Initialize the program's main window
void
TShowBitApp::InitMainWindow()
{
  MainWindow = new TShowBitWin(0, FILENAME);
}

#pragma argsused
```

```
// Main program
int
OwlMain(int argc, char* argv[])
{
  TShowBitApp app("ShowBit");
  return app.Run();
}
```

As in the preceding program, SHOWBIT declares a private TBitmap pointer in its main window class, TShowBitWin. To load the bitmap image identified by constant FILENAME (use another name to display a different bitmap file), the class constructor executes these three statements:

```
TDib* pdib = new TDib(FILENAME);
bitmap = new TBitmap(*pdib);
delete pdib;
```

The first line loads the image into a TDib object, which is used by the second line to construct a device-dependent TBitmap object, addressed by the bitmap pointer. After that step, the TDib object addressed by pdib is deleted.

To enable scrollers, the window's Style attribute is modified to include WS_VSCROLL and WS_HSCROLL. Another statement constructs a TScroller object, and assigns the object's address to the inherited Scroller pointer:

```
Scroller = new TScroller(this,
  1, 1, bitmap->Width(), bitmap->Height());
```

Remember, you don't have to delete the constructed object because the statement passes this to the constructor—an indication that the owning class automatically deletes the TScroller object. Also, because the window's data is in memory at this point, it is appropriate to specify the scroller's unit and range values when constructing the object. Even so, it is still necessary to adjust these settings if the window's size changes, as demonstrated by response function EvSize, which calls AdjustScrollers.

The AdjustScrollers function calls SetRange and SetScrollPos. The functions configure the scrollers so the image stops scrolling when its edges become visible. (The mark of a sloppy Windows program is one that permits you to scroll data completely out of view. It is amazing how many such programs manage to survive in the marketplace.)

SHOWBIT's Paint function displays the bitmap image using the same technique shown in RESBIT. First, the function constructs a memory device context of type TMemoryDC:

```
TMemoryDC memdc(tdc);
```

Paint then selects the bitmap into the device context:

```
memdc.SelectObject(*bitmap);
```

When using a pointer to address a bitmap, you must dereference it with an asterisk. You pass *objects*, not pointers, to SelectObject. Lastly, call the encapsulated BitBlt function in reference to the device context passed to Paint:

```
dc.BitBlt(0, 0,
  bitmap->Width(), bitmap->Height(), memdc, 0, 0, SRCCOPY);
```

That transfers the bitmap selected into the memory device context to the window associated with dc. In this example, I did not call RestoreBitmap because the memory device-context object does that when Paint ends, at which time memdc goes out of scope. Compare this version of Paint with the one in RESBIT. You could also display an expanded bitmap image (or a shrunken one) by calling StretchBlt.

DRAWBIT (Offscreen Bitmaps)

Finally in this chapter is a much improved version of the SKETCH program from the Chapter 7. The new program, DRAWBIT, repairs an intentional bug in SKETCH that causes overlapping windows to erase your drawing, a problem caused by not saving the image for redrawing in response to a WM_PAINT message.

There are several ways to fix that problem, but drawing into an offscreen bitmap is the easiest solution. The game plan is simple. When the program draws a line or other shape on screen, the program also draws a mirror image of that graphic into an offscreen bitmap. On receiving a WM_PAINT message, the program repaints the image by copying the in-memory bitmap to the window's display context. As a bonus, to save the image to disk, the program simply writes the in-memory bitmap to a file.

Listings 8.9 (DRAWBIT.RH), 8.10 (DRAWBIT.H), 8.11 (DRAWBIT.RC), and 8.12 (DRAWBIT.CPP) implement the improved sketch program. Compile and run the demonstration by opening its DRAWBIT.IDE project file, sketch some figures into the window, and use the scrollers to view different parts of the window's contents. Try shrinking and expanding the window. If your display's resolution is larger than 640-by-480, you see blackened areas outside of the defined bitmap, indicating that you can't draw there. Think of the bitmap's white surface as sheet of paper. For a larger "paper size," increase the values of BMP_WIDTH and BMP_HEIGHT in SKETCH.H. Decrease the bitmap width and height for a smaller image. Also try covering and uncovering a sketch with another program's window. Unlike SKETCH, DRAWBIT properly updates the window when a window on top moves aside.

Listing 8.9. DRAWBIT.RH.

```
// drawbit.rh -- Resource header file

#define ID_MENU 100      // Menu resource identifier
#define CM_ERASE 101     // Demo¦Erase command identifier
```

Listing 8.10. DRAWBIT.H.

```
// drawbit.h -- Program header file

#define BMP_WIDTH 640    // Bitmap minimum width
#define BMP_HEIGHT 480   // Bitmap minimum height
```

Listing 8.11. DRAWBIT.RC.

```
#include <owl\window.rh>
#include "drawbit.rh"

ID_MENU MENU
BEGIN
  POPUP "&Demo"
  BEGIN
    MENUITEM "&Erase", CM_ERASE
    MENUITEM "E&xit", CM_EXIT
  END
END
```

Listing 8.12. DRAWBIT.CPP.

```
/* ============================================================ *\
**   drawbit.cpp -- Draw into an offscreen bitmap              **
** ============================================================ **
**                                                             **
** ============================================================ **
**     Copyright  1994 by Tom Swan. All rights reserved.       **
\* ============================================================ */

#include <owl\applicat.h>
#include <owl\framewin.h>
#include <owl\dc.h>
```

continues

Listing 8.12. continued

```
#include <owl\gdiobjec.h>
#include <owl\scroller.h>
#pragma hdrstop
#include "drawbit.rh"
#include "drawbit.h"

// Return true if TRect ra is larger than rb in either
// its width OR its height
// This function is not a class member
inline BOOL
RectIsLarger(TRect& ra, TRect& rb)
{
  return ((ra.Width() > rb.Width()) ||
          (ra.Height() > rb.Height()));
}

// ==========================================================
// The application's main window
// ==========================================================

class TDrawWin: public TFrameWindow {
public:
  TDrawWin(TWindow* parent, const char far* title,
    int w = BMP_WIDTH, int h = BMP_HEIGHT);
  ~TDrawWin();
  void AdjustScrollers();
  void EraseImage();
protected:
  void CmErase();
  void GetWindowClass(WNDCLASS &wndClass);
  char far* GetClassName() { return "TDrawWin"; }
  void SetupWindow();
  void EvSize(UINT sizeType, TSize& size);
  void EvLButtonDown(UINT modKeys, TPoint& point);
  void EvMouseMove(UINT modKeys, TPoint& point);
  void EvLButtonUp(UINT modKeys, TPoint& point);
  void EvLButtonDblClk(UINT modKeys, TPoint& point);
  virtual void Paint(TDC& dc, BOOL erase, TRect& rect);
private:
  BOOL dragging;       // True if clicking and dragging mouse
  int width, height;   // Bitmap width and height in pixels
  TClientDC* cdc;      // Pointer to client-area device context
  TMemoryDC* mdc;      // Pointer to memory device context
  TBitmap* bitmap;     // Pointer to offscreen bitmap
  TPen* pen;           // Drawing pen
DECLARE_RESPONSE_TABLE(TDrawWin);
};
```

```
DEFINE_RESPONSE_TABLE1(TDrawWin, TFrameWindow)
  EV_COMMAND(CM_ERASE, CmErase),
  EV_WM_SIZE,
  EV_WM_LBUTTONDOWN,
  EV_WM_MOUSEMOVE,
  EV_WM_LBUTTONUP,
  EV_WM_LBUTTONDBLCLK,
END_RESPONSE_TABLE;

// Constructor
TDrawWin::TDrawWin(TWindow* parent, const char far* title,
  int w, int h)
  : TFrameWindow(parent, title),
    TWindow(parent, title),
    width(w), height(h)
{
  AssignMenu(ID_MENU);
  if (w < BMP_WIDTH) w = BMP_WIDTH;
  if (h < BMP_HEIGHT) h = BMP_HEIGHT;
  Attr.Style |= WS_HSCROLL | WS_VSCROLL;
  Attr.X = 0;
  Attr.Y = 0;
  Attr.H = height;
  Attr.W = width;
  Scroller = new TScroller(this, 1, 1, width, height);
  dragging = FALSE;
  cdc = 0;            // Valid while clicking and dragging
  mdc = 0;            // Memory device context
  bitmap = 0;         // Bitmap object selected into mdc
  pen = new TPen(TColor::Black, 3);  // Solid black pen, width 3
}

// Destructor
TDrawWin::~TDrawWin()
{
  delete cdc;
  delete mdc;
  delete bitmap;
  delete pen;
}

// Adjust scrollers to match bitmap and window sizes
void
TDrawWin::AdjustScrollers()
{
  TRect r;    // Rectangle for client area dimensions
  int h, w;   // Bitmap size minus window in display units

  GetClientRect(r);
  w = width - (r.right - r.left);
```

continues

Listing 8.12. continued

```
  h = height - (r.bottom - r.top);
  Scroller->SetRange(w / Scroller->XUnit, h / Scroller->YUnit);
  SetScrollPos(SB_HORZ, (int)Scroller->XPos);
  SetScrollPos(SB_VERT, (int)Scroller->YPos);
}

// Erase drawing (on and offscreen)
void
TDrawWin::EraseImage()
{
  TRect r(0, 0, width, height);
  mdc->FillRect(r, TBrush(TColor(255, 255, 255)));
  Invalidate(FALSE);
}

// Respond to Demo¦Erase command
void
TDrawWin::CmErase()
{
  EraseImage();
}

// Modify registered window class to use black background
void
TDrawWin::GetWindowClass(WNDCLASS &wndClass)
{
  TFrameWindow::GetWindowClass(wndClass);
  wndClass.hbrBackground = (HBRUSH)GetStockObject(BLACK_BRUSH);
}

// Perform additional window initializations requiring HWindow
void
TDrawWin::SetupWindow()
{
  TFrameWindow::SetupWindow();  // Default actions

// 1. Get temporary device context for window
// 2. Create offscreen bitmap
// 3. Create a "memory display context" for offscreen drawing
// 4. Attach offscreen bitmap hMemDC and erase to white
// 5. Clear garbage bits out of in-memory image

  TClientDC* tempdc = new TClientDC(*this);
  bitmap = new TBitmap(*tempdc, width, height);
  width = bitmap->Width();
  height = bitmap->Height();
  mdc = new TMemoryDC(*tempdc);
  delete tempdc;
  mdc->SelectObject(*bitmap);
```

```
   EraseImage();
}

// Respond to changes in the window's size
void
TDrawWin::EvSize(UINT sizeType, TSize& size)
{
  TFrameWindow::EvSize(sizeType, size);
  AdjustScrollers();
}

// Respond to left-mouse-button click
void
TDrawWin::EvLButtonDown(UINT /*modKeys*/, TPoint& point)
{
  if (!dragging) {
    dragging = TRUE;
    SetCapture();
    cdc = new TClientDC(*this);
    cdc->SelectObject(*pen);
    mdc->SelectObject(*pen);
    cdc->MoveTo(point);
    mdc->MoveTo(
        (int)Scroller->XPos + point.x,
        (int)Scroller->YPos + point.y);
  }
}

// Respond to mouse movement
void
TDrawWin::EvMouseMove(UINT /*modKeys*/, TPoint& point)
{
  if (dragging) {
    cdc->LineTo(point);
    mdc->LineTo(
        (int)Scroller->XPos + point.x,
        (int)Scroller->YPos + point.y);
  }
}

// Respond to release of left mouse button
void
TDrawWin::EvLButtonUp(UINT /*modKeys*/, TPoint& /*point*/)
{
  if (dragging) {
    ReleaseCapture();
    mdc->RestorePen();
    cdc->RestorePen();
    delete cdc;
```

continues

Listing 8.12. continued

```
    cdc = 0;   // (Because the destructor also deletes cdc)
    dragging = FALSE;
  }
}

// Erase window on double-click of left mouse button
void
TDrawWin::EvLButtonDblClk(UINT /*modKeys*/, TPoint& /*point*/)
{
  EraseImage();
}

// Paint or repaint window contents
void
TDrawWin::Paint(TDC& dc, BOOL /*erase*/, TRect& /*rect*/)
{
  dc.BitBlt(0, 0, width, height, *mdc, 0, 0, SRCCOPY);
}

// ================================================================
// The application class
// ================================================================

class TDrawApp: public TApplication {
public:
  TDrawApp(const char far* name)
    : TApplication(name) {};
  void InitMainWindow();
};

// Initialize the program's main window
void
TDrawApp::InitMainWindow()
{
  MainWindow = new TDrawWin(0, "Draw Into Offscreen Bitmap");
}

#pragma argsused

// Main program
int
OwlMain(int argc, char* argv[])
{
  TDrawApp app("DrawBit");
  return app.Run();
}
```

DRAWBIT's main window class, TDrawWin, declares several private data members. For better display speed, the class declares two pointers to device-context objects. A TClientDC pointer, cdc, addresses a device context for drawing in the program's window. A TMemoryDC pointer, mdc, addresses a memory device context into which the offscreen bitmap is selected. Creating the two device-context objects ahead of time avoids having to recreate them every time Paint is called.

The class also declares a TBitmap pointer for referring to the offscreen bitmap, which holds a copy of the onscreen image. A TPen pointer addresses the on- and offscreen pen selected into both contexts.

Function SetupWindow in the TDrawWin class prepares the offscreen image by first creating a TClientDC object:

```
TClientDC* tempdc = new TClientDC(*this);
```

That can't be done in the class constructor because the object must be initialized using a valid window handle. (You receive an exception error if you attempt to construct a TClientDC object in a TWindow derived-class constructor.) The TBitmap object is next created using the client device context, specifying the bitmap's desired width and height:

```
bitmap = new TBitmap(*tempdc, width, height);
```

That creates a fresh device-dependent bitmap in memory, ready for selecting into a memory device context. For simplicity, the bitmap's width and height are copied into two data members:

```
width = bitmap->Width();
height = bitmap->Height();
```

Then, the program creates a memory device context, deletes the temporary context object, and selects the bitmap into the object addressed by mdc:

```
mdc = new TMemoryDC(*tempdc);
delete tempdc;
mdc->SelectObject(*bitmap);
```

Finally, SetupWindow calls EraseImage to set the offscreen bitmap's bits to all white. Freshly created bitmaps are filled with random bits. For a clean page, erase it by calling FillRect as shown in EraseImage.

315

To draw into the offscreen bitmap, call GDI commands in reference to the memory device context. For example, this draws a rectangle in the offscreen bitmap:

```
mdc->Rectangle(10, 10, 100, 150);
```

You don't see that rectangle until the offscreen bitmap is transferred to an output device's context—a TClientDC or TPaintDC object, for example.

It should now be clearer why you have to select a bitmap into a memory device context. There aren't any commands in Windows for drawing inside bitmaps. There are only commands for drawing in a device context. By constructing a bitmap, and selecting it into a *memory* device context, *you create the equivalent of a display window in memory.* Drawing into the memory device context directs GDI output to the offscreen image— just as drawing into a TPaintDC object directs output to a visible window on a display device.

Other examples of offscreen drawing appear in three response functions, EvLButtonDown, EvMouseMove, and EvLButtonUp. The functions are similar to those in SKETCH, but in this case, DRAWBIT's response functions perform two new operations:

- They call the same GDI commands twice—once to draw in the window, and again to draw the offscreen bitmap selected into the memory device context.
- They account for the scroller's thumb positions when drawing into the offscreen bitmap, because only Paint's TPaintDC context is automatically adjusted to account for scroller thumb positions.

The program's Paint function is extremely simple, executing only one statement:

```
dc.BitBlt(0, 0, width, height, *mdc, 0, 0, SRCCOPY);
```

Paint calls BitBlt to copy the offscreen bitmap held by the TMemoryDC object addressed by tmdc to the window associated by the TPaintDC object tdc, passed to Paint. This single statement properly restores the display in response to a WM_PAINT message.

Drawing in Bitmap Files

DRAWBIT shows the basic techniques used by Paint programs to draw over images stored in bitmap files. The process is easier than you might imagine. Simply by adding the device-independent bitmap techniques explained earlier in this chapter, you can convert DRAWBIT into a simple bitmap editor. Make the following changes to DRAWBIT.CPP.

In `SetupWindow`, construct the `TBitmap` object as follows (replace the assignment to `bitmap` with the following two statements):

```
TDib dib("..\\data\\picture.bmp");
bitmap = new TBitmap(dib);
```

Also comment out, or remove, the call to `EraseImage` at the end of `SetupWindow`—otherwise, the bitmap would be erased to all white before being displayed. Change the final statement in `SetupWindow` to this:

```
// EraseImage();
```

Recompile and run DRAWBIT to load a bitmap file. Instead of a blank sheet of paper, you now see the bitmap's image. Click and drag the mouse to draw over the bitmap. Of course, a finished bitmap editor needs additional features such as colored pens, commands to save edited images, and so on, but the sample listings here provide most of the necessary basics for a bitmap editor. To save a bitmap, construct a `TDib` object from the offscreen image, and use the `TDib` class's `WriteFile` function to save the image to disk. It's that easy!

Looking Ahead

A window is, of course, the fundamental component of Windows software. In the next chapter, you look more closely at classes for creating window interface objects. As you will discover, there's a lot more to a window than its simple on-screen appearance suggests.

9

Bringing Up Windows

The obvious focal point of all Windows software is the *window*. I like to think of a window as a kind of fluid output terminal—a software CRT that gives me full control over every aspect of my programs' output. I can display a single window, or I can construct as many *child windows* as my program needs. A button control, for example, is just a highly specialized child window. Buttons and other controls add visually attractive, efficient interface devices for manipulating data, selecting options, and performing other jobs.

In this chapter, you learn:

- How window class objects interface with window elements.
- How to create child windows.
- How to insert controls in windows.
- How to construct frame windows and derivatives.
- How to merge menu resources in a frame window.
- How to use decorated frames to create gadgets, toolbars, and status bars.

Window-Interface Classes

All BC4 window classes are based on the TWindow class. To use BC4's window classes effectively, you need to understand the relationship between the TWindow class objects(on which all window classes are based) and their associated Windows elements. You also need to understand that a window is not just a box with scrollers and a menu. A control object such as a button, a status bar that displays online help, a dialog box, and other interface elements are also windows.

In all Windows software, window features (their title strings, display options, and so on) are stored internally as *window elements,* structures maintained by Windows. The characteristics of window elements are given by *window registration classes* (not C++ classes), which are passed to Windows by programs during startup. When a program constructs a new window—to display a main window, for example, or to bring up an OK button control—Windows uses a registration class to construct a window element for that new window. You can construct many window elements from the same registration class, similar to the way you can construct many program objects (integers, floating-point values, and so forth) of types such as int and float.

The ObjectWindows Library (OWL) adds an additional programming layer to these concepts. Window *classes,* derived from TWindow, encapsulate data and functions that you can use to control window elements. A window object (meaning any object of a class derived from TWindow) serves as an interface to the window element maintained internally by the Windows operating system. The TWindow class automatically registers the necessary information with Windows, and it automatically constructs an associated window element for every window object. In most cases, all you need to do is create a variable of a TWindow class and let OWL do the rest.

It's important to understand the relationship between window objects and window elements. But in your code, you can usually communicate with window objects *as though they actually were the elements they represent.* Window objects simplify message-handling, and they encapsulate Windows API functions. Using object-oriented programming, you don't pass windows to functions; instead, you call encapsulated class functions in reference to window objects.

Window Construction

Every window object is associated with one window element (which is constructed from a registered window class). The link between a window object and a window element is a *handle,* an integer value that Windows uses to find window elements in memory. Every class derived from TWindow inherits a member HWindow, which if nonnull, stores a window objects's window element handle.

In past chapters, you learned how to create a program's main window using the TFrameWindow class (derived from TWindow). You construct most other TWindow-derived classes similarly. In general terms, you:

- Perform object initializations (assigning values to class data members, for example) in the class constructor
- Perform other initializations requiring a window handle (calling Windows API functions, for example) in a replacement SetupWindow member function
- Write a CanClose function that returns true if the window may be safely closed (after checking that file data is saved, for example)
- Delete any dynamically allocated data and perform other shutdown duties in the class destructor

You met examples of these techniques in previous chapters. Keep them in mind as you learn more about the TWindow class and its derivatives in this chapter.

TWindow Classes

TWindow is a prolific ancestor class that has spawned many other classes in the ObjectWindows library. TWindow is derived from two other classes, TStreamableBase (which adds file-stream capabilities) and TEventHandler (which enables calling member functions in response to Windows messages). All classes derived from TWindow are therefore streamable (able to be written to file streams) and can respond to messages. In most cases, using TWindow derived classes requires filling in a few member functions, or writing some new ones, and constructing a message-response table for the messages to which objects of the class are required to respond. You also can add streaming features for writing class objects to disk, but you can ignore this detail. TWindow classes can be streamable, but they don't have to be. (Chapter 12 introduces streamable classes.)

Following are the main classes derived from TWindow. You can use some of these classes directly (TDialog and TTinyCaption, for example), but you are more likely to derive your own classes from them or to use other provided derivations. For example, you never construct a TControl object—you instead construct an object of a *specific* control such as TButton, derived from TControl. The following classes are *directly* derived from TWindow (as I note here, some classes are discussed in other chapters):

- TControl—For control objects, buttons, scrollbars, list boxes, and other controls inserted in a window. TControl objects are child windows that a parent window owns. Using a TControl object makes it easy to communicate with a window's controls—the object serves as an interface to the control's window element (also called a control element) created and maintained by Windows.

- **TFrameWindow**—Adds keyboard handling, menu-command processing, and icon support to the **TWindow** class. Restores the input focus for reactivated windows.

- **TGadgetWindow**—Organizes tiled gadgets such as toolbar buttons. Usually incorporated into a window's border to provide visually interactive commands, or to provide information such as function key settings, status messages, and the like.

- **TLayoutWindow**—Defines layout metrics for a window (usually a child window owned by another). The **TDecoratedFrame** class, for example, is derived from **TFrameWindow** and **TLayoutWindow**, and is used to create *decorated main windows* that can hold toolbars and status lines. The **TLayoutWindow** controls the positions and sizes of these child windows.

- **TTinyCaption**—Known as a *mix-in class,* this highly specialized **TWindow** derivative creates a tiny caption bar in a window, useful when display space is at a premium, but generally best for users under 40 who don't need reading glasses.

- **TDialog**—For constructing dialog boxes (see Chapter 10, "Dealing with Dialog Boxes").

- **TMDIClient**—For Multiple Document Interface (MDI) client windows (see Chapter 12, "Writing MDI Applications").

- **TWindowView**—For creating window document/views (see Chapter 12, "Writing MDI Applications").

- **TPreviewPage**—For print preview windows (see Chapter 13, "Printing Text and Graphics").

- **TClipboardViewer**—For clipboard viewer windows (see Chapter 15, "Finishing Touches").

TWindow Members

All **TWindow** classes have data members and functions that you can use to set various window features, and to interrogate window properties. Construct **TWindow** objects using one of two constructors. The first is the simplest—it requires a window handle of type HWND and optionally accepts a pointer to the window's module:

```
TWindow(HWND hWnd, TModule* module = 0);
```

If **module** is null, the class uses a default module, usually the window's parent module—in other words, the application object. (The **TApplication** class is derived from **TModule**.) You can use this constructor to create a window object as an interface to an existing window—in a dynamic link library (DLL), for example:

```
TMyWin *myWinPtr = new TMyWin(hWnd);
```

In most cases, however, you should create a new window object and its internal element. For that, use TWindow's second constructor:

```
TWindow(TWindow* parent, const char far* title = 0,
  TModule* module = 0);
```

The first parameter is a pointer to the window's parent object. Because main windows have no parents, this pointer is null for a program's main window. When inserting child windows into parent windows, set parent to the parent window object's address. You may optionally pass a caption string to the constructor's title parameter. You can also pass a module pointer as in the first constructor, but you rarely need to do that.

A window's *caption* is simply a string that, in the case of common windows, is displayed as the window's title. The caption, however, may also be text associated with a child window—a control, for instance. Call TWindow's SetCaption function to change the window's title. To retrieve the current title, access the Title data member (a char pointer). For example:

```
string oldtitle(Title);
SetCaption("Press Enter or Click OK");
MessageBox("Pause", "Refreshing");
SetCaption(oldtitle.c_str());
```

The first line preserves the current window title in a string object, oldtitle (include the CSTRING.H header). Call SetCaption to change the window's caption, which also changes the Title pointer. I inserted a call to MessageBox just to demonstrate operations that follow the title change. To reset the title to its original text, call SetCaption again. In this case, I passed the C-style string equivalent of oldtitle to the function.

If you suspect that a window's caption (maintained internally as part of the window element) is not the same text addressed by TWindow object's Title, call GetWindowTextTitle to synchronize. The function sets TWindow's Title pointer to a copy of the string used as the windows caption.

> **NOTE**
>
> TWindow's Title pointer always addresses a copy of the windows caption. Call SetCaption to change the addressed string. Assigning strings to Title, or changing an addressed string by other means, does not automatically update the window's caption.

You've already seen other TWindow members. For example, you can call SetCursor to assign a dynamically changing cursor to a window object. When the mouse cursor passes over the window, it changes to the assigned design.

You also saw examples of the Attr structure, which has members that configure a window's position, size, and other attributes. Attr is defined in WINDOW.H as

```
struct TWindowAttr {
  DWORD      Style;
  DWORD      ExStyle;
  int        X, Y, W, H;
  TResId     Menu;
  int        Id;
  char far*  Param;
  TResId     AccelTable;
};
```

Style contains window style attribute bits. ExStyle contains extended window styles. X, Y, W, and H define the window's initial position and size. Menu equals a main window's menu resource. Id is a child window's optional integer identifier. (You may, for example, search for a child window by calling ChildWithId, which returns a TWindow pointer to a child window identified by a unique Id value.) Param addresses optional application-specific window-element creation parameters (see the Windows API function CreateWindowEx for more information—Attr.Param is passed to that function's lpvCreateParams parameter.) Most times, you can leave Param set to its null default value. AccelTable holds the resource identifier for an accelerator table.

During construction, TWindow constructors call an overloaded member function, Init, which initializes Attr members. To change any member, assign new values in your derived class constructor *after* calling the base class constructor. For example, to set a window's position and size, design your constructor like this (assume that TMainWin is a derived class of TFrameWindow, which is in turn derived from TWindow):

```
TMainWin::TMainWin(TWindow* parent, const char far* title)
  : TFrameWindow(parent, title),
    TWindow(parent, title)
{
  AssignMenu(ID_MENU);
  // ... Other initializations
  Attr.X = 345;
  Attr.Y = 260;
  Attr.W = 150;
  Attr.H = 200;
}
```

Use similar programming to select attributes for any window object of any class derived from TWindow. To set and reset window style bits, you can modify the Attr structure's Style member. The following code, for example, turns off the WS_MAXIMIZEBOX and WS_THICKFRAME default settings:

```
Attr.Style &= ~(WS_MAXIMIZEBOX ¦ WS_THICKFRAME);
```

For keeping track of windows of different kinds, TWindow maintains a private DWORD member, Flags. A TWindow object that is constructed from an existing window, for example, sets the wfAlias flag. This might be important to know if another process created the window element associated with a window object. If the object is a main window, the wfMainWindow flag is set, and so on. Flag values are constants of the TWindowFlag enumerated data type, defined in WINDOW.H as:

```
enum TWindowFlag {
  wfAlias           = 0x0001,
  wfAutoCreate      = 0x0002,
  wfFromResource    = 0x0004,
  wfShrinkToClient  = 0x0008,
  wfMainWindow      = 0x0010,
  wfStreamTop       = 0x0020,
  wfPredefinedClass = 0x0040,
  wfTransfer        = 0x0080,
  wfUnHidden        = 0x0100,
  wfUnDisabled      = 0x0200,
};
```

Use functions SetFlag, ClearFlag, and IsFlagSet to change and view these values. Given a TWindow pointer wp, for example, you can determine whether the window object is an alias (it was created from an existing window element) with the statement:

```
if (wp->IsFlagSet(wfAlias))
  DoSomething();
```

Frame Windows

A frame window is a specialized TWindow object that is used as a program's main window. Frame windows are objects of the TFrameWindow class (or a class derived from TFrameWindow), which is derived from TWindow. To its inheritance from TWindow, TFrameWindow adds keyboard handling, menu-command processing, and icon support. Objects of the TFrameWindow class also automatically restore the input focus for reactivated windows, simplifying keyboard operations.

You've already seen numerous examples of TFrameWindow objects used as main windows. In simple programs, a TFrameWindow might simply display some text or graphics, as in most of the sample programs presented so far. In more sophisticated applications, TFrameWindow objects perform two key services:

- They provide methods for changing a program's menus dynamically at runtime.
- They provide a program's output, either directly or through one or more attached client windows.

The following two sections describe these aspects of TFrameWindow programming.

Menu Handling in Frame Windows

Call TFrameWindow's AssignMenu function to assign a menu resource to a program's main window. Normally, you do that in the constructor of your class derived from TFrameWindow. For example, open the SKETCH.CPP file from the SKETCH application (listed in Chapter 7). The program's TSketchWin class, derived from TFrameWindow, constructs a main window and assigns its menu with the statement in bold:

```
// Constructor
TSketchWin::TSketchWin(TWindow* parent, const char far* title)
  : TFrameWindow(parent, title),
    TWindow(parent, title)
{
  AssignMenu(ID_MENU);
  dragging = FALSE;
  ...
}
```

You may call AssignMenu at other times, not only in a window's constructor. For example, a menu command can change the program's menu to a new one. Just call AssignMenu with the menu resource's id:

```
AssignMenu(ID_MENU2);
```

You can define as many menu resources as you need in the program's .RC script (or by using Resource Workshop). Changing menus completely, however, is rarely convenient. Instead, to implement *dynamic menus,* you probably need to keep some menus around while changing others. For example, in a program that edits files, you may want to display a Search menu only if a file is opened. You want the other menus—File and Help, for instance—to remain active at all times.

Instead of calling AssignMenu to change menus dynamically in response to commands or other conditions, you can prepare and insert a TMenuDescr object into a frame window. You can then select among a program's *menu groups,* as demonstrated by the next set of listings. TMenuDescr is a structure declared in FRAMEWIN.H (which also declares the `TFrameWindow` class). The structure simplifies the task of merging menus at runtime, usually after a menu command.

To use `TMenuDescr`, first write down your program's complete menu. Then, assign values to each of `TMenuDescr`'s six groups:

```
FileGroup, EditGroup, ContainerGroup,
ObjectGroup, WindowGroup, HelpGroup
```

It's your choice how many menus to assign to each group. For example, suppose the full menu looks like this:

```
File Edit Search View Tool Options Window Help
```

Divide the menus into groups. The `FileGroup` might have just one menu: *File*. The `EditGroup` might have two: *Edit* and *Search*. The `ContainerGroup` might have one: *View*. The `ObjectGroup` might have two: *Tool* and *Options*. The `WindowGroup` might have one: *Window*. And the `HelpGroup` might have one: *Help*. As a series of integer values, those groupings are:

```
1, 2, 1, 2, 1, 1
```

From those values, you can define partial menu sets. On startup, for instance, the program might display the shortened menu:

```
File Tool Options Help
```

That menu corresponds to the grouping:

```
1, 0, 0, 2, 0, 1
```

Zeros represent placeholders in the complete menu. The preceding series therefore represents one menu from the `FileGroup`, no menus from the `Edit-` and `ContainerGroups` (a total of three menus), two menus from the `ObjectGroup`, and one menu from the `HelpGroup`. Conversely, the following series represents the menus that fit into the "holes" (the zero values) in the preceding pattern:

```
0, 2, 1, 0, 1, 0
```

After laying the groundwork, you can design menu resources that correspond to the partial menu sets. You can then use the `TMenuDescr` structure along with three `TFrameWindow` member functions—`SetMenuDescr`, `MergeMenu`, and `RestoreMenu`—to create a dynamic menu that expands and shrinks in response to menu commands.

Listings 9.1 (MENUDEMO.RH), 9.2 (MENUDEMO.RC), and 9.3 (MENUDEMO.CPP) put the preceding techniques to the test. Run the program (open its MENUDEMO.IDE project) and select *File|Test* to expand the program's startup menu to its full configuration. Select the *Help\About* command, read the instructions, and select the message box's OK button to reset the menu to its partial size.

Listing 9.1. MENUDEMO.RH.

```
// menudemo.rh -- Resource header file

#define ID_MENU1      100
#define ID_MENU2 101
#define CM_TEST 101
#define CM_EDIT_COMMAND 102
#define CM_SEARCH_COMMAND 103
#define CM_VIEW_COMMAND 104
#define CM_TOOL_COMMAND 105
#define CM_OPTION_COMMAND 106
#define CM_WINDOW_COMMAND 107
#define CM_INSTRUCT 999
```

Listing 9.2. MENUDEMO.RC.

```
#include <owl\window.rh>
#include "menudemo.rh"

ID_MENU1 MENU
BEGIN
  POPUP "&File"
  BEGIN
    MENUITEM "&Test", CM_TEST
    MENUITEM "E&xit", CM_EXIT
  END
  POPUP "&Tools"
  BEGIN
    MENUITEM "Tool &command", CM_TOOL_COMMAND
  END
  POPUP "&Options"
  BEGIN
    MENUITEM "Option &command", CM_OPTION_COMMAND
  END
  POPUP "&Help"
  BEGIN
    MENUITEM "&Instructions", CM_INSTRUCT
  END
END

ID_MENU2 MENU
BEGIN
  POPUP "&Edit"
```

```
BEGIN
  MENUITEM "Edit &command", CM_EDIT_COMMAND
END
POPUP "&Search"
BEGIN
  MENUITEM "Search &command", CM_SEARCH_COMMAND
END
POPUP "&View"
BEGIN
  MENUITEM "View &command", CM_VIEW_COMMAND
END
POPUP "&Window"
BEGIN
  MENUITEM "Window &command", CM_WINDOW_COMMAND
END
END
```

Listing 9.3. MENUDEMO.CPP.

```
/* ============================================================ *\
** menudemo.cpp -- Demonstrate dynamic menus with TMenuDescr  **
** ============================================================ **
**                                                            **
** ============================================================ **
**     Copyright  1994 by Tom Swan. All rights reserved.      **
\* ============================================================ */

#include <owl\applicat.h>
#include <owl\framewin.h>
#pragma hdrstop
#include "menudemo.rh"


// ============================================================
// The application's main window
// ============================================================

class TDemoWin: public TFrameWindow {
public:
  TDemoWin(TWindow* parent, const char far* title);
protected:
  void CmTest();
  void CmInstruct();
private:
  BOOL merged;
```

continues

329

Listing 9.3. continued

```
DECLARE_RESPONSE_TABLE(TDemoWin);
};

DEFINE_RESPONSE_TABLE1(TDemoWin, TFrameWindow)
  EV_COMMAND(CM_TEST, CmTest),
  EV_COMMAND(CM_INSTRUCT, CmInstruct),
END_RESPONSE_TABLE;

// Constructor
TDemoWin::TDemoWin(TWindow* parent, const char far* title)
  : TFrameWindow(parent, title),
    TWindow(parent, title)
{
  merged = FALSE;
}

// Menu command function
void
TDemoWin::CmTest()
{
  if (!merged) {
    MergeMenu(TMenuDescr(ID_MENU2,0,2,1,0,1,0));
    merged = TRUE;
  }
}

// Display help window
void
TDemoWin::CmInstruct()
{
  string msg;
  string newline('\n');
  msg += "Menu Demonstration" + newline + newline;
  msg += "Selecting this command from the help" + newline;
  msg += "menu resets the menu to its startup" + newline;
  msg += "configuration. Selecting File¦Test" + newline;
  msg += "expands the menu to full size.";
  MessageBox(msg.c_str(), "About Box", MB_OK);
  RestoreMenu();
  merged = FALSE;
}

// ==============================================================
// The application class
// ==============================================================

class TMenuDemoApp: public TApplication {
public:
```

```
  TMenuDemoApp(const char far* name)
    : TApplication(name) {};
  void InitMainWindow();
};

// Initialize the program's main window
void
TMenuDemoApp::InitMainWindow()
{
// Standard method:
//  MainWindow = new TDemoWin(0, "Main Window");
// Alternate TMenuDescr method:
  TDemoWin *win = new TDemoWin(0, "Main Window");
  SetMainWindow(win);
  GetMainWindow()->
    SetMenuDescr(TMenuDescr(ID_MENU1,1,0,0,2,0,1));
}

#pragma argsused

// Main program
int
OwlMain(int argc, char* argv[])
{
  TMenuDemoApp app("MenuDemo");
  return app.Run();
}
```

For a better understanding of how the menu demonstration works, examine the resource script file, MENUDEMO.RC. The script defines two menus identified as ID_MENU1 and ID_MENU2. Notice that the menu items are not sequential—to create the final full menu with all its pieces in the proper order, portions of menu 2 must be *inserted* into menu 1. Normally, Windows programs do that by calling API functions such as AppendMenu, InsertMenu, DeleteMenu, GetSubMenu, and others—a complex chore that often requires painstaking debugging sessions to achieve reliable results. With TMenuDescr, you don't need to go to so much trouble. Instead, initialize your program's frame window as demonstrated in MENUDEMO.CPP at function InitMainWindow.

Normally, that function constructs a main window object and assigns its address to MainWindow like this:

```
MainWindow = new TDemoWin(0, "Main Window");
```

Using TMenuDescr, the process is a bit more complex. First, construct the window object, and save its pointer:

```
TDemoWin *win = new TDemoWin(0, "Main Window");
```

Make that object the program's main window by calling SetMainWindow, a function in the TApplication class:

```
SetMainWindow(win);
```

Finally, construct a TMenuDescr object for the program's initial menu resource—the one you want to have displayed when the program begins. Pass the object to the frame window by calling the window's SetMenuDescr function (defined in TFrameWindow):

```
GetMainWindow()->
  SetMenuDescr(TMenuDescr(ID_MENU1,1,0,0,2,0,1));
```

The menu pattern (1, 0, 0, 2, 0, 1) corresponds to the first partial menu set. This has the same effect as calling AssignMenu, but prepares the TFrameWindow object to merge another menu into the one described by the TMenuDescr object. For example, when you select the demonstration's *File|Test* command, the message-response function CmTest executes this code:

```
if (!merged) {
  MergeMenu(TMenuDescr(ID_MENU2,0,2,1,0,1,0));
  merged = TRUE;
}
```

If the frame window's merged flag is false, the program passes a second TMenuDescr object to TFrameWindow's MergeMenu function. The second partial menu, identified by ID_MENU2 in the program's resources, uses the pattern 0, 2, 1, 0, 1, 0, which tells MergeMenu which menus to merge into the existing menu bar. The result is a full menu composed of submenus from the second resource. Setting the merged flag true prevents merging the same menu twice.

To reset the menu to its startup configuration, CmInstruct (executed in the demonstration by selecting *Help|About*), calls TFrameWindow's RestoreMenu function. This resets the program's menu to the resource stored in the window's Attr structure.

TIP

Because this is just a demonstration, I did not provide response functions for all commands in MENUDEMO—a fact that is also true for a large program under development in which many functions might be unfinished. In classic Windows programming, unfinished menu commands need placeholder functions or their resources should be temporarily disabled to prevent the commands from being selected. Using OWL, however, commands without response functions are automatically grayed, preventing their selection. Just design your menu resource and fill in the response functions at your leisure.

Client Windows in Frame Windows

You can program output operations in a frame window—by using a Paint function, for example—or you can create a *client window* that you attach to a frame. This modularizes the program's output operations, simplifying their programming, and also makes it possible to create multiple clients for different jobs.

Create client windows by deriving one or more classes from TWindow. Construct objects of your client-window classes, and pass one of them to the TFrameWindow constructor when you create your program's main window. Call TFrameWindow's SetClientWindow function to change from one client to another. For example, declare a client window class like this:

```
class TClientWin: public TWindow {
public:
  TClientWin() : TWindow(0, "") {}
  // ... other members
};
```

Insert a Paint function, response functions, and other items in the class—whatever you need this client to do. Create other client classes similarly. Next, in your program's TApplication-derived class, attach a client object to the frame window. For example, in the application class's InitMainWindow function, you can use code such as this:

```
TWindow* client = new TClientWin;
MainWindow = new TFrameWindow(0, "Test", client, TRUE);
```

The first line defines a client window object of type TClientWin. The second line creates the program's frame window, and passes the client window object pointer as the third argument. The fourth argument, TRUE, tells the frame to shrink or expand to fit the client object's size. Set this argument to FALSE if you don't want the frame to automatically adjust its size.

Elsewhere, you can switch to another client window using code such as this:

```
TWindow* otherClient = new TOtherClientWin;
TWindow* client = MainWindow->GetClientWindow();
if (!client) return;
client->Show(SW_HIDE);
MainWindow->SetClientWindow(otherClient);
```

There are some other details in the process, but those are the essential steps. Function GetClientWindow returns the address of the frame's current client window object (if any). You can hide or delete the current client, and then attach a new one to the frame by calling TFrameWindow's SetClientWindow function.

## NINE

The following listings demonstrate how to write a program that toggles between two client window objects. This is a great way to organize a program that needs to switch among multiple output operations—easier than, for example, calling subfunctions from a single window's Paint method. Listings 9.4 (CLIENT.RH), 9.5 (CLIENT.RC), and 9.6 (CLIENT.CPP) form the demonstration. Compile and run the program by opening its CLIENT.IDE project file on disk and pressing Ctrl+F9. Then select the Demo|Test menu to toggle between the two clients. Client #1 displays a simple message (see Figure 9.1). Client #2 also displays some graphics just to show that another client object is in charge of the program's output (see Figure 9.2).

FIGURE 9.1.
Client #1.

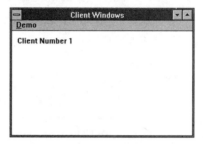

FIGURE 9.2.
Client #2.

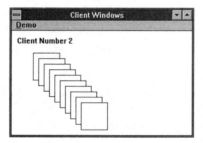

Listing 9.4. CLIENT.RH.

```
// client.rh -- Resource header file

#define ID_MENU      100
#define CM_TEST 101
```

Listing 9.5. CLIENT.RC.

```
#include <owl\window.rh>
#include "client.rh"

ID_MENU MENU
BEGIN
  POPUP "&Demo"
  BEGIN
    MENUITEM "&Test", CM_TEST
    MENUITEM "E&xit", CM_EXIT
  END
END
```

Listing 9.6. CLIENT.CPP.

```cpp
/* ========================================================== *\
**   client.cpp -- Attach client windows to a frame window    **
** ========================================================== **
**                                                            **
** ========================================================== **
**      Copyright  1994 by Tom Swan. All rights reserved.     **
\* ========================================================== */

#include <owl\applicat.h>
#include <owl\framewin.h>
#include <owl\dc.h>
#pragma hdrstop
#include "client.rh"

// ==========================================================
// The application's client window #1
// ==========================================================

class TClientWin1: public TWindow {
public:
  TClientWin1();
protected:
  void Paint(TDC& dc, BOOL erase, TRect& r);
};

// Constructor
TClientWin1::TClientWin1()
 : TWindow(0, "")
{
  Attr.X = GetSystemMetrics(SM_CXSCREEN) / 8;
```

continues

Listing 9.6. continued

```
  Attr.Y = GetSystemMetrics(SM_CYSCREEN) / 8;
  Attr.H = Attr.Y * 6;
  Attr.W = Attr.X * 6;
}

// Respond to update events for client #1
void
TClientWin1::Paint(TDC& dc, BOOL /*erase*/, TRect& /*r*/)
{
  dc.TextOut(10, 10, (const char far*)"Client Number 1");
}

// ============================================================
// The application's client window #2
// ============================================================

class TClientWin2: public TWindow {
public:
  TClientWin2() : TWindow(0, "") {}
protected:
  void Paint(TDC& dc, BOOL erase, TRect& r);
};

// Respond to update events for client #2
// Display some graphics just for fun
void
TClientWin2::Paint(TDC& dc, BOOL /*erase*/, TRect& /*r*/)
{
  dc.TextOut(10, 10, (const char far*)"Client Number 2");
  TSize s(50, 50);
  TPoint p(40, 40);
  for (int i = 0; i < 10; i++) {
    dc.Rectangle(p, s);
    p += TSize(10, 10);
  }
}

// ============================================================
// The application's main window
// ============================================================

class TFrame: public TFrameWindow {
public:
  TFrame(TWindow* parent, const char far* title,
    TWindow* clientWnd, BOOL shrinkToClient);
};
```

336

```
// Constructor
TFrame::TFrame(TWindow* parent, const char far* title,
  TWindow* clientWnd, BOOL shrinkToClient)
  : TFrameWindow(parent, title, clientWnd, shrinkToClient),
    TWindow(parent, title)
{
  AssignMenu(ID_MENU);
}

// ============================================================
// The application class
// ============================================================

class TClientApp: public TApplication {
public:
  TClientApp(const char far* name);
  ~TClientApp();
  void InitMainWindow();
protected:
  void CmTest();
private:
  TWindow* client1;  // Pointer to client #1 object
  TWindow* client2;  // Pointer to client #2 object
DECLARE_RESPONSE_TABLE(TClientApp);
};

DEFINE_RESPONSE_TABLE1(TClientApp, TApplication)
  EV_COMMAND(CM_TEST, CmTest),
END_RESPONSE_TABLE;

// Constructor
TClientApp::TClientApp(const char far* name)
  : TApplication(name)
{
  client1 = client2 = 0;
};

// Destructor
TClientApp::~TClientApp()
{
  MainWindow->SetClientWindow(0);  // Remove current client
  delete client1;
  delete client2;
}
```

continues

Listing 9.6. continued

```
// Initialize the program's main window
void
TClientApp::InitMainWindow()
{
  client1 = new TClientWin1;
  client2 = new TClientWin2;
  MainWindow = new TFrame(0, "Client Windows", client1, TRUE);
}

// Toggle between the two client windows
void
TClientApp::CmTest()
{
  TWindow* client = MainWindow->GetClientWindow();
  if (!client) return;      // Exit if no client is active
  client->Show(SW_HIDE);    // Hide current client window
  if (client == client1)    // Test which client is active
    client = client2;       // If #1 is active, switch to #2
  else                      // else...
    client = client1;       // If #2 is active, switch to #1
  MainWindow->SetClientWindow(client);  // Set new client
}

#pragma argsused

// Main program
int
OwlMain(int argc, char* argv[])
{
  TClientApp app("ClientApp");
  return app.Run();
}
```

Child Windows and Controls

Child windows add specialized interface elements to other windows. For example, a control such as a button or a scrollbar is a *child window* that a *parent window* owns. A program's main window object of type TFrameWindow (or a client window of a class derived from TWindow and assigned to the frame) might own various control objects of type TControl. Each of these objects is related through its common TWindow ancestry, and as a result, you program parent and child windows in many of the same ways.

Parent windows can also have other kinds of children. You can *decorate* a window with toolbars and status lines—but more on those subjects later in this chapter. In this section, you investigate child windows, and you learn how to use them to insert controls of various kinds in a program's window.

Child Windows

A parent window keeps track of its children through a private data member, `ChildList`, a `TWindow` pointer. Children also keep track of their parents—each child window has a public `Parent` pointer, also a `TWindow` pointer. You may access a child window's `Parent` pointer directly. You must call a member function, however, to access a parent window's children.

The relationships between parent and child window *objects* mirror the similar relationships among their internal window elements. Generally, however, you can ignore this fact and just deal with the objects. Internal window elements are maintained automatically for each object, and there's usually no need to access them directly.

The best place to construct child windows (a set of buttons, for instance) is in the parent window's constructor. That way, the child window elements are automatically created and displayed along with the parent. If you create child windows outside of the parent's constructor, then it's your responsibility to create their internal window elements (usually by calling `TWindow`'s `Create` function.). Two functions, `DisableAutoCreate` and `EnableAutoCreate`, make it possible to construct child window objects but *not* have them appear automatically along with their parent window. You can construct all of your child windows, and designate some of them to appear along with the parent, but save others to appear in response to various program operations. Usually, this is the best plan.

When the parent window closes, it automatically closes all of its child windows. All objects are deleted—you don't have to delete child windows by using the C++ `delete` operator. In addition, every child window object's `CanClose` function must return true, or the parent window will not close. `CanClose` normally returns true, so you normally can ignore this detail. When, however, you need to prevent a parent window from closing due to the condition of one or more child windows, simply implement a `CanClose` function in the child object. The parent will not close, nor will it delete any of its children, until all `CanClose` functions return true.

A few examples show how to put these concepts into action. First, declare a child window class based on `TWindow`:

```
class TChild: public TWindow {
public:
  TChild(TWindow* parent, const char far* title);
protected:
  void Paint(TDC& dc, BOOL erase, TRect& rect);
};
```

The class constructor can specify various attributes, and it can set the child's position and size by assigning values to the `Attr` structure:

```
TChild::TChild(TWindow* parent, const char far* title)
  : TWindow(parent, title)
{
  Attr.Style = (WS_POPUP | WS_VISIBLE | WS_OVERLAPPEDWINDOW);
  Attr.X = 0;
  Attr.Y = 0;
  Attr.W = 200;
  Attr.H = 300;
}
```

Use a Paint function to insert text and graphics in the child window's client area:

```
// Respond to update events
void
TChild::Paint(TDC& dc, BOOL /*erase*/, TRect& /*rect*/)
{
  dc.TextOut(10, 10, "Child window contents");
}
```

Next, create a main window class derived from TFrameWindow as you normally do. Create the child window object in the frame's constructor, as demonstrated here:

```
TFrame::TFrame(TWindow* parent, const char far* title)
  : TFrameWindow(parent, title),
    TWindow(parent, title)
{
  AssignMenu(ID_MENU);
  TChild* p = new TChild(this, "Child Window");
  p->SetCursor(0, IDC_CROSS);
}
```

The call to SetCursor just shows that you can access child window objects at the parent level, or you can program capabilities directly in the child. (The child object could have a SetupWindow function, for example, that calls SetCursor.) Passing this to the TChild constructor automatically sets the relationships among the parent and child. Because the parent owns the child object, the child window closes automatically—and its associated object is deleted—when the parent closes.

Child Window Controls

You can create child windows as demonstrated in the preceding section, but most children are specialized *control windows*. Controls have many features that make them easier to program than plain child windows. For example, you can insert a text-input control into a window. To do the same with a plain child window requires you to write text-editing functions from scratch, which is no easy job.

In the next two chapters, you investigate dialog boxes and child window controls along with dialog boxes, so I'll postpone a detailed explanation of control objects for the moment. Following are general techniques that you can use to insert controls of any type into windows.

Control classes are derived from TControl, a derived class of TWindow. All control class objects, then, inherit TWindow's members, and you program them just as you do other windows. Control classes are highly specialized, however, for different kinds of interface requirements. A TButton control, for example, is a TWindow class object extended to display a pushbutton, and to permit that button's selection using the mouse or keyboard.

To add a control to a window, first define a symbolic constant that uniquely identifies the control among all child windows owned by the parent. To add OK and Cancel buttons to a window, you might first define these two constants:

```
#define ID_OK_BUTTON 100;
#define ID_CANCEL_BUTTON 101;
```

The exact values are unimportant—just be sure to uniquely identify all controls and other child windows are uniquely identified. Next, define TButton pointers in the window class (it can be any class derived from TWindow, or it can be the program's main window class, derived from TFrameWindow). First include the BUTTON.H header:

```
#include <owl\button.h>
```

Then, declare the window class:

```
class TButtonWin: public TFrameWindow {
public:
  TButtonWin(TWindow* parent, const char far* title);
protected:
  void OkButtonResponse();
  void CancelButtonResponse();
private:
  TButton* okButton;
  TButton* cancelButton;
DECLARE_RESPONSE_TABLE(TButtonWin);
};
```

The two private TButton pointers, okButton and cancelButton, listed in bold, have corresponding response functions, OkButtonResponse and CancelButtonResponse. Define a response table listing the button ID constants and these functions. When you select a button, the response table handles the resulting message by calling the associated function:

```
DEFINE_RESPONSE_TABLE1(TButtonWin, TFrameWindow)
  EV_COMMAND(ID_OK_BUTTON, OkButtonResponse),
  EV_COMMAND(ID_CANCEL_BUTTON, CancelButtonResponse),
END_RESPONSE_TABLE;
```

In the window's constructor, create the two button objects and assign their addresses to the TButton pointers:

```
// Constructor
TButtonWin::TButtonWin(TWindow* parent, const char far* title)
  : TFrameWindow(parent, title),
    TWindow(parent, title)
{
  AssignMenu(ID_MENU);
  okButton = new TButton(this, ID_OK_BUTTON, "OK",
    50, 40, 100, 40, TRUE);
  cancelButton = new TButton(this, ID_CANCEL_BUTTON, "Cancel",
    50, 100, 100, 40, FALSE);
}
```

Because the program passes this to the TButton constructor, the objects become children of the parent frame window. When the window is created, it automatically creates window elements for each of its children. The buttons are therefore automatically displayed, and because they are child windows, they "stick" to their parent. Move the parent, and its children tag along.

Actually, you don't have to save the TButton object addresses in pointers as shown here. The only reason to do so is to provide a means to access the objects elsewhere. If all you need is a button that calls a response function, you don't need to save the button object's pointer. Parent windows automatically delete their child windows at the appropriate time, and you can safely discard a TButton object's pointer even though you constructed the object with the C++ new operator.

Of course, you also have to write the OkButtonResponse and CancelButtonResponse functions to perform operations for button selections. The actions of selecting a button are limited only by your imagination. You might, for example, want to create *dynamic controls* that affect one another, as demonstrated by the next set of listings. The program inserts two buttons in a window, *Help* and *Enable Exit*. Click the *Help* button for instructions (or select the *Demo\Help* command). Click *Enable Exit* to display a third button, *Exit,* which you can select to end the program. When *Exit* is visible, the *Enable Exit* button's label changes to *Disable Exit*. Click that button to remove the *Exit* button from the display. You can use the technique demonstrated by the sample program to enable advanced features or other options upon selecting a certain button—a good way to reduce the clutter in a busy display.

Listings 9.7 (BUTTON.RH), 9.8 (BUTTON.RC), and 9.9 (BUTTON.CPP) list the program's source files. As usual, open the BUTTON.IDE project on disk and press Ctrl+F9 to compile and run. Figure 9.3 shows the program's window with the *Exit* button displayed. I explain more about the program after the BUTTON.CPP listing.

FIGURE 9.3.
BUTTON's display.

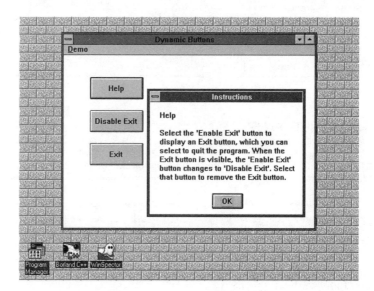

Listing 9.7. BUTTON.RH.

```
// button.rh -- Resource header file

// Menu resource and command ID
#define ID_MENU        100
#define CM_HELP 101

// Button IDs
#define ID_HELP 201
#define ID_ENABLE 202
#define ID_EXIT 203
```

Listing 9.8. BUTTON.RC.

```
#include <owl\window.rh>
#include "button.rh"

ID_MENU MENU
BEGIN
  POPUP "&Demo"
  BEGIN
    MENUITEM "&Help...", CM_HELP
  END
END
```

Listing 9.9. BUTTON.CPP.

```
/* ============================================================ *\
**   button.cpp -- Demonstrate button child controls           **
** ============================================================ **
**                                                              **
** ============================================================ **
**      Copyright  1994 by Tom Swan. All rights reserved.       **
\* ============================================================ */

#include <owl\applicat.h>
#include <owl\framewin.h>
#include <owl\button.h>
#include <cstring.h>
#pragma hdrstop
#include "button.rh"

// ==========================================================
// The application's main window
// ==========================================================

class TButtonWin: public TFrameWindow {
public:
  TButtonWin(TWindow* parent, const char far* title);
protected:
  void CmHelp();
  void EnableExit();
  void ExitProgram();
private:
  TButton* helpButton;
  TButton* enableButton;
  TButton* exitButton;
DECLARE_RESPONSE_TABLE(TButtonWin);
};
```

```
DEFINE_RESPONSE_TABLE1(TButtonWin, TFrameWindow)
  EV_COMMAND(CM_HELP, CmHelp),
  EV_COMMAND(ID_HELP, CmHelp),
  EV_COMMAND(ID_ENABLE, EnableExit),
  EV_COMMAND(ID_EXIT, ExitProgram),
END_RESPONSE_TABLE;

// Constructor
TButtonWin::TButtonWin(TWindow* parent, const char far* title)
  : TFrameWindow(parent, title),
    TWindow(parent, title)
{
  AssignMenu(ID_MENU);
  Attr.X = GetSystemMetrics(SM_CXSCREEN) / 8;
  Attr.Y = GetSystemMetrics(SM_CYSCREEN) / 8;
  Attr.H = Attr.Y * 6;
  Attr.W = Attr.X * 6;

  helpButton = new TButton(this, ID_HELP, "Help",
    50, 40, 100, 40, TRUE);

  enableButton = new TButton(this, ID_ENABLE, "Enable Exit",
    50, 100, 100, 40, FALSE);

  exitButton = new TButton(this, ID_EXIT, "Exit",
    50, 160, 100, 40, FALSE);
  exitButton->DisableAutoCreate();
}

// Respond to "Help" button and menu command selections
void
TButtonWin::CmHelp()
{
  string msg;
  string newline('\n');
  msg += "Select the 'Enable Exit' button to" + newline;
  msg += "display an Exit button, which you can" + newline;
  msg += "select to quit the program. When the" + newline;
  msg += "Exit button is visible, the 'Enable Exit'" + newline;
  msg += "button changes to 'Disable Exit'. Select" + newline;
  msg += "that button to remove the Exit button.";
  MessageBox(msg.c_str(), "Instructions", MB_OK);
}
```

continues

Listing 9.9. continued

```
// Respond to "Enable Exit" button selection
void
TButtonWin::EnableExit()
{
  if (exitButton->IsWindow()) {
    exitButton->Destroy();
    enableButton->SetCaption("Enable Exit");
  } else {
    exitButton->Create();
    enableButton->SetCaption("Disable Exit");
  }
}

// Respond to "Exit" button selection
void
TButtonWin::ExitProgram()
{
  CloseWindow();
}

// ============================================================
// The application class
// ============================================================

class TButtonApp: public TApplication {
public:
  TButtonApp(const char far* name)
    : TApplication(name) {};
  void InitMainWindow();
};

// Initialize the program's main window
void
TButtonApp::InitMainWindow()
{
  MainWindow = new TButtonWin(0, "Dynamic Buttons");
}

#pragma argsused

// Main program
int
OwlMain(int argc, char* argv[])
{
  TButtonApp app("ButtonApp");
  return app.Run();
}
```

BUTTON's resource header defines two menu resource identifiers. ID_MENU identifies the menu resource as it does for most of this book's sample programs. CM_HELP identifies the *Help* command in the *Demo* menu.

Three other constants identify each of three buttons displayed in the program's main window (see Figure 9.3). ID_HELP identifies the *Help* button (and causes the same action as the *Help* command). ID_ENABLE identifies the *Enable Exit* button. ID_EXIT identifies the *Exit* button, displayed by selecting *Enable Exit.*

In the program's source file, BUTTON.CPP, class TButtonWin, derived from TFrameWindow for the program's main window, defines three TButton pointers, one for each button control: helpButton, enableButton, and exitButton. Three member functions—CmHelp, EnableExit, and ExitProgram—are called in response to button selections. Selecting the *Demo\Help* command also calls CmHelp, showing how one function can respond to more than one event.

The class's response table associates the menu command and button identifiers with the appropriate response functions. All that remains is to construct the buttons and write the function statements. The TButtonWin constructor creates the three TButton objects, and assigns their addresses to the private pointers. The following statement constructs the *Help* button:

```
helpButton = new TButton(this, ID_HELP, "Help",
  50, 40, 100, 40, TRUE);
```

As usual, passing this to the TButton constructor causes the object to become a child of the parent window. The second constructor argument identifies the button as ID_HELP. The third argument assigns the button label. After that, four integer values give the button's position (50, 40) relative to the window, and its width and height (100, 40) in display units. TRUE makes this the default button (which doesn't matter in this case since keyboard support is lacking in the demo). Change the last argument to FALSE for all other child controls.

The program constructs the second and third buttons similarly. The *Exit* button, however, adds a new twist:

```
exitButton = new TButton(this, ID_EXIT, "Exit",
  50, 160, 100, 40, FALSE);
exitButton->DisableAutoCreate();
```

Normally, a parent window automatically creates window elements for all of its child window objects. Because those window elements usually have their WS_VISIBLE attribute bit set, the child windows are also automatically displayed along with the parent. When you don't want a window element to be created automatically—and thus, the child window remains hidden even though its window *object* is fully constructed—call that object's DisableAutoCreate function as shown here. In the demonstration, the *Exit* button object addressed by exitButton is ready for use, but it lacks an associated window element, and therefore, the button isn't displayed in the parent window. (The corresponding function,

`EnableAutoCreate`, prepares child windows for automatic creation of their window elements.)

Call TWindow's `Create` function to create a window element for a TWindow object (or an object of a derived class). Call the `Delete` function to delete a window element for any TWindow object. The functions do not affect the object in any way—they merely create and destroy the object's associated window elements. In the sample program, for example, the `EnableExit` function (called when you select the *Enable Exit* button) executes the following if statement:

```
if (exitButton->IsWindow()) {
  exitButton->Destroy();
  enableButton->SetCaption("Enable Exit");
} else {
  exitButton->Create();
  enableButton->SetCaption("Disable Exit");
}
```

Function `IsWindow` returns true if a TWindow object has a valid window element. (As I've mentioned, when I say "TWindow object," I mean any object of the TWindow class or of a derived class such as TButton here.). Calling `Destroy` removes the window element from the object addressed by `exitButton`, and therefore, also removes the *Exit* button from the window. The object, however, remains ready to use. The next time you select *Enable Exit*, the program calls the `Create` function to create a window element for the object. This also redisplays the button. Notice also how `SetCaption` changes the *Enable* button's label.

Decorated Frame Windows

By using a class derived from TFrameWindow, you can add *gadgets* such as toolbars and status lines to a program's main window. You might think of gadgets as *exceptional child windows* that perform highly sophisticated interface tasks. In the following sections, you build a demonstration program, listed at the end of the chapter, that produces the window shown in Figure 9.4.

Just under the menu bar is a *toolbar* of icons that you can select with a mouse to perform operations. To the right is a *toolbox* of the same icons (in another program, a paint application, for instance, a toolbox might list various drawing tools). At the bottom of the window is a *statusline,* which shows online help messages for menu and toolbar selections. The statusline also shows the states of the *CapsLock, NumLock, ScrLock,* and *Ins* keys. Obviously, there's a lot happening in this program's busy display, but the programming is relatively simple, as the next sections explain.

FIGURE 9.4.

Sample decorated window.

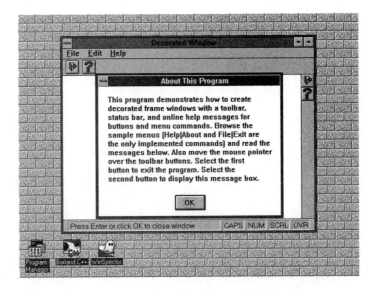

Laying Out Child Windows

The TLayoutWindow class is the cement that holds a decorated frame window and its child windows in place. You probably won't ever use TLayoutWindow directly, but you should understand in general terms what this class does.

A TLayoutWindow object organizes a frame window's child windows according to various *layout metrics.* The metrics consist of coordinate, width, and height values that position and size child windows. Layout metrics also define *constraints* that, for example, anchor a child window to another window's border, or that specify a child window's size as a percentage of its parent. Layout metrics are objects of the TLayoutMetrics class.

Defining your own child window layouts is a difficult task, but fortunately, you probably won't need to use the TLayoutWindow and TLayoutMetrics classes directly. For most programs, you can define your main window using the TDecoratedFrame class described in the next section. Derived from TFrameWindow and TLayoutWindow, the TDecoratedFrame class can maintain child-window gadgets (a toolbar, for example) that you construct using various supplied classes. The following section explains how to construct a program's main window with the TDecoratedFrame class.

349

Decorating Frame Windows

Use the TDecoratedFrame class to construct your program's main window. For example, derive your program's main-window class from TDecoratedFrame like this:

```
class TDecWin: public TDecoratedFrame {
public:
  TDecWin(TWindow* parent, const char far* title);
};
```

Of course, you can add other members to the class. I used only a constructor for the demonstration. The constructor must call the TDecoratedFrame and TWindow base-class constructors as follows:

```
// Constructor
TDecWin::TDecWin(TWindow* parent, const char far* title)
  : TDecoratedFrame(parent, title, 0, TRUE),
    TWindow(parent, title)
{
  AssignMenu(ID_MENU);
  // ... other statements
}
```

You can pass up to five arguments to the TDecoratedFrame constructor. The first argument is a TWindow pointer to the parent window. The second is the caption you want to have appear in the window's top border. The third parameter (0 in the example) can be the address of a client window, not used in this case. The fourth parameter, TRUE, tells the decorated window to track highlighted menu commands and to attempt to display a message in the window's statusline. Each message must be identified in a string-table resource by the same identifier used by the menu command. Set the fourth parameter to FALSE if you do not want statusline messages. (You *must* set it FALSE if the windows doesn't have a statusline.) You can also pass a fifth argument to the TDecoratedFrame constructor as the address of the application's TModule object. Most often, you can leave out this argument, which defaults to 0.

Inserting Gadgets into Decorated Frames

Construct an object of your TDecoratedFrame class in the same way you construct a nondecorated frame of type TFrameWindow. In the application's InitMainWindow function, for instance, use code such as this to create a decorated frame window (assume that TAnyApp is the application's class derived from TApplication):

```
void
TAnyApp::InitMainWindow()
{
  TDecWin* frame = new TDecWin(0, "Decorated Window");
  // .. Insert gadgets here
  MainWindow = frame;
}
```

First, construct an object of the TDecoratedFrame class (TDecWin in the example). To use that object as the program's main window, assign its address to MainWindow. In between those two steps, at the comment *Insert gadgets here,* you can also construct and insert *gadget windows* of five varieties, each a class that is derived from TGadgetWindow:

- TControlBar—For a toolbar of icons, usually displayed at the top of a window, just under the menu bar (as in the sample window shown in Figure 9.4).

- TToolBox—For a toolbox of icons, displayed as a multicolumn matrix, usually along a window's right or left border. A paint program, for example, might use a TToolBox object to provide selectable icons for line, circle, pen, and other drawing tools. (The sample application in Figure 9.4 has a single-column toolbox anchored to the main window's right edge.)

- TMessageBar—For a simple message bar, usually displayed at the bottom of a main window. You can display any text in this child window, and you also can have the decorated frame display online help messages automatically for highlighted menu commands and for toolbar buttons pointed to and selected by a mouse.

- TStatusBar—For a more complex message bar that, in addition to all the capabilities of TMessageBar, can also display the states of *CapsLock, NumLock, ScrLock,* and *Ins* keys (Figure 9.4 shows a sample at the window's bottom-right corner). The TStatusBar class is derived from TMessageBar.

Objects of those types can hold one or more *gadgets,* each an object of a TGadget class. Gadgets, in other words, are owned by a gadget window, which is inserted as a child window into the decorated frame. That frame uses a layout window to arrange the gadget windows according to various constraints that you specify when constructing the gadget windows. You can construct these gadget objects (each a class derived from TGadget):

- TBitmapGadget—Displays a bitmap in a gadget window. Use this gadget to show colors, patterns, and other noninteractive objects.

- TButtonGadget—Displays clickable buttons that appear to be up or down. Use this gadget to create selectable option buttons in toolbars.

- TTextGadget—Displays text within a defined region. Use this gadget for custom message lines.

351

- **TSeparatorGadget**—Displays blank space. Use this gadget to separate other gadgets from one another in a gadget window.
- **TControlGadget**—Displays control objects in a gadget window. Use this gadget as a "surrogate" for TControl for inserting control buttons, checkbox, even Visual BASIC controls (VBX), in a gadget window. (See other chapters in this book for more information on the TControl class and on VBX controls.)

How To Create a Toolbar

Using gadget windows and gadget objects, you can construct a toolbar of icons. Users can select the icons, which appear to move up and down. Selecting an icon issues a command event, the same as selecting a menu command. A window class can respond to the event with a message response function.

To create a toolbar, first define menu commands and their identifiers. You might, for example, define these two commands in a resource header file:

```
#define CM_FILEEXIT 24340
#define CM_HELPABOUT 24346
```

I borrowed those constants from other OWL header files, but you don't have to use the default values listed here. (The defaults, however, are associated with standard online help strings.) Also define constants for your toolbar icons:

```
#define IDB_EXIT 600
#define IDB_HELP 601
```

In the resource file, define your program's menu commands as you normally do. In addition, create icons (usually 20-by-20 pixels in size) for each toolbar button. Here's a partial sample as it might appear in the resource script (look ahead to DECORATE.RC in this chapter for complete sample icons):

```
IDB_EXIT BITMAP
{
 '42 4D 66 01 00 00 00 00 00 00 76 00 00 00 28 00'
 ...
}
```

With those preliminary steps out of the way, you are ready to construct the toolbar. Include the CONTROLB.H header file:

```
#include <owl\controlb.h>
```

Then, in the application's TApplication class, define a pointer to address the toolbar object:

```
TControlBar* toolbar;
```

Next, in the application's `InitMainWindow` function, after constructing the `TDecoratedFrame` object, construct a toolbar of the `TControlBar` class, and assign the object's address to `toolbar`:

```
toolbar = new TControlBar(frame);
```

That completes the construction of the toolbar gadget child window. You next insert gadget objects into the child window, one object for each icon plus any separators between the images. Call the toolbar's `Insert` function to insert each object. The following statements, for example, insert two `TButtonGadget` objects and one `TSeparatorGadget`:

```
toolbar->Insert(*new TButtonGadget(IDB_EXIT, CM_FILEEXIT));
toolbar->Insert(*new TSeparatorGadget(6));
toolbar->Insert(*new TButtonGadget(IDB_HELP, CM_HELPABOUT));
```

In each gadget, specify the icon and command identifiers from the program's resource header. The application also needs a response table for each command. At runtime, selecting an icon from the toolbar issues a `WM_COMMAND` message for the appropriate command, and calls the proper response function. You don't have to intercept that message in any special way—just program command-response functions as you do for menu commands.

Finally, after inserting the gadgets you want in the toolbar, insert the toolbar gadget window into the frame:

```
frame->Insert(*toolbar, TDecoratedFrame::Top);
```

Pass the toolbar *object,* not its address, in the first argument. Pass a `TDecoratedFrame` enumerated value—`Left`, `Top`, `Right`, or `Bottom`—as the second argument. (This is how you specify a layout metric constraint for the child window.)

In addition, you might also want to enable automatic *hints*—online help messages that appear in a status line when the mouse pointer passes over a toolbar icon. You do not have to click the button to see these messages. To enable this feature, you must prepare a status line and associated message strings (I explain how in the next section). Use this statement before inserting the toolbar into the frame window:

```
toolbar->SetHintMode(TGadgetWindow::EnterHints);
```

How To Create a Status Line

You can also construct a status line gadget window for messages and to display the states of the *CapsLock* and other keys. You can also have messages appear in a status line for highlighted commands and selected toolbar buttons (see the sample application at the end of this chapter for details on how to link all these features together).

Include the MESSAGEB.H header file:

```
#include <owl\messageb.h>
```

Then, in your TApplication class, define a TMessageBar pointer:

```
TMessageBar* statusLine;
```

In InitMainWindow, construct a TMessageBar object, and assign its address to the statusLine pointer. Insert the status line gadget window into the TDecoratedFrame object (addressed in these examples by a frame pointer). Usually, the status line should go at the bottom of a window, but you could change Bottom to Top if you prefer:

```
statusLine = new TMessageBar(frame);
frame->Insert(*statusLine, TDecoratedFrame::Bottom);
```

You can now display text in the status line gadget window. Simply call the TMessageBar class's SetText function:

```
statusLine->SetText("Press Enter to continue...");
```

For a more complex status line, define the statusLine pointer using the TStatusBar class instead of TMessageBar. Include the STATUSBA.H header:

```
#include <owl\statusba.h>
```

Then, define the pointer like this:

```
TStatusBar* statusLine;
```

In the application class's InitMainWindow function, construct the status line object and insert it into the frame window using statements such as:

```
statusLine = new TStatusBar(frame, TGadget::Recessed,
  TStatusBar::CapsLock ¦ TStatusBar::NumLock ¦
  TStatusBar::ScrollLock ¦ TStatusBar::Overtype);
frame->Insert(*statusLine, TDecoratedFrame::Bottom);
```

To the TStatusBar constructor, pass the parent window address in the first argument (frame addresses the TDecoratedFrame object). Pass an enumerated value such as TGadget::Recessed to select a border style (you may change Recessed to None, Plain, Raised, or Embossed). Finally, to add keyboard status indicators to the status line, pass the logical-OR combination of one or more TModeIndicator values such as TStatusBar::CapsLock. You may use any combination of the values ExtendSelection, CapsLock, NumLock, ScrollLock, Overtype, and RecordingMacro. Because the TModeIndicator enumerated type is a member of the TStatusBar class, you must precede each value with the class name as shown in the sample.

Combining Toolbars and Status Lines

You may also want to combine a toolbar and status line to show online help messages (also called *hints*) for highlighted menu selections and toolbar buttons. Each message must be a string in a string-table resource. Identify each message using the command identifier from the menu resource. For example, you might add this string table resource to your program's .RC script:

```
STRINGTABLE LOADONCALL MOVEABLE DISCARDABLE
{
  CM_FILEEXIT, "Quits the application"
  CM_HELPABOUT, "Displays message box"
}
```

In your decorated frame class constructor, be sure to pass TRUE as the fourth argument when calling the `TDecoratedFrame` base class. This tells the object to enable its `trackMenuSelection` flag, which enables online help messages for highlighted menu commands:

```
TDecWin::TDecWin(TWindow* parent, const char far* title)
  : TDecoratedFrame(parent, title, 0, TRUE),
    TWindow(parent, title)
{
}
```

Those steps enable online help messages for toolbar buttons—you don't need to take any additional steps. (Toolbar buttons are already linked to menu commands—in fact, they *are* menu commands displayed in icon form.) If, however, you want online messages to appear when the mouse pointer merely passes over the toolbar's icons—you don't have to click the mouse—also call the toolbar's `SetHintMode` function like this:

```
toolbar->SetHintMode(TGadgetWindow::EnterHints);
```

Change `EnterHints` to `PressHints` (the default setting) if you want a message to appear only when clicking the mouse pointer on a button. Use `NoHints` to disable messages.

You can make these changes at any time—in response to an option command, for example, often provided in Windows programs to turn off online help for experienced users.

Understanding the Sample Application

The foregoing notes about layout windows, decorated frames, gadget windows, and gadget objects, will be much clearer after you study a sample application that puts all of these features into action. Because this program is larger than most in the book, I explain each listing separately. Listing 9.10, DECORATE.RH, defines the program's resource identifiers.

Listing 9.10. DECORATE.RH.

```
// decorate.rh -- Resource header file

// Menu resource and command identifiers
#define ID_MENU 100

// File menu commands
#define CM_FILENEW 24331
#define CM_FILEOPEN 24332
#define CM_FILESAVE 24333
#define CM_FILESAVEAS 24334
#define CM_FILEPRINT 24337
#define CM_FILEPAGESETUP 24338
#define CM_FILEPRINTERSETUP 24339
#define CM_FILEEXIT 24340


// Edit menu commands
#define CM_EDITUNDO 24321
#define CM_EDITCUT 24322
#define CM_EDITCOPY 24323
#define CM_EDITPASTE 24324


// Help menu commands
#define CM_HELPINDEX 24341
#define CM_HELPKEYBOARD 24342
#define CM_HELPCOMMANDS 24343
#define CM_HELPPROCEDURES 24344
#define CM_HELPUSINGHELP 24345
#define CM_HELPABOUT 24346


// Toolbar button icon identifiers
#define IDB_EXIT 600
#define IDB_HELP 601
```

I borrowed most of the values in DECORATE.RH from .RH and .RC files included with BC4. The identifiers are used by various help-message strings and functions, and are automatically inserted by Resource Workshop commands. You don't have to use the default values—you can define your own menu command constants. For this demonstration, however, I wanted to include several sample commands, so I used the defaults. (Most commands have no corresponding functions—they are just for show.)

Listing 9.11, DECORATE.RC, is the program's resource script, created by Resource Workshop.

NOTE

Unlike most other .RC files in this book, curly braces { and } delimit the beginnings and ends of various resources. You may use the key words BEGIN and END interchangeably with braces, inserted by Resource Workshop.

Listing 9.11. DECORATE.RC.

```
#include <owl\window.rh>
#include "decorate.rh"

ID_MENU MENU
{
 POPUP "&File"
 {
  MENUITEM "&New", CM_FILENEW
  MENUITEM "&Open...", CM_FILEOPEN
  MENUITEM "&Save", CM_FILESAVE
  MENUITEM "Save &as...", CM_FILESAVEAS
  MENUITEM SEPARATOR
  MENUITEM "&Print...", CM_FILEPRINT
  MENUITEM "Page se&tup...", CM_FILEPAGESETUP
  MENUITEM "P&rinter setup...", CM_FILEPRINTERSETUP
  MENUITEM SEPARATOR
  MENUITEM "E&xit", CM_FILEEXIT
 }
```

continues

Listing 9.11. continued

```
POPUP "&Edit"
{
 MENUITEM "&Undo\tCtrl+Z", CM_EDITUNDO
 MENUITEM "&Cut\tCtrl+X", CM_EDITCUT
 MENUITEM "&Copy\tCtrl+C", CM_EDITCOPY
 MENUITEM "&Paste\tCtrl+V", CM_EDITPASTE
}

POPUP "&Help"
{
 MENUITEM "&Index\tF1", CM_HELPINDEX
 MENUITEM "&Keyboard", CM_HELPKEYBOARD
 MENUITEM "&Commands", CM_HELPCOMMANDS
 MENUITEM "&Procedures", CM_HELPPROCEDURES
 MENUITEM "&Using help", CM_HELPUSINGHELP
 MENUITEM SEPARATOR
 MENUITEM "&About...", CM_HELPABOUT
}

}

IDB_EXIT BITMAP
{
 '42 4D 66 01 00 00 00 00 00 00 76 00 00 00 28 00'
 '00 00 14 00 00 00 14 00 00 00 01 00 04 00 00 00'
 '00 00 F0 00 00 00 00 00 00 00 00 00 00 00 00 00'
 '00 00 10 00 00 00 00 00 00 00 00 00 BF 00 00 BF'
 '00 00 00 BF BF 00 BF 00 00 00 BF 00 BF 00 BF BF'
 '00 00 C0 C0 C0 00 80 80 80 00 00 00 FF 00 00 FF'
 '00 00 00 FF FF 00 FF 00 00 00 FF 00 FF 00 FF FF'
 '00 00 FF FF FF 00 77 77 77 77 77 77 77 77 77 77'
 '00 00 77 77 77 77 77 77 77 77 77 77 00 00 77 77'
 '77 77 70 77 77 77 77 77 00 00 77 77 77 77 00 77'
 '77 77 77 77 00 00 77 77 77 70 80 77 77 77 77 77'
 '00 00 77 77 77 08 80 77 77 77 77 77 00 00 77 77'
 '70 88 80 00 07 77 77 77 00 00 77 77 70 88 80 FF'
 '07 07 77 77 00 00 77 77 70 88 80 FF 00 07 77 77'
 '00 00 77 77 70 88 80 FF 00 80 00 77 00 00 77 77'
 '70 88 80 F0 08 88 80 77 00 00 77 77 70 88 80 00'
 '88 88 80 77 00 00 77 77 70 88 80 F0 08 88 80 77'
 '00 00 77 77 70 88 80 FF 00 80 00 77 00 00 77 77'
 '70 88 0F FF 00 07 77 77 00 00 77 77 70 80 FF FF'
 '07 07 77 77 00 00 77 77 70 0F FF FF 07 77 77 77'
 '00 00 77 77 70 00 00 00 07 77 77 77 00 00 77 77'
 '77 77 77 77 77 77 77 77 00 00 77 77 77 77 77 77'
 '77 77 77 77 00 00'
}

IDB_HELP BITMAP
{
 '42 4D 66 01 00 00 00 00 00 00 76 00 00 00 28 00'
```

```
'00 00 14 00 00 00 14 00 00 00 01 00 04 00 00 00'
'00 00 F0 00 00 00 00 00 00 00 00 00 00 00 00 00'
'00 00 10 00 00 00 00 00 00 00 00 00 BF 00 00 BF'
'00 00 00 BF BF 00 BF 00 00 00 BF 00 BF 00 BF BF'
'00 00 C0 C0 C0 00 80 80 80 00 00 00 FF 00 00 FF'
'00 00 00 FF FF 00 FF 00 00 00 FF 00 FF 00 FF FF'
'00 00 FF FF FF 00 77 77 77 70 00 07 77 77 77 77'
'00 00 77 77 77 06 66 60 77 77 77 77 00 00 77 77'
'77 0E 66 60 77 77 77 77 00 00 77 77 77 0E E6 60'
'77 77 77 77 00 00 77 77 77 70 00 07 77 77 77 77'
'00 00 77 77 77 70 00 07 77 77 77 77 00 00 77 77'
'77 06 66 60 77 77 77 77 00 00 77 77 77 06 66 60'
'77 77 77 77 00 00 77 77 77 06 E6 60 77 77 77 77'
'00 00 77 77 77 70 E6 66 07 77 77 77 00 00 77 77'
'77 77 06 E6 60 07 77 77 00 00 77 77 77 77 70 6E'
'66 60 77 77 00 00 77 77 77 77 77 06 E6 66 07 77'
'00 00 77 70 00 07 77 77 06 E6 60 77 00 00 77 06'
'66 60 77 77 06 E6 60 77 00 00 77 06 66 60 77 77'
'06 66 60 77 00 00 77 70 E6 66 00 00 66 66 60 77'
'00 00 77 70 6E 66 66 66 66 66 07 77 00 00 77 77'
'00 EE 66 66 66 60 77 77 00 00 77 77 77 00 00 00'
'00 07 77 77 00 00'
}

STRINGTABLE LOADONCALL MOVEABLE DISCARDABLE
{
  CM_FILEPAGESETUP, "Selects page output options"
  CM_FILEPRINTERSETUP, "Selects printer options"
  CM_FILEEXIT, "Quits the application"
}

STRINGTABLE LOADONCALL MOVEABLE DISCARDABLE
{
  CM_HELPINDEX, "Displays help-system index"
  CM_HELPKEYBOARD, "Displays keyboard instructions"
  CM_HELPCOMMANDS, "Displays help with menu commands"
  CM_HELPPROCEDURES, "Displays help on procedures"
  CM_HELPUSINGHELP, "Displays help-system instructions"
  CM_HELPABOUT, "Displays message box"
}
```

DECORATE.RC lists three types of resources. A menu resource defines the text for the program's menu commands. Two BITMAP resources define icons for the toolbar buttons. Two string-table resources define online help messages for commands that do not have default strings. I used two tables to organize the strings for each menu. Compiling the resource script (using RW, the IDE, or the stand-alone BRCC compiler), combines the two string tables into one resource.

Finally, Listing 9.12, DECORATE.CPP, lists the program's source code, and shows how to construct toolbar, status line, and toolbox gadget windows (refer back to Figure 9.4 for a sample of the program's display).

Listing 9.12. DECORATE.CPP.

```cpp
/* ============================================================ *\
**   decorate.cpp -- Demonstrate decorated windows             **
** ============================================================ **
**                                                             **
** ============================================================ **
**      Copyright  1994 by Tom Swan. All rights reserved.      **
\* ============================================================ */

#include <owl\applicat.h>
#include <owl\decframe.h>
#include <owl\controlb.h>
#include <owl\gadget.h>
#include <owl\buttonga.h>
#include <owl\messageb.h>
#include <owl\toolbox.h>
#include <owl\statusba.h>
#pragma hdrstop
#include "decorate.rh"


// ============================================================
// The application's main window
// ============================================================

class TDecWin: public TDecoratedFrame {
public:
  TDecWin(TWindow* parent, const char far* title);
};

// Constructor
TDecWin::TDecWin(TWindow* parent, const char far* title)
  : TDecoratedFrame(parent, title, 0, TRUE),
    TWindow(parent, title)
{
  AssignMenu(ID_MENU);
  Attr.X = GetSystemMetrics(SM_CXSCREEN) / 8;
  Attr.Y = GetSystemMetrics(SM_CYSCREEN) / 8;
  Attr.H = Attr.Y * 6;
  Attr.W = Attr.X * 6;
}

// ============================================================
// The application class
// ============================================================

class TDecApp: public TApplication {
public:
  TDecApp(const char far* name)
    : TApplication(name) {};
  void InitMainWindow();
```

```
protected:
  void CmFileExit();
  void CmHelpAbout();
private:
  TControlBar* toolbar;
  TToolBox* toolBox;
//  TMessageBar* statusLine; // Enable this and delete following
  TStatusBar* statusLine;    // line for a simpler status line
DECLARE_RESPONSE_TABLE(TDecApp);
};

DEFINE_RESPONSE_TABLE1(TDecApp, TApplication)
  EV_COMMAND(CM_FILEEXIT, CmFileExit),
  EV_COMMAND(CM_HELPABOUT, CmHelpAbout),
END_RESPONSE_TABLE;

// Initialize the program's main window
void
TDecApp::InitMainWindow()
{
// Construct the appliction's frame window
  TDecWin* frame = new TDecWin(0, "Decorated Window");

// Construct a toolbar with two icons
  toolbar = new TControlBar(frame);
  toolbar->Insert(*new TButtonGadget(IDB_EXIT, CM_FILEEXIT));
  toolbar->Insert(*new TSeparatorGadget(6));
  toolbar->Insert(*new TButtonGadget(IDB_HELP, CM_HELPABOUT));

// Enable status line messages when mouse touches a button
  toolbar->SetHintMode(TGadgetWindow::EnterHints);

// Insert the toolbar into the frame window
  frame->Insert(*toolbar, TDecoratedFrame::Top);

// Construct a simple statusline object for messages
//  statusLine = new TMessageBar(frame);
//  frame->Insert(*statusLine, TDecoratedFrame::Bottom);

// Delete the following four lines and enable the preceding
// two statements for a simple, text-only status line. Also
// define statusLine as a TMessageBar pointer in the
// TDecApp class declaration.
  statusLine = new TStatusBar(frame, TGadget::Recessed,
    TStatusBar::CapsLock | TStatusBar::NumLock |
    TStatusBar::ScrollLock | TStatusBar::Overtype);
  frame->Insert(*statusLine, TDecoratedFrame::Bottom);

// Construct a toolbox using same icons as toolbar
```

continues

361

Listing 9.12. continued

```
  toolBox = new TToolBox(frame, 1);   // one column toolbox
  toolBox->Insert(*new TButtonGadget(IDB_EXIT, CM_FILEEXIT));
  toolBox->Insert(*new TButtonGadget(IDB_HELP, CM_HELPABOUT));
  frame->Insert(*toolBox, TDecoratedFrame::Right);

// Assign the decorated frame as the program's main window
  MainWindow = frame;
}

// Exit program
void
TDecApp::CmFileExit()
{
  MainWindow->CloseWindow();
}

// Menu command function
void
TDecApp::CmHelpAbout()
{
  statusLine->SetText("Press Enter or click OK to close window");
  string msg;
  string newline('\n');
  msg += "This program demonstrates how to create" + newline;
  msg += "decorated frame windows with a toolbar," + newline;
  msg += "status bar, and online help messages for" + newline;
  msg += "buttons and menu commands. Browse the" + newline;
  msg += "sample menus (Help|About and File|Exit are" + newline;
  msg += "the only implemented commands) and read the" + newline;
  msg += "messages below. Also move the mouse pointer" + newline;
  msg += "over the toolbar buttons. Select the first" + newline;
  msg += "button to exit the program. Select the" + newline;
  msg += "second button to display this message box.";
  MainWindow->
    MessageBox(msg.c_str(), "About This Program", MB_OK);
  statusLine->SetText("");
}

#pragma argsused

// Main program
int
OwlMain(int argc, char* argv[])
{
  TDecApp app("DecApp");
  return app.Run();
}
```

Rather than base its main window class on TFrameWindow, the sample program derives TDecWin from TDecoratedFrame. To that class's constructor, TDecWin's constructor passes the usual parent pointer and title string arguments. It also passes 0 (indicating there's no client window in this example), and TRUE (enabling automatic message tracking for showing online help messages in the status bar).

The application's class, TDecApp, derived from TApplication, defines pointers for three gadget windows—toolBar, toolBox, and statusLine. The status line is the more complex variety with CapsLock and other key settings. For a simpler message-only status line, enable the TMessageBar* definition and delete the TStatusBar* pointer (or turn it into a comment). The class also defines a message response table for two of the sample menu commands. To save space here, I implemented only those two commands.

TDecApp's InitMainWindow function constructs the program's main window, but in this case, using the TDecWin class derived from TDecoratedFrame. After constructing the object, the function creates a toolbar, a status bar, and a toolbox, calling the frame object's Insert function to insert each child window. The last statement assigns the frame-window object's address to MainWindow.

All activities involving the toolbar, menu commands, status line messages, CapsLock and other key settings, occur automatically. No other programming is needed. You may, however, want to display other messages in the status line as demonstrated in the CmHelpAbout function, which displays the program's instructions in a message box window. Before displaying that window, the program displays a message in the status line by executing the statement:

```
statusLine->SetText("Press Enter or click OK to close window");
```

That text becomes the default for the status line, and is displayed at times when no other message is visible. To display no default message, set the default text to a null string:

```
statusLine->SetText("");
```

Looking Ahead

Another common interface object used in practically every Windows program is a *dialog box*. Inside dialog boxes are *controls* that you can use to select program options, enter text, and display progress reports—among other tasks. In Chapter 10, coming up next, you learn how to program dialog boxes. Chapter 11 explains how to program controls.

10

Dealing with Dialog Boxes

In days of old, most software interfaces were little more than a series of text prompts that scrolled up on a terminal and elicited responses from users. Certain answers led to other prompts, wending a twisted (and often thorny) path through the program's logic, which might seem like some kind of devious insect cleverly enticing its victims into the depths of its lair. Old answers scrolled away, never to be seen again, and it was difficult to know how to back out through your previous responses once you got yourself snared in the web of the program's interrelated menus and commands.

Visual operating systems like Windows put users in control of software interfaces, making it possible to switch more or less randomly among tasks the way humans were meant to do—that is, in whatever order seems most appealing at the time. I don't mean to suggest that Windows interfaces are never complex or that users must be given scatterbrained control over a program's tasks, but interface elements such as dialog boxes and controls go a long way in making software friendlier and easier to use, primarily by giving users a great deal of authority over the program's operation.

One of the primary goals, then, in a well written Windows interface, is to develop programs that *respond* to user's demands. Dialog boxes are key tools in achieving that goal. A dialog box provides a kind of electronic form, like a tax form, in which you check off boxes, enter values, and supply other information. Dialog boxes can also reveal important facts—how many records a database contains, for example, or how much memory is available. Many dialog boxes appear as the result of selecting menu commands that end with an ellipsis, as in the *Open...* command. The ellipsis indicates that selecting the command opens a dialog box. When you see such a command, you know that selecting it gives you access to additional choices in the form of a dialog box. In this way, dialog boxes serve as *menu extenders,* or advanced command systems, to which users gain access through the menu bar.

Dialog boxes can also be informational, serving as bulletin boards where programs post information about events and happenings. Dialogs can be read-only, merely showing users facts and figures, or they can be interactive, permitting users to enter new information. All of a program's options, for example, can usually fit into one or two dialog boxes, making it easy to choose among the program's features and to see all current selections.

In this chapter, you learn:

- How to use the TDialog class.
- How to design dialog box resources.
- How to program modal and modeless dialogs.
- How to use a dialog box as a program's main window.
- How to use Windows' common dialog boxes.

Dialog Boxes

There are two kinds of dialog boxes: those that Windows (or another source) provides in ready-to-use form, and those you create yourself. Ready-made dialogs include Windows common dialog boxes such as the ever-present *File|Open...* dialog. Those you create yourself are limited only by your imagination. In all cases, you can program interfaces to dialogs by constructing objects of the TDialog class.

The *TDialog* Class

Dialogs are specialized windows, and therefore, the TDialog class is naturally derived from TWindow. A dialog object (that is, any TDialog or derived class object) provides programs with a well defined interface to the internal dialog element maintained by

Windows. Rather than manipulate that element directly, as you would have to do in a plain C program, you can more easily use the TDialog class's member functions, data items, and response tables to perform dialog-related operations.

Those operations are mostly concerned with sending and receiving information to a dialog's controls. For that, TDialog provides a *data transfer mechanism,* which greatly simplifies initializing control values and receiving user input. (More on this in the next chapter.)

You can program dialogs to be modal or modeless. A modal dialog places the program in dialog mode, which requires users to close the dialog before they can select other program operations. A modeless dialog operates more like a child window. As a dialog, a modeless dialog is the same as a modal one, but does not prohibit users from selecting menu commands and performing other operations. A *File|Open...* dialog is a modal dialog—you must select a file and close the dialog before you can use other program commands. A text-file *Find...* dialog is usually implemented as a modeless dialog—you may enter commands or type changes into documents while the dialog is active as it is during a search for a word.

Dialog boxes are child windows owned, usually, by the program's main window (the parent). In the simplest case, you construct a TDialog object in a command response function of the parent window's class. You *execute* the dialog—not to kill it off, but to kick its internal mechanisms into gear. Executing a dialog makes it visible, displays the dialog's controls, and enables users to enter information into those controls. Most dialogs also have buttons such as *OK* that accepts new input, or *Cancel* that resets the dialog's control values.

Dialog Box Resources

The first step in creating a dialog box is to design its layout using Resource Workshop (RW) or by typing resource script commands into your program's resource script file (.RC). You may identify the dialog, as you may other resources, by a string or numeric value. Into the dialog's window, you can insert various control objects—buttons, static text, list boxes, and so on—and identify these subelements numerically.

To create a dialog, select RW's *Resource|New...* command and choose *Dialog* for the type. You can then select standard Windows style dialogs with OK, Close, and Help buttons on the right or bottom, or you can select a Borland style dialog with similar buttons. I'll use Borland style dialogs here—they give dialogs and controls a three-dimensional look, like a chiseled steel panel in a rack of electronic gear (see Figure 10.1).

FIGURE 10.1.

Sample Borland-style dialog box.

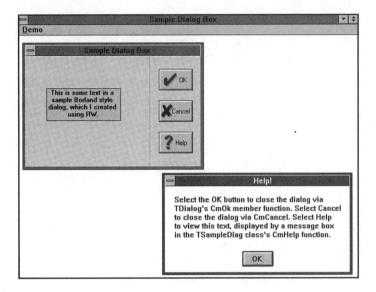

To create the dialog in the figure, I entered a text box into the dialog window, using RW's *T* tool in the dialog editor's *Tools*. I also renamed the dialog resource ID_DIALOG, using the numeric identifier 100, and I stored the #define statement for that identifier in my program's .RH resource header. Because I don't need to access the dialog's text control, I left its identifier set to the default value -1, the traditional value for controls that have no associated resource identifier. I also double-clicked the dialog border and entered a new title for the caption bar.

> **WARNING**
>
> Never save new identifiers to BC4 header files such as OWL\WINDOW.RH, or you might lose the ability to compile resource scripts that include that file. RW has a bad habit of making such modifications without warning. If you find that you cannot open resource script files, the cause might be a damaged WINDOW.RH or other .RH header file. Recover the lost file by reinstalling BC4. (For safety, it's a good idea to keep a separate copy of all .RH files in C:\BC4\INCLUDE\OWL.)

The easiest way to create a dialog box is to construct an object of the TDialog class and call its Execute function. For example, a menu command-response function in the parent window's class could execute this code:

```
TDialog *dp;
string s;
dp = new TDialog(this, ID_DIALOG);
if (dp->Execute() == IDOK)
  s = "You selected Ok";
else
  s = "You selected Cancel";
MessageBox(s.c_str(),GetApplication()->GetName(),MB_OK);
```

Calling Execute for the TDialog object addressed by pointer dp returns IDOK if the user selected the OK button or IDCANCEL for the Cancel button. The dialog box object is closed and deleted by Execute—you don't need to delete the memory allocated by new to the pointer. This sample demonstrates how the parent window can respond to dialog events, but its also possible to program responses into a class derived from TDialog.

Listings 10.1 (DIAGAPP.RH), 10.2 (DIAGAPP.RC), and 10.3 (DIAGAPP.CPP) demonstrate how to add response functions to TDialog class. The functions can respond directly to the selection of buttons and other controls in the dialog window (see Figure 10.1 for a sample of the program's display). Open the program's DIAGAPP.IDE project file on the supplied disk, then press Ctrl+F9 to compile and run the demonstration.

NOTE

I listed the DIAGAPP.RC resource file to show the format of a dialog resource in script form, but the lines in the file are too long to accurately reproduce here. Refer to the file on this book's disk for the actual resource commands. Because of this problem, future sample programs in this book do not list resource files that contain dialog and other lengthy resource script commands. All files are, of course, provided on the disk supplied with this book.

Listing 10.1. DIAGAPP.RH.

```
// diagapp.rh -- Resource header file

#define ID_MENU 100
#define ID_DIALOG 100
#define CM_TEST 101
#define IDHELP 998
```

Listing 10.2. DIAGAPP.RC.

```
#include <owl\window.rh>
#include "diagapp.rh"

ID_MENU MENU
BEGIN
  POPUP "&Demo"
  BEGIN
    MENUITEM "&Test...", CM_TEST
    MENUITEM "E&xit", CM_EXIT
  END
END


ID_DIALOG DIALOG 6, 15, 189, 124
STYLE DS_MODALFRAME ¦ WS_POPUP ¦ WS_VISIBLE ¦
  WS_CAPTION ¦ WS_SYSMENU
CLASS "bordlg"
CAPTION "Sample Dialog Box"
FONT 8, "MS Sans Serif"
{
 CONTROL "", -1, "BorShade", BSS_VDIP ¦ BSS_LEFT ¦
WS_CHILD ¦ WS_VISIBLE, 135, 0, 1, 124
 CONTROL "", IDOK, "BorBtn", BS_DEFPUSHBUTTON ¦ WS_CHILD ¦
WS_VISIBLE ¦ WS_TABSTOP, 144, 14, 37, 25
 CONTROL "", IDCANCEL, "BorBtn", BS_PUSHBUTTON ¦ WS_CHILD ¦
WS_VISIBLE ¦ WS_TABSTOP, 144, 49, 37, 25
 CONTROL "", IDHELP, "BorBtn", BS_PUSHBUTTON ¦ WS_CHILD ¦
WS_VISIBLE ¦ WS_TABSTOP, 144, 84, 37, 25
 CONTROL "This is some text in a sample Borland style dialog,
which I created using RW.", -1, "BorStatic", SS_CENTER ¦
WS_CHILD ¦ WS_VISIBLE ¦ WS_BORDER ¦ WS_GROUP, 23, 36, 81, 36
}
```

Listing 10.3. DIAGAPP.CPP.

```
/* ============================================================ *\
** diagapp.cpp -- How to create and use a dialog box           **
** ============================================================ **
**                                                              **
** ============================================================ **
**     Copyright  1994 by Tom Swan. All rights reserved.        **
\* ============================================================ */

#include <owl\applicat.h>
#include <owl\framewin.h>
```

```
#include <owl\dialog.h>
#pragma hdrstop
#include "diagapp.rh"

// ==============================================================
// Sample dialog
// ==============================================================

class TSampleDiag: public TDialog {
public:
  TSampleDiag(TWindow* parent, TResId resId)
    : TDialog(parent, resId) {}
protected:
  void CmHelp();
DECLARE_RESPONSE_TABLE(TSampleDiag);
};

DEFINE_RESPONSE_TABLE1(TSampleDiag, TDialog)
  EV_COMMAND(IDHELP, CmHelp),
END_RESPONSE_TABLE;

void
TSampleDiag::CmHelp()
{
  string s;
  string newline('\n');
  s += "Select the OK button to close the dialog via" + newline;
  s += "TDialog's CmOk member function. Select Cancel" + newline;
  s += "to close the dialog via CmCancel. Select Help" + newline;
  s += "to view this text, displayed by a message box" + newline;
  s += "in the TSampleDiag class's CmHelp function.";
  MessageBox(s.c_str(), "Help!", MB_OK);
}

// ==============================================================
// The application's main window
// ==============================================================

class TDiagWin: public TFrameWindow {
public:
  TDiagWin(TWindow* parent, const char far* title);
protected:
  void CmTest();
DECLARE_RESPONSE_TABLE(TDiagWin);
};

DEFINE_RESPONSE_TABLE1(TDiagWin, TFrameWindow)
  EV_COMMAND(CM_TEST, CmTest),
END_RESPONSE_TABLE;
```

continues

371

Listing 10.3. continued

```cpp
// Constructor
TDiagWin::TDiagWin(TWindow* parent, const char far* title)
  : TFrameWindow(parent, title),
    TWindow(parent, title)
{
  AssignMenu(ID_MENU);
}

// Construct and execute a modal dialog box
void
TDiagWin::CmTest()
{
  TSampleDiag *dp;
  string s;

  dp = new TSampleDiag(this, ID_DIALOG);
  if (dp->Execute() == IDOK)
    s = "You selected Ok";
  else
    s = "You selected Cancel";
  MessageBox(s.c_str(),GetApplication()->GetName(),MB_OK);
}

// ============================================================
// The application class
// ============================================================

class TDiagApp: public TApplication {
public:
  TDiagApp(const char far* name)
    : TApplication(name) {}
  void InitMainWindow();
};

// Initialize the program's main window
void
TDiagApp::InitMainWindow()
{
  EnableBWCC();  // Loads custom control DLL
  MainWindow = new TDiagWin(0, "Sample Dialog Box");
}

#pragma argsused

// Main program
int
OwlMain(int argc, char* argv[])
```

```
{
  TDiagApp app("DiagApp");
  return app.Run();
}
```

A dialog box is just a fancy window, and it can respond to messages just like a window can. In the sample DIAGAPP.CPP listing, for example, class `TDiagWin` defines a message-response function `CmHelp`, and it declares that it requires a response table. That table uses the `EV_COMMAND` macro to relate the command identifier `IDHELP` with the `CmHelp` member function in the class. Selecting the *Help* button calls the function, which displays the message box shown in Figure 10.1.

You can also override `TDialog`'s `CmOk` and `CmCancel` functions to trap those button selections. For example, rather than respond to those buttons *after* the dialog box closes, you can trap those events inside the dialog box object. Add these two response functions to the `TSampleDiag` class:

```
void CmOk();
void CmCancel();
```

Also add these lines to the class's response table:

```
EV_COMMAND(IDOK, CmOk),
EV_COMMAND(IDCANCEL, CmCancel),
```

`TDialog`'s `CmOk` and `CmCancel` functions are not virtual, so you have to direct events to them in your own class as explained here by using a response table. You can now implement the message response functions. First, do `CmOk`:

```
void
TSampleDiag::CmOk()
{
  MessageBox("You selected Ok", "Message", MB_OK);
  CloseWindow(IDOK);
}
```

CmOk should close the dialog box by calling CloseWindow as shown. Next, do CmCancel:

```
void
TSampleDiag::CmCancel()
{
  MessageBox("You selected Cancel", "Message", MB_OK);
  Destroy(IDCANCEL);
}
```

CmCancel should destroy the dialog box as shown. This prevents any changes made to control values from being saved using the automated data transfer mechanism described later in this chapter.

After modifying the class, you can rewrite the main window's CmTest function to construct and execute the dialog as follows. Because the dialog class directly responds to the selection of its Ok and Cancel buttons, the modified program ignores the value returned by Execute:

```
TSampleDiag *dp;
dp = new TSampleDiag(this, ID_DIALOG);
dp->Execute();
```

Modal Dialogs

The dialog box programming examples you've seen so far create modal dialogs—those that require users to close the dialog window before selecting other program commands and operations. Call the TDialog Execute function to bring up a modal dialog.

Modeless Dialogs

A modeless dialog is just a child window with controls. It can remain on screen while the user selects other program operations. You design modeless dialogs as you do modal ones—create a resource using RW, write .RC script commands, insert controls, and so on.

The difference between a modal and modeless dialog is not in its design but in how the dialog window is created. Instead of calling the TDialog class's Execute function, to create a modeless dialog, call Create like this (assume that TMyDialog is derived from TDialog):

```
TMyDialog *dp = new TMyDialog(this, ID_MYDIALOG);
dp->Create();
```

Closing the dialog automatically deletes the memory allocated to dp provided that the dialog is closed via CmOk or CmCancel as explained for modal dialogs. Override those functions, but call DestroyWindow to close the dialog if you want to retain the object addressed by dp. That way, a window's constructor could execute the preceding code, and then display the dialog when needed rather than repeatedly create the TMyDialog object.

> **NOTE**
>
> Because dialog boxes are child windows, they are automatically deleted when the parent window is closed. You therefore don't have to take any extra steps to delete TDialog objects created in a parent window's class constructor.

You also have to take one of two steps to make the dialog visible—an action that Create performs only if the dialog's window includes the WS_VISIBLE attribute. Dialogs created by RW normally have that attribute switched on by default, but if your modeless dialog doesn't appear, check that setting in RW's dialog editor.

Alternatively, you can create the dialog, but make it appear at a later time. In that case, switch off WS_VISIBLE in the resource, and then, after calling Create, call the ShowWindow function inherited from TWindow:

```
dp->ShowWindow(SW_SHOW);
```

Main Window Dialogs

A popular trick is to use a dialog box as a program's main window. Typically, the program does not have a menu bar but instead makes all commands and operations available through the dialog's controls. (It can have a menu, however, if you want.) The window usually lacks scrollers and it also cannot be maximized to full screen, but it can be minimized as an icon on the Windows desktop. You might use this technique for a configuration utility that selects among various hardware and software options, or you might design a calculator or similar tool with buttons that resemble real-life objects.

Three special steps enable any TDialog object to serve as a program's main window. First, design your dialog as you normally do, by using RW or by typing resource script statements into a file ending in .RC, but select WS_CHILD for the dialog's STYLE options as follows (the statement should be on one line in the script):

```
STYLE DS_MODALFRAME | WS_CHILD | WS_VISIBLE |
  WS_CAPTION | WS_SYSMENU
```

In RW, double-click the dialog's caption, and change *Window type* to *Child*. As a child, the dialog follows its parent when the parent moves or is resized—thus, by making the dialog exactly the same size as the parent window, it appears to be the only window there when in fact the dialog overlays its parent on screen. Normally, dialogs are popup windows (style WS_POPUP), which are also child windows, but are more independent minded and do not follow their parents. Overlapped dialogs can also be main windows.

Second, construct an object of a class derived from TDialog, using the dialog's resource identifier. If TMyDiag is the name of your class and ID_DIALOG the resource identifier, create the object like this:

```
TMyDiag *dp;
dp = new TMyDiag(0, ID_DIALOG);
```

If you identify resources using strings, change the second line to something like this:

```
dp = new TMyDiag(0, "MainDialog");
```

Third, construct your program's main window as an object of the TFrameWindow class (or of a class derived from TFrameWindow). Assign the dialog object as the frame's client window:

```
MainWindow = new TFrameWindow(
  0, "My Program", dp, TRUE);
```

The first argument, 0, signifies that the TFrameWindow object has no parent. The second argument assigns a window title, the third addresses the dialog object to be used as the frame's client, and the fourth must be TRUE to automatically size the client to fit within the frame window's borders. Figure 10.2 shows an example of a Borland-style dialog used as a program's main window.

FIGURE 10.2.

A Borland-style dialog used as the main window.

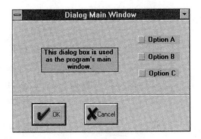

Listings 10.4 (DIAGMAIN.RH) and 10.5 (DIAGMAIN.CPP) demonstrate how to put these ideas into practice. I did not list the program's .RC script file because of the lengthy dialog box commands (see file DIAGMAIN.RC on the book's disk). As usual, open the program's DIAGMAIN.IDE project file on the disk's DIAGMAIN directory, and press

Ctrl+F9 to create the window in Figure 10.2. Just for fun, I programmed the three option buttons to display some messages, and in the case of Option C, to switch off Option B by sending that control a message. After the listing, I explain how the program works.

Listing 10.4. DIAGMAIN.RH.

```
// diagmain.rh -- Resource header file

#define ID_DIALOG     100
#define ID_OPTIONA    101
#define ID_OPTIONB    102
#define ID_OPTIONC    103
```

Listing 10.5. DIAGMAIN.CPP.

```
/* ============================================================ *\
**   diagmain.cpp -- Use a dialog as a program's main window    **
** ============================================================ **
**                                                              **
** ============================================================ **
**      Copyright  1994 by Tom Swan. All rights reserved.       **
\* ============================================================ */

#include <owl\applicat.h>
#include <owl\framewin.h>
#include <owl\dialog.h>
#include <cstring.h>
#pragma hdrstop
#include "diagmain.rh"

// ============================================================
// The dialog client window class
// ============================================================

class TDiagClient: public TDialog {
public:
  TDiagClient(TWindow *parent, TResId resId);
protected:
  void CmOptionA();
  void CmOptionB();
  void CmOptionC();
private:
  BOOL optionA, optionB, optionC;
DECLARE_RESPONSE_TABLE(TDiagClient);
};
```

continues

377

Listing 10.5. continued

```
DEFINE_RESPONSE_TABLE1(TDiagClient, TDialog)
  EV_COMMAND(ID_OPTIONA, CmOptionA),
  EV_COMMAND(ID_OPTIONB, CmOptionB),
  EV_COMMAND(ID_OPTIONC, CmOptionC),
END_RESPONSE_TABLE;

// Constructor
TDiagClient::TDiagClient(TWindow *parent, TResId resId)
  : TWindow((TWindow*)0),
    TDialog(parent, resId)
{
  optionA = optionB = optionC = FALSE;
}

// Button response functions
void
TDiagClient::CmOptionA()
{
  optionA = ~optionA;
  if (!optionA) return;
  string s = "Beep!";
  MessageBeep(0);
  MessageBox(s.c_str(), "Option A", MB_OK);
}

void
TDiagClient::CmOptionB()
{
  optionB = ~optionB;
  if (!optionB) return;
  string s = "Displays a message.";
  MessageBox(s.c_str(), "Option B", MB_OK);
}

void
TDiagClient::CmOptionC()
{
  optionC = ~optionC;
  if (!optionC) return;
  string s = "Turns off B";
  MessageBox(s.c_str(), "Option C", MB_OK);
  SendDlgItemMessage(
    ID_OPTIONB,          // Control identifier
    BM_SETCHECK,         // Message to send to control
    0);                  // State (0-off, 1-on)
  optionB = FALSE;       // Because we just forced it to off
}
```

```
// ============================================================
// The application class
// ============================================================

class TDiagMainApp: public TApplication {
public:
  TDiagMainApp(const char far* name)
    : TApplication(name) {}
  void InitMainWindow();
};

// Initialize the program's main window
void
TDiagMainApp::InitMainWindow()
{
// Enable Borland Custom Controls
  EnableBWCC();

// Construct client window object from dialog resource
  TDiagClient *cp;
  cp = new TDiagClient(0, ID_DIALOG);

// Create main frame window and pass it the client object
  MainWindow =
    new TFrameWindow(
        0,                         // No parent window
        "Dialog Main Window",      // Caption
        cp,                        // Client window pointer
        TRUE);                     // Shrink to client

// Select attribute styles for frame window
  MainWindow->Attr.Style &= ~(WS_MAXIMIZEBOX | WS_THICKFRAME);
}

#pragma argsused

// Main program
int
OwlMain(int argc, char* argv[])
{
  TDiagMainApp app("DiagMainApp");
  return app.Run();
}
```

Be sure to include the DIALOG.H header file so you can derive your dialog's class from
TDialog. In the DIAGMAIN.CPP listing, I named my class TDiagClient. The class
declares a public constructor, three protected member functions, and three private BOOL

variables. It also declares its intention to use a response table. In the response table's definition following the class, three EV_COMMAND macros relate the dialog option control identifiers (ID_OPTIONA, ID_OPTIONB, and ID_OPTIONC) with the three protected member functions. By using a response table, selecting the control buttons automatically calls the associated function.

The class constructor calls the TWindow and TDialog constructors, passing null to TWindow and the two arguments, parent and resId, to TDialog. The constructor also initializes the private variables to FALSE—each variable represents the state of one option button.

Next, I implemented the three member functions. CmOptionA, which is called when you select the *Option A* button, sounds a beep by calling the Windows *MessageBeep* function. The function also displays a message. CmOptionB simply displays a message. So does CmOptionC, which also sends the *Option B* button a message to switch that button off. This demonstrates how one control can affect another. This statement calls the TDialog class's SendDlgItemMessage function:

```
SendDlgItemMessage(
  ID_OPTIONB,
  BM_SETCHECK,
  0);
```

The first argument is the resource identifier of the control to which you want to send a message. The second is the message value, defined in the WINDOWS.H header file. BM_SETCHECK is a "Button Message" that sets a checkbox's state to on and displays a small checkmark in the button's box. (Look up other BM_ constants in a Windows reference for other messages you can send to button controls.) The final argument to SendDlgItemMessage sets the checkbox's state to off. Change this to 1 to turn on a checkbox.

Finally in DIAGMAIN.CPP, the application class's InitMainWindow function constructs the program's frame window using an object of the TDiagClient class as a client. This makes the dialog box appear as the program's main window. Note the final statement in InitMainWindow that removes the frame's WS_MAXIMIZEBOX and WS_THICKFRAME styles.

DIAGMAIN.CPP demonstrates all the required steps to use a dialog box as a program's main window, but the program uses questionable methods for keeping track of the dialog's control values. In other words, for simplicity in the demonstration, I cheated. A better program would not keep track of checkbox states using separate variables such as the TDiagClient's private BOOL members, but would take additional steps to program interfaces for the checkboxes and other controls, and to transfer data to and from those objects. In the next chapter, I explain better techniques for communicating with a dialog's controls. First, however, there's one more dialog-box subject to cover.

Common Windows Dialogs

Windows 3.1 provides several common dialogs that can dress up a program with features such as open-save dialogs and color selectors. Because many Windows programs use these same dialogs, experienced users might be able to run your programs more easily if you employ common dialogs for standard operations. Besides, why reinvent the wheel when you can use an existing common dialog? Believe me, writing your own open-save dialog is no easy task—you will save time and aggravation by using common dialogs whenever possible. ObjectWindows provides classes that you can use to interface with all Windows common dialogs. There isn't enough space here to go into each class in detail—common dialog classes contain a treasure-house of functions and data members that you can use for a variety of purposes. My objective here is to explain fully how to use one common dialog class. You program the others using similar techniques. All classes are, of course, documented in your BC4 printed references and in online help files. Also, future programs in this book show additional examples.

All common dialog classes are derived from the `TCommonDialog` class, which is derived from `TDialog` (see header file OWL\COMMDIAL.H). The `TOpenSaveDialog` class, for example, is derived from `TCommonDialog`. You build a file menu's *Open...*, *Save*, and *Save as...* dialogs using an object of a class derived from `TOpenSaveDialog`—`TFileOpenDialog` for selecting existing filenames, or `TFileSaveDialog` for entering new filenames. Both dialogs permit users to change to other directories and drives. Table 10.1 lists these and other common dialog classes and their associated header files.

Table 10.1. Common dialog classes and header files.

Class	Base class	Header file	Purpose
TChooseColorDialog	TCommonDialog	CHOOSECO.H	Color selections
TChooseFontDialog	TCommonDialog	CHOOSEFO.H	Font selections
TCommonDialog	TDialog	COMMDIAL.H	Base class for other common dialog classes.
TFindReplaceDialog	TCommonDialog	FINDREPL.H	Base class for `TFindDialog` and `TReplaceDialog`.
TFindDialog	TFindReplaceDialog	FINDREPL.H	Modeless Find dialog boxes.

continues

381

Table 10.1. continued

Class	Base class	Header file	Purpose
TReplaceDialog	TFindReplaceDialog	FINDREPL.H	Modeless Find and Replace dialog boxes.
TOpenSaveDialog	TCommonDialog	OPENSAVE.H	Base class for TFileOpenDialog and TFileSaveDialog.
TFileOpenDialog	TOpenSaveDialog	OPENSAVE.H	Existing file selections and directory changes.
TFileSaveDialog	TOpenSaveDialog	OPENSAVE.H	New file selections and directory changes.
TPrintDialog	TCommonDialog	PRINTDIA.H	Printer option selections.

Include the appropriate header file, then construct and use a common dialog class object. To activate the dialog, call its Execute member function, inherited from TDialog, just as you do for other modal dialog objects. To construct a modeless common dialog, use the Create function as explained in this chapter.

Common dialog classes such as TOpenSaveDialog include a nested TData subclass that stores various dialog options and information. The TData subclass is different for each common dialog. In TOpenSaveDialog, for example, TData defines char pointers for FileName (obviously a selected file's name), and for Filter, which specifies strings that specify wild card filters such as *.CPP and *.RH to limit the types of files displayed in the dialog window. You access a common dialog's information by referring to the TData class's public members.

For example, in Chapter 6, program WLIST uses a common TOpenDialog object to display the file-selection dialog in Figure 10.3. To create this dialog, the program's

WLIST.CPP file includes the OPENSAVE.H header file, which declares the `TOpenSaveDialog`, `TFileOpenDialog`, and `TFileSaveDialog` classes:

```
#include <owl\opensave.h>
```

FIGURE 10.3.

Common file-selection dialog from WLIST in Chapter 6.

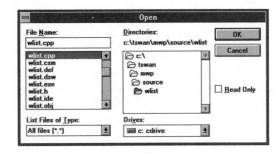

The program's main-window class, `TListWin` (derived from `TFrameWindow`), declares two data members for use with the common dialog:

```
string* filename;
TOpenSaveDialog::TData filenameData;
```

The `filename` pointer addresses an object of the C++ `string` class. The `filenameData` variable is an object of the `TData` subclass, nested in `TOpenSaveDialog`. You must specify the outer class, a scope resolution operator (`::`), and the `TData` class name to declare the `filenameData` object. The window's constructor initializes `filenameData` with this statement:

```
filenameData(OFN_FILEMUSTEXIST|OFN_PATHMUSTEXIST,
  "All files (*.*)|*.*|Text files (*.txt)|*.txt|",
  0, "", "*")
```

The `OFN_` constants select various dialog options—in this case specifying that selected file- and pathnames must actually exist on disk. If you didn't specify these options, users would be able to enter filenames that referred to nonexistent files—perhaps useful in some applications, but not in this one.

The string argument passed to the `TData` constructor specifies a set of wild cards, also called filters. The common dialog (see Figure 10.3) lists these strings, which users may select to alter the types of displayed files. Each filter string has two parts, separated with a vertical bar. First is the filter's description that you want the dialog to list (*All files (*.*)*), and next is the actual wild card specification (*.*). You may list as many filter strings as you wish.

The final three arguments are string pointers (the first is null) that select custom filters, an initial directory, and a default extension. Try changing these arguments to see the effect they have on the common dialog.

To display the dialog, construct an object of the TFileOpenDialog class. Pass the TData object (filenameData in this case) to the class constructor, and call the resulting object's Execute function. If that function returns IDOK, the dialog was closed by its *OK* button, and the program should obtain the selected filename. If Execute does not return IDOK, you should abort the file-open command—the dialog was closed by selecting its *Cancel* button, or it was closed by a system menu command. For example, WLIST executes the following code in response to its *File|Open...* command in function CmFileOpen:

```
if ((new TFileOpenDialog(this,
  filenameData))->Execute() == IDOK) {
  if (filenameData.Error == 0) { // no error and not cancelled
    delete filename;
    filename = new string(filenameData.FileName);
    OpenNamedFile();
  }
}
```

If Execute returns IDOK, and if filenameData.Error indicates no other errors in the file's selection, the program deletes the current string object addressed by filename. Then, the expression filenameData.FileName obtains the char pointer in the dialog's TData subclass, used here to construct a new string object, assigned to filename. Finally, OpenNamedFile, a function in WLIST, opens the selected file.

As I mentioned, you program other common dialogs using similar techniques, but of course, specifying different TData arguments. To use a common font dialog, for instance, you construct an object of the TChooseFontDialog's TData subclass. Then, to activate the dialog, you construct a TChooseFontDialog object, pass it the TData subclass object, and call the resulting object's Execute function. If that function returns ID_OK, you extract the necessary font information from the TData object.

Looking Ahead

For better control over a dialog's controls, you can construct objects of classes derived from TControl. You can also use TControl objects to insert controls into other windows as well as dialog boxes. In the next chapter, you explore many kinds of controls— checkboxes, lists, combo boxes, pushbuttons, gauges, and more. You also learn how to use an important dialog-box technique that automatically transfers control values to and from a buffer, which you can use to store program options or other information.

Inserting Controls in Windows and Dialogs

Everybody who has used Windows software, even for a short time, recognizes standard controls such as pushbuttons, checkboxes, radio buttons, listboxes, and other visual interface elements. You may not realize, however, that controls are just windows, of a highly specialized form, but with all the characteristics of more familiar window varieties. Controls have window handles, and as objects, you construct them as instances of the TControl class, itself a derivative of TWindow.

You also may not realize that Controls are not limited for use in dialog boxes. In fact, a control may appear in any window or dialog. Controls are actually child windows of their parents, and controls can communicate with their parents by sending and receiving messages.

In this chapter, you learn:

- How to use the TControl class.
- How to construct buttons, listboxes, gauges, and other controls.

● How to enable and use Borland Custom Controls.

● How to interface with controls in windows.

● How to interface with controls in dialog boxes.

● How to transfer information to and from a dialog's controls.

Control Classes

Interface elements such as scrollbars, checkboxes, and radio buttons are called *controls* because they make it possible for users to control aspects of a program's operation. Controls are also windows—that is, they have window elements, just as all windows do, that are maintained internally by Windows. In your program, to manipulate controls, you can create an interface object of a class derived from TControl, which is derived from TWindow.

You can also communicate with controls by sending them messages, and by receiving messages sent by controls as users manipulate them. But the TControl class encapsulates all control operations, and by using response tables, the class simplifies control message handling.

Controls are also child windows that belong to a parent. Typically, a main window owns one or more controls that appear in the parent window as buttons, boxes, and other visual devices. The controls stick to the window's client area. Move the window, and the controls move right along.

The *TControl* Class

The TControl class wraps up the basic operational characteristics for seven types of Windows controls: scrollbar, gauges, group boxes, static text items, buttons, Visual BASIC extended (VBX) controls, and listboxes. Variations on these basic controls include sliders (horizontal and vertical), editable text items, checkboxes, radio buttons, and combination listboxes (or "combo boxes"). All of these controls have TControl-derived classes that you can use to construct interface objects for creating and manipulating controls. You may use the controls and their classes in windows and in dialog boxes.

> **NOTE**
>
> See Chapter 15 for information about using VBX controls in BC4 and ObjectWindows programs.

Derived Classes

Table 11.1 lists ObjectWindows' control classes derived from TControl. The table also shows the header files that declare the controls. To use a control class, include its header file into your program.

Table 11.1. Control classes and header files.

Class	Base class	Header file	Purpose
TButton	TControl	BUTTON.H	Pushbuttons such as OK or Cancel
TCheckBox	TButton	CHECKBOX.H	Checkboxes (any or none of a group may be selected)
TComboBox	TListBox	COMBOBOX.H	Combination input and listboxes
TEdit	TStatic	EDIT.H	Input text boxes (editable text controls)
TEditFile	TEditSearch	EDITFILE.H	File-editing windows
TEditSearch	TEdit	EDITSEAR.H	Text-editing controls for *Find and Replace* commands
TGauge	TControl	GAUGE.H	Progress reports
TGroupBox	TControl	GROUPBOX.H	Group boxes for organizing checkboxes and radio buttons
THSlider	TSlider	SLIDER.H	Customized horizontal scrollbars
TListBox	TControl	LISTBOX.H	Listboxes (no input area)
TRadioButton	TCheckBox	RADIOBUT.H	Radio buttons (only one of a group may be selected)
TScrollBar	TControl	SCROLLBA.H	Classic horizontal and vertical scrollbars
TSlider	TScrollBar	SLIDER.H	Base class for custom scrollbars (see THSlider and TVSlider)

continues

387

Table 11.1. continued

Class	Base class	Header file	Purpose
TStatic	TControl	STATIC.H	Labels and information only text items (can't be edited)
TVbxControl	TControl	VBXCTL.H	Visual BASIC Extended (VBX) Control object interfaces
TVSlider	TSlider	SLIDER.H	Customized vertical scrollbars

Controls in Windows

The following sections give examples of most types of controls, and shows how to insert them into windows. I extracted the sample programming listed here from files in the CONTROLS subdirectory on this book's disk. (I did not list every file of the program in this chapter, but of course, all files are supplied on the book's disk.) As usual, use the IDE to open the CONTROLS.IDE project file, and press Ctrl+F9 to compile and run the example. Use the commands in the program's *Demo* menu to open windows that demonstrate various controls.

> **WARNING**
>
> Compiling the CONTROLS program creates a compiled-symbol (.CSM) file that may occupy several megabytes of disk space. The file saves time when recompiling the program—after making changes suggested in this chapter, for example—but, to save disk space, you may elect not to create the file. To do that, open the project file, select the *Options/Project...* command, open the *Compiler* topic (by clicking its plus sign), and highlight *Precompiled headers.* Toggle on the radio button labeled *Do not generate or use.*

TButton

For pushbuttons—an *OK* button, for example—use the TButton class declared in BUTTON.H. For checkboxes, use TCheckBox, which is derived from TButton and declared in CHECKBOX.H. For radio buttons (so named because they resemble the buttons on an automobile radio), use TRadioButton, which is derived from TCheckBox and declared in RADIOBUT.H. You can also group checkboxes and radio buttons in a group box as an object of the TGroupBox class, declared in GROUPBOX.H.

First, define some pointers to address the button and group box objects, usually in a private section in the parent window's class. For example, see Listing 11.1, BNCHILD.H. The file declares a child window class, TButtonChild, which the main program uses to build the window shown in Figure 11.1.

> **NOTE**
>
> The CONTROLS program uses the multiple document interface (MDI) to display sample controls in child windows. Chapter 12 explains more about how to write MDI applications.

FIGURE 11.1.

Button controls.

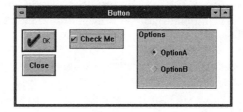

Listing 11.1. BUTTON.H.

```
// bnchild.h -- TButtonChild header file

class TButtonChild: public TMDIChild {
public:
  TButtonChild(TMDIClient& parent);
protected:
  void CmOkButton();
  void CmCloseButton();
  void SetupWindow();
private:
  TButton* okButton;
  TButton* closeButton;
  TCheckBox* checkBox;
  TRadioButton* radioButtonA;
  TRadioButton* radioButtonB;
  TGroupBox* radioGroup;
DECLARE_RESPONSE_TABLE(TButtonChild);
};
```

To create a button, the program executes the following statement in the constructor of the child window in which the control appears (see file BNCHILD.CPP on disk):

```
okButton =
  new TButton(this, IDOK, "OK",
    10, 20, 50, 35, TRUE);
```

The `this` argument supplies the address of the parent window object that owns the button. `IDOK` is a predefined identifier for a standard OK button, but you can also define your own button identifiers like this:

```
#define ID_CLOSEBUTTON 100
```

The *OK* string gives the button a label, and the four integer values represent the control's position and size parameters, `X`, `Y`, `width`, and `height`. `TRUE` makes the button the default, displayed with a heavy border and selected by pressing Enter. By the way, to enable keyboard support for buttons in windows, call `EnableKBHandler` in the parent window's constructor. Pressing Tab will then move the focus from control to control in their creation order. You can also press the Spacebar to toggle checkmarks, and use the cursor keys to manipulate radio buttons. For Borland-style controls, also call `EnableBWCC` in the application's `InitMainWindow` function.

Checkboxes look best with a border. Add one by executing code such as this:

```
checkBox =
  new TCheckBox(this, ID_CHECKBOX, "Check Me",
    100, 20, 100, 35);
checkBox->Attr.Style |= WS_BORDER;
```

Most often, you should insert radio buttons into a group, with an appropriate border. First, construct the group object:

```
radioGroup =
  new TGroupBox(this, ID_RADIOGROUP, "Options",
    225, 20, 150, 108);
radioGroup->Attr.Style |= WS_BORDER;
```

Then, construct some radio button objects, and pass each one the pointer to the `TGroupBox` object:

```
radioButtonA =
  new TRadioButton(this, ID_RADIOA, "OptionA",
    250, 50, 110, 24, radioGroup);
radioButtonB =
  new TRadioButton(this, ID_RADIOB, "OptionB",
    250, 80, 110, 24, radioGroup);
```

This organizes the radio buttons in a good-looking border, and also enables proper keyboard support for the control group. Press Tab to move the keyboard input focus to the current radio button in a group, then use the cursor keys to select a button. Of course, it's easier just to use the mouse to select buttons, but well written Windows programs should also be operable from the keyboard.

When creating radio-button groups, you must have one button toggled on, or keyboard support won't operate correctly. (If all radio buttons in a group are toggled off, the only way to select any button is by using a mouse. After doing that, keyboard support begins to work correctly for the controls. Avoid this minor bug in Windows by always preselecting one control in each radio-button group.) You may construct control objects in the parent window's constructor as shown here. But you should initialize those objects in the parent window's SetupWindow function. In the parent's constructor, the associated window elements for child controls have not yet been created. Those window elements come into being only *after* SetupWindow calls its ancestor functions. For example, here's how CONTROLS turns on one of the sample radio buttons:

```
void
TButtonChild::SetupWindow()
{
// Control window elements are not yet created!
  TMDIChild::SetupWindow();
// Control window element have been created, and
// it is now Okay to initialize controls.
// For example, this turns on a radio button:
  radioButtonA->SetCheck(BF_CHECKED);
}
```

The preceding example shows one way to communicate with controls—by calling a class member function such as SetCheck. Another method is to send a control a message. For example, you could write a function that calls the TWindow HandleMessage function:

```
radioButtonA->HandleMessage(BM_SETCHECK, BF_CHECKED);
```

This differs from the normal Windows method of calling SendMessage to send messages. If you want to do that, however, you may call SendMessage as follows:

```
radioButtonA->SendMessage(BM_SETCHECK, BF_CHECKED, 0);
```

You can also broadcast a message to all controls using the parent window's ChildBroadCastMessage function. This statement, which can go in the parent's SetupWindow or another member function (but not a constructor) checks all buttons in the window:

```
ChildBroadcastMessage(BM_SETCHECK, BF_CHECKED);
```

Parent windows can also receive messages from their child window controls. For example, the parent window might define a response table for a couple of buttons:

```
DEFINE_RESPONSE_TABLE1(TButtonChild, TMDIChild)
  EV_COMMAND(IDOK, CmOkButton),
  EV_COMMAND(ID_CLOSEBUTTON, CmCloseButton),
END_RESPONSE_TABLE;
```

You can then implement the member functions, CmOkButton and CmCloseButton in the example, to perform whatever action you want when a button is selected:

```
void
TButtonChild::CmCloseButton()
{
  CloseWindow();
}
```

Find out whether a checkbox is checked by calling its GetCheck function. For example, the response function CmOkButton, which responds to OK-button selections, beeps only if the window's checkbox is selected:

```
if (checkBox->GetCheck())
  MessageBeep(0);
```

TListBox

One of the most versatile controls is a listbox. To create one, include the LISTBOX.H header file and define a TListBox pointer as in Listing 11.2, LBCHILD.H. The sample class also defines a TStatic object to list text in a window. Figure 11.2 shows the controls in their parent window.

FIGURE 11.2.

Listbox and static text controls.

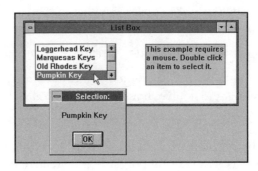

Listing 11.2. LBCHILD.H.

```
// lbchild.h -- TListBoxChild header file
class TListBoxChild: public TMDIChild {
public:
  TListBoxChild(TMDIClient& parent);
protected:
  void SetupWindow();
  void SelectAnItem();
private:
  TListBox* listbox;
  TStatic* instructions;
DECLARE_RESPONSE_TABLE(TListBoxChild);
};
```

In the constructor of the window in which the control appears (see file LBCHILD.CPP on disk), enable keyboard support by calling EnableKBHandler, then construct the listbox:

```
EnableKBHandler();
listbox = new TListBox(this, ID_LISTBOX,
  20, 20, 150, 75);
```

The first two parameters specify the parent object's address and a unique ID for the listbox control. (Most controls require similar arguments.) The integer values position and size the control. Construct a static text item similarly, but turn on its WS_BORDER style to give it a frame:

```
instructions = new TStatic(this, -1, "Instructions",
  225, 20, 150, 75);
instructions->Attr.Style |= WS_BORDER;
```

Because the program doesn't need to refer to the static text item, I set its identifier to -1.

A listbox without a list is like a scarecrow without any straw—so, add some items to the listbox in the parent window's SetupWindow function:

```
void
TListBoxChild::SetupWindow()
{
  TMDIChild::SetupWindow();
  listbox->AddString("Pumpkin Key");
  listbox->AddString("Old Rhodes Key");
  listbox->AddString("Rodriguez Key");
  ...
}
```

> **NOTE**
>
> Never add strings to a listbox control, or perform any other actions that affect a control, in the constructor of the window in which the control appears. The window constructor may create a TControl or derived-class object for a control, but any actions involving that control must go in SetupWindow or in another function, not in the window's constructor. The reason for this rule is simple: calling the ancestor SetupWindow function (as done in the first statement of the preceding example) creates the window elements associated with all of a window's children (including that window's controls). Until then, *the control window elements do not exist,* and you cannot use the control.

Also assign some text to the static control. For example, use a string class object to initialize the TStatic object addressed by the window's instructions pointer:

```
string s;
s += "This example requires a mouse.";
s += " Double click an item to select it.";
instructions->SetText(s.c_str());
```

You probably also need a function to respond to listbox selections. The function needs no arguments and it must return void. Declare it like this in the parent window's class:

```
void SelectAnItem();
```

Then, define a response table for the class, and use the EV_LBN_DBLCLK macro (defined in WINDOWEV.H) to call the function in response to the listbox's *notification message* that an item has been selected:

```
DEFINE_RESPONSE_TABLE1(TListBoxChild, TMDIChild)
  EV_LBN_DBLCLK(ID_LISTBOX, SelectAnItem),
END_RESPONSE_TABLE;
```

Look up other EV_LBN macros in Borland's references and online help for additional listbox operations you can use. Use them the same as EV_LBN_DBLCLK. For example, macro EV_LBN_SETFOCUS calls a function when any item in the listbox receives the focus due to a mouse click (single or double) or by pressing the Tab key.

TComboBox

A combo box combines an input text item with a listbox for a handy selection tool of which there are three varieties—a *simple* box (CBS_SIMPLE) that always shows its list and permits users to select listed items or enter new ones, a *drop down box* (CBS_DROPDOWN) that initially hides its listbox but otherwise works like a simple box, and a *drop down listbox* (CBS_DROPDOWNLIST) that also hides its listbox and permits users to select only listed items.

All three types of combo boxes are available as objects of the TComboBox class, declared in the COMBOBOX.H header. Include that header file, then define a TComboBox pointer in the parent window class as Listing 11.3, CBCHILD.H, demonstrates. I also defined a static text item to display strings selected from the combo box control. Figure 11.3 shows the controls in their parent window.

FIGURE 11.3.

Combo box and static text controls.

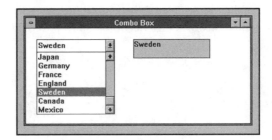

Listing 11.3. CBCHILD.H.

```
// cbchild.h -- TComboBoxChild header file

class TComboBoxChild: public TMDIChild {
public:
  TComboBoxChild(TMDIClient& parent);
protected:
  void SetupWindow();
  void EvCbnSelChange();
private:
  TComboBox* combobox;
  TStatic* selection;
DECLARE_RESPONSE_TABLE(TComboBoxChild);
};
```

In the constructor of the window in which the control appears, enable keyboard handling and create a TComboBox object using statements such as these:

```
EnableKBHandler();
combobox = new TComboBox(this, ID_COMBOBOX,
  20, 20, 145, 150,
  CBS_DROPDOWNLIST, TEXT_LEN);
```

As in all controls, the this pointer refers to the parent window object. ID_COMBOBOX is any unique resource identifier that you can use to refer to the control. The four integer values position and size the control, CBS_DROPDOWNLIST selects a control style (try other CBS_ constants for a different look and feel), and TEXT_LEN sets the maximum length for listed strings. To provide a place for displaying selected items, I also defined a static text item:

```
selection = new TStatic(this, -1, "No selection",
  200, 20, 145, 35);
selection->Attr.Style |= WS_BORDER;
```

Initialize combo boxes as you do listboxes, usually in the parent window's SetupWindow function. For example, the sample CONTROLS program (see disk file CBCHILD.CPP) initializes the combo box with this function (I show only a portion here):

```
void
TComboBoxChild::SetupWindow()
{
  TMDIChild::SetupWindow();
  combobox->AddString("U.S.A.");
  combobox->AddString("Japan");
...
}
```

Use a macro such as EV_CBN_SELCHANGE in the parent window's response table to intercept notification events from the combo box control. (See Borland's COMBOBOX.H header file for a complete list of macros.) For example, the sample program defines the following response table, which causes the program to call the parent window's EvCbnSelChange function every time an action changes the current combo box selection.

```
DEFINE_RESPONSE_TABLE1(TComboBoxChild, TMDIChild)
  EV_CBN_SELCHANGE(ID_COMBOBOX, EvCbnSelChange),
END_RESPONSE_TABLE;
```

Implement the function to respond to the notification event. The sample program extracts the selected item, and sends it to the static text control for display. (Despite its name, a *static* control's text may be changed under program control. Users, however, cannot enter new text into static text controls.) Here's the function implementation from file CBCHILD.CPP:

```
void
TComboBoxChild::EvCbnSelChange()
{
  int i = combobox->GetSelIndex();
  if (i >= 0) {
    char seltext[TEXT_LEN];
    combobox->GetSelString(seltext, sizeof(seltext));
    selection->SetText(seltext);
  }
}
```

TEdit

The TEdit class, derived from TStatic, wraps up a complete text editor into a single control. Use TEdit to create single- and multiline input boxes into which users can type strings. The class implements all the usual *Edit* menu options: *Undo, Cut, Copy, Paste, Delete,* and *Clear,* and fully supports keyboard and mouse operations.

Declare pointers to TEdit objects in the parent window class—the one that is to own the text editing controls. For example, Listing 11.4, TXCHILD.H (part of the CONTROLS demonstration), declares two TEdit pointers: oneLiner and multiLiner. The class also declares a TButton pointer for an OK button that closes the window at which time the program extracts and displays the text in the oneLiner control. Figure 11.4 shows the two controls in their parent's window.

FIGURE 11.4.

Single- and multiline text edit controls.

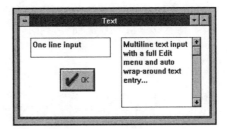

Listing 11.4. TXCHILD.H.

```
// txchild.h -- TTextChild header file

class TTextChild: public TMDIChild {
public:
  TTextChild(TMDIClient& parent);
protected:
  void CmOkButton();
private:
  TButton* okButton;
  TEdit* oneLiner;
  TEdit* multiLiner;
DECLARE_RESPONSE_TABLE(TTextChild);
};
```

Construct TEdit control objects much as you do other controls. For example, the
CONTROLS demonstration creates a single-line edit control with the following statement (see file TXCHILD.CPP on the book's disk):

```
oneLiner = new TEdit(this, ID_ONELINER,
  "One line input",
  20, 20, 150, 35,
  MAX_TEXTLEN, FALSE);
```

As with other controls, this addresses the parent window object, ID_ONELINER is any
identifier (numeric or string) that other processes can use to access this control. The
string initializes the control's contents. The four integer values position and size the
control, MAX_TEXTLEN limits the amount of text users can type into the control, and FALSE
selects single-line style.

Create multiline text-edit controls similarly, but change FALSE to TRUE:

```
multiLiner = new TEdit(this, ID_MULTILINER,
  "Multiline text input",
  190, 20, 150, 125,
  MAX_TEXTLEN, TRUE);
```

By default, multiline TEdit control windows have the following edit-style options (all
of which begin with ES_ and are defined in WINDOWS.H in the BC4\INCLUDE
directory):

```
ES_LEFT, ES_MULTILINE, ES_AUTOHSCROLL, ES_AUTOVSCROLL
```

In addition, multiline edit controls also have the following window-style options:

```
WS_CHILD, WS_VISIBLE, WS_BORDER, WS_VSCROLL, WS_HSCROLL, WS_TABSTOP
```

These settings result in a control with horizontal and vertical scrollbars, making the
control look like a text-editor window. The horizontal scrollbars, however, interfere with
the control's capability to automatically wrap around lines of text, breaking at spaces
between words. To enable auto-wraparound for text-edit controls, you must turn off
both the ES_AUTOHSCROLL and WS_HSCROLL options. Do that after constructing the control object by using this statement:

```
multiLiner->Attr.Style &= ~(WS_HSCROLL | ES_AUTOHSCROLL);
```

When you type, the text automatically wraps around to fit inside the control's border.
The entered text is formatted as a single string—it does not have carriage returns added
at the ends of lines. If you want carriage returns added, however, enable them with this
statement:

```
multiLiner->FormatLines(TRUE);
```

As with all control initializations (other than constructing the control object and setting its attributes), such statements should be placed in the parent window's `SetupWindow` or other member function, *never* in the parent window's constructor because, as I mentioned, the control's associated window element doesn't exist until your window's `SetupWindow` function call its ancestor `SetupWindow`.

Edit controls implement common *Edit* menu commands. To take advantage of this feature, simply add an *Edit* menu to your program's menu resource. Include the EDIT.RH resource header file and use the predefined `CM_` identifiers shown in Listing 11.5, extracted from the sample program's resource script file, CONTROLS.RC. (The complete file is on the book's disk.)

Listing 11.5. CONTROLS.RC (Edit menu).

```
POPUP "&Edit"
BEGIN
  MENUITEM "&Undo\tCtrl+Z", CM_EDITUNDO
  MENUITEM SEPARATOR
  MENUITEM "Cu&t\tCtrl+X", CM_EDITCUT
  MENUITEM "&Copy\tCtrl+C", CM_EDITCOPY
  MENUITEM "&Paste\tCtrl+V", CM_EDITPASTE
  MENUITEM "&Delete\tDel", CM_EDITDELETE
  MENUITEM "C&lear", CM_EDITCLEAR
END
```

To extract text from an edit control, call the `TEdit` class's `GetText` function, inherited from `TStatic`. For example, when you select the OK button, the message response function `CmOkButton` executes these statements to get and display the text entered into the sample single-line control (use the same programming to extract multiline text):

```
char line[MAX_TEXTLEN];
oneLiner->GetText(line, sizeof(line));
MessageBox(line, "One line entry:", MB_OK);
CloseWindow();
```

TScrollBar, TSlider, THSlider, and *TVSlider*

Unlike objects of the `TScroller` class, which interfaces with window scrollers attached to the right and bottom window borders, `TScrollBar` objects are true controls that you can place anywhere in a window. These versatile controls are useful in a variety of applications that require selecting value ranges. For example, a scrollbar might select the volume of a sound-output device, or it could select a color value component.

Sliders of the TSlider class, derived from TScrollBar, are highly specialized scrollbar objects that you can use to create thermometers and other visually interesting scrollbars. Two derived classes, TVSlider and THSlider select between vertical and horizontal slider styles. Sliders also demonstrate how to customize the TScrollBar class for special visual effects.

Construct scrollbar controls by first declaring TScrollBar pointers in the parent window class. Construct sliders by declaring TVSlider or THSlider pointers. Listing 11.6, SBCHILD.H (part of the CONTROLS program) demonstrates. Figure 11.5 shows the final result. The three horizontal scrollbars select red, green, and blue color components for the rectangle at their left. The vertical slider changes the numeric value at its right. These actions demonstrate how to use scrollbars and sliders to perform interactive tasks in response to user selections with the mouse and keyboard.

FIGURE 11.5.

Scrollbar and slider controls.

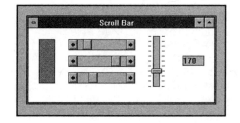

Listing 11.6. SBCHILD.H.

```
// sbchild.h -- TScrollBarChild header file

class TScrollBarChild: public TMDIChild {
public:
  TScrollBarChild(TMDIClient& parent);
protected:
  void SetupWindow();
  void EvHScroll(UINT scrollCode, UINT thumbPos, HWND hWndCtl);
  virtual void Paint(TDC& dc, BOOL erase, TRect& rect);
  void ShowSlideValue(UINT code = 0);
private:
  int redValue;
  int grnValue;
  int bluValue;
  TScrollBar* redBar;
  TScrollBar* grnBar;
  TScrollBar* bluBar;
  TRect colorRect;
  TVSlider* slide;
```

```
    TStatic* slideValue;
DECLARE_RESPONSE_TABLE(TScrollBarChild);
};
```

In the parent window's constructor, create a scrollbar as an object of the `TScrollBar` class, and save the object's address in a pointer. Here's how the sample program creates a scrollbar to select the red component of a red-green-blue color value:

```
redBar = new TScrollBar(this, ID_REDBAR,
  75, 20, 125, 20, TRUE);
```

As with other controls, `this` is a pointer to the parent window object, `ID_REDBAR` is a constant that uniquely identifies the control among others in the same window, the four integer values position and size the control, and `TRUE` selects horizontal style. For a vertical scrollbar, change `TRUE` to `FALSE`.

You might also want to initialize the control. For example, in the parent window's `SetupWindow` or another member function (but never in the parent's constructor) you can change a scrollbar's range (normally set to 1...100) by calling the `SetRange` function:

```
redBar->SetRange(0, MAX_RANGE);
```

Construct sliders using similar code. In the parent window's constructor, create a `TVSlider` object and assign its address to a pointer (`slide` in the sample):

```
slide = new TVSlider(this, ID_SLIDE,
  225, 10, 32, 100);
```

Construct horizontal sliders similarly but specify the `THSlider` class. In the parent's `SetupWindow` or other member function, initialize the control by calling `TSlider` and `TVSlider` (or `THSlider` for horizontal controls) functions. For instance, the sample program configures its slider with these three statements:

```
slide->SetRange(100, 200);    // Top & bottom ranges
slide->SetRuler(10, TRUE);    // Grid-spacing and snap
slide->SetPosition(150);      // Initial thumb position
```

Call `SetRange` to change the slider's minimum and maximum range. Call `SetRuler` with two arguments: the first to set the spacing between slider movements (shown as grid dots next to the control), and the second to select snapping (`TRUE`) or no snapping (`FALSE`). With snapping enabled, the slider thumb box jumps between grid dots, and it cannot be set to other positions. With snapping disabled, the thumb box moves smoothly to all positions. Call `SetPosition` to display the thumb box at a specific location within the control's defined range.

To respond to scrollbar notification events, define a response table for the parent window's class and insert the macro EV_WM_HSCROLL for horizontal scrollbars or EV_WM_VSCROLL for vertical controls. The macros require the class to declare a function named EvHScroll as follows:

```
void EvHScroll(UINT scrollCode, UINT thumbPos, HWND hWndCtl);
```

Use EvVScroll for vertical scrollbars. Scrollbar events call EvVScroll or EvHScroll with a code that distinguishes among various notification messages such as SB_LINEUP and SB_PAGEDOWN. (See other SB_ constants in the ObjectWindows SCROLLBA.H header file.) You may inspect the scrollCode parameter to limit the EvHScroll function to responding to certain events, or ignore the code to respond to all notifications (this is usually the best course of action). You can also use the thumbPos parameter to determine the thumb box's position and hWndCtl if you need a handle to the scrollbar window element.

The sample program ignores those EvHScroll parameters and simply updates the color rectangle for all scrollbar actions. In file SBCHILD.CPP (supplied on the book's disk), for example, the EvHScroll function is implemented as follows:

```
void
TScrollBarChild::EvHScroll(
  UINT scrollCode, UINT thumbPos, HWND hWndCtl)
{
// Call ancestor method
  TMDIChild::EvHScroll(scrollCode, thumbPos, hWndCtl);
// Get scroll bar position as color values
  redValue = redBar->GetPosition();
  grnValue = grnBar->GetPosition();
  bluValue = bluBar->GetPosition();
// Force update event to repaint color box in window
  InvalidateRect(colorRect, FALSE);
}
```

The replacement function should call the ancestor EvHScroll function to ensure proper visual effects. After that, you may perform whatever actions you want in response to the scrollbar's movements. In this case, the program calls the GetPosition function to obtain each scrollbar's thumb positions (these values are limited to the defined range for the controls). Then, InvalidateRect tells Windows to generate an update event for the portion of the window in which the colored rectangle appears. To handle that event, the parent window implements this Paint function:

```
void
TScrollBarChild::Paint(TDC& dc, BOOL /*erase*/, TRect& /*rect*/)
{
  TColor color(redValue, grnValue, bluValue);
  TBrush* brush = new TBrush(color);
  dc.SelectObject(*brush);
  dc.Rectangle(colorRect);
  dc.RestoreBrush();
  delete brush;
}
```

You may also write similar code to respond to slider events. Or, you can do as I did in the sample program to trap all notification codes generated by the use of the slider control. To do that, declare a function such as ShowSlideValue (you can use a different name) in the parent window class. The function must declare one UINT (unsigned integer) parameter, optionally initialized to a default value (0 in the sample):

```
void ShowSlideValue(UINT code = 0);
```

As in the preceding example, code represents the notification code generated by the use of the control. You can inspect the code to, say, limit the response to specific events—SB_PAGEUP (thumb was moved up one "page" value) or SB_TOP (thumb was moved to the top). Or, you can ignore the code parameter and simply respond to all notifications, as in the sample listing (see file SBCHILD.CPP supplied on the book's disk). The sample program implements ShowSlideValue to get the slide's numeric position, convert that value to text, and pass the result to a static text control for display (shown at far right in the window—refer back to Figure 11.5):

```
void
TScrollBarChild::ShowSlideValue(UINT /*code*/)
{
  char s[10];
  int p = slide->GetPosition();
  wsprintf(s, "%d", p);
  slideValue->SetText(s);
}
```

TGauge

Surprisingly, there's no standard gauge control in Windows, even though just about every Windows program—or, at least, every utility that installs Windows software—uses a gauge to display a progress report of goings on such as files copied from a floppy disk to a hard drive. The standard gauge is a horizontal bar (or it can be vertical), with some text inside and a colored band that moves from one end of the bar to the other. When the bar is half way across the control, you know the job is about half done—a purely visual device, but an important one to provide users with feedback about what a program is doing behind the scenes.

The TGauge class fills in the missing gap in Windows standard controls. Use the class, declared in GAUGE.H, to construct gauge objects that you can update during the course of other processes. Listing 11.7, GACHILD.H (from the CONTROLS demonstration program) shows how to declare a pointer to a TGauge control object. Figure 11.6 shows the resulting parent window with a simple gauge, updated by a timer to simulate an ongoing process.

FIGURE 11.6.

Gauge control.

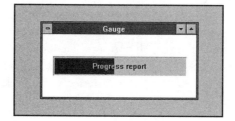

Listing 11.7. GACHILD.H.

```
// gachild.h -- TGuageChild header file

class TGaugeChild: public TMDIChild {
public:
  TGaugeChild(TMDIClient& parent);
  ~TGaugeChild();
protected:
  void SetupWindow();
  void EvTimer(UINT timerId);
private:
  TGauge* gauge;
DECLARE_RESPONSE_TABLE(TGaugeChild);
};
```

Construct the gauge, as you do other control objects, in the constructor of the window in which the control appears:

```
gauge = new TGauge(this, "Progress report",
  ID_GAUGE, 20, 40, 250, 35, TRUE,  // FALSE for vertical
  MARGIN);
```

Pass the parent window object's address (this), a string to display inside the control, an identifier value constant, position and size values, and TRUE for a horizontal control; FALSE for a vertical design. Pass also a value that selects a margin (border) style.

After constructing the control, you may call its member functions to initialize the gauge and to update its interior. For example, in the parent window's SetupWindow or another member function, set the control's range and its initial value with these statements:

```
gauge->SetRange(0, 100);
gauge->SetValue(0);
```

For a building-block kind of effect—rather than a smoothly growing bar, the control shows its progress by displaying successive squares—call the SetLed function:

```
gauge->SetLed(LEDS);
```

To update the control's bar, pass a value within the defined range to the SetValue function:

```
gauge->SetValue(value++);
```

Calling SetValue invalidates the control, causing Windows to issue an update event, which is handled by a TGauge Paint function. Set the control value back to zero (or its other minimum range value) to clear the control—before starting another process, for example.

To change the color of the control's bar (it's normally blue), construct a TColor object (include the COLOR.H header) and pass the object to SetColor. The following, for example, creates a bright red gauge:

```
gauge->SetColor(TColor(255, 0, 0));
```

Controls in Dialog Boxes

In this chapter, you've leaned how to design dialog boxes as resources, and how to construct TDialog interface objects. By calling the Execute member function for those objects, you bring up a modal dialog box that operates completely on its own. For modeless dialogs, you can call the Create function instead.

These are the simplest methods for creating and using dialogs, but for more sophisticated tasks, you might also need to program special actions for a dialog's controls. Although it's possible to communicate with controls by sending and receiving messages—the classic method used by Windows software written in C—ObjectWindows provides far easier (and I think better) support for handling a dialog's controls. (The same techniques work in nondialog windows, too.) In general, you design and use your dialog boxes as you normally do, but you derive a new class from TDialog into which you insert member functions to perform whatever tasks you need. To communicate with the dialog's controls, your class constructs objects of classes derived from TControl. Rather than building those objects as explained in the preceding sections—specifying the parent window object address (this), an identifying value, position and size information, strings, and so on—you construct the control objects by passing their resource identifiers to the class constructors. The constructors take the control object's information directly from the dialog's resource that you designed with Resource Workshop or by typing commands into a script file.

The result is a TDialog object with a set of TControl objects, one for each control in the dialog. You may call member functions for the control objects, pass them data, receive notification messages, and perform other operations as the CONTROLS demonstration showed for using control objects in common windows. In addition, you can also use the ObjectWindows *data transfer mechanism* to automate the transfer of information to and from all of a dialog's controls. The next section explains how to program data transfers. But first, you need to learn how to construct control objects for a dialog box.

Declare a class derived from TDialog. At a minimum, your class (named TMyDialog here) needs a constructor, but it can have other functions and data members. Also declare control class pointers for each control to which you want special access:

```
class TMyDialog: public TDialog }
public:
  TMyDialog(TWindow* parent, TResId resId);
private:
  TComboBox* myComboBox;
  TEdit* myInputBox;
};
```

In the constructor, create control objects and assign their addresses to the class pointers. Initialize each control by passing its resource identifier to the appropriate control-class constructor:

```
TMyDialog::TMyDialog(TWindow* parent, TResId resId)
  : TDialog(parent, resId)
{
  myComboBox = new TComboBox(this, ID_MYCOMBOBOX);
  myInputBox = new TEdit(this, ID_MYINPUTBOX);
}
```

The dialog box may have other controls for which you do not create TControl object interfaces. Those controls work on their own as controls normally do. You need to create TControl objects only for controls that you want to reference as objects. In other TMyDialog functions, you can call member functions for the controls, prepare response tables to handle notification events, and so on.

When using this technique to interface with dialog controls, you might also want to derive your own classes for each control. Listings 11.8 (DIAGCTL.RH) and 11.9 (DIAGCTL.CPP) demonstrate how, with this method, a control can respond to its own events, and in that way, act as an autonomous object (usually a good plan in object-oriented programming). I did not list the sample program's resource script file because it contains dialog box commands that are too long to reproduce here. See the file DIAGCTL.RC on this book's disk. You might also want to open that file using Resource Workshop to inspect how I constructed the program's sample dialog box, shown in Figure 11.7. (The sample program's *OK, Cancel,* and *Help* buttons are just for show. You may select *OK* or *Cancel* to close the dialog. *Help* does nothing.)

FIGURE 11.7.
Dialog box from the DIAGCTL program.

Listing 11.8. DIAGCTL.RH.

```
// diagctl.rh -- Resource header file

// Menu resource identifiers
#define ID_MENU 100
#define CM_TEST 101

// Dialog resource identifer
#define ID_DIALOG 100

// Dialog control identifiers
#define ID_OPTION_GROUP 999
#define ID_ENABLE_REACTOR 101
#define ID_PREVENT_MELTDOWN 102
#define ID_LOCK_CONTROL_RODS 103
#define ID_SOUND_ALARM 104
```

Listing 11.9. DIAGCTL.CPP.

```
/* ============================================================ *\
**   diagctl.cpp -- Control objects in dialog boxes            **
** ============================================================ **
**                                                             **
** ============================================================ **
**      Copyright   1994 by Tom Swan. All rights reserved.     **
\* ============================================================ */

#include <owl\applicat.h>
#include <owl\framewin.h>
#include <owl\dialog.h>
#include <owl\checkbox.h>
#pragma hdrstop
#include "diagctl.rh"


// ============================================================
// CheckBox control class
// ============================================================

class TAlarmCheck: public TCheckBox {
public:
  TAlarmCheck(TWindow* parent)
    : TCheckBox(parent, ID_SOUND_ALARM) { }
protected:
  void BNClicked();
DECLARE_RESPONSE_TABLE(TAlarmCheck);
};

// Response table notifies the check
DEFINE_RESPONSE_TABLE1(TAlarmCheck, TCheckBox)
  EV_NOTIFY_AT_CHILD(BN_CLICKED, BNClicked),
END_RESPONSE_TABLE;

// Respond to checkbox selections--note that the
// control itself does this, not its parent window.
void
TAlarmCheck::BNClicked()
{
  char *s;

  TCheckBox::BNClicked();  // Call ancestor function
  if (GetCheck() == BF_CHECKED)
    s = "Alarm is enabled!";
  else
    s = "Alarm is disabled";
  MessageBox(s, "An alarming event", MB_OK);
}
```

```
// ============================================================
// Dialog box class
// ============================================================

class TOptions: public TDialog {
public:
  TOptions(TWindow* parent);
private:
  TCheckBox* alarmOption;
};

// Constructor

TOptions::TOptions(TWindow* parent)
  : TDialog(parent, ID_DIALOG)
{
// Construct interface object for one of the
// dialog's checkbox controls.
  alarmOption = new TAlarmCheck(this);
}

// ============================================================
// The application's main window
// ============================================================

class TDCtlWin: public TFrameWindow {
public:
  TDCtlWin(TWindow* parent, const char far* title);
protected:
  void CmTest();
DECLARE_RESPONSE_TABLE(TDCtlWin);
};

DEFINE_RESPONSE_TABLE1(TDCtlWin, TFrameWindow)
  EV_COMMAND(CM_TEST, CmTest),
END_RESPONSE_TABLE;

// Constructor
TDCtlWin::TDCtlWin(TWindow* parent, const char far* title)
  : TFrameWindow(parent, title),
    TWindow(parent, title)
{
  AssignMenu(ID_MENU);
}
```

continues

409

Listing 11.9. continued

```
// Menu command function
void
TDCtlWin::CmTest()
{
  TOptions* dialog;
  dialog = new TOptions(this);
  dialog->Execute();
}


// ============================================================
// The application class
// ============================================================

class TDCtlApp: public TApplication {
public:
  TDCtlApp(const char far* name)
    : TApplication(name) {}
  void InitMainWindow();
};

// Initialize the program's main window
void
TDCtlApp::InitMainWindow()
{
// Enable Borland Custom Controls
  EnableBWCC();

// Construct demonstration's main window
  MainWindow = new TDCtlWin(0, "Controls in Dialogs");
}

#pragma argsused

// Main program
int
OwlMain(int argc, char* argv[])
{
  TDCtlApp app("DiagCtlApp");
  return app.Run();
}
```

Imagine that you need to create a checkbox that responds to its own notification messages—that is, selecting the box should also perform an action. To demonstrate one solution, I declared a class TAlarmCheck from TCheckBox. Notice how the class constructor passes the control's resource identifier, ID_SOUND_ALARM, to the TCheckBox constructor. Constructing an object of TAlarmCheck initializes the object from the resource. I also declared a function, BnClicked, and a response table that includes the macro statement:

`EV_NOTIFY_AT_CHILD(BN_CLICKED, BNClicked),`

Use similar programming to have a child window (a control, for example) receive its own notification messages. In this case, when the control generates a BN_CLICKED message, that message is bounced back to the control for handling in function BNClicked.

That function is inherited from TCheckBox, so in the new implementation, the first job is to call the ancestor function:

```
TCheckBox::BNClicked();  // Call ancestor function
```

After that, the control is free to perform any other action in response to its selection. In the sample, the control tests whether it is checked by calling its GetCheck function. Just for show, the demonstration displays a message box that confirms the checkbox setting.

The sample program also derives class TOptions from TDialog. To create the control object for the alarm checkbox, the class constructor executes the statement:

```
alarmOption = new TAlarmCheck(this);
```

In this example, the TAlarmCheck object operates completely on its own, and for that reason, the alarmOption pointer is redundant. You can remove the pointer's declaration from the TOptions class, and change the preceding statement to:

```
new TAlarmCheck(this);
```

Because the control object is a child of its parent window (the dialog box object, that is), you do not have to save the control object's address. You also do not need to delete the memory allocated by new. When you close the dialog, it destroys its control objects automatically.

Data Transfer Mechanism

Many times, you need a dialog box that presents a number of controls that represent various settings. An example is an *Options* dialog, typically used in Windows programs to select program features. Designing and programming the dialog box is the easy part— just use the techniques explained in this chapter. But you also need a convenient method for storing and initializing the dialog's control values.

You could initialize each control separately, and you could write code to interrogate each control for its final value when the dialog is closed by its *OK* button. These methods are tedious to program, however, especially in complex dialogs with many controls of different types. In such cases, a better plan is to use TWindow's *data transfer mechanism,* which can copy one or more control values from a dialog box or a window to a *transfer buffer.* The mechanism can also copy information from a transfer buffer to a set of controls.

A transfer buffer is a structure that has one member for each control that is to participate in data transfers. Buttons, group boxes, static text controls, and gauges normally
do not participate in transfers (there's nothing to transfer in a button because it doesn't
hold any information). Other controls such as TListBox objects are ready to perform
transfers on demand. Table 11.2 lists data transfer types for the control classes described
in this chapter.

Table 11.2. Data transfer types.

TControl Class	Data transfer type
TButton	none
TCheckBox	WORD
TRadioButton	WORD
TListBox	TListBoxData
TComboBox	TComboBoxData
TEdit	char array
TScrollBar	TScrollBarData
TGauge	none

To create a data transfer buffer, declare a structure with members of the types in the
table. Include a member for each control that is to participate in data transfers. A dialog
may also have other controls that don't have corresponding members in the buffer. For
example, you could declare the struct:

```
struct TMyOptions {
  TComboBoxData *mylist;
  TEdit* myinput;
};
```

Also define the buffer variable, usually as a private or protected member of the parent
window or dialog box class:

```
class TMyDialog: public TDialog {
...
private:
  TMyOptions transferBuffer;
};
```

Next, the parent window (the dialog box object, for example) must construct objects
for each control. Use the techniques illustrated in the preceding section to initialize the
control objects from the dialog resource. You don't need to save pointers to the class

objects unless you plan to call member functions or use the objects in other ways. You need only construct the control objects as children of their parent window (the dialog):

```
new TComboBoxData(this, ID_MYLIST);
new TEdit(this, ID_MYINPUT);
```

You must construct the control objects in their declaration order in the transfer buffer structure. You also need to enable data transfers for the parent window. Do that by calling `SetTransferBuffer`, usually in the parent's constructor:

```
SetTransferBuffer(&transferBuffer);
```

Data transfers are automatic. When you construct the dialog box, the transfer buffer's members are passed to each control, initializing their values. When you close the dialog by selecting its *OK* button (or by any other means that closes the dialog via a command message identified as `IDOK`) control values are transferred back to the buffer. You can save the buffer in a disk file or use it in any other way you wish.

To exclude a control from the transfer mechanism (but to still be able to construct an object interface for the control), call the control's `DisableTransfer` function. To include a control, call `EnableTransfer`. Both functions are inherited from `TWindow`. You can enable transfer for a static text item, for example, perhaps used to display interactive information in a dialog box or window. Normally, static text controls do not participate in data transfers.

You can also transfer information to and from the transfer buffer at any time by calling the `TransferData` function inherited from `TWindow`. Pass a direction constant as follows:

```
TransferData(tdGetData);    // From controls to transfer buffer
TransferData(tdSetData);    // From transfer buffer to controls
```

As an example of how to create and use data transfer buffers, the next set of listings implements an *Options* dialog box. You can use the dialog to change the program's title, select an auto-save feature, and cause the program's window to stay on top of other windows. I explain more about using the program and how it works after the listings. Figure 11.8 shows the program's option dialog. The program's declarations and statements are in Listings 11.10 (OPTION.RH), 11.11 (OPTION.H), and 11.12 (OPTION.CPP). A resource file, OPTION.RC, is not listed here—the file is included on the book's disk.

Listing 11.10. OPTION.RH.

```
// option.rh -- Resource header file

// Menu resource and command identifiers
#define ID_MENU 100
#define CM_OPTIONS 101
#define CM_SAVE 102

// Options dialog resource
#define ID_OPTIONS 100

// Window title input box
#define ID_WINDOW_TITLE 101

// Preferences check box identifiers
#define ID_CONFIRM_EXIT 201
#define ID_AUTO_SAVE 202
#define ID_MAXIMIZE_WINDOW 203

// Sound radio button identifiers
#define ID_SOUND_ON 301
#define ID_SOUND_OFF 302

// Stay-on-top check box identifier
#define ID_STAY_ON_TOP    401
```

FIGURE 11.8.

Sample Options dialog.

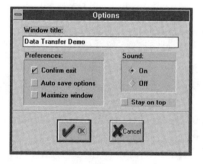

Listing 11.11. OPTION.H.

```
// option.h -- Program header file

#define TITLE_LEN 41
#define TITLE_SIZE 42   // TITLE_LEN + 1
#define DEFAULT_TITLE "Data Transfer Demo"
#define WINCLASSNAME "TOptionWin"
```

```
#define FILENAME "option.dat"

struct OptionBuffer {
// Title string
  char windowTitle[TITLE_SIZE];

// Preferences check boxes
  WORD confirmExit;
  WORD autoSaveOptions;
  WORD maximizeWindow;

// Sound option radio buttons
  WORD soundOn;
  WORD soundOff;

// Stay-on top check box
  WORD stayOnTop;
};
```

Listing 11.12. OPTION.CPP.

```
/* =========================================================== *\
**   option.cpp -- Demonstrates data transfer mechanism        **
** =========================================================== **
**                                                             **
** =========================================================== **
**      Copyright  1994 by Tom Swan. All rights reserved.      **
\* =========================================================== */

#include <stdio.h>
#include <string.h>
#include <owl\applicat.h>
#include <owl\framewin.h>
#include <owl\dialog.h>
#include <owl\edit.h>
#include <owl\checkbox.h>
#include <owl\radiobut.h>
#pragma hdrstop
#include "option.rh"
#include "option.h"

// ===========================================================
// The options dialog
// ===========================================================

class TOptionDialog: public TDialog {
public:
  TOptionDialog(TWindow* parent, OptionBuffer* options);
};
```

Listing 11.12. continued

```
// Constructor
TOptionDialog::TOptionDialog(
  TWindow* parent, OptionBuffer* options)
  : TDialog(parent, ID_OPTIONS)
{
// Construct control object interfaces in the same
// order of their members in the OptionBuffer structure
  new TEdit(this, ID_WINDOW_TITLE, TITLE_SIZE);
  new TCheckBox(this, ID_CONFIRM_EXIT);
  new TCheckBox(this, ID_AUTO_SAVE);
  new TCheckBox(this, ID_MAXIMIZE_WINDOW);
  new TRadioButton(this, ID_SOUND_ON);
  new TRadioButton(this, ID_SOUND_OFF);
  new TCheckBox(this, ID_STAY_ON_TOP);

// Enable data transfers between options buffer and controls
  SetTransferBuffer(options);
}

// ============================================================
// The application's main window
// ============================================================

class TOptionWin: public TFrameWindow {
public:
  TOptionWin(TWindow* parent);
  const OptionBuffer* GetOptions() { return &options; }
protected:
  void SetupWindow();
  virtual char far* GetClassName() { return WINCLASSNAME; }
  BOOL CanClose();
  void CmOptions();
  void CmSave();
  BOOL LoadOptions();
  void InitOptions();
  void SetOnTop();
  void EvActivate(UINT active, BOOL minimized, HWND hWndOther);
private:
  OptionBuffer options;  // Data transfer buffer
DECLARE_RESPONSE_TABLE(TOptionWin);
};

DEFINE_RESPONSE_TABLE1(TOptionWin, TFrameWindow)
  EV_COMMAND(CM_OPTIONS, CmOptions),
  EV_COMMAND(CM_SAVE, CmSave),
  EV_WM_ACTIVATE,
END_RESPONSE_TABLE;
```

```
// Constructor
TOptionWin::TOptionWin(TWindow* parent)
  : TFrameWindow(parent, ""),
    TWindow(parent, "")
{
  AssignMenu(ID_MENU);
  InitOptions();
}

// Initialize window
void
TOptionWin::SetupWindow()
{
  TFrameWindow::SetupWindow();
  SetCaption(options.windowTitle);
  SetOnTop();
}

// Return True if okay to close window
BOOL
TOptionWin::CanClose()
{
  BOOL result = TFrameWindow::CanClose();
  if ((result) && (options.confirmExit)) {
    if (options.soundOn)
      MessageBeep(0);
    result = (MessageBox("Exit program?",
      GetApplication()->GetName(),
      MB_OKCANCEL | MB_ICONQUESTION) == IDOK);
  }
  return result;
}

// Display options dialog
void
TOptionWin::CmOptions()
{
  TOptionDialog* optionsDialog =
    new TOptionDialog(this, &options);
  if (options.soundOn)
    MessageBeep(0);
  if (optionsDialog->Execute() == IDOK) {
    SetCaption(options.windowTitle);
    SetOnTop();
    if (options.autoSaveOptions)
      CmSave();
  }
}
```

continues

417

Listing 11.12. continued

```
// Save options to disk file
void
TOptionWin::CmSave()
{
  BOOL okay;    // True if no errors detected
  int mbopts;   // MessageBox button and icon options
  char *s;      // Pointer to MessageBox string
  FILE *f = fopen(FILENAME, "wb");
  if (!f)
    okay = FALSE;
  else {
    okay = (fwrite(&options, sizeof(options), 1, f) == 1);
    fclose(f);
  }
  if (!okay) {
    s = "Save failed";
    mbopts = MB_OK | MB_ICONSTOP;
  } else {
    s = "Options saved";
    mbopts = MB_OK | MB_ICONINFORMATION;
  }
  if (options.soundOn)
    MessageBeep(0);
  MessageBox(s, GetApplication()->GetName(), mbopts);
}

// Return true if options are loaded from disk
BOOL
TOptionWin::LoadOptions()
{
  FILE *f = fopen(FILENAME, "rb");
  if (!f) return FALSE;
  BOOL okay = (fread(&options, sizeof(options), 1, f) == 1);
  fclose(f);
  return okay;
}

// Load options from disk or use default settings
void
TOptionWin::InitOptions()
{
  if (!LoadOptions()) {
    strcpy(options.windowTitle, DEFAULT_TITLE);
    options.confirmExit = TRUE;
    options.autoSaveOptions = FALSE;
    options.maximizeWindow = FALSE;
    options.soundOn = TRUE;
    options.soundOff = FALSE;
    options.stayOnTop = FALSE;
  }
}
```

```cpp
// Change on-top status
void
TOptionWin::SetOnTop()
{
  HWND hwndInsertAfter;
  if (options.stayOnTop)
    hwndInsertAfter = HWND_TOPMOST;
  else
    hwndInsertAfter = HWND_NOTOPMOST;
  SetWindowPos(hwndInsertAfter, 0, 0, 0, 0,
    SWP_NOMOVE | SWP_NOSIZE);
}

// Respond to WM_ACTIVATE messages. Bring last program window
// that was on top (the main window or a dialog box, for
// example) back on top if stay-on-top status selected.
void
TOptionWin::EvActivate(UINT /*active*/,
  BOOL /*minimized*/, HWND /*hWndOther*/)
{
  if (options.stayOnTop)
    ::BringWindowToTop(GetLastActivePopup());
  DefaultProcessing();
}

// ============================================================
// The application class
// ============================================================

class TOptionApp: public TApplication {
public:
  TOptionApp(const char far* name)
    : TApplication(name) {}
  void InitMainWindow();
  void InitInstance();
};

// Initialize the program's main window
void
TOptionApp::InitMainWindow()
{
  TOptionWin* optionWin = new TOptionWin(0);
  if (optionWin->GetOptions()->maximizeWindow)
    nCmdShow = SW_SHOWMAXIMIZED;
  MainWindow = optionWin;
}

// Initialize each program instance. Only one instance is
```

continues

419

Listing 11.12. continued

```
// allowed in this case because of the stay-on-top option.
// (Two copies of the program would otherwise have to compete
// for on-top status.)
void
TOptionApp::InitInstance()
{
  if (hPrevInstance) {
    HWND hwnd = ::FindWindow(WINCLASSNAME, 0);
    if (hwnd) {
      hwnd = GetLastActivePopup(hwnd);
      BringWindowToTop(hwnd);
      ShowWindow(hwnd, SW_RESTORE);
    }
    PostAppMessage(GetCurrentTask(), WM_QUIT, 0, 0);
  } else
    TApplication::InitInstance();
}

#pragma argsused

// Main program
int
OwlMain(int argc, char* argv[])
{
  TOptionApp app("OptionApp");
  return app.Run();
}
```

Compile OPTION.CPP by opening its IDE project and pressing Ctrl+F9. Run the resulting OPTION.EXE file from the File Manager. You can run the program directly from the IDE, but due to OPTION's capability to force its window to stay on top, the program is restricted to one instance. Try running a second copy of the program without closing the first—instead of a second window, you are returned to the program's current one. Obviously, only one window can be on top at a time, so it wouldn't make sense to permit two instances of the same code to run simultaneously.

Use the program's *Options* menu to modify various runtime features. Here's a summary of the options you can select:

- *Window title*—Enter any string for the program's window title.

- *Confirm exit*—Check this box to display a confirmation dialog for the *File\Exit* command. Uncheck this box to exit immediately on using that command.

- *Auto save options*—Check this box to save options in a file named OPTION.DAT when you select the Options dialog's OK button. Uncheck this box to turn off the auto-save feature.

- *Maximize window*—Check this box to display the program's window in full screen size when the program first starts running. Uncheck this box to let Windows choose a size and position for the window. Any change to this option takes effect the *next* time you start the OPTION demonstration.

- *Sound on* and *Sound off*—Toggle these radio buttons to sound a tone at various times—when displaying a dialog box, for example.

- *Stay on top*—Check this box to force the program's window to stay on top of other windows. Uncheck this box for a normal overlapping window style. If other application windows are also configured to stay on top, OPTION's window and those other windows revert to normal overlapping styles.

Try selecting various options, close the *Options* dialog box, exit the program, rerun it, change its title, and so on. Options are automatically loaded at runtime from OPTION.DAT, which you may delete from the current directory to restore the original program settings.

I designed the *Options* dialog (refer back to Figure 11.8) using Resource Workshop and Borland Custom Controls. To store control values, I declared a structure, OptionBuffer, in the OPTION.H header file. This structure is the dialog's transfer buffer—it has one member for each control in the dialog that participates in transfers. The window title is a char array, the checkboxes are WORD variables, and the radio buttons are also WORD variables.

In the program's main listing, OPTION.CPP, I derived a new class, TOptionDialog, from TDialog. The class has only a constructor, declared as

```
TOptionDialog(TWindow* parent, OptionBuffer* options);
```

To use the options dialog, the program constructs an object of the TOptionDialog class, passing the parent window object's address and the address of a transfer buffer structure. The dialog's constructor calls its TDialog ancestor, specifying the ID_OPTIONS resource identifier to initialize the dialog object from the program's resources. After that, the constructor creates control objects, one for each control in the transfer buffer, in the same order those controls appear in the OptionBuffer structure. Because I didn't need to access those controls, I did not save their object pointers. They are child windows, and as such, are automatically handled and deleted by their parent dialog window. Finally in the dialog constructor, I call SetTransferBuffer, passing the address of the transfer buffer. This enables data transfers between the dialog's controls and the buffer. When creating a dialog object, the controls are initialized using the buffer's data. When the dialog is closed by selecting its *OK* button, control values are copied back to the buffer.

If the dialog is closed by its *Cancel* button, the original buffer's contents are not changed.

The program's main window uses the *Options* dialog by declaring a private data member of the OptionBuffer structure in the main window class, TOptionWin. The window constructor calls InitOptions to load the current settings from file OPTION.DAT, or to assign default values if that file doesn't exist. (You must run the program and save its options to create OPTION.DAT.)

Other functions in the TOptionWin class respond to various settings, which you may select by using the dialog. For example, CanClose requests permission to end the program if the confirmExit option is set to TRUE in the options structure.

The program's most difficult task enables a feature that may be useful in other applications. Function SetOnTop changes the main window's status as a normal overlapping to one that stays on top of other windows. To do that, the function calls SetWindowPos, passing a window handle value HWND_TOPMOST or HWND_NOTOPMOST depending on the stayOnTop member of the options structure. That alone, however, is not enough to create a stay-on-top window. The program also must respond to WM_ACTIVATE messages, sent to the window when it is reactivated after switching to a different application. To respond to this message, the window class inserts an EV_WM_ACTIVATE macro in its response table. This macro requires the window class to implement a member function defined as:

```
void EvActivate(UINT active, BOOL minimized, HWND hWndOther);
```

When the program receives a WM_ACTIVATE message, EvActivate tests whether options.stayOnTop setting is TRUE. If so, the function calls the global Windows API function, BringWindowToTop, passing to that function the result of the encapsulated function GetLastActivePopup. These actions ensure that the correct window is reactivated in case, for example, you switch away from the program while a dialog box, rather than the main window, is active.

The sample program's application class also has extra duties to perform. For example, InitMainWindow constructs the program's main window object of type TOptionWin. After that, if the program's options indicate that the window should be maximized at startup, InitMainWindow assigns SW_SHOWMAXIMIZED to the TApplication variable, nCmdShow.

Because of the program's capability to have its window stay on top of other windows, I also implemented the application's InitInstance function to prevent more than one copy of the program from running at the same time. If the hPrevInstance handle indicates that the program is already running, InitInstance calls the global API function,

FindWindow, to locate that instance's window. If the window is found, three steps bring the window (or one of its child windows such as a dialog box and the child's parent) to the front of other windows. Thus if the window is hidden when you rerun the program, its window appears. The three steps to bring the window back to the font are:

```
hwnd = GetLastActivePopup(hwnd);
BringWindowToTop(hwnd);
ShowWindow(hwnd, SW_RESTORE);
```

First, call GetLastActivePopup to retrieve the handle of the parent or child window that was last active when you switched to another application. Next, call BringWindowToTop to make that window (and its parent if the window is a child) to the front. Finally, call ShowWindow to display the window in case it was shrunk to an icon. This last step isn't strictly necessary, but is recommended.

Looking Ahead

Programs that operate on single documents are often inconvenient to use—imagine, for example, how difficult it would be to write a computer program if the Borland C++ IDE could open only one file at a time. Editors, database managers, compilers, and other file-related software benefit greatly by being able to open multiple documents, one per window, a design technique known as the *multiple document interface,* or MDI, explained in the next chapter.

12

Writing MDI Applications

Most Windows programs that work with file-based data can use the *multiple document interface* (MDI) to great advantage. MDI applications use child windows to display file data so that users can open, view, and edit multiple documents and switch easily among them. MDI applications include text editors, word processors, drawing and painting software, compilers, database managers, and other programs that work with files. The chapter ends with the complete listings for *MDIDraw,* an object-drawing application that demonstrates MDI techniques.

In this chapter, you learn:

- How the multiple document interface (MDI) simplifies multiple-window programming.
- How to use MDI frame, client, and child window classes to create MDI applications.
- How to create decorated MDI frame windows with toolbars and status lines.

- How to create streamable classes.
- How to use streamable classes and file streams for document input and output in MDI applications.

The Multiple Document Interface

Writing MDI applications requires you to follow some additional rules and to learn a few new terms. Much of the programming of an MDI application's parts and pieces is the same as it is for other Windows programs, but the interface elements, windows, and menus need special handling. There are three basic components to every MDI application:

- A *frame window* serves as the application's main window.
- A *client window,* owned by the frame window, handles operations that apply generally to the application and that create new document windows.
- One or more *document windows* display file-based or other information. Usually, each opened file, known generally as a document, is assigned to an individual document window.

The frame window's primary job is to own a client window and to provide the visual parts of the program's main window. The frame window shows the program's menu bar (required in all MDI applications), and it may also own child-window objects such as toolbars and status lines. There is only one frame window in an MDI application.

The client window attaches to the frame, and provides all global operations—those that apply to the application as a whole or that create new child windows or open existing files. A command to open an options dialog, for example, might be handled by the client window. There is only one client window in an MDI application.

Document windows—also called *MDI child windows*—display document information. Each document window is a child of the MDI client window, and each may respond individually to menu commands and other events such as mouse clicks and keyboard operations. The client window handles any events that are not processed by a document window. Those events include standard window operations that can cascade, tile, close, and rearrange document window icons.

The next two sections show how to put these concepts into practice, using ObjectWindow classes to create MDI applications.

MDI Classes

ObjectWindows provides three classes that you can use to develop MDI applications. The classes and their header files are:

- `TMDIFrame`—Use this class, declared in MDI.H, to construct MDI frame window objects, which serve as the program's main window.

- `TMDIClient`—Use this class, also declared in MDI.H, to construct MDI client window objects. A `TMDIFrame` object must own an object of the `TMDIClient` class.

- `TMDIChild`—Use this class, declared in MDICHILD.H, to construct document child window objects. Each document object is owned by an object of the `TMDIClient` class.

You might also want to include the MDI.RH resource header file, which declares several standard Window menu command constants such as `CM_CASCADECHILDREN`. You can use these constants to build a Window menu with *Cascade, Tile,* and other commands commonly used in MDI applications. You don't have to implement these commands—they are handled automatically by the `TMDIClient` object. Most applications should use these #include directives:

```
#include <owl\applicat.h>
#include <owl\mdi.h>
#include <owl\mdichild.h>
#include <owl\mdi.rh>
```

Use the `TApplication` class, declared in APPLICAT.H, for MDI applications. This is the same application class used in single-window programs.

Each MDI class has several member functions you can call to perform various tasks. `TMDIFrame` doesn't have much to do in MDI applications, so you'll rarely need to use this class except to build the program's main window. The `TMDIClient` class, however, has several functions you might want to call. For example, if `client` addresses the program's `TMDIClient` object, this statement cascades all document child windows:

```
client->CascadeChildren();
```

To tile document windows in adjacent blocks, call the `TileChildren` function to which you can pass one of three constants defined in WINDOWS.H (located in the BC4\INCLUDE directory):

```
client->TileChildren(MDITILE_VERTICAL);     // Vertical tile
client->TileChildren(MDITILE_HORIZONTAL);   // Horizontal tile
client->TileChildren(MDITILE_SKIPDISABLED); // Skip disabled windows
```

To close all document windows, call `CloseChildren` for the client window:

```
client->CloseChildren();
```

To obtain the address of the currently active document child window, call `GetActiveMDIChild` and use a type-cast to convert the function's returned address to the address of your child window:

```
TYourMDIChild* cp;
cp = (TYourMDIChild*)client->GetActiveMDIChild();
```

Probably the most important `TMDIClient` function you'll need is `InitChild`, which you should replace in a derived class. `InitChild` creates new document child windows, and is called when the client window receives a `CM_CREATECHILD` command message, usually associated with the program's *File|New* command. In its simplest form, `InitChild` constructs and returns the address of an instance of your `TMDIChild`-derived class (named `TYourChild` here):

```
TMDIChild*
TYourClient::InitChild()
{
  return new TYourChild(*this);
}
```

The client window automatically creates an associated window element for the `TYourChild` (or other `TMDIChild`-derived class) object. In another function—one that opens an existing document, for example—you have to carry out that task by calling the `Create` function inherited from `TWindow`. For instance, here's how you can write a *File|Open...* function (minus details such as displaying a file-open dialog and so on):

```
void
TYourClient::CmFileOpen()
{
  char *filename;
  // Obtain file name here, perhaps from a dialog
  // and assign the name's address to filename, then...
  TYourChild* cp = new TYourChild(filename);
  cp->Create();
}
```

MDI Applications

A sample MDI application makes the preceding techniques clearer. The following listings show how to use the `TMDIFrame`, `TMDIClient`, and `TMDIChild` classes. Figure 12.1 shows the program's window with three sample document windows (labeled *Untitled*), and with the Window menu open. Most MDI applications should have a similar

Window menu. Listing 12.1 (MDIDEMO.RH) declares the program's resource identifiers. Listing 12.2 (MDIDEMO.RC) shows the program's menu resource, including a Window menu you can copy to your own .RC script. Listing 12.3 (MDIDEMO.CPP) lists the program's statements and shows how to use the three MDI classes.

FIGURE 12.1.
MDIDEMO window.

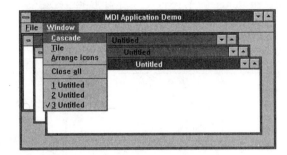

Listing 12.1. MDIDEMO.RH.

```
// mdidemo.rh -- Resource header file

#define ID_MENU 100
#define CM_FILEEXIT 24338
#define CM_FILESAVEAS 24334
#define CM_FILESAVE 24333
#define CM_FILEOPEN 24332
```

Listing 12.2. MDIDEMO.RC.

```
#include <owl\window.rh>
#include <owl\mdi.rh>
#include "mdidemo.rh"

ID_MENU MENU
BEGIN
  POPUP "&File"
  BEGIN
    MENUITEM "&New", CM_CREATECHILD
    MENUITEM "&Open...", CM_FILEOPEN
    MENUITEM "&Save", CM_FILESAVE
    MENUITEM "Save &as...", CM_FILESAVEAS
    MENUITEM SEPARATOR
    MENUITEM "E&xit", CM_EXIT
  END
```

continues

429

Listing 12.2. continued

```
  POPUP "&Window"
  BEGIN
    MENUITEM "&Cascade", CM_CASCADECHILDREN
    MENUITEM "&Tile", CM_TILECHILDREN
    MENUITEM "&Arrange icons", CM_ARRANGEICONS
    MENUITEM SEPARATOR
    MENUITEM "Close &all", CM_CLOSECHILDREN
  END
END
```

Listing 12.3. MDIDEMO.CPP.

```
/* ============================================================ *\
** mdidemo.cpp -- How to write an MDI application              **
** ============================================================ **
**                                                             **
** ============================================================ **
**      Copyright (c) 1994 by Tom Swan. All rights reserved.   **
\* ============================================================ */

#include <owl\applicat.h>
#include <owl\mdi.h>
#include <owl\mdichild.h>
#include <owl\mdi.rh>
#include <cstring.h>
#pragma hdrstop
#include "mdidemo.rh"


// ============================================================
// The MDI child window class
// ============================================================

class TDemoChild: public TMDIChild {
public:
  TDemoChild(TMDIClient& parent);  // Default constructor
  TDemoChild(TMDIClient& parent, const char far *name);
  void ChangeName(const char far *name);
  int Unnamed() { return filename.length() == 0; }
  int OpenFile() { return TRUE; }
  int SaveFile() { return TRUE; }
private:
  string filename;
};

// Default constructor for File|New
TDemoChild::TDemoChild(TMDIClient& parent)
```

```
  : TMDIChild(parent, "Untitled")
{
  filename = "";
}

// Alternate constructor for File|Open
TDemoChild::TDemoChild(TMDIClient& parent, const char far *name)
  : TMDIChild(parent, name)
{
  filename = name;
}

// Change window file name
void
TDemoChild::ChangeName(const char far *name)
{
  filename = name;
  SetCaption(name);
}

// =============================================================
// The MDI client window class
// =============================================================

class TDemoClient: public TMDIClient {
public:
  TDemoClient(): TMDIClient() {}
protected:
  virtual TMDIChild* InitChild();
  void CmFileOpen();
  void CmFileSave();
  void CmFileSaveAs();
DECLARE_RESPONSE_TABLE(TDemoClient);
};

DEFINE_RESPONSE_TABLE1(TDemoClient, TMDIClient)
  EV_COMMAND(CM_FILEOPEN, CmFileOpen),
  EV_COMMAND(CM_FILESAVE, CmFileSave),
  EV_COMMAND(CM_FILESAVEAS, CmFileSaveAs),
END_RESPONSE_TABLE;

// Construct a child window object for File|New command
TMDIChild*
TDemoClient::InitChild()
{
  return new TDemoChild(*this);
}
```

continues

431

Listing 12.3. continued

```cpp
// Open an existing file for File¦Open command
void
TDemoClient::CmFileOpen()
{
  TMDIChild* cp = new TDemoChild(*this, "File Name");
  cp->Create();
}

// Save window's information for File¦Save command
void
TDemoClient::CmFileSave()
{
  TDemoChild* cp = (TDemoChild *)GetActiveMDIChild();
  if (!cp) return;
  if (cp->Unnamed())
    CmFileSaveAs();
  else
    cp->SaveFile();
}

// Name and save window's information for File¦Save as command
void
TDemoClient::CmFileSaveAs()
{
  TDemoChild* cp = (TDemoChild *)GetActiveMDIChild();
  if (!cp) return;
  cp->ChangeName("Save as name");
  cp->SaveFile();
}

// ============================================================
// The MDI application class
// ============================================================

class TDemoApp: public TApplication {
public:
  TDemoApp(const char far* name)
    : TApplication(name) {}
  void InitMainWindow();
private:
  TDemoClient* client;
};

// Initialize the program's main window
void
TDemoApp::InitMainWindow()
{
  client = new TDemoClient;
  MainWindow = new TMDIFrame("MDI Application Demo",
```

```
      ID_MENU, *client);
}

#pragma argsused

// Main program
int
OwlMain(int argc, char* argv[])
{
  TDemoApp app("MDIDemoApp");
  return app.Run();
}
```

Browse the MDIDEMO.CPP listing—it shows the basic steps required by all MDI applications. First, derive one or more classes from TMDIChild. Objects of your classes become the program's document child windows. Insert whatever functions and data members you need to open, save, edit, and display document data. You may derive as many TMDIChild classes as you need—usually, one for each document type your program handles. Because the sample program doesn't actually use any real documents, it derives only one document child window class, TDemoChild.

The class has two constructors—a default constructor, which should create a new document window (usually in memory, not on disk), and most often titled *Untitled*. The alternate constructor receives the name of a file to open, and it should use that name to initialize the child window object with the document's contents. The only required parameter is a reference to the child's TMDIClient object parent. Pass this parameter to the TMDIClient base-class constructor.

I added some other functions just to show a few of the duties that a document child window might need to perform. I also stored a fictitious filename in a string-class object. In your own programs, you might add a response table to handle messages directed to the document window, and you might use a Paint member function to update the window's contents.

TIP

The TMDIChild class is derived from TFrameWindow, which is normally used as a single-window application's main window object. Because document child window objects are actually frame windows, they can have their own client windows and they operate just as single windows do in non MDI applications. Any operation that

---

you can perform in a single-window application's TFrameWindow object, you can perform equally well, and using the identical programming, in a document child window object derived from the TMDIChild class.

MDI child windows are more independent than other child windows such as pushbuttons and other controls. An MDI child window is an overlapping window that is restricted to its parent's borders, but it may be resized, shrunk to an icon, or expanded to fill the parent frame window. MDI child windows cannot be moved outside of their parent window's borders. MDI child windows also cannot have menus, but they can be controlled by commands in the frame window's menu bar.

Most often, MDI child window titles are set to the filenames of documents. If you want to name your child windows something else, however, that's okay, but the result might be confusing to users who are familiar with other MDI programs.

After programming your TMDIChild-derived classes, the next step is to derive a client window class from TMDIClient. Every MDI application needs only one such derived class, named TDemoClient in the MDIDEMO.CPP listing.

The client window class can have a simple, default constructor, as shown in the listing. The MDI frame window owns the client window, but the client doesn't need to refer to its parent window, so the constructor needs no parameters. (Of course, if you need to initialize a client window with values important to your application, you can pass them to your class's constructor.)

The client window class normally provides a replacement function for InitChild, inherited from TMDIClient. It also normally provides message response functions for *File* menu command that open and save documents. Relate these command functions in a response table for the appropriate menu command resource identifiers as shown in the listing. For example, function CmFileOpen is called to respond to the *File|Open...* command, identified by constant CM_FILEOPEN.\

Function InitChild should *not* call its ancestor function, which constructs a default TMDIChild object. Such an object is merely a bare cupboard and has no practical use. Instead, in your InitChild function, construct an object of your TMDIChild-derived class. If you have more than one such class, construct whichever one makes sense in response to your program's *File|Open...* command (perhaps distinguishing between different documents, for example, by their filename extensions). Return the document child object's address as InitChild's return value. You do not need to save this address, but you may if you wish. Remember, however, that InitChild is called to create *each* new child window, of which there might several instances. If you save your child window object addresses, you need to figure out a way to store an unknown number of pointers, and to access the correct pointers in other applications.

In other functions, you have to perform one additional step to construct a document child window object. Function `CmFileOpen`, for example, which is called when you select the program's *File|Open...* command, executes these two statements:

```
TMDIChild* cp = new TDemoChild(*this, "File Name");
cp->Create();
```

The first statement constructs the child window object, in this case, as an instance of the `TDemoChild` class (derived from `TMDIChild`). The second statement calls the `TWindow` `Create` function to create a window element for the object. `InitChild` doesn't need to do that because the `TMDIClient` function that calls `InitChild` performs this step automatically. Notice also that the first statement calls the alternate `TDemoChild` constructor, simulating how a program can initialize a document child with a file name, perhaps returned from a file dialog box.

> **NOTE:**
>
> In case you are interested, the function that calls `InitChild` is `CreateChild`, which you might want to look up in `TMDIClient`'s source code in file MDICLIEN.CPP, located in the BC4\SOURCE\OWL directory—if, that is, you installed BC4's source files. Menu commands identified by CM_CREATECHILD call the `TMDIClient` class's `CmCreateChild` inline function, which calls `CreateChild`, which calls your replacement `InitChild` function.

As demonstrated here, `InitChild` and `CmFileOpen` do not save the addresses of the document child window objects the functions create. Other operations need those addresses, however, to know where to direct commands and data to the currently active child window. Call `GetActiveMDIChild` to find that address. For example, the sample program's `CmFileSave` function, which in your own code might save a document to a disk file, begins with the statements:

```
TDemoChild* cp = (TDemoChild *)GetActiveMDIChild();
if (!cp) return;
```

After those statements, you can call member functions for the child object addressed by cp. For example, the sample listing calls functions to save the windows data. (The example doesn't actually write any files to disk—this is just a simulation.)

Function `CmFileSaveAs` performs similar tasks. In most cases, `CmFileSave` should test whether the window has been given a real filename. If not, `CmFileSave` should call

CmFileSaveAs, which should prompt users to enter a new filename. (I didn't complete all the steps to display the appropriate dialogs boxes because those techniques are covered elsewhere in the book and demonstrated by other sample listings on this book's disk.)

Finally, you need an application class, derived from TApplication. This class is no different from the application class that a single-window program needs. As in those programs, you need to replace function InitMainWindow to create the program's main window. There is one difference, however, in an MDI program's application class— you should declare a private (it could also be public or protected) pointer to a TMDIClient object, which will become the program's client window.

Construct that window inside InitMainWindow as shown in the sample listing. First, construct the object, and save its address in the class's TMDIClient pointer. (Actually, you need to save this object's address only for referring to the client object in other functions, which the demonstration program doesn't do.) Next, construct an instance of the TMDIFrame class, to which you should pass the program's title (displayed in the frame's caption bar), a menu resource identifier (ID_MENU), and a reference to the client window object. The TMDIFrame class requires a menu resource because, by design, all MDI applications must have a menu bar. MDI frame windows never have parent windows.

> **NOTE**
>
> You may derive a new class from TMDIFrame, and you may construct an object of your class for an MDI application's main window. Because frame windows have very little to do in MDI programs, however, you can usually use the ObjectWindows TMDIFrame class as shown here. In keeping with the MDI guidelines, the client window, not the frame, should handle global operations—creating new document child windows, for example. For that reason, you should add your own programming to classes derived from TMDIClient and TMDIChild, but not from TMDIFrame.

Constructing an object of the TMDIFrame initiates a search for a window menu. If the object finds that menu, it automatically attaches the titles of document child windows to the bottom of the menu. When you close a document window, its name is automatically removed from the menu. You don't have to take any special steps to enable this feature—just add a window menu at any position to your program's menu bar.

Decorated MDI Frame Windows

Sophisticated Windows users expect features such as toolbars and status lines in their software. In the past, those features have been major stumbling blocks for Windows programmers, but with *decorated windows* (introduced in Chapter 9), it's easy to implement these useful interface devices for frame windows.

With the help of the TDecoratedMDIFrame class, you also can decorate MDI frame windows. The following demonstrates how to use the class to create an MDI application complete with a toolbar and status line. The completed program is stored on this book's disk in directory MDIDECO. Much of the programming in this directory is the same as in the MDIDEMO program listed in this chapter—I discuss only the parts that differ between the two similar demonstrations. Figure 12.2 shows the program's final result, which has many of the features of a finished Windows applications, including a status line with function key legends and a toolbar of command icons.

FIGURE 12.2.

MDIDECO's decorated MDI frame window.

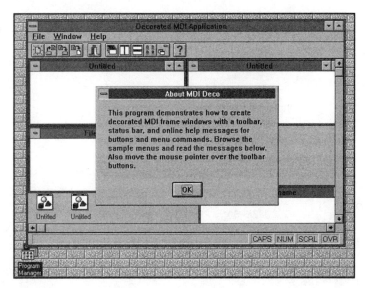

NOTE

You might recognize some of MDIDECO's icons—I borrowed them from BC4's IDE. To extract the icons, I used Resource Workshop to open file BCWRES.DLL located in C:\BC4\BIN. After locating the icon I wanted, I selected RW's *Resource/Edit as text...* command, copied the icon in text form to the Windows clipboard, and pasted it into the

MDIDECO.RC resource script. I assigned new resource identifiers to each icon. Of course, you'll probably want to invent custom icons, but you can extract existing ones for temporary use or use the icons as templates for writing your own.

Identify each icon and menu command with numeric or string values defined in the resource header file. Toolbar icons issue the same command messages as menus—they are just visually different, and usually more convenient, ways for users to select among a program's commands. In Listing 12.4, MDIDECO.RH, I defined several identifiers, some of which (such as CM_FILESAVE) are duplicated in ObjectWindows. Using the standard identifiers automatically displays hints in the status bar when those commands are selected. You can create your own command identifiers, but then it's your responsibility to write all status-line hint strings.

Listing 12.4. MDIDECO.RH.

```
// mdideco.rh -- Resource header file

// Menu resource identifier
#define ID_MENU      100

// Menu command identifiers
#define CM_FILESAVEAS 24334
#define CM_FILESAVE   24333
#define CM_FILEOPEN   24332
#define CM_HELPABOUT 24346

// Toolbar button icon identifiers
#define IDB_FILENEW 600
#define IDB_FILEOPEN 601
#define IDB_FILESAVE 602
#define IDB_FILESAVEAS 603
#define IDB_FILEEXIT 604
#define IDB_WINDOWCASCADE 605
#define IDB_WINDOWTILEH 606
#define IDB_WINDOWTILEV 607
#define IDB_WINDOWARRANGE 608
#define IDB_WINDOWCLOSE 609
#define IDB_HELPABOUT 610
```

With the menu command and icon resource identifiers defined, create your resource script file as you normally do. You can use Resource Workshop, or enter the items using the IDE text editor as I did for this example. Listing 12.5, MDIDECO.RC shows a portion of the program's resource script, including one of the 11 icons in the complete file on the book's disk. Each icon resource has the identical form, but of course, different values. The partial listing also shows the status-line hints in a string table resource for those menu commands that don't have hints built into ObjectWindows.

Listing 12.5. MDIDECO.RC (partial).

```
#include <owl\window.rh>
#include <owl\mdi.rh>
#include "mdideco.rh"

ID_MENU MENU
BEGIN
  POPUP "&File"
  BEGIN
    MENUITEM "&New", CM_CREATECHILD
    MENUITEM "&Open...", CM_FILEOPEN
    MENUITEM "&Save", CM_FILESAVE
    MENUITEM "Save &as...", CM_FILESAVEAS
    MENUITEM SEPARATOR
    MENUITEM "E&xit", CM_EXIT
  END
  POPUP "&Window"
  BEGIN
    MENUITEM "&Cascade", CM_CASCADECHILDREN
    MENUITEM "&Tile vertical", CM_TILECHILDREN
    MENUITEM "&Tile horizontal", CM_TILECHILDRENHORIZ
    MENUITEM "&Arrange icons", CM_ARRANGEICONS
    MENUITEM SEPARATOR
    MENUITEM "Close &all", CM_CLOSECHILDREN
  END
  POPUP "&Help"
  BEGIN
    MENUITEM "&About...", CM_HELPABOUT
  END
END

// File¦New icon
IDB_FILENEW BITMAP
{
 '42 4D 66 01 00 00 00 00 00 00 76 00 00 00 28 00'
 '00 00 14 00 00 00 14 00 00 00 01 00 04 00 00 00'
 '00 00 F0 00 00 00 00 00 00 00 00 00 00 00 00 00'
 '00 00 00 00 00 00 00 00 00 00 00 00 80 00 00 80'
 '00 00 00 80 80 00 80 00 00 00 80 00 80 00 80 80'
 '00 00 80 80 80 00 C0 C0 C0 00 00 00 FF 00 00 FF'
```

continues

Listing 12.5. continued

```
'00 00 00 FF FF 00 FF 00 00 00 FF 00 FF 00 FF FF'
'00 00 FF FF FF 00 88 88 88 88 88 88 88 88 88 88'
'29 49 88 88 88 88 80 88 88 88 88 88 77 C1 88 08'
'88 88 80 88 88 88 80 88 66 57 88 80 88 88 88 88'
'88 88 08 88 6E 0E 88 88 80 00 00 00 00 08 88 88'
'6F 43 88 88 80 FE FE FE FE 08 88 88 DF 94 88 88'
'80 EF EF EF EF 08 88 88 BB 69 88 88 80 FE FE FE'
'FE 08 88 88 67 4B 88 88 80 EF EF EF EF 08 88 88'
'DF 94 88 88 80 FE FE FE FE 08 80 08 BB 69 80 08'
'80 EF EF EF EF 08 88 88 66 5A 88 88 80 FE FE FE'
'FE 08 88 88 09 FB 88 88 80 EF EF E0 00 08 88 88'
'02 F6 88 88 80 FE FE F0 E0 88 88 88 04 FD 88 88'
'80 EF EF E0 08 88 88 88 08 CA 88 88 80 00 00 00'
'88 88 88 88 89 84 88 80 88 88 88 88 88 08 88'
'4D 2F 88 08 88 88 88 08 88 88 80 88 99 58 88 88'
'88 88 88 08 88 88 88 88 21 A1 88 88 88 88 88 88'
'88 88 88 88 99 5C'
}

STRINGTABLE LOADONCALL MOVEABLE DISCARDABLE
{
  CM_CREATECHILD, "Creates new document window"
  CM_EXIT, "Quits the application"
  CM_HELPABOUT, "Displays message box"
  CM_TILECHILDRENHORIZ, "Tiles open windows horizontally"
}
```

With the resources identified and defined, it's time to write the code. I began with a copy of the MDIDEMO.CPP file listed earlier in this chapter. I modified the listing, creating the decorated MDIDECO.CPP example in Listing 12.6.

Listing 12.6. MDIDECO.CPP.

```
/* ============================================================ *\
**   mdideco.cpp -- Decorated MDI applications                 **
** ============================================================ **
**                                                             **
** ============================================================ **
**      Copyright (c) 1994 by Tom Swan. All rights reserved.   **
\* ============================================================ */

#include <owl\applicat.h>
#include <owl\decmdifr.h>
#include <owl\mdi.h>
#include <owl\mdichild.h>
#include <owl\mdi.rh>
```

```
#include <cstring.h>
#include <owl\controlb.h>
#include <owl\gadget.h>
#include <owl\buttonga.h>
#include <owl\messageb.h>
#include <owl\toolbox.h>
#include <owl\statusba.h>
#pragma hdrstop
#include "mdideco.rh"

// ============================================================
// The MDI child window class
// ============================================================

class TDecoChild: public TMDIChild {
public:
  TDecoChild(TMDIClient& parent);  // Default constructor
  TDecoChild(TMDIClient& parent, const char far *name);
  void ChangeName(const char far *name);
  int Unnamed() { return filename.length() == 0; }
  int OpenFile() { return TRUE; }
  int SaveFile() { return TRUE; }
private:
  string filename;
};

// Default constructor for File|New
TDecoChild::TDecoChild(TMDIClient& parent)
  : TMDIChild(parent, "Untitled")
{
  filename = "";
}

// Alternate constructor for File|Open
TDecoChild::TDecoChild(TMDIClient& parent, const char far *name)
  : TMDIChild(parent, name)
{
  filename = name;
}

// Change window file name
void
TDecoChild::ChangeName(const char far *name)
{
  filename = name;
  SetCaption(name);
}
```

continues

441

Listing 12.6. continued

```cpp
// ================================================================
// The MDI client window class
// ================================================================

class TDecoClient: public TMDIClient {
public:
  TDecoClient(): TMDIClient() {}
protected:
  virtual TMDIChild* InitChild();
  void CmFileOpen();
  void CmFileSave();
  void CmFileSaveAs();
  void CmHelpAbout();
DECLARE_RESPONSE_TABLE(TDecoClient);
};

DEFINE_RESPONSE_TABLE1(TDecoClient, TMDIClient)
  EV_COMMAND(CM_FILEOPEN, CmFileOpen),
  EV_COMMAND(CM_FILESAVE, CmFileSave),
  EV_COMMAND(CM_FILESAVEAS, CmFileSaveAs),
  EV_COMMAND(CM_HELPABOUT, CmHelpAbout),
END_RESPONSE_TABLE;

// Construct a child window object for File¦New command
TMDIChild*
TDecoClient::InitChild()
{
  return new TDecoChild(*this);
}

// Open an existing file for File¦Open command
void
TDecoClient::CmFileOpen()
{
  TMDIChild* cp = new TDecoChild(*this, "File Name");
  cp->Create();
}

// Save window's information for File¦Save command
void
TDecoClient::CmFileSave()
{
  TDecoChild* cp = (TDecoChild *)GetActiveMDIChild();
  if (!cp) return;
  if (cp->Unnamed())
    CmFileSaveAs();
  else
    cp->SaveFile();
```

```
}

// Name and save window's information for File¦Save as command
void
TDecoClient::CmFileSaveAs()
{
  TDecoChild* cp = (TDecoChild *)GetActiveMDIChild();
  if (!cp) return;
  cp->ChangeName("Save as name");
  cp->SaveFile();
}

// Display help message box
void
TDecoClient::CmHelpAbout()
{
  string msg;
  string newline('\n');
  msg += "This program demonstrates how to create" + newline;
  msg += "decorated MDI frame windows with a toolbar," + newline;
  msg += "status bar, and online help messages for" + newline;
  msg += "buttons and menu commands. Browse the" + newline;
  msg += "sample menus and read the messages below." + newline;
  msg += "Also move the mouse pointer over the toolbar" + newline;
  msg += "buttons.";
  MessageBox(msg.c_str(), "About MDI Deco", MB_OK);
}

// ============================================================
// The MDI application class
// ============================================================

class TDecoApp: public TApplication {
public:
  TDecoApp(const char far* name)
    : TApplication(name) {}
  void InitMainWindow();
private:
  TDecoClient* client;
  TControlBar* toolbar;
  TStatusBar* statusLine;
};

// Initialize the program's main window
void
TDecoApp::InitMainWindow()
{
  EnableCtl3d(TRUE);
  EnableBWCC();
```

continues

Listing 12.6. continued

```
// Construct the MDI client window
  client = new TDecoClient;

// Construct MDI frame, passing client window object
  TDecoratedMDIFrame * frame = new TDecoratedMDIFrame(
    "Decorated MDI Application",  // Caption
    ID_MENU,        // Required menu resource identifier
    *client,        // Required client window object
    TRUE);          // Optional track menu selections

// Construct a toolbar with icons for various commands
  toolbar = new TControlBar(frame);

  toolbar->Insert(
   *new TButtonGadget(IDB_FILENEW, CM_CREATECHILD));
  toolbar->Insert(
   *new TButtonGadget(IDB_FILEOPEN, CM_FILEOPEN));
  toolbar->Insert(
   *new TButtonGadget(IDB_FILESAVE, CM_FILESAVE));
  toolbar->Insert(
   *new TButtonGadget(IDB_FILESAVEAS, CM_FILESAVEAS));
  toolbar->Insert(
   *new TSeparatorGadget(8));
  toolbar->Insert(
   *new TButtonGadget(IDB_FILEEXIT, CM_EXIT));
  toolbar->Insert(
   *new TSeparatorGadget(8));
  toolbar->Insert(
   *new TButtonGadget(IDB_WINDOWCASCADE, CM_CASCADECHILDREN));
  toolbar->Insert(
   *new TButtonGadget(IDB_WINDOWTILEV, CM_TILECHILDREN));
  toolbar->Insert(
   *new TButtonGadget(IDB_WINDOWTILEH, CM_TILECHILDRENHORIZ));
  toolbar->Insert(
   *new TButtonGadget(IDB_WINDOWARRANGE, CM_ARRANGEICONS));
  toolbar->Insert(
   *new TButtonGadget(IDB_WINDOWCLOSE, CM_CLOSECHILDREN));
  toolbar->Insert(
   *new TSeparatorGadget(6));
  toolbar->Insert(
   *new TButtonGadget(IDB_HELPABOUT, CM_HELPABOUT));

// Enable status line messages when mouse touches a button
  toolbar->SetHintMode(TGadgetWindow::EnterHints);

// Insert the toolbar into the frame window
  frame->Insert(*toolbar, TDecoratedFrame::Top);
```

```
// Create status line with function keys legend
  statusLine = new TStatusBar(frame, TGadget::Recessed,
    TStatusBar::CapsLock | TStatusBar::NumLock |
    TStatusBar::ScrollLock | TStatusBar::Overtype);
  frame->Insert(*statusLine, TDecoratedFrame::Bottom);

// Assign the decorated MDI frame as the program's main window
  MainWindow = frame;
}

#pragma argsused

// Main program
int
OwlMain(int argc, char* argv[])
{
  TDecoApp app("MDIDecoApp");
  return app.Run();
}
```

Include the DECMDIFR.H header file, which declares the `TDecoratedMDIFrame` class. The class is derived from `TMDIFrame` and from `TDecoratedFrame`, effectively combining the encapsulated elements of MDI frame windows with single-window decorated frames that can own toolbars and other gadgets. Also include the gadget headers that you need—BUTTONGA.H and MESSAGEB.H, for example. (Refer back to Chapter 9 for more information on these and other headers and classes.)

Child windows are the same in decorated and traditional MDI applications. The MDI client window also requires no new programming, but in this example, I added a function, `CmHelpAbout`, to display brief instructions in response to selecting the program's *Help\About* command.

Mostly unchanged also is the program's application class, `TDecoApp` in the demonstration. Derived from `TApplication`, the class requires a constructor and `InitMainWindow` to initialize the frame and client window objects. New in `TDecoApp` are two additional private pointers—`toolbar` for an icon toolbar, and `statusLine` for online hint text and function key legends.

Most of the differences between traditional and decorated MDI applications occur in the application class's `InitMainWindow` function. Construct the client window object normally, but construct the frame as an object of the `TDecoratedMDIFrame` class. Pass a window caption, menu resource identifier, and client object to the class constructor. Also pass `TRUE` and the fourth argument to automatically track menu selections in the status line. If you don't implement online hints for selected menu items, set the fourth argument to `FALSE`.

Next, construct a toolbar as an object of the TControlBar class, to which you pass the frame window object's address. Insert various icon button gadgets as shown into the toolbar, specifying an icon's resource identifier and the menu command that should be issued when users select the button. Use the TSeparatorGadget class to create space between button groups. Call the SetHintMode function as shown to enable online hints for buttons touched (but not necessarily clicked) by the mouse pointer. Finally, insert the toolbar into the decorated MDI frame window object. Create a status line similarly, and insert it also into the frame. Finally, assign the frame window object address to MainWindow, completing the program's window initializations.

MDI Document Handling

Although this chapter is about the multiple document *interface,* it wouldn't be complete without some information about techniques you can use to handle document input and output in MDI applications. This chapter ends with a medium-size MDI application that uses *file streams* to read and write graphics information in disk files. *MDIDraw* has many of the features of a full-scale object-drawing program. It's not a finished program—that would take too much room to list in a book. But it is more than a bare beginning, and after studying the listing, you might want to expand the code into a complete drawing application. Figure 12.3 shows the finished program's display with two graphics documents open in child windows. Notice that the program uses a toolbar and status line with a function key legend.

FIGURE 12.3.
MDIDraw's display.

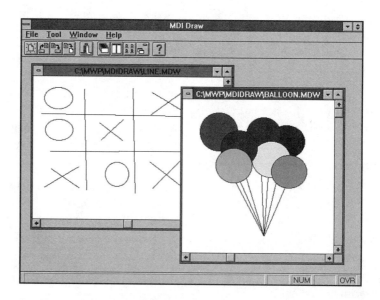

File Streams

A *stream* is a series of bytes that travel from one place to another. A *file stream* is a series of bytes that travel to and from disk files. By creating *streamable classes,* you can perform file input and output operations with relatively simple C++ stream statements such as these:

```
os << mydata;   // Write to output stream os
is >> mydata;   // Read from input stream is
```

Objects written to a stream are called *persistent objects* because they persist outside of their defining scope. For example, an object defined as an automatic variable in a function is normally destroyed when the function ends. By writing that object to a disk file, it is made to persist beyond its normal life span. Persistent objects can also be sent to reserved memory areas for safekeeping, or they might be passed among the nodes of a network, but in this chapter, I focus on using file streams to save persistent objects in disk files.

To create a persistent object, include the OBJSTRM.H header file, one of several files in BC4's general-purpose class library:

```
#include <classlib\objstrm.h>
```

The header file declares several classes, but to create streamable classes, you need only one: TStreamableBase. Derive your own class from TStreamableBase, using multiple inheritance if necessary, and usually specifying the base class to be public and virtual:

```
class TYourClass: public virtual TStreamableBase {
public:
  TYourClass();           // Default constructor
  TYourClass(TData d);    // Alternate constructor
  ~TYourClass();          // Destructor
// ...                    // Other member functions
private:
  TData data;   // Data member
DECLARE_STREAMABLE( , TYourClass, 1);
};
```

Your class probably needs a default constructor, plus a constructor to initialize the class with passed data. (Those aren't requirements, however, and your constructors can do whatever is needed to create class objects.) Your class may also need a destructor. Classes for any data objects must have default constructors. In the example, for instance, TData must have a default constructor. After all other members, use the DECLARE_STREAMABLE macro as shown to add several items needed in streamable classes. (Any class that uses this macro must be derived from TStreamableBase.) If your class is abstract (that is, if it declares any pure virtual member functions in the form void f()=0), use this macro instead:

```
DECLARE_ABSTRACT_STREAMABLE( , TGraphTool, 1);
```

The two macros each require three arguments. The first may be another macro that expands to __import or __export if the class is in a dynamic link library (DLL). If not, leave the first argument empty as in these examples. The second argument is the class name, which must be the same name as the class in which the macro appears. The third and final argument is a version number, which can be any integer. If you don't want to use version numbers, set this argument to 1.

In a derived-class hierarchy, only one base class needs to be derived from TStreamableBase. For example, *MDIDraw* defines the TGraphTool abstract class like this (minus its members):

```
class TGraphTool: public virtual TStreamableBase {
public:
  // ... Constructors, member functions, data, etc.
DECLARE_ABSTRACT_STREAMABLE( , TGraphTool, 1);
};
```

The class is derived from TStreamableBase, and because TGraphTool is abstract, it uses the DECLARE_ABSTRACT_STREAMABLE macro to add various required items to the class for use by stream statements. Other classes derived from TGraphTool inherit TStreamableBase, but each class to be read or written in stream statements must use the DECLARE_STREAMABLE macro. For example, *MDIDraw*'s line tool is based on the abstract TGraphTool:

```
class TLine: public TGraphTool {
public:
  // ... Constructors, member functions, data, etc.
DECLARE_STREAMABLE( , TLine, 1);
};
```

You could derive other classes from TGraphTool, creating a hierarchy of streamable classes. *MDIDraw,* for example, declares the classes TRectangle and TEllipse for its rectangle and ellipse drawing tools.

The DECLARE_STREAMABLE macro automatically adds the necessary operator<< and operator>> member functions to your class so you can read and write class objects, references, and pointers to objects in stream statements. The macro also adds a constructor to your class to create a blank object into which stream data is read.

After declaring your streamable classes, you next have to implement functions for use in stream statements. For each abstract streamable class (those that use the DECLARE_ABSTRACT_STREAMABLE macro), insert the following macro in your program's source file:

```
IMPLEMENT_ABSTRACT_STREAMABLE(TGraphTool);
```

Specify the abstract class name in parentheses. For each nonabstract streamable class (those that use the DECLARE_STREAMABLE macro), insert one of several macros named IMPLEMENT_STREAMABLEx, where x is the total number of direct and all virtual base classes. For example, TLine (which has one base class, TGraphTool), uses this macro:

```
IMPLEMENT_STREAMABLE1(TLine, TGraphTool);
```

Next, you must implement two functions, Read and Write, for each abstract and nonabstract streamable class. Here's the Write function for *MDIDraw*'s TGraphTool class:

```
void
TGraphTool::Streamer::Write(opstream& os) const
{
  os << GetObject()->startPt.x;
  os << GetObject()->startPt.y;
  os << GetObject()->endPt.x;
  os << GetObject()->endPt.y;
  os << GetObject()->pen->GetColor();
  os << GetObject()->brush->GetColor();
}
```

Function Write is a member of the Streamer class, nested in TGraphTool by the streamable macro. Write is const (it is not permitted to change any class data members), and it receives a reference to an opstream object, which represents the output file stream. Inside the function, use stream statements to write the object's data members to the stream. For each such statement, call the GetObject function to obtain the address of the TGraphTool object being written to disk. (Because Write is a member of a nested class, statements in the function cannot access any of the parent class's private or protected members. That's why you have to call GetObject.) You may write the class's data members in any order, and you don't have to write them all. You may write members directly as shown for the startPt and endPt TPoint objects, or you may call member functions such as GetColor in the example to obtain object data. Write returns no value.

Also implement a Read function, which returns a generic pointer of type void*. Like Write, Read is also a member of the nested Streamer class, and it is also const. (The function reads data into its parent class, but changes no Streamer members.) Read receives two arguments: a reference to an ipstream object (the input stream), and an unsigned 32-bit integer that you can optionally use as a version number. If you don't use class versioning, you may ignore the second parameter, but you still must declare it. Here's *MDIDraw*'s Read function for the abstract TGraphTool class:

```
void*
TGraphTool::Streamer::Read(ipstream& is, uint32) const
{
  COLORREF penColor, brushColor;
  is >> GetObject()->startPt.x;
  is >> GetObject()->startPt.y;
  is >> GetObject()->endPt.x;
  is >> GetObject()->endPt.y;
  is >> penColor;
  is >> brushColor;
  GetObject()->pen = new TGraphPen(TColor(penColor));
  GetObject()->brush = new TGraphBrush(TColor(brushColor));
  return GetObject();
}
```

Input stream statements read data from the stream identified here as is in the same order that data was written to the stream in function Write. The Read function may read some values directly (such as the startPt and endPt values), and it may read other values (such as color values) for creating dynamic objects with new, and assigning those objects' addresses to pointers such as pen and brush. Read must return the address of the object for which it is called—simply return the value of GetObject as shown here.

In a hierarchy of derived classes, each class must have its own Write and Read functions. For example, the TLine class, derived from TGraphTool, implements Write like this:

```
void
TLine::Streamer::Write(opstream& os) const
{
  WriteBaseObject((TGraphTool *)GetObject(), os);
}
```

The first statement in a derived class should call WriteBaseObject as shown. The statement calls the base class's Write member function, which in this example, writes all graphics tool data members to the stream. TLine's Write function, therefore, has nothing else to do. If, however, TLine declared its own data members in addition to those inherited from TGraphTool, you would write those members to the output stream after calling WriteBaseObject.

Implement a derived class's Read function similarly. For example, here's TLine's Read function:

```
void*
TLine::Streamer::Read(ipstream& is, uint32) const
{
  ReadBaseObject((TGraphTool *)GetObject(), is);
  return GetObject();
}
```

In this case, `ReadBaseObject` calls the base class's `Read` member function. Because `TLine` does not declare any new data members, the function simply returns `GetObject`. If `TLine` had its own data members, you would read them from the input stream by inserting statements between the call to `ReadBaseObject` and the function's `return` statement.

At this stage, you have completed the necessary foundations for all of your streamable classes. You can now create objects of those classes (`TLine`, for example) and write those objects to a stream. You can also read `TLine` and other streamable class objects from a stream. The objects are reconstructed in memory automatically as a result of reading them from the stream.

In most cases, you will need a function that writes one or more streamable objects of various types—in other words, a window's document. Here's the `WriteDocument` function from `TDrawChild`, the class that *MDIDraw* uses for each of its MDI child windows:

```
int
TDrawChild::WriteDocument()
{
  ofpstream os(fileName.c_str());
  if (os.bad())
    return FALSE;
  string signature(SIGNATURE);
  os << signature;
  unsigned count = image->GetItemsInContainer();
  os << count;
  image->ForEach(WriteTool, &os);
  fileSaved = TRUE;
  return TRUE;
}
```

First, construct an output file stream of the `ofpstream` class, passing the file's name as an argument. After that step, if `os.bad()` is true, the file could not be opened, and the function should end. (As shown, the function may return a value indicating the problem.) After opening the output file stream, use stream statements to write information to disk. For example, this statement writes a signature string set to *"MDIDRAW"*:

```
os << signature;
```

The signature provides a simple method for determining whether an opened file belongs to the program. *MDIDraw* uses a container class to store graphics shapes, and for simplicity in reading an image, the function also writes the number of objects in the image:

```
unsigned count = image->GetItemsInContainer();
os << count;
```

You don't need any special programming to write strings and integer values (and values of other simple types) to output streams. These values are already streamable. Of course, you will also write your streamable class objects to the file. *MDIDraw* does that by calling the container object's ForEach function:

```
image->ForEach(WriteTool, &os);
```

To ForEach, pass the address of a local (nonmember) function and the address of the output file stream object. Implement the local function like this:

```
void WriteTool(TGraphTool& tool, void * os)
{
  *(ofpstream *)os << &tool;
}
```

The function's lone statement writes one TGraphTool object in the container to the output file stream. The stream argument is passed as a void pointer, and it therefore must be recast and dereferenced as shown. The statement calls the tool's Write function inherited from the abstract TGraphTool class.

Of course, you also need programming that reads a document from disk into memory. For example, take a look at TDrawChild's ReadDocument function:

```
void
TDrawChild::ReadDocument()
{
  ifpstream is(fileName.c_str());
  if (is.bad())
    throw "Can't open file";
  string signature;
  is >> signature;
  if (signature != SIGNATURE)
    throw "Bad file format";
  unsigned count;
  is >> count;        // Get count of objects in file
  for (unsigned i = 0; i < count; i++) {
    TGraphTool* p;    // Pointer to each tool read from file
    is >> p;          // Read TGraphTool object
    image->Add(p);    // Add object to image collection
  }
}
```

The first two statements construct and verify an input file stream object. In this case, the function throws an exception if it can't open the file—but more on that later. (Whether to use exceptions is your choice—you may return values as in WriteDocument or throw exceptions for errors as in ReadDocument. I use both methods here for illustration. In your own program, you should adopt and stick to one or the other method.)

Always read a document's information in the same order the program writes it to a stream. In this example, the first job is to verify that the file belongs to the program. Do that by reading the signature string:

```
string signature;
is >> signature;
```

If the signature doesn't equal *"MDIDRAW"*, throw an exception (or use another kind of error mechanism) to prevent accidentally opening the wrong kinds of files.

For simplicity in reconstructing a document, the program next reads the count of graphics objects in the file:

```
unsigned count;
is >> count;
```

After that comes the key step in the reconstruction process—reading the persistent objects into the window's container. *MDIDraw* uses this for loop:

```
for (unsigned i = 0; i < count; i++) {
  TGraphTool* p;    // Pointer to each tool read from file
  is >> p;          // Read TGraphTool object
  image->Add(p);    // Add object to image collection
}
```

Carefully study the three statements inside the loop—they show the necessary steps to read a persistent object. First, define a pointer to the object's base class—TGraphTool in this example. *Do not initialize the pointer in any way.* Read the object from the stream to the pointer as shown. By virtue of the elements you added to your streamable classes derived from TStreamable, the input statement constructs the object of the proper type, and calls that object's Read function to read data members from the stream. The last statement adds the constructed object to the container addressed by image. You might also store objects in other ways—in a simple array, for example, or on a list.

MDIDraw: A Sample Application

Keep the preceding background information on persistent objects and file streams in mind as you browse the following listings for the *MDIDraw* sample application. This is the largest program in this book, but despite its size, all of the source code is listed for reference—the program also makes a useful guide to writing your own multifile

Windows programs. To compile and run the program, open its project file (MDIDRAW.IDE) and press F9. You can run the program from the Windows File Manager, or press Ctrl+F9 to run it from the BC4 environment.

> **WARNING**
>
> Compiling the MDIDRAW program creates a compiled-symbol (.CSM) file that may occupy several megabytes of disk space. The file saves time when recompiling the program—after making changes suggested in this chapter, for example—but, to save disk space, you may elect not to create the file. To do that, open the project file, select the *Options/Project...* command, open the *Compiler* topic (by clicking its plus sign), and highlight *Precompiled headers.* Toggle on the radio button labeled **Do** *not generate or use.*

Listing 12.7, MDIDRAW.DEF, increases the usual heap and stack sizes to 10K and 32K respectively.

Listing 12.7. MDIDRAW.DEF.

```
EXETYPE WINDOWS
CODE PRELOAD MOVEABLE DISCARDABLE
DATA PRELOAD MOVEABLE MULTIPLE
HEAPSIZE 10000
nSTACKSIZE 32000
```

Listing 12.8, MDIDRAW.RH, defines resource and toolbar button identifiers, and also menu command values. The program's source and resource files include MDIDRAW.RH so they can refer to various resources by their defined names.

Listing 12.8. MDIDRAW.RH.

```
// mdidraw.rh -- Resource header file

// Menu resource identifier
#define ID_MENU      100

// Menu command identifiers
#define CM_FILESAVEAS 24334
#define CM_FILESAVE   24333
#define CM_FILEOPEN   24332
#define CM_TOOLLINE 201
```

```
#define CM_TOOLELLIPSE 202
#define CM_TOOLRECTANGLE 203
#define CM_TOOLPENCOLOR 204
#define CM_TOOLBRUSHCOLOR 205
#define CM_HELPABOUT 24346

// Toolbar button icon identifiers
#define IDB_FILENEW 600
#define IDB_FILEOPEN 601
#define IDB_FILESAVE 602
#define IDB_FILESAVEAS 603
#define IDB_FILEEXIT 604
#define IDB_WINDOWCASCADE 605
#define IDB_WINDOWTILE 606
#define IDB_WINDOWARRANGE 607
#define IDB_WINDOWCLOSE 608
#define IDB_HELPABOUT 609
```

Listing 12.9, MDIDRAW.RC, defines the program's resources. The program uses three types of resources: a menu, several bitmaps for toolbar buttons, and a string table for status-line "hints" (help messages).

Listing 12.9. MDIDRAW.RC.

```
#include <owl\window.rh>
#include <owl\mdi.rh>
#include "mdidraw.rh"

ID_MENU MENU
BEGIN
  POPUP "&File"
  BEGIN
    MENUITEM "&New", CM_CREATECHILD
    MENUITEM "&Open...", CM_FILEOPEN
    MENUITEM "&Save", CM_FILESAVE
    MENUITEM "Save &as...", CM_FILESAVEAS
    MENUITEM SEPARATOR
    MENUITEM "E&xit", CM_EXIT
  END
  POPUP "&Tool"
  BEGIN
    MENUITEM "&Line", CM_TOOLLINE, CHECKED
    MENUITEM "&Ellipse", CM_TOOLELLIPSE
    MENUITEM "&Rectangle", CM_TOOLRECTANGLE
    MENUITEM SEPARATOR
    MENUITEM "&Pen color...", CM_TOOLPENCOLOR
    MENUITEM "&Brush color...", CM_TOOLBRUSHCOLOR
  END
```

continues

455

Listing 12.9. continued

```
  POPUP "&Window"
  BEGIN
    MENUITEM "&Cascade", CM_CASCADECHILDREN
    MENUITEM "&Tile", CM_TILECHILDREN
    MENUITEM "&Arrange icons", CM_ARRANGEICONS
    MENUITEM SEPARATOR
    MENUITEM "Close &all", CM_CLOSECHILDREN
  END
  POPUP "&Help"
  BEGIN
    MENUITEM "&About...", CM_HELPABOUT
  END
END

// File¦New icon
IDB_FILENEW BITMAP
{
  '42 4D 66 01 00 00 00 00 00 00 76 00 00 00 28 00'
  '00 00 14 00 00 00 14 00 00 00 01 00 04 00 00 00'
  '00 00 F0 00 00 00 00 00 00 00 00 00 00 00 00 00'
  '00 00 00 00 00 00 00 00 00 00 00 00 80 00 00 80'
  '00 00 00 80 80 00 80 00 00 00 80 00 80 00 80 80'
  '00 00 80 80 80 00 C0 C0 C0 00 00 00 FF 00 00 FF'
  '00 00 00 FF FF 00 FF 00 00 00 FF 00 FF 00 FF FF'
  '00 00 FF FF FF 00 88 88 88 88 88 88 88 88 88 88'
  '29 49 88 88 88 88 80 88 88 88 88 88 77 C1 88 08'
  '88 88 80 88 88 88 80 88 66 57 88 80 88 88 88 88'
  '88 88 08 88 6E 0E 88 88 80 00 00 00 00 08 88 88'
  '6F 43 88 88 80 FE FE FE FE 08 88 88 DF 94 88 88'
  '80 EF EF EF EF 08 88 88 BB 69 88 88 80 FE FE FE'
  'FE 08 88 88 67 4B 88 88 80 EF EF EF EF 08 88 88'
  'DF 94 88 88 80 FE FE FE FE 08 80 08 BB 69 80 08'
  '80 EF EF EF EF 08 88 88 66 5A 88 88 80 FE FE FE'
  'FE 08 88 88 09 FB 88 88 80 EF EF E0 00 08 88 88'
  '02 F6 88 88 80 FE FE F0 E0 88 88 88 04 FD 88 88'
  '80 EF EF E0 08 88 88 88 08 CA 88 88 80 00 00 00'
  '88 88 88 88 89 84 88 80 88 88 88 88 88 88 08 88'
  '4D 2F 88 08 88 88 88 08 88 88 80 88 99 58 88 88'
  '88 88 88 08 88 88 88 88 21 A1 88 88 88 88 88 88'
  '88 88 88 88 99 5C'
}

// File¦Open icon
IDB_FILEOPEN BITMAP
{
  '42 4D 66 01 00 00 00 00 00 00 76 00 00 00 28 00'
  '00 00 14 00 00 00 14 00 00 00 01 00 04 00 00 00'
  '00 00 F0 00 00 00 00 00 00 00 00 00 00 00 00 00'
  '00 00 00 00 00 00 00 00 00 00 00 00 80 00 00 80'
```

```
    '00 00 00 80 80 00 80 00 00 00 80 00 80 00 80 80'
    '00 00 80 80 80 00 C0 C0 C0 00 00 00 FF 00 00 FF'
    '00 00 00 FF FF 00 FF 00 00 00 FF 00 FF 00 FF FF'
    '00 00 FF FF FF 00 88 88 88 88 88 88 88 88 88 88'
    'BB 09 80 00 00 00 00 00 88 88 88 88 73 61 80 87'
    '77 77 77 70 88 88 88 88 6F 4A 80 F8 88 88 88 70'
    '88 88 88 88 DD B4 80 F9 98 88 88 70 88 88 88 88'
    'BB 2D 80 FF FF FF FF 80 88 88 88 88 04 FC 80 00'
    '00 00 00 00 88 88 88 88 64 40 88 88 88 88 88 88'
    '88 88 88 88 84 55 88 80 08 88 88 88 88 88 88 88'
    '6F 3E 88 80 08 88 88 88 88 88 88 88 45 95 88 80'
    '08 88 88 80 00 00 00 08 2A E0 88 80 08 80 88 80'
    'EF EF EF 08 9C D5 88 80 07 80 08 80 F4 44 4E 08'
    '4C 0C 88 87 00 00 00 80 EF EF EF 08 98 D5 88 88'
    '70 00 00 80 F4 44 4E 08 00 00 88 88 88 80 08 80'
    'EF EF EF 08 00 00 88 88 88 80 88 80 F4 4E 00 08'
    '00 00 88 88 88 88 88 80 EF EF 00 88 00 00 88 88'
    '88 88 88 80 00 00 08 88 00 00 88 88 88 88 88 88'
    '88 88 88 88 01 12'
}

// File¦Save icon
IDB_FILESAVE BITMAP
{
    '42 4D 66 01 00 00 00 00 00 00 76 00 00 00 28 00'
    '00 00 14 00 00 00 14 00 00 00 01 00 04 00 00 00'
    '00 00 F0 00 00 00 00 00 00 00 00 00 00 00 00 00'
    '00 00 00 00 00 00 00 00 00 00 00 00 80 00 00 80'
    '00 00 00 80 80 00 80 00 00 00 80 00 80 00 80 80'
    '00 00 80 80 80 00 C0 C0 C0 00 00 00 FF 00 00 FF'
    '00 00 00 FF FF 00 FF 00 00 00 FF 00 FF 00 FF FF'
    '00 00 FF FF FF 00 88 88 88 88 88 88 88 88 88 88'
    'B7 00 88 88 88 88 00 00 00 00 00 08 62 F9 88 88'
    '88 88 08 77 77 77 77 08 36 85 88 88 88 88 0F 88'
    '88 88 87 08 CC 75 88 88 88 88 0F 99 88 88 87 08'
    '00 00 88 88 88 88 0F FF FF FF F8 08 00 C4 88 88'
    '88 88 00 00 00 00 00 08 11 12 88 88 88 88 88 88'
    '88 88 88 88 02 A8 88 88 88 88 88 88 88 00 88 88'
    '10 01 88 88 88 88 88 88 80 00 08 88 10 00 80 00'
    '00 00 08 88 00 00 00 88 00 00 80 EF EF EF 08 88'
    '88 00 88 88 00 00 80 F4 44 4E 08 88 88 00 88 88'
    '00 00 80 EF EF EF 08 88 87 00 88 88 00 00 80 F4'
    '44 4E 08 00 00 07 88 88 00 00 80 EF EF EF 08 00'
    '00 78 88 88 01 12 80 F4 4E 00 08 88 88 88 88 88'
    '42 64 80 EF EF 00 88 88 88 88 88 88 1D 49 80 00'
    '00 08 88 88 88 88 88 88 0B B2 88 88 88 88 88 88'
    '88 88 88 88 46 64'
}
```

continues

Listing 12.9. continued

```
// File¦Save as icon
IDB_FILESAVEAS BITMAP
{
  '42 4D 66 01 00 00 00 00 00 00 76 00 00 00 28 00'
  '00 00 14 00 00 00 14 00 00 00 01 00 04 00 00 00'
  '00 00 F0 00 00 00 00 00 00 00 00 00 00 00 00 00'
  '00 00 00 00 00 00 00 00 00 00 00 00 80 00 00 80'
  '00 00 00 80 80 00 80 00 00 00 80 00 80 00 80 80'
  '00 00 80 80 80 00 C0 C0 C0 00 00 00 FF 00 00 FF'
  '00 00 00 FF FF 00 FF 00 00 00 FF 00 FF 00 FF FF'
  '00 00 FF FF FF 00 88 88 88 88 88 88 88 88 88 88'
  '00 D0 88 88 88 88 88 80 00 00 00 00 08 22 90 88 88'
  '88 88 88 80 FF FF FF 08 26 02 88 88 88 88 88 80'
  'FF FF FF 08 44 94 88 88 88 88 88 80 FF FF FF 08'
  'BB 09 88 88 88 88 88 80 FF FF FF 08 73 61 88 88'
  '88 88 88 80 FF FF FF 08 6F 4A 88 88 88 88 88 80'
  'FF FF 00 08 DD B4 88 88 88 88 88 80 FF FF 00 88'
  'BB 2D 88 88 88 88 88 80 00 00 08 88 04 FC 80 00'
  '00 00 08 88 88 88 88 88 64 40 80 EF EF EF 08 88'
  '88 00 88 88 84 55 80 F4 44 4E 08 88 80 00 08 88'
  '6F 3E 80 EF EF EF 08 88 00 00 00 88 45 95 80 F4'
  '44 4E 08 88 88 00 88 88 2A E0 80 EF EF EF 08 88'
  '87 00 88 88 9C D5 80 F4 4E 00 08 00 00 07 88 88'
  '4C 0C 80 EF EF 00 88 00 00 78 88 88 98 D5 80 00'
  '00 08 88 88 88 88 88 88 00 00 88 88 88 88 88 88'
  '88 88 88 88 00 00'
}

// File¦Exit icon
IDB_FILEEXIT BITMAP
{
  '42 4D 66 01 00 00 00 00 00 00 76 00 00 00 28 00'
  '00 00 14 00 00 00 14 00 00 00 01 00 04 00 00 00'
  '00 00 F0 00 00 00 00 00 00 00 00 00 00 00 00 00'
  '00 00 00 00 00 00 00 00 00 00 00 00 80 00 00 80'
  '00 00 00 80 80 00 80 00 00 00 80 00 80 00 80 80'
  '00 00 80 80 80 00 C0 C0 C0 00 00 00 FF 00 00 FF'
  '00 00 00 FF FF 00 FF 00 00 00 FF 00 FF 00 FF FF'
  '00 00 FF FF FF 00 77 77 77 77 77 77 F8 F8 F8 77'
  '29 49 77 77 77 77 77 78 8F 8F 87 77 77 C1 44 44'
  '44 00 77 7F FF 44 44 44 66 57 88 88 84 D5 00 8F'
  'FF 48 88 88 6E 0E 88 88 84 5D 50 FF FF 48 88 88'
  '6F 43 88 88 84 D5 D0 FF FF 48 88 88 DF 94 88 88'
  '84 5D 50 FE FE 48 88 88 BB 69 88 88 84 D5 D0 FF'
  'FF 48 88 88 67 4B 88 88 84 5D 50 FE FE 48 88 88'
  'DF 94 88 88 84 D5 D0 FF FF 48 88 88 BB 69 88 88'
  '84 5D 50 FE FE 48 88 88 66 5A 88 88 84 D5 D0 EF'
  'EF 48 88 88 09 FB 88 88 84 5D 50 FE FE 48 88 88'
  '02 F6 88 88 84 D5 D0 EF EF 48 88 88 04 FD 88 88'
```

```
'84 44 44 44 44 48 88 88 08 CA 88 88 88 88 88 88'
'88 88 88 88 89 84 88 88 88 80 00 00 08 88 88 88'
'4D 2F 88 88 88 80 AA AA 08 88 88 88 99 58 88 88'
'88 80 00 00 08 88 88 88 21 A1 88 88 88 88 88 88'
'88 88 88 88 99 5C'
}

// Window¦Cascade icon
IDB_WINDOWCASCADE BITMAP
{
'42 4D 66 01 00 00 00 00 00 00 76 00 00 00 28 00'
'00 00 14 00 00 00 14 00 00 00 01 00 04 00 00 00'
'00 00 F0 00 00 00 00 00 00 00 00 00 00 00 00 00'
'00 00 00 00 00 00 00 00 00 00 00 00 80 00 00 80'
'00 00 00 80 80 00 80 00 00 00 80 00 80 00 80 80'
'00 00 80 80 80 00 C0 C0 C0 00 00 00 FF 00 00 FF'
'00 00 00 FF FF 00 FF 00 00 00 FF 00 FF 00 FF FF'
'00 00 FF FF FF 00 88 88 88 88 88 88 88 88 88 88'
'BB 09 88 88 88 88 88 88 88 88 88 88 73 61 88 88'
'80 00 00 00 00 00 00 08 6F 4A 88 88 80 FF FF FF'
'FF FF FF 08 DD B4 88 88 80 FF FF FF FF FF FF 08'
'BB 2D 88 80 00 FF FF FF FF FF FF 08 04 FC 88 80'
'F0 FF FF FF FF FF FF 08 64 40 88 80 F0 FF FF FF'
'FF FF FF 08 84 55 80 00 F0 FF FF FF FF FF FF 08'
'6F 3E 80 F0 F0 FF FF FF FF FF FF 08 45 95 80 F0'
'F0 00 00 00 00 00 00 08 2A E0 80 F0 F0 F0 CC CC'
'CC 0F 0F 08 9C D5 80 F0 F0 00 00 00 00 00 00 08'
'4C 0C 80 F0 00 00 00 00 00 00 08 88 98 D5 80 F0'
'F0 CC CC CC 0F 0F 08 88 00 00 80 F0 00 00 00 00'
'00 00 08 88 00 00 80 00 00 00 00 00 00 08 88 88'
'00 00 80 F0 CC CC CC 0F 0F 08 88 88 00 00 80 00'
'00 00 00 00 00 08 88 88 00 00 88 88 88 88 88 88'
'88 88 88 88 01 12'
}

// Window¦Tile icon
IDB_WINDOWTILE BITMAP
{
'42 4D 66 01 00 00 00 00 00 00 76 00 00 00 28 00'
'00 00 14 00 00 00 14 00 00 00 01 00 04 00 00 00'
'00 00 F0 00 00 00 00 00 00 00 00 00 00 00 00 00'
'00 00 00 00 00 00 00 00 00 00 00 00 80 00 00 80'
'00 00 00 80 80 00 80 00 00 00 80 00 80 00 80 80'
'00 00 80 80 80 00 C0 C0 C0 00 00 00 FF 00 00 FF'
'00 00 00 FF FF 00 FF 00 00 00 FF 00 FF 00 FF FF'
'00 00 FF FF FF 00 88 88 88 88 88 88 88 88 88 88'
'BB 09 80 00 00 00 00 00 00 00 00 08 73 61 80 FF'
'FF FF F0 0F FF FF FF 08 6F 4A 80 FF FF FF F0 0F'
'FF FF FF 08 DD B4 80 FF FF FF F0 0F FF FF FF 08'
```

continues

Listing 12.9. continued

```
'BB 2D 80 FF FF FF F0 0F FF FF FF 08 04 FC 80 FF'
'FF FF F0 0F FF FF FF 08 64 40 80 FF FF FF F0 0F'
'FF FF FF 08 84 55 80 FF FF FF F0 0F FF FF FF 08'
'6F 3E 80 FF FF FF F0 0F FF FF FF 08 45 95 80 FF'
'FF FF F0 0F FF FF FF 08 2A E0 80 FF FF FF F0 0F'
'FF FF FF 08 9C D5 80 FF FF FF F0 0F FF FF FF 08'
'4C 0C 80 FF FF FF F0 0F FF FF FF 08 98 D5 80 FF'
'FF FF F0 0F FF FF FF 08 00 00 80 FF FF FF F0 0F'
'FF FF FF 08 00 00 80 00 00 00 00 00 00 00 00 08'
'00 00 80 F0 CC C0 F0 0F 0C CC 0F 08 00 00 80 00'
'00 00 00 00 00 00 00 08 00 00 88 88 88 88 88 88'
'88 88 88 88 01 12'
}

// Window¦Arrange icons
IDB_WINDOWARRANGE BITMAP
{
'42 4D 66 01 00 00 00 00 00 00 76 00 00 00 28 00'
'00 00 14 00 00 00 14 00 00 00 01 00 04 00 00 00'
'00 00 F0 00 00 00 00 00 00 00 00 00 00 00 00 00'
'00 00 00 00 00 00 00 00 00 00 00 00 80 00 00 80'
'00 00 00 80 80 00 80 00 00 00 80 00 80 00 80 80'
'00 00 80 80 80 00 C0 C0 C0 00 00 00 FF 00 00 FF'
'00 00 00 FF FF 00 FF 00 00 00 FF 00 FF 00 FF FF'
'00 00 FF FF FF 00 88 88 88 88 88 88 88 88 88 88'
'00 00 88 88 88 88 88 88 88 88 88 88 03 00 88 44'
'44 44 88 88 44 44 44 88 00 00 88 88 88 88 88 88'
'88 88 88 88 00 00 88 80 00 08 88 88 80 00 08 88'
'00 00 88 80 AA 08 88 88 80 DD 08 88 03 00 88 80'
'AA 08 88 88 80 DD 08 88 00 00 88 80 A0 08 88 88'
'80 D0 08 88 00 00 88 80 00 88 88 88 80 00 88 88'
'00 00 88 88 88 88 88 88 88 88 88 88 22 22 88 88'
'88 88 88 88 88 88 88 88 11 11 88 44 44 44 88 88'
'44 44 44 88 00 00 88 88 88 88 88 88 88 88 88 88'
'00 00 88 80 00 08 88 88 80 00 08 88 00 00 88 80'
'EE 08 88 88 80 BB 08 88 22 22 88 80 EE 08 88 88'
'80 BB 08 88 11 11 88 80 E0 08 88 88 80 B0 08 88'
'00 00 88 80 00 88 88 88 80 00 88 88 88 88 88 88'
'88 88 88 88 88 88 88 88 00 00 88 88 88 88 88 88'
'88 88 88 88 00 00'
}

// Window¦Close all icon
IDB_WINDOWCLOSE BITMAP
{
'42 4D 66 01 00 00 00 00 00 00 76 00 00 00 28 00'
'00 00 14 00 00 00 14 00 00 00 01 00 04 00 00 00'
'00 00 F0 00 00 00 00 00 00 00 00 00 00 00 00 00'
'00 00 00 00 00 00 00 00 00 00 00 00 80 00 00 80'
```

```
 '00 00 00 80 80 00 80 00 00 00 80 00 80 00 80 80'
 '00 00 80 80 80 00 C0 C0 C0 00 00 00 FF 00 00 FF'
 '00 00 00 FF FF 00 FF 00 00 00 FF 00 FF 00 FF FF'
 '00 00 FF FF FF 00 88 88 88 88 88 88 88 88 88 88'
 'BB 09 88 88 00 00 00 00 08 88 88 88 73 61 88 88'
 '0F FF FF FF 08 88 88 88 6F 4A 88 88 0F FF FF FF'
 '08 88 88 88 DD B4 80 00 0F FF FF FF 08 88 88 88'
 'BB 2D 80 FF 0F FF FF FF 08 88 88 88 04 FC 80 FF'
 '0C CC CC CC 08 88 88 88 64 40 80 FF 00 00 00 00'
 '08 88 88 88 84 55 80 FF FF FF F0 88 88 88 88 88'
 '6F 3E 80 CC CC CC C0 88 88 88 88 88 45 95 80 00'
 '00 00 00 88 88 88 88 88 2A E0 88 88 88 88 88 88'
 '88 88 88 88 9C D5 88 88 88 88 88 88 88 88 88 88'
 '4C 0C 88 88 88 88 88 88 88 88 88 88 98 D5 88 88'
 '88 88 88 88 88 88 88 88 00 00 88 88 88 88 88 88'
 '77 77 77 78 00 00 88 88 88 88 88 80 00 00 00 78'
 '00 00 88 88 88 88 88 80 FF FF F0 78 00 00 88 88'
 '88 88 88 80 00 00 00 88 00 00 88 88 88 88 88 88'
 '88 88 88 88 01 12'
}

// Help¦About icon
IDB_HELPABOUT BITMAP
{
 '42 4D 66 01 00 00 00 00 00 00 76 00 00 00 28 00'
 '00 00 14 00 00 00 14 00 00 00 01 00 04 00 00 00'
 '00 00 F0 00 00 00 00 00 00 00 00 00 00 00 00 00'
 '00 00 00 00 00 00 00 00 00 00 00 00 80 00 00 80'
 '00 00 00 80 80 00 80 00 00 00 80 00 80 00 80 80'
 '00 00 80 80 80 00 C0 C0 C0 00 00 00 FF 00 00 FF'
 '00 00 00 FF FF 00 FF 00 00 00 FF 00 FF 00 FF FF'
 '00 00 FF FF FF 00 88 88 88 88 88 88 88 88 88 88'
 '00 00 88 88 88 88 88 77 78 88 88 88 00 00 88 88'
 '88 88 86 44 78 88 88 88 00 00 88 88 88 88 8E 64'
 '78 88 88 88 00 00 88 88 88 88 8E E6 88 88 88 88'
 '00 00 88 88 88 88 88 88 88 88 88 88 00 00 88 88'
 '88 88 88 77 78 88 88 88 00 00 88 88 88 88 86 44'
 '78 88 88 88 00 00 88 88 88 88 8E 64 78 88 88 88'
 '00 00 88 88 88 88 8E 64 77 88 88 88 00 00 88 88'
 '88 88 8E 66 47 78 88 88 00 00 88 88 88 88 88 E6'
 '64 77 88 88 08 33 88 88 88 88 88 8E 66 47 88 88'
 '00 00 88 88 88 77 78 88 E6 47 88 88 11 00 88 88'
 '86 44 78 88 E6 47 88 88 09 10 88 88 8E 64 77 77'
 'E6 47 88 88 65 F0 88 88 8E 66 44 44 66 48 88 88'
 '65 F0 88 88 88 EE 66 66 66 88 88 88 65 F0 88 88'
 '88 88 EE EE E8 88 88 88 65 F0 88 88 88 88 88 88'
 '88 88 88 88 65 F0'
}
```

continues

Listing 12.9. continued

```
STRINGTABLE LOADONCALL MOVEABLE DISCARDABLE
{
  CM_CREATECHILD, "Creates new document window"
  CM_EXIT, "Quits the application"
  CM_TOOLLINE, "Selects line drawing tool"
  CM_TOOLELLIPSE, "Selects ellipse drawing tool"
  CM_TOOLRECTANGLE, "Selects rectangle drawing tool"
  CM_HELPABOUT, "Displays message box"
}
```

Listing 12.10, MDIDRAW.CPP, is the program's main module. The module declares and implements the application class, TDrawApp. The class has a constructor, the ever-present InitMainWindow function, plus three private data member pointers. The client pointer addresses the MDI application's client window of the derived class TDrawClient. The toolbar pointer addresses the toolbar of icons under the frame window's menu bar. The statusLine pointer addresses the frame's status line at the window's bottom.

Listing 12.10. MDIDRAW.CPP.

```
/* ============================================================ *\
**    mdidraw.cpp -- Object drawing demonstration               **
** ============================================================ **
**                                                              **
** ============================================================ **
**      Copyright (c) 1994 by Tom Swan. All rights reserved.    **
\* ============================================================ */

#include <owl\applicat.h>
#include <owl\decmdifr.h>
#include <owl\controlb.h>
#include <owl\buttonga.h>
#include <owl\messageb.h>
#include <owl\statusba.h>

#include "tools.h"
#include "child.h"
#include "client.h"
#include "mdidraw.rh"


// ============================================================
// The MDI application class
// ============================================================

class TDrawApp: public TApplication {
public:
```

```cpp
  TDrawApp(const char far* name)
    : TApplication(name) {}
  void InitMainWindow();
private:
  TDrawClient* client;
  TControlBar* toolbar;
  TStatusBar* statusLine;
};

// Initialize the program's main window
void
TDrawApp::InitMainWindow()
{
  EnableCtl3d(TRUE);
  EnableBWCC();

// Construct the MDI client window
  client = new TDrawClient;

// Construct MDI frame, passing client window object
  TDecoratedMDIFrame * frame = new TDecoratedMDIFrame(
    "MDI Draw",    // Caption
    ID_MENU,       // Required menu resource identifier
    *client,       // Required client window object
    TRUE);         // Optional track menu selections

// Give client window frame window pointer
  client->SetFrame(frame);

// Construct a toolbar with icons for various commands
  toolbar = new TControlBar(frame);

  toolbar->Insert(
   *new TButtonGadget(IDB_FILENEW, CM_CREATECHILD));
  toolbar->Insert(
   *new TButtonGadget(IDB_FILEOPEN, CM_FILEOPEN));
  toolbar->Insert(
   *new TButtonGadget(IDB_FILESAVE, CM_FILESAVE));
  toolbar->Insert(
   *new TButtonGadget(IDB_FILESAVEAS, CM_FILESAVEAS));
  toolbar->Insert(
   *new TSeparatorGadget(8));
  toolbar->Insert(
   *new TButtonGadget(IDB_FILEEXIT, CM_EXIT));
  toolbar->Insert(
   *new TSeparatorGadget(8));
  toolbar->Insert(
   *new TButtonGadget(IDB_WINDOWCASCADE, CM_CASCADECHILDREN));
  toolbar->Insert(
```

continues

Listing 12.10. continued

```
 *new TButtonGadget(IDB_WINDOWTILE, CM_TILECHILDREN));
 toolbar->Insert(
  *new TButtonGadget(IDB_WINDOWARRANGE, CM_ARRANGEICONS));
 toolbar->Insert(
  *new TButtonGadget(IDB_WINDOWCLOSE, CM_CLOSECHILDREN));
 toolbar->Insert(
  *new TSeparatorGadget(6));
 toolbar->Insert(
  *new TButtonGadget(IDB_HELPABOUT, CM_HELPABOUT));

// Enable status line messages when mouse touches a button
 toolbar->SetHintMode(TGadgetWindow::EnterHints);

// Insert the toolbar into the frame window
 frame->Insert(*toolbar, TDecoratedFrame::Top);

// Create status line with function keys legend
 statusLine = new TStatusBar(frame, TGadget::Recessed,
  TStatusBar::CapsLock | TStatusBar::NumLock |
  TStatusBar::ScrollLock | TStatusBar::Overtype);
 frame->Insert(*statusLine, TDecoratedFrame::Bottom);

// Assign the decorated MDI frame as the program's main window
 MainWindow = frame;
}

#pragma argsused

// Main program
int
OwlMain(int argc, char* argv[])
{
  TDrawApp app("MDIDrawApp");
  return app.Run();
}
```

Next are two listings that declare and implement the MDI application's client window class. The frame window owns an object of the client window class, which in turn owns the program's child windows—the ones that display and edit graphics documents. Listing 12.11, CLIENT.H, declares TDrawClient, derived from TMDIClient. Listing 12.12, CLIENT.CPP, implements the TDrawClient class.

NOTE

This is a typical arrangement in a large program. A header file declares one or more classes, implemented separately in a source file, usually of the same name, but ending in .CPP.

Listing 12.11. CLIENT.H.

```
// client.h -- TDrawClient header file

#ifndef __CLIENT_H
#define __CLIENT_H

#ifndef __MDI_H
  #include <owl\mdi.h>
#endif
#ifndef __DECMDIFR_H
  #include <owl\decmdifr.h>
#endif
#ifndef __COLOR_H
  #include <owl\color.h>
#endif

enum TTool {LINETOOL, ELLIPSETOOL, RECTANGLETOOL};

class TDrawClient: public TMDIClient {
public:
  TDrawClient();
  void SetFrame(TDecoratedMDIFrame * fp)
    { frame = fp; }
  TTool GetSelectedTool()
    { return selectedTool; }
  TColor GetPenColor()
    { return penColor; }
  TColor GetBrushColor()
    { return brushColor; }
protected:
  virtual TMDIChild* InitChild();
  void AddMenuCheck(WORD MenuCommand);
  void RemoveMenuCheck(WORD MenuCommand);
  void CmFileOpen();
  void CmFileSave();
  void CmFileSaveAs();
  void CmToolLine();
```

continues

465

Listing 12.11. continued

```
  void CmToolEllipse();
  void CmToolRectangle();
  void CmToolPenColor();
  void CmToolBrushColor();
  void CmHelpAbout();
private:
  TTool selectedTool;    // Line, ellipse, or rectangle tool id
  TColor penColor;       // Pen (outline) color
  TColor brushColor;     // Brush (interior) color
  TDecoratedMDIFrame * frame;  // Pointer to client's frame
DECLARE_RESPONSE_TABLE(TDrawClient);
};

#endif // __CLIENT_H
```

Listing 12.12. CLIENT.CPP.

```
// client.cpp -- TDrawClient implementation

#include <owl\opensave.h>
#include <owl\chooseco.h>
#include "client.h"
#include "child.h"
#include "mdidraw.rh"

DEFINE_RESPONSE_TABLE1(TDrawClient, TMDIClient)
  EV_COMMAND(CM_FILEOPEN, CmFileOpen),
  EV_COMMAND(CM_FILESAVE, CmFileSave),
  EV_COMMAND(CM_FILESAVEAS, CmFileSaveAs),
  EV_COMMAND(CM_TOOLLINE, CmToolLine),
  EV_COMMAND(CM_TOOLELLIPSE, CmToolEllipse),
  EV_COMMAND(CM_TOOLRECTANGLE, CmToolRectangle),
  EV_COMMAND(CM_TOOLPENCOLOR, CmToolPenColor),
  EV_COMMAND(CM_TOOLBRUSHCOLOR, CmToolBrushColor),
  EV_COMMAND(CM_HELPABOUT, CmHelpAbout),
  EV_COMMAND_ENABLE(CM_FILESAVE, CmChildActionEnable),
  EV_COMMAND_ENABLE(CM_FILESAVEAS, CmChildActionEnable),
  EV_COMMAND_ENABLE(CM_TOOLLINE, CmChildActionEnable),
  EV_COMMAND_ENABLE(CM_TOOLELLIPSE, CmChildActionEnable),
  EV_COMMAND_ENABLE(CM_TOOLRECTANGLE, CmChildActionEnable),
END_RESPONSE_TABLE;

// Constructor
TDrawClient::TDrawClient()
  : TMDIClient(),
```

```
    selectedTool(LINETOOL),
    penColor(TColor::Black),
    brushColor(TColor::White),
    frame(0)  // Initialized by InitMainWindow
{
}

// Add checkmark to menu command
// Requires parent frame to call SetFrame
void
TDrawClient::AddMenuCheck(WORD menuCommand)
{
  if (!frame) return;
  ::CheckMenuItem(frame->GetMenu(), menuCommand,
    MF_BYCOMMAND | MF_CHECKED);
}

// Remove checkmark from menu command
// Requires parent frame to call SetFrame
void
TDrawClient::RemoveMenuCheck(WORD menuCommand)
{
  if (!frame) return;
  ::CheckMenuItem(frame->GetMenu(), menuCommand,
    MF_BYCOMMAND | MF_UNCHECKED);
}

// Construct a child window object for File|New command
TMDIChild*
TDrawClient::InitChild()
{
  return new TDrawChild(*this);
}

// Open an existing file for File|Open command
// Catch possible exception thrown by TDrawChild constructor
void
TDrawClient::CmFileOpen()
{
  TDrawChild* cp;  // Child window pointer

  TOpenSaveDialog::TData filenameData(
    OFN_FILEMUSTEXIST | OFN_PATHMUSTEXIST | OFN_HIDEREADONLY,
    "Draw files (*.mdw)|*.mdw|All files (*.*)|*.*||",
    0, "", "mdw");
  TFileOpenDialog *fileDialog
    = new TFileOpenDialog(this, filenameData);
  if (!fileDialog) return;
  if (fileDialog->Execute() == IDOK) {
```

continues

467

Listing 12.12. continued

```
    if (filenameData.Error == 0) { // No error and not canceled
      try {
        cp = new TDrawChild(*this, filenameData.FileName);
      }
      catch (TXOwl error) {
        MessageBox(error.why().c_str(),
          "Error!", MB_OK | MB_ICONSTOP);
        delete fileDialog;
        return;
      }
      if (cp) cp->Create();
    }
  }
  delete fileDialog;
}

// Save window's information for File|Save command
void
TDrawClient::CmFileSave()
{
  TDrawChild* cp = (TDrawChild *)GetActiveMDIChild();
  if (!cp) return;
  cp->SaveFile();
}

// Name and save window's information for File|Save-as command
void
TDrawClient::CmFileSaveAs()
{
  TDrawChild* cp = (TDrawChild *)GetActiveMDIChild();
  if (!cp) return;
  cp->SaveAsFile();
}

// Select line drawing tool
void
TDrawClient::CmToolLine()
{
  RemoveMenuCheck(CM_TOOLLINE + (int)selectedTool);
  selectedTool = LINETOOL;
  AddMenuCheck(CM_TOOLLINE);
}

// Select ellipse drawing tool
void
TDrawClient::CmToolEllipse()
{
  RemoveMenuCheck(CM_TOOLLINE + (int)selectedTool);
  selectedTool = ELLIPSETOOL;
```

```
    AddMenuCheck(CM_TOOLELLIPSE);
}

// Select rectangle drawing tool
void
TDrawClient::CmToolRectangle()
{
  RemoveMenuCheck(CM_TOOLLINE + (int)selectedTool);
  selectedTool = RECTANGLETOOL;
  AddMenuCheck(CM_TOOLRECTANGLE);
}

// Called by CmToolPenColor in ForEach statement
// p == pointer to child window; d == pointer to pen color data
void SetChildPenColor(TWindow *p, void *d)
{
  TYPESAFE_DOWNCAST(p, TDrawChild)->
    SetPenColor(*(TColor *)d);
}

// Select pen color from common color dialog
void
TDrawClient::CmToolPenColor()
{
// Palette of 16 selected colors shown in dialog
// Declared static to save palette between function calls
  static TColor palette[16];

// Construct data structure for the TChooseColorDialog class
  TChooseColorDialog::TData colorData;
  colorData.Flags = CC_RGBINIT;
  colorData.Color = penColor;
  colorData.CustColors = palette;

// Execute dialog and, if closed with the Ok button,
// set all child window pen colors to selected color
  TChooseColorDialog *colorDialog
    = new TChooseColorDialog(this, colorData);
  if (!colorDialog) return;
  int resultIsOkay = (colorDialog->Execute() == IDOK);
  delete colorDialog;   // So ForEach doesn't attempt to use it
  if (resultIsOkay) {
    if (colorData.Error == 0) {
      penColor = colorData.Color;
      ForEach(SetChildPenColor, &penColor);
    }
  }
}
```

continues

469

Listing 12.12. continued

```
// Called by CmToolBrushColor in ForEach statement
// p == pointer to child window; d == pointer to brush color data
void SetChildBrushColor(TWindow *p, void *d)
{
  TYPESAFE_DOWNCAST(p, TDrawChild)->
    SetBrushColor(*(TColor *)d);
}

// Select brush color from common color dialog
// (Same as preceding function, but changes tool's brush color)
void
TDrawClient::CmToolBrushColor()
{
  static TColor palette[16];
  TChooseColorDialog::TData colorData;
  colorData.Flags = CC_RGBINIT;
  colorData.Color = brushColor;
  colorData.CustColors = palette;
  TChooseColorDialog *colorDialog
    = new TChooseColorDialog(this, colorData);
  if (!colorDialog) return;
  int resultIsOkay = (colorDialog->Execute() == IDOK);
  delete colorDialog;  // So ForEach doesn't attempt to use it
  if (resultIsOkay) {
    if (colorData.Error == 0) {
      brushColor = colorData.Color;
      ForEach(SetChildPenColor, &brushColor);
    }
  }
}

// Display help message box
void
TDrawClient::CmHelpAbout()
{
  string msg;
  string newline('\n');
  msg += "MDI Draw Demonstration" + newline + newline;
  msg += "from Mastering Windows Programming" + newline;
  msg += "_ 1994 by Tom Swan" + newline;
  msg += "All rights reserved";
  MessageBox(msg.c_str(), "About MDI Draw", MB_OK);
}
```

The TDrawClient class overrides InitChild to construct new child windows—those that
begin with an empty document. The class also declares response functions for each menu
command, plus some other member functions to add checkmarks to commands and to

return object data members. All of those members are private. The `selectedTool` equals one of the `TTool` constants in the enumerated statement that precedes the class declaration. This indicates which drawing tool (line, rectangle, or ellipse) is selected. The two `TColor` variables, `penColor` and `brushColor`, select foreground and background colors for the selected tool. The `frame` member provides a handy way for the client to call functions in its parent window.

The `TDrawClient` class's response table (see CLIENT.CPP) associates each response function with the appropriate menu command resource identifier. The table also uses the `EV_COMMAND_ENABLE` macro to enable and disable various commands depending on whether any child windows are open. (Toolbar icons are similarly enabled and disabled.)

Two of the client window's primary jobs are creating new child windows (which empty documents) and opening existing documents. `InitChild` creates new child windows by calling the `TDrawChild` class's default constructor. `CmFileOpen`, the response function for the *File|Open...* command, uses the common file-open dialog box to prompt for a file name and to allow users to browse directories.

Any exceptions in the construction of a `TDrawChild` object—attempting to read a file that doesn't belong to *MDIDraw*, for example—are caught by the `catch` statement following `try`, which attempts to construct a child window by passing it a file name. Exceptions that cause an object's constructor to fail result in no object being formed, therefore, the `cp` pointer must not be deleted in the event that `TDrawChild`'s constructor fails in the `try` block. The `catch` statement intercepts any exceptions, and calls the `why` function for the thrown `TXOwl` object to display a message about the trouble before returning. The file dialog is deleted beforehand.

NOTE

To see the result of the exception handling code in CLIENT.CPP, run *MDIDraw* and attempt to open the provided BADFILE.MDW file, which is purposely corrupted. If that file doesn't exist, open file CHILD.CPP, and locate the two lines:

```
  string signature(SIGNATURE);
// string signature("BADFILE");
```

Turn the first into a comment, and enable the second. Recompile and run the program, create a test window, and save it to BADFILE.MDW. Restore the preceding statements and recompile. (You could also use a file utility to alter a test file's signature string, *"MDIDRAW"*.) Figure 12.4 shows the resulting dialog box displayed as a result of `TDrawChild`'s throwing an exception for a file in the wrong format.

FIGURE 12.4.

*Error message displayed
as a result of a
TDrawChild
exception.*

CLIENT.CPP demonstrates some other useful MDI techniques. For example, the
CmFileSave and CmFileSaveAs response functions use these statements to obtain the
address of the active child window (if any):

```
TDrawChild* cp = (TDrawChild *)GetActiveMDIChild();
if (!cp) return;
```

Another function, SetChildPenColor, demonstrates how to downcast a TWindow pointer
to a derived class object. You must take special pains to do that because TWindow is virtually inherited by the derived class, creating a potential ambiguity for the usual casting
you can use to convert the types of relatively simple objects (a void pointer, for example,
into a typed pointer). SetChildPenColor needs to change the color of a child window's
pen. To do that, the function executes the statement:

```
TYPESAFE_DOWNCAST(p, TDrawChild)->
  SetPenColor(*(TColor *)d);
```

The TYPESAFE_DOWNCAST macro ensures that p, a TWindow pointer, is properly converted
to a TDrawChild object pointer. The result of the macro is a pointer, which in this case
is dereferenced by the -> operator for calling the child object class's SetPenColor member function. A normal C++ cast expression converts the void data pointer d to a TColor
object—you don't need to use the downcast macro for every cast, just for those involving virtual base classes such as TWindow.

Function CmToolPenColor demonstrates how to prepare and use a common color dialog, in this case, to select drawing colors. The program's *Tool\Pen color...* and *Tool\Brush
color...* command display the dialog, illustrated in Figure 12.5. Select the dialog's *Define Custom Colors...* button to open the dialog to its full width as shown here.

For storing the dialog's **Custom Colors,** which you configure by choosing color values in
the full dialog and then selecting the *Add to Custom Colors* button, function
CmToolPenColor defines a static array of TColor objects:

```
static TColor palette[16];
```

FIGURE 12.5.

Common color selection dialog.

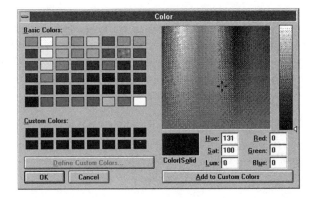

Next, the function prepares a data structure for use by the dialog—similar to the data structure, but with different members, used in the program's file-open and file-save dialogs. In this case, the object is of type `TChooseColorDialog::TData`—in other words, it's an object of the class `TData` nested inside `TChooseColorDialog`. (All common dialog classes have similar nested data structure classes.) The program initializes the data structure with these statements:

```
TChooseColorDialog::TData colorData;
colorData.Flags = CC_RGBINIT;
colorData.Color = penColor;
colorData.CustColors = palette;
```

The rest of function `CmToolPenColor` executes the color dialog. If that dialog is closed by selecting its OK button, the program extracts the selected color value from the `TData` structure's `Color` member, and passes that color to every child window with the statements:

```
penColor = colorData.Color;
ForEach(SetChildPenColor, &penColor);
```

Each child window could have individual color settings, in which case only the active child's pen color would need to be changed. You might want to make this change in a revision of the program. Function `CmToolBrushColor` works just like `CmToolPenColor`, but of course, sets the child window brush colors, used for painting filled rectangles and ellipses shapes.

The next two listings declare and implement graphics tool classes. Objects of these classes form drawing images, and as explained, the classes are streamable so they can be read and written using C++ stream statements. Listing 12.13, TOOL.H, declares the `TGraphTool` abstract class and three derived classes, `TLine`, `TRectangle`, and `TEllipse`. Listing 12.14, TOOL.CPP, implements the classes.

Listing 12.13. TOOLS.H.

```
// tools.h -- TGraphTool and derived tool classes header file

#ifndef __TOOLS_H
#define __TOOLS_H

#if !defined( __CLASSLIB_OBJSTRM_H )
  #include <classlib\objstrm.h>
#endif
#ifndef __POINT_H
  #include <owl\point.h>
#endif
#ifndef __DC_H
  #include <owl\dc.h>
#endif
#ifndef __GDIOBJEC_H
  #include <owl\gdiobjec.h>
#endif

// TGraphPen adds a default constructor to TPen,
// required for streaming TGraphTool objects
class TGraphPen: public TPen {
public:
  TGraphPen(): TPen(TColor::Black), color(TColor::Black) { }
  TGraphPen(TColor c): TPen(c), color(c) { }
  TColor GetColor() const { return color; }
private:
  TColor color;
};

// TGraphBrush adds a default constructor to TBrush,
// also required for streaming TGraphTool objects
class TGraphBrush: public TBrush {
public:
  TGraphBrush(): TBrush(TColor::White), color(TColor::White) { }
  TGraphBrush(TColor c): TBrush(c), color(c) { }
  TColor GetColor() const { return color; }
private:
  TColor color;
};

// Abstract base class for object-drawing tools
class TGraphTool: public virtual TStreamableBase {
public:
  TGraphTool();
  TGraphTool(TPoint p1, TPoint p2,
    TColor penColor, TColor brushColor);
  ~TGraphTool();
  void SetStartPt(TPoint p) { startPt = p; }
  void SetEndPt(TPoint p) { endPt = p; }
```

```
    void OffsetPoints(long xofs, long yofs);
    virtual TGraphTool * Clone() = 0;   // Pure virtual function
    virtual void Draw(TDC& dc) = 0;      // Pure virtual function
    void SelectAttributes(TDC& dc);
    void DeselectAttributes(TDC& dc);
    const TGraphPen* GetPen() const { return pen; }
    const TGraphBrush* GetBrush() const { return brush; }
    void SetPenColor(TColor color);
    void SetBrushColor(TColor color);
    int operator== (const TGraphTool& tool);
protected:
  TPoint startPt;
  TPoint endPt;
private:
  TGraphPen* pen;        // Pointer to tool's outline color
  TGraphBrush* brush;    // Pointer to tool's interior color
DECLARE_ABSTRACT_STREAMABLE( , TGraphTool, 1);
};

class TLine: public TGraphTool {
public:
  TLine(TPoint p1, TPoint p2,
    TColor penColor, TColor brushColor)
    : TGraphTool(p1, p2, penColor, brushColor) {};
  virtual TGraphTool * Clone();
  virtual void Draw(TDC& dc);
DECLARE_STREAMABLE( , TLine, 1);
};

class TEllipse: public TGraphTool {
public:
  TEllipse(TPoint p1, TPoint p2,
    TColor penColor, TColor brushColor)
    : TGraphTool(p1, p2, penColor, brushColor) {};
  virtual TGraphTool * Clone();
  virtual void Draw(TDC& dc);
DECLARE_STREAMABLE( , TEllipse, 1);
};

class TRectangle: public TGraphTool {
public:
  TRectangle(TPoint p1, TPoint p2,
    TColor penColor, TColor brushColor)
    : TGraphTool(p1, p2, penColor, brushColor) {};
  virtual TGraphTool * Clone();
  virtual void Draw(TDC& dc);
DECLARE_STREAMABLE( , TRectangle, 1);
};

#endif // __TOOLS_H
```

Listing 12.14. TOOLS.CPP.

```cpp
// tools.cpp -- TGraphTool and derived class implementations

#include "tools.h"

// ===========================================================
// TGraphTool
// ===========================================================

// Default constructor
TGraphTool::TGraphTool()
  : startPt(0, 0),
    endPt(0, 0)
{
  pen = new TGraphPen(TColor::Black);
  brush = new TGraphBrush(TColor::White);
}

// Alternate constructor
TGraphTool::TGraphTool(TPoint p1, TPoint p2,
  TColor penColor, TColor brushColor)
  : startPt(p1),
    endPt(p2)
{
  pen = new TGraphPen(penColor);
  brush = new TGraphBrush(brushColor);
}

IMPLEMENT_ABSTRACT_STREAMABLE(TGraphTool);

// Destructor
TGraphTool::~TGraphTool()
{
  delete pen;
  delete brush;
}

// Offset starting and ending points by passed amounts to
// account for scoller thumb position
void
TGraphTool::OffsetPoints(long xofs, long yofs)
{
  startPt.x += (int)xofs;
  startPt.y += (int)yofs;
  endPt.x += (int)xofs;
  endPt.y += (int)yofs;
}

// Read object from stream
void*
```

```
TGraphTool::Streamer::Read(ipstream& is, uint32) const
{
  COLORREF penColor, brushColor;

  is >> GetObject()->startPt.x;
  is >> GetObject()->startPt.y;
  is >> GetObject()->endPt.x;
  is >> GetObject()->endPt.y;
  is >> penColor;
  is >> brushColor;
  GetObject()->pen = new TGraphPen(TColor(penColor));
  GetObject()->brush = new TGraphBrush(TColor(brushColor));
  return GetObject();
}

// Write object to stream
void
TGraphTool::Streamer::Write(opstream& os) const
{
  os << GetObject()->startPt.x;
  os << GetObject()->startPt.y;
  os << GetObject()->endPt.x;
  os << GetObject()->endPt.y;
  os << GetObject()->pen->GetColor();
  os << GetObject()->brush->GetColor();
}

// Insert tool's attributes into dc.
void
TGraphTool::SelectAttributes(TDC& dc)
{
  dc.SelectObject(*pen);
  dc.SelectObject(*brush);
}

// Restore old DC and delete the current Pen and Brush
void
TGraphTool::DeselectAttributes(TDC& dc)
{
  dc.RestorePen();
  dc.RestoreBrush();
}

// Change tool's pen color
void
TGraphTool::SetPenColor(TColor color)
{
  delete pen;
```

continues

477

Listing 12.14. continued

```
  pen = new TGraphPen(color);
}

// Change tool's brush color
void
TGraphTool::SetBrushColor(TColor color)
{
  delete brush;
  brush = new TGraphBrush(color);
}

// Implement == operator for TGraphTool objects
// Required by array template that holds image
int
TGraphTool::operator== (const TGraphTool& tool)
{
  return &tool == this;
}

// =============================================================
// TLine
// =============================================================

// Return pointer to TLine object clone
TGraphTool *
TLine::Clone()
{
  return new TLine(startPt, endPt,
    GetPen()->GetColor(), GetBrush()->GetColor());
}

IMPLEMENT_STREAMABLE1(TLine, TGraphTool);

// Read object from stream
void*
TLine::Streamer::Read(ipstream& is, uint32) const
{
  ReadBaseObject((TGraphTool *)GetObject(), is);
  // Nothing else to read for a TLine object,
  // but if TLine declared its own data members,
  // you would read them here.
  return GetObject();
}

// Write object to stream
void
TLine::Streamer::Write(opstream& os) const
{
  WriteBaseObject((TGraphTool *)GetObject(), os);
```

```
  // Nothing else to write for a TLine object
  // but if TLine declared its own data members,
  // you would write them here.
}

// Draw a TLine object
void TLine::Draw(TDC& dc)
{
  SelectAttributes(dc);
  dc.MoveTo(startPt);
  dc.LineTo(endPt);
  DeselectAttributes(dc);
}


// ============================================================
// TEllipse
// ============================================================

// Return pointer to TEllipse object clone
TGraphTool *
TEllipse::Clone()
{
  return new TEllipse(startPt, endPt,
    GetPen()->GetColor(), GetBrush()->GetColor());
}

IMPLEMENT_STREAMABLE1(TEllipse, TGraphTool);

// Read object from stream
void*
TEllipse::Streamer::Read(ipstream& is, uint32) const
{
  ReadBaseObject((TGraphTool *)GetObject(), is);
  return GetObject();
}

// Write object to stream
void
TEllipse::Streamer::Write(opstream& os) const
{
  WriteBaseObject((TGraphTool *)GetObject(), os);
}

// Draw a TEllipse object
void
TEllipse::Draw(TDC& dc)
{
  SelectAttributes(dc);
  dc.Ellipse(startPt, endPt);
```

continues

479

Listing 12.14. continued

```
  DeselectAttributes(dc);
}

// ==============================================================
// TRectangle
// ==============================================================

// Return pointer to TRectangle object clone

TGraphTool *
TRectangle::Clone()
{
  return new TRectangle(startPt, endPt,
    GetPen()->GetColor(), GetBrush()->GetColor());
}

IMPLEMENT_STREAMABLE1(TRectangle, TGraphTool);

// Read object from stream
void*
TRectangle::Streamer::Read(ipstream& is, uint32) const
{
  ReadBaseObject((TGraphTool *)GetObject(), is);
  return GetObject();
}

// Write object to stream
void
TRectangle::Streamer::Write(opstream& os) const
{
  WriteBaseObject((TGraphTool *)GetObject(), os);
}

// Draw a TRectangle object
void
TRectangle::Draw(TDC& dc)
{
  SelectAttributes(dc);
  dc.Rectangle(startPt, endPt);
  DeselectAttributes(dc);
}
```

I've already described most of the stream programming in TOOL.CPP. Because ob-jects of the class are stored in a container object, the abstract class defines the operator function operator==, required by Borland's class templates. In this case, two TGraphTool objects are considered to be equal only if their addresses are the same. (Two distinct objects with the same values, in other words, are not equal.) It's up to you how to implement the operator== function, but this is the simplest approach.

Each graphics tool class—TLine, for example—overrides the pure virtual Draw member function declared in the abstract TGraphTool base class. To draw an image, the program simply calls the Draw function for each object in the image's container.

The program's final two listings declare and implement the TDrawChild class, used to create each child window, and to draw and edit graphics. Listing 12.15, CHILD.H, declares the TDrawChild class. Listing 12.16, CHILD.CPP, implements the class.

Listing 12.15. CHILD.H.

```
// child.h -- TDrawChild header file

#ifndef __CHILD_H
#define __CHILD_H

#if !defined( __CLASSLIB_OBJSTRM_H )
  #include <classlib\objstrm.h>
#endif
#ifndef __MDICHILD_H
  #include <owl\mdichild.h>
#endif
#ifndef __DC_H
  #include <owl\dc.h>
#endif
#ifndef __POINT_H
  #include <owl\point.h>
#endif
#ifndef __CLASSLIB_ARRAYS_H
  #include <classlib\arrays.h>
#endif
#ifndef __CSTRING_H
  #include <cstring.h>
#endif
#ifndef __TOOLS_H
  #include "tools.h"
#endif

// Data file signature stored as first object in .MDW files
#define SIGNATURE "MDIDRAW"

class TDrawChild: public TMDIChild {
public:
```

continues

Listing 12.15. continued

```cpp
  TDrawChild(TMDIClient& parent);  // Default constructor
  TDrawChild(TMDIClient& parent, const char far *name);
  ~TDrawChild();
  void SetPenColor(TColor c)
    { if (currentTool) currentTool->SetPenColor(c); }
  void SetBrushColor(TColor c)
    { if (currentTool) currentTool->SetBrushColor(c); }
  void SaveAsFile();
  void SaveFile();
protected:
  void InitDrawChild();
  virtual BOOL CanClose();
  void ReadDocument();
  int WriteDocument();
  void SetCurrentTool(TGraphTool* p);
  virtual void BeginDragging(TDC& dc, TPoint p);
  virtual void DragMouse(TDC& dc, TPoint p);
  virtual void EndDragging(TDC& dc);
  void EvLButtonDown(UINT modKeys, TPoint& pt);
  void EvMouseMove(UINT modKeys, TPoint& pt);
  void EvLButtonUp(UINT modKeys, TPoint& pt);
  void DrawImage(TDC& dc);
  void Paint(TDC &dc, BOOL erase, TRect& rect);
private:
  BOOL dragging;     // True when clicking and dragging
  TClientDC* cdc;    // Passed to dragging functions
  BOOL fileSaved;    // TRUE if window contents saved
  string fileName;   // File name as a C++ string object
  TIArrayAsVector<TGraphTool> * image;  // The drawing
  TGraphTool* currentTool;  // Current drawing tool
DECLARE_RESPONSE_TABLE(TDrawChild);
};

#endif  // __CHILD_H
```

Listing 12.16. CHILD.CPP.

```cpp
// child.cpp -- TDrawChild implementation

#include <owl\applicat.h>
#include <owl\scroller.h>
#include <owl\opensave.h>
#include <cstring.h>
#include "tools.h"
#include "client.h"
#include "child.h"
```

```
DEFINE_RESPONSE_TABLE1(TDrawChild, TMDIChild)
  EV_WM_LBUTTONDOWN,
  EV_WM_MOUSEMOVE,
  EV_WM_LBUTTONUP,
END_RESPONSE_TABLE;

// Default constructor for File¦New
TDrawChild::TDrawChild(TMDIClient& parent)
  : TMDIChild(parent, "Untitled"),
    fileName("")
{
  InitDrawChild();  // Initialize various members
}

// Alternate constructor for File¦Open
// Throw exception if file cannot be opened
// Because this is a constructor, an exception causes the
// object not to be constructed.
TDrawChild::TDrawChild(TMDIClient& parent, const char far *name)
  : TMDIChild(parent, name),
    fileName(name)
{
  InitDrawChild();
  try {
    ReadDocument();
  }
  catch (const char *msg) {
    delete image;      // Because InitDrawChild creates it
    throw TXOwl(msg);
  }
}

// Destructor
TDrawChild::~TDrawChild()
{
  if (dragging)
    delete cdc;
  delete image;
  delete currentTool;
}

// Constructors call this to initialize objects
void
TDrawChild::InitDrawChild()
{
  dragging = FALSE;
  cdc = 0;
  fileSaved = TRUE;
```

continues

Listing 12.16. continued

```
  Attr.Style = Attr.Style ¦ (WS_VSCROLL ¦ WS_HSCROLL);
  Scroller = new TScroller(this, 1, 1, 200, 200);
  image = new TIArrayAsVector<TGraphTool>(100, 25);
  currentTool = 0;
}

// Save file under a new name
void
TDrawChild::SaveAsFile()
{
  TOpenSaveDialog::TData filenameData(
    OFN_OVERWRITEPROMPT ¦ OFN_PATHMUSTEXIST ¦ OFN_HIDEREADONLY,
    "Draw files (*.mdw)¦*.mdw¦All files (*.*)¦*.*¦¦",
    0, "", "mdw");
  if ((new TFileSaveDialog(this,
    filenameData))->Execute() == IDOK) {
    if (filenameData.Error == 0) { // no error and not cancelled
      string tempName = fileName;
      fileName = filenameData.FileName;
      if (!WriteDocument())
        fileName = tempName;  // Restore original name on error
      SetCaption(fileName.c_str());  // Set title to file name
    }
  }
}

// Unconditionally write document to disk file
void
TDrawChild::SaveFile()
{
  if (fileName.length() == 0)
    SaveAsFile();     // Default to SaveAsFile if file unnamed
  else
    WriteDocument();  // Write to current fileName
}

// Read document from named file.
// Assumes fileName is initialized.
// Throw string exception for file error.
void
TDrawChild::ReadDocument()
{
  ifpstream is(fileName.c_str());
  if (is.bad())
    throw "Can't open file";
  string signature;
  is >> signature;
  if (signature != SIGNATURE)
```

```
    throw "Bad file format";
  unsigned count;
  is >> count;          // Get count of objects in file
  for (unsigned i = 0; i < count; i++) {
    TGraphTool* p;    // Pointer to each tool read from file
    is >> p;            // Read TGraphTool object
    image->Add(p);    // Add object to image collection
  }
}

// Write one graphics object (tool) to file
// Called by WriteDocument.
// Local function. Not a member of TDrawChild.
void WriteTool(TGraphTool& tool, void * os)
{
  *(ofpstream *)os << &tool;
}

// Write document to named file. Closes file after.
// Assumes fileName is initialized.
// Returns TRUE for success; FALSE for failure
int
TDrawChild::WriteDocument()
{
  ofpstream os(fileName.c_str());
  if (os.bad())
    return FALSE;
  string signature(SIGNATURE);
//  string signature("BADFILE");
  os << signature;
  unsigned count = image->GetItemsInContainer();
  os << count;
  image->ForEach(WriteTool, &os);
  fileSaved = TRUE;
  return TRUE;
}

// Change current drawing tool to object addressed by p
void
TDrawChild::SetCurrentTool(TGraphTool* p)
{
  if (currentTool)
    delete currentTool;
  currentTool = p;
}

// Returns TRUE if okay to close this document window
// Gives user the chance to save changes to document.
BOOL
```

continues

485

Listing 12.16. continued

```cpp
TDrawChild::CanClose()
{
  BOOL result;  // Temporary function result

  if (fileSaved)
    result = TRUE;
  else {
    string msg;
    string newline('\n');
    if (fileName.length() == 0)
      msg = "Untitled file";
    else
      msg = fileName;
    msg += newline + "has not been saved.";
    msg += newline + "Save file before closing?";
    int answer = MessageBox(msg.c_str(),
      GetApplication()->GetName(), MB_YESNOCANCEL);
    if (answer == IDCANCEL)
      result = FALSE;       // Abort window close
    else if (answer == IDNO)
      result = TRUE;        // Throw away document changes
    else /* answer == IDYES */ {
      SaveFile();           // Attempt to save file before close
      result = fileSaved;   // True if preceding worked
    }
  }
  if (result)
    result = TMDIChild::CanClose();
  return result;
}

// Start drawing a new object with the current tool
void
TDrawChild::BeginDragging(TDC& dc, TPoint p)
{
  TGraphTool* tool;    // Temporary pointer to graphics object
  TDrawClient* client; // Pointer to child's parent window

  client = TYPESAFE_DOWNCAST(Parent, TDrawClient);
  switch (client->GetSelectedTool()) {
    case LINETOOL:
      tool = new TLine(p, p,
        client->GetPenColor(), client->GetBrushColor());
      break;
    case ELLIPSETOOL:
      tool = new TEllipse(p, p,
        client->GetPenColor(), client->GetBrushColor());
      break;
    case RECTANGLETOOL:
```

```
        tool = new TRectangle(p, p,
          client->GetPenColor(), client->GetBrushColor());
        break;
      default:
        tool = 0;
    }
  SetCurrentTool(tool);
  if (currentTool) {
    ::SetCursor(LoadCursor(0, IDC_CROSS));
    dc.SetROP2(R2_NOTXORPEN);
    currentTool->Draw(dc);
    fileSaved = FALSE;
  }
}

// Continue drawing a new object with the current tool
void
TDrawChild::DragMouse(TDC& dc, TPoint p)
{
  if (currentTool) {
    currentTool->Draw(dc);       // Erase
    currentTool->SetEndPt(p);    // Set new end point
    currentTool->Draw(dc);       // Draw
  }
}

// End drawing a new object with the current tool
void
TDrawChild::EndDragging(TDC& dc)
{
  if (currentTool) {
    currentTool->Draw(dc);       // Erase
    dc.SetROP2(R2_COPYPEN);      // Change drawing mode
    currentTool->Draw(dc);       // Fix in image
    ::SetCursor(LoadCursor(0, IDC_ARROW));
    currentTool->OffsetPoints(Scroller->XPos, Scroller->YPos);
    image->Add(currentTool->Clone());
  }
}

// Respond to WM_LBUTTONDOWN
void
TDrawChild::EvLButtonDown(UINT /*modKeys*/, TPoint& pt)
{
  if (!dragging) {
    cdc = new TClientDC(*this);
    SetCapture();
    dragging = TRUE;
    BeginDragging(*cdc, pt);
```

continues

487

Listing 12.16. continued

```cpp
    }
}

// Respond to WM_MOUSEMOVE
void
TDrawChild::EvMouseMove(UINT /*modKeys*/, TPoint& pt)
{
  if (dragging)
    DragMouse(*cdc, pt);
}

// Respond to WM_LBUTTONUP
void
TDrawChild::EvLButtonUp(UINT /*modKeys*/, TPoint& /*pt*/)
{
  if (dragging) {
    EndDragging(*cdc);
    ReleaseCapture();
    delete cdc;
    cdc = 0;  // So cdc isn't deleted again in destructor
    dragging = FALSE;
  }
}

// Draw one tool (local function called by DrawImage)
// Not a member of TDrawChild
void DrawTool(TGraphTool& tool, void * dc)
{
  tool.Draw(*(TDC *)dc);
}

// Draw all graphics tools stored in this image
void
TDrawChild::DrawImage(TDC& dc)
{
  if (image)
    image->ForEach(DrawTool, &dc);
}

// Draw image in response to a wm_Paint message from Windows
void
TDrawChild::Paint(TDC &dc, BOOL /*erase*/, TRect& /*rect*/)
{
  DrawImage(dc);
}
```

TDrawChild class members handle graphical operations in *MDIDraw* child windows, which also manage each open document. The program's client window constructs TDrawChild objects in response to the *File\New* or *File\Open...* commands. The class therefore needs two constructors. One to create a blank child window initially labeled *Untitled,* and another that opens a named file and displays its contents in a window. Other class functions set brush and pen colors, read and write documents, and respond to mouse movements and left button clicks.

For storing a document's graphical shapes, TDrawChild uses a container class object addressed by a pointer, image. (See the class's private: section in CHILD.H.) The container is constructed using a C++ template with the declaration:

```
TIArrayAsVector<TGraphTool> * image;  // The drawing
```

The image consists of TGraphTool and derived class objects, stored in an array of vectors (pointers). The image pointer addresses the array. To initialize the array, TDrawChild's constructors call an initializing function, InitDrawChild (see CHILD.CPP), which constructs the array container with the statement:

```
image = new TIArrayAsVector<TGraphTool>(100, 25);
```

Initially, the array can hold up to 100 graphics objects, but if more are needed, the array automatically expands by blocks of 25 additional shapes. Two of TDrawChild's main duties are reading and writing graphical shapes stored in the image array. For saving files under new names, function SaveAsFile presents a file-save dialog, similar to the file-open dialog displayed by the client window. (It's appropriate for child windows to perform their own file-saving operations, but because file-open commands create new child windows, the client window must handle those jobs.) The file-save dialog works just like file-open, but has some different options. In this case, for example, I specify OFN_OVERWRITEPROMPT to display a warning that requests permission to overwrite an existing file.

Two other functions, however, take care of the class's real file input and output chores. ReadDocument reads an existing *MDIDraw* document file. WriteDocument writes a document to disk. WriteDocument calls a local function, WriteTool, to write each graphical shape to the file. WriteTool is not a class member.

You examined these functions earlier in the tutorial in C++ file streams, so I won't explain them again. Take a look, though, at how ReadDocument uses C++ exceptions for error handling. If the function cannot open a file, it *throws* an exception:

```
ifpstream is(fileName.c_str());
if (is.bad())
  throw "Can't open file";
```

The thrown object is a string that describes the problem. Throwing an exception immediately ends the function, just as though it had executed a `return` statement, but returning a different type of object—the one thrown. The function throws a different exception if the file doesn't begin with the signature string *MDIFILE:*

```
is >> signature;
if (signature != SIGNATURE)
  throw "Bad file format";
```

In this program, the only way to open a document is to construct a child window using the alternate `TDrawChild` constructor—the one that accepts a file name argument. That constructor, therefore, might fail if `ReadDocument` throws an exception. To guard against that possibility, the constructor calls `ReadDocument` in a `try` block, followed by a `catch` statement for string-exception objects (the type of object that `ReadDocument` throws):

```
try {
  ReadDocument();
}
catch (const char *msg) {
  delete image;      // Because InitDrawChild creates it
  throw TXOwl(msg);
}
```

If `ReadDocument` throws an exception, the `catch` statement deletes the container addressed by `image` (because that container has already been allocated memory), and *rethrows the exception,* this time as an object of the `TXOwl` class, initialized by the string message that `ReadDocument` reported. The constructor, in other words, passes the exception upward in the chain of events that led to the windows construction—but, because the constructor throws an exception, that construction is not completed, and the end result is as though the child window had never been created.

The client window (which attempted to open the document by creating a child window) further handles the exception in another `try` block and `catch` statement (see CLIENT.CPP, function `CmFileOpen`):

```
try {
  cp = new TDrawChild(*this, filenameData.FileName);
}
catch (TXOwl error) {
  MessageBox(error.why().c_str(),
    "Error!", MB_OK | MB_ICONSTOP);
  delete fileDialog;
  return;
}
```

There are a few other interesting sights to see in CHILD.CPP. Function `CanClose` prompts whether to save document changes when you close a window or end the program. The function inspects a `fileSaved` flag, set to `FALSE` if any changes are made to a window's graphical shapes, and to `TRUE` after saving the file. It's important for `CanClose` to call its ancestor function, which takes care of calling any other subwindows owned by this one. (There aren't any such windows in this case, but it's still a good idea to write `CanClose` correctly.) The general rule is: if your `CanClose` will return true, return the ancestor `CanClose` instead, but if your `CanClose` will return false, you may simply return that value (preventing the window from closing) without calling the ancestor function. Here's how `TDrawChild`'s `CanClose` follows that rule (`result` holds the function's temporary return value):

```
if (result)
  result = TMDIChild::CanClose();
return result;
```

Other functions in `TDrawChild` respond to mouse movements and left button clicks, similar to programming you examined elsewhere in this book. (See the files in the RUBBER directory on this book's disk.) The only significant difference here is the way the program stores new graphical shapes. Function `EndDragging`, called when you release the left mouse button after drawing a shape, adds that shape to the image with the statement:

```
image->Add(currentTool->Clone());
```

The container's `Add` function inserts the new object, constructed as a clone of the current drawing tool. Function `Clone` in each `TGraphTool` derived class returns a copy of its own object for insertion in the container array.

Because all graphics shapes are stored in the container, it's a simple matter to redisplay an image. To do that, `TDrawChild`'s `DrawImage` function executes the statements:

```
if (image)
  image->ForEach(DrawTool, &dc);
```

Calling the container's `ForEach` function passes each graphical shape to a local function, `DrawTool`, and also passes the address of the device context object `dc`. `DrawTool` calls the tool's `Draw` function to display individual shapes:

```
tool.Draw(*(TDC *)dc);
```

As a result of all this advance work, the child windows' Paint function (which responds to WM_PAINT messages) has very little to do. TDrawChild's Paint function simply calls DrawImage to display and redisplay graphical documents, no matter how many shapes they contain:

```
DrawImage(dc);
```

Looking Ahead

In this chapter, you learned input and output techniques using file streams for document handling. Many Windows programs also need to generate another kind of output—documents printed on paper. The next chapter explains how to implement printing commands in Windows programs.

13

Printing Text and Graphics

One of the most demanding tasks in any computer system is getting a decent printout. How many times do you select a program's *Print* command and obtain perfect results on the first print run? Probably not often—printing good-looking text and graphics is much harder than it should be.

Windows 3.1 eases the pain of printing by providing device-independent functions in the graphics device interface (GDI). The same commands that display text and graphics on-screen also can print information by directing output to a GDI-compatible printer driver.

Windows comes with a wide variety of standard drivers for dozens of popular printers. Many printer manufacturers and graphics software providers also provide optimized drivers with their products. Because actual printer drivers differ in quality, however, printed results are not always perfectly independent of a specific device's quirks and peculiarities. In general, though, printing in Windows tends to be easier and more reliable than in computer systems without a similar GDI.

In this chapter, you learn:

- How to add *Print...* and *Printer setup...* commands to your Windows programs.
- How to use the TPrinter and TPrintout classes.
- How to print single- and multiple-page documents.
- How to use printer dialogs.

Printer Classes

Writing code that communicates with printer device drivers is one of the most tedious chores you are likely to face in Windows programming. But don't despair. ObjectWindows provides two classes, TPrinter and TPrintout, that completely eliminate the need to use *escape* codes and other archaic techniques explained in Windows programming tutorials for plain C. With the help of C++ classes, you can add printing commands to any program simply by creating a few objects and filling in a couple of functions.

The two classes, TPrinter and TPrintout, provide the capabilities that most programs need for printing commands. This section introduces these two printer classes and their associated header files.

Header Files

Include the PRINTER.H header file in your program's main module, or in any module that uses TPrinter or TPrintout. Use the directive:

```
#include <owl\printer.h>
```

Printer classes make use of some additional symbols, an "abort-printing" dialog box, and a few strings defined in two other files, PRINTER.RH and PRINTER.RC. Include both files in your program's resource script with the directives:

```
#include <owl\printer.rh>
#include <owl\printer.rc>
```

You can also include PRINTER.RH in a program module if you need to refer to symbols defined there as identifiers for the abort-printing dialog and string resources. (In most cases, you don't need to do that.)

Another header file, PRINTDIA.H, declares a common dialog class, TPrintDialog, that you can use to interface with printer setup dialog boxes.

TPrinter

The TPrinter class encapsulates operations provided by Windows printer drivers. In simple terms, you construct an object of the TPrinter class, usually belonging to the program's frame window. (Multiple windows may own their own TPrinter objects, but usually, one object is adequate for the entire program's use.) The TPrinter object displays printer configuration dialogs (provided in part by Windows and in part by the printer driver itself), and it also provides the capabilities for users to configure some aspects of printed output such as resolution, gray scale shading, and landscape (horizontal) or portrait (vertical) page orientations.

> **NOTE**
>
> Specific features depend on the driver selected through a setup dialog or the Windows Control Panel. Simple drivers may have limited features. Sophisticated laser-printer drivers may have many related dialogs that require much study to learn how to use. You don't have to program these dialogs—they are provided by the printer drivers and are activated by the TPrinter class.

To use the TPrinter class, declare a TPrinter* pointer variable in your program's frame window:

```
class TYourWin: public TFrameWindow {
public:
  TYourWin(TWindow* parent, const char far* title);
  ~TYourWin();
// ... Other members
private:
  TPrinter* printer;
};
```

A multiple document interface (MDI) program could declare the printer pointer in the client window class, or each child window could have its own printer. Construct the TPrinter object in the window's constructor:

```
TYourWin::TYourWin(TWindow* parent, const char far* title)
  : TFrameWindow(parent, title),
    TWindow(parent, title)
{
  AssignMenu(ID_MENU);  // ... Plus other initializations
  printer = new TPrinter;
}
```

The TPrinter class constructor requires no parameters. It uses the system's default printer as specified in the WIN.INI initialization file (located in C:\WINDOWS), and modified by the Windows Control Panel. Users can select a different driver though a printer setup dialog, so there's no need to specify which driver to use when constructing the TPrinter object. (Later in the chapter, I explain how to change to a different driver under program control.)

Unlike many classes, TPrinter is not derived from TWindow, and therefore, the constructed object is not automatically deleted when the window closes. The TPrinter object, in other words, is not a child window, and for that reason, it is your responsibility to delete the object in the window's destructor.

```
TYourWin::~TYourWin()
{
  delete printer;
}
```

You may construct multiple TPrinter objects—to provide access to more than one printer, for example. If you need to do that, see "Printer Device Selections" in this chapter for information about how to configure TPrinter objects to use specific drivers. For most applications, one TPrinter object is all you need.

The TPrinter class provides several useful member functions. You can call ClearDevice to reset the printer before starting a print run:

```
printer->ClearDevice();
```

To display a common printer configuration dialog, call the TPrinter class's Setup function, and pass the address of the dialog's parent window (usually it's easiest to pass the C++ this pointer). Use the following statement, usually in a response function for a menu's *Printer setup...* command:

```
printer->Setup(this);
```

Figure 13.1 shows the result of that statement, which constructs and executes an object of the TPrintDialog command-dialog class. The dialog provides users with a list of installed printer drivers, as well as some other specific features such as page orientation and paper size. By selecting the dialog's *Options...* button, users can open the selected driver's configuration dialog (or dialogs), provided by the printer driver software.

To retrieve setup information, call TPrinter's GetSetup function, which returns a reference to the TPrintDialog's nested TData class object. (See section "TPrintDialog" in this chapter for more information on using the common dialog.)

FIGURE 13.1.

Printer configuration dialog.

Print Setup		
Printer		**OK**
⦿ Default Printer		**Cancel**
[currently HP LaserJet Series II on FILE:]		**Options...**
○ Specific Printer:		
HP LaserJet Series II on FILE:		

Orientation: ⦿ Portrait ○ Landscape

Paper — Size: Letter 8 1/2 x 11 in Source: Upper Tray

TPrinter's most important function, Print, does exactly what you might expect—it prints a document by directing GDI output statement in your program to the selected printer. How that works, however, requires you to first examine the class that provides those output operations, TPrintout, described next.

TPrintout

An object of the TPrintout class represents a printed document—that is, it encapsulates the commands needed to print a document's text and graphics. In general terms, in an object of the TPrintout class, you insert statements to draw your document on a printer device, similar to the way you program a TWindow or a derived class's Paint function to display text and graphics on-screen. In fact, you can use the *identical* output statements in both instances—as a later example shows. But you still need a TPrintout document to represent the printed form of your program's information.

To print a document, you construct an object of a class derived from TPrintout. Derive your class like this:

```
class TYourPrintout: public TPrintout {
public:
  TYourPrintout(TWindow* window, const char* title);
protected:
  void PrintPage(int page, TRect& rect, unsigned flags);
private:
  TWindow* parentWindow;
};
```

At a minimum, the derived class needs a constructor and a replacement for function PrintPage, inherited from TPrintout. Optionally, define a pointer to a TWindow object so you can refer to the window that created the TYourPrintout object. Implement the constructor by calling the ancestor TPrintout constructor and saving the parent window object's address:

```
TRulerPrintout::TRulerPrintout(
  TWindow* window, const char* title)
  : TPrintout(title)
{
  parentWindow = window;
}
```

By saving the parent window's address, `PrintPage` can simply call the window's `Paint` function to print a window's contents:

```
void
TRulerPrintout::PrintPage(
  int /*page*/, TRect& rect, unsigned /*flags*/)
{
  parentWindow->Paint(*DC, FALSE, rect);
}
```

The `TPrinter` class object calls the `TPrintout` class's `PrintPage` function for each page to be sent to the printer device. This simple example ignores the page number and `flags` arguments passed to `PrintPage`, but passes the second argument `rect`, which defines the output area, to `Paint`. The `DC` argument passed to `Paint` is the printer's device context, and passing that context to `Paint` directs output to the printer rather than its normal window destination.

After laying the groundwork, you are ready to create a print command response function. In your function, to print a document, simply pass your `TPrintout` derived class object to the `TPrinter` object's `Print` function:

```
TYourPrintout printout(this, "Your Printout");
printer->Print(this, printout, TRUE);
```

The `this` argument gives the printout object the address of the parent window object, The `TPrintout` object also needs a name (used by the printer driver or the Windows Print Manager to queue up multiple print jobs). You can name the printout anything you like, but if the information comes from a file, the disk file name would be a better choice than *Your Printout*. Pass the `TPrintout`-derived class object to the `TPrinter` object's `Print` function. Also pass the window object's address (`this`), and `TRUE` if you want users to be prompted with the setup dialog shown in Figure 13.2 before printing begins. Change `TRUE` to `FALSE` if you don't want users to see this dialog before printing—if, for example, your program executes the same dialog via another menu command. (See the next section for more on this topic.)

`TPrintout` has a number of other functions that you meet later in this chapter. For simple print jobs, however, the preceding steps will help you add printing commands to your programs with a minimum of work.

FIGURE 13.2.

Pre-printing setup dialog.

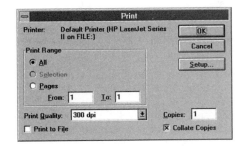

TPrintDialog

For sophisticated print jobs, you might want to provide a separate *Printout configuration...* command (you can call it something else). The command provides users with a standard method for selecting pages to print and for configuring other aspects of printed output. You still need a *Printer setup...* command, which configures the printer *device*. A *Printout configuration...* command selects options related to a document, but also gives access to printer hardware features.

> **NOTE**
>
> There's considerable overlap among the various dialogs that configure printed output and printer device drivers. To lessen confusion, instruct users that the *Printer setup...* command is strictly for selecting hardware features, and that *Printout configuration...* is mostly for selecting document-related items.

Follow these steps to display a printout configuration dialog. First, define any variables you need in your window's class. For example, you might keep `fromPage` and `toPage` variables to represent a range of pages that users want to print:

```
class TAnyWin: public TFrameWindow {
public:
  TAnyWin(TWindow* parent, const char far* title);
private:
  int fromPage, toPage;
};
```

Initialize the variables in the class constructor. In another function, perhaps one that responds to a *Print configuration...* menu command, initialize a `TPrintDialog::TData` structure for use by the dialog:

```
TPrintDialog::TData printData;
printData.Flags = PD_ALLPAGES;
printData.FromPage = fromPage;
printData.ToPage = toPage;
```

Construct the dialog object, and pass the window's address (this) and the TData structure:

```
TPrintDialog* printDialog
  = new TPrintDialog(this, printData);
```

Execute the dialog by calling the Execute member function. If that function returns IDOK, extract the setup information you need from the TData structure:

```
if (printDialog->Execute() == IDOK) {
  fromPage = printData.FromPage;
  toPage = printData.ToPage;
}
```

Refer back to Figure 13.2 for a sample of the dialog's display. This is the same dialog displayed when you pass TRUE to the TPrinter class's Print function. Use the preceding techniques only if you want a separate menu command to bring up the dialog.

Don't forget to delete the dialog object when you're done with it:

```
delete printDialog;
```

Single-Page Printouts

You've studied a lot of new information in the preceding sections, so let's review the required steps to print graphics and text. After that, I list a sample application that puts the techniques into practice.

Required Steps

Keep in mind that the goal in printing under Windows is to achieve true device independence. Write your program's display output functions first, then use those *same* functions to print. Always pass TDC object references, and call GDI functions for those objects. That way, other functions can direct output to a window (by using a TClientDC class, for example) or to the printer (by using TPrintDC).

To add printing capabilities to any program, you need to:

● Include the PRINTER.H header file.

- Derive a class from `TPrintout` and provide a replacement `PrintPage` function. The function may call the parent window's `Paint` or another output function.

- Declare a `TPrinter` pointer in your window's class (usually the program's frame window or the client window in MDI applications).

- Construct an object of the `TPrinter` class and assign the object's address to the `TPrinter` pointer. Most often, you can use `TPrinter` as provided—you do not need to derive a class from it.

- Delete the `TPrinter` object in your window's constructor. The object is not a child window, and therefore, you must delete it before the window closes.

- Provide a *Printer setup...* command, which can simply call the `TPrinter` class's `Setup` function for configuring the printer device, or selecting a different device.

- Optionally provide a *Print configuration...* command that displays a `TPrintDialog` common dialog box. Include the PRINTDIA.H header if you use this method.

- To print, construct an object of your `TPrintout`-derived class (the one that replaces `PrintPage`). Pass this object to the `TPrinter` class's `Print` function.

Sample Application

The next three listings implement the preceding printing techniques in a sample program that displays and prints a 6-inch ruler. On-screen, the ruler may or may not appear true to scale, depending on how well your system's display driver implements the display-mapping methods that the program uses. On some screens, the ruler may be smaller than real size; on others, it may be larger. Consider yourself lucky if the results match perfectly! On paper, however, the ruler should be close to real-life measurements—if, that is, your printer driver is working correctly.

Listing 13.1, RULER.RH, lists the program's resource identifiers. Listing 13.2, RULER.RC, lists the program's resource script. Listing 13.3, RULER.CPP, lists the program's source code. I explain more about the program after the listings. Figure 13.3 shows the program's display.

FIGURE 13.3.
RULER's display.

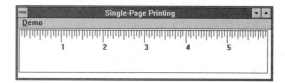

Listing 13.1. RULER.RH.

```
// ruler.rh -- Resource header file

#define ID_MENU   100
#define CM_PRINT 101
#define CM_PRINTERSETUP 102
```

Listing 13.2. RULER.RC.

```
#include <owl\window.rh>
#include <owl\printer.rh>
#include "ruler.rh"
#include <owl\printer.rc>

ID_MENU MENU
BEGIN
  POPUP "&Demo"
  BEGIN
    MENUITEM "&Print...", CM_PRINT
    MENUITEM "P&rinter setup...", CM_PRINTERSETUP
    MENUITEM SEPARATOR
    MENUITEM "E&xit", CM_EXIT
  END
END
```

Listing 13.3. RULER.CPP.

```
/* ============================================================ *\
** ruler.cpp -- Demonstrates single-page printing            **
** ============================================================ **
**                                                              **
** ============================================================ **
**       Copyright (c) 1994 by Tom Swan. All rights reserved.   **
```

```
\* ============================================================ */

#include <owl\applicat.h>
#include <owl\framewin.h>
#include <owl\printer.h>
#include <owl\scroller.h>
#include <owl\dc.h>
#include <classlib\stacks.h>
#include <string.h>
#include <cstring.h>
#include <stdio.h>
#pragma hdrstop
#include "ruler.rh"

// ============================================================
// Printout class (represents printed document)
// ============================================================

class TRulerPrintout: public TPrintout {
public:
  TRulerPrintout(TWindow* window, const char* title);
protected:
  void PrintPage(int page, TRect& rect, unsigned flags);
private:
  TWindow* parentWindow;
};

// Constructor
TRulerPrintout::TRulerPrintout(
  TWindow* window, const char* title)
  : TPrintout(title)
{
  parentWindow = window;
}

// Print pages of document (there's only one page in this case)
void
TRulerPrintout::PrintPage(
  int /*page*/, TRect& rect, unsigned /*flags*/)
{
  parentWindow->Paint(*DC, FALSE, rect);
}

// ============================================================
// The application's main window
// ============================================================

class TRulerWin: public TFrameWindow {
public:
```

continues

Listing 13.3. continued

```cpp
    TRulerWin(TWindow* parent, const char far* title);
    ~TRulerWin();
protected:
    BOOL StackEmpty()
        { return stack.IsEmpty(); }
    void Line(int x1, int y1, int x2, int y2)
        { dc->MoveTo(x1, y1); dc->LineTo(x2, y2); }
    void Rectangle(int left, int top, int right, int bottom)
        { dc->Rectangle(left, top, right, bottom); }
    void TextAt(int x, int y, const char *s)
        { dc->TextOut(x, y, s, strlen(s)); }
    void InchRuler(int xOutline, int yOutline, int numInches);
    void Ruler(int l, int r, int h, int level);
    void Push(int l, int r, int m, int h, int level);
    void Pop(int& l, int& r, int& m, int& h, int& level);
    void CmPrint();
    void CmPrinterSetup();
    void Paint(TDC& paintDC, BOOL erase, TRect& rect);
private:
    TPrinter* printer;      // Printer-device object pointer
    TDC* dc;                // Device context for member functions
    int unitsPerInch;       // Display scale
    int numDivisions;       // Number of ruler marker divisions
    int largeMarkerSize;    // Size of main markers at labels
    int smallMarkerIncr;    // Size of sub marker increments
    int smallMarkerSize;    // Size of largest sub marker
    int left, top, right, bottom;  // Ruler outline coordinates
    TStackAsVector<int> stack;     // Push-down stack
DECLARE_RESPONSE_TABLE(TRulerWin);
};

DEFINE_RESPONSE_TABLE1(TRulerWin, TFrameWindow)
    EV_COMMAND(CM_PRINT, CmPrint),
    EV_COMMAND(CM_PRINTERSETUP, CmPrinterSetup),
END_RESPONSE_TABLE;

// Constructor
TRulerWin::TRulerWin(TWindow* parent, const char far* title)
    : TFrameWindow(parent, title),
      TWindow(parent, title)
{
// Window initializations
    AssignMenu(ID_MENU);
    Attr.Style |= WS_VSCROLL | WS_HSCROLL;
    Scroller = new TScroller(this, 1, 1, 2000, 2000);
// Constant initializations
    dc = 0;                 // Set pointer to null
    unitsPerInch = 100;     // 1 pixel == 1/100 inch
    numDivisions = 4;       // Recursion level (i.e. to 1/16-inch)
```

```
    smallMarkerIncr = 4;   // In units per inch (i.e. 0.04 inch)
    left = top = right = bottom = 0;   // Ruler coordinates
// Position dependent initializations
    smallMarkerSize =      // Size of largest sub marker
      smallMarkerIncr + (smallMarkerIncr * numDivisions);
    largeMarkerSize =      // Size of markers at digit labels
      smallMarkerSize + (smallMarkerIncr * 2);
// Create printer interface object
    printer = new TPrinter;
}

// Destructor
TRulerWin::~TRulerWin()
{
  delete printer;
}

// Print window contents
void
TRulerWin::CmPrint()
{
  if (printer) {
    TRulerPrintout printout(this, "Ruler");
    printer->Print(this, printout, TRUE);
  }
}

// Display printer setup dialog
void
TRulerWin::CmPrinterSetup()
{
  if (printer)
    printer->Setup(this);
}

// Draw ruler markings on device context dc at coordinate (l,r)
// and with a submarker height of h. The function is a
// nonrecursive adaptation of a recursive ruler algorithm,
// described in my June 1994 Dr. Dobb's column, Algorithm Alley.
// The level parameter controls the recursion (which is
// controlled internally by this version of the function).
void
TRulerWin::Ruler(int l, int r, int h, int level)
{
  int m;
  Push(l, r, 0, h, level);   // 0 == m, which is uninitialized
  while (!StackEmpty()) {
    Pop(l, r, m, h, level);
    while (level > 0) {
```

continues

Listing 13.3. continued

```
      if (h <= 0)
        throw "Levels incomplete";
      m = (l + r) / 2;
      Line(m, -top, m, -(top + h));
      h -= smallMarkerIncr;
      level--;
      Push(m, r, m, h, level);
      r = m;
    }
  }
}

// Draw ruler with all its miscellaneous parts--a border,
// digit labels, and so on.
void
TRulerWin::InchRuler(int xOutline, int yOutline, int numInches)
{
  int i;      // For-loop control variable
  int x, y;   // Working coordinate variables
  char s[4];  // Holds ruler digits in text form

// Initialize and draw ruler outline
  left = xOutline;
  top = yOutline;
  right = left + (numInches * unitsPerInch);
  bottom = top + (largeMarkerSize * 3);
  Rectangle(left, -top, right, -bottom);
// Label main ruler markers at every inch
  y = top + largeMarkerSize;
  x = left;
  for (i = 1;  i < numInches; i++) {
    x += unitsPerInch;
    Line(x, -top, x, -y);
    sprintf(s, "%d", i);
    TextAt(x, -y, s);
  }
// Call Ruler() function to display ruler markings
  x = left;
  for (i = 0; i < numInches; i++) {
    try {
      Ruler(x, x + unitsPerInch, smallMarkerSize, numDivisions);
    }
    catch (const char *msg) {
      throw TXOwl(msg);
    }
    x += unitsPerInch;
  }
}
```

```
// Push integer arguments onto stack
void
TRulerWin::Push(int l, int r, int m, int h, int level)
{
  stack.Push(l);
  stack.Push(r);
  stack.Push(m);
  stack.Push(h);
  stack.Push(level);
}

// Pop integer arguments from stack
void
TRulerWin::Pop(int& l, int& r, int& m, int& h, int& level)
{
  level = stack.Pop();
  h = stack.Pop();
  m = stack.Pop();
  r = stack.Pop();
  l = stack.Pop();
}

// Respond to WM_PAINT messages
void
TRulerWin::Paint(TDC& paintDC, BOOL /*erase*/, TRect& /*rect*/)
{
  dc = &paintDC;   // Address paintDC with object's private dc

// Initialize device context
  dc->SaveDC();
  dc->SetMapMode(MM_LOENGLISH);
  InchRuler(3, 3, 6);   // x == 3, y == 3, length = 6 inches

// Restore changes made to device context
  dc->RestoreDC();
}

// ============================================================
// The application class
// ============================================================

class TRulerApp: public TApplication {
public:
  TRulerApp(const char far* name)
    : TApplication(name) {}
  void InitMainWindow();
};

// Initialize the program's main window
```

continues

507

Listing 13.3. continued

```
void
TRulerApp::InitMainWindow()
{
  EnableCtl3d();  // Use Windows 3D controls and dialogs
  MainWindow = new TRulerWin(0, "Single-Page Printing");
}

#pragma argsused

// Main program
int
OwlMain(int argc, char* argv[])
{
  TRulerApp app("RulerApp");
  return app.Run();
}
```

Class TRulerPrintout, derived from TPrintout, represents the program's printed document. By "document," in this case, I mean the sample ruler displayed in the window. The TRulerPrintout constructor saves its parent window's address in a private TWindow pointer named parentWindow. The class also replaces function PrintPage, inherited from TPrintout.

That function in its base class performs no operations, but is called by other functions to print each page of a document. Your implementation of PrintPage (as demonstrated in the TRulerPrintout class) does not need to call the base class function. Instead, simply call your window's function that generates output by calling GDI functions in reference to a device context. Usually, the easiest solution is to call the window's Paint function as shown here.

The application's main window, TRulerWin, derived from TFrameWindow, declares a TPrinter pointer, named printer, initialized in the class constructor and deleted in its destructor. The TRulerWin class also provides two menu-command response functions—CmPrint and CmPrinterSetup—plus a Paint function that displays and prints the sample ruler.

Function CmPrint, called when you select the *Demo\Print...* command, constructs an object of the TRulerPrintout class, and then passes that object to the TPrinter class Print function. The first argument to that function represents the parent window's address (this). The second parameter is the TRulerPrintout object. The third is TRUE to display a printer configuration dialog before printing.

Function CmPrinterSetup displays a printer setup dialog to configure features in the printer device driver. As I mentioned, this dialog differs among different drivers.

Finally in RULER is the heart of the program—the function, Paint, that prints and displays the window's contents. There's nothing new in the function—it simply calls various GDI commands in reference to the passed device context. If that context refers to a window, output appears on-screen. If it refers to a printer device, output is directed to that device.

One final note: If you want your dialogs to look like those printed in this chapter, call EnableCtl3d in the application's InitMainWindow function. This gives the dialogs a shaded background and a "chiseled steel" appearance to its controls. For a plain Window dialog with a white background and two-dimensional controls, delete the EnableCtl3d statement.

Multiple-Page Printouts

Although printing and displaying text and graphics are similar—you call the same GDI functions to do both—two concerns complicate printing:

- Printer output is nonrandom. On-screen, you can display part of a graphical shape in the lower left corner, move to another location, and display something else. On the printer, all output is generated in lines from top to bottom.

- Paper sizes limit output size. On-screen, you have one large "sheet of paper" on which you can display graphics anywhere within a window's maximum dimensions. On the printer, you must divide your output into pages.

The TPrinter class automates the first concern. Just replace your TPrintout-derived class's PrintPage function (called by the TPrinter object) and draw your graphics as you do when displaying them. Output is automatically buffered and sent to the printer in serial fashion. Output can also be further sectioned into *bands,* which can conserve memory on supporting devices by sending portions of full pages to the printer, a process called *banding.*

The second concern, however, requires more work to conquer. When printing multiple-page documents, your program must determine the printer's page size, calculate the number of pages in a document (whatever that means to your application), and determine how much of that document to print on a given page. These facts complicate the job of writing a PrintPage function.

Required Steps

Printing a multipage document is similar to printing only one page, but you need to add some additional programming to your TPrintout derived class. In general terms, you need to perform these extra steps:

- Prepare information for the *Print* dialog optionally displayed before printing begins.
- Determine how many pages your document requires.
- Optionally enable banding to conserve memory.
- Output a selected page of graphics or text.
- Indicate when all pages have been printed.

To handle the first concern—preparing dialog information—replace this function in your TPrintout derived class:

```
void GetDialogInfo(int& minPage, int& maxPage,
  int& selFromPage, int& selToPage);
```

The function sets the minimum and maximum page ranges, and also indicates selected pages, displayed in the *Print* dialog. Implement the dialog something like this (assume that pagesToPrint equals the total number of document pages):

```
void
TYourPrintout::GetDialogInfo(int& minPage, int& maxPage,
 int& selFromPage, int& selToPage)
{
  minPage = 1;
  maxPage = pagesToPrint;
  selFromPage = minPage;
  selToPage = maxPage;
}
```

Handle the second concern—determining how many pages your document requires—by replacing another function in your TPrintout derived class, declared as:

```
void SetPrintParams(TPrintDC* dc, TSize pageSize);
```

The dc parameter refers to the selected printer device. The pageSize parameter equals the size in printer units (dots on a dot matrix printer, for example) of one page. Use this information to calculate how many pages your document requires and to prepare any other variables you need during printing.

As originally designed, ObjectWindows is supposed to call `GetDialogInfo` *after* calling `SetPrintParams`. Apparently, however, due to last-minute changes to the `TPrinter` class, that order is reversed, and consequently, `GetDialogInfo` cannot use the number of pages calculated in `SetPrintParams`. Also, setting the dialog's minimum and maximum page values does not properly initialize the *Print* dialog's `TData` object, causing the page values not to show up properly in the dialog. Later in this chapter, I show temporary workarounds for these problems, which we can only hope will be repaired in a future ObjectWindows release.

You might also want to enable *banding*, mostly so you can print large bitmaps on dot-matrix printers with limited memory. With banding enabled, Windows sends portions of printed output in horizontal chunks, called *bands*, in place of entire pages. The minimum band size is a single printer scan line—the maximum band size is a full page. Not all printers support banding. Many laser printers, for example, must have enough memory to form an entire page before printing. If you attempt to send the printer more data than the printer's memory can hold, printing will fail. The only solution in that event is to add more memory to the printer's page buffer. Banding will not help.

Windows automatically bands output to supporting printers, but you can gain better control over the process using the techniques described here. You might want to do that, for example, to size each band yourself—to prevent, for instance, a band's border from cutting through a line of text, which might produce output problems on some types of printers. To enable banding, add this public function to your `TPrintout` class:

```
void EnableBanding() { Banding = TRUE; }
```

The `Banding` flag is a protected member of the `TPrintout` class, and for that reason, it can be changed only by a member function such as `EnableBanding`. Call that function after constructing your `TPrintout` object, and before calling the `TPrinter` class's `Print` function:

```
TYourPrintout printout("Your Document");
printout.EnableBanding();
printer->Print(this, printout, TRUE);
```

> **TIP**
>
> Not all printers support banding, but you can safely ignore that fact and enable banding for all devices. The TPrinter class uses banding, whether enabled or not, only if the selected printer supports this feature. Banding, however, is disabled by default.

The fourth new concern for multipage printing is how to print a selected page. You must do this in your replacement PrintPage function, which every TPrintout derived class requires. The function, declared as follows, receives three parameters that you can use to print a selected page:

```
void PrintPage(int page, TRect& rect, unsigned flags);
```

Parameter page equals the page to be printed. Your function should output only the information on this page. Parameter rect equals the dimensions of the banding rectangle. Parameter flags contains the bit settings pfGraphics (if the current band accepts graphics), pfText (if the current band accepts text), or pfBoth (if the current band accepts graphics and text). In most cases, you can use the page parameter and ignore the other two PrintPage parameters, but you can use the extra banding information to limit output to a specific band on a page.

Dealing with the fifth and final multipage concern—indicating whether all pages have been printed—is the easiest of all. Just replace the inherited TPrintout function, HasPage, with your own version:

```
BOOL HasPage(int pageNumber);
```

Parameter pageNumber equals the number of the page that will next be printed. HasPage should return TRUE if there are any pages not yet printed. The function should return FALSE if pageNumber indicates that all pages have not been printed. Assuming your TPrintout class contains a variable, pagesToPrint, equal to the total number of pages to print in the document (or the highest page number in a selected range), you can write HasPage as follows:

```
BOOL
TListPrintout::HasPage(int pageNumber)
{
  return pageNumber <= pagesToPrint;
}
```

Sample Application

The TPrinter class's Print function calls your TPrintout object's PrintPage function for each of the document's pages. Writing a successful multipage PrintPage function depends largely on how well you prepare your document and related variables, a process best shown by example, as demonstrated by the following listings.

The program, WLIST, is similar to the program of that name in Chapter 6. The revised program, located on this book's disk in directory WPRINT, adds *Print...* and *Printer setup...* commands to the *File* menu. Because most of the program is listed in Chapter 6, I list only the new programming here. The complete listings are, of course, on the book's disk.

Listing 13.4, WLIST.RH, adds identifiers for the program's menu resource.

Listing 13.4. WLIST.RH.

```
// wlist.rh -- Resource header file

#define ID_MENU 100
#define CM_FILE_OPEN 101
#define CM_FILE_PRINT 102
#define CM_FILE_SETUP 103
```

Listing 13.5, WLIST.RC, adds printing commands to the *File* menu. The resource script includes the PRINTER.RH resource header file and also the PRINTER.RC script file, provided with BC4 in the INCLUDE\OWL directory. If you don't include these files, printing will fail with an error message when the TPrinter class object attempts to display the *Print* dialog box.

Listing 13.5. WLIST.RC.

```
#include <owl\window.rh>
#include <owl\printer.rh>
#include "wlist.rh"

#include <owl\printer.rc>

ID_MENU MENU
BEGIN
  POPUP "&File"
  BEGIN
```

continues

Listing 13.5. continued

```
    MENUITEM "&Open...", CM_FILE_OPEN
    MENUITEM SEPARATOR
    MENUITEM "&Print...", CM_FILE_PRINT
    MENUITEM "Printer &setup...", CM_FILE_SETUP
    MENUITEM SEPARATOR
    MENUITEM "E&xit", CM_EXIT
  END
END
```

Finally, Listing 13.6, WLIST.CPP, shows the new programming that implements printing for this text-file lister. As I mentioned, I show only the new additions here. Ellipses in the listing show sections already listed and explained in Chapter 6. (For reference, and to make the listing easier to read, I duplicated a few lines here and there—the OwlMain function, for example.)

Listing 13.6. WLIST.CPP (partial).

```
/* =============================================================== *\
**  wlist.cpp -- list and print text files                       **
** =============================================================== **
**  This is the same program found in directory WLIST, but       **
**  with Print... and Printer setup... commands in the File      **
**  menu. Demonstrates multipage printing.                       **
** =============================================================== **
**      Copyright (c) 1994 by Tom Swan. All rights reserved.     **
\* =============================================================== */

#include <owl\applicat.h>
#include <owl\framewin.h>
#include <owl\color.h>
#include <owl\dc.h>
#include <owl\gdiobjec.h>
#include <owl\scroller.h>
#include <owl\opensave.h>
#include <owl\printer.h>
#include <classlib\arrays.h>
#include <classlib\stdtempl.h>
#include <stdio.h>
#include <cstring.h>
#include <string.h>
#include <mem.h>
#pragma hdrstop
#include "wlist.h"
#include "wlist.rh"
```

```
// =============================================================
// Printout class (represents printed document)
// =============================================================

class TListPrintout: public TPrintout {
public:
  TListPrintout(const char* title, int rows,
    TIArrayAsVector<string>& sArrayRef,
    TPrinter* printer);
  ~TListPrintout();
  void EnableBanding() { Banding = TRUE; }
protected:
  BOOL HasPage(int pageNumber);
  void PrintPage(int page, TRect& rect, unsigned flags);
  void GetDialogInfo(int& minPage, int& maxPage,
    int& selFromPage, int& selToPage);
  void SetPrintParams(TPrintDC* dc, TSize pageSize);
private:
  int numRows;             // Total number of rows in document
  TFont* pfont;            // Pointer to printer font
  int glyphH;              // Character glyph height
  int rowSep;              // Units separation between text rows
  int pagesToPrint;        // Number of printed pages
  int linesPerPage;        // Lines to print on each page
  TIArrayAsVector<string>& sa;  // Reference to string array
  TPrintDialog::TData& Data;    // Reference to dialog data
};

// Constructor
TListPrintout::TListPrintout(
  const char* title, int rows,
  TIArrayAsVector<string>& sArrayRef,
  TPrinter* printer)
  : Data(printer->GetSetup()),
    sa(sArrayRef),
    TPrintout(title)
{
  numRows = rows;     // Save number of rows from parent window

// Initialized prior to each print run
  pfont = 0;
  glyphH = 0;
  rowSep = 0;
  pagesToPrint = 0;
  linesPerPage = 0;
}

// Destructor
TListPrintout::~TListPrintout()
{
```

continues

515

Listing 13.6. continued

```cpp
  delete pfont;
}

// Returns false if pageNumber is the last page, ending
// the print run after printing that page
BOOL
TListPrintout::HasPage(int pageNumber)
{
  return pageNumber <= pagesToPrint;
}

// Print pages of document
void
TListPrintout::PrintPage(
  int page, TRect& /*rect*/, unsigned /*flags*/)
{
  int x, y, row;
  const char* cp;

// Calculate starting and ending lines for this page
// Print lines from string array (sa)
  int startRow = (page - 1) * linesPerPage;
  int endRow = min(numRows, startRow + linesPerPage) - 1;
  for (row = startRow; row <= endRow; ++row) {
    x = 0;
    y = (rowSep + glyphH) * (row - startRow);
    cp = sa[row]->c_str();
    DC->TextOut(x, y, cp, strlen(cp));
  }

// The following function demonstrates a bug in ObjectWindows
// which is supposed to call SetPrintParams BEFORE GetDialogInfo.
// Since the number of pages to print aren't known until
// after SetPrintParams calculates the correct figure,
// GetDialogInfo is unable to list a correct maximum page number
// value. For that reason, I set maxPage to 999, but the
// preceding statement would be correct if GetDialogInfo were
// called AFTER SetPrintParams as it should be.

// Called prior to printing.
// Initializes print dialog parameters.
void
TListPrintout::GetDialogInfo(int& minPage, int& maxPage,
 int& selFromPage, int& selToPage)
{
  minPage = 1;
//  maxPage = pagesToPrint;  // pagesToPrint is not initialized!!
  maxPage = 999;             // Use literal value instead
  selFromPage = minPage;
```

```
    selToPage = maxPage;

// Temporary fix to above problem. Required to make page
// range show up correctly in dialog.
    Data.FromPage = minPage;
    Data.ToPage = maxPage;
}

// Called prior to printing.
// Initializes document parameters.
void
TListPrintout::SetPrintParams(TPrintDC* dc, TSize pageSize)
{
    TEXTMETRIC tm;        // Text (font) information

// Call ancestor function (required!)
    TPrintout::SetPrintParams(dc, pageSize);

// Delete old font if previously created. Create printer font
    if (pfont)
        delete pfont;
    int yUnits = dc->GetDeviceCaps(LOGPIXELSY);
    pfont = new TFont(
        "Courier New",
        -::MulDiv(FONT_POINTSIZE, yUnits, 72),
        0, 0, 0,
        FW_NORMAL,
        FIXED_PITCH,
        FALSE, FALSE, FALSE,
        ANSI_CHARSET,
        OUT_TT_PRECIS,
        CLIP_DEFAULT_PRECIS,
        PROOF_QUALITY
    );

// Select font into printer device context
    dc->SelectObject(*pfont);

// Calculate height of one line
    dc->GetTextMetrics(tm);
    glyphH = tm.tmHeight;
    rowSep = tm.tmExternalLeading;

// Calculate number of lines per page and pages to print
    linesPerPage = max(1, pageSize.cx / (glyphH + rowSep));
    pagesToPrint = max(1, numRows / linesPerPage);
    if (linesPerPage < numRows && numRows % linesPerPage != 0)
        pagesToPrint++;  // Add one for last partial page
}
```

continues

517

Listing 13.6. continued

```cpp
// ============================================================
// The application's main window
// ============================================================

class TListWin: public TFrameWindow {
public:
  TListWin(TWindow* parent, const char far* title,
    BOOL autoOpen);
  ~TListWin();
protected:
...
  void CmFilePrint();
  void CmFileSetup();
...
private:
  TIArrayAsVector<string> sArray;  // Array of string objects
...
  TPrinter* printer;   // Printer-device object pointer
DECLARE_RESPONSE_TABLE(TListWin);
};

DEFINE_RESPONSE_TABLE1(TListWin, TFrameWindow)
  EV_WM_SIZE,
  EV_WM_KEYDOWN,
  EV_COMMAND(CM_FILE_OPEN, CmFileOpen),
  EV_COMMAND(CM_FILE_PRINT, CmFilePrint),
  EV_COMMAND(CM_FILE_SETUP, CmFileSetup),
END_RESPONSE_TABLE;

// Constructor
TListWin::TListWin(TWindow* parent, const char far* title,
  BOOL autoOpen)
  : TFrameWindow(parent, title),
    TWindow(parent, title),
    sArray(SARRAY_HIGH, SARRAY_LOW, SARRAY_DELTA),
    filenameData(OFN_FILEMUSTEXIST|OFN_PATHMUSTEXIST,
      "All files (*.*)|*.*|Text files (*.txt)|*.txt|",
      0, "", "*")
{
...
  printer = new TPrinter;
...
}

// Destructor
TListWin::~TListWin()
{
...
```

```
    delete printer;
}

...

// Print file
void
TListWin::CmFilePrint()
{
  if (numRows == 0) return;  // Exit if nothing to print
  if (printer) {
    TListPrintout printout(filename->c_str(), numRows,
      sArray, printer);
//    printout.EnableBanding();  // Optional
    printer->Print(this, printout, TRUE);
  }
}

// Display printer setup dialog
void
TListWin::CmFileSetup()
{
  if (printer)
    printer->Setup(this);
}

...

#pragma argsused

// Main program
int
OwlMain(int argc, char* argv[])
{
  TListApp app("WList");
  return app.Run();
}
```

The TListPrintout class, derived from TPrintout, is completely new to the program. The class has a constructor, a destructor, and a public function, EnableBanding, that sets the inherited Banding flag to true. To provide access to the *Print* dialog's TData object, the class constructor requires a pointer to the TPrinter object owned by the parent window. The constructor uses that pointer to call the TPrinter class's GetSetup function, which returns a reference to the TData object. The reference is saved in a private variable, declared as:

```
TPrintDialog::TData& Data;    // Reference to dialog data
```

519

Also passed to the constructor is a reference to the data array that stores a file's text lines. The TListPrintout constructor stores this reference in a variable, sa, declared as:

```
TIArrayAsVector<string>& sa;  // Reference to string array
```

The TListPrintout class also replaces the inherited HasPage, PrintPage, GetDialogInfo, and SetPrintParams functions for the reasons given in the preceding section. In addition, the class declares several private variables used during printing.

Function HasPage returns FALSE after the last page has been printed. As written, the function requires pagesToPrint to equal the total number of pages in the document.

Skip PrintPage for now, and turn to function GetDialogInfo, which is preceded by a comment that complains about a bug in ObjectWindows. As I mentioned, GetDialogInfo is supposed to be called *after* SetPrintParams, but is in fact, called before. For this reason, it is not possible for GetDialogInfo to use the page information calculated in SetPrintParams. To work around that problem, you can set maxPage to a high value such as 999 as I do here. (You could also write an initialization function similar to SetPrintParams that calculates the number of pages in your document, or if that information is already available, use the correct figure here.)

A second bug fails to pass the minPage and maxPage information to the dialog. To do that, insert the values in the Data object's FromPage and ToPage variables as shown at the end of the sample GetDialogInfo.

Function `SetPrintParams` determines several facts about the document being printed, and also initializes some base class variables. Always call the ancestor `TPrintout` function as shown here. After that step, the example function creates a font to be used during printing. That font's characteristics depend on the currently selected printer, referenced by the passed device context, `dc`. Compare the programming here with that used to prepare a font for on-screen display (see the WLIST.CPP listing in Chapter 6 or on the book's disk). The programming is different, but the resulting fonts are configured for their respective output devices.

`SetPrintParams` continues by selecting the prepared font into the printer's device context. The function then performs a number of calculations to determine the height of one text line, and from that, the number of lines on one page. These statements resemble the kind of programming needed to optimize scrolling, also demonstrated by WLIST, by limiting the number of lines displayed in the window's `Paint` function. In fact, writing printer functions requires much of the same kind of effort, but rather than using scrolling units, you deal with pages and bands.

Return now to function `PrintPage`, which precedes `GetDialogInfo`. The function calculates the line numbers, `startRow` and `endRow`, of each line to print on the specified page, using the `linesPerPage` value initialized by `SetPrintParams`. With these values, it's a simple matter to print the correct lines by calling the GDI `TextOut` function in reference to the printer device context. That context, `DC`, is a protected member of the `TPrintout` class—any derived class function may therefore access `DC` directly as shown here.

> **NOTE**
>
> WLIST doesn't show how to print graphical shapes, but the steps are no different from printing text. To draw shapes on a printed page, simply call the GDI functions you need—`Rectangle`, for example, or `Ellipse`—in reference to the `DC` printer device context.

Special Printing Techniques

There are a few other printing techniques you might need in special circumstances, described in the following sections.

Device Capabilities

Of all the pieces of hardware you can purchase for a computer, printers offer the widest variety of features. Not all printers, however, support the same capabilities. A plotter, for example, cannot print a bitmap.

If your program needs a particular printer features, or if you need to determine facts about a printer such as its page size, call the GetDeviceCaps function (*Caps* stands for *Capabilities*). The function returns various flag values that tell you all sorts of facts and figures about a printer device. Actually, the function works with any device for which you can create a device context, but the steps for using GetDeviceCaps with printer contexts are more complicated than for display contexts. First include the DC.H, PRINTER.H, and PRINTDIA.H header files:

```
#include <owl\dc.h>
#include <owl\printer.h>
#include <owl\printdia.h>
```

Next, construct a TPrinter object (or, you can use the one you create for a window object):

```
TPrinter* printer = new TPrinter;
```

The TPrinter object contains a nested-class TPrintDialog::TData object that you can use to construct the printer device context. Do that with this statement:

```
TPrintDC* dc = new TPrintDC(
  printer->GetSetup().GetDriverName(),
  printer->GetSetup().GetDeviceName(),
  printer->GetSetup().GetOutputName(),
  printer->GetSetup().GetDevMode());
```

The GetSetup calls return a reference to the TPrinter object's TData class structure. Calling the GetDriverName, GetDeviceName, and GetOutputName functions for that structure obtains the default printer information from WIN.INI required by the TPrintDC context. For example, the three functions might return these strings:

```
"HPPCL"
"HP LaserJet Series II"
"FILE:"
```

The GetDevMode function, also called for the printer's nested-class TData structure, returns a pointer to a DEVMODE structure, defined by Windows (look it up in BC4's API reference or online help). The structure contains over a dozen additional fields that describe a device's capabilities.

After constructing the TPrintDC object, you can use it to call GetDeviceCaps. For example, this statement obtains the printer driver's version number:

```
int version = dc->GetDeviceCaps(DRIVERVERSION);
```

To determine the type of device, pass TECHNOLOGY to GetDeviceCaps in a statement such as this:

```
int technology = dc->GetDeviceCaps(TECHNOLOGY);
```

The result in technology equals one of the following values:

```
DT_PLOTTER      Vector plotter
DT_RASDISPLAY   Raster display
DT_RASPRINTER   Raster printer
DT_RASCAMERA    Raster camera
DT_CHARSTREAM   Character stream
DT_METAFILE     Metafile
DT_DISPFILE     Display file
```

A *Raster printer* can print a bitmap, but a *Vector plotter* cannot. Pass the constant RASTERCAPS to GetDeviceCaps, and use the resulting value to determine whether a selected printer can handle your program's text and graphics printing requirements.

To determine the output device's horizontal and vertical resolutions—for calculating how much information to output in a PrintPage function, for example—call GetDeviceCaps as follows:

```
int horzres = dc->GetDeviceCaps(HORZRES);
int vertres = dc->GetDeviceCaps(VERTRES);
```

Look up other GetDeviceCaps parameters in BC4's API references and online help. Don't forget to delete the device context and printer pointers when you are done using them:

```
delete dc;
delete printer;
```

Printout Initializations

When you call your TPrinter object's Print function to start printing, you still have two more opportunities to perform special initializations before printing actually begins. The TPrintout class provides two functions, BeginPrinting and BeginDocument that you can use to perform initializations at different stages of printing. The corresponding EndPrinting and EndDocument functions can perform deinitializations after printing.

Print calls the printout's BeginPrinting function one time before starting to print one or more copies of a document. It calls EndPrinting after printing all copies of a document.

Print calls the printout's BeginDocument function one time before starting to print *each* copy of a document. It calls EndDocument after printing each copy.

Replace these functions in your TPrintout-derived class. The inherited functions are placeholders that contain no statements. You don't have to call the ancestor functions. They are declared in TPrintout as:

```
virtual void BeginPrinting();
virtual void BeginDocument(int startPage, int endPage, unsigned flags);
virtual void EndDocument();
virtual void EndPrinting();
```

Three of the functions receive no parameters. BeginDocument receives three values indicating the starting and ending page numbers and any banding flags. You can ignore these values, or use them to configure your document's output in some special fashion. (For example, when printing a limited page range, you might save time by preparing output only for those pages.)

Page Order

Normally, pages print in sequential order, from low page numbers to high. In some instances, it might be advantageous to exercise better control over the order in which pages are printed. You could, for example, print all even numbered pages before odd ones, print pages in reverse order, or collate multiple copies in some special way.

Use the BeginDocument and EndDocument functions in the TPrintout class to alter page order. As I mentioned in the preceding section, BeginDocument receives three parameters:

```
virtual void BeginDocument(int startPage, int endPage, unsigned flags);
```

Use the startPage and endPage variables to prepare a table or other structure that translates page numbers to those you want. For example, for a page number range of 4 through 8, the table could reverse page order:

```
Printout   Translated
Page       Page
4          8
5          7
6          6
7          5
8          4
```

Next, in your `PrintPage` function, when you receive a request to output page 5, for example, you actually print page 7. When `PrintPage` receives a request for page 8, you actually output page 4.

Use `EndDocument`, called after printing each copy of a document, to undo any structures (deleting dynamic memory allocations, for instance) that you prepare in `BeginDocument`.

Printer Device Selections

In most programs, you can use the default printer selection for output. Users can run the Windows Control Panel to install and configure their printers—you don't have to provide any special configuration code. Also, the *Print* dialog permits selecting among installed printers.

If your program needs better control over output device selections, you can prepare specific printer devices by following the notes in this section. You might need to do this to support more than one printer without requiring users to switch among them. Or, you can force a program to use a printer other than the default—so, for example, text output normally goes to a dot matrix, but your program's high-resolution graphics print on a color laser device without requiring reconfiguration with the Control Panel.

As you've learned in this chapter, constructing a `TPrinter` object normally selects the default output device:

```
TPrinter* printer = new TPrinter;
// ... use printer
delete printer;
```

To permit users to select their own printer in a `TPrintDialog` box, use this alternate code:

```
TPrinter* printer = new TPrinter;
printer->Setup(this);
// ... use selected printer
delete printer;
```

To use a specific printer other than the default, call the `TPrinter` class's `SetPrinter` function. Because the function is a protected member of the class (it probably should have been made public), you can't call it directly as you can `Setup`. Instead, derive a new class from `TPrinter`:

```
class TLaserPrinter: public TPrinter {
public:
  TLaserPrinter();
};
```

In your class's constructor, call `SetPrinter`:

```
TLaserPrinter::TLaserPrinter()
  : TPrinter()
{
  SetPrinter("HPPCL", "HP LaserJet Series II", "LPT1:");
}
```

Then, construct a object of your class and use it as you do a default `TPrinter` object:

```
TLaserPrinter* laser = new TLaserPrinter;
// ... use special printer
delete laser;
```

Looking Ahead

Dynamic Link Libraries (DLLs), the subject of the next chapter, provide shared resources and functions to programs. You've already used several DLLs to enable Windows 3D controls, and to display Borland Custom Controls. In fact, most of Windows is stored in DLL form—a DLL is just a common module that other programs can share. In the next chapter, you learn how to write your own object-oriented DLLs.

14

CHAPTER

Using and Creating Dynamic Link Libraries

A dynamic link library (DLL) provides resources and functions that one or more programs can share. DLLs conserve memory by consolidating common subroutines into a single module rather than linking multiple copies of those subroutines into each program that needs them. DLLs also can provide resources (bitmaps, string tables, and so on) for sharing among multiple applications. Typical DLLs include custom control libraries, specialized child windows, function and resource libraries.

In this chapter, you learn:

- How to use a DLL in a Windows program.
- How to write your own object-oriented DLLs.
- How to export a class from a DLL.
- How to create a resource-only DLL.
- How to use resource DLLs to write multinational software.

How To Use a DLL

In general terms, to use the functions and resources stored in a DLL (usually in a file named with the extension .DLL), your program needs to *import* the DLL's components. You probably also need to include a header file that identifies elements in the DLL.

In straight C programming, to use a DLL, call the Windows LoadLibrary function to load a DLL by its filename. The function returns an instance handle to the loaded library, or a value less than HINSTANCE_ERROR (defined in WINDOWS.H as 32) if it cannot load the library successfully:

```
HINSTANCE hInstance;
hInstance = ::LoadLibrary(filename);
if (hInstance <= HINSTANCE_ERROR)
  throw "Unable to load library";
```

When done using the library, call FreeLibrary to unload the library from memory:

```
FreeLibrary(hInstance);
```

After loading a library, you can retrieve the addresses of library functions by name. For example, if the library has an integer function named IntFunction (you get the name from the library's documentation or a header file), first define a pointer to that function:

```
int (FAR *lpfnIntFunction)(double d1, double d2);
```

Then, locate the function's address in the DLL by calling the Windows GetProcAddress function, passing the DLL's instance handle and function name as arguments:

```
(FARPROC)lpfnIntFunction =
  GetProcAddress(hInstance, "IntFunction");
```

You can then call the function by using the address assigned to the function pointer, lpfnIntFunction.

In ObjectWindows programs, there's a better way to accomplish these same tasks with an instance of the TModule class—but more on that later. First, let's review some of the DLL's you've already used in this book's sample programs.

Custom Control DLLs

BC4 comes with an updated version of Borland's Window Custom Controls, stored in the BWCC.DLL dynamic link library file. Installing BC4 copies this file, plus several related files (and a 32-bit version in BWCC32.DLL) to your WINDOWS\SYSTEM directory. Loading a BWCC library makes custom buttons, checkboxes, radio boxes, shaded boxes, separators, and other items available to windows, dialogs, and to Resource Workshop.

> **TIP**
>
> I store a copy of BWCC.DLL as BWCC.BC4 in case other programs overwrite the DLL with an earlier version. You must use the newest release of this library with BC4 and with all BC4-developed applications.

Windows 3.1 supplies a similar control library in CTL3D.DLL, or for 32-bit applications, in CTL3D32.DLL. Loading a CTL3D library makes better-looking message box and standard controls (pushbuttons, checkboxes, and so on) available to programs.

> **NOTE**
>
> Future releases of Windows will incorporate the CTL3D library (or an updated, compatible version), replacing old style controls and dialogs—those with white backgrounds and plain buttons. You can make your programs more compatible with future Windows releases by using the CTL3D library now.

To use the Borland Windows Custom Control and Windows 3D control libraries in 16- and 32-bit applications, add these statements to your application's InitMainWindow function:

```
EnableCtl3d();
EnableBWCC();
```

The ObjectWindows DLL

BC4 also comes with all of its standard, class, and runtime libraries in static and DLL forms. Use the *TargetExpert* dialog to select among these libraries—select the program's .EXE code filename in the IDE's project window, click the right mouse button (or press Alt+F10), and select the resulting popup menu's **T**argetExpert... command. Choose the *Standard Libraries* that you need (**O**WL, **C**lass Library, **R**untime, or **B**WCC). To use DLL forms of these libraries, select the **D**ynamic radio button. To use static forms, select the **S**tatic button.

Static libraries are linked into your program's code file, which grows accordingly in size. This option is the most convenient because every subroutine your program uses is contained in its .EXE code file. Unfortunately, however, those subroutines are for your program's private use—another program cannot call them. Thus, if you run three programs with static-linked libraries, three copies of the library subroutines are loaded into memory, wasting space.

Dynamic libraries are linked at runtime, making it possible for two or more programs to share the *same* copies of the library's subroutines and resources. Only one copy of those libraries is loaded into memory for all programs to share, conserving memory. The only disadvantage is a slightly longer load time for the first application that loads the DLL.

> **NOTE**
>
> If you distribute dynamic-linked applications, be sure to provide the necessary BWCC.DLL, OWL.DLL, and related files to your customers. To make sure your program will run correctly on other systems, close the BC4 IDE before testing, which unloads any of these libraries used by the IDE.

The *TModule* Class

The easiest way to load and use a DLL is to construct an instance of the TModule class, declared in MODULE.H. The class encapsulates the operations and data for all Windows code files, including executable applications and DLLs. As you know from most of this book's sample programs, an application is embodied in an object of the TApplication class. That class is derived from TModule.

For easy access to a DLL's components, define a global static pointer to an object of the TModule class in your program's source file. Initialize the pointer to null (because it's a global variable, it is initialized to zero anyway, but the following form makes that fact perfectly clear):

```
static TModule* dllPointer = 0;
```

Construct the TModule object by passing its constructor the DLL's filename. Usually, the best place to do this is in the program's OwlMain function as demonstrated here for a fictitious library named YOURLIB.DLL:

```
int
OwlMain(int argc, char* argv[])
{
  dllPointer = new TModule("yourlib.dll");
  TYourApp app("YourApp");
  int ret = app.Run();
  delete dllPointer;
  return ret;
}
```

If the DLL cannot be loaded, Windows displays an error message and halts the program. All DLLs that an application uses must be loaded and initialized without error before Windows allows the application to run.

> **NOTE**
>
> Supply only the DLL's filename, without drive or path information. Windows searches for DLL's in the following places and in this order:
>
> 1. The current directory.
>
> 2. The Windows directory that contains WIN.COM (for example, C:\WINDOWS).
>
> 3. The Windows system directory (for example, C:\WINDOWS\SYSTEM).
>
> 4. The directory that contains the executable file for the current task (for example, the directory where you store the program's .EXE code file).
>
> 5. All directories listed in the DOS PATH environment variable.
>
> 6. Directories mapped by a network.

Functions in your application and window classes can call functions exported from the DLL as though those functions were global to the application. In other words, if the DLL provides a function `Calculate`, your program can simply call that function the same way it calls functions defined in the program—that is, by referring to the function by its name in a statement:

```
result = Calculate(data1, data2);
```

The BC4 linker automatically creates and links all the necessary elements required to import DLL functions—you don't need to create definition files, procedure addresses, or fuss with other low-level concerns that you would otherwise need in plain C.

Also, because the DLL is encapsulated in a `TModule` object, you can call the `TModule` class's member functions to perform operations on the DLL. For example, to obtain the DLL's instance handle (perhaps needed to call a Windows API function), use the statement:

```
HINSTANCE dllInstance = dllPointer->GetInstance();
```

To determine whether a DLL is loaded, call `IsLoaded`:

```
if (dllPointer->IsLoaded)
  doSomethingWithDll();
```

You can load a resource of any type by calling the `TModule` `FindResource` and `LoadResource` functions, which operate the same as the global Windows API functions of those names (look them up in your API printed and online references). It's easier, however, to use other `TModule` functions to load resources of specific types. For example, this loads a bitmap stored as a resource in a DLL and identified by `ID_BITMAP`:

```
HBITMAP hBitmap = dllPointer->LoadBitmap(ID_BITMAP);
```

The result is a handle to the bitmap element. To construct a `TBitmap` class object from that element, pass the handle to the `TBitmap` constructor:

```
TBitmap* bmp = new TBitmap(hBitmap);
```

You can then use the `bmp` pointer to access the bitmap as a class object rather than as a standard Windows element identified by a handle. This technique creates a class-object *alias* for the bitmap element, but also introduces a potential problem that you must consider. The question is: Should the element be deleted from memory when you delete the object? For example, when you are done using the bitmap, you delete its pointer:

```
delete bmp;
```

That statement deletes the `TBitmap` object that `bmp` addresses. You must also decide, however, whether that statement should delete the original bitmap element that you used to construct the class object. Normally, class object aliases do *not* perform this service because they assume that, as aliases, they are mere interfaces for existing elements created and deleted by some other process.

For example, if you obtain a bitmap handle from a DLL (or from any process or task), you can construct the `TBitmap` object like this:

```
TBitmap* bmp = new TBitmap(hBitmap);
```

Deleting `bmp` leaves the element intact because alias objects do not normally delete their associated elements. To delete *both* the object and its element requires two steps:

```
delete bmp;  // Delete object
::DeleteObject(hBitmap);  // Delete element
```

If instead, you want the object to delete the element, you may construct the object using this alternate form:

```
TBitmap* bmp = new TBitmap(hBitmap, AutoDelete);
```

Constructed like that, the object automatically deletes its associated element when you delete the object or when that object goes out of scope. Constructed with only a bitmap handle, the object does not delete its associated element. The following two statements are equivalent:

```
TBitmap* bmp = new TBitmap(hBitmap);
TBitmap* bmp = new TBitmap(hBitmap, NoAutoDelete);
```

Include the GDIBASE.H header file (included automatically by including GDIOBJEC.H) to define the AutoDelete and NoAutoDelete enumerated constants:

```
enum TAutoDelete { NoAutoDelete, AutoDelete };
```

You must take similar pains to construct class-object aliases for other types of resources such as menus and cursors, which a DLL also can provide. Be sure to consider carefully whether the object should delete its initializing element, or whether the program should do that by calling DeleteObject.

How To Create a DLL

There has been a lot of information published on how to write DLLs using the C language. In fact, you can find entire books on this subject, which is too extensive to cover completely in a single chapter. For these reasons, I concentrate here on the less-well-known techniques of writing *object-oriented* DLLs that export classes. By using this method, you construct DLLs by writing class objects as you normally do. You then program your application to import and use those objects, call member functions, access object data elements, and so on. This approach greatly simplifies DLL design and construction.

Sample Application

The next set of listings demonstrate how to write a DLL, how to export a class from a DLL, and how to import and use that class in an application. The sample DLL provides a bitmap window that any application can use to display bitmaps in child windows. The DLL encapsulates all of the operational details concerning loading the bitmap, creating and using window scrollers, and responding to WM_PAINT and WM_SIZE messages. The result is a finished, easy-to-use *bitmap engine* that multiple programs can share.

You can use similar techniques to create other DLL engines—to compress data, for example, or for database work. The key is to create useful classes that applications import as interfaces to the DLL's functions and data members. To better understand the steps required for accomplishing these goals, it's helpful to convert an an existing application to DLL form. The following listings are therefore based on the DRAWBIT program listed in Chapter 8.

Starting with that program's main window class, I created the TBitWin class declared in Listing 14.1, DLLWIN.H. The DLL and application (both listed later in this chapter) include this same header to declare the class, derived from TWindow. (The original class was derived from TFrameWindow because it served as the program's main window. The new class serves as a child-window interface, and is therefore derived from TWindow.)

> **NOTE**
>
> All listings in this section are stored on the book's disk in directory DLLBIT.

Listing 14.1. DLLWIN.H.

```
// dllwin.h -- DLL TBitWin header file

#ifndef __DLLWIN_H
#define __DLLWIN_H

#if defined(MWP_DLL)
  #define _MWPCLASS _export
#elif defined(MWP_APP)
  #define _MWPCLASS _import
#else
  #define _MWPCLASS
#endif

class _MWPCLASS TBitWin: public TWindow {
public:
  TBitWin(TWindow* parent, const char far* title, TModule* mod);
  ~TBitWin();
protected:
  void AdjustScrollers();
  virtual void Paint(TDC& dc, BOOL erase, TRect& rect);
```

```
    void EvSize(UINT sizeType, TSize& size);
private:
  TBitmap* bitmap;
DECLARE_RESPONSE_TABLE(TBitWin);
};

#endif  // __DLLWIN_H
```

The DLLWIN.H header file defines the symbol __DLLWIN_H to prevent the header from being recompiled in case multiple files include it more than once. The header file also recognizes two externally defined symbols, MWP_DLL and MWP_APP. When compiling the DLL module, include the header with these directives:

```
#define MWP_DLL      // Compile DLL
#include "dllwin.h"
```

In the header, upon detecting that MWP_DLL is defined (the symbol doesn't have to be assigned any value), the header defines another symbol, _MWPCLASS (for *Mastering Windows Programming Class*) as equivalent to the BC4 symbol, _export.

To include this same class in an application that uses the DLL, the application module includes the header using these directives:

```
#define MWP_APP      // Compile application
#include "dllwin.h"
```

This time, the header defines _MWPCLASS as equivalent to the BC4 symbol _import. If neither MWP_DLL nor MWP_APP is defined, the header defines _MWPCLASS as equivalent to nothing. You can use this third alternative in an application that doesn't use the DLL, but declares the class and implements the class's member functions—a test program, for example, used for developing the DLL's subroutines.

The result of these definitions is a class, TBitWin, that is declared three different ways. The class declaration specifies the _MWPCLASS symbol after the class keyword:

```
class _MWPCLASS TBitWin: public TWindow {...
```

When compiling the DLL module, because _MWPCLASS is equivalent to _export, the class is declared as:

```
class _export TBitWin: public TWindow {...
```

When compiling an application that uses the DLL, because _MWPCLASS is equivalent to _import, the class is declared as:

```
class _import TBitWin: public TWindow {...
```

In cases where _MWPCLASS is defined as equivalent to nothing, the class is declared as:

```
class TBitWin: public TWindow {...
```

In every case, the class declaration remains the same, but the _import and _export BC4 symbols instruct the compiler and linker to configure the generated code differently. In the DLL, the compiler and linker export the class name and all public function members so an application can use them. In the application, the compiler and linker import the class functions so you can call them in reference to a class object. You use the class as you do any other, but its members' code reside in the DLL, and can therefore be shared by two or more applications that load the DLL as a TModule instance.

> **NOTE**
>
> DLLs have a global data segment, but they use the application's stack. For that reason, it's usually best to limit a DLL's global data and to create any large structures dynamically with the new operator.

After declaring the class, implement the DLL module as you do any other module to be combined in an application. Listing 14.2, DLLWIN.CPP, provides implementations for the class member functions declared in DLLWIN.H. The module needs no special programming, but you must compile it as explained at the end of this section.

Listing 14.2. DLLWIN.CPP.

```
/* ============================================================ *\
**   dllwin.cpp -- Create a Window with bitmap in a DLL        **
** ============================================================ **
**                                                              **
** ============================================================ **
**      Copyright  1994 by Tom Swan. All rights reserved.       **
\* ============================================================ */

#include <owl\applicat.h>
#include <owl\framewin.h>
#include <owl\dc.h>
#include <owl\gdiobjec.h>
#include <owl\scroller.h>
#pragma hdrstop

#define MWP_DLL          // Exports class from DLL
#include "dllwin.h"      // Include class declaration
```

```
// ================================================================
// The bitmap window
// ================================================================

DEFINE_RESPONSE_TABLE1(TBitWin, TWindow)
  EV_WM_SIZE,
END_RESPONSE_TABLE;

// Constructor
TBitWin::TBitWin(TWindow* parent, const char far* title,
  TModule* mod)
  : TWindow(parent, title, mod)
{
  Attr.Style |= WS_POPUPWINDOW | WS_CAPTION | WS_THICKFRAME |
                WS_VSCROLL | WS_HSCROLL |
                WS_MINIMIZEBOX | WS_MAXIMIZEBOX;
  Attr.X = GetSystemMetrics(SM_CXSCREEN) / 8;
  Attr.Y = GetSystemMetrics(SM_CYSCREEN) / 8;
  Attr.H = Attr.Y * 6;
  Attr.W = Attr.X * 6;
  TDib* pdib = new TDib(title);        // Load DIB file
  bitmap = new TBitmap(*pdib);         // Convert DIB to DDB bitmap
  delete pdib;                         // Done with DIB, so delete it
  Scroller = new TScroller(this,
    1, 1, bitmap->Width(), bitmap->Height());
}

// Destructor
TBitWin::~TBitWin()
{
  delete bitmap;
}

// Paint or repaint window contents
// Scrolling is automatic
void
TBitWin::Paint(TDC& dc, BOOL /*erase*/, TRect& /*rect*/)
{
  TMemoryDC memdc(dc);
  memdc.SelectObject(*bitmap);
  dc.BitBlt(0, 0,
    bitmap->Width(), bitmap->Height(), memdc, 0, 0, SRCCOPY);
}
```

continues

537

Listing 14.2. continued

```
// Respond to WM_SIZE message
// Limit scroller ranges to window and bitmap sizes
void
TBitWin::EvSize(UINT sizeType, TSize& size)
{
  TWindow::EvSize(sizeType, size);
  AdjustScrollers();
}

// Adjust horizontal and vertical scroller ranges
void
TBitWin::AdjustScrollers()
{
  TRect tr;    // Rectangle for client area dimensions
  long H, W;   // Document size minus window in display units

  GetClientRect(tr);
  W = bitmap->Width() - (tr.right - tr.left);
  H = bitmap->Height() - (tr.bottom - tr.top);
  Scroller->SetRange(W / Scroller->XUnit, H / Scroller->YUnit);
  SetScrollPos(SB_HORZ, (int)Scroller->XPos, TRUE);
  SetScrollPos(SB_VERT, (int)Scroller->YPos, TRUE);
}
```

Compare DLLWIN.CPP with the DRAWBIT.CPP listing in Chapter 8. The two listings are nearly identical, but the DLL version has a few subtle and important differences. First, the module includes the DLLWIN.H header after defining MWP_DLL This ensures that the TBitWin class is declared with the _export symbol:

```
#define MWP_DLL
#include "dllwin.h"
```

The DLLWIN module defines a response table for the class, just as in an application. Using response tables greatly simplifies message handling in DLLs—another good reason to use C++ classes in constructing your libraries.

The TBitWin constructor changes the window attributes used in the original example from Chapter 8. Because the class will be used to construct child windows, it initializes its attribute styles with the statement:

```
Attr.Style |= WS_POPUPWINDOW | WS_CAPTION | WS_THICKFRAME |
             WS_VSCROLL | WS_HSCROLL |
             WS_MINIMIZEBOX | WS_MAXIMIZEBOX;
```

The class also assigns position and size values to the Attr structure's X, Y, H, and W variables.

The rest of the listing is the same as it is in the original example. By using C++ classes, you write DLLs in nearly the same way you write modules that are linked statically into executable code files.

Next, you can write an application, sometimes called the *host* program, that uses the DLL to create bitmap child windows. For completeness, I list every source file for the sample application, which you can use as a guide to writing your own DLL host programs.

Listing 14.3, DLLAPP.DEF, provides linker information for the application. This file is the same as the default .DEF files used by most of this book's example programs. I include the file here, however, to point out that no similar .DEF file is needed for the DLL module (it would be needed in plain C). BC4's linker can construct DLLs without a definition file.

Listing 14.3. DLLAPP.DEF.

```
EXETYPE WINDOWS
CODE PRELOAD MOVEABLE DISCARDABLE
DATA PRELOAD MOVEABLE MULTIPLE
HEAPSIZE 4096
STACKSIZE 5120
```

Listing 14.4, DLLAPP.RH, defines the application's resource identifiers. The only resource is a menu, identified as ID_MENU, with a single command, identified as CM_TEST.

Listing 14.4. DLLAPP.RH.

```
// bitapp.rh -- Resource header file

#define ID_MENU 100
#define CM_TEST 101
```

Listing 14.5, DLLAPP.RC, defines the application's resources in script form. As I mentioned, the only resource is a menu, which uses the identifiers from DLLAPP.RH.

Listing 14.5. DLLAPP.RC.

```
#include <owl\window.rh>
#include "dllapp.rh"

ID_MENU MENU
BEGIN
  POPUP "&Demo"
  BEGIN
    MENUITEM "&Test", CM_TEST
    MENUITEM SEPARATOR
    MENUITEM "E&xit", CM_EXIT
  END
END
```

The application's header file, Listing 14.6, DLLAPP.H, defines the filename for a sample bitmap. You can change the bitmap name and directory if you want. (I use a relative path to refer to the DATA subdirectory on this book's disk.)

Listing 14.6. DLLAPP.H.

```
// bitapp.h -- Header file for bitapp.cpp

#define FILENAME "..\\data\\picture.bmp"
```

Finally, Listing 14.7, DLLAPP.CPP, lists the host program's source code. The listing demonstrates how to write an application that uses a DLL to import a class, in this case, to create one or more child windows. You can also write multiple applications similar to DLLAPP.CPP that use the *same* DLL module, sharing the TBitWin class member functions. Notes after the listing explain how the program works. I also give hints for compiling the DLL and application. Figure 14.1 shows the program's window with three bitmap child windows managed by the DLL. (For simplicity, the sample program uses the same bitmap for all windows, but it could just as easily open different bitmap files.)

FIGURE 14.1.
DLLAPP's display with three bitmap child windows.

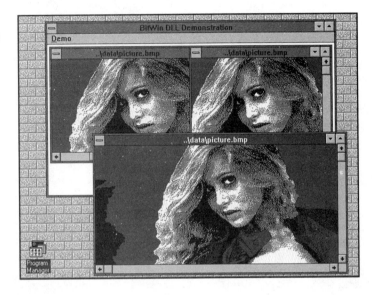

Listing 14.7. DLLAPP.CPP.

```
/* ============================================================ *\
** dllapp.cpp -- Use dllwin DLL to display bitmaps             **
** ============================================================ **
**                                                             **
** ============================================================ **
**      Copyright  1994 by Tom Swan. All rights reserved.      **
\* ============================================================ */

#include <owl\module.h>
#include <owl\applicat.h>
#include <owl\framewin.h>
#include <owl\dc.h>
#include <owl\gdiobjec.h>
#include <owl\scroller.h>
#pragma hdrstop

#include "dllapp.h"
#include "dllapp.rh"

#define MWP_APP          // Imports class from DLL
#include "dllwin.h"       // Include class declaration

static TModule* bitWinDll = 0;
```

continues

Listing 14.7. continued

```cpp
// =============================================================
// The application's main window
// =============================================================

class TBitAppWin: public TFrameWindow {
public:
  TBitAppWin(TWindow* parent, const char far* title);
protected:
  void CmTest();
DECLARE_RESPONSE_TABLE(TBitAppWin);
};

DEFINE_RESPONSE_TABLE1(TBitAppWin, TFrameWindow)
  EV_COMMAND(CM_TEST, CmTest),
END_RESPONSE_TABLE;

// Constructor
TBitAppWin::TBitAppWin(TWindow* parent, const char far* title)
  : TFrameWindow(parent, title),
    TWindow(parent, title)
{
  AssignMenu(ID_MENU);
}

// Test command (calls DLL to create child window)
void
TBitAppWin::CmTest()
{
  TBitWin* bitwin =
    new TBitWin(this, FILENAME, GetApplication());
  if (bitwin) bitwin->Create();
}

// =============================================================
// The application class
// =============================================================

class TBitApp: public TApplication {
public:
  TBitApp(const char far* name)
    : TApplication(name) {};
  void InitMainWindow();
};

// Initialize the program's main window
void
TBitApp::InitMainWindow()
{
```

```
  MainWindow = new TBitAppWin(0, "BitWin DLL Demonstration");
}

#pragma argsused

// Main program
int
OwlMain(int argc, char* argv[])
{
  bitWinDll = new TModule("dllwin.dll");
  TBitApp app("BitApp");
  int ret = app.Run();
  delete bitWinDll;
  return ret;
}
```

In most respects, the DLLAPP.CPP application file resembles a normal ObjectWindows application. It differs, however, in its use of the DLLWIN.DLL dynamic link library to construct child windows for displaying bitmaps. To create those windows, the application includes the TBitWin class declaration using these directives:

```
#define MWP_APP
#include "dllwin.h"
```

Defining the MWP_APP symbol compiles the class with the BC4 _import symbol, which instructs the compiler and linker that the class's members are external to the program and will be linked at runtime from the DLL. The DLL and application use the *same* class declaration, modified only by the _import and _export symbols.

The application also defines a static TModule pointer, bitWinDll, for addressing the BITWIN dynamic link library as a TModule object. Skip to the end of the listing where OwlMain loads the DLL, and initializes the bitWinDll pointer, with the statement:

```
bitWinDll = new TModule("dllwin.dll");
```

In the first application that uses DLLWIN.DLL, that statement loads and initializes the library, constructs the TModule object, and assigns the object's address to bitWinDll. In subsequent applications, the statement constructs new and distinct TModule objects, but uses the existing copy of the DLL in memory. Only one copy of a DLL's resources, data, and code are loaded into memory. (A 32-bit DLL, however, receives separate global data segments, one for each host program that uses the DLL. 16-bit DLLs have only a single shared data segment.)

543

Turn to the CmTest function, which responds to the program's **D**emo|**T**est command, for an example of how to use the imported TBitWin class. The function constructs a child window, opened to a bitmap file, with the statements:

```
TBitWin* bitwin =
  new TBitWin(this, FILENAME, GetApplication());
if (bitwin) bitwin->Create();
```

Because the child window might be opened for different applications, I pass function GetApplication's result to the constructor's TModule pointer parameter in addition to the usual parent window object's address (this) and the window's title, which in this example is set equal to the bitmap's filename. Also, because the program creates the child window after the parent object has been created, I call the resulting window's Create function to create an associated window element for the object. This step also displays the window.

> **NOTE**
>
> You may run two or more instances of the sample application, demonstrating how multiple programs can share the same DLL.

How To Compile the Sample Application

To compile the sample application, open the program's project file, DLLAPP.IDE (in the DLLBIT directory on the book's disk) using the BC4 IDE's **P**roject|**O**pen project... command. Press F9 to compile both the DLL and application code files. You can then run the application's .EXE file using the File or Program Managers. (You can also run the program by pressing Ctrl+F9 in the IDE, but you may run only one instance with that method.)

The DLLAPP.IDE file demonstrates how to create a multiple-target project, necessary in this case to compile the two separate code files. You could compile the code files separately, but when developing your own DLLs, you'll probably write a test host program anyway, so it's easiest to create a multiple-target project and compile that program along with the DLL. To learn the proper steps, follow these suggestions to recreate the sample program's project file:

1. Copy all .DEF, .CPP, .H, .RH, and .RC files from the book-disk's DLLBIT directory to a new, empty directory.

2. Close any open project in the IDE, then select the **P**roject|**N**ew project... command.

3. Select the resulting dialog box's **B**rowse... button, and change to the directory to which you copied the program's files. Enter **dllapp** into the *File* **N**ame input box, then select *OK* to close the browsing dialog.

4. Check that *Target Type* is set to *Application [.exe]*, and that *Platform* equals *Windows 3.x (16)*. Also select *Large* for the *Target* **M**odel, check (turn on) the **O**WL, **C**lass Library, and **R**untime Standard Libraries, and select **D**ynamic just below those names. Some or all of these options may already be selected.

5. Close the *New Project* dialog box by selecting the OK button, which creates the application's project file. You should see files DLLAPP.EXE (the target) and the files on which the target depends: DLLAPP.CPP, DLLAPP.RC, and DLLAPP.DEF, in the project window.

6. To that project, you next have to add a second target for the DLL. Highlight the DLLAPP.EXE line in the project window, then select the IDE's **P**roject*New* **t**arget... command, which displays a *New Target* dialog box.

7. Enter **dllwin.dll** into the dialog box's **T**arget Name input box. Then, select the *OK* button. Once again, you see the same dialog box in which you configured the application's code file. This time, however, the dialog is named *Add Target*, and the **T**arget Name should be set to DLLWIN.DLL.

8. To instruct the project that this target is a DLL, set *Target Type* to *Dynamic Library [.dll]*. The other settings should be the same as they were for the application's .EXE code file. Close the dialog by selecting the *OK* button.

> **WARNING**
>
> If an application uses the ObjectWindows dynamic DLL (and the class and runtime library DLLs), any DLL used by that application must also use the dynamic forms of these libraries. In other words, a DLL and host application must *both* use the same library forms, either static or dynamic.

9. You should now see a project window listing two code file targets: DLLAPP.EXE and DLLWIN.DLL. The default application filenames, inserted by the IDE's project manager, are correct, but the DLL files include DLLWIN.DEF, which the BC4 linker does not need. Highlight DLLWIN.DEF and press Del to delete it from the project, leaving only DLLWIN.CPP under its target, DLLWIN.DLL.

10. Click and drag the small dot to the left of the DLLWIN.DLL target (its file automatically tags along) until DLLWIN.EXE is highlighted, then release the

mouse button. This makes the DLL a subelement of the application, and automatically creates an import library file, DLLWIN.LIB, used during linking to import the DLL's functions into the application.

11. The multiple-target project is complete. Press F9 to compile the DLL and .EXE code files, then use **P**roject|*Close project...* to close the project window and save the project's .IDE file to disk.

DLL Debugging

Debugging DLLs with Turbo Debugger is similar to debugging nonDLL applications, but there's an added complication that needs mentioning. To locate function, variable, and other names in a program, TD loads the program's *symbol table,* part of the information generated when you elect to include debugging information in object- and executable-code files. (See Chapter 2 for more information on these topics.)

Because a DLL is a separate code module, it has its own symbol table. TD can load only one symbol table at a time, which means you can debug a DLL or its host program, but not both simultaneously because you must switch between the modules' symbol tables. This isn't difficult to do, but you must do it to view a DLL's code and data symbolically. Follow these steps to learn how to load a DLL's symbols into the debugger:

1. Open the DLLAPP.IDE project file and press F9 to compile.

2. When finished compiling, select the **T**ool|**T**urbo Debugger command to run TD and load the sample application.

3. At this time, the application's symbol table is loaded into TD, and you may view the application's variables, set breakpoints inside functions, and so on. If you want to debug the host application, you need to take no further steps.

4. To debug a DLL used by the application, select TD's **V**iew|**M**odule... command. Highlight the DLL you want to debug from those listed under *DLLs & programs.* If you are following along, highlight DLLWIN.DLL. (You can select only DLLs that you compiled with debugging information. Selecting another DLL used by the program—one supplied by Windows, for example—is allowed but because those DLLs don't have symbol tables, you can't view them symbolically.)

5. Make sure *Load symbols* is set to *Yes,* then select the *Sy**m**bol load* button to load the DLL's symbol table.

6. You now see the DLL's source code in TD. You can set breakpoints on DLL statements, and you can view variables. (You can view only variables in scope—true for applications and DLLs. Set a breakpoint, run the program to that

location, then view the variables that exist at that stage in the program's execution.)

7. Use the same techniques starting with step 4 to return to debugging the application, but select the program's executable-code filename (DLLAPP.EXE in this case). You may switch among application and DLL code files as often as you wish.

Resource DLLs

DLLs make perfect depositories for popular resources that your programs use. You can store icons, bitmaps, menus, cursors, strings, and other resources inside DLLs for all of your programs to share. This approach to resource management eliminates redundant resources across multiple applications, a common problem for developers who write and maintain multiple software systems that share many of the same resource elements.

Resource-Only Projects

A resource-only DLL contains resources in its code file, but has no code. It *can* have code, but that would complicate the works with no real benefits. Follow these steps to create a resource-only DLL in an IDE project:

1. Create an application project as you normally do, similar to the way you created one for the DLLAPP project in this chapter.

2. Use the **P**roject|*New* **t**arget... command and enter the DLL's name— **resource.dll**, for example—in the resulting dialog box. Make sure also that *Target Type* is set to *Standard.*

3. Select *Dynamic Library [.dll]* from the *TargetExpert* dialog (which may have a different title depending on how you open the dialog) as you did when creating the multiple-target project for DLLAPP.

4. Click and drag the small dot to the left of the RESOURCE.DLL target in the project window to the application's .EXE code file target, making the DLL a subelement of the application.

5. Finally, delete every file associated with RESOURCE.DLL *except* for the resource script file, in this case, RESOURCE.RC. (You may name the target and its resource script something else if you want.)

By following those steps, you create a multiple-target project with a resource-only DLL that consists solely of a resource script file. Insert your resources into that script as you do in an application's resources. (The application may have its own script as well.) Compiling the project creates a RESOURCE.DLL file that has only resources, and no code.

Sample Application

The next several listings demonstrate how to create and use a resource-only DLL, using a project that I created as explained in the preceding section. Even though some listings duplicate information presented elsewhere in this book, all listings are printed here for reference so you can see exactly how the program and DLL fit together.

> **NOTE**
>
> All listings in this section are stored on the book's disk in directory DLLRES.

Listing 14.8, RESOURCE.RH, defines several identifiers for the resource DLL. Each identifier refers to one resource stored in the DLL file.

Listing 14.8. RESOURCE.RH.

```
// resource.rh -- DLL resource header file

// Define error message string-resource identifiers
#define IDS_ERROR1 101
#define IDS_ERROR2 102
#define IDS_ERROR3 103

// Define system icon resource identifier
#define ID_SYSICON 100
```

Listing 14.9, RESOURCE.RC, lists the script commands that define each of the DLL's resources. The script includes the RESOURCE.RH header file, and it defines two types of resources: a string table and an icon. The icon is stored in binary form in the file RESOURCE.ICO on this book's disk. If you have other resources to store in the DLL, place them in the RESOURCE.RC script exactly as you would for an application's resources (but be sure to define any identifiers in RESOURCE.RH, *not* in the application's resource header).

Listing 14.9. RESOURCE.RC.

```
// resource.rc -- DLL resource script

#include "resource.rh"

STRINGTABLE
BEGIN
 IDS_ERROR1, "Bad vibes";
 IDS_ERROR2, "Bad whiskey"
 IDS_ERROR3, "Bad language"
END

ID_SYSICON ICON "resource.ico"
```

Next, write a host application to test the resource-only DLL. Listing 14.10, DLLRES.DEF, gives the sample application's linker definition file. As in the preceding sample application, the definition file is the same as the ones used by most of this book's examples. The DLL does not require a definition file.

Listing 14.10. DLLRES.DEF.

```
EXETYPE WINDOWS
CODE PRELOAD MOVEABLE DISCARDABLE
DATA PRELOAD MOVEABLE MULTIPLE
HEAPSIZE 4096
STACKSIZE 5120
```

Listing 14.11, DLLRES.RH, defines more resource identifiers, but this time, for resources stored in the application's code file.

Listing 14.11. DLLRES.RH.

```
// dllres.rh -- Resource header file

#define ID_MENU   100
#define CM_ERROR1 101
#define CM_ERROR2 102
#define CM_ERROR3 103
```

549

Listing 14.12, DLLRES.RC, lists the application's resource script, which in this case has only a menu resource. This file and the preceding one demonstrate that an application may have its own resources in addition to those it imports from a resource-only DLL.

Listing 14.12. DLLRES.RC.

```
#include <owl\window.rh>
#include "dllres.rh"

ID_MENU MENU
BEGIN
  POPUP "&Demo"
  BEGIN
    MENUITEM "Error &1", CM_ERROR1
    MENUITEM "Error &2", CM_ERROR2
    MENUITEM "Error &3", CM_ERROR3
    MENUITEM SEPARATOR
    MENUITEM "E&xit", CM_EXIT
  END
END
```

Finally, Listing 14.13, DLLRES.CPP, lists the program's source code, and demonstrates how to load and use the resource-only DLL. After the listing, I explain how the program works. Compile it along with RESOURCE.DLL by opening the DLLRES.IDE project file and pressing F9, or press Ctrl+F9 to compile and run. Figure 14.2 shows the program's display with a message box that shows a fictitious error message supplied by one of the DLL's string resources.

FIGURE 14.2.
DLLRES display and message box.

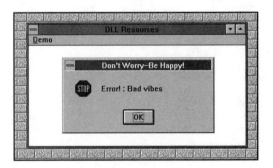

Listing 14.13. DLLRES.CPP.

```
/* ============================================================ *\
**   dllres.cpp -- Demonstrates resources in DLLs              **
** ============================================================ **
**                                                             **
** ============================================================ **
**      Copyright  1994 by Tom Swan. All rights reserved.      **
\* ============================================================ */

#include <owl\module.h>
#include <owl\applicat.h>
#include <owl\framewin.h>
#pragma hdrstop
#include "dllres.rh"     // Main program's resource identifiers
#include "resource.rh"   // DLL's resource identifiers

#define RES_STRLEN 256

// Global DLL module interface
static TModule* resModule = 0;


// ============================================================
// The application's main window
// ============================================================

class TDllResWin: public TFrameWindow {
public:
  TDllResWin(TWindow* parent, const char far* title);
protected:
  void ShowError(UINT errorCode);
  void CmError1();
  void CmError2();
  void CmError3();
DECLARE_RESPONSE_TABLE(TDllResWin);
};

DEFINE_RESPONSE_TABLE1(TDllResWin, TFrameWindow)
  EV_COMMAND(CM_ERROR1, CmError1),
  EV_COMMAND(CM_ERROR2, CmError2),
  EV_COMMAND(CM_ERROR3, CmError3),
END_RESPONSE_TABLE;

// Constructor
TDllResWin::TDllResWin(TWindow* parent, const char far* title)
  : TFrameWindow(parent, title),
    TWindow(parent, title)
{
  AssignMenu(ID_MENU);
}
```

continues

551

Listing 14.13. continued

```
// Display error message identified by errorCode
void
TDllResWin::ShowError(UINT errorCode)
{
  char far* s = new char[RES_STRLEN];
  resModule->LoadString(errorCode, s, RES_STRLEN);
  string msg("Error! : ");
  msg += s;
  MessageBox(msg.c_str(), "Don't Worry--Be Happy!",
    MB_OK | MB_ICONSTOP);
  delete s;
}

// Respond to Demo|Error1 command
void
TDllResWin::CmError1()
{
  ShowError(IDS_ERROR1);
}

// Respond to Demo|Error2 command
void
TDllResWin::CmError2()
{
  ShowError(IDS_ERROR2);
}

// Respond to Demo|Error3 command
void
TDllResWin::CmError3()
{
  ShowError(IDS_ERROR3);
}

// ============================================================
// The application class
// ============================================================

class TDllResApp: public TApplication {
public:
  TDllResApp(const char far* name)
    : TApplication(name) {}
  void InitMainWindow();
};

// Initialize the program's main window
void
TDllResApp::InitMainWindow()
```

```
{
  EnableCtl3d();
  EnableBWCC();
  MainWindow = new TDllResWin(0, "DLL Resources");
  MainWindow->SetIcon(resModule, ID_SYSICON);
}

#pragma argsused

// Main program
int
OwlMain(int argc, char* argv[])
{
  resModule = new TModule("resource.dll");
  TDllResApp app("DllResApp");
  int ret = app.Run();
  delete resModule;
  return ret;
}
```

For an interface to the resource-only DLL, the program defines a TModule pointer as a static global variable with the declaration:

```
static TModule* resModule = 0;
```

Function OwlMain (at the end of the DLLRES.CPP listing) loads the resource-only DLL by constructing a TModule object, initializing that object with the DLL's filename:

```
resModule = new TModule("resource.dll");
```

These are the same techniques used to load this chapter's bitmap child-window DLL. You use the same methods to load a resource-only DLL.

Because the DLL has only resources and no code, however, you use it somewhat differently. Of course, there are no functions in the DLL, but you *can* call functions for the TModule interface, which you might think of as a shell that envelopes the resource DLL. To load a string resource from the DLL, for example, call the TModule object's LoadString function as demonstrated in function ShowError:

```
char far* s = new char[RES_STRLEN];
resModule->LoadString(errorCode, s, RES_STRLEN);
```

The application module (DLLRES.CPP in this example) should include the RESOURCE.RH header file so statements such as those can refer to the DLL's resources by name. The first line defines a string variable to hold the loaded string. The second line calls TModule's LoadString function to load the string identified in the string-table resource by variable errorCode. Other functions—CmError1, for instance—call ShowError to load and display strings tagged by identifiers such as IDS_ERROR1 and IDS_ERROR2.

Load other resources similarly. Icon resources, however, require a slightly different approach, as demonstrated in the sample application's InitMainWindow function. There, this statement loads the icon, identified as ID_SYSICON in the resource-only DLL, with the statement:

```
MainWindow->SetIcon(resModule, ID_SYSICON);
```

That statement calls the SetIcon function for the program's main window, an object of type TFrameWindow. SetIcon is declared as:

```
SetIcon(TModule* iconModule, TResId iconResId);
```

Normally, you pass the current application's module pointer to the first parameter and the icon's resource identifier to the second. For example, if the system icon is stored in the program's .EXE code file, you would use this statement to set the icon:

```
MainWindow->SetIcon(this, ID_SYSICON);
```

In this case, however, the icon resource is stored in the RESOURCE.DLL, addressed as a TModule object by the resModule global pointer. This statement, then, extracts the icon from the DLL simply by specifying to SetIcon which TModule object to use:

```
MainWindow->SetIcon(resModule, ID_SYSICON);
```

International Resources

By storing resources in DLLs, you can create multinational software—with menu commands, for example, in French, Spanish, German, Swedish, Danish, and English. (I hope I've included all of this book's "multinational" readers in that list!)

> **NOTE**
>
> BC4 comes with a complete example that demonstrates the technique explained here. See the files in directory C:\BC4\EXAMPLES in the subdirectory OWL\OWLAPPS\INTLDEMO. You must have installed BC4's examples to create this directory and its files.

To create a multinational application, follow the steps in the preceding section to create a resource-only DLL for each supported language. The DLL, for example, might have menus, string tables, dialogs, controls and other resources in a variety of languages—one language per DLL. You might name your DLLs as in the BC4 example:

```
apieng.dll  // English resource DLL
apifra.dll  // French resource DLL
apiger.dll  // German resource DLL
```

For best results, *all* string information used by the program should be stored in your DLLs. Obviously, this step takes a lot of work, and probably, much help from translators who are expert in your target languages. Writing multinational software should be no more difficult than developing applications in single languages, but writing the actual text for those applications requires painstaking testing and debugging. (Just to mention one problem: the same strings in different languages will probably differ in length, complicating string display and use.)

In most cases, you can use a startup command to identify which language to use, and create a TModule object for that DLL, as demonstrated in this chapter's sample applications. To switch languages, perhaps in response to a menu command, delete the current TModule, and create another for the language resource-only DLL you need:

```
delete pResModule;
pResModule = new TModule(newDLLname);
```

You also need to redraw text in windows, reset the program's menu, and perform other actions to completely change an application from one language to another. (BC4's INTLDEMO sample program demonstrates the necessary techniques.) For example, to change menus, you can execute statements such as:

```
delete tMenu;  // Pointer to current menu
tMenu = new TMenu(pResModule->LoadMenu(ID_MENU), AutoDelete);
SetMenu(*tMenu);
```

In addition, you can switch to an international version of Borland Custom Controls, supplied with BC4 in the DLLs:

```
bwcc0007.dll
bwcc0009.dll
bwcc000c.dll
```

The hexadecimal values correspond to these definitions, which you can insert into your program's source code:

```
#define LANG_ENGLISH 0x09
#define LANG_FRENCH  0x0C
#define LANG_GERMAN  0x07
```

Include the BWCC.H header file, located in BC4\INCLUDE:

```
#include <bwcc.h>
```

Then, to initialize your application to use BWCC controls for a specific language, call EnableBWCC as you normally do to enable custom controls, but supply two additional arguments:

```
EnableBWCC(TRUE, LANG_GERMAN);
```

The TRUE argument enables the controls for immediate use (which you normally should do unless you want to load the DLL but not use it immediately). The second argument specifies which language to use for control buttons and other labels.

To switch between supported languages at runtime, terminate the current control DLL by calling BWCCIntlTerm, then call BWCCIntlInit with the new country code as an argument:

```
BWCCIntlTerm();
BWCCIntlInit(LANG_FRENCH);
```

Figure 14.3 shows a sample Borland Custom Control dialog box that uses the German DLL. I took this illustration from BC4's INTLDEMO application.

> **NOTE**
>
> The concept of *locales,* which define numeric, date, monetary, and other formats for different national locations, is only just being supported by C++ compilers. Currently, BC4 supports locales only for English, French, and German. Other locales are planned for future Borland C++ releases.

FIGURE 14.3.
*INTLDEMO's
German locale dialog.*

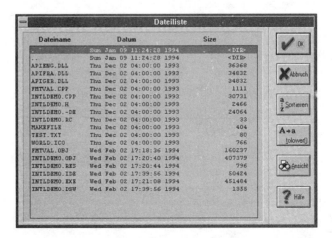

Looking Ahead

Every book needs a chapter to present information, tips, tidbits, and sundry facts that don't seem to fit anywhere else. The next, and last, chapter in this book is such a place. Turn to it for a variety of techniques that you can use to put the finishing touches on your Windows applications.

15

Adding the Finishing Touches

Anybody can learn how to write a program, but writing a finished *application* requires adding numerous finishing touches that place heavy demands on programmers. In this book's preceding 14 chapters, you've met key Windows programming techniques for getting your program up and running. In this chapter, you learn a variety of subjects for developing that program into a finished application, including:

- How to validate user input.
- How to use menu objects.
- How to add a command to a window's system menu.
- How to create a floating popup menu.
- How to use Visual BASIC Extended (VBX) Controls.
- How to use exceptions in ObjectWindows programs.
- How to write 32-bit Windows applications.
- How to detect operating system types and version numbers.

Input Validations

Everybody makes mistakes, but errors in data input can cause headaches for database administrators. Make life easy for your database systems (and for the people who maintain them) by validating user input in your database entry dialogs.

There are two basic approaches. One, check all input fields for errors when the dialog is closed by selecting its *OK* button. Or, two, validate input in each field during data entry. This second method is far preferable, but more difficult to program. By validating data during entry, users can fix their mistakes immediately. Two classes, TValidator and TEdit, make data-entry validations as easy as creating a couple of objects and specifying what kind of validations you need to perform.

The next several listings demonstrate how to use those classes in a data-entry dialog that validates several different types of input fields. Figure 15.1 shows the dialog. Listing 15.1, VALIDATE.RH, defines the program's resource identifiers. Listing 15.2, VALIDATE.RC, lists the program's resources, including a menu and the illustrated dialog. (The dialog resource's lines wrap around here to fit on the page. See the disk file for the proper format of these statements.) Listing 15.3, VALIDATE.CPP, shows how to program the validated input fields and also how to use the dialog's data-transfer mechanism to extract validated information from the dialog's edit controls.

FIGURE 15.1.

VALIDATE's dialog box of validated entry fields.

NOTE

Files in this section are located in the book disk's VALIDATE directory.

Listing 15.1. VALIDATE.RH.

```
// validate.rh -- Resource header file

// Menu resource and command identifiers
#define ID_MENU      100
#define CM_TEST 101

// Dialog resource identifier
#define ID_DIALOG    100

// Input string control identifiers
#define ID_LETTERS   101
#define ID_DIGITS    102
#define ID_RANGE     103
#define ID_STATE     104
#define ID_SOCSEC    105
#define ID_PHONE     106


// Dialog Help button
#define IDHELP 998
```

Listing 15.2. VALIDATE.RC.

```
#include <owl\window.rh>
#include <owl\validate.rh>
#include "validate.rh"

#include <owl\validate.rc>

ID_MENU MENU
BEGIN
  POPUP "&Demo"
  BEGIN
    MENUITEM "&Test", CM_TEST
    MENUITEM "E&xit", CM_EXIT
  END
END

ID_DIALCG DIALOG 6, 15, 189, 165
STYLE DS_MODALFRAME ¦ WS_POPUP ¦ WS_VISIBLE ¦
 WS_CAPTION ¦ WS_SYSMENU
CLASS "bordlg"
CAPTION "Validations"
FONT 8, "MS Sans Serif"
```

continues

Listing 15.2. continued

```
{
  EDITTEXT ID_LETTERS, 92, 14, 83, 12
  EDITTEXT ID_DIGITS, 92, 31, 83, 12
  EDITTEXT ID_RANGE, 92, 48, 83, 12
  EDITTEXT ID_STATE, 92, 65, 83, 12
  EDITTEXT ID_SOCSEC, 92, 82, 83, 12
  EDITTEXT ID_PHONE, 92, 99, 83, 12
  CONTROL "", IDOK, "BorBtn", 1 ¦ WS_TABSTOP, 20, 137, 37, 25
  CONTROL "", IDCANCEL, "BorBtn", WS_TABSTOP, 76, 137, 37, 25
  CONTROL "", IDHELP, "BorBtn", WS_TABSTOP, 132, 137, 37, 25
  CONTROL "Letters only (A-Z,a-z)", -1, "BorStatic",
   SS_LEFT ¦ WS_CHILD ¦ WS_VISIBLE ¦ WS_GROUP, 13, 16, 72, 8
  CONTROL "Digits only (0-9)", -1, "BorStatic",
   SS_LEFT ¦ WS_CHILD ¦ WS_VISIBLE ¦ WS_GROUP, 13, 33, 72, 8
  CONTROL "Range (1-100)", -1, "BorStatic",
   SS_LEFT ¦ WS_CHILD ¦ WS_VISIBLE ¦ WS_GROUP, 13, 50, 72, 8
  CONTROL "State (ex. Texas)", -1, "BorStatic",
   SS_LEFT ¦ WS_CHILD ¦ WS_VISIBLE ¦ WS_GROUP, 13, 67, 72, 8
  CONTROL "Soc Sec (xxx-xx-xxxx)", -1, "BorStatic",
   SS_LEFT ¦ WS_CHILD ¦ WS_VISIBLE ¦ WS_GROUP, 13, 84, 72, 8
  CONTROL "Phone (xxx-xxx-xxxx)", -1, "BorStatic",
   SS_LEFT ¦ WS_CHILD ¦ WS_VISIBLE ¦ WS_GROUP, 13, 101, 72, 8
  CONTROL "", -1, "BorShade",
   BSS_GROUP ¦ BSS_LEFT ¦ WS_CHILD ¦ WS_VISIBLE, 8, 7, 173, 112
  CONTROL "", -1, "BorShade",
   BSS_HDIP ¦ BSS_LEFT ¦ WS_CHILD ¦ WS_VISIBLE, 0, 128, 189, 3
}
```

Listing 15.3. VALIDATE.CPP.

```
/* ============================================================ *\
** validate.cpp -- Demonstrates TValidator objects             **
** ============================================================ **
**                                                              **
** ============================================================ **
**      Copyright  1994 by Tom Swan. All rights reserved.       **
\* ============================================================ */

#include <owl\applicat.h>
#include <owl\framewin.h>
#include <owl\dialog.h>
#include <owl\edit.h>
#include <owl\validate.h>
#include <mem.h>
#include <cstring.h>
#pragma hdrstop
```

```
#include "validate.rh"

// ================================================================
// Dialog box transfer-buffer struct
// ================================================================

// Structure string-member sizes (including null terminators)
#define LETTERS_SIZE   11
#define DIGITS_SIZE    11
#define RANGE_SIZE     4
#define STATE_SIZE     21
#define SOCSEC_SIZE    12
#define PHONE_SIZE     13

struct TValidBuffer {
  char letters[LETTERS_SIZE];  //  Letters only (A-Z, a-z)
  char digits[DIGITS_SIZE];    //  Digits only (0-9)
  char range[RANGE_SIZE];      //  Range (1-100)
  char state[STATE_SIZE];      //  State (ex. Texas)
  char socSec[SOCSEC_SIZE];    //  Soc Sec (xxx-xx-xxxx)
  char phone[PHONE_SIZE];      //  Phone (xxx-xxx-xxxx)
};

// ================================================================
// Dialog box class
// ================================================================

class TValidDialog: public TDialog {
public:
  TValidDialog(TWindow* parent, TValidBuffer* buffer);
  ~TValidDialog();
protected:
  void CmHelp();
private:
// WARNING: The TStringLookupValidator class deletes
// the states array (unfortunately). Deleting states
// in the class destructor causes a GPF!
  TSortedStringArray* states;
DECLARE_RESPONSE_TABLE(TValidDialog);
};

DEFINE_RESPONSE_TABLE1(TValidDialog, TDialog)
  EV_COMMAND(IDHELP, CmHelp),
END_RESPONSE_TABLE;

// Constructor
TValidDialog::TValidDialog(
  TWindow* parent, TValidBuffer* buffer)
  : TDialog(parent, ID_DIALOG)
{
```

continues

Listing 15.3. continued

```
  TEdit* e;   // Temporary pointer for creating TEdit objects

// Allocate and initialize partial states string array
// (You can complete the list if you want)
  states = new TSortedStringArray(50);
  states->Add("Arizona");
  states->Add("California");
  states->Add("Florida");
  states->Add("Maryland");
  states->Add("Pennsylvania");
  states->Add("Texas");
  states->Add("Virginia");

  e = new TEdit(this, ID_LETTERS, LETTERS_SIZE);
  e->SetValidator(new TFilterValidator("A-Za-z"));
  e = new TEdit(this, ID_DIGITS, DIGITS_SIZE);
  e->SetValidator(new TFilterValidator("0-9"));
  e = new TEdit(this, ID_RANGE, RANGE_SIZE);
  e->SetValidator(new TRangeValidator(1, 100));
  e = new TEdit(this, ID_STATE, STATE_SIZE);
  e->SetValidator(new TStringLookupValidator(states));
  e = new TEdit(this, ID_SOCSEC, SOCSEC_SIZE);
  e->SetValidator(new TPXPictureValidator("###-##-####"));
  e = new TEdit(this, ID_PHONE, PHONE_SIZE);
  e->SetValidator(new TPXPictureValidator("###-###-####"));

  SetTransferBuffer(buffer);
}

// Destructor
TValidDialog::~TValidDialog()
{
//  delete states;   // Don't do this! Causes GPF.
}

// Display help message
void
TValidDialog::CmHelp()
{
  string msg;         // Message box string
  string nl('\n');    // New line

  msg += "Enter valid information into the input boxes" + nl;
  msg += "as labeled. Improper values display an error" + nl;
  msg += "message if you attempt to move away from an" + nl;
  msg += "input field or if you select OK. You can close" + nl;
  msg += "the dialog, even if it contains invalid data," + nl;
  msg += "by selecting the Cancel button.";
  MessageBox(msg.c_str(), "ValidApp Help",
    MB_OK | MB_ICONINFORMATION);
```

```
}

// ============================================================
// The application's main window
// ============================================================

class TValidWin: public TFrameWindow {
public:
  TValidWin(TWindow* parent, const char far* title);
protected:
  void CmTest();
private:
  TValidBuffer buffer;  // Dialog transfer buffer
DECLARE_RESPONSE_TABLE(TValidWin);
};

DEFINE_RESPONSE_TABLE1(TValidWin, TFrameWindow)
  EV_COMMAND(CM_TEST, CmTest),
END_RESPONSE_TABLE;

// Constructor
TValidWin::TValidWin(TWindow* parent, const char far* title)
  : TFrameWindow(parent, title),
    TWindow(parent, title)
{
  AssignMenu(ID_MENU);
  memset(&buffer, 0, sizeof(buffer));
}

// Execute the dialog box
void
TValidWin::CmTest()
{
  TValidDialog* validDialog =
    new TValidDialog(this, &buffer);
  if (validDialog->Execute() == IDOK) {
    // Use strings in buffer
  }
}

// ============================================================
// The application class
// ============================================================

class TValidApp: public TApplication {
public:
  TValidApp(const char far* name)
    : TApplication(name) {}
  void InitMainWindow();
};
```

continues

Listing 15.3. continued

```
// Initialize the program's main window
void
TValidApp::InitMainWindow()
{
  EnableBWCC();
  MainWindow = new TValidWin(0, "TValidator Objects");
}

#pragma argsused

// Main program
int
OwlMain(int argc, char* argv[])
{
  TValidApp app("ValidApp");
  return app.Run();
}
```

To make use of the TValidator and TEdit classes, the program includes the EDIT.H and VALIDATE.H header files (among others):

```
#include <owl\edit.h>
#include <owl\validate.h>
```

Structure TValidBuffer holds character arrays for each of the dialog's input fields. The program uses the structure for the dialog's transfer buffer. In a database program, a similar structure could represent one record. Be sure to allocate enough space for each field plus a null terminator. The best way to do that is to define constants equal to the complete size of the string, including the null, then use those constants in the structure's declaration:

```
struct TValidBuffer {
  char letters[LETTERS_SIZE];  // Letters only (A-Z, a-z)
  char digits[DIGITS_SIZE];    // Digits only (0-9)
  char range[RANGE_SIZE];      // Range (1-100)
  char state[STATE_SIZE];      // State (ex. Texas)
  char socSec[SOCSEC_SIZE];    // Soc Sec (xxx-xx-xxxx)
  char phone[PHONE_SIZE];      // Phone (xxx-xxx-xxxx)
};
```

Create the dialog using Resource Workshop (or another method if you prefer), and insert one text-edit control for each field in the transfer buffer structure. Back in the program, derive a class from TDialog to serve as an interface to the dialog box at runtime (see class TValidDialog in the VALIDATE.CPP listing). At a minimum, the class needs a constructor and a destructor. It also can have member functions such as the example's CmHelp function, which displays a message when you select the dialog's *Help* button. You also need a response table to associate that function with the message, ID_HELP, generated by that button. The sample dialog class also defines an array of strings:

```
TSortedStringArray* states;
```

The VALIDATE.H header file defines TSortedStringArray as an alias for the template class declaration from the ARRAYS.H header file in BC4's class library:

```
typedef TSArrayAsVector<string> TSortedStringArray;
```

The sorted array stores C++ string objects for use in validating one of the dialog's input fields. Users must enter one of the strings in this array before the dialog's data is accepted. (I explain more about this technique a bit later.)

The dialog class constructor plays a key role in creating validated input fields. As usual when creating control objects for an automated transfer buffer (the TValidBuffer structure in this example), the constructor creates one control object of a class derived from TControl for each field in the buffer. Each edit control, for example, is created with a statement such as:

```
e = new TEdit(this, ID_LETTERS, LETTERS_SIZE);
```

Variable e is a TEdit pointer that the program doesn't need to keep because the constructed edit control object is a child of its parent, and the parent takes care of deleting that control when the dialog box closes. We need the pointer, however, to attach a *validator object* to the control. For the first control, which accepts only alphabetic letters, the dialog constructor creates a validator of type TFilterValidator:

```
e->SetValidator(new TFilterValidator("A-Za-z"));
```

Calling SetValidator for the edit control attaches a validator object of any class derived from TValidator. The TFilterValidator class in this example receives a string argument that specifies the range of acceptable ASCII characters (*A* to *Z* and *a* to *z*). Simply attaching the validator object to the edit control ensures that no other characters may be entered into that field.

The dialog constructor creates a second filter validator, but this time accepting only digit characters, with the statements:

```
e = new TEdit(this, ID_DIGITS, DIGITS_SIZE);
e->SetValidator(new TFilterValidator("0-9"));
```

The first statement constructs the TEdit object for the second input field in the dialog. The second statement constructs a TFilterValidator object limited to the digits 0 to 9. Users may type only those characters into the validated control.

Another kind of validator limits input to a numeric range. Again, first the dialog constructor creates a TEdit control associated with a dialog box input field. Then, the constructor attaches a validator object to the control:

```
e = new TEdit(this, ID_RANGE, RANGE_SIZE);
e->SetValidator(new TRangeValidator(1, 100));
```

This time, a TRangeValidator object limits entries into the control to value from 1 to 100. If you enter a value outside of this range, you cannot move to another control and you cannot close the dialog by selecting its *OK* button. (You can always close the dialog, however, by selecting its *Cancel* button.)

Filter and range validators are useful for simple validations. More sophisticated data entry tasks require limiting input to a known set of values. For that, you can use a TStringLookupValidator, a class derived from the more general TLookupValidator class, which verifies that a control's value is equal to an entry in an array of values. With the TStringLookupValidator class, those values must be an array of string objects, stored in the template array class TSortedStringArray, a member of this program's dialog class. To prepare the strings, the dialog constructor first allocates the array with the statement:

```
states = new TSortedStringArray(50);
```

Next, call Add to insert strings into the array:

```
states->Add("Arizona");
states->Add("California");
states->Add("Florida");
```

To save space, I didn't enter all 50 state names. Feel free to complete the array if you want.

For validating input against the array of strings, the dialog constructor creates an edit control and attaches a validator object of type TStringLookupValidator with these statements:

```
e = new TEdit(this, ID_STATE, STATE_SIZE);
e->SetValidator(new TStringLookupValidator(states));
```

The result is a validated input field into which users must type one of the strings in the states array.

> **WARNING**
>
> The validator deletes the string array when the dialog box is closed, a fact that became painfully obvious from the General Protection Faults (GPF) I received when I deleted states in the dialog class destructor. I left the faulty programming as a comment to

punctuate this warning. (It would be better for the validator *not* to delete the string array so that array could be prepared and deleted by some other process. As designed, you must recreate the array on *each* entry to the dialog, which wastes time for lengthy lookup tables.)

Two other validator objects in the sample dialog use a *picture* to limit input to a styled pattern. For validating social security numbers, for example, which must be in the form 000-00-0000 (where 0s stand for any digits), the dialog constructor executes the statements:

```
e = new TEdit(this, ID_SOCSEC, SOCSEC_SIZE);
e->SetValidator(new TPXPictureValidator("###-##-####"));
```

The picture string ###-##-#### instructs the TPXPictureValidator class to limit input to digits at every pound sign, and to insist on literal dashes at the specified locations.

For validating telephone numbers, the program creates a similar edit control and picture validator with the statements:

```
e = new TEdit(this, ID_PHONE, PHONE_SIZE);
e->SetValidator(new TPXPictureValidator("###-###-####"));
```

Picture strings in TPXPictureValidator objects are the same as used by Borland's Paradox database manager. You can use any of the characters in Table 15.1 in a picture string—other characters are taken literally (that is, they must be entered as typed in the picture string).

Table 15.1. TPXPictureValidator picture string characters.

Character	Purpose in picture string
#	Digit required
?	Any letter required
&	Uppercase letter required
@	Any character
!	Any character, converted to uppercase
;	Next character is literal
*	Repeat count
[ ]	Option
{ }	Group
,	Set separator

The final step in the process of creating a series of validated input strings is to assign a transfer buffer to the dialog. In the sample listing, the dialog constructor ends with the statement:

```
SetTransferBuffer(buffer);
```

> **NOTE**
>
> Strictly speaking, you don't have to use a transfer buffer along with validated edit controls. If you want to use a different method for initializing and extracting information in the dialog's controls, that's fine, but a transfer buffer is the easiest way to send data to a dialog's controls and to extract validated entries after the dialog is closed.

The rest of the program is straightforward. To execute the dialog and copy the transfer buffer's string data to the dialog's controls, function `CmTest` constructs a `TValidDialog` object and calls its `Execute` function:

```
TValidDialog* validDialog =
  new TValidDialog(this, &buffer);
if (validDialog->Execute() == IDOK) {
  // Use strings in buffer
}
```

All input validations are handled automatically—there are no other functions to call or buttons to push. If the user closes the dialog by selecting its *OK* button (or by selecting a system menu command or pressing that command's associated hot keys), the transfer `buffer` contains all validated input strings. Closing the dialog by selecting the *Cancel* button (or by pressing Esc) restores the transfer buffer to its original contents.

Menu Objects

Simple menus, such as those used by most of this book's example programs, work well enough in most cases. Just create a menu resource, declare and define menu-response functions, and associate those functions with the corresponding menu resource identifiers in a window's message-response table. The rest is automatic.

In sophisticated applications, however, you might need better control over a window's menu bar. In particular, you might need to:

- Check and uncheck menu commands.
- Insert new commands into the window's system menu.

- Add and delete menus and commands dynamically at runtime.
- Create floating popup menus.

To simplify these advanced menu tasks, you can use objects of the TMenu class, declared in the MENU.H header file. The next listings show how to use TMenu to program each of the preceding four menu techniques. Figure 15.2 shows the final program's display with the cursor poised at a floating popup menu's second command.

FIGURE 15.2.
MENUOBJ's display with floating popup menu.

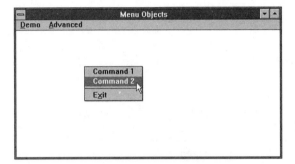

NOTE

The files in this section are located in the book disk's MENUOBJ directory.

Listing 15.4. MENUOBJ.RH.

```
// menuobj.rh -- Resource header file

#define ID_MENU     100
#define ID_ADVANCED 200

#define CM_ADVANCED 101
#define CM_NEWCMD1  201
#define CM_NEWCMD2  202
#define CM_HELP 999
```

Listing 15.5. MENUOBJ.RC.

```
#include <owl\window.rh>
#include "menuobj.rh"

ID_MENU MENU
BEGIN
  POPUP "&Demo"
  BEGIN
    MENUITEM "&Advanced", CM_ADVANCED
    MENUITEM SEPARATOR
    MENUITEM "E&xit", CM_EXIT
  END
END
```

Listing 15.6. MENUOBJ.CPP.

```
/* ============================================================ *\
**   menuobj.cpp -- Demonstrates dynamic, popup, system menus  **
** ============================================================ **
**                                                             **
** ============================================================ **
**      Copyright  1994 by Tom Swan. All rights reserved.      **
\* ============================================================ */

#include <owl\applicat.h>
#include <owl\framewin.h>
#include <owl\menu.h>
#pragma hdrstop
#include "menuobj.rh"

// ============================================================
// The application's main window
// ============================================================

class TMenuObjWin: public TFrameWindow {
public:
  TMenuObjWin(TWindow* parent, const char far* title);
  ~TMenuObjWin();
protected:
  void SetupWindow();
  void CmAdvanced();
  void CmNewCmd1();
  void CmNewCmd2();
  void EvSysCommand(UINT cmdType, TPoint& p);
  void EvRButtonDown(UINT modkeys, TPoint& p);
private:
  TMenu* windowMenu;         // Pointer to window's menu
  TPopupMenu* popupMenu;     // Popup menu
```

```
  BOOL advanced;            // TRUE if advanced menu is displayed
DECLARE_RESPONSE_TABLE(TMenuObjWin);
};

DEFINE_RESPONSE_TABLE1(TMenuObjWin, TFrameWindow)
  EV_COMMAND(CM_ADVANCED, CmAdvanced),
  EV_COMMAND(CM_NEWCMD1, CmNewCmd1),
  EV_COMMAND(CM_NEWCMD2, CmNewCmd2),
  EV_WM_SYSCOMMAND,
  EV_WM_RBUTTONDOWN,
END_RESPONSE_TABLE;

// Constructor
TMenuObjWin::TMenuObjWin(TWindow* parent, const char far* title)
  : TFrameWindow(parent, title),
    TWindow(parent, title)
{
  AssignMenu(ID_MENU);
  advanced = FALSE;  // Start with simple menu
}

// Initialize window object
void
TMenuObjWin::SetupWindow()
{
  TFrameWindow::SetupWindow();

// Create menu object interface for this window's menu
  windowMenu = new TMenu(HWindow);

// Add Help command to bottom of system menu
  TSystemMenu sysMenu(HWindow);
  sysMenu.AppendMenu(MF_SEPARATOR, 0, (LPSTR)0);
  sysMenu.AppendMenu(MF_STRING, CM_HELP, "&Help");

// Initialize popup menu object
  popupMenu = new TPopupMenu();
  popupMenu->AppendMenu(MF_STRING, CM_NEWCMD1, "Command 1");
  popupMenu->AppendMenu(MF_STRING, CM_NEWCMD2, "Command 2");
  popupMenu->AppendMenu(MF_SEPARATOR, 0, 0);
  popupMenu->AppendMenu(MF_STRING, CM_EXIT, "E&xit");
}

// Destructor
TMenuObjWin::~TMenuObjWin()
{
  delete windowMenu;
  delete popupMenu;
}
```

continues

573

Listing 15.6. continued

```
// Toggle between advanced and simple menus
void
TMenuObjWin::CmAdvanced()
{
  if (advanced) {
    windowMenu->DeleteMenu(1, MF_BYPOSITION);
    windowMenu->CheckMenuItem(CM_ADVANCED,
      MF_BYCOMMAND | MF_UNCHECKED);
    advanced = FALSE;
  } else {
    TPopupMenu newMenu(NoAutoDelete);
    windowMenu->AppendMenu(
      MF_POPUP, (UINT)(HMENU)newMenu, "&Advanced");
    newMenu.AppendMenu(
      MF_STRING | MF_ENABLED, CM_NEWCMD1, "Command 1");
    newMenu.AppendMenu(
      MF_STRING | MF_ENABLED, CM_NEWCMD2, "Command 2");
    windowMenu->CheckMenuItem(CM_ADVANCED,
      MF_BYCOMMAND | MF_CHECKED);
    advanced = TRUE;
  }
  DrawMenuBar();
}

// Do advanced or popup command #1
void
TMenuObjWin::CmNewCmd1()
{
  MessageBox("New command #1", "MenuObjApp",
    MB_OK | MB_ICONINFORMATION);
}

// Do advanced or popup command #2
void
TMenuObjWin::CmNewCmd2()
{
  MessageBox("New command #2", "MenuObjApp",
    MB_OK | MB_ICONINFORMATION);
}

// Do system commands
void
TMenuObjWin::EvSysCommand(UINT cmdType, TPoint& p)
{
  if (cmdType == CM_HELP) {
    MessageBox("System menu help command", "Help!",
      MB_OK | MB_ICONINFORMATION);
  } else {
    TFrameWindow::EvSysCommand(cmdType, p);
  }
}
```

```
// Display popup menu for right mouse button click
void
TMenuObjWin::EvRButtonDown(UINT /*modkeys*/, TPoint& p)
{
  TPoint mouseLocation(p);
  ClientToScreen(mouseLocation);
  popupMenu->TrackPopupMenu(
    TPM_LEFTALIGN | TPM_RIGHTBUTTON, mouseLocation, 0, HWindow);
}

// ==========================================================
// The application class
// ==========================================================

class TMenuObjApp: public TApplication {
public:
  TMenuObjApp(const char far* name)
    : TApplication(name) {}
  void InitMainWindow();
};

// Initialize the program's main window
void
TMenuObjApp::InitMainWindow()
{
  EnableCtl3d();
  EnableBWCC();
  MainWindow = new TMenuObjWin(0, "Menu Objects");
}

#pragma argsused

// Main program
int
OwlMain(int argc, char* argv[])
{
  TMenuObjApp app("MenuObjApp");
  return app.Run();
}
```

The TMenu class has many functions that you can call to perform various operations on a window's menu. You can use an object of the class as an interface to your program's entire menu, and you can create multiple TMenu objects for a variety of purposes—to access the window's system menu, for example, to create a floating popup menu, or to add and delete popup menus from the menu bar.

To construct a TMenu object as an interface for a window's entire menu bar, create the object by passing it the window's HWindow handle:

```
windowMenu = new TMenu(HWindow);
```

Don't do that in the window's constructor, where HWindow has not yet been initialized. You may construct the menu object in the window's SetupWindow function (as in the sample listing), or in another member function. After constructing the TMenu object, you can call functions to operate on the menu's commands. For example, to add a checkmark to the *Advanced* command in the sample *Demo* menu, the CmAdvanced function uses the statement:

```
windowMenu->CheckMenuItem(CM_ADVANCED,
  MF_BYCOMMAND | MF_CHECKED);
```

Change MF_CHECKED to MF_UNCHECKED to remove a checkmark.

Add a new command to a window's system menu by constructing an object of the TSystemMenu class, derived from TMenu. First, construct a TSystemMenu object, passing the window's handle as an argument:

```
TSystemMenu sysMenu(HWindow);
```

Next, call AppendMenu, a function inherited from TMenu, to add a separator line and a command, named *Help* in this case, to the bottom of the menu:

```
sysMenu.AppendMenu(MF_SEPARATOR, 0, (LPSTR)0);
sysMenu.AppendMenu(MF_STRING, CM_HELP, "&Help");
```

To associate the CM_HELP message with a member function, declare EvSysCommand in the window class (TMenuObjWin in the sample listing) exactly as shown here:

```
void EvSysCommand(UINT cmdType, TPoint& p);
```

Insert the macro EV_WM_SYSCOMMAND in the window's response table. The macro expects to find a function, EvSysCommand, declared as shown. In the function's implementation, compare cmdType with the command identifier you added to the system menu.

If, for example, `cmdType` equals `CM_HELP`, the program responds by displaying a message box (see function `EvSysCommand` in the listing). To handle other commands normally, call the ancestor's `EvSysCommand`:

```
TFrameWindow::EvSysCommand(cmdType, p);
```

Some programs benefit from a menu that changes dynamically in response to other commands. The sample program, for example, begins with a simple menu that has only two commands: *Advanced* and *Exit*. Selecting *Advanced* adds another menu with two more commands (which, if you select them, display message boxes for confirmation). Selecting *Advanced* again restores the original menu bar.

First, create an object of the `TPopupMenu` class, derived from `TMenu`. The object is a *submenu* that you can use to attach a new popup menu to the menu bar:

```
TPopupMenu newMenu(NoAutoDelete);
```

To append `newMenu` to the window's menu bar (interfaced by another `TMenu` object addressed by `windowMenu`), call the `AppendMenu` member function as you did to add a command to the system menu:

```
windowMenu->AppendMenu(
  MF_POPUP, (UINT)(HMENU)newMenu, "&Advanced");
```

In this case, the first parameter, `MF_POPUP`, dictates that the second parameter be a menu handle. Unfortunately, the `AppendMenu` function requires an unsigned integer value, required a double type cast that first translates `newMenu` as a menu handle (using a class operator function of type `HMENU`), and second translates that value to `UINT`, the one the function requires. (Better overloading of `TMenu` functions would prevent having to take this painful route to pass a submenu object to `AppendMenu`.) The final parameter specifies the new menu's name.

You can now use the submenu object `newMenu` to add commands to the menu added to the menu bar. For example, to add a command, again call `AppendMenu`, but this time in reference to `newMenu` rather than the object addressed by `windowMenu`:

```
newMenu.AppendMenu(
  MF_STRING ¦ MF_ENABLED, CM_NEWCMD1, "Command 1");
```

To delete a menu, call the `DeleteMenu` function like this:

```
windowMenu->DeleteMenu(1, MF_BYPOSITION);
```

Parameter 1 indicates the menu's position, with 0 for the first popup menu in the bar. `MF_BYPOSITION` indicates that the first parameter is a position. Use `MF_BYCOMMAND` to identify menus by their resource names.

When making any changes to a menu that affect its appearance—adding or deleting popup menus, for example—always call the window's DrawMenuBar function to update the display:

```
DrawMenuBar();
```

Creating a floating popup menu requires more work, but the results are truly worth the effort. Popup menus make it possible for users to select context-sensitive commands that change according to the mouse position, or perhaps, according to other conditions. Most Windows designers assign the right mouse button to the task. Point the mouse at something and click that button to display a floating popup menu of additional commands—sometimes called *local commands* because they are localized to the mouse position.

To create a floating popup menu, construct a TPopupMenu object and save its pointer in a variable, popupMenu here:

```
popupMenu = new TPopupMenu();
```

Call AppendMenu to add menu commands and separators to the menu object. Identify commands as you normally do with resource identifiers, and associate those identifiers in a response table with member functions. You may create entirely new commands for a floating popup menu, or you may create commands for functions associated with other menu-bar commands as I did for *Exit,* which appears in the program's *Demo* menu and also in the sample floating popup.

To activate the floating popup menu when you click the right mouse button, add a function of this exact design to your window class:

```
void EvRButtonDown(UINT modkeys, TPoint& p);
```

Also insert the EV_WM_RBUTTONDOWN macro in the window class's response table, associating the Windows WM_RBUTTONDOWN message with the function. Implement the function as shown in the listing. First, construct a TPoint object and call the window's ClientToScreen function to convert the mouse coordinates, passed by reference to EvRButtonDown, to global screen values:

```
TPoint mouseLocation(p);
ClientToScreen(mouseLocation);
```

Then, call the floating popup menu object's TrackPopupMenu function, passing alignment values, the mouse location, 0 for a reserved (unused) parameter, and the window's

`HWindow` handle. Windows displays and uses the menu, generating a message if the user selects any of the menu's commands. Pressing Esc or clicking a mouse button outside of the menu erases the floating popup menu without further action.

> **TIP**
>
> To create a context-sensitive floating popup menu, examine the mouse location in `EvRButtonDown`, then select an appropriate menu object to pass and call its `TrackPopupMenu` function.

Visual BASIC (VBX) Controls

> **NOTE**
>
> Some of the text in this section first appeared in my PC Techniques Dec/Jan 1993/1994 column, *Shades of Windows.*

A VBX control extends the Visual BASIC toolbox. To use a control in a VB program, you simply select it from the tool palette. In C++, VBX controls are used differently, but the end results are similar.

In a typical application, you add VBX controls to a dialog just as you do any other control by using Resource Workshop (or another resource editor) to insert the control at just the right spot. RW lets you select the control's properties—a valuable feature for configuring color attributes, cursor shapes, and other aspects of individual controls. To add VBX controls to RW, use the *Install Control Library* command to open a .VBX file before creating your program's resource file. You can also manually type VBX control statements into a resource script text file. Or, you can use VBX controls the "hard" way—by opening the control's file at runtime.

Typical VBX controls include custom gauges, graphics, and also multimedia and pen objects. Each control is identified by an *Object Type,* analogous to a C++ class name. Table 15.2 lists some of the controls in the Visual Control Pack, provided with Microsoft's Custom Control Development Kit and also Visual BASIC and Visual C++ professional editions. Dozens of other controls are available from third-party vendors.

Table 15.2. VBX Controls from the Visual Control Pack.

Control	Object Type	Required File(s)
3D checkbox	SSCheck	THREED.VBX
3D command button	SSCommand	THREED.VBX
3D frame	SSFrame	THREED.VBX
3D group pushbutton	SSRibbon	THREED.VBX
3D option button	SSOption	THREED.VBX
3D panel	SSPanel	THREED.VBX
Animated button	AniPushButton	ANIBUTON.VBX
Common dialog	CommonDialog	CMDIALOG.VBX COMMDLG.DLL
Communications	MSComm	MSCOMM.VBX
Gauge	Gauge	GAUGE.VBX
Graph	Graph	GRAPH.VBX GSW.EXE GSWDLL.DLL
Key status	MhState	KEYSTAT.VBX
Multimedia MCI	MMControl	MCI.VBX
Pen BEdit	VBedit	PENCTRLS.VBX
Pen HEdit	VHedit	PENCTRLS.VBX
Pen ink-on-bitmap	InkOnBitmap	PENCTRLS.VBX
Pen on-screen keyboard	SKBButton	PENCTRLS.VBX
Picture clip	PictureClip	PICCLIP.VBX
Spin button	SpinButton	SPIN.VBX

A VBX control has three basic characteristics: properties, events, and methods. A *property* is a value stored and used by the control. An *event* is represented as a message sent to the window that owns the control. A *method* resembles an encapsulated class member function that the application may call. On disk, VBX controls are stored in files, ending in .VBX, that are actually DLLs (dynamic link libraries) in disguise. A .VBX file may contain one or several controls, and in some cases, a control may require additional library, bitmap, and other supporting files. Usually, the control's .VBX file should be stored in WINDOWS\SYSTEM by the application's installation utility, but the file may instead be placed in the application's .EXE path.

VBX controls share many common properties, events, and methods. Most controls, for example, define Visible and Width properties. Controls may also define unique properties, events, and error messages. A SpinButton control, for instance, defines a SpinOrientation property that selects between vertical and horizontal styles. It's possible to interrogate a control to find its property names, but to use a control effectively, you need its documentation.

To communicate with an application, a VBX control "fires" an event, received as a message by the owning window. Like properties, some events are shared by all controls; other events are unique. The SpinButton control, for example, defines SpinUp and SpinDown events, triggered by clicking on the button's triangles. Sometimes, merely changing a property value causes the control to fire an associated event—thus VBX controls may be used interactively (by clicking, dragging, and so forth), or they may be manipulated by program statements. These are truly versatile objects!

Lastly, VBX controls may define methods such as Move, Refresh, AddItem, and RemoveItem. ObjectWindows simplifies the task of calling a control's methods by providing class functions of those names. Vendors may also add an About-Box dialog to a control, displayed in the resource editor, but not normally used by applications.

VBX Class Interface

That explains what a VBX control is; using one in a C++ program is another matter. Until recently, that job was next to impossible because of the intimate relationship between VBX controls and the Visual BASIC runtime system. ObjectWindows 2.0 supplants that system with low-level code and a couple of classes, making it possible to use VBX controls directly in C++ programs. Follow these steps to add VBX control capabilities to any OWL application:

- Include the VBXCTL.H header file, which defines some classes and other items you'll need. Use this statement to include the header, located in the BC4\INCLUDE\OWL subdirectory:

  ```
  #include <owl\vbxctl.h>
  ```

- VBXCTL.H includes two other headers: OWL\CONTROL.H and BIVBX.H. The CONTROL.H file declares the TControl class, from which TVbxControl is derived. A window or dialog uses that class to create objects for interfacing with VBX controls. The BIVBX.H file defines several related items that also can be used in a non-OWL program by hearty programmers who prefer to program Windows the hard way using straight C.

● In OwlMain, construct an object of the TBIVbxLibrary class, which loads and initializes VBX support code:

```
TBIVbxLibrary vbxlib;        // Initialize VBX controls
```

● In the program's source code, derive a dialog or window class from TDialog or TFrameWindow (or a similar TWindow derivative). Using multiple inheritance, also derive your class from TVbxEventHandler, which adds VBX awareness to the window. This step enables the class to set VBX properties, to respond to control events, and to call control methods.

● For each control used in the dialog or window class, define a TVbxControl pointer or object (a pointer is usually best). Create or initialize the control object in the dialog or window class constructor. Because the control objects are owned by their parent, they are automatically deleted along with the parent window. You don't have to delete VBX controls in the dialog or window destructor. A typical control is constructed simply by specifying its parent window pointer (this) and a resource identifier:

```
Spin1 =
  new TVbxControl(this, IDC_SPIN1);
```

● Finally, declare and define a message response table for any control events to be intercepted by the window. Program event functions as you do other message handlers. Use the EV_VBXEVENTNAME or EV_VBXEVENTINDEX message-cracking macros for each control event for which you intend to provide a class function.

Sample VBX Application

The next several listings show the source for an application with a dialog box that uses a SpinButton VBX control. You also need the SPIN.VBX file installed in WINDOWS\SYSTEM. Figure 15.3 shows the program's display with the mouse cursor positioned on the button's "down" panel. The "50" next to the control is a common text-edit control object, typically used in conjunction with a SpinButton VBX control.

FIGURE 15.3.

*VBXDEMO's sample
VBX SpinButton
control.*

Listing 15.7, VBXDEMO.RH, defines the program's resource identifiers.

NOTE

Listings in this section are located in the book disk's VBXDEMO directory.

Listing 15.7. VBXDEMO.RH.

```
// vbxdemo.rh -- Resource header file

#define ID_MENU 100
#define CM_DEMO_TEST 101
#define ID_DIALOG 100
#define IDC_SPIN1 101
#define IDC_VALUE 102
```

I used Resource Workshop to add the SpinButton to the sample dialog. Listing 15.8, VBXDEMO.RC, shows the resulting resource script.

Listing 15.8. VBXDEMO.RC.

```
#include <owl\window.rh>
#include "vbxdemo.rh"

ID_DIALOG DIALOG 32, 34, 123, 94
STYLE DS_MODALFRAME ¦ WS_POPUP ¦ WS_VISIBLE ¦
 WS_CAPTION ¦ WS_SYSMENU
CAPTION "Test VBX Control"
FONT 8, "MS Sans Serif"
{
 EDITTEXT IDC_VALUE, 65, 39, 16, 12
 DEFPUSHBUTTON "Ok", IDOK, 59, 71, 50, 14
 CONTROL "SPIN.VBX;SpinButton;Spin101", IDC_SPIN1, "VBControl",
  0 ¦ WS_CHILD ¦ NOT WS_VISIBLE ¦ WS_TABSTOP, 42, 36, 15, 17
 CTEXT "Click Me", -1, 31, 22, 35, 8
}


ID_DIALOG DLGINIT
{
    101, 0x0400, 80L,
0x0400, 0x7053, 0x6e69, 0x6501, 0x0200, 0xff06, 0xff07,
  0x0108, 0x000a,
```

continues

Listing 15.8. continued

```
0x000c, 0x050d, 0x0000, 0x0e80, 0x0008, 0x8000, 0x000f,
  0x1000, 0xffff,
0x00ff, 0x8011, 0x8080, 0x1200, 0x0001, 0x0013, 0x0000,
  0x1400, 0x0032,
0x0015, 0x1600, 0x8080, 0x0080, 0xff17, 0xffff, 0x1800,
  0x1901, 0x0000,
0x0000, 0xc01a, 0xc0c0, 0xff00,
    0
}

ID_MENU MENU
{
 POPUP "&Demo"
 {
  MENUITEM "&Test dialog...", CM_DEMO_TEST
  MENUITEM SEPARATOR
  MENUITEM "E&xit", CM_EXIT
 }
}
```

The relevant control statement in the dialog resource (entered as a single line) is:

```
CONTROL "SPIN.VBX;SpinButton;Spin101", IDC_SPIN1, "VBControl",
 0 ¦ WS_CHILD ¦ NOT WS_VISIBLE ¦ WS_TABSTOP, 42, 36, 15, 17
```

You can insert similar statements directly in resource script files, but it's easier to let Resource Workshop create the command. As VBXDEMO.RC also shows, additional dialog initialization data is provided in hexadecimal for the VBX control's properties. To edit a property, double click on the control in Resource Workshop—to select between horizontal or vertical button styles, for example.

Listing 15.9 shows the sample program's source code, which demonstrates how to create and use a class object to interface with a VBX control.

Listing 15.9. VBXDEMO.CPP.

```
/* ============================================================ *\
**  vbxdemo.cpp -- Demonstrates VBX Controls                    **
** ============================================================ **
**  Uses the SPIN.VBX custom control supplied with Visual       **
**  Basic 1.0. SPIN.VBX must be in the current directory or     **
**  it must be installed in WINDOWS\SYSTEM.                      **
** ============================================================ **
**     Copyright  1994 by Tom Swan. All rights reserved.        **
**           First appeared in PC Techniques                    **
\* ============================================================ */
```

```cpp
#include <owl\applicat.h>
#include <owl\framewin.h>
#include <owl\dialog.h>
#include <owl\edit.h>
#include <owl\vbxctl.h>
#include "vbxdemo.rh"

#define MINVALUE 0     // Minimum SpinButton value
#define MAXVALUE 99    // Maximum SpinButton value
#define EDITLEN 4      // Buffer size for editing value as text

// =============================================================
// TVbxDialog class
// =============================================================

class TVbxDialog: public TDialog, public TVbxEventHandler {
public:
  TVbxDialog(TWindow *parent, TResId resId, int &v);
protected:
  void SetupWindow();
  BOOL CanClose();
  void EvSpinUp(VBXEVENT far *event);
  void EvSpinDown(VBXEVENT far *event);
  void LimitValue();
  void GetValue();
  void SetValue();
  void AdjustValue(int k);
private:
  int &value;             // Reference to caller's value v
  TVbxControl *Spin1;     // Pointer to VBX SpinButton Control
  TEdit *Edit1;           // Pointer to text edit control
DECLARE_RESPONSE_TABLE(TVbxDialog);
};

DEFINE_RESPONSE_TABLE2(TVbxDialog, TDialog, TVbxEventHandler)
  EV_VBXEVENTNAME(IDC_SPIN1,"SpinUp",EvSpinUp),
  EV_VBXEVENTNAME(IDC_SPIN1,"SpinDown",EvSpinDown),
END_RESPONSE_TABLE;

// Constructor
TVbxDialog::TVbxDialog(TWindow *parent, TResId resId, int &v)
  : TDialog(parent, resId),  // Call TDialog constructor
    TWindow(parent),         // Call TWindow constructor
    value(v)                 // Set value to caller's int v
{
  Spin1 = new TVbxControl(this, IDC_SPIN1);
  Edit1 = new TEdit(this, IDC_VALUE, EDITLEN);
}
```

continues

585

Listing 15.9. continued

```
// Extract current value; return ancestor CanClose
BOOL
TVbxDialog::CanClose()
{
  // Optional: Test edit control for errors here
  GetValue();
  return TDialog::CanClose();
}

// Initialize dialog window
void
TVbxDialog::SetupWindow()
{
  TDialog::SetupWindow();
  SetValue();  // Make edit control and int value agree
}

// Respond to SpinButton SpinUp event
void
TVbxDialog::EvSpinUp(VBXEVENT far * /*event*/)
{
  AdjustValue(1);          // Increment text edit control
  Edit1->UpdateWindow();   // Show new edit control value
  Spin1->Refresh();        // Animate VBX SpinButton Control
}

// Respond to SpinButton SpinDown event
void
TVbxDialog::EvSpinDown(VBXEVENT far * /*event*/)
{
  AdjustValue(-1);         // Decrement text edit control
  Edit1->UpdateWindow();   // Show new edit control value
  Spin1->Refresh();        // Animate VBX SpinButton Control
}

// Limit value to allowed range MINVALUE ... MAXVALUE
void
TVbxDialog::LimitValue()
{
  if (value < MINVALUE)
    value = MAXVALUE;
  else if (value > MAXVALUE)
    value = MINVALUE;
}
```

```
// Extract current Text Edit control value
void
TVbxDialog::GetValue()
{
  char buffer[EDITLEN];
  Edit1->GetText(buffer, EDITLEN);
  value = atoi(buffer);
  LimitValue();
}

// Set Text Edit control value
void
TVbxDialog::SetValue()
{
  char buffer[EDITLEN];
  LimitValue();
  wsprintf(buffer, "%d", value);
  Edit1->SetText(buffer);
}

// Add k to edit control value
void
TVbxDialog::AdjustValue(int k)
{
  GetValue();
  value += k;
  SetValue();
}

// =============================================================
// The application's main window
// =============================================================

class TVbxDemoWin: public TFrameWindow {
public:
  TVbxDemoWin(TWindow* parent, const char far* title);
protected:
  void CmDemoTest();
DECLARE_RESPONSE_TABLE(TVbxDemoWin);
};

DEFINE_RESPONSE_TABLE1(TVbxDemoWin, TFrameWindow)
  EV_COMMAND(CM_DEMO_TEST, CmDemoTest),
END_RESPONSE_TABLE;

// Constructor
TVbxDemoWin::TVbxDemoWin(TWindow* parent, const char far* title)
  : TFrameWindow(parent, title),
    TWindow(parent, title)
{
```

continues

587

Listing 15.9. continued

```cpp
  AssignMenu(ID_MENU);
}

// Respond to Demo¦Test command; show final value
void
TVbxDemoWin::CmDemoTest()
{
  int value = 50;  // Dialog directly modifies this object
  TVbxDialog *dialog = new TVbxDialog(this, ID_DIALOG, value);
  dialog->Execute();
  delete dialog;
  char buffer[EDITLEN];
  wsprintf(buffer, "%d", value);
  MessageBox(buffer, "Final Value", MB_OK);
}

// ============================================================
// The application class
// ============================================================

class TVbxDemoApp: public TApplication {
public:
  TVbxDemoApp(const char far* name)
    : TApplication(name) {};
  void InitMainWindow();
};

// Initialize the program's main window
void
TVbxDemoApp::InitMainWindow()
{
  EnableCtl3d();
  EnableBWCC();
  MainWindow = new TVbxDemoWin(0, "VBX Control Demonstration");
}

#pragma argsused

// Main program
int
OwlMain(int argc, char* argv[])
{
  TBIVbxLibrary vbxlib;             // Initialize VBX controls
  TVbxDemoApp app("VbxDemo");       // Construct application object
  int runResult = app.Run();        // Run app and save result
  return runResult;                 // Return app run result
}
```

To respond to VBX control events, the dialog class, TVbxDialog is derived from TDialog and also from TVbxEventHandler. The class declares a response table using the macro:

```
DECLARE_RESPONSE_TABLE(TVbxDialog);
```

That tells the compiler to prepare the TVbxDialog class for using a response table. Define that table with the DEFINE_RESPONSE_TABLE2 macro as shown in the listing below the class declaration. (The 2 in the macro name indicates that the class inherits two base classes.) The class should intercept SpinUp and SpinDown messages, generated by clicking the mouse pointer on the SpinButton control. All VBX control events are identified by index and name. Here, I used the EV_VBXEVENTNAME macros to specify the two events as strings. If I knew the event index numbers, I could use the EV_VBXEVENTINDEX instead. It's easier to identify properties and events by name as I did, but it's faster to use the index values.

Each response table entry specifies three pieces of information: the VBX control's resource ID (IDC_SPIN1 or IDC_SPIN2), the name of the event as a string (*SpinUp* or *SpinDown*), and the class function that should be called in response to those events (EvSpinUp or EvSpinDown). It's then a simple matter to program the event functions to perform whatever action you want in response to clicking on the SpinButton—updating a text edit control, for example, or extending a bar on a gauge.

To communicate with the SpinButton, the class constructs an object of type TVbxControl, addressed by a pointer, Spin1. To show the results of the control as a number in a text edit box, I also defined a pointer to a text-edit control object of the TEdit class.

To see how the two controls cooperate, examine the EvSpinUp and EvSpinDown functions. For each click of the SpinButton—or repeatedly while you hold down the mouse button—the control fires events intercepted by the two functions. Statements in the functions increment or decrement the value of the text edit control, into which you can also enter values with the keyboard. There's a lot going on behind the scenes in this seemingly simple example! The edit control, for example, fully supports cut, copy, paste, and undo operations.

It's important to update any controls affected by a VBX control event. For instance, in addition to setting the edit control's text for each change of value, the program also calls that control's UpdateWindow function, inherited from TWindow by the TEdit class. Similarly, each response function also calls the SpinButton's Refresh method—the VBX equivalent of OWL's UpdateWindow. If your controls don't seem to update their values when you think they should, try calling UpdateWindow (for an OWL control) or Refresh (for a VBX control).

Other VBX Notes

An event response function, such as EvSpinUp or EvSpinDown in the sample program, receives a pointer to a structure of type VBXEVENT that describes a control event. The following shows this structure's members:

```
typedef struct VBXEVENT {
   HCTL    Control;    // VBX control handle (not a window handle)
   HWND    Window;     // VBX control window handle
   int     ID;         // Resource or other ID
   int     EventIndex; // Index value of this event
   LPCSTR  EventName;  // Pointer to string value of this event
   int     NumParams;  // Number of parameters attached to event
   LPVOID  ParamList;  // Parameter pointers
} VBXEVENT;
```

Every control is identified by two handles—one for the control object, and one for the control's window. The control is also identified by its resource ID. In addition, the event index and name are passed in the structure. Last are two values not used by every control. NumParams indicates the number of optional parameters associated with this event. Each parameter is stored as a pointer in the following ParamList table. You must use type-casting to extract any addressed information as described in the control's documentation—a significant drawback in the VBX design, as the compiler can't prevent errors caused by incorrectly referencing the passed information. (Ah well, we live in an imperfect world. It's not that big of a problem if you're careful.)

You may also construct objects of the TVbxControl class without inserting VBX controls into dialog resources. Instead, you can use the class's alternate constructor to load a control directly from its .VBX file. You might do that, for example, to display a control inside a window. First, define a pointer:

```
TVbxControl *p;
```

Then, construct an object, specifying the control's filename and other parameters (the this parameter refers to the parent window object):

```
p = new TVbxControl(this,
 123,           // Abitrary ID number
 "SPIN.VBX",    // Control file name
 "SpinButton",  // Object Type
 "VBControl",   // Control title
 42, 36, 15, 17); // Coordinates
```

Compare that with the resource statement in VBXDEMO.RC and the parameters will make better sense. Whatever method you use to construct the control object, you may use the resulting pointer to set properties and to call methods. Use a response table and define class member functions as shown in the sample listing to respond to control events just as you do for VBX controls in a resource. Suppose the control defines an integer property named Temperature. Set that value like this:

```
int k = 123;
p->SetProp("Temperature", k);
Retrieve the control's value by calling GetProp:
int q;
p->GetProp("Temperature", q);
```

The TVbxControl functions SetProp and GetProp are overloaded to the hilt and then some. Use them to set and get control properties of various types. You may also specify a property's index value rather than its name. If the control's Temperature property is identified as the index value 5, for instance, the preceding statements become:

```
p->SetProp(5, k);
p->GetProp(5, k);
```

Call the control's methods as you do other member functions. For example, to refresh a control's contents, call the Refresh function defined by the TVbxControl class:

```
p->Refresh();
```

Exception Handling

Exception handling is the new darling of C++, and like most newfangled vehicles, this one will take time before you are ready to take it out for a spin around the block. Exception handling may seem difficult, but its really just an alternate return mechanism—a method, that is, for functions to return errors as different *types* rather than as reserved *values* (such as the ubiquitous -1 that many functions return to indicate something has gone wrong).

Chapter 3 introduced exceptions and showed how to use them in C++ programs. Up to now, however, I've purposely avoided using exceptions in example programs. Like all error-reporting mechanisms, exceptions are "ugly"—they obscure statements with a layer of error-handling, making it hard to see what's going on below. Exceptions, however, are much better at handling errors that might occur at various levels in a complex program's execution—an especially difficult chore in event-driven operating systems such as Windows.

All of ObjectWindows 2.0 is "exception aware," and by using exceptions in your OWL programs, you can trap your own errors as well as those of a system nature—the inability to construct a child window object, for example, or the failure of the new operator to allocate a requested amount of memory. Because you can now use the same error-reporting mechanism to handle your errors and the system's, in theory at least, error-handling is simpler than ever before. The truth is, writing robust error-handling code is never easy, but perhaps it is a teensy bit easier with C++ exceptions than without.

To demonstrate how to use exceptions in ObjectWindows programs, the following listings force some errors to occur. The sample program's OwlMain function also demonstrates how you can write an OWL program that traps all unhandled exceptions—those that are thrown as a result of a critical condition but are not caught by your statements or by OWL's. Listing 15.10, OWLEX.RH, defines the program's resource identifiers. Listing 15.11, OWLEX.RC, lists the program's resource script. Listing 15.12, OWLEX.CPP, shows the program's source code, explained following the listing.

> **NOTE**
>
> Listings in this section are located in the book disk's OWLEX directory.

Listing 15.10. OWLEX.RH.

```
// owlex.rh -- Resource header file

#define ID_MENU 100
#define CM_TEST 101
#define CM_BLOWUP 102
```

Listing 15.11. OWLEX.RC.

```
#include <owl\window.rh>
#include "owlex.rh"

ID_MENU MENU
BEGIN
  POPUP "&Demo"
  BEGIN
    MENUITEM "&Test", CM_TEST
    MENUITEM "&Blow up", CM_BLOWUP
    MENUITEM SEPARATOR
    MENUITEM "E&xit", CM_EXIT
  END
END
```

Listing 15.12. OWLEX.CPP.

```cpp
/* ============================================================ *\
**  owlex.cpp -- Demonstrates ObjectWindows exceptions         **
** ============================================================ **
**                                                             **
** ============================================================ **
**      Copyright  1994 by Tom Swan. All rights reserved.      **
\* ============================================================ */

#include <owl\applicat.h>
#include <owl\framewin.h>
#include <cstring.h>
#pragma hdrstop
#include "owlex.rh"

// ============================================================
// Bad class (cannot be instantiated)
// ============================================================

class TBadObject {
public:
  TBadObject();
};

// Constructor (always fails)
TBadObject::TBadObject()
{
  throw "TBadObject construction failed";
}

// ============================================================
// The application's main window
// ============================================================

class TOwlExWin: public TFrameWindow {
public:
  TOwlExWin(TWindow* parent, const char far* title);
protected:
  void DoSomethingBad();
  void CmTest();
  void DoBlowup();
  void CmBlowup();
DECLARE_RESPONSE_TABLE(TOwlExWin);
};

DEFINE_RESPONSE_TABLE1(TOwlExWin, TFrameWindow)
  EV_COMMAND(CM_TEST, CmTest),
  EV_COMMAND(CM_BLOWUP, CmBlowup),
END_RESPONSE_TABLE;
```

continues

593

Listing 15.12. continued

```
// Constructor
TOwlExWin::TOwlExWin(TWindow* parent, const char far* title)
  : TFrameWindow(parent, title),
    TWindow(parent, title)
{
  AssignMenu(ID_MENU);
}

// Force an exception
void
TOwlExWin::DoSomethingBad()
{
  throw "Forced exception error";
}

// Call a function that throws an exception. Rethrow any
// error messages as a TXOwl exception object.
void
TOwlExWin::CmTest()
{
  MessageBeep(0);
  try {
    DoSomethingBad();
  }
  catch (const char *s) {
    throw TXOwl(s);
  }
}

// Force object-construction failure
void
TOwlExWin::DoBlowup()
{
  TBadObject* p;
  try {
    p = new TBadObject();
  }
  catch (xalloc x) {
    throw "Memory allocation failure";
  }
  catch (...) {
    throw "Object construction failure";
  }
  delete p;
}
```

```
// Respond to Blow up command. Calls DoBlowup to force
// an exception by attempting to construct an object of
// the TBadObject class.
void
TOwlExWin::CmBlowup()
{
  try {
    DoBlowup();
  }
  catch (const char *s) {
    throw TXOwl(s);
  }
}


// ============================================================
// The application class
// ============================================================

class TOwlExApp: public TApplication {
public:
  TOwlExApp(const char far* name)
    : TApplication(name) {}
  void InitMainWindow();
};

// Initialize the program's main window
void
TOwlExApp::InitMainWindow()
{
  EnableCtl3d();
  EnableBWCC();
  MainWindow = new TOwlExWin(0, "Exceptions");
}

#pragma argsused

// Main program. Catches all unhandled exceptions and gives
// user the option of continuing the program, exiting, or
// restarting.
int
OwlMain(int argc, char* argv[])
{
  TOwlExApp* app;
  int status;
  int done;
  do {
    try {
      app = new TOwlExApp("OwlExApp");
      status = app->Run();
      done = TRUE;
      if (status) {
        char s[40];
```

continues

595

Listing 15.12. continued

```
        wsprintf(s, "Run returned %i", status);
        done = HandleGlobalException(xmsg(string(s)),
          "Abnormal Termination", "RunAgain?");
      }
    }
    catch (xmsg& x) {
      done = status = HandleGlobalException(x,
        "Abnormal Termination, uncaught xmsg", "RunAgain?");
    }
    catch(...) {
      done = status = HandleGlobalException(xmsg(string()),
        "Abnormal Termination, uncaught ...", "RunAgain?");
    }
    delete app;
  } while (!done);
  return status;
}
```

Function CmTest, executed when you select the program's *Demo|Test* command, calls another function, DoSomethingBad, which *throws an exception,* simulating a function that reports an error condition. DoSomethingBad simply executes the statement:

```
throw "Forced exception error";
```

To *catch* that exception, CmTest calls DoSomethingBad inside a try block:

```
try {
  DoSomethingBad();
}
```

If you don't call a function in a try block, any exceptions the function throws are passed upward in the program's call chain until reaching one of the global exception handlers discussed in Chapter 3. (You can also catch unhandled exceptions by writing a special OwlMain function as I explain later.) In most cases, however, you should try to catch the exceptions that a function might throw. For example, in CmTest, the try block is immediately followed by a catch statement:

```
catch (const char *s) {
  throw TXOwl(s);
}
```

The catch statement lists the type of exception—const char *—that the tried function throws. If the function throws an exception of that type, the catch statement is executed. In this case, that statement *rethrows the exception,* converting the string message to an object of the TXOwl class.

This is the best all around way to handle exceptions. In essence, you design your exceptions as strings, then pass them on to ObjectWindows, which knows how to deal with TXOwl objects. (Other classes define their own exception classes, many of which are based on TXOwl.) Figure 15.4 shows the message box that ObjectWindows displays for the exception.

FIGURE 15.4.

*ObjectWindows
exception message box.*

If you want to handle an exception locally, just catch it and display your own message box. In that case, the exception is handled—it goes no farther up the call chain, and ObjectWindows never learns of the exception's existence. It's always up to you whether to handle an exception locally or let ObjectWindows take care of reporting the problem for you.

Exceptions that make it all the way out of the program are called *unhandled exceptions*. To deal sensibly with these serious problems, which might be caused, for example, by an out-of-memory condition or by a failure to construct a window object due to a lack of some system resource in Windows, write an OwlMain function as shown in OWLEX.CPP (see the end of the listing).

The revised OwlMain constructs the program's application object—of type TOwlExApp in this case—inside a try block. OwlMain also calls the application's Run function in the block. This technique catches one of three possible error conditions: a nonzero value returned by Run, an xmsg exception object thrown by a function, or another exception object of some other type. To catch all possible exceptions other than those the program knows about, the final catch statement uses a three-dot ellipsis in parentheses, which stands for "all exception types:"

```
catch(...) {
}
```

Figure 15.5 shows the message box displayed by any exceptions that make it back to OwlMain. To force this type of error to occur, the sample program attempts to construct an object of the TBadObject class, in which a constructor always throws an exception. (Throwing an exception from a constructor results in that object *not* being constructed, and its destructor, if any, is not called.) Calling HandleGlobalException at this stage gives users the chance to resume operation or to restart the program.

FIGURE 15.5.

Unhandled exception message box.

Windows 32-Bit Programming

The big headlines in Windows programming today usually have the phrase *32-bit* in them. Yes, it's time to join the 32-bit bandwagon, but don't jump into the cart without carefully considering the consequences to your programs. Be sure that you *need* 32-bit code before compiling it. Many Windows applications continue to be perfectly suited to 16-bit operation.

I've already gone over the major concerns in Chapter 2, so I won't rehash the basics here. The key fact to remember is: 32-bit-wide integers don't guarantee faster running times. In fact, converting 16-bit values to 32 bits might waste memory, and could result in slower code.

Remember also that there is only one 32-bit Windows operating system, namely, Windows NT. So that NT executable programs can run under Windows 3.1, Microsoft makes available the Win32s subset of NT, which fools Windows 3.1 into thinking that an NT code file is a run-of-the-mill 16-bit .EXE program. That doesn't mean you can run NT programs under Windows 3.1—not every NT capability is available in Win32s. But to target the largest possible market for your 32-bit programs, you can write to the Win32s standard and be sure that Windows 3.1 *and* NT users can run your applications.

> **NOTE**
>
> I call Win32s and Windows NT program's *32-bit Windows* here.

It's easy to create 32-bit Windows programs—just select the Win32 target using the IDE's *TargetExpert* dialog accessed through the local popup menu for a project's .EXE code file or when you create a new project. (See Chapter 2 for a review of these methods.)

The next listings demonstrate a few techniques that you'll find useful in your own 32-bit code. Listing 15.13, WINDEMO.RH, identifies the program's resources. Listing 15.14, WINDEMO.RC, lists the program's resource script. Listing 15.15, WINDEMO.CPP, shows the program's source code.

> **NOTE**
>
> The listings in this section are located in the book disk's WIN32 directory.

Listing 15.13. WINDEMO.RH.

```
// windemo.rh -- Resource header file

#define ID_MENU     100
#define CM_VERSION 101
#define CM_MEMORY 102
#define CM_SIZE 103
```

Listing 15.14. WINDEMO.RC.

```
#include <owl\window.rh>
#include "windemo.rh"

ID_MENU MENU
BEGIN
  POPUP "&Demo"
  BEGIN
    MENUITEM "&Version", CM_VERSION
    MENUITEM "&Memory", CM_MEMORY
    MENUITEM "&Sizes", CM_SIZE
    MENUITEM SEPARATOR
    MENUITEM "E&xit", CM_EXIT
  END
END
```

Listing 15.15. WINDEMO.CPP.

```
/* ============================================================ *\
**   windemo.cpp -- Win32s 32-bit example program              **
** ============================================================ **
**                                                             **
**   Open this program's IDE project file, highlight the file, **
**   WINDEMO.EXE, and press Alt+F10 or click the right mouse   **
**   button to open a local menu. Select TargetExpert from the **
**   menu, and change the Platform to either Windows 3.x (16)  **
**   or to Win32. Select the Project¦Build all command after   **
```

continues

Listing 15.15. continued

```
**   selecting a different platform. You must have Win32s or    **
**   Windows NT installed to run the 32-bit code file.          **
**                                                              **
** ============================================================ **
**      Copyright  1994 by Tom Swan. All rights reserved.       **
\* ============================================================ */

#include <owl\applicat.h>
#include <owl\framewin.h>
#include <owl\dc.h>
#include <owl\gdiobjec.h>
#include <owl\point.h>
#include <bwcc.h>
#include <stdlib.h>
#include <time.h>
#pragma hdrstop
#include "windemo.rh"

#ifdef __WIN32__
#define ARRAY_SIZE 128000    // 128K buffer under 32-bit Windows
#else
#define ARRAY_SIZE 64000L    // 64K buffer under 16-bit Windows
#endif

// ============================================================
// The application's main window
// ============================================================

class TWDemoWin: public TFrameWindow {
public:
  TWDemoWin(TWindow* parent, const char far* title);
protected:
  void CmVersion();
  void CmMemory();
  void CmSize();
  void Paint(TDC &dc, BOOL erase, TRect& rect);
DECLARE_RESPONSE_TABLE(TWDemoWin);
};

DEFINE_RESPONSE_TABLE1(TWDemoWin, TFrameWindow)
  EV_COMMAND(CM_VERSION, CmVersion),
  EV_COMMAND(CM_MEMORY, CmMemory),
  EV_COMMAND(CM_SIZE, CmSize),
END_RESPONSE_TABLE;

// Constructor
TWDemoWin::TWDemoWin(TWindow* parent, const char far* title)
  : TFrameWindow(parent, title),
    TWindow(parent, title)
{
```

```
  AssignMenu(ID_MENU);
  randomize();
}

// Display operating system versions
void
TWDemoWin::CmVersion()
{
  char s[80];
  string msg;
  string nl('\n');
  DWORD version = GetVersion();

// Determine Windows version for 16- and 32-bit GetVersion
  wsprintf(s, "Windows version %d.%d",
    LOBYTE(LOWORD(version)),
    HIBYTE(LOWORD(version)));
  msg = nl + s;

// Determine DOS version for 16-bit GetVersion only
#ifndef __WIN32__
  wsprintf(s, "MS-DOS version %d.%d",
    HIBYTE(HIWORD(version)),
    LOBYTE(HIWORD(version)));
  msg += nl + s;
#endif

// Detect Windows NT or Win32s for 32-bit GetVersion only
#ifdef __WIN32__
  if (HIWORD(version) & 0x8000)
    msg += nl + "Win32s Operating System";
  else
    msg += nl + "Windows NT Operating System";
#endif
  MessageBox(msg.c_str(), "WinDemoApp",
    MB_OK | MB_ICONINFORMATION);
}

// Don't warn about loss of significant digits in CmMemory
#pragma warn -sig

// Allocate some memory to a big buffer
// Size = 128K under 32-bit Windows; 64K under 16-bit Windows
void
TWDemoWin::CmMemory()
{
  char buf[80];  // For MessageBox
  char* bigArray = new char[ARRAY_SIZE];  // Allocate memory
  unsigned sz = &bigArray[ARRAY_SIZE - 1] - &bigArray[0];
```

continues

601

Listing 15.15. continued

```
  sz++;
  wsprintf(buf, "Size of bigArray = %u bytes", sz);
  MessageBox(buf, "WinDemoApp", MB_OK | MB_ICONINFORMATION);
  delete[] bigArray;
}

// Don't warn about unused variables in CmSize
#pragma warn -use

// Display sizes of common variables
void
TWDemoWin::CmSize()
{
  char c;
  short s;
  int i;
  long l;
  float f;
  double d;
  long double ld;
  char buf[80];
  string msg;
  string nl('\n');

  wsprintf(buf, "char -- %2d byte(s)", sizeof);
  msg = buf + nl;
  wsprintf(buf, "short -- %2d byte(s)", sizeof(s));
  msg += buf + nl;
  wsprintf(buf, "int -- %2d byte(s)", sizeof(i));
  msg += buf + nl;
  wsprintf(buf, "long -- %2d byte(s)", sizeof(l));
  msg += buf + nl;
  wsprintf(buf, "float -- %2d byte(s)", sizeof(f));
  msg += buf + nl;
  wsprintf(buf, "double -- %2d byte(s)", sizeof);
  msg += buf + nl;
  wsprintf(buf, "long -- %2d byte(s)", sizeof(ld));
  msg += buf;
  MessageBox(msg.c_str(), "WinDemoApp",
    MB_OK | MB_ICONINFORMATION);
}

// Paint (a rather odd) shape in window
// Works the same for 16- and 32-bit programs
void
TWDemoWin::Paint(TDC &dc, BOOL /*erase*/, TRect& /*rect*/)
{
  TRect r(10, 10, 150, 250);
  TPoint p1(20, 75);
```

```
    TPoint p2(125, 150);
    TSize s1(1, 2);
    TSize s2(2, 1);
    for (int i = 1; i <= 25; ++i) {
      TPen pen(TColor(random(256), random(256), random(256)));
      dc.SelectObject(pen);
      r += s1;
      p1 += s1;
      p2 += s1;
      dc.Arc(r, p1, p2);
      dc.RestorePen();
    }
    for (int j = 1; j <= 25; ++j) {
      TPen pen(TColor(random(256), random(256), random(256)));
      dc.SelectObject(pen);
      r += s2;
      p1 -= s2;
      p2 -= s2;
      dc.Arc(r, p1, p2);
      dc.RestorePen();
    }
}

// ============================================================
// The application class
// ============================================================

class TWDemoApp: public TApplication {
public:
  TWDemoApp(const char far* name)
    : TApplication(name) {}
  void InitMainWindow();
};

// Initialize the program's main window
void
TWDemoApp::InitMainWindow()
{
  EnableCtl3d();
  EnableBWCC();
  BWCCRegister(GetInstance());
  MainWindow = new TWDemoWin(0, "Win32s Demonstration");
}

// Don't warn about unused arguments in OwlMain
#pragma argsused

// Main program
int
```

continues

603

Listing 15.15. continued

```
OwlMain(int argc, char* argv[])
{
  TWDemoApp app("WDemoApp");
  return app.Run();
}
```

The WINDEMO 32-bit demonstration program displays an odd graphical shape just to demonstrate that you write 32-bit output as you do in 16-bit programs. Unfortunately, under Win32s, you cannot call Bezier and a few other advanced graphics functions available only under NT. (If you do call them, nothing bad happens, if that is, no output is "nothing bad.")

To determine whether Win32s, Windows 3.1, or Windows NT is running, use the technique demonstrated in function CmVersion. Call the GetVersion function and assign its result to a DWORD variable:

```
DWORD version = GetVersion();
```

The low and high bytes of that value's low word give the 16- and 32-bit Windows version numbers. The low and high bytes of that value's high word give the DOS version, but not if you call GetVersion while Win32s or Windows NT is running. If either of those systems is running, the high word of that value indicate in the high bit if the system in Win32s (high bit is 1) or Windows NT (high bit is 0).

If that seems confusing, just use the code as listed in CmVersion. Be sure to use the _ _WIN32_ _ symbol, defined only when compiling for 32-bit Windows, to conditionally compile statements intended for 32-bit operation. Figure 15.6 shows the dialog box created when running the program under Win32s and selecting the *Demo|Version* command. (You don't have to start Win32s—running the 32-bit program automatically does that for you. But you do have to *install* Win32s on top of Windows 3.1, which the BC4 installation utility does unless you told it otherwise.)

FIGURE 15.6.

Operating system identification and version message box.

One great advantage of 32-bit Windows is the ability to create large arrays—or, I should say, the advantage is the *lack* of 64K memory segments that have hampered DOS and Windows programmers for many years. As function CmMemory demonstrates, you can create large structures under 32-bit Windows.

When you compile the program for 32 bits, symbol ARRAY_SIZE is defined as 128000. Under 16-bit compilation, that symbol equals 64000. The resulting message box shows the allocated array size, calculated by subtracting the address of the first and last array bytes (and adding one). Figure 15.7 shows the function's dialog box for the program running under Win32s.

FIGURE 15.7.

Function CmMemory's dialog box, showing a large array's size.

When writing 32 bit code, be aware that any assumptions you may have made about the sizes of variables may no longer be correct. Integers, for example, are four bytes long in 32 bit code—not two bytes as they are in 16-bit programs. As you are probably aware, assuming that data types are specific sizes is a dangerous practice. But, as you may also realize, that rule is broken more often than a politician's campaign promises.

Function CmSize illustrates the sizes of common C++ data types for a 32-bit Windows program. Figure 15.8 shows the message box displayed by the function when running under Win32s.

FIGURE 15.8.

C++ variable sizes under 32-bit Windows.

You might want to compile the sample program for 16-bit operation and compare the dialog boxes with those printed in this chapter. Under 16-bit operation, the program displays the Windows and DOS version numbers, it allocates a smaller "big" array, and it shows variable sizes for 16-bit Windows programs. Follow these steps to recompile the program:

1. Use *Project|Open* to open the WINDEMO.IDE project file.
2. Highlight the WINDEMO.EXE filename.
3. Click the right mouse button or press Alt+F10 to open a floating popup menu.
4. Select the *TargetExpert...* command.
5. Change *Platform* to *Windows 3.x (16)*. (Change to Win32 if you are rebuilding for 32-bit operation.) Close the dialog by selecting the OK button.
6. Rebuild all files by selecting the *Project|Build all* command or by selecting the folder toolbar icon with the exclamation point and an arrow pointing to a binary value.

> **NOTE**
>
> When switching between 16- and 32-bit compilation, you must rebuild all files. Pressing F9 or attempting to compile only a portion of a program under this circumstance will fail.

Looking Ahead

This may be the end of the last chapter in this book, but it's hardly the end of what you can do with Borland C++ 4.0 and Windows 16- and 32-bit programming. No single book can cover every Windows programming topic, but I've tried to explain those subjects that will help you get started quickly programming your own Windows applications with BC4. If there are any areas of Windows programming that you'd like to know more about, please write to me in care of the publisher and let us know what subjects you want to have in a future edition of *Mastering Windows Programming*.

Compilation Instructions

After installing the book's diskette (see the page facing the inside back cover), read the following notes for hints about compiling and running the book's listings. The sample programs have the same system requirements as BC4—if you can run the compiler, you should be able to compile and run all of the book's programs. Read these notes, however, if you receive errors during compilation or when running programs.

> **NOTE**
>
> If a README.TXT file is on the book's diskette, open it with a text editor such as the Windows Notepad for additional notes and instructions. Your disk might not have a README.TXT file.

Required Files

You must install Borland C++ 4.0 (BC4) to compile and run this book's sample programs. BC4's BIN directory must be on the system path. Be sure your system's AUTOEXEC.BAT file contains a path statement such as

```
path c:\windows;c:\dos;c:\bc4\bin
```

Type that command exactly as shown with no extra spaces or punctuation. Of course, if your installation uses different pathnames or drive letters, change the command accordingly. You may insert other pathnames, but in case of trouble, try this minimum configuration.

Also specify at least 40 buffers and 60 files in your system's CONFIG.SYS file, which should have two commands such as these:

```
buffers=40
files=60
```

All sample ObjectWindows programs use BC4's dynamic link library, OWL.DLL, which must be available at runtime. Some compiled programs also require other DLLs such as BWCC.DLL (Borland Windows Custom Controls) and CTL3D.DLL (the Windows 3-D control library).

> **NOTE**
>
> For best results, install BC4 before installing and attempting to use this book's diskette.

Compiling from the IDE

If you installed the compiler in the default C:\BC4 directory, and if you specified BC4's default subdirectory names, you should be able to compile and run the sample programs without making any changes. From BC4's integrated development environment (IDE), select the *Project|Open project...* command, change to one of the installed directories (C:\MWP\POLYFLOW, for example), and open the .IDE project file in that directory. After opening a program's project file, press Ctrl+F9 to compile and run the example. Or, press F9 to compile, and then run the program using the Windows File or Program Managers.

> **NOTE**
>
> Three directories do not have .IDE project files. These are DATA (support files used by some of the sample programs), MISC (miscellaneous batch files), and MAKEDEMO (command-line demonstrations).

Compiling from a DOS Prompt

You may compile programs from a DOS prompt with or without Windows running. Change to one of the installed directories, and run BC4's MAKE utility by typing commands such as

```
c:
cd \mwp\polyflow
make
```

Run the resulting .EXE code file by typing win filename at a DOS prompt, or if you are running Windows, by selecting the filename from the Windows File Manager. You can also run programs by entering their path- and filenames with the File or Program Manager *File|Run...* commands, or by dragging the .EXE filename to a Program Manager window and selecting the program's icon.

> **NOTE**
>
> The HOWL (Hello OWL) directory does not have a MAKEFILE, which Chapter 2 explains how to create. The DATA and MISC directories, which do not contain sample programs, also do not have MAKEFILEs.

Configuring Resource Workshop

If Resource Workshop reports errors when opening a program's .RC resource script file, configure RW by following these steps:

1. Run Workshop from the Program Manager or by selecting Resource Workshop from the IDE's Tool menu.

2. Select the *File\Preferences...* command and enter the compiler's installation INCLUDE directory in the Include path input box. For example, I set my path to C:\BC4\INCLUDE;. Unlike pathnames in the IDE, RW's include-pathname ends with a semicolon.

3. Toggle on the *Generate* identifiers automatically checkbox.

4. Select an appropriate Target Windows version option. Most readers should set this option to Windows 3.1.

> **NOTE**
>
> Step 3 works around a bug in RW that causes automatic menu-generation commands in the menu editor to fail. Contact Borland if you experience this trouble. If not, you can toggle off automatic identifier generation. Be aware also that this option affects RW's startup operations. When the option is on and you start a new resource project, RW prompts you for a resource header filename (in which new identifier #define statements are inserted). When the option is off, you must create a resource header file using the *File\Add to project...* command.

Modifying Project Files

All projects on the diskette assume you installed the compiler in the default drive and directory, C:\BC4. Follow these steps to update the book's MAKEFILE and project files if you installed BC4 in a different location:

1. Use the IDE's *Project\Open project...* command to open a program's .IDE project file.

2. Select the *Options\Project...* command, and highlight the Directories topic from the Topics list in the Project Options dialog.

3. Change Source Directories to your compiler's INCLUDE and LIB subdirectories. For example, if you installed the compiler in D:\BC4, change the Include directory to D:\BC4\INCLUDE and change Library to D:\BC4\LIB.

4. Select OK to close the dialog and accept your changes, then close the project file with the *Project|Close project* command. Repeat these steps for each .IDE project file.

Modifying MAKEFILEs

If you compile from a DOS prompt, you can use one of two methods to update the book's MAKEFILEs if you did not install the compiler in the default C:\BC4 drive and directory. Follow these steps:

1. Use the IDE to modify each project file as explained in the preceding section, but don't close the project.

2. Select the *Project|Generate makefile* command to create a new file named with the extension .MAK.

3. Close the project and answer Yes when prompted whether to save the generated file.

4. Rename the original MAKEFILE in the directory to MAKEFILE.BAK, then rename the newly generated file to MAKEFILE.

> **NOTE**
>
> BC4 occasionally fails to create a proper MAKEFILE from an IDE project. When recreating MAKEFILEs, save the original file for comparison in case the results do not work. In a few cases, I hand-edited the supplied MAKEFILEs to remove faulty commands inserted by the IDE.

Rather than modify the project files and regenerate each MAKEFILE, you might find it easier to use a text editor to change the pathnames in the files. Simply load each MAKEFILE into your editor, and globally replace C:\BC4 with your compiler's installation drive and path.

Cleaning Directories

After compiling, running, and examining a program, you might want to delete the many files created by the IDE, the command-line compiler, MAKE, and Resource Workshop. These files can occupy lots of room, which you can recover by running the supplied batch files explained here. (You can delete the extra files manually, but using the batch files is much easier.)

Of all generated files, precompiled headers take the most room. Because all of this book's sample programs use precompiled headers to save compilation time, you might have to delete one or more of these files to make room for compiling other programs. Precompiled headers, named with the extension .CSM (compiled symbol), store declarations (classes, #define directives, and so on) in fast-loading binary form. The first time you compile a program, the compiler creates a precompiled header file for use during subsequent compilations. This saves time by not recompiling declarations that haven't changed.

Unfortunately, precompiled header files can take acres of disk space—as much as seven or eight megabytes in some cases. If your disk is short on free space, you might want to delete precompiled headers and other files after compiling each sample program.

For easier clean ups, the installed C:\MWP directory has two batch files, CLEAN.BAT and CLEANUP.BAT (see Listings A.1 and A.2), which you can run from a DOS prompt. Run CLEAN file to restore a specified directory to its original installed state. Run CLEANUP to restore all directories to their installed states.

To clean a specified directory, from a DOS prompt, change to C:\MWP and run the CLEAN batch file. To clean the POLYFLOW directory, for example, enter the commands:

```
c:
cd \mwp
clean polyflow
```

To clean all directories, run CLEANALL, which calls CLEAN for each of the book disk's subdirectories. Enter these commands to restore all directories to their installed states:

```
c:
cd \mwp
cleanall
```

> **NOTE**
>
> Before running CLEAN or CLEANALL, examine the list of files that CLEAN deletes. You can modify the commands to delete fewer or additional file types. For example, if you don't want to delete .EXE files, simply comment out that del instruction by prefacing the line with REM. Or, you can delete the instruction.

Listing A.1. CLEAN.BAT.

```
@echo off
rem
rem clean.bat -- erase unneeded files (called by cleanall.bat)
rem ex. call clean mdidemo
rem
if "%1"=="" goto ERROR
if exist %1\NUL goto CONTINUE
goto ERROR
:CONTINUE
cd %1
echo Cleaning %1
rem
rem Add new files to delete here:
rem
if exist *.bak del *.bak
if exist *.cfg del *.cfg
if exist *.csm del *.csm
if exist *.dll del *.dll
if exist *.dsk del *.dsk
if exist *.dsw del *.dsw
```

continues

613

Listing A.1. continued

```
if exist *.err del *.err
if exist *.exe del *.exe
if exist *.lib del *.lib
if exist *.lst del *.lst
if exist *.map del *.map
if exist *.pdl del *.pdl
if exist *.obj del *.obj
if exist *.obr del *.obr
if exist *.res del *.res
if exist *.rws del *.rws
if exist *.scr del *.scr
if exist *.tdr del *.tdr
if exist *.tdw del *.tdw
if exist *.trw del *.trw
if exist *.t2r del *.t2r
if exist *.tr2 del *.tr2
if exist *.td2 del *.td2
if exist *.~*  del *.~*
rem
rem Go back one directory level and end
rem
cd ..
goto END
:ERROR
echo Error! No directory or directory invalid.
echo Directory specified: %1
pause
:END
```

Listing A.2. CLEANALL.BAT.

```
@echo off
rem
rem cleanall.bat -- call clean.bat for all source directories
rem
echo working...
if exist *.bak del *.bak
call clean appstart
call clean args
call clean bar
call clean button
call clean client
call clean controls
call clean data
call clean decorate
call clean diagapp
```

```
call clean diagctl
call clean diagmain
call clean dllbit
call clean dllres
call clean drawbit
call clean except
call clean howl
call clean makedemo
call clean mdideco
call clean mdidemo
call clean mdidraw
call clean menudemo
call clean menuobj
call clean misc
call clean option
call clean owlex
call clean painter
call clean pdemo
call clean polyflow
call clean resbit
call clean resdemo
call clean rubber
call clean ruler
call clean scroll
call clean shell
call clean showbit
call clean sketch
call clean validate
call clean vbxdemo
call clean wback
call clean win32
call clean winsize
call clean wlist
call clean wprint
echo done
:END
```

TIP

You can save additional disk space by stripping debugging and browsing information from compiled code files. First, compile the program, then, to reduce the code file's size, from a DOS prompt, enter a command such as: `tdstrip polyflow`

B

File Finder

Installing the accompanying diskette (see instructions on the page facing the inside back cover) creates the following subdirectories and files. All of this book's printed listings, along with many related support files, are included on disk.

Use this appendix to confirm that your installation is complete, to restore a directory to its installation state (by deleting files created by the compiler and linker, for example), and to determine how much space on disk a particular file or directory requires. I used the following DOS command to create this directories listed here:

```
dir /ONEG /S >dir.txt
```

> **NOTE**
>
> Directory and file times are set to 4:00a, which matches the Borland C++ version number 4.0. Directory dates and times will differ on your system.

MWP Directories and Files

```
Volume in drive C is CDRIVE
Volume Serial Number is 0FD8-1422
```

Directory of C:\MWP

```
.                <DIR>         03-21-94    4:00a
..               <DIR>         03-21-94    4:00a
APPSTART         <DIR>         03-21-94    4:00a
ARGS             <DIR>         03-21-94    4:00a
BAR              <DIR>         03-21-94    4:00a
BUTTON           <DIR>         03-21-94    4:00a
CLEAN    BAT       1054        03-21-94    4:00a
CLEANALL BAT        973        03-21-94    4:00a
CLIENT           <DIR>         03-21-94    4:00a
CONTROLS         <DIR>         03-21-94    4:00a
DATA             <DIR>         03-21-94    4:00a
DECORATE         <DIR>         03-21-94    4:00a
DIAGAPP          <DIR>         03-21-94    4:00a
DIAGCTL          <DIR>         03-21-94    4:00a
DIAGMAIN         <DIR>         03-21-94    4:00a
DLLBIT           <DIR>         03-21-94    4:00a
DLLRES           <DIR>         03-21-94    4:00a
DRAWBIT          <DIR>         03-21-94    4:00a
EXCEPT           <DIR>         03-21-94    4:00a
HOWL             <DIR>         03-21-94    4:00a
MAKEDEMO         <DIR>         03-21-94    4:00a
MDIDECO          <DIR>         03-21-94    4:00a
MDIDEMO          <DIR>         03-21-94    4:00a
MDIDRAW          <DIR>         03-21-94    4:00a
MENUDEMO         <DIR>         03-21-94    4:00a
MENUOBJ          <DIR>         03-21-94    4:00a
MISC             <DIR>         03-21-94    4:00a
OPTION           <DIR>         03-21-94    4:00a
OWLEX            <DIR>         03-21-94    4:00a
PAINTER          <DIR>         03-21-94    4:00a
PDEMO            <DIR>         03-21-94    4:00a
POLYFLOW         <DIR>         03-21-94    4:00a
RESBIT           <DIR>         03-21-94    4:00a
RESDEMO          <DIR>         03-21-94    4:00a
RUBBER           <DIR>         03-21-94    4:00a
RULER            <DIR>         03-21-94    4:00a
SCROLL           <DIR>         03-21-94    4:00a
SHELL            <DIR>         03-21-94    4:00a
SHOWBIT          <DIR>         03-21-94    4:00a
SKETCH           <DIR>         03-21-94    4:00a
VALIDATE         <DIR>         03-21-94    4:00a
VBXDEMO          <DIR>         03-21-94    4:00a
WBACK            <DIR>         03-21-94    4:00a
WIN32            <DIR>         03-21-94    4:00a
```

```
WINSIZE       <DIR>      03-21-94    4:00a
WLIST         <DIR>      03-21-94    4:00a
WPRINT        <DIR>      03-21-94    4:00a
         47 file(s)         2027 bytes
```

Subdirectories and Files

APPSTART

Directory of C:\MWP\APPSTART

```
.             <DIR>      03-21-94    4:00a
..            <DIR>      03-21-94    4:00a
APPSTART CPP        1816 03-21-94    4:00a
APPSTART DEF         117 03-21-94    4:00a
APPSTART IDE       34604 03-21-94    4:00a
APPSTART RC          137 03-21-94    4:00a
APPSTART RH           72 03-21-94    4:00a
MAKEFILE            1368 03-21-94    4:00a
          8 file(s)        38114 bytes
```

ARGS

Directory of C:\MWP\ARGS

```
.             <DIR>      03-21-94    4:00a
..            <DIR>      03-21-94    4:00a
ARGS     CPP        1162 03-21-94    4:00a
ARGS     DEF         115 03-21-94    4:00a
ARGS     IDE       33558 03-21-94    4:00a
MAKEFILE            1122 03-21-94    4:00a
          6 file(s)        35957 bytes
```

BAR

Directory of C:\MWP\BAR

```
.             <DIR>      03-21-94    4:00a
..            <DIR>      03-21-94    4:00a
BAR      CPP        5384 03-21-94    4:00a
BAR      DEF         115 03-21-94    4:00a
BAR      H          1107 03-21-94    4:00a
BAR      IDE       36842 03-21-94    4:00a
BAR      RC          133 03-21-94    4:00a
BAR      RH          100 03-21-94    4:00a
MAKEFILE            1203 03-21-94    4:00a
          9 file(s)        44884 bytes
```

619

BUTTON

Directory of C:\MWP\BUTTON

```
.             <DIR>      03-21-94   4:00a
..            <DIR>      03-21-94   4:00a
BUTTON   CPP    3414 03-21-94   4:00a
BUTTON   DEF     115 03-21-94   4:00a
BUTTON   IDE   34950 03-21-94   4:00a
BUTTON   RC      146 03-21-94   4:00a
BUTTON   RH      203 03-21-94   4:00a
MAKEFILE        1304 03-21-94   4:00a
        8 file(s)     40132 bytes
```

CLIENT

Directory of C:\MWP\CLIENT

```
.             <DIR>      03-21-94   4:00a
..            <DIR>      03-21-94   4:00a
CLIENT   CPP    4198 03-21-94   4:00a
CLIENT   DEF     115 03-21-94   4:00a
CLIENT   IDE   35986 03-21-94   4:00a
CLIENT   RC      174 03-21-94   4:00a
CLIENT   RH       88 03-21-94   4:00a
MAKEFILE        1304 03-21-94   4:00a
        8 file(s)     41865 bytes
```

CONTROLS

Directory of C:\MWP\CONTROLS

```
.             <DIR>      03-21-94   4:00a
..            <DIR>      03-21-94   4:00a
BNCHILD  CPP    1772 03-21-94   4:00a
BNCHILD  H       426 03-21-94   4:00a
CBCHILD  CPP    1512 03-21-94   4:00a
CBCHILD  H       301 03-21-94   4:00a
CONTROLS CPP    3680 03-21-94   4:00a
CONTROLS DEF     115 03-21-94   4:00a
CONTROLS IDE   76678 03-21-94   4:00a
CONTROLS RC     1034 03-21-94   4:00a
CONTROLS RH      214 03-21-94   4:00a
GACHILD  CPP    1358 03-21-94   4:00a
GACHILD  H       284 03-21-94   4:00a
LBCHILD  CPP    1533 03-21-94   4:00a
LBCHILD  H       296 03-21-94   4:00a
```

```
MAKEFILE              4366 03-21-94   4:00a
SBCHILD   CPP         2844 03-21-94   4:00a
SBCHILD   H            577 03-21-94   4:00a
TXCHILD   CPP         1133 03-21-94   4:00a
TXCHILD   H            275 03-21-94   4:00a
        20 file(s)        98398 bytes
```

DATA

Directory of C:\MWP\DATA

```
.              <DIR>        03-21-94   4:00a
..             <DIR>        03-21-94   4:00a
PICTURE  BMP   153718 03-21-94   4:00a
SAMPLE   ICO      766 03-21-94   4:00a
         4 file(s)       154484 bytes
```

DECORATE

Directory of C:\MWP\DECORATE

```
.              <DIR>        03-21-94   4:00a
..             <DIR>        03-21-94   4:00a
DECORATE CPP    4773 03-21-94   4:00a
DECORATE DEF     115 03-21-94   4:00a
DECORATE IDE   39340 03-21-94   4:00a
DECORATE RC     3877 03-21-94   4:00a
DECORATE RH      792 03-21-94   4:00a
MAKEFILE        1368 03-21-94   4:00a
         8 file(s)        50265 bytes
```

DIAGAPP

Directory of C:\MWP\DIAGAPP

```
.              <DIR>        03-21-94   4:00a
..             <DIR>        03-21-94   4:00a
DIAGAPP  CPP    3013 03-21-94   4:00a
DIAGAPP  DEF     115 03-21-94   4:00a
DIAGAPP  IDE   35146 03-21-94   4:00a
DIAGAPP  RC      937 03-21-94   4:00a
DIAGAPP  RH      132 03-21-94   4:00a
MAKEFILE        1358 03-21-94   4:00a
         8 file(s)        40701 bytes
```

DIAGCTL

Directory of C:\MWP\DIAGCTL

```
.                <DIR>      03-21-94    4:00a
..               <DIR>      03-21-94    4:00a
DIAGCTL  CPP      3382 03-21-94    4:00a
DIAGCTL  DEF       115 03-21-94    4:00a
DIAGCTL  IDE     35708 03-21-94    4:00a
DIAGCTL  RC       1394 03-21-94    4:00a
DIAGCTL  RH        362 03-21-94    4:00a
MAKEFILE          1336 03-21-94    4:00a
        8 file(s)      42297 bytes
```

DIAGMAIN

Directory of C:\MWP\DIAGMAIN

```
.                <DIR>      03-21-94    4:00a
..               <DIR>      03-21-94    4:00a
DIAGMAIN CPP      3291 03-21-94    4:00a
DIAGMAIN DEF       115 03-21-94    4:00a
DIAGMAIN IDE     34728 03-21-94    4:00a
DIAGMAIN RC       1031 03-21-94    4:00a
DIAGMAIN RH        143 03-21-94    4:00a
MAKEFILE          1368 03-21-94    4:00a
        8 file(s)      40676 bytes
```

DLLBIT

Directory of C:\MWP\DLLBIT

```
.                <DIR>      03-21-94    4:00a
..               <DIR>      03-21-94    4:00a
DLLAPP   CPP      2301 03-21-94    4:00a
DLLAPP   DEF       115 03-21-94    4:00a
DLLAPP   H         93 03-21-94    4:00a
DLLAPP   IDE     43332 03-21-94    4:00a
DLLAPP   RC       198 03-21-94    4:00a
DLLAPP   RH        86 03-21-94    4:00a
DLLWIN   CPP      2694 03-21-94    4:00a
DLLWIN   H        594 03-21-94    4:00a
MAKEFILE          2145 03-21-94    4:00a
       11 file(s)      51558 bytes
```

DLLRES

Directory of C:\MWP\DLLRES

```
.                  <DIR>         03-21-94    4:00a
..                 <DIR>         03-21-94    4:00a
DLLRES   CPP        2922 03-21-94    4:00a
DLLRES   DEF         115 03-21-94    4:00a
DLLRES   IDE       37008 03-21-94    4:00a
DLLRES   RC          275 03-21-94    4:00a
DLLRES   RH          136 03-21-94    4:00a
MAKEFILE           2222 03-21-94    4:00a
RESOURCE ICO         766 03-21-94    4:00a
RESOURCE RC          212 03-21-94    4:00a
RESOURCE RH          242 03-21-94    4:00a
        11 file(s)      43898 bytes
```

DRAWBIT

Directory of C:\MWP\DRAWBIT

```
.                  <DIR>         03-21-94    4:00a
..                 <DIR>         03-21-94    4:00a
DRAWBIT  CPP        6788 03-21-94    4:00a
DRAWBIT  DEF         115 03-21-94    4:00a
DRAWBIT  H           142 03-21-94    4:00a
DRAWBIT  IDE       36502 03-21-94    4:00a
DRAWBIT  RC          171 03-21-94    4:00a
DRAWBIT  RH          158 03-21-94    4:00a
MAKEFILE           1336 03-21-94    4:00a
         9 file(s)      45212 bytes
```

EXCEPT

Directory of C:\MWP\EXCEPT

```
.                  <DIR>         03-21-94    4:00a
..                 <DIR>         03-21-94    4:00a
EXCEPT   CPP        2907 03-21-94    4:00a
EXCEPT   DEF         115 03-21-94    4:00a
EXCEPT   IDE       23378 03-21-94    4:00a
MAKEFILE           1087 03-21-94    4:00a
         6 file(s)      27487 bytes
```

623

HOWL

Directory of C:\MWP\HOWL

```
.              <DIR>        03-21-94    4:00a
..             <DIR>        03-21-94    4:00a
CHOWL16   BAT       173 03-21-94    4:00a
CHOWL32   BAT       156 03-21-94    4:00a
HOWL      CPP       237 03-21-94    4:00a
HOWL      DEF       117 03-21-94    4:00a
HOWL      IDE     32228 03-21-94    4:00a
          7 file(s)       32911 bytes
```

MAKEDEMO

Directory of C:\MWP\MAKEDEMO

```
.              <DIR>        03-21-94    4:00a
..             <DIR>        03-21-94    4:00a
DEMO      CPP      1072 03-21-94    4:00a
DEMO      DEF       117 03-21-94    4:00a
DEMO      H          79 03-21-94    4:00a
DEMO      RC        253 03-21-94    4:00a
DEMO      RH        108 03-21-94    4:00a
DEMOWIN   CPP       253 03-21-94    4:00a
DEMOWIN   H         193 03-21-94    4:00a
MAKE16    MAK      5806 03-21-94    4:00a
MAKE32    MAK      5540 03-21-94    4:00a
MAKEFILE           5806 03-21-94    4:00a
          12 file(s)      19227 bytes
```

MDIDECO

Directory of C:\MWP\MDIDECO

```
.              <DIR>        03-21-94    4:00a
..             <DIR>        03-21-94    4:00a
MAKEFILE           1336 03-21-94    4:00a
MDIDECO   CPP      6909 03-21-94    4:00a
MDIDECO   DEF       115 03-21-94    4:00a
MDIDECO   IDE     42954 03-21-94    4:00a
MDIDECO   RC      14373 03-21-94    4:00a
MDIDECO   RH        580 03-21-94    4:00a
          8 file(s)       66267 bytes
```

MDIDEMO

Directory of C:\MWP\MDIDEMO

```
.               <DIR>      03-21-94    4:00a
..              <DIR>      03-21-94    4:00a
MAKEFILE              1336 03-21-94    4:00a
MDIDEMO  CPP         3627 03-21-94    4:00a
MDIDEMO  DEF          115 03-21-94    4:00a
MDIDEMO  IDE        35348 03-21-94    4:00a
MDIDEMO  RC           579 03-21-94    4:00a
MDIDEMO  RH           178 03-21-94    4:00a
        8 file(s)        41183 bytes
```

MDIDRAW

Directory of C:\MWP\MDIDRAW

```
.               <DIR>      03-21-94    4:00a
..              <DIR>      03-21-94    4:00a
BADFILE  MDW          511 03-21-94    4:00a
BALLOON  MDW          858 03-21-94    4:00a
CHILD    CPP         7521 03-21-94    4:00a
CHILD    H           1890 03-21-94    4:00a
CLIENT   CPP         6108 03-21-94    4:00a
CLIENT   H           1243 03-21-94    4:00a
ELLIPSE  MDW          759 03-21-94    4:00a
LINE     MDW          764 03-21-94    4:00a
MAKEFILE             1672 03-21-94    4:00a
MDIDRAW  CPP         3387 03-21-94    4:00a
MDIDRAW  DEF          117 03-21-94    4:00a
MDIDRAW  IDE        63016 03-21-94    4:00a
MDIDRAW  RC         13443 03-21-94    4:00a
MDIDRAW  RH           693 03-21-94    4:00a
RECT     MDW         1019 03-21-94    4:00a
TOOLS    CPP         5253 03-21-94    4:00a
TOOLS    H           2881 03-21-94    4:00a
       19 file(s)       111135 bytes
```

MENUDEMO

Directory of C:\MWP\MENUDEMO

```
.               <DIR>      03-21-94    4:00a
..              <DIR>      03-21-94    4:00a
MAKEFILE             1368 03-21-94    4:00a
MENUDEMO CPP         2655 03-21-94    4:00a
MENUDEMO DEF          115 03-21-94    4:00a
```

625

```
MENUDEMO IDE       34212 03-21-94    4:00a
MENUDEMO RC          781 03-21-94    4:00a
MENUDEMO RH          318 03-21-94    4:00a
         8 file(s)       39449 bytes
```

MENUOBJ

Directory of C:\MWP\MENUOBJ

```
.              <DIR>      03-21-94    4:00a
..             <DIR>      03-21-94    4:00a
MAKEFILE             1336 03-21-94    4:00a
MENUOBJ  CPP         4667 03-21-94    4:00a
MENUOBJ  DEF          115 03-21-94    4:00a
MENUOBJ  IDE        36278 03-21-94    4:00a
MENUOBJ  RC           206 03-21-94    4:00a
MENUOBJ  RH           187 03-21-94    4:00a
         8 file(s)       42789 bytes
```

MISC

Directory of C:\MWP\MISC

```
.              <DIR>      03-21-94    4:00a
..             <DIR>      03-21-94    4:00a
C16      BAT          165 03-21-94    4:00a
C32      BAT          148 03-21-94    4:00a
         4 file(s)         313 bytes
```

OPTION

Directory of C:\MWP\OPTION

```
.              <DIR>      03-21-94    4:00a
..             <DIR>      03-21-94    4:00a
MAKEFILE             1304 03-21-94    4:00a
OPTION   CPP         6632 03-21-94    4:00a
OPTION   DEF          115 03-21-94    4:00a
OPTION   H            509 03-21-94    4:00a
OPTION   IDE        37762 03-21-94    4:00a
OPTION   RC          1870 03-21-94    4:00a
OPTION   RH           546 03-21-94    4:00a
         9 file(s)       48738 bytes
```

OWLEX

Directory of C:\MWP\OWLEX

```
.               <DIR>        03-21-94    4:00a
..              <DIR>        03-21-94    4:00a
MAKEFILE              1272 03-21-94    4:00a
OWLEX    CPP         3899 03-21-94    4:00a
OWLEX    DEF          115 03-21-94    4:00a
OWLEX    IDE        34430 03-21-94    4:00a
OWLEX    RC           232 03-21-94    4:00a
OWLEX    RH           110 03-21-94    4:00a
        8 file(s)        40058 bytes
```

PAINTER

Directory of C:\MWP\PAINTER

```
.               <DIR>        03-21-94    4:00a
..              <DIR>        03-21-94    4:00a
MAKEFILE              1336 03-21-94    4:00a
PAINTER  CPP         5921 03-21-94    4:00a
PAINTER  DEF          115 03-21-94    4:00a
PAINTER  IDE        36030 03-21-94    4:00a
PAINTER  RC           139 03-21-94    4:00a
PAINTER  RH            62 03-21-94    4:00a
        8 file(s)        43603 bytes
```

PDEMO

Directory of C:\MWP\PDEMO

```
.               <DIR>        03-21-94    4:00a
..              <DIR>        03-21-94    4:00a
MAKEFILE              1272 03-21-94    4:00a
PDEMO    CPP         1838 03-21-94    4:00a
PDEMO    DEF          115 03-21-94    4:00a
PDEMO    IDE        36010 03-21-94    4:00a
PDEMO    RC           139 03-21-94    4:00a
PDEMO    RH            62 03-21-94    4:00a
        8 file(s)        39436 bytes
```

POLYFLOW

Directory of C:\MWP\POLYFLOW

```
.               <DIR>        03-21-94    4:00a
..              <DIR>        03-21-94    4:00a
```

627

```
MAKEFILE            1368 03-21-94   4:00a
POLYFLOW CPP        7367 03-21-94   4:00a
POLYFLOW DEF         115 03-21-94   4:00a
POLYFLOW H           210 03-21-94   4:00a
POLYFLOW IDE       36768 03-21-94   4:00a
POLYFLOW RC          140 03-21-94   4:00a
POLYFLOW RH           98 03-21-94   4:00a
         9 file(s)       46066 bytes
```

RESBIT

Directory of C:\MWP\RESBIT

```
.               <DIR>        03-21-94   4:00a
..              <DIR>        03-21-94   4:00a
MAKEFILE            1304 03-21-94   4:00a
RESBIT   CPP        3093 03-21-94   4:00a
RESBIT   DEF         115 03-21-94   4:00a
RESBIT   H           146 03-21-94   4:00a
RESBIT   ICO         766 03-21-94   4:00a
RESBIT   IDE       37148 03-21-94   4:00a
RESBIT   RC         8337 03-21-94   4:00a
RESBIT   RH          274 03-21-94   4:00a
        10 file(s)       51183 bytes
```

RESDEMO

Directory of C:\MWP\RESDEMO

```
.               <DIR>        03-21-94   4:00a
..              <DIR>        03-21-94   4:00a
MAKEFILE            1336 03-21-94   4:00a
RESDEMO  CPP        2481 03-21-94   4:00a
RESDEMO  DEF         115 03-21-94   4:00a
RESDEMO  ICO         766 03-21-94   4:00a
RESDEMO  IDE       35686 03-21-94   4:00a
RESDEMO  RC          879 03-21-94   4:00a
RESDEMO  RH          215 03-21-94   4:00a
         9 file(s)       41478 bytes
```

RUBBER

Directory of C:\MWP\RUBBER

```
.               <DIR>        03-21-94   4:00a
..              <DIR>        03-21-94   4:00a
```

```
DRAG      CPP       1697 03-21-94   4:00a
DRAG      H         1056 03-21-94   4:00a
MAKEFILE            1542 03-21-94   4:00a
RUBBER    CPP       1796 03-21-94   4:00a
RUBBER    H          905 03-21-94   4:00a
TESTRUB   CPP       3460 03-21-94   4:00a
TESTRUB   DEF        115 03-21-94   4:00a
TESTRUB   H          103 03-21-94   4:00a
TESTRUB   IDE      46556 03-21-94   4:00a
TESTRUB   RC         136 03-21-94   4:00a
TESTRUB   RH          96 03-21-94   4:00a
         13 file(s)      57462 bytes
```

RULER

Directory of C:\MWP\RULER

```
.              <DIR>      03-21-94   4:01a
..             <DIR>      03-21-94   4:01a
MAKEFILE            1447 03-21-94   4:00a
RULER     CPP       7691 03-21-94   4:00a
RULER     DEF        115 03-21-94   4:00a
RULER     IDE      40098 03-21-94   4:00a
RULER     RC         306 03-21-94   4:00a
RULER     RH         117 03-21-94   4:00a
          8 file(s)      49774 bytes
```

SCROLL

Directory of C:\MWP\SCROLL

```
.              <DIR>      03-21-94   4:01a
..             <DIR>      03-21-94   4:01a
MAKEFILE            1304 03-21-94   4:00a
SCROLL    CPP       3166 03-21-94   4:00a
SCROLL    DEF        115 03-21-94   4:00a
SCROLL    H          112 03-21-94   4:00a
SCROLL    IDE      36468 03-21-94   4:00a
SCROLL    RC         136 03-21-94   4:00a
SCROLL    RH         103 03-21-94   4:00a
          9 file(s)      41404 bytes
```

629

SHELL

Directory of C:\MWP\SHELL

```
.                 <DIR>      03-21-94    4:01a
..                <DIR>      03-21-94    4:01a
MAKEFILE              1304   03-21-94    4:00a
XSHELL    CPP        2128    03-21-94    4:00a
XSHELL    DEF         115    03-21-94    4:00a
XSHELL    H            55    03-21-94    4:00a
XSHELL    IDE       34664    03-21-94    4:00a
XSHELL    RC          174    03-21-94    4:00a
XSHELL    RH           88    03-21-94    4:00a
          9 file(s)       38528 bytes
```

SHOWBIT

Directory of C:\MWP\SHOWBIT

```
.                 <DIR>      03-21-94    4:01a
..                <DIR>      03-21-94    4:01a
MAKEFILE              1336   03-21-94    4:00a
SHOWBIT   CPP        3379    03-21-94    4:00a
SHOWBIT   DEF         115    03-21-94    4:00a
SHOWBIT   H            95    03-21-94    4:00a
SHOWBIT   IDE       25358    03-21-94    4:00a
SHOWBIT   RC          139    03-21-94    4:00a
SHOWBIT   RH           64    03-21-94    4:00a
          9 file(s)       30486 bytes
```

SKETCH

Directory of C:\MWP\SKETCH

```
.                 <DIR>      03-21-94    4:01a
..                <DIR>      03-21-94    4:01a
MAKEFILE              1304   03-21-94    4:00a
SKETCH    CPP        3624    03-21-94    4:00a
SKETCH    DEF         115    03-21-94    4:00a
SKETCH    IDE       36050    03-21-94    4:00a
SKETCH    RC          175    03-21-94    4:00a
SKETCH    RH           89    03-21-94    4:00a
          8 file(s)       41357 bytes
```

VALIDATE

Directory of C:\MWP\VALIDATE

```
.                <DIR>      03-21-94    4:01a
..               <DIR>      03-21-94    4:01a
MAKEFILE          1549 03-21-94    4:00a
VALIDATE CPP      5447 03-21-94    4:00a
VALIDATE DEF       115 03-21-94    4:00a
VALIDATE IDE     37314 03-21-94    4:00a
VALIDATE RC       1640 03-21-94    4:00a
VALIDATE RH        406 03-21-94    4:00a
        8 file(s)      46471 bytes
```

VBXDEMO

Directory of C:\MWP\VBXDEMO

```
.                <DIR>      03-21-94    4:01a
..               <DIR>      03-21-94    4:01a
MAKEFILE          1832 03-21-94    4:00a
SPIN     VBX     22528 03-21-94    4:00a
VBXDEMO  CPP      5662 03-21-94    4:00a
VBXDEMO  DEF       115 03-21-94    4:00a
VBXDEMO  IDE     37294 03-21-94    4:00a
VBXDEMO  RC        986 03-21-94    4:00a
VBXDEMO  RH        157 03-21-94    4:00a
        9 file(s)      68574 bytes
```

WBACK

Directory of C:\MWP\WBACK

```
.                <DIR>      03-21-94    4:01a
..               <DIR>      03-21-94    4:01a
MAKEFILE          1272 03-21-94    4:00a
WBACK    CPP      2750 03-21-94    4:00a
WBACK    DEF       115 03-21-94    4:00a
WBACK    IDE     36046 03-21-94    4:00a
WBACK    RC        139 03-21-94    4:00a
WBACK    RH         97 03-21-94    4:00a
        8 file(s)      40419 bytes
```

WIN32

Directory of C:\MWP\WIN32

```
.                 <DIR>      03-21-94    4:01a
..                <DIR>      03-21-94    4:01a
MAKEFILE            1379 03-21-94    4:00a
WINDEMO  CPP        5818 03-21-94    4:00a
WINDEMO  DEF         115 03-21-94    4:00a
WINDEMO  IDE       36748 03-21-94    4:00a
WINDEMO  RC          272 03-21-94    4:00a
WINDEMO  RH          136 03-21-94    4:00a
        8 file(s)       44468 bytes
```

WINSIZE

Directory of C:\MWP\WINSIZE

```
.                 <DIR>      03-21-94    4:01a
..                <DIR>      03-21-94    4:01a
MAKEFILE            1200 03-21-94    4:00a
WINSIZE  CPP        2955 03-21-94    4:00a
WINSIZE  DEF         115 03-21-94    4:00a
WINSIZE  IDE       33566 03-21-94    4:00a
        6 file(s)       37836 bytes
```

WLIST

Directory of C:\MWP\WLIST

```
.                 <DIR>      03-21-94    4:01a
..                <DIR>      03-21-94    4:01a
MAKEFILE            1272 03-21-94    4:00a
WLIST    CPP        9571 03-21-94    4:00a
WLIST    DEF         117 03-21-94    4:00a
WLIST    H           210 03-21-94    4:00a
WLIST    IDE       38776 03-21-94    4:00a
WLIST    RC          176 03-21-94    4:00a
WLIST    RH          150 03-21-94    4:00a
        9 file(s)       50272 bytes
```

WPRINT

Directory of C:\MWP\WPRINT

```
.                 <DIR>      03-21-94    4:01a
..                <DIR>      03-21-94    4:01a
```

```
MAKEFILE            1447 03-21-94    4:00a
WLIST    CPP       14873 03-21-94    4:00a
WLIST    DEF         117 03-21-94    4:00a
WLIST    H           276 03-21-94    4:00a
WLIST    IDE       40342 03-21-94    4:00a
WLIST    RC          370 03-21-94    4:00a
WLIST    RH          144 03-21-94    4:00a
         9 file(s)        57569 bytes
```

Total files listed:

```
       428 file(s)     2066411 bytes
```

Symbols

C

D

I

INDEX

MDIDEMO SUBDIRECTORY

S

T

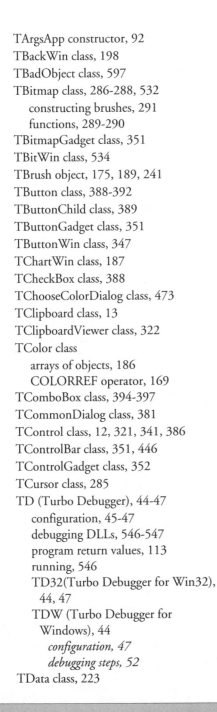

X-Y-Z

GO AHEAD. PLUG YOURSELF INTO
PRENTICE HALL COMPUTER PUBLISHING.
Introducing the PHCP Forum on CompuServe®

Yes, it's true. Now, you can have CompuServe access to the same professional, friendly folks who have made computers easier for years. On the PHCP Forum, you'll find additional information on the topics covered by every PHCP imprint—including Que, Sams Publishing, New Riders Publishing, Alpha Books, Brady Books, Hayden Books, and Adobe Press. In addition, you'll be able to receive technical support and disk updates for the software produced by Que Software and Paramount Interactive, a division of the Paramount Technology Group. It's a great way to supplement the best information in the business.

WHAT CAN YOU DO ON THE PHCP FORUM?

Play an important role in the publishing process—and make our books better while you make your work easier:

- Leave messages and ask questions about PHCP books and software—you're guaranteed a response within 24 hours
- Download helpful tips and software to help you get the most out of your computer
- Contact authors of your favorite PHCP books through electronic mail
- Present your own book ideas
- Keep up to date on all the latest books available from each of PHCP's exciting imprints

JOIN NOW AND GET A FREE COMPUSERVE STARTER KIT!

To receive your free CompuServe Introductory Membership, call toll-free, **1-800-848-8199** and ask for representative **#597**. The Starter Kit Includes:

- Personal ID number and password
- $15 credit on the system
- Subscription to CompuServe Magazine

HERE'S HOW TO PLUG INTO PHCP:

Once on the CompuServe System, type any of these phrases to access the PHCP Forum:

GO PHCP   **GO BRADY**
GO QUEBOOKS   **GO HAYDEN**
GO SAMS   **GO QUESOFT**
GO NEWRIDERS   **GO PARAMOUNTINTER**
GO ALPHA

Once you're on the CompuServe Information Service, be sure to take advantage of all of CompuServe's resources. CompuServe is home to more than 1,700 products and services—plus it has over 1.5 million members worldwide. You'll find valuable online reference materials, travel and investor services, electronic mail, weather updates, leisure-time games and hassle-free shopping (no jam-packed parking lots or crowded stores).

Seek out the hundreds of other forums that populate CompuServe. Covering diverse topics such as pet care, rock music, cooking, and political issues, you're sure to find others with the sames concerns as you—and expand your knowledge at the same time.

Add to Your Sams Library Today with the Best Books for Programming, Operating Systems, and New Technologies

The easiest way to order is to pick up the phone and call

1-800-428-5331

between 9:00 a.m. and 5:00 p.m. EST.

For faster service please have your credit card available.

ISBN	Quantity	Description of Item	Unit Cost	Total Cost
0-672-30441-4		Borland C++ 4 Developer's Guide (book/disk)	$45.00	
0-672-30471-6		Teach Yourself Advanced C in 21 Days (book disk)	$34.95	
0-672-30177-6		Windows Programmer's Guide to Borland C++ Tools (book/disk)	$39.95	
0-672-30030-3		Windows Programmer's Guide to Serial Communications (book/disk)	$39.95	
0-672-30097-4		Windows Programmer's Guide to Resources (book/disk)	$34.95	
0-672-30226-8		Windows Programmer's Guide to OLE/DDE (book/disk)	$34.95	
0-672-30364-7		Win32 API Desktop Reference (book/CD)	$49.95	
0-672-30287-X		Tom Swan's Code Secrets	$39.95	
0-672-30236-5		Windows Programmer's Guide to DLLs and Memory Management (book/disk)	$34.95	
0-672-30338-8		Inside Windows File Formats (book/disk)	$29.95	
0-672-30299-3		Uncharted Windows Programming (book/disk)	$34.95	
0-672-30239-X		Windows Developer's Guide to Application Design (book/disk)	$34.95	
❏ 3 ½" Disk		Shipping and Handling: See information below.		
❏ 5 ¼" Disk		TOTAL		

Shipping and Handling: $4.00 for the first book, and $1.75 for each additional book. Floppy disk: add $1.75 for shipping and handling. If you need to have it NOW, we can ship product to you in 24 hours for an additional charge of approximately $18.00, and you will receive your item overnight or in two days. Overseas shipping and handling adds $2.00 per book and $8.00 for up to three disks. Prices subject to change. Call for availability and pricing information on latest editions.

201 W. 103rd Street, Indianapolis, Indiana 46290

1-800-428-5331 — Orders   1-800-835-3202 — FAX   1-800-858-7674 — Customer Service

How To Install the Disk

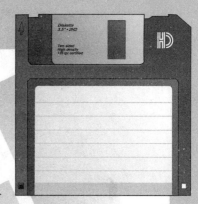

The accompanying diskette provides this book's sample listings in a compressed, self-extracting archive file. You must decompress the files before you can use them. Check that your hard drive has about 3.5 megabytes of free space. (After installation, the unpacked files occupy about 2.5 megabytes.) Then, follow these instructions:

1. If you are running Windows, open a DOS-prompt window.

2. From the DOS prompt, create a directory to hold the decompressed files. You may use any directory name and drive. To create the recommended MWP directory on drive C:, enter:

   ```
   md c:\mwp
   ```

3. Copy MWP.EXE from the diskette to the new directory:

   ```
   copy a:\mwp.exe c:\mwp
   ```

4. Change to the installation drive and directory, and run the self-extracting archive file, MWP.EXE, by typing its name:

   ```
   c:
   cd \mwp
   mwp
   ```

5. Running MWP.EXE creates numerous subdirectories and decompresses all listings and other files. When the DOS prompt returns, you may delete MWP.EXE (keep a backup copy, however, in case you need to reinstall the listings).

NOTE

See Appendix A for compilation instructions. See Appendix B for an inventory of installed directories and files.